SUSTAINABILISM
Exposing the Sustainability Illusion

SUSTAINABILISM
Exposing the Sustainability Illusion

The Authentic Sustainability Framework
A radical paradigm for regenerative and enduring systems

ASHKAN TASHVIR
Best-selling author of BEING, HUMAN BEING and METACONTENT

First published 2025 by Engenesis Publications

Copyright © Ashkan Tashvir 2025

Ashkan Tashvir asserts the moral right to be identified as the author of *SUSTAINABILISM* and all associated products.

ISBN 978-1-922433-21-3   Paperback (Australian Print)
ISBN 978-1-922433-22-0   Paperback (POD)
ISBN 978-1-922433-23-7   Hardcover (POD)
ISBN 978-1-922433-24-4   EPUB
ISBN 978-1-922433-25-1   Audio book

publications.engenesis.com

All rights reserved. No part of this publication may be reproduced or transmitted, copied, stored in a retrieval system, distributed or otherwise made available by any person or entity (including Google, Amazon or similar organisations), in any form (electronic, digital, optical, mechanical or otherwise), or by any means (photocopying, recording, scanning or otherwise) without prior written permission from the publisher, except in the case of brief quotations embodied in critical reviews and certain other non-commercial uses permitted by copyright law. For permission requests, contact the publisher on +61 (02) 9188 0844 or email publications@engenesis.com

 A catalogue record for this book is available from the National Library of Australia

Edited by Phaedra Pym – awaywithwords.net.au
Sub-edited by Caroline New – quantumvalues.com
Cover design and diagrams by Odette Abrenica
Book design and production by Eric and Thymen Hoek – exlibris.com.au

Disclaimer: This book is intended to give general information only. The material herein does not represent professional advice. The author expressly disclaims all liability to any person arising directly or indirectly from the use of, or for any errors or omissions in, the information in this book. The adoption and application of the information in this book is at the reader's discretion and is his or her sole responsibility.

I dedicate this book to my dear friend John Lowe,
and to all those who honour the quiet resilience of renewal,
who trust in the rhythm of what endures,
and who shape the future, not through force,
but through flow.

Acknowledgements

Some say that only storms bring transformation, that only thunder shapes destiny, and that solitude must be armour for those who walk uncommon paths. Yet there comes a season where a gentler truth reveals itself, where struggle is not the sole proof of depth, nor solitude the only companion of truth.

Often growth arrives through steady presence, clear sight and the calm rhythm of work done with care. Wisdom teaches us that creation moves not with noise, but with stillness; that meaning can arrive like dawn across an untouched field – quiet, yet all-encompassing.

This work was shaped not through defiance, but through devotion. Devotion to coherence, to responsibility and to the sacred task of stewarding what is entrusted to us. It was written not to claim, but to serve; not to conquer the world around us, but to cultivate the world within.

It did not emerge from a sense of urgency to prove anything, but from a responsibility to contribute to the long arc of building a sustainable civilisation.

To those who walked beside me with patience, discernment, curiosity and goodwill, thank you. Your questions refined the ideas, your encouragement strengthened the long arc of creation, and your integrity made the path lighter. You stood not as observers, but as fellow travellers committed to clarity and contribution.

To those who challenged me through resistance, distance or silence, know that your role also mattered. You reminded me of the world we must grow, one shaped by understanding rather than assumption, where progress is measured not by noise, but by depth, capacity and continuity.

To my team at Engenesis, especially Odette Abrenica for her role in designing the front cover of the book, thank you. Your loyalty, sincerity and unwavering spirit have walked beside this vision as guardians of what is true.

To each of you, and others who have stood in steadfast commitment, your presence has been a sanctuary of clarity and goodwill.

To those who played a direct role in shaping and refining this work, I offer my heartfelt gratitude.

To Ariya Chittasy, Jacqueline Hofste, Marlous Teh, Lucy Faulconer and Aydin Yassemi, your thoughtful engagement, care and commitment helped ensure this book stands with clarity and strength.

To Caroline New and Jeanette Mundy, your discerning eyes, feedback and willingness to challenge and uplift the work have been invaluable.

To my editor and right hand throughout this journey, Phaedra Pym, whose dedication has travelled with me across several books: you have refined language, safeguarded meaning and ensured these ideas remain accessible to the reader. Your presence has been nothing short of instrumental.

Many others may not have contributed directly to the book's production, yet their conversations, questions and shared thinking quietly planted seeds and shaped the conceptual ground from which this work grew.

To John Smallwood, Dr Anna Carr, Dr Jordan Marijana Alexander, Wayne Stickel, Kevin Holloway, Dr Ehssan Sakhaee and Anthea Stevanovic, your perspectives and thoughtful exchanges nourished the ideas long before they took root here.

To the many more people whose names may not appear, yet whose influence lives on these pages, please know that my appreciation extends to you as well.

To my family, whose love is a shelter and whose patience is a blessing, thank you for the grace you bring to my life.

To Atefeh, my wife, you have been the quiet hearth where meaning gathers and steadiness grows.

To my children, Diana and Diyan, your laughter and light are constant reminders of what truly matters. You have been my living proof that the future is not something we merely speak of, but something we raise, nurture and behold with awe. Even in your young years, you have offered a joy that steadies and a love that deepens the purpose behind every word on these pages.

To the readers who have journeyed through my earlier works and now arrive here, I honour your courage to seek, to question, to rise. There is a sacredness in your sincerity and a light in your inquiry. May these pages be a companion to your becoming.

Last, but by no means least, I honour my beloved friend, John Lowe. John would have been the person I asked to write the foreword to this book. His absence from these opening pages is not a sign of forgetting, but the quiet mark of a presence that no longer speaks in words. His wisdom, generosity and ontological clarity shaped this work more than he ever knew. Though the foreword is missing, his voice remains in the scaffolding of the ideas, in the refinement of the distinctions, and in the tone of this journey. Thank you, John, for the path we walked side by side, for the map you helped shape, and for the grace of your being. What you cultivated lives on here – in the lines, in the spaces between them, and in the hearts of those who read and carry this work forward.

In the hush of evening, dogs resting at my feet, pipe smoke lifting like a whispered offering to the night sky, I often sat in quiet gratitude. In that stillness, I learned again that the most enduring creations are not forced; they are allowed. They unfold with grace, as all things aligned with truth eventually do.

If even one earnest soul finds light, steadiness or a sense of inner covenant in these pages, the work has been blessed and fulfilled – not as a statement of arrival, but as a humble offering towards what may yet become.

This work stands not as a monument to effort, but as an offering: a companion for those who choose to build systems, relationships and futures guided by Being, responsibility and care. If it brings clarity, courage or steadiness to even one thoughtful soul navigating the complexities of our time, the journey has already been worthwhile.

Preface

Beyond first impressions: The crisis of thinking we know

Sustainability has been misunderstood. For most people, the word conjures images of recycling, emissions targets and environmental campaigns. Yet sustainability, in its truest sense, was never meant to be confined to ecology or policy. It is a meta-framework for understanding how systems of every kind – individual, organisational, environmental and civilisational – maintain integrity and the capacity to regenerate over time. This book is about that deeper meaning: the architecture of authentic sustainability.

In an age of endless information, we seem to have perfected the art of instant perception – the ability to glance at something, form a hasty opinion and move on with complete confidence that we have *understood* it. A few lines of a news article, a viral clip, a tweet or a cleverly edited documentary are enough for many of us to feel like we grasp the full picture.

But here's the problem: what we perceive as understanding is often just a well-wrapped illusion. This tendency does not stop at trivial or minor topics; it extends to how we interpret capitalism, postmodernism, religious scriptures, scientific statements, political movements and even children's movies. We assume that because we have seen something, we comprehend it. Because we have heard something, we can pass judgement. And because we have assigned it meaning – often one that aligns with our own ideological or emotional biases – it must be true.

Religious believers and non-believers alike claim to know what the scriptures say. Yet studying its content in depth is a rarer endeavour. A surface read leaves only initial impressions or confirms pre-existing biases. In contrast, an intentional read engages with the words with the aim of discovery rather than merely validating what is already believed. True depth situates the text in its historical and cultural setting, attends to whether its language is poetic, metaphorical, or literal, and discerns the metacontent beneath the content. It weighs contextual variables – for instance, whether a term such as 'law' refers to modern civil legislation or to the principles, norms and practices of a faith tradition. It seeks perspectives from multiple angles to form a more complete horizon of understanding, and it considers the paradigms and schools of interpretation that have shaped meaning across time. A shallow reading may yield only unprocessed impressions, while deeper study works those insights through a process of reflection and reason until they become a coherent argument.

Capitalists and anti-capitalists speak confidently about capitalism, relying on economic structures far more nuanced than the slogans they parrot. Postmodernism? Ask 10 people, get 10 different answers: each delivered with unshakable conviction. Beyond merely thinking we understand, we act. We pass judgement, create policies, enforce cultural norms and take to activism, all based on interpretations that may be incomplete, distorted or fundamentally incongruent with reality.

These distortions – assumed, reinforced and acted upon – are what I refer to as 'shadows'. Shadows are lived delusions that shape systems, institutions and ways of being. When left unexamined, they give rise to misery: not as an abstract concept, but as a tangible condition where dysfunction spirals into self-sustaining chaos. When misery becomes deeply embedded, it solidifies into entrenchment: a state where dysfunction feels both inescapable and inevitable. Suffering, then, is the lived experience of distress and hardship that arises from existing within a state of misery, whether consciously or unconsciously.

Why 'sustainabilism'?

If there is one thing the modern world does not need, it's another *-ism*. The suffix has been stretched, repurposed and overworked, applied to nearly every intellectual proposition, political ideology or economic framework. Capitalism, socialism, liberalism, scientism, feminism, environmentalism: each neatly packaged and wielded as blunt instruments against dissenters.

Yet here I am, introducing yet another *-ism*. Let me clarify: sustainabilism is not a new intellectual orthodoxy or a rallying cry for factional disputes. It's precisely the opposite. Sustainabilism, as I use it, is intentionally ironic. It's a word explicitly used to critique how genuine sustainability has been reduced to bureaucratic agendas, compliance forms and institutional mandates.

Sustainability as it was always meant to be

As mentioned, sustainability is not merely an environmental, economic or social framework. It is a meta-theory or theory about theories. It operates at a higher ontological level, providing the organising principles and conceptual scaffolding within which other theories are developed and interpreted. Rather than addressing a specific domain or problem, a meta-theory guides how we structure knowledge, meaning and coherence across multiple systems and frameworks. As a meta-theory then, sustainability is meant to guide how we think about coherence, integrity, resilience and long-term viability across all domains of existence.

However, sustainability has been distorted into an imposed agenda: a checklist of green policies, marketing slogans, image-driven campaigns or corporate compliance requirements. I refer to that bureaucratic, compliance-driven version as 'sustainabilism'. Sustainabilism is sustainability stripped of depth, reduced to institutional mandates and regulated into submission, losing its capacity as a lens to understand genuinely stable and regenerative systems.

Sustainability should have always been about the creation and nurture of inherently adaptive, regenerative and self-sustaining systems – systems that require minimal external interference to thrive. True sustainability – referred to in this book as 'authentic sustainability' – emerges organically from structural coherence, not from endless top-down regulations or perpetual oversight.

What is authentic sustainability?

Authentic sustainability is a state of dynamic coherence where systems naturally evolve, regenerate and maintain their structural integrity without constant external enforcement. It's about designing systems that are intrinsically aligned with their environment and purpose: allowing adaptability, resilience and genuine growth to emerge from within. Authentic sustainability recognises that true stability is not achieved through rigid control but through embracing the natural processes and cyclical nature of transformation and renewal.

To pursue authentic sustainability is to shift from a mindset of imposition to one of alignment – to understand that enduring systems are not manufactured through bureaucratic frameworks but cultivated through dynamic coherence and integrity. This book is about reclaiming that understanding and challenging the distortions that have reduced sustainability to a box-ticking exercise.

Sustainabilism as a critique

The reason for naming the distorted form of sustainability as an *-ism* is twofold. Firstly, the authentic sustainability discourse directly challenges institutionally enforced, performative narratives – particularly those promoted by global bodies, progressive institutions, multinational corporations and hedge funds – that have reduced sustainability to a prescriptive doctrine managed through spreadsheets, metrics and regulatory oversight. By framing sustainability as something to be imposed and measured rather than understood and integrated, these entities perpetuate a superficial approach that often prioritises compliance over coherence.

Secondly, sustainabilism critiques the assumption that sustainability must be actively imposed rather than allowed to emerge organically from structurally coherent systems. This approach raises two crucial questions. First: where has sustainability emerged organically and what does it look like? Consider the Subak system in Bali: a centuries-old, community-based irrigation practice that arose without bureaucratic enforcement. It sustained both agriculture and social harmony by aligning spiritual, ecological and cooperative principles.

Where the Subak system was left structurally intact, sustainability endured. But when top-down modernisation intervened, the system's coherence collapsed. A foundational study[1] showed that the Subak irrigation system functioned as a self-organising, adaptive and sustainable social-ecological network, requiring no centralised control. It is just one example of what becomes possible when sustainability is permitted to emerge organically and maintain itself with minimal intervention.

The second question that arises is: can authentic sustainability ever emerge from externally enforced compliance? The short answer is: no, it can't. Ironically, the persistent need to regulate sustainability only highlights the inherent unsustainability of our systems. The more we attempt to enforce sustainability through rigid frameworks, the further we move away from its authentic expression.

This critique is not limited to progressive-leaning institutions. It applies equally to libertarian and conservative camps, who, in their resistance to bureaucratic overreach, often dismiss sustainability altogether rather than confronting its underlying principles. Authentic sustainability sits uneasily with both extremes, as it rejects both the bureaucratic enforcement of sustainability doctrines and the naive belief that market forces alone can resolve systemic fragilities. Instead, it calls for a deeper, more coherent approach that transcends ideological boundaries.

A word on words

Before we dive deeper, it's worth noting an important truth: language is both our greatest gift and our biggest limitation. As human beings, we have the remarkable ability to articulate, explain and express. But let's be honest – we often intend to say one thing and end up saying another. We reach for meaning, only to find that the words we've selected barely scratch the surface of what we meant. And sometimes, we don't even know what we meant until after we've said it.

---

1   Lansing, J. S., & Kremer, J. N. (1993) Emergent Properties of Balinese Water Temple Networks: Coadaptation on a Rugged Fitness Landscape. *American Anthropologist*, 95(1), pp. 97–114. https://anthrosource.onlinelibrary.wiley.com/doi/abs/10.1525/aa.1993.95.1.02a00050

Consider this: many of our most profound experiences and perceptions don't yet have names. Entire regions of consciousness, emotional nuance and subtle knowing remain unmapped. So what do we do? We improvise. We wrap metaphor around intuition, borrow language from other domains and stretch definitions until they almost fit. Sometimes it works. Other times, not so much – and meanings become misconstrued.

Even when the words are technically accurate, the message is still filtered. First, there's the gap between what I meant to say and what I actually managed to articulate. Then there's your side – where what you hear is shaped by your own assumptions, expectations and prior knowledge. That invisible interpretive framework is what I call your **metacontent**: the underlying architecture that shapes how you make sense of things and, ultimately, attach meaning to them.

Communication, then, is not a perfect transfer of understanding from one mind to another. It's more like two travellers trying to meet in a fog, using a hand-drawn map that got smudged in the rain. And yet (somehow) we manage.

So, as you read this book, I invite you to bring a sense of openness and lightness. Don't treat every sentence as a rigid formula or a final word. Consider it a gesture, a direction, a point of contact. Let it challenge your own metacontent. Let it land where it needs to. And when something feels unclear or incomplete, let your curiosity fill the space and know that it might not be a flaw, but the natural consequence of trying to describe what resists being pinned down.

Beyond doctrine: A call for clarity

This book is about accountability and clarity. I will explain why authentic sustainability cannot simply be mandated and why it must be allowed to emerge naturally from systems built on coherence, alignment and authentic human agency. Attempting to enforce sustainability through rigid doctrines only ensures its distortion. Genuine sustainability arises by creating conditions where alignment and coherence are achieved organically, not through prescriptive control.

By clearly separating sustainabilism (the imposed, prescribed, bureaucratic version of sustainability) from authentic sustainability (genuine, regenerative and lasting sustainability), I aim not merely to critique, but also to encourage deeper reflection and meaningful transformation. This approach allows us to ask vital questions like:

- If a system constantly requires external correction, is it truly sustainable?
- Are we sustaining something simply because it exists, regardless of whether it serves any real purpose?
- Are we intervening out of necessity or because we refuse to accept our limitations?

A respectful invitation

I invite you to read this book in sequence, from beginning to end. Each chapter builds on the last, with the later insights depending on the groundwork laid earlier.

The opening chapters may seem more foundational than immediately practical – and that is intentional. They set the stage for the applied material that follows. By approaching the book as a whole, with patience from the beginning, its coherence and practical application will emerge, allowing the later chapters to carry their full weight.

How do we participate meaningfully in existence?

For all our grandiosity, modern humanity often behaves as if we are the undisputed rulers of existence, self-appointed architects of reality and custodians of universal wisdom – or, at least, some like to think so. On the other extreme, there are those who insist that human agency is an illusion, that we are nothing but passive recipients of life, swept along by fate, divine decree or the cold indifference of the cosmos. Some demand complete submission to an ideology, a deity or an historical inevitability, insisting that we are mere specks, powerless and insignificant, whose only duty is obedience.

But what if neither of these narratives is quite right?

What if we are neither masters nor mere passengers, but something altogether more interesting – participants? Not gods, not helpless subjects, but conscious, sentient and uniquely self-aware beings capable of understanding, shaping and coexisting with existence itself. Unlike any other known species, we possess a rare combination of autonomy, moral and cogent reasoning and the ability to choose beyond our impulses. Although we are flawed, we are also capable of great coherence, profound ethical conduct and systemic integrity when we stop mistaking ideological dogma for wisdom.

This is not the hollow individualism of unchecked self-interest, nor the rigid collectivism of enforced submission. It is a radical reorientation: one that neither treats humanity as supreme overlords nor as irrelevant background noise in the grand play of existence. We are part of it all, intrinsically connected, yet responsible for discerning our role within it.

So, the question is not whether we must control the world or surrender to it entirely, but rather: how do we participate? How do we navigate the balance of agency and interdependence, autonomy and responsibility, intelligence and humility?

To participate meaningfully in existence requires more than knowledge or good intentions. It demands authenticity in its most expansive form. Authenticity, in the way it is understood and lived throughout this discourse, is neither a lifestyle choice nor a momentary feeling of being seen or heard. It is not found in personality tests, social media bios or the encouragement to simply 'be yourself'. That is the popular version: what the world settles for when it has forgotten what it means to simply *be*.

In its most expansive sense, authenticity is a *way of being*. It is the unbroken continuity between who one is, how one is and what one is across time, context and circumstance. It is not fixed in temperament or expression, but rather in ontological coherence: the inner consistency between what one is (essence), how one is (attunement), and how one engages with existence (participation) across all contexts. It expands beyond mere emotional honesty or personal expression into a deep alignment with truth, integrity and the reality of existence.

Authenticity, in this form, is an existential and experiential choice. It is the fundamental decision we make – moment by moment – about *how* we choose to interact with existence and all the content within it. Whether in silence or speech, action or inaction, we are always participating. Authenticity shapes *how* we participate: Do we engage in life and with content from a place of distortion or clarity, performance or presence, borrowed scripts or grounded awareness?

The choice to engage with life and content authentically is not made once but continuously. Authenticity demands a *living participation* in what is real. It asks how we show up, how we speak, how we listen, how we relate: not only to others but to the truth of the moment, to systems, to relationships, to meaning, to life itself. It is not only what we say, but the *ontological posture* from which we say it: the internal orientation of our Being, shaped by how we are relating to truth, presence and meaning in that moment.

Authenticity as a way of being cannot be reduced to a set of behaviours or moral preferences. It is an emergent property of a human being who strives to be undistorted in their awareness and intention, who has seen through the layers of inherited identity, internalised scripts and performative adaptations. It is not tribal. It is not rebellious for rebellion's sake. It is the natural unfolding of a being who no longer wishes to fracture themself to conform.

To be authentic in this expansive sense is to allow one's entire field of consciousness – cognitive, emotional, relational and ontological – to participate in truth-making, not merely truth-telling. It is to see clearly, act deliberately and live integrally, even when the world offers more comfortable and socially acceptable alternatives. It is to remain whole in the face of fragmentation and remain true in a world addicted to image, performance and consensus.

Authenticity, then, is not just about being true to oneself; it is about becoming one's truest self through an ongoing, often uncomfortable act of discernment and disclosure. It is not an act of rebellion. It is an act of returning to the source of one's Being, to the clarity that preceded the noise, roles and pretences. It is a form of existential elegance: quiet, firm, unshakable.

In this light, authenticity is not a personality trait. It is not even a virtue. It is a state of coherence between what is, what matters and how we, as individuals, show up in the world. It expands with our awareness. The more we see, the more we must adjust to remain whole. And in that sense, authenticity is a continuously expanding frontier: a deepening commitment to truth in all its forms and a deliberate way of participating in the unfolding of existence itself.

This distinction of authenticity is the very foundation of the authentic sustainability discourse discussed in this book. Just as authenticity is not imposed through external prescriptions or superficial performances, authentic sustainability cannot be achieved through top-down interventions, mandates or coercive frameworks. Instead, it must arise naturally from systems that are coherent, adaptive and aligned with their ontological foundations.

Authentic sustainability, like authenticity itself, is an emergent property: one that is structured to thrive through alignment rather than control, coherence rather than correction. It requires the same commitment to clarity, integrity and continuous adaptation that defines an authentic way of being.

Figuring out how to participate in existence – without the arrogance of utopian planners or the passivity of those who reject all agency – is the real journey. If the authentic sustainability discourse introduced in this book challenges existing dogmas: good. If it makes sustainability ideologues uncomfortable: even better. Because nothing is more unsustainable than entrenched arrogance masquerading as wisdom, and nothing is more vital than the courage to show up with integrity, coherence and authenticity.

Introduction – An Invitation to Awaken

The world today feels like a balancing act on a tightrope stretched across the chasms of uncertainty. We marvel at the dizzying heights of human achievement, only to realise that beneath it all lies a foundation that's crumbling: fractured by political disunity, divisive ideologies, cultural conflicts and the relentless hum of crises spanning environmental degradation, economic disparity and the erosion of trust in our institutions. We live in a world obsessed with 'progress', yet that progress often feels as fragile as a house of cards in a wind tunnel. One small shift – a global pandemic, a market crash, a social reckoning or even AI writing poetry – and the whole structure threatens to collapse.

At its core, what we are witnessing is not merely struggle but disintegration: the gradual breakdown, recalibration and restructure of meaning, cohesion and integrity at every level. Disintegration goes beyond dysfunction; it is a state of fragmentation where shadows, misery, suffering and entrenchment erode coherence, leading to systemic breakdown and a profound loss of agency.

Disintegration is not an intentional act but an inevitable reality: an 'is-ness' rather than an 'ought-ness'. It can create space for renewal, reinvention and new structures to emerge, much like a forest fire that clears the way for new growth. However, disintegration is not inherently constructive. If shadows, misery, suffering and entrenchment remain unaddressed, they may lead to further disintegration rather than renewal. The distinction lies in whether disintegration is engaged with clarity and intention or whether it remains a reactive breakdown without recalibration.

In contrast, integrity is a state of dynamically sustained wholeness and coherence, where intention, trust, sovereignty and Being function in harmony to support resilience, adaptation and meaningful engagement with life. Integrity and disintegration are not binary conditions or fixed opposites; rather, they form a fluid continuum, with societies, individuals and institutions always in some degree of transition between them – a major premise of the discussion in this book. Movements towards disintegration are not random; they follow patterns shaped by deep-seated forces that remain largely unexamined, often serving as precursors to structural recalibration. If we fail to recognise and address these underlying fractures, we risk not just temporary turbulence but an accelerating descent into systemic breakdown and collective disarray.

While many experts diligently dissect the problems within their domains of environmental science, medicine, economics, governance, finance or psychology – including the slow, tragic demise of dinner table conversations – the more significant concern lies in the foundation beneath it all. These problems are not merely isolated failures within their respective disciplines; they are symptoms of a deeper, structural fracture that stems from the forces shaping either the coherence (integrity) or fragmentation (disintegration) of human systems at large.

Instead of simply relying on problem-solving within each domain, we need a fundamental way to map, diagnose and adjust the underlying dynamics that either sustain coherence or drive fragmentation. In other words, we need the ability to modulate: to actively influence, regulate, calibrate and refine the foundational structures that shape coherence and fragmentation. This requires an ontology – a set of concepts and categories that reveals the properties and relationships at play within a domain – one that explains why societies either sustain integrity or disintegrate into dysfunction.

But we also need to go deeper. Why? Because the fracture isn't just within isolated domains. It runs through the very platform that underpins them all: the dominant metacontent – the intellectual substrate through which we interpret all content and the bedrock upon which all constructs, sciences and institutions are built.

This book introduces a structured framework called the **Authentic Sustainability Framework (ASF)**, an overarching paradigm that brings together the key elements developed throughout this work into a single, coherent architecture. Central to the ASF is the **Unified Ontology of Systemic Integrity (UOSI)**. The UOSI does not consider the states of integrity and disintegration as rigid binary opposites, where systems – from individuals and relationships to organisations, institutions, cultures and societies – must be either wholly functional or entirely fractured. Instead, it considers them as dynamic states on a continuum shaped by the ongoing interplay of various external and internal forces. In other words, instead of a mere dichotomy, the states of integrity and disintegration exist in *dynamic modulation*, where systems oscillate between coherence and fragmentation, adapting in response to internal and external conditions: sometimes stabilising, sometimes shifting.

So, rather than viewing systems – including the manufactured systems we human beings create – as thriving or collapsing, we must recognise that they often exist in a delicate flux, with certain elements reinforcing integrity while others gradually erode it. All of this matters because the instability we are witnessing in the world is not random. It follows clear, structural patterns of coherence and fragmentation.

Issues in the world are typically examined through the lens of specific disciplines or domains, focusing on symptoms rather than underlying causes. The UOSI is different. Far from just a theory, it is a practical map of reality's coherence and collapse. It enables us to see the bigger picture from a pluralistic perspective and move beyond surface-level quick fixes towards foundational reconstruction.

Institutions, like all manufactured systems, permanently exist on a continuum between integrity and disintegration or dysfunction. When the stabilising underpinnings of integrity (trust, intention, sovereignty and Being) erode, the mechanisms of dysfunction (shadows, misery, suffering and entrenchment) take hold. Understanding this interplay is essential if we are to engage meaningfully with the root causes of dysfunction rather than just its symptoms.

As mentioned, it is not merely various domains that are unstable; the very substrate upon which they are built – the metacontent underpinning them – is also in a state of flux. The consequences of this instability are not just economic downturns or political upheaval; they include social disintegration, segregation and the fragmentation of humanity itself. Without a structured understanding of why human systems either sustain or collapse, we remain trapped in cycles of crisis management rather than evolving into systemic transformation.

While certain aspects of the existing metacontent may be authentic and capable of withstanding the test of time, history shows that inauthentic, misaligned or unsustainable elements inevitably give way to more congruent and enduring structures. The UOSI provides a framework for navigating this interplay, ensuring that transformation remains structured, yet adaptable. It enables us to look beyond individual failures and examine the deeper architecture governing all human progress and dysfunction. By shifting focus from reacting to symptoms to addressing the fundamental conditions, this unique ontological framework offers a path towards building systems where societies can genuinely thrive rather than merely survive.

Why it matters

Cultural conflicts, ideological battles and deepening political divisions all contribute to an unravelling that threatens our collective ability to function as a society. If we fail to engage with these deeper structural forces, we risk intensifying cycles of fragmentation, which amplify instability and accelerate the conditions for systemic collapse and entrenchment rather than guide transformation towards recalibration and coherence.

But here's the kicker: while these threats appear to be lurking 'out there' like some cosmic villain plotting our downfall, the truth is far less cinematic (but just as unsettling). Much of what we call 'external dysfunction' is, in great part, a messy projection of our own unresolved baggage. It is the *integrity of individuals* – or lack thereof – that is the true test. Our fears, desires, biases and unresolved tensions shape the crises we see unfolding in the world. They lie in the shadows we cast as individuals, societies and within the very systems we've created. These shadows – the fears, desires and unresolved tensions that lurk beneath the surface – are masters of disguise. They shape our thoughts, drive our actions and distort our perceptions without us even realising it. And, if left unchecked, they quietly fester, turning our personal struggles into societal dysfunction through misery, suffering and, eventually, entrenchment.

Let's briefly examine what I mean by this in relation to disintegration or dysfunction.

Shadows are unseen distortions: unresolved aspects of individuals and societies that quietly distort how we perceive, interpret and prioritise. Though subtle, their impact is far-reaching. When left unacknowledged, shadows skew our sense-making and decision-making, leading us to construct lives, systems and cultures upon foundations that are fundamentally misaligned. What begins as a distortion in perception can gradually harden into a condition of sustained dysfunction.

That condition is **misery**, which does not merely descend upon us as a passing state, but takes root when we leave shadows unexamined and allow dysfunction to solidify into identity. Misery is sustained not only by what happens to us, but by how we choose – or fail – to respond. When misalignments are tolerated and distorted behaviours and beliefs are repeated without question, dysfunction becomes familiar – even inevitable. Over time, misery forms a closed loop, perpetuated by our own patterns of disempowerment, false certainty and cycles of stagnation. It is not just how we feel, but how we function when misperception is lived out as normal.

We do not simply observe misery: we participate in it. We sustain it in ourselves, in our relationships, and in the systems we build. **Suffering** is the direct and often painful experience of inhabiting that condition. It shows itself in the body, echoes in the mind and weighs on meaning and purpose. While suffering may appear triggered externally, it intensifies when we internalise dysfunction, inherit false narratives or collude in collective denial. It is both deeply personal and strikingly universal.

Entrenchment is the phenomenon that allows this entire cycle to persist. It is how shadows become embedded, how misery is maintained, and how suffering becomes normalised. It infiltrates identities, ideologies and institutions when we defend dysfunction rather than disrupt it. Entrenchment does not always impose itself overtly. More often, it endures subtly, through the stories we repeat and the choices we stop questioning. Entrenchment doesn't just preserve dysfunction; we participate in its evolution, making it more enduring, less visible and harder to escape.

Unlike suffering, which can be fleeting, both misery and entrenchment are self-reinforcing and self-sustaining. Misery is the lived condition; entrenchment is its machinery. Together, they endure because we collude – actively or passively – in weaving shadows into the fabric of our lives and our systems.

Shadows, misery, suffering and entrenchment make up the 'Disintegration Sphere', which will be explored in detail later in the book when the UOSI is introduced and fully unpacked from Part II.

The dance between dysfunction and integrity

Just as dysfunction is sustained through shadows, misery, suffering and entrenchment, integrity emerges through the dynamic interplay of dysfunction's antidotes – intention, trust, sovereignty and Being. These forces make up the UOSI's 'Integrity Sphere', with each one reinforcing the others in a tangible way.

Intention drives action and engagement, shaping choices with either clarity and sincerity or distortion and coercion. But intention alone is fragile without **trust**, which stabilises coherence, enabling meaningful interaction and reliable engagement. Trust gives intention a foundation to function effectively, ensuring integrity holds firm in both personal and collective contexts.

For trust to thrive, **sovereignty** is essential. Sovereignty is an expansive state that allows intention to be expressed authentically and without distortion. It dissolves internal and external constraints that hinder self-determination, ensuring intention and trust aren't undermined by fear, control or self-imposed limits. Sovereignty is knowing you have the freedom, autonomy and liberty to stay true to who you are, even when faced with internal or external pressure.

At the core lies **Being**, which is not just a state but a cluster construct encompassing how human beings relate to and embody key primal qualities such as authenticity, courage, commitment, assertiveness and resourcefulness, as well as how we *act upon them* in shaping our lives. Being integrates intention, trust and sovereignty into a cohesive whole, determining whether individuals realise their potential and navigate complexity with clarity or suppress it, leading to disintegration. Without alignment in Being, intention can be misplaced, trust can be blind and sovereignty can be reckless.

These four elements don't operate in isolation, but function as a *unified system*. When in harmony, they sustain integrity. When they are fractured, dysfunction takes root, eroding coherence at every level: personal, relational and systemic.

Modulation – The inner stabilisers of coherence

Between the forces that drive disintegration and those that anchor integrity lies a quieter, often overlooked domain: the 'Modulation Sphere', which comprises the subtle human capacities of patience, tolerance, adaptability and surrender. These qualities function like inner stabilisers of coherence, helping us navigate the thresholds where reaction can turn into repression or resilience. It's the ability to sit with discomfort without reacting (**patience**), hold space for others without agreement (**tolerance**), recalibrate when the world shifts beneath us (**adaptability**) and yield without resignation (**surrender**). While these modulating qualities don't resolve dysfunction on their own, without them, our ability to meaningfully engage with complexity diminishes. In many ways, they are the qualities that allow us to remain in conversation with life rather than retreating into dogma or denial.

Ultimately, the essence of authentic sustainability is the recognition that sustainability is not just about environmental concerns or economic longevity; it's about the very structures that govern coherence and fragmentation: integrity, disintegration and the modulating forces that enable systems (including human beings) to transition between the two and self-regulate.

A preview of the key concepts and models explored in this book

As this book unfolds, I will introduce and expand on several critical concepts that form the foundation of authentic sustainability and its application to leadership, governance and systemic renewal. This discourse is an evolution of the philosophical and ontological inquiries explored in my previous works. Due to the complexity of these ideas and how they build upon one another, they are unpacked in detail throughout the chapters. Towards the final sections, you will be introduced to various solutions in depth, exploring each of these components in greater detail. There is also an Appendix, which describes how this discourse evolved. For now, here is a brief introduction to some of the key concepts and models introduced in this book.

What is meant by 'system'?

In this body of work, the word 'system' is not confined to technology, processes or organisational structures. It is used in a broader and more fundamental sense.

Here, a system is defined as a set of interconnected parts that influence one another towards a purpose, pattern or outcome – whether consciously designed or unconsciously evolved.

Within this context, a system may take many forms: an organisation, a team, a family, a culture, a nation, a relationship, a leadership group, a belief structure, a market, a framework of meaning, or even a single human being, as each of us is an internal system of values, emotions, intentions and actions.

Therefore, sustainability in this book is not limited to environmental systems or corporate mechanisms. It addresses the total ecology of human existence – how people think, relate, govern, create, decide, organise and sustain meaning and integrity.

The Authentic Sustainability Framework (ASF)

From the outset, this book draws a distinction between **authentic sustainability** and the prescriptive, performative versions referred to here as **sustainabilism**. Sustainabilism has long dominated the discourse, reducing renewal into compliance checklists, corporate branding or policy optics. However, authentic sustainability is not merely a counter-discourse. It is a structured framework – one that integrates ontological precision, methodological clarity and practical tools for both diagnosis and transformation.

The ASF is an overarching framework that brings together the key elements developed throughout this work into a single, coherent and multidimensional architecture consisting of:

- **The Unified Ontology of Systemic Integrity (UOSI)** – The backbone of the framework, providing a map of 16 systemic qualities (including Being from the Being Framework™)[2] across four Spheres: the Architectonic, Integrity, Disintegration and Modulation Spheres.
- **The Systemic Subversion Cycle (SSC)** – A diagnostic model that reveals how systems slide into dysfunction, entrenchment and collapse, and why timely intervention is vital to avoid irreversible breakdown.
- **The Reconstructive Ontology of Sustainability (ROS)** – The reconstructive dimension of the ASF, moving us beyond critique into actionable renewal. ROS integrates the Being Framework, Metacontent Discourse and its associated Nested Theory of Sense-making,[3] Minalogy (meaning-making) and the Being Framework's Transformation Methodology™ into a generative paradigm for systemic reconstruction.
- **The Sustainability Profile** – An ontometric tool that makes visible a system's relationship with the 16 UOSI qualities, offering leaders structured insights for assessment, measurement and practical action.

---

2 Tashvir, A. (2021) *Being – The Source of Power*. Sydney: Engenesis Publications.
3 Tashvir, A. (2024) *Metacontent: The Intellectual Substrates for Sense-making*. Sydney: Engenesis Publications.

- **The Fulfilment Pyramid** – A multidimensional model that shows how intention matures into fulfilment through three interlocking dimensions – Developmental, Phenomenological and Relational. It operationalises the ASF by translating coherence from meaning to action, ensuring that commitments are formed with depth, enacted with integrity and sustained across relationships, structures and time.

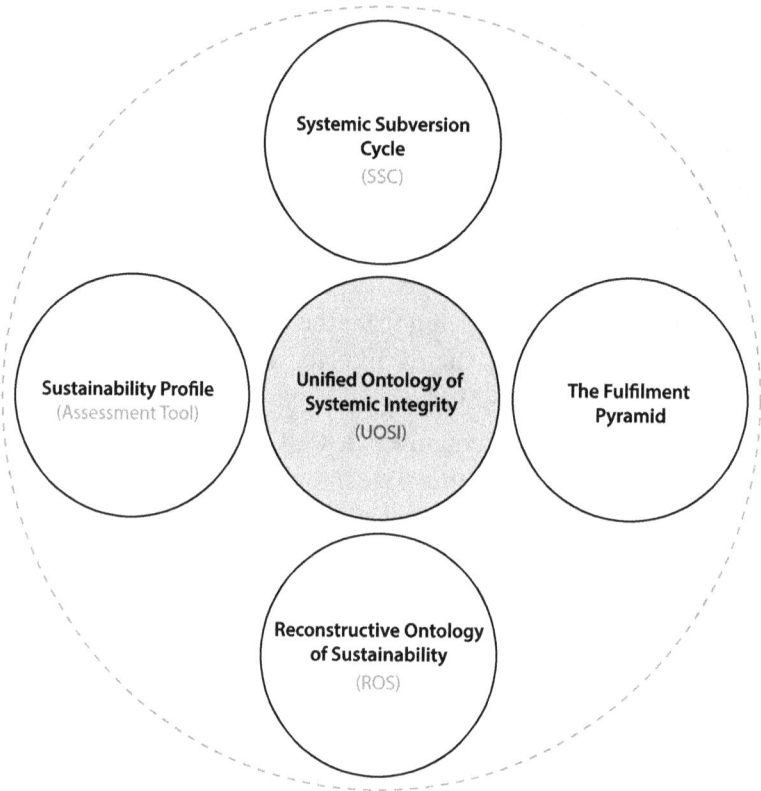

Figure 1 – Authentic Sustainability Framework.

Together, these components form more than a collection of ideas. They are an interdependent whole – a practical, systemic pathway for building, assessing and sustaining integrity across individuals, relationships, teams, organisations, institutions, communities, cultures and societies.

Why the ASF matters

The importance of the ASF lies not only in its structure, but in how it reshapes the very principles and practice of sustainability. Too often, sustainability has been approached as a technical or managerial problem, reduced to dashboards, metrics or symbolic gestures that fail to address the ontological roots of dysfunction.

Most approaches to systems – whether in ecology, economics or governance – have been framed as if we could stand outside them as detached observers analysing moving parts. This has been useful, but also limited. Human beings are never outside the systems we describe. Our beliefs, intentions, awareness and ways of being are themselves constitutive forces within every system. We are simultaneously shaping and being shaped by the very structures we study.

This gap has been identified before. In his Integral Theory, Ken Wilber pointed to the limitations of systems thinking and ecology in prioritising only what can be observed and measured – the 'exterior' world – while neglecting the equally vital 'interior' dimensions of human experience, meaning and value.[4] Western thought, he argued, has long reduced complex realities to what can be seen, leaving the felt, shared and cultural dimensions underexplored. The ASF directly addresses this omission. It bridges the interior and exterior domains by offering a rigorous ontological model that accounts not only for systems 'out there', but also for the inner architecture of human beings who live, act and decide within them. In doing so, ASF provides a pathway for moving from individual integrity to systemic integrity – and ultimately towards authentic sustainability.

Consider, for example, an organisation that celebrates its reduced emissions as proof of sustainability. On the surface, this appears commendable. Yet when assessed through the ASF lens, the organisation may reveal systemic shadows – exploitative labour practices, displacement of their carbon footprint onto outsourced countries or factories, performative leadership or a culture sustained by fear. By integrating UOSI (including the Being Framework), SSC and ROS,

---

4   Wilber, K. (2000) *Integral Psychology: Consciousness, Spirit, Psychology, Therapy*. Boston, MA: Shambhala; Wilber, K. (2001) *Sex, Ecology, Spirituality: The Spirit of Evolution*. 2nd edn. Boston, MA: Shambhala.

the ASF exposes such fractures and offers a reconstructive pathway for transformation.

Similarly, an executive may succeed in driving a team to deliver a project on time and to specification, presenting this as evidence of effective leadership. Yet beneath the surface, such success may come at the cost of jeopardising the team's sustained effectiveness and long-term sustainability. Yes, the deliverable was achieved – but at what price? If the process eroded trust, strained relationships or left individuals depleted, then the very foundations of ongoing collaboration have been undermined. The critical question is not only whether the project was delivered, but whether the team still wants to work together, or whether unresolved fractures will soon manifest in disengagement and retention problems.

On a larger scale, consider a government that, in a rushed response to a growing housing crisis, enables first-home buyers to purchase property with only a 5% deposit. While this may deliver momentary satisfaction for some and appear favourable in optics, the policy risks generating far greater systemic problems. A sudden influx of buyers with artificially lowered barriers fuels demand without increasing supply, driving housing prices even higher. Those who once could not 'afford' a $1.5 million home may now appear able to do so, yet in reality, sellers simply raise their prices to match the surge. Beyond inflated property values, many new buyers may find themselves unable to sustain repayments, leading to defaults, foreclosures and long-term financial distress. In attempting to solve one issue – if it can even be called a solution – the policy risks destabilising the broader economy and society. Such measures are often delivered under the banner of authority – 'experts said' – but what kind of expertise produces outcomes that deepen the very fractures they claim to heal? The issue was never simply the deposit requirement; it was the underlying purchasing power, which remains unaddressed.

At the end of the day, if a system must be continuously and significantly manipulated or artificially 'maintained' – like interest rates that are perpetually adjusted to keep the system afloat – then it is inherently unsustainable. Anything that requires constant artificial maintenance cannot be called sustainable.

At the societal level, governments could use the ASF to design policies that go beyond short-term fixes and embed trust, sovereignty and systemic coherence into governance. And communities could leverage the ASF to design regenerative practices that hold together diversity without collapsing into polarisation.

The ASF therefore serves three critical functions:

- **A Discourse** – providing new language and distinctions that free us from the limits of prescriptive sustainability (sustainabilism).
- **A Framework** – integrating multiple ontological models into a unified architecture.
- **A Practical Methodology** – equipping us with the tools, processes and practices needed to translate insight into execution.

In this sense, the ASF is both conceptual and practical. It critiques, reconstructs and enables. It provides leaders, communities and societies with a way of not only imagining authentic sustainability but actually living it. Unlike sustainabilism, which reduces renewal into compliance and performance, the ASF embeds sustainability into the very Being of individuals and the structural coherence of the systems we humans design, engage with and inhabit, from organisations and institutions to communities, cultures, religions and societies.

Critically, it all starts with who and how we are being. More specifically, how we, as individuals, relate to fundamental qualities like trust, sovereignty, meta-awareness, adaptability, intention, tolerance and surrender determines the nature of the systems we create. The ways we embody these qualities in thought, emotion and action, whether within a team, relationship, organisation or society, are ultimately mirrored in the collective structures that emerge from us. Every system, in this sense, is a reflection of the relational coherence – or incoherence – of its participants.

The ASF is not an endpoint. It is a living architecture – one that evolves as systems evolve, adapts as contexts shift and sustains itself through the ongoing interplay of analysis, meaning-making, intention, commitment, modulation and practice.

As shown, the ASF comes to life through its constituent parts. What follows is a closer look at each of these elements – how they work individually, and how together they form a coherent architecture for authentic sustainability.

Metacontent and the Nested Theory of Sense-making

Our understanding of reality is not based on raw information alone, but on 'metacontent' – a term first introduced in *Metacontent – The Intellectual Substrates for Sense-making*.[5] Metacontent represents the intellectual bedrock for making sense of any content through a structured meta-analysis. The Nested Theory of Sense-making, as introduced and explored in the *Metacontent* book, identifies seven layers through which we interpret reality, from basic assumptions to broad societal paradigms. Without examining content through these layers, misconceptions and biases arise, leading to flawed decisions.

The Being Framework

First introduced in *Being*,[6] the Being Framework, provides a structured model to help you understand why individuals – including yourself – think, act and perform the way they do. It consists of three elements:

- The **Being Framework Ontological Model**: An ontological model that identifies and maps out the metadata for 31 Aspects of Being linked to our performance, leadership and wellbeing.
- The **Being Profile**®: The core assessment tool associated with the Being Framework, which accurately measures an individual's relationship with all 31 Aspects of Being.
- The **Transformation Methodology**™: A model and series of processes and principles designed to lead an individual on a transformational journey in relation to each of the 31 Aspects of Being identified in the ontological model.

---

[5] Tashvir, A. (2024) *Metacontent: The Intellectual Substrates for Sense-making*. Sydney: Engenesis Publications.

[6] Tashvir, A. (2021) *Being: The Source of Power*. Sydney: Engenesis Publications.

Leadership and performance are not just about skills, but about who and how a person is being. The Being Framework and its associated tools enable leaders and organisations to develop resilience, integrity and impact in a structured and actionable way.

The Unified Ontology of Systemic Integrity (UOSI)

As discussed earlier, the UOSI explains why systems either sustain themselves or collapse. Introduced for the first time in this book, the framework consists of four interconnected spheres:

- **Architectonic Sphere**: The meta-governing layer responsible for the design, evolution and overarching coherence of systems. It determines the foundational logic, purpose and direction that guide all other spheres. Without architectonic alignment, systems drift, fragment or become rigid.
- **Integrity Sphere**: The qualities required for coherence to emerge and be sustained – intention, trust, sovereignty and Being.
- **Disintegration Sphere**: The forces that lead to (or keep) a system in a state of dysfunction – shadows, misery, suffering, entrenchment.
- **Modulation Sphere**: The forces that regulate integrity and disintegration – patience, tolerance, adaptability, surrender – ensuring responsiveness rather than stagnation or collapse.

All systems – from individuals, relationships and businesses to governments, cultures and societies – exist within this dynamic interplay. Understanding these forces is essential for sustaining meaningful progress.

The Systemic Subversion Cycle (SSC)

Also introduced for the first time in this book, the SSC describes how crises are manufactured, exploited and perpetuated within failing systems. It identifies a recurrent pattern where a crisis destabilises a system, triggering structural breakdown, social fractures and opportunistic exploitation. Institutional inertia then prevents meaningful intervention, allowing dysfunction to self-perpetuate and fuel future instability. Understanding this cycle enables leaders and decision-makers to break free from destructive loops rather than applying temporary fixes that only prolong systemic collapse.

The Fulfilment Pyramid

Originally introduced in Human Being[7], the Fulfilment Pyramid described how care matures into intention, intention relies on integrity and effectiveness, and effectiveness culminates in fulfilment. It also demonstrated that awareness of the constituent dimensions of our Being is essential to sustaining integrity itself. In this book, the Fulfilment Pyramid has been expanded into a tri-dimensional structure that not only represents the individual pathway towards fulfilment, but also illuminates the developmental, phenomenological and relational dimensions required to form, enact and coherently sustain intention at a systemic level over time.

The Reconstructive Ontology of Sustainability (ROS)

ROS is another novel approach that brings together metacontent, the Being Framework and the UOSI into a practical model for sustainable leadership, governance and systemic renewal. While many critical theories deconstruct failing systems without offering alternatives, ROS provides a structured process for reconstruction, ensuring solutions are coherent, regenerative and genuinely sustainable. It moves beyond critique by offering a methodology for designing systems that can sustain themselves with minimal external intervention: the epitome of genuine sustainability.

These six key components – metacontent (including the Nested Theory of Sense-making), the Being Framework, UOSI, SSC, the Fulfilment Pyramid and ROS – form the foundation of this book's argument and recommended solutions. You will learn how they interconnect as part of the overarching Authentic Sustainability Framework (ASF) to create a new approach for sustainable leadership, governance, systemic renewal and authentic sustainability.

---

7 Tashvir, A. (2022) *Human Being – Illuminating the Reality Beneath the Facade.* Engenesis Publications: Sydney.

The architecture of 'wholeness'

Before we can meaningfully explore sustainability, we must first understand what it means for something to be whole. In this book, the term **integrity** is not used in its moral sense, as in honesty or ethical virtue. It is used in its ontological sense: **the state of being whole and undivided**. This definition – consistent with the *Oxford English Dictionary* – is foundational to how we examine systems, structures, performance and sustainability.

Across both the physical and abstract domains of existence, we observe a consistent pattern: transcendence and inclusion. That is, parts come together to form a higher-order whole, and once formed, that whole – including its constituent parts – becomes a new entity with properties the parts alone did not possess. Atoms come together to form molecules. Molecules gather and transcend into the emergence of cells. Cells form tissues, tissues form organs, and organs constitute living systems. Each layer transcends what was there before and includes it as a constituent part of a greater whole.

This principle applies not only to material structures but to abstract constructs as well. Consider a complex idea like 'justice'. Justice is not a single element, but an interwoven whole composed of underlying concepts such as fairness, equity, law, reparation and societal order. These parts cohere to form an emergent structure: a system of meaning and application that includes and transcends its elements.

In this book, when we refer to a **system**, we mean any configuration of interdependent parts that functions to produce outcomes or maintain equilibrium. This includes physical systems like ecosystems or machines, as well as abstract and social systems – individuals, families, teams, organisations, institutions, communities and entire societies. In other words, a system (as referred to in this body of work) is anything that generates outcomes, operates through interdependencies and is capable of design and evolution. It may be an individual, a family, a relationship, a business, a team, a government, an institution, a movement or a society.

Every system, regardless of its form, has **integrity** when its constituent parts work in harmony to maintain its structure and purpose.

Take a mechanical watch: its cogs, springs and gears must function together with precision for it to operate. If even one part is misaligned or deteriorates, the whole system becomes inaccurate or breaks down. Similarly, in the human body, integrity is expressed through homeostasis, the optimal functioning of its subsystems, such as the nervous, cardiovascular and digestive systems. If any one of these falls out of alignment or function, the entire organism is affected.

However, in the context of sustainability, wholeness is not just an abstract condition. It must be observable in function, design and consequence. This leads us to the more structured concept used throughout this work: systemic integrity.

Systemic integrity is the condition in which a system maintains coherence between its inherent or intended purpose, how it is designed or co-created, what it does and its impact. Systemic integrity is not a fixed state. It is dynamic, recursive and must be continuously cultivated and recalibrated. This view is consistent with established system theories: dynamic equilibrium in General Systems Theory,[8] homeostasis in Cybernetics,[9] and resilience in ecology,[10] all of which emphasise that systems sustain themselves through ongoing adaptation and recalibration. The Being Framework and UOSI build on these foundations by extending the inquiry into the ontological domain of human systems, where coherence and fragmentation are continuously modulated by the qualities articulated in the UOSI.

Systems – both human beings and the systems they design and manufacture – that neglect their own design principles or fail to evolve in accordance with their purpose will eventually lose coherence, erode performance and collapse into a state of disintegration under the weight of internal or external pressure. Sustainability simply cannot be achieved without systemic integrity.

---

8   Bertalanffy, L. von (1968) *General System Theory: Foundations, Development, Applications*. New York: George Braziller.
9   Wiener, N. (1948) *Cybernetics: Or Control and Communication in the Animal and the Machine*. Cambridge, MA: MIT Press; Ashby, W.R. (1956) *An Introduction to Cybernetics*. London: Chapman & Hall.
10 Holling, C.S. (1973) 'Resilience and Stability of Ecological Systems', *Annual Review of Ecology and Systematics*, 4(1), pp. 1–23.

Within this broader systemic view, the human being is one of the most complex and consequential systems in existence. For example, Kenneth Boulding proposed a nine-level hierarchy of systems,[11] with the upper levels corresponding to human beings, social organisations and even transcendental systems as the most complex forms. A person's **Being** (their inner architecture) is also a system with constituent parts. This is where the **Being Framework,** as defined earlier, becomes relevant to our discussion.

Within the Unified Ontology of Systemic Integrity, **Being** is one of 16 primary systemic qualities. It refers to the architecture of presence, consciousness and action: the internal system that governs how a person relates to self, others, the world and meaning itself. And just as any system must maintain integrity to perform and sustain itself, a person must also cultivate integrity (wholeness) within their Being.

This is what we mean when we refer to a person's **integrity of Being** – not a performance of moral virtue, but the coherence of the internal qualities that constitute their Being. The Being Framework Ontological Model, as discussed, identifies 31 core qualities such as authenticity, responsibility, courage, commitment, compassion and presence that together form the constituent anatomy of one's Being. These qualities are not external behaviours or traits. They are ontological stances, faculties and postures that shape how one *is being* in the world.

When these qualities are fragmented, suppressed, distorted or misaligned, a person's Being slides out of integrity. They may appear functional or successful on the outside, but they are divided, exhausted or directionless internally. Conversely, when these qualities are consciously cultivated and aligned – when they transcend and include one another as a coherent whole – the individual's Being has integrity (wholeness) and becomes a generative force for sustainable leadership, creativity, connection and transformation.

A quality within the Being Framework Ontological Model that is critical in the authentic sustainability discourse is **authenticity**.

---

11   Boulding, K.E. (1956) 'General Systems Theory – The Skeleton of Science', *Management Science*, 2(3), pp. 197–208.

Authenticity is not merely self-expression or being honest. Ontologically, it is the quality that governs one's relationship with reality: the degree to which one's perception, understanding and communication are congruent with how things actually are. A person with a healthy relationship with authenticity does not merely express opinions, but engages reality without distortion. They are capable of refining their sense-making in response to feedback and are open to truth, even when it disrupts their prior assumptions. In this sense, authenticity safeguards integrity by grounding Being in reality, rather than illusion or image.

To summarise:

- **Integrity**, in this book, refers to the ontological condition of wholeness, coherence and structural alignment, not moral virtue.
- **Systemic Integrity** is the generic technical term used throughout this work to describe whether a system of any kind maintains coherence across its claims, design, function and impact.
- **Integrity of Being** refers to a person's inner systemic coherence, based on the health of their relationship with the constituent parts (ontological qualities) – including authenticity – that lead to a state of wholeness (integrity).

Authentic sustainability emerges through the dynamic interaction between authenticity, integrity of Being and systemic integrity. Each one reinforces or erodes the others.

- **Authenticity** enables integrity of Being by ensuring that one's perception and expression remain congruent with reality.
- **Systemic integrity** reinforces integrity of Being by creating environments that support coherence and discourage fragmentation.
- **Integrity of Being** supports systemic integrity by contributing whole, grounded human beings into the systems they shape and influence.

When authenticity breaks down, integrity begins to fracture because the individual is no longer relating to reality as it is. When integrity of Being weakens, authenticity becomes performative, because the person lacks the internal structure to act congruently. When systemic integrity collapses, even coherent individuals are pulled into dysfunction, often experiencing burnout, disillusionment and resistance as they attempt to navigate misaligned systems.

These three elements form an interdependent chain of coherence:

Authenticity → Integrity of Being → Systemic Integrity

Each is distinct, but all are essential for authentic sustainability. Without authenticity, the individual becomes unstable. Without integrity, systems lose the ability to sustain trust. Without systemic integrity, even coherent individuals are pulled towards fragmentation.

Consider the case of a mid-level leader in a large organisation. This individual is deeply committed to truth, responsibility and purpose. They listen actively, take ownership of outcomes, and lead their team with care and clarity. In this sense, they demonstrate both authenticity and integrity of Being. However, what if the organisation they work within is structurally incoherent? It rewards political conformity over principled decision-making, prioritises short-term optics over long-term purpose, and punishes those who challenge the status quo. Despite the leader's internal coherence, they are operating within a misaligned system. Over time, their energy erodes, their sense of purpose dims, and they experience burnout and frustration. Systemic integrity collapses, dragging even a grounded individual into dysfunction.

Now consider a grassroots social movement that begins with a sincere commitment to justice and equity. At its inception, its participants are aligned, authentic and deeply grounded in purpose. Integrity of Being is strong across the group. But as the movement grows, its internal dynamics change. Image overtakes substance. Public signalling becomes more important than structural alignment or long-term coherence. Differences of opinion lead to infighting and alienation. What began as a sincere expression of authenticity becomes performative. As authenticity fractures, integrity weakens. Eventually, the movement fragments. Its systemic integrity unravels.

In both cases, we see how the breakdown of one layer impacts the others. Whether in an individual, a movement or an institution, authenticity, integrity of Being and systemic integrity must remain in conversation. When they reinforce each other, sustainability becomes possible. When any one collapses, the entire system is at risk.

A unified inquiry

Just as the Nested Theory of Sense-making reveals how distorted metacontent leads to flawed interpretations of reality, the authentic sustainability discourse exposes how rigid, prescriptive and centralised approaches to sustainability – what this book refers to as **sustainabilism** – can produce the very dysfunctions they aim to solve.

In the Being Framework, integrity is not something externally imposed. It is not a performance. It is an emergent quality that arises when there is alignment within the human system. It is not just a desirable characteristic, but an ontological axiom: a foundational principle from which sustainable systems, ethical conduct and coherent leadership naturally emerge.

The authentic sustainability discourse presented in this book does not exist outside these inquiries. It is their application at scale. It brings the principles of Being, systemic design and ontological coherence into the realm of governance, institutions and shared human systems.

An alternative meta-theory, lens and frameworks

The sustainability discourse unpacked in this book offers an alternative meta-theory, lens, frameworks and pathways to move beyond cycles of suffering and dysfunction towards a state of enduring integrity, alignment and meaningful progress.

The distinction between authentic sustainability and sustainabilism functions as a meta-theory because it does not offer a singular model of sustainability, but instead provides a higher-order framework for analysing, integrating and critiquing diverse sustainability narratives. By examining the assumptions, intentions and structures behind existing sustainability paradigms, it reveals how ideological, cultural and systemic forces influence the way sustainability is conceptualised and practised. In this sense, the discourse does not simply present an alternative view. Instead, it operates at the level of theory about theories, enabling reflection on how sustainability frameworks emerge, what they prioritise or obscure, and how they impact meaning-making, ethics and systemic integrity. This qualifies it as a meta-theory because it situates competing discourses within a broader evaluative and integrative context.

This book is not about offering shallow optimism or promising an escape from pain. Instead, it is about developing the awareness and clarity to prevent suffering from consuming us: enabling us to break free from cycles of misery, suffering and entrenchment and, ultimately, build something better in its place.

While we can criticise the systems, including the political system or method of government we live under, we must recognise a fundamental truth: manufactured systems are not as real as we are. They are not autonomous entities with independent existence. They are initiated, designed, further developed, implemented and followed by us human beings. We continuously choose to participate in them, and without our participation, they would cease to exist. In other words, they are manufactured constructs; we are the ones who give birth' to them, sustain them and grant them legitimacy.

This raises a crucial question: who decided that these institutions, constructs and the substrates beneath them are axiomatic[12] or universally accepted as a foundational principle? Why must they exist in the exact form they do now? We often assume that because something has been in place for generations, it must remain unchanged. Yet, history has repeatedly shown that structures and paradigms evolve. The conservative stance seeks to preserve the status quo, regardless of how many people resist or question it. The radical, progressive stance aims to dismantle and disrupt it entirely. But is there another way?

What if, instead of blindly clinging to tradition or indiscriminately destroying it, we exercised the discernment to assess what remains

---

12 Axiomatic means *self-evident, foundational, or universally accepted as true without needing proof.* It refers to a principle so fundamental that other ideas are built upon it.

valuable and relevant while recognising that some aspects must transform or, in some cases, transcend or be let go? After all, some things are not meant to go on forever. In fact, some things *should not* go on forever. The assumption that everlasting survival is inherently good, that a system deserves to persist simply because it exists, is a delusion. Survival at all costs is not a virtue – it is often a parasite's dream. When a system festers in dysfunction, relying not on genuine sustainability but on the exhaustion of a few, its collapse is not a tragedy. It is a *correction*.

Collapse is not always the end. Sometimes, it is the long-overdue reckoning for a structure that has outlived its legitimacy or the necessary release of resources, energy and human potential that had been locked into something that should have disintegrated long ago. There are times when collapse is the only way forward because what came before was never truly viable to begin with. For example, many self-proclaimed entrepreneurs spend enormous energy optimising something that arguably should not even exist in the first place, let alone be scaled or refined. This reflects a deeper issue: when the fundamental premise is flawed, no amount of optimisation can make it meaningful or valuable.

But beyond the collapse of misguided efforts, a deeper question emerges: Are we, as humanity, truly learning from these failures, or are we merely repeating old patterns under new disguises? Are we developing authentic awareness,[13] clarity and discernment in our choices and decisions, or are we blindly perpetuating systems that should have been left behind? The reality we collectively shape is not the result of a single ideology or faction; it emerges from the interaction of all these seemingly opposing forces. The challenge before us is not merely to take sides but to recognise the deeper mechanisms at play and engage with them consciously rather than as passive participants in a system we assume is inevitable.

---

13 Authentic awareness is an asymptotic ideal – a horizon we can approach but never fully reach. As human beings, our perceptions are always mediated by cognitive, emotional and cultural filters; we do not have unmediated access to reality. Like integrity, authentic awareness is not a quality to be possessed but a practice to be continually cultivated. It serves as a guiding orientation – shaping how we perceive, interpret and act in coherence with what is, rather than what we wish to see.

A pathway towards transformation

This is far from a book about doom and gloom. If you're expecting a bleak diagnosis of humanity's fate, you're in for a surprise (and maybe a bit of relief). Instead, this book is an invitation to do something bold: to look those shadows square in the eye, confront them and (critically) begin to make sense of them. This isn't just a call to action; it's a call to awaken. It's a call to wake up to the visible and hidden patterns shaping our lives for centuries: patterns we often inherit without question, like family heirlooms no one ever asked for, yet which continue to be passed down.

Whether you're aware of it or not, these patterns influence everything – from the exhaustion you feel after a long day of performing to the quiet resentment that builds when you realise life has become a race with no finish line. You may already recognise some of these patterns. Maybe you've found yourself trapped in the tyranny of metrics, where your worth is reduced to KPIs and productivity reports, each number stripping away a little more of your intrinsic value. Or perhaps you've encountered the performance paradox, where the harder you work, the less accomplished you feel, as if success is always just out of reach.

Sound familiar? It should. We live in a society that treats burnout like an Olympic sport – gold medals all around! But at what cost? We've mistaken constant output for purpose, equating busyness with worth, and have become so entrenched in the grind that we've forgotten how to be human beings, not just human doings. We need a better way. And that's exactly what this book seeks to offer.

At its core, this book is about illuminating the ontology of integrity and disintegration, including its constituent parts. For instance, by breaking misery down to understand its structure and the unstable foundations it rests upon, we can also dismantle its grip on us. And more importantly, once we identify what has been misconstructed or poorly built within the whole, we can begin the work of reconstructing something more authentic, resilient and aligned with what truly matters. This book shows you how you do that too.

You won't find grand conspiracy theories in this book about how 'they' are out to get us or how some hidden elite is pulling the strings of civilisation. It's not about finger-pointing or playing the blame game – there's already an oversupply of that and no shortage of takers. Instead, this book is about *accountability* – ours and everyone else's. We will turn the lens both inward and outward, asking tough questions like:

- What intentions shape your life?
- What shadows are you complicit in nurturing because you fear change?
- How do the systems we all rely on, from corporations to governments, perpetuate dysfunction?

As we progress, we'll explore the many paradoxes of performance, purpose and leadership that define modern life. Why do we chase mastery, yet remain unfulfilled? Why do we divide life into 'work' and 'life' as if they are opposing forces? Why does trust – perhaps the most precious commodity of all – collapse so quickly and easily, yet take years to rebuild?

Throughout the book, you will encounter case studies and examples drawn from a range of personal, organisational and societal contexts. These are designed for learning and reflection, not as definitive solutions or simplified representations of complex realities. Each example distils intricate dynamics to make core ontological principles visible and usable. They should be read as illustrations of pattern, not as prescriptions – lenses through which to explore coherence, not formulas to copy. Authentic sustainability, by its nature, resists reduction. The intent here is not to oversimplify, but to illuminate what is often unseen, and to invite deeper discernment in your own context.

Ultimately, one truth stands firm: transformation is possible. The systems and structures that seem immovable are, in reality, shaped by human intention. Dysfunction, while pervasive, is not an immutable law of nature; it is a pattern. And patterns can be unravelled and reconstructed with courage, curiosity and integrity. Shadows shrink when exposed to light, and light comes from awareness, meaning and authentic connection.

A shared responsibility

The notion that, as individuals, we are powerless, is one of the greatest illusions of our time. It is this illusion that keeps dysfunction alive – our belief that systems govern us rather than the reality that we continuously shape and sustain them. This recognition is not novel; it echoes a lineage of systemic thought across disciplines. Second-order Cybernetics (Heinz von Foerster)[14] dismantled the myth of detached objectivity, insisting that observers are always participants in the systems they study. Maturana and Varela's Theory of Autopoiesis[15] further showed that the observer and the observed co-evolve, making knowledge inseparable from its historical and embodied context. In *The Systems Approach*,[16] Churchman highlighted that any system's description carries the perspective and value commitments of its designer. Likewise, Complexity Theorists emphasise co-evolution and emergence; as van der Leeuw notes:[17] knowing itself arises through participation, with no rigid boundary between knower and known.

Together, these insights affirm the premise at the heart of this book – that systems are not external forces acting upon us, but living structures we continuously shape, sustain and transform. This is where the authentic sustainability discourse comes in. At its core, it challenges the illusion that systems govern us by asserting that sustainability is not just an institutional concern, but a deeply personal and systemic responsibility: one that begins with each and every one of us. This book is an invitation to reclaim your role in shaping the future.

The antidote to social disintegration and humanity's greatest challenges rests on the integrity of individuals – on how we choose to BE. The authentic sustainability discourse holds that governance, markets and ecological balance are not abstract forces beyond our control, but dynamic systems shaped by the alignment (or misalignment) of

---

14   von Foerster, H. (2003) *Understanding Understanding: Essays on Cybernetics and Cognition*. New York: Springer.

15   Maturana, H.R. and Varela, F.J. (1980) *Autopoiesis and Cognition: The Realization of the Living*. Dordrecht: D. Reidel.

16   Churchman, C.W. (1968) *The Systems Approach*. New York: Delacorte Press.

17   van der Leeuw, S.E. & McGlade, J. (eds.) (1997) *Time, Process and Structured Transformation in Archaeology*. London: Routledge.

individual and collective integrity. It is through our choices, actions and ability to stand firm in authenticity that we either perpetuate dysfunction or become a force that helps dissolve it. Institutions, policies and global systems may set the conditions, but it is the integrity of individuals that determines whether those conditions lead to destruction or transformation.

Consider also that you are not just a person. You are a community of individuals distributed across time. Every past version of you, every decision you've made and every belief you've held have shaped the present moment. Likewise, who you are is not fixed. Your Being is unfolding, continuously shaped by how you engage with your shadows, choices and the structures you either uphold or challenge. So, we are not merely in a state of Being, but in a dynamic, ever-unfolding state of *becoming*, existing within a continuum.The authentic sustainability discourse recognises this continuum. It acknowledges that systemic change does not emerge from sudden disruption alone but through the continuous transformation of individuals who, in turn, shape the integrity of their environments.

To move forward, we must do more than just examine shadows. We must strengthen their antidotes: intention, trust, sovereignty and an authentic and integrous way of being. This isn't just about diagnosing what's 'wrong'; it's about embodying what's 'right'. A world governed by disconnection, fear and manipulation won't fix itself, just like a gym membership won't get you in shape if you never go. We must actively lay the groundwork for a life built on integrity, meaning and connection. This is the essence of authentic sustainability – not merely surviving within broken systems, but fostering the integrity that sustains human and societal wellbeing. And that means asking the hard questions:

- What is wrong with the world and how did it get this way?
- What role do we, as individuals, play in sustaining or challenging dysfunction?
- And perhaps most importantly: What can we do about it?

The answers won't be simple, and the journey won't be easy. But transformation never is. It demands courage, discomfort and an unflinching commitment to authenticity and authentic awareness. Yet the rewards – living a life of purpose and helping to build a society grounded in integrity – are immeasurable. By embracing authentic sustainability with integrity, we move beyond resignation and into conscious, ongoing transformation: a process that reclaims individual and collective agency in shaping a truly sustainable future.

Ultimately, the goal of this book is to restore the true meaning of sustainability, not as a doctrine, but as dynamic coherence and meaningful engagement with reality. It urges us to awaken to the hidden patterns shaping our lives, to consciously participate in our collective future, and to reclaim sustainability from institutional distortion. If this makes people uncomfortable, perhaps that's precisely why it's needed now more than ever.

Let this work serve as both a mirror and a guide: a mirror to reveal the truths you may have been avoiding, and a guide to support you in navigating towards purpose, authenticity and hope. Yet, amid the gravity of the topics covered, I encourage you not to lose your sense of humour and optimism. After all, life is as absurd as it is profound. For every tragedy, there's also a moment of unexpected levity – a reminder that we are resilient, capable of laughter even in the darkest times.

Together, let's embark on this journey, not just to understand the ontology of integrity and disintegration, but to reimagine what it truly means to thrive in a world that often feels broken. Let's uncover the possibilities of a brighter, more authentic future – a future where we do not passively inherit dysfunction, but actively shape the world with clarity, systemic integrity and courage.

Contents

Acknowledgements   vii
Preface   xi
Introduction – An Invitation to Awaken   xxi

PART I : Humanity at a Crossroads   1

    Chapter 1 : The Weight of the Moment   5
    Chapter 2 : Sentience and Society   24
    Chapter 3 : Bad Faith and its Impact   39
    Chapter 4 : The Breakdown of Trust   50
    Chapter 5 : Shadows – The Unseen Forces   64
    Chapter 6 : The Systemic Subversion Cycle (SSC)   81
    Chapter 7 : The Shadow Trap –
                    How Dysfunction Undermines Sustainability   96
    Chapter 8 : The Cost of Ignoring Shadows   103
    Chapter 9 : The Power of Intentions
                    and The Shadows That Shape Them   114
    Chapter 10 : The Shadows of Traditional Economics   127
    Chapter 11 : The Production-Consumption Paradigm   134
    Chapter 12 : The Influence of Critical Theory
                     and Postmodernism   145
    Chapter 13 : Substantial Motion – Beyond Static Sustainability   157
    Chapter 14 : Sustainability – Rethinking the Foundations   164

Chapter 15 : A Radical Departure From Sustainabilism	186
Chapter 16 : Sustainability – A shared responsibility	202
Chapter 17 : The Role of Authenticity in Systemic Integrity	210

PART II : The Ontological Basis for Sustainability — 227

Chapter 18 : The Ontological Triad Schema	231
Chapter 19 : The Unified Ontology of Systemic Integrity (UOSI)	240
Chapter 20 : The Architectonic Sphere	255
Chapter 21 : The Disintegration Sphere	266
Chapter 22 : The Integrity Sphere	280
Chapter 23 : The Modulation Sphere	293
Chapter 24 : Sustaining Coherence and Mitigating Dysfunction in the Real World	306
Chapter 25 : The Expansive Nature of Transformation	320

PART III : The Architectonic Sphere — 347

Chapter 26 : Meta-awareness	351
Chapter 27 : Systemic Integrity	369
Chapter 28 : Sustained Effectiveness	381
Chapter 29 : Normativity	393

PART IV : The Disintegration Sphere — 413

Chapter 30 : Shadows	418
Chapter 31 : Misery	436
Chapter 32 : Suffering	459
Chapter 33 : Entrenchment	484

PART V : The Integrity Sphere — 501

Chapter 34 : Intention	504
Chapter 35 : Trust	520
Chapter 36 : Sovereignty	534
Chapter 37 : Being	549

PART VI : The Modulation Sphere — 569

    Chapter 38 : Patience — 573

    Chapter 39 : Tolerance — 585

    Chapter 40 : Adaptability — 597

    Chapter 41 : Surrender — 608

Part VII : From Insight to Design – Pathways to Authentic Sustainability — 621

    Chapter 42 : From Cause to Consequence – The UOSI's Emergent Forces — 629

    Chapter 43 : Analysing Systems through the UOSI — 662

    Chapter 44 : The Power of Meta-Awareness and Metacontent in Analysis — 671

    Chapter 45 : Applying the SSC to Diagnose Systemic Dysfunction — 684

    Chapter 46 : Minalogy – From Sense-making to Meaning-Making — 693

    Chapter 47 : From Desire to Direction – The Sources of Intention — 713

    Chapter 48 : The Flow of Coherence – From Meaning to Action — 721

    Chapter 49 : The Architecture of Fulfilment – The Fulfilment Pyramid — 740

    Chapter 50 : Gauging Authentic Sustainability — 768

    Chapter 51 : The Reconstructive Ontology of Sustainability (ROS) — 791

    Chapter 52 : From Vision to Blueprint – Designing Sustainable Futures — 805

Part VIII : From Plan to Practice – Executing Authentic Sustainability — 839

    Chapter 53 : From Blueprint to Practice – The Leap into Action — 842

    Chapter 54 : Leveraging the UOSI – The Compass of Execution — 856

Chapter 55 : Measuring What Matters –
        The Sustainability Profile   867

Chapter 56 : Executing Transformation –
        The Methodology in Practice   890

Chapter 57 : Modulation and Mastering Transitions   901

Chapter 58 : Expanding Sustainability – The Ripple Effect   917

Chapter 59 : Coherence by Design – Applying the ASF   937

Chapter 60 : Leveraging the ASF as a Systemic Lens
        for Analysis and Renewal   949

Epilogue : The Bright Horizon –
        Humanity Beyond Sustainabilism   981

APPENDIX : Authentic Sustainability Framework White Paper   989

Background   991

Summary – How this Work was Developed   993

Introduction   999

Philosophical Grounding and Practical Imperative   1002

Insights from Ontometric Data and Practitioner Dialogue   1004

Integration with the Existing Body of Work   1007

The Program Context   1012

Research Methodology and Approach   1023

Data Gathering and Iterative Refinement   1028

Testing the Sustainability Profile (Ontometric Tool)   1032

The Nature of the Work – Philosophy Meets Phenomenology   1036

Beyond the Program – Broader Validation   1044

Global Sustainability Literature and Practitioner Discourse   1049

Distinction from 'Sustainabilism'   1052

Conclusion – A Work in Motion   1056

References   1061

About the Author   1066

Pathways to Further Exploration   1068

PART I

Humanity at a Crossroads

Every age has faced challenges, but rarely has humanity stood so starkly at a crossroads. The crises of our time are not isolated events to be solved in silos. They are entangled and systemic, reverberating across ecological, political, economic, cultural and personal domains. What makes this moment decisive is not just the scale of these challenges, but the way they converge, amplify one another and expose fractures in the very systems we created to sustain us.

Part I of this book explores the conditions that brought us here. It examines the forces that destabilise trust, corrode integrity and entrench dysfunction, often beneath the surface of everyday life. From the unseen influence of shadows to the self-perpetuating cycle of systemic subversion, these chapters unpack how crises are compounded when bad faith, dishonesty and denial shape our responses. Alongside this, we trace the paradigms – economic, cultural and intellectual – that have too often prescribed shallow versions of sustainability, neglecting the deeper structures required for genuine renewal.

This part of the book is not simply an inventory of problems. It is a map of distortions and illusions – from the false comforts of traditional economics to the seductions of postmodern critique – that must be confronted if we are to navigate towards authentic sustainability. Each chapter illuminates another dimension of the crossroads we face, revealing both the costs of ignoring systemic shadows and the possibilities that emerge when we begin to engage with integrity, authenticity and intention.

By the end of Part I, the aim is not only to understand the weight of this moment, but also to see more clearly the responsibility that rests with each of us. The choice before humanity is not abstract. It is immediate, personal and systemic: either we remain trapped in the patterns that sustain dysfunction, or we step into the possibility of authentic sustainability – a path that requires us to see, name and transform the forces shaping our shared future.

CHAPTER 1

The Weight of the Moment

We are living through a moment heavy with consequence. The signs of fracture are everywhere: ecological systems pushed past their limits, widening inequalities, escalating conflicts and the quiet erosion of meaning that leaves cultures adrift. These are not abstract headlines. They are conditions shaping our daily lives and futures.

But what makes this moment so precarious isn't just the crises themselves. It's our collective disconnection from reality. An unsettling cocktail of denial, bad faith – where stated intentions are distorted, masking self-interest, coercion or avoidance of responsibility – inauthenticity and systemic dishonesty turns challenges into catastrophes. We are not simply facing dysfunction; we are entangled in it, often unconsciously reinforcing structures that exacerbate suffering. Shadows left unexamined do not just linger; they compound and solidify into entrenchment, ensuring dysfunction is sustained rather than confronted.

And yet, the very weight of this moment also reveals our capacity to act differently. Seeing the distortions clearly – and confronting the illusion that systems govern us rather than recognising our role in shaping them – opens the door to recalibration. This chapter begins by facing the gravity of where we are and the responsibility that clarity demands.

Imagine you're driving a car speeding towards dangerous terrain, yet instead of adjusting course, you're busy working out which playlist fits the moment: classical for the drama, rock for the rebellion, or maybe jazz, because nothing says 'graceful descent into chaos' quite like a smooth saxophone solo. Doesn't make sense, does it? And yet, humanity's perfect storm stems, in great part, from our refusal to confront crises with clarity and integrity. And the irony? Many of the systems we created to address these problems – states, governments, corporations, educational institutions and so on – frequently amplify rather than mitigate them. Without intentional recalibration, dysfunction becomes industrial in scale.

The ripple effects of avoidance

The consequences of avoidance are both immediate and long-term. Rising sea levels don't just threaten to swallow distant islands – they could engulf entire cities, displacing millions and turning homes into histories lost beneath the tide. So, it's not just physical landscapes at risk. Entire cultures face erasure as communities are uprooted and traditions dissolve with them.

Look closer and you'll see the erosion of something even more fragile: trust. Trust in institutions, leaders and even in each other is disintegrating. Corruption scandals, corporate greed and political polarisation gnaw away at our collective faith, leaving behind a society where cynicism and disengagement become the norm. The more fractured our trust becomes, the more dysfunction takes root, unless actively confronted through intentional recalibration and structural renewal. Misery is not just the consequence of dysfunction – it is the state that ensures dysfunction continues as individuals and systems become trapped in cycles of stagnation, distorted certainty and avoidance.

We are not just innocent bystanders to these crises. We are active participants. And yet, as humans, we are masters of avoidance. It is deeply ingrained in us to seek comfort and defer pain. We distract ourselves with the latest streaming series, bury ourselves in endless work or lose hours to mindless scrolling, not realising that the shadows we refuse to face don't disappear. They multiply. They become the silent architects of even greater dysfunction. Ironically, avoidance fuels the very crises we fear, making their resolution more difficult, until intervention or realignment disrupts the cycle. This is the cycle of misery – a condition that is not merely felt, but structurally reinforced, ensuring that suffering remains a lived experience rather than a momentary state, especially when the cycle of misery becomes entrenched.

The collapse of meaning

Meaninglessness has quietly emerged as a silent yet profoundly destructive force in the modern world. This gradual collapse of meaning permeates both individual and societal life, driving disconnection, apathy and conflict. Without a strong sense of significance to anchor life, people and communities become untethered, struggling to find purpose amid a relentless pace of change. While meaninglessness may appear as a subtle malaise, its systemic impact is both deep and wide-reaching. It can cause various underlying issues, from fractured communities to mental health crises and global tensions.

Though the phenomenon of meaninglessness is not new, its scale and intensity have grown in response to rapid societal transformations. Hyper-consumerism, technological dependency and the drive for short-term gratification have widened the gap between human aspirations and the systems meant to support them. In this landscape of transient distractions, individuals risk becoming trapped in cycles of alienation, discontent and existential confusion.

At the heart of this collapse lies a crisis of alignment between values, goals and actions. Modern life often promotes decisions driven by external pressures – social status, material gain and surface-level validation – rather than grounded principles or axiomatic laws.[18] Over time, these misaligned pursuits accumulate, leaving individuals and institutions disconnected from their core purpose.

---

18 Axiomatic laws are deep truths that don't need to be invented or agreed upon. They reveal themselves through life. When trust is broken, systems collapse. When integrity is absent, dysfunction follows. These aren't social rules; they are foundational patterns that govern the sustainability of all human systems.

For example, professionals may dedicate decades to career advancement, achieving financial success and societal recognition, only to find themselves feeling numb and empty. Despite outward achievements, they experience a void of purpose, realising that their authentic aspirations have been sacrificed in pursuit of externally imposed expectations.

This misalignment is mirrored at the institutional level. Systems that prioritise superficial metrics often exacerbate the disconnection and alienation experienced by individuals. For example, urban development projects may prioritise economic growth without considering the social impact on long-standing communities. Displacement, loss of identity and weakened community ties are frequent consequences of such initiatives.

Economic systems that prioritise GDP and profit over wellbeing contribute to ecological degradation, social fragmentation and inequity. The focus on short-term financial success neglects critical human needs such as cultural preservation, social trust and environmental stewardship. Consequently, trust in these systems deteriorates, as individuals perceive them as mechanisms of exploitation rather than progress.

Similarly, education systems that focus on the bottom line rather than holistic growth perpetuate disconnection. Students are often prepared to enter the workforce with limited attention to values, critical thinking and emotional wellbeing. As a result, many individuals excel professionally but lack the tools to navigate life's deeper existential challenges.

In the face of this collapse, many descend into nihilism, resigning from the inquiry altogether and abandoning the question of *'what does it all mean?'* Others, with equal fervour, sip the intoxicating brew of hedonism – a cocktail of radical pleasure-seeking that numbs but never nourishes, delivering stimulation without joy. Between these poles lies a wider multitude, grasping at ideologies in a fickle and lenient way as one might clutch a dummy or pacifier – not because it feeds them, but because it soothes for a moment, dulling the deeper hunger for meaning. These systemic failures create a reinforcing cycle, where short-term gains are prioritised at the expense of long-term purpose and sustainability. Without a foundation of shared meaning, societies become fragmented and vulnerable to division, extremism and manipulation.

It is here, with humility and without pretence of final answers, that the kind of inquiry undertaken in this work seeks to offer a different path: not a doctrine to swallow, but a framework for rediscovering coherence or integrity and the possibility of a life that is both purposeful and sustainable.

Materialism and the illusion of fulfilment

Materialism epitomises the consequences of meaninglessness. It seduces individuals with the promise that happiness and identity can be attained through the accumulation of possessions. Cultural norms and media reinforce this narrative, fostering an endless cycle of consumption and dissatisfaction.

Take the fashion industry as a case in point. Fast fashion encourages consumers to make frequent, impulsive purchases to remain fashionable. While this provides momentary gratification, it also leads to environmental degradation, exploitative labour practices and emotional emptiness. Clothes that once symbolised success quickly lose their appeal, prompting another round of consumption to fill the void.

Materialism reshapes not only consumption, but also self-worth. Individuals often equate their value with the ability to accumulate wealth and social status, leading to chronic comparison, insecurity and isolation. Instead of fostering deeper connections and wellbeing, this mindset drives people into an endless quest for external validation.

The struggle for wellbeing in a world of manufactured realities

Let's talk about the everyday struggles that touch all of us. You don't need to be an environmental scientist or a political activist to feel the cracks in the system. Think about your last power bill. Did it leave you shaking your head, wondering if you'd need a second job just to keep the lights on? Or maybe you've spent hours battling hidden fees from your bank or telecommunications provider, questioning when transparency became a relic of the past.

The issue here isn't just about material frustrations. It's also about dignity. We crave systems that honour fairness, transparency and justice. We long for transportation networks that work, healthcare that doesn't bankrupt us and groceries priced reasonably enough to nourish every family. Yet, for many, these aspirations remain just that – aspirations. Instead, we are trapped in a vortex of broken promises and systemic inefficiencies, caught between institutions that claim to serve us and realities that tell a different story.

And what about transparency? That was meant to be a cornerstone of public trust. But what happens when we can no longer distinguish transparency from surveillance? We are supposed to be private citizens, yet we have almost no privacy left. A lack of privacy has become normalised and we have been desensitised to this. Our data, thoughts and personal content are being manufactured, tracked and monetised. And we allow it to happen! Our lives are catalogued, sold and repurposed without our informed consent.

We don't even have clarity on where our taxes go. Are they funding education, healthcare and infrastructure? Or are they funnelling money into conflicts, corruption or even terrorism? In their sustainabilistic zeal, they even dared to raise the suggestion of taxing spare bedrooms – as if the air in an unused room were a planetary offence! The so-called public servants who were meant to govern on our behalf – where is their transparency? It appears to operate on a need-to-know basis. But somehow, we're never the ones who need to know. Transparency only miraculously resurfaces during election campaigns, when accountability becomes the word of the hour alongside grand promises of prosperity and reform. Then, as if transparency were allergic to daylight, it promptly vanishes again. Meanwhile, the public servants' personal wealth remains conveniently hidden while they demand absolute disclosure from the rest of us. Many act more like the ruling elite of the past – kings and aristocrats in everything but name.

And what about the media? It was supposed to deliver unbiased facts, enabling us to form our own opinions. But now, it is openly funded by interest groups, lobbyists, corporate backers and political agendas. Instead of presenting reality, it manufactures narratives

– cherry-picked, self-selected, carefully arranged half-truths and strategic omissions. The burden of extracting the truth now falls on us as we sift through a maze of opinions disguised as journalism.

If you're reading this with relief that it's *them* (the media, the corporations, the politicians) causing our woes, you're about to be disappointed. Because here's the catch: there is no *them*. This is about *us* – ourselves, our uncles and aunts, parents and children, friends, neighbours and colleagues. We are not merely passive outsiders to the system. We give it life, shape it, participate in it and reinforce it. The dysfunction we see is not some distant force; it's woven into the fabric of our collective decisions, actions and inactions. There's no point resenting any of this. That in itself has its own consequences.

Resentment: A hidden force with widespread impact

Resentment is a powerful undercurrent that shapes both individual lives and societal dynamics in profound ways. Born from unresolved grievances, unmet expectations and perceived injustices, it fosters a narrative of blame that isolates individuals and groups in cycles of hostility and division. Left unchecked, resentment corrodes relationships, stifles collaboration and obstructs meaningful progress, becoming a significant barrier to achieving a harmonious and flourishing existence.

Resentment is unique in how it anchors people to the past. It ties them to moments of pain and injustice, compelling them to relive those experiences and reinforcing negative perceptions. This attachment impedes emotional and cognitive flexibility, preventing both individuals and societies from moving forward and creating new possibilities. When resentment becomes entrenched, it gives rise to lasting patterns of dysfunction and alienation. It also serves as fertile ground for manipulation by opportunistic leaders and institutions.

The individual cost: Stagnation, isolation and lost potential

At a personal level, resentment manifests as bitterness, a distorted lens that alters how individuals perceive and respond to their circumstances. This fixation on perceived slights or injustices traps people in cycles of negativity and stagnation, emotionally anchoring them to grievances and preventing them from engaging fully with the present or envisioning a hopeful future.

Imagine an individual who feels undervalued at their workplace. Over time, resentment festers as they dwell on every perceived insult, snub or inequity. Their outlook becomes tainted, shaping how they interpret interactions with colleagues and supervisors, reinforcing their sense of victimhood. Rather than seeking resolution through constructive dialogue, they withdraw emotionally, becoming increasingly disengaged and alienated. This detachment diminishes their opportunities for collaboration, recognition and growth.

The same pattern unfolds in intimate relationships and family dynamics. When one partner or family member feels unseen or unappreciated, unresolved feelings can quietly harden into bitterness. Everyday moments become coloured by suspicion or defensiveness, and gestures of care may be overlooked or misinterpreted. Instead of fostering connection through honest conversation, they may retreat, creating emotional distance that weakens trust and intimacy over time.

The psychological toll of resentment is considerable. It hinders self-reflection and personal development by externalising blame. When individuals become consumed by the belief that others are solely responsible for their dissatisfaction, they lose the opportunity to examine their own role in perpetuating negative patterns. This avoidance fosters a self-reinforcing cycle of blame, where growth is sacrificed for self-justification.

Furthermore, unresolved resentment has tangible effects on health. Various studies show that chronic negative emotions contribute to stress-related conditions such as high blood pressure, suppressed immune systems and heart disease.[19] Studies have also shown that

---

19 Brosschot, J. F., Pieper, S., & Thayer, J. F. (2005) The Perseverative Cognition Hypothesis: Prolonged Activation and Worry as Mediators of Stress-related Illness, *Journal of Psychosomatic Research*, 58(1), pp.163–169. Ravi, M., Miller, A. H., & Michopoulos, V. (2021) Immunology of Stress and the Impact of Inflammation on the Brain and Behaviour, *BJPsych Advances*, 27(3), pp. 158–165.

the inability to forgive or release past grievances leads to prolonged psychological strain, exacerbating anxiety, depression and social isolation.[20] This emotional burden reduces a person's capacity for creativity, empathy and mental resilience.

The societal toll: Division, polarisation and instability

On a societal scale, resentment operates as a potent destabilising force. It often stems from historical grievances, systemic inequities and power imbalances, creating fertile ground for collective resentment. Opportunistic actors – whether political leaders, media outlets or interest groups – exploit this sentiment to consolidate power or advance divisive agendas. As a result, polarisation deepens, mistrust proliferates and collaboration becomes increasingly difficult.

Consider societies where historical injustices, such as colonialism, racial discrimination or economic exploitation, have not been adequately addressed. Marginalised groups may harbour deep resentment towards those in positions of power, while dominant groups may feel defensive or threatened by calls for equity and inclusion. This cycle of blame and defensiveness prevents meaningful dialogue and perpetuates division.

Divisive rhetoric exacerbates these dynamics. The media often thrives on framing issues through an 'us versus them' narrative. Social media echo chambers further reinforce resentment, amplifying hostility and mistrust. In extreme cases, these tensions erupt into widespread unrest, violence and institutional instability.

History is filled with examples of resentment-driven conflict. After World War I, the Treaty of Versailles imposed severe reparations on Germany, sowing deep resentment that was compounded by widespread economic hardship and social dislocation. These conditions created fertile ground for extremism and, eventually, World War II. While multiple factors contributed to this outcome, unresolved resentment and systemic inequities played a decisive role. The violent break-up of Yugoslavia in the 1990s illustrated how suppressed

---

20   Kim, I.-B., Lee, J.-H., & Park, S.-C. (2022). *The Relationship between Stress, Inflammation, and Depression.* Biomedicines, 10(8), p.1929.

ethnic grievances and territorial disputes, once inflamed, could lead to cycles of mass violence, displacement and instability. Similarly, unresolved ethnic and territorial disputes across the world continue to fuel cycles of violence and division.

The ripple effects of resentment

As you can see, resentment is not confined to individuals or isolated communities. Its influence extends into institutions, organisations and global systems.

- In **workplaces**, resentment between employees and management creates toxic environments where collaboration, innovation and productivity suffer. Leaders who ignore grievances often find themselves presiding over disengaged, fractured teams.
- **Globally**, resentment fuels distrust in international institutions. Nations that have historically experienced economic exploitation often view international agreements as mechanisms of dominance rather than opportunities for genuine cooperation.
- In **geopolitical conflicts**, historical resentment over land, resources and cultural suppression continues to spark diplomatic breakdowns and regional instability, which can escalate into long-term geopolitical crises.

Resentment may be the emotional residue of perceived injustice, but it also signals something deeper: a breakdown in structural coherence. When individuals, communities and systems feel betrayed, ignored or manipulated, they don't just react emotionally; they begin to fragment. And this fragmentation, if left unaddressed, becomes a silent force of disintegration that corrodes trust, erodes integrity and undermines the very foundations of sustainable coexistence.

Fragmentation and systemic disintegration

Before we can reclaim our values and align our systems with authentic sustainability, we must confront a deeper and more elusive threat – fragmentation and systemic disintegration. Fragmentation occurs when individuals, institutions and societies become disconnected from a coherent sense of purpose, identity or truth. It shows up as misalignment between values and actions, between aspirations and behaviours, and between inner convictions and outer conformity. And it is this fragmentation that silently feeds systemic disintegration.

The notion of fragmentation is not unique to this discourse; it has deep roots in other fields. In ecology, fragmentation is recognised as a threat to biodiversity and resilience, typically examined through three lenses: structural fragmentation, the physical division of a continuous whole; functional fragmentation, where the coordinated operation of system components breaks down despite structural links remaining; and informational fragmentation, where disrupted flows create isolated pools of knowledge that hinder collective response.[21] Network science studies similar patterns through metrics of cohesion, modularity and connectivity.[22] Likewise, governance studies highlight 'governance fragmentation' as a growing concern in addressing global challenges.[23] These diverse perspectives all converge on a single truth: fragmentation weakens coherence, making systems brittle, misaligned and prone to collapse.

You can see it in:

- **Individuals** who project success while feeling empty inside,
- **Institutions** that promote wellbeing while burning out their own people, and
- **Governments** that speak of integrity while enacting policies rooted in fear, short-termism and control.

Fragmentation is not simply personal confusion; it is a structural condition that erodes meaning and coherence across every level of

---

21   Fahrig, L. (2003) 'Effects of Habitat Fragmentation on Biodiversity', *Annual Review of Ecology, Evolution, and Systematics*, 34, pp. 487–515.

22   Newman, M.E.J. (2010) *Networks: An Introduction*. Oxford: Oxford University Press.

23   Biermann, F., Pattberg, P., van Asselt, H. and Zelli, F. (2009) 'The Fragmentation of Global Governance Architectures: A framework for Analysis', *Global Environmental Politics*, 9(4), pp. 14–40; Tosun, J. and Peters, B.G. (2018) 'Intergovernmental Organizations' Normative Discourses in the Global Energy Transition: The International Energy Agency and the International Renewable Energy Agency', *Energy Research & Social Science*, 41, pp. 83–91.

life. At its core, it fractures the relationship between sentience and society: between our deep, inner awareness and the structures we co-create. We lose not only our connection to truth but our capacity to integrate it. And without integration, values, systems and people become performative. We mimic, echo and conform – not out of conviction, but out of fear, fatigue or a desperate need to belong.

This leads to systemic disintegration: a state where systems collapse, not just because they are flawed but because they are hollow. Their foundations of trust, purpose and coherence have eroded. And when systems disintegrate, so too does the possibility of genuine sustainability. You cannot sustain what has already lost its structural integrity.

Disintegration also masks itself in seemingly functional systems. An education system may produce graduates, but if it disempowers critical thought and creativity, it is dysfunctional. A business may generate profits, but if it does so by exploiting people or the planet, it is eroding at its core. A society may function on paper, but if it runs on fear, division or false narratives, it is already unravelling beneath the surface.

If sustainability is to be more than a slogan – if it is to become a lived reality – it must begin with reintegration: the restoration of coherence between our inner awareness, our shared values and the systems we shape. Otherwise, no matter how much we optimise or innovate, we will simply be reinforcing the fragmentation that led us here.

The erosion of structural integrity is not always obvious. Many of the systems we rely on still appear to be delivering results – providing education, administering healthcare, enforcing policy, and so on. But outcomes alone can be misleading. When underlying dynamics are misaligned with human values, even seemingly successful systems can become engines of harm. This brings us to the hidden architecture of systemic dysfunction.

Systemic dysfunction: When structure betrays purpose

Fragmented systems don't always look broken. In fact, many appear to be functioning smoothly, including the generation of healthy profits. But beneath the appearance of order, something is off. When systems lose coherence with human values, their very structure becomes part of the problem.

Systemic dysfunction arises when the structures designed to support human flourishing perpetuate harm and disconnection instead. In modern societies, this dysfunction often remains hidden beneath layers of complexity, disguised by the language of progress, efficiency and success. Institutions – whether in government, business or education – may outwardly appear functional but suffer internally from entrenched misalignments that undermine trust, authenticity and collective wellbeing.

This section explores two major patterns of dysfunction: the tyranny of metrics and the collapse of trust capital. Each reveals how distorted systems can reinforce fragmentation and erode our collective capacity to thrive.

The tyranny of metrics: When numbers govern meaning

Modern systems are increasingly governed by metrics: quantifiable outputs designed to measure performance, efficiency and progress. While data-driven approaches offer important insights, overreliance on measurable outcomes has led to a distortion of meaning and priorities. This phenomenon creates environments where what can be measured is prioritised over what truly matters.

In organisations, key performance indicators (KPIs) and productivity metrics frequently become proxies for success. For example, a healthcare institution may prioritise reducing patient wait times over improving quality of care. Educational systems may focus on test scores rather than critical thinking and creativity. While metrics provide a sense of control and accountability, they fail to capture the nuanced, long-term aspects of human development and wellbeing.

This fixation on metrics often leads to unintended consequences. Employees may manipulate data or prioritise short-term targets at the expense of ethical decision-making. Leaders under pressure to deliver measurable success may cut corners or neglect areas that cannot be quantified, such as workplace morale, organisational culture or community wellbeing. In a metrics-driven culture, people internalise the belief that their worth is defined by quantifiable achievements, leading to anxiety, perfectionism and fear of failure. This reductionist mindset creates a world where numbers dictate value, distorting the broader purpose of institutions, organisations and individual aspirations.

The collapse of trust capital: Eroding the foundations of collaboration

Trust is the invisible currency that underpins all human systems. It enables cooperation, innovation and resilience in the face of challenges. However, in many modern systems, trust capital – the accumulated reservoir of trust within a relationship, organisation or society – is in decline, eroded by dynamics that prioritise productivity over relationships. This collapse creates environments of suspicion, competition and disengagement, undermining both individual and collective performance.

One of the most significant factors in the erosion of trust capital is the commodification of human relationships. Many workplaces treat employees as interchangeable resources, reinforcing practices such as:

- Excessive micromanagement
- Arbitrary performance reviews
- Hierarchical control over collaboration

As a result, employees feel dehumanised and disconnected from their organisation's mission, leading to lower engagement, higher turnover and declining morale.

Beyond workplaces, societal trust capital is further compromised by:

- Misinformation and polarisation
- Government failures in transparency and accountability
- Perceived corporate exploitation

Citizens lose faith in political leaders, media outlets and regulatory bodies when these institutions fail to demonstrate fairness. Once trust capital is depleted, it becomes increasingly difficult to rebuild, leaving people sceptical of any initiative claiming to prioritise the common good.

The erosion of trust capital is particularly evident in crises. During events such as economic downturns, natural disasters and public health emergencies, systems with high trust capital are better able to mobilise resources, coordinate responses and maintain social cohesion. In contrast, the erosion of trust capital leads to fragmentation, delays and internal conflict, worsening the very crises institutions are meant to address.

The dynamics of trust creation and disintegration

Trust is both fragile and dynamic. It is built over time through consistent actions that demonstrate integrity, competence and care. However, it can be rapidly destroyed by:

- **A lack of transparency**: Withholding information breeds suspicion and fear.
- **Inconsistent leadership**: Leaders who fail to uphold commitments weaken confidence in governance.
- **Exploitation of power**: When institutions prioritise self-interest, they weaken the social contract that sustains trust.
- **Inauthenticity:** When perception, words, or motives are distorted or merely performative rather than congruent with reality, relationships fracture and trust quickly erodes.

Conversely, trust can be strengthened through:

- Transparent communication: Clear and timely information-sharing.
- Consistency and integrity: Aligning words with actions.
- Empowerment and inclusion: Encouraging participation and shared decision-making.
- Authenticity: Relating with coherence between inner stance, perception and outward expression – engaging reality as it is, without distortion or sentimentality, and ensuring that alignment is lived rather than performed.

Organisations with high trust capital experience stronger employee engagement, customer loyalty and adaptability. Similarly, societies with strong trust networks are more resilient and collaborative in the face of change.

Balancing productivity and relationships

The collapse of trust capital highlights a fundamental tension between productivity and relationships. In many systems, the pursuit of efficiency and output comes at the expense of human connection and wellbeing. This trade-off is neither inevitable nor sustainable. Long-term success depends on integrating both dimensions, recognising that relationships are essential to meaningful and enduring performance.

This integration is evident in how effective teams and societies function:

- **Teams with high psychological safety** – where members feel respected, valued and able to take risks – outperform those driven by competitive pressures alone.
- **Organisations that prioritise employee wellbeing** experience higher retention, innovation and overall performance.
- **Societies that invest in trust-building policies** – such as equitable healthcare, education and justice systems – experience greater stability and prosperity.

Trust capital functions as a multiplier, enhancing the effectiveness of systems and enabling them to achieve their goals sustainably. But when trust capital erodes, even the most sophisticated systems falter. Collaboration breaks down, motivation declines and the pursuit of shared goals becomes fractured and fragile.

Confronting shadows to reclaim values

What drives all this dysfunction? Shadows. Examined in detail in the coming chapters, shadows aren't just poetic abstractions. They're the unseen distortions that quietly steer our thoughts, decisions and systems towards dysfunction – like a faulty compass that keeps pointing us towards disaster. But dysfunction doesn't thrive in isolation. It is the lack of clear, aligned intention, the erosion of trust, the loss of sovereignty and the disintegration of an embodied way of being that allows shadows to run the show. When integrity is missing, dysfunction fills the gap like weeds taking over an untended garden. Governments betray the trust of their citizens, organisations prioritise profits over people and individuals become prisoners of resentment, complaints and blame. Left unchecked, shadows corrode not just institutions, but the very foundation of a coherent and thriving civilisation.

It's up to each and every one of us to confront those shadows with unwavering resolve. Only then can we revive values often dismissed as archaic – integrity, virtue and honour. Far from being quaint relics of a bygone era, these values are anchors that ground us in authenticity and truth. They are the antidote to disconnection, manipulation and dysfunction. They are essential if we are to navigate the complexities of our world with clarity and conviction.

Nothing erodes more quickly than values when convenience, fear or self-interest demand their sacrifice. A state may claim to uphold justice, human rights or democracy. Yet to maintain alliances with powerful actors, it may turn a blind eye when its ally commits atrocities. It may justify violations of its core principles for the sake of diplomacy or economic gain. However, an ally without accountability eventually becomes a liability.

This isn't just about states. We see the same pattern at every level of human life. We subscribe to political parties, ideologies, academia, media or religious institutions, even when they betray the very values they claim to represent. We justify our silence in the face of corruption, cruelty or dysfunction – not because we support it, but because challenging it feels inconvenient and overwhelming. Often, many don't know where to start, so they give up before even trying. Even in our intimate relationships, we may submit to violence, coercion or manipulation just to avoid looking bad, to fit in, or to maintain a fragile sense of belonging.

We tell ourselves we're being diplomatic, loyal or pragmatic. But in reality, our actions or inactions are often negligence, naivety or conformity disguised as virtue. And this is how values erode – not through sudden, dramatic betrayals, but through the small, quiet compromises we make every day. But here's the catch. The erosion of values starts within. The dysfunctions we observe externally mirror the fragmentation within ourselves. If we cannot confront the dissonance between who we are and how we live, we will continue to perpetuate the very dysfunctions we decry. Fortunately, the renewal of values also starts within. Change does not begin with dismantling the external world. It begins by bringing light to the shadows within ourselves.

The profound interconnectedness of global and personal issues

It's easy to feel overwhelmed, powerless and disarmed in the face of large-scale crises. After all, what can one person do in the face of war, corruption or environmental collapse? However, global and personal issues are deeply interconnected. Decisions made in the corridors of power ripple outward, shaping our homes, workplaces and relationships. At the same time, the choices we make – what we consume, how we vote and how we treat others – feed back into those larger systems. So, it turns out we can do something.

Take climate action, for example. Policies to curb carbon emissions are critical, but so are the everyday choices we make about resource consumption, sustainability and accountability. Together, these actions – systemic and individual – shape the future. Recognising this interconnectedness is both daunting and empowering. It reveals that we are not passive spectators in history. We are co-creators of the world in which we live.

Reflection

Take a moment to reflect on the following:

1. **Where do you see avoidance in your own life?**

   - Are there uncomfortable truths – personal or societal – that you have ignored, deferred or rationalised away?
   - What fears, conveniences or habits keep you from confronting them?

2. **In what ways are you reinforcing dysfunction?**
   - Are there systems, institutions or relationships where you conform to practices you know are unsustainable, unjust or misaligned with your values?
   - What would it take for you to challenge them, even in small ways?

3. **How do you engage with information?**
   - Do you critically question the information you consume, or do you accept convenient narratives without deeper scrutiny?
   - How might you cultivate a greater commitment to truth in how you seek information?

Life is not just a personal journey. It is inseparable from the structures and forces that shape us. As sentient beings, we do not exist in isolation. Our awareness, choices and sense of purpose are deeply intertwined with the societies we inhabit. The tension between self-realisation and social responsibility is not a flaw; it is a defining aspect of our existence. If we are to move towards a truly sustainable future, we must first understand the forces that govern this dynamic – how human sentience creates both extraordinary opportunities and profound burdens.

CHAPTER 2

Sentience and Society

At the heart of the human condition lies a fascinating paradox: we are sentient beings, capable of complex thought, analysis, imagination and reflection. And yet we are also profoundly social creatures, shaped by and shaping the world around us. These two aspects of our nature – sentience and social interconnectedness – define us as human beings. They offer us extraordinary opportunities for meaning, purpose and growth. But they also create a profound tension. How do we honour our individuality while fulfilling our responsibilities to the collective?

Often celebrated as the crown jewel of human existence, sentience enables us to not only survive, but continuously refine and expand our engagement with existence. It enables us to contemplate life's purpose, envision a better future and leave a meaningful legacy. But with this gift comes a burden: a responsibility to navigate our social environments with integrity and intentionality. Ignore either one – our inner world or our obligations to others – and we risk tilting towards fragmentation, where dysfunction slowly takes root.

We see this struggle everywhere. Consider the overworked executive who neglects their family in the pursuit of professional success. The result? Material wealth, status and a collection of unread self-help books combined with an aching sense of alienation and lost time with loved ones that no bonus package can ever buy back. Or think of the person who sacrifices every personal dream to serve others, only to find themselves trapped in chronic burnout and resentment.

The tension created by this struggle between self-realisation and social responsibility is not a flaw. It is a defining characteristic of our species. And it is within this balancing act that we discover who we truly are and, more importantly, how we can create a world that reflects our highest aspirations.

The paradoxes of performance

Human beings have always strived to perform: to push boundaries, achieve greatness and leave a lasting legacy. However, this quest for excellence is fraught with paradoxes. While performance is often framed as a pathway to fulfilment, recognition and self-actualisation, it can also become a source of profound dysfunction.

When performance is driven by fear, the need for external validation or misaligned aspirations, it leads to burnout, anxiety and disconnection from intrinsic values. Modern culture reinforces these contradictions through relentless demands for productivity, perfection and constant self-optimisation. Let's explore four core paradoxes that undermine human performance, revealing how they contribute to cycles of frustration, disillusionment and underachievement.

1. **The performance paradox: When fear undermines flourishing**

    The first paradox lies in the relationship between ambition and wellbeing. Conventional wisdom suggests that ambition fuels success, and that greater performance leads to greater rewards. Yet when ambition is rooted in fear – fear of failure, irrelevance or inadequacy – it often has the opposite effect.

    Individuals consumed by fear-driven ambition push themselves beyond healthy limits, sacrificing wellbeing in the process. They become trapped in cycles of overwork and diminishing returns, where greater effort yields less satisfaction. Over time, this paradox erodes creativity, collaboration and resilience – the very qualities essential to sustainable performance.

Consider a leader driven by the fear of appearing weak. To compensate, they micromanage their team, over-exert control and demand constant perfection. Ironically, this insecurity stifles trust, autonomy and innovation, making it harder for the team to perform at their best. The anxiety created by fear-based ambition ultimately undermines the very success it seeks to secure.

This 'win at all costs' mentality has become one of the most corrosive features of modern performance culture. It treats exhaustion as a badge of honour and sacrifice as proof of commitment, even when the sacrifice is wellbeing, relationships or integrity itself. In such environments, individuals push themselves and others to the brink, mistaking burnout for dedication. Systems and organisations built on this logic may deliver short-term victories, but they hollow out the very structures needed for long-term resilience. A culture obsessed with winning at all costs eventually loses sight of what is worth winning in the first place.

The antidote to this paradox lies in cultivating a mindset of abundance rather than scarcity. This shift involves embracing failure as a learning opportunity, valuing progress over perfection and decoupling self-worth from external validation. By reframing performance as a journey of growth rather than a relentless race, individuals can sustain their ambition without compromising their wellbeing.

2. **The burden of becoming: The exhaustion of endless self-improvement**

The second paradox emerges from the cultural obsession with self-improvement. While growth is an essential part of life, modern society has distorted this principle, turning it into an unrelenting pursuit of an ever-elusive ideal. Individuals are bombarded with messages urging them to optimise every aspect of their lives: career, health, relationships, finances, productivity and more.

This burden of becoming creates a sense of perpetual inadequacy. No matter how much one achieves, there is always a higher standard to reach, a new goal to conquer. Rather than empowering, this pressure leads to exhaustion, self-doubt and disillusionment. People find themselves asking, 'When will I finally be enough?'

The paradox is that self-improvement – intended to enhance life – often diminishes it by fostering a sense of chronic insufficiency. Individuals lose touch with their intrinsic worth, becoming trapped in cycles of self-criticism and comparison.

Breaking free from this paradox requires shifting from extrinsic to intrinsic motivation. Growth must be seen not as a linear climb, but as a dynamic interplay of reflection, learning and renewal. Cultivating self-compassion and celebrating incremental progress alongside occasional, more ambitious leaps of transformation supports most individuals to sustain their growth without falling into the trap of endless striving – unless their chosen path requires the pursuit of excellence, where sustained discipline and commitment become essential.

3. **The illusion of mastery: Superficial achievement versus deep expertise**

In an era of instant information and rapid success, mastery has become both more accessible and more elusive. Many people chase the appearance of mastery, accumulating titles, certifications and accolades without fully committing to the long, often arduous process of deep expertise.

Superficial mastery is encouraged by societal structures that prioritise efficiency, immediate results and short-term success. Educational and professional systems reward people for meeting benchmarks rather than for fostering critical thinking, curiosity and sustained inquiry. As a result, individuals may rise quickly in their careers, only to later encounter limitations due to shallow expertise.

In contrast, true mastery requires:

- **Humility**, acknowledging gaps in knowledge and embracing the learning process.
- **Patience**, understanding that expertise takes time and effort.
- **A commitment to continuous learning**, rather than relying on a fixed set of credentials.

4. **Performance by proxy: The erosion of intrinsic motivation**

The final paradox involves the loss of intrinsic motivation through performance by proxy. This occurs when individuals adopt goals and behaviours that reflect external expectations rather than their authentic desires. Over time, they become disconnected from their true purpose, leading to emotional exhaustion and disengagement. This erosion echoes what Self-Determination Theory highlights: when autonomy, competence and relatedness are undermined, intrinsic motivation withers.[24]

Performance by proxy is particularly prevalent in highly standardised environments. For example:

- Students may prioritise grades over genuine learning, memorising facts rather than developing understanding.
- Employees may focus on meeting arbitrary performance targets, sacrificing creativity and innovation.
- Artists, writers or entrepreneurs may tailor their work solely to market trends, losing touch with their original passion.

This misalignment creates a cycle of demotivation and underperformance, as people struggle to find meaning in their work. Reclaiming intrinsic motivation involves reconnecting with personal values,

---

[24] Deci, E.L. and Ryan, R.M. (1985) *Intrinsic Motivation and Self-Determination in Human Behavior.* New York: Springer Science & Business Media. https://doi.org/10.1007/978-1-4899-2271-7; Ryan, R.M. and Deci, E.L. (2000) 'Self-Determination Theory and the Facilitation of Intrinsic Motivation, Social Development, and Well-being', *American Psychologist*, 55(1), pp. 68–78. https://doi.org/10.1037/0003-066X.55.1.68

cultivating curiosity and giving ourselves permission to redefine success on our own terms.

Each of these paradoxes reflects the deeper ontological tension explored in this chapter: how to remain true to oneself while fulfilling social roles and expectations. Performance, in all its forms, becomes the crucible in which this tension is tested. By confronting these paradoxes with honesty and courage, we move closer to the kind of coherence that honours both our sentience and our shared humanity.

Navigating circumstance and choice

Life can sometimes feel like a story written by forces beyond our control. We are each born into specific circumstances – a family, culture and environment – that shape our early experiences. Our thoughts and emotions can seem to arise uninvited and without warning, influenced by trauma, genetics and social conditioning. These forces can be powerful, even overwhelming, making it easy to see ourselves as passive participants in an ongoing drama.

Yet here lies a crucial reality: while we may not be able to choose our circumstances, we have the power to shape how we *respond* to them. This is the essence of agency and ownership, not as burdens, but as opportunities for self-empowerment.

In the Being Framework, one of the defining qualities of Being is responsibility, but not as a weight to carry. Rather, responsibility, as a way of being, means that we are 'response-able': we possess the ability to respond. No matter how dire our situation, we are never completely without choice. Ownership, in this sense, is not about blame or guilt. It is about recognising that, even in the face of adversity, we have the ability to reframe challenges, make meaningful choices and carve a path towards purpose.

The opposite of being response-able is being locked into victimhood: a state that, if left unexamined, can become self-reinforcing, deepening cycles of disempowerment. Sometimes this looks trivial, like 'accidentally' subscribing to yet another streaming service and then wondering why your bank account is slowly evaporating. But in more serious contexts, when we experience suffering – especially when it is profound, historical or deeply personal – it is tempting to anchor our identity in being the aggrieved party.

Victimhood offers a powerful psychological escape. It absolves us of responsibility and justifies cycles of resentment, retaliation or inaction. It allows us to externalise blame rather than confront the difficult question of how we choose to respond to injustice, hardship or oppression. While victimhood might offer temporary validation, in reality, it is a double-edged sword. When sustained over time, it transforms into entrenchment – a state where dysfunction no longer requires external reinforcement, but becomes self-sustaining, embedding disempowerment into identity, culture and institutions.

When an individual or a group remains trapped in the narrative of victimhood, it becomes a cycle that feeds itself – further conflict, deepening divisions and ensuring that misery remains the governing condition of their reality. Misery is not the result of suffering; it is the structure that sustains dysfunction, reinforcing entrenchment and ensuring suffering remains chronic rather than episodic. The past may shape us, but when we allow it to dictate our future, we surrender the very agency that defines our sentience.

Throughout history, we see countless examples of individuals, communities or nations who refused to succumb to victimhood despite adversity, oppression or hardship. They could have allowed their circumstances to define them. Instead, they chose ownership over despair, agency over resentment.

Viktor Frankl, a Holocaust survivor, endured unimaginable suffering in Nazi concentration camps, losing his family and facing constant dehumanisation. Yet, he refused to succumb to victimhood. In his book, *Man's Search for Meaning*,[25] Frankl argued that between stimulus and response lies our power to choose. Instead of surrendering to despair while imprisoned, he found purpose in helping fellow prisoners. He later developed logotherapy – a form of psychotherapy focused on the future and on our ability to endure hardship and suffering through a search for purpose – proving that even in extreme suffering, we can reclaim agency.

---

25   Frankl, V.E. (2004) *Man's Search for Meaning*. Rev. edn. London: Rider.

Similarly, Behrouz Boochani, an Iranian-Kurdish journalist who was imprisoned for years in Australia's offshore detention system on Manus Island, chose responsibility over victimhood. Rather than resigning to victimhood, Boochani documented his ordeal in *No Friend but the Mountains*,[26] smuggling the manuscript out via WhatsApp. His decision to go from being a victim to being responsible turned oppression into a powerful literary protest, ultimately earning him asylum and global recognition. Refusing to let injustice define him, he transformed his suffering into a force for change.

Many of the world's most influential leaders, thinkers and creators have shared this pattern, whether in politics, science, philosophy or the arts. They did not passively resign themselves to the roles or circumstances shaped by their past or environment. Instead, they engaged with these realities, modulating them into pathways for transformation. They reframed their narratives, embraced growth and used their experiences as catalysts for transformation. Their decisions not only shaped their own lives, but also inspired and uplifted others.

These examples embody the power of choosing response over reaction and victimhood, of owning our capacity to shape our future rather than being bound by our past. It is not about denying suffering; it's about refusing to be ruled by it.

Metacontent – The intellectual substrates for sense-making

Our capacity to respond is deeply shaped by the layers of metacontent we have access to. In the metacontent discourse, as explored in detail in *Metacontent – The intellectual substrates for sense-making*,[27] all content is embedded within a multi-layered reality. The way we interpret and engage with the world is not simply a matter of raw perception, but is shaped by metacontent – the contextual structures, stories, perspectives and paradigms that frame sense-making and understanding.

---

26   Boochani, B. (2018) *No Friend but the Mountains: Writing from Manus Prison*. Translated by O. Tofighian. Sydney: Picador.

27   Tashvir, A. (2024) *Metacontent: The Intellectual Substrates for Sense-making*. Sydney: Engenesis Publications.

In this sense, responsibility is not just about willpower; it's about sense-making. If we lack the right metacontent to develop our understanding and interpret reality, our ability to respond with clarity and alignment is limited. This is where the 'Nested Theory of Sense-making', as introduced and unpacked in *Metacontent*, is highly beneficial.

At the most immediate level, our **cognitive maps** – mental representations of how we perceive and navigate experiences (what things are for me) – shape our understanding of reality. From there, the **perspectives** we adopt – the angles or standpoints from which we approach an issue – influence what comes into focus and what remains unseen. Beyond that, the **stories** we inherit shape what we see as possible. Our **mental models** – internal frameworks that guide thinking, decision-making and interpretation of how things work – define how we engage with problems and opportunities. At an even broader level, the **paradigms** we adopt – dominant systems of thought within a domain that define what is considered valid knowledge and practice – determine how we structure our understanding of complex issues.

Notably, all of these layers rest upon a bedrock of context – the ground beneath sense-making. Context can be further broken down into factors, such as the era (timing in which something takes place), culture and environmental, subjective and intersubjective influences. These **contextual variables** play a major role in how we make sense of things. Ultimately, this comprehensive process of sense-making directs us to cultivate understanding through the use of cognitive tools, such as analysis, comparison, contemplation, dialogue and consensus, rather than relying solely on **initial insight** – the raw, immediate information apprehended at first glance.

So, the difference between victimhood and ownership is not just a matter of thinking positively. It's about having suitable, relevant and effective tools – like the Nested Theory of Sense-making – to reframe and engage with reality beyond its superficial, surface-level content. We often assume that everyone is trained and capable of thinking. However, what many refer to as 'thought' is often just an initial insight or a repetitive thought pattern rather than a well-polished, educated or credible conception of a fragment of reality or an idea.

Instead, a quick conclusion about the content in question is formed without engaging in a deeper inquiry to consider different perspectives, examine the surrounding narratives or even correctly identify which domain the topic belongs to. In many cases, people fail to even assess what the most relevant paradigm within that domain would be for making sense of the issue at hand.

For instance, those trapped in distorted metacontent (narratives of helplessness, ideological entrenchment or socially conditioned victimhood), find it nearly impossible to shift their orientation. Entrenchment operates at the level of metacontent distortion, ensuring that even when external conditions change, the internalised framework of dysfunction remains intact, shaping new experiences through the same distorted lens. Without an accurate and evolving metacontent structure, one's response to life becomes either rigid or reactive rather than intentional and adaptive. In contrast, those who refine their sense-making capacity by actively improving their cognitive maps and mental models are not bound by their initial conditions. They *expand* their ability for intentionality, reframing suffering as a catalyst for meaning rather than an inescapable fate.

For all the reasons outlined above, integrating the metacontent discourse into personal growth is not optional; it's essential if you want to be an active agent in your life rather than a victim. The ability to navigate adversity does not come from raw determination or sheer persistence alone, but from developing the cognitive, narrative and ontological tools to engage with reality authentically.

Beyond victimhood: becoming creators

Imagine an artist standing before a blank canvas. At first, the vast emptiness might feel overwhelming, much like the daunting challenges we face in life. Yet that same blank canvas holds infinite possibilities. With each stroke of paint, the artist transforms what was once nothing into something filled with meaning and beauty.

We, too, hold the capacity to create through the choices we make each day. Victimhood keeps us locked in reactivity, while creation moves us towards intentionality. A seemingly small act, like planting a tree or mentoring a colleague, can ripple outward in ways we may never fully comprehend. Take Martin Luther King Jr., whose decision to lead through nonviolent resistance in the face of injustice helped spark a movement that reshaped civil rights in America and inspired struggles for justice worldwide. On their own, his marches, speeches and acts of defiance might have seemed inadequate against entrenched systems of segregation and oppression. Yet they ignited a transformation of conscience and policy. In this way, he epitomises what it means to be a creator instead of a victim.

Stepping into the role of creator does not require grand, heroic gestures. It begins with cultivating intention, trust, freedom and an embodied way of being. Awareness of dysfunction, patterns or possibilities alone is not enough. What matters is how we translate that awareness into choices that reinforce coherence rather than perpetuate dysfunction. Recognising where your choices, beliefs and actions shape not just your personal experience, but the very structures in which you exist is the first step. The real challenge is ensuring that what you create is not merely a reaction to dysfunction but an intentional step towards integrity.

The past may have shaped us, but it does not have to define us. The creator's role is to make intentional, values-driven choices that transcend immediate circumstances. It's about recognising that, while we cannot singlehandedly solve the world's problems, our actions contribute to a larger collective shift. Every meaningful act reinforces the narrative that agency matters.

Choosing creation and responsibility over victimhood is not about denying suffering; it's refusing to be ruled by it. It's about choosing to engage with the world, not as a helpless by-product of history, but as an active force in shaping what comes next.

The social context of sentience

Human beings do not exist in isolation. Our wellbeing is profoundly shaped by the communities, institutions and cultural norms that surround us. At its best, society provides essential structures, such as healthcare, education and justice systems, to support individuals to thrive, not just survive. But when these systems become distorted by bad faith, misaligned intentions or self-serving agendas, they no longer fulfil their purpose. Instead of fostering growth, connection and integrity, they reinforce dysfunction.

Consider the current state of public discourse. Misinformation, polarisation and ideological echo chambers have eroded our ability to engage in constructive dialogue. At the heart of this dysfunction is not just the presence of 'bad' ideas, but the erosion of trust, intention and the sovereignty to engage meaningfully. When trust is broken, even the best ideas are met with scepticism. When intention is distorted, conversations become battlegrounds rather than explorations of truth. And when sovereignty is reduced to reactive defiance rather than the space for authentic engagement, discourse crumbles into hostility, leaving little room for nuance, reflection or the creative synthesis of various perspectives.

While intellectuals may treat their ideas as if they were safely contained within academic forums or theoretical debates, ideas rarely stay confined. Once released, they enter the public sphere, where they can be misunderstood, taken out of context or inflamed into social unrest and even bloodshed. This is not an argument against free expression, but a reminder that freedom of speech does not equate to freedom from consequence. Phenomenologically, the reality is that ideas live in the world and shape it, for better or worse. Responsibility therefore accompanies expression. Moreover, it is a mistake to assume that governments alone determine the bounds of free speech. In practice, no government holds absolute control over expression. The real measure lies in the tolerance of society itself – how willing a culture is to hold space for opposing ideas without collapsing into censorship or violence.

Take social media, for example. Once hailed as a tool for connection and free expression, it has become a breeding ground for outrage, oversimplification and performative virtue-signalling. The more nuanced a conversation, the less likely it is to gain traction in an environment that rewards speed, emotional reactivity and tribal allegiance over thoughtful inquiry. This climate has left many people believing it is safer to disengage entirely than to risk being misunderstood, attacked or ostracised.

Our sentience holds the key to change in this social context. Unlike any other species, we possess metacognition – the ability to think about our own thinking. This gives us the power to pause, reflect and consciously *choose* how we engage with the world. It is this inner awareness that allows us to break free from reactionary cycles and step into deliberate, thoughtful interaction.

By embracing empathy, humility and curiosity, we can rebuild spaces where dialogue thrives. Sentience, when used with intentionality and integrity, becomes more than just a cognitive advantage. It becomes a tool for bridging divides, restoring trust and reshaping society towards something more authentic and meaningful.

Sentience is both a burden and a gift

Sentience grants us the capacity for deep reflection, self-awareness and vision. However, it also confronts us with existential tension: the weight of choice, responsibility and the reality of our own limitations. This is why intention, trust, sovereignty and an embodied way of being are critical. Without clear intention, sentience becomes scattered or misdirected, pulled in every direction by impulse or distraction. Without trust, the burden of choice becomes paralysing, as fear of betrayal or failure undermines action. Without sovereignty, awareness is suffocating rather than empowering, because seeing what is happening clearly without the capacity to act or choose differently traps us in helplessness. And without an embodied way of being, reflection remains disembodied, disconnected from meaningful action. Yet, sentience alone is not enough. To truly navigate existence with integrity, we must move beyond surface perceptions, question assumptions and engage in rigorous, ongoing sense-making that refines itself through cycles of integration and recalibration.

The world is not as it first appears, and our ability to perceive reality with greater accuracy depends on our willingness to investigate, challenge biases and hold space for multiple perspectives — not as a final achievement, but as a continual striving towards less distortion. Sense-making is not passive. It requires an active, conscious decision to explore all angles, seek coherence and refine our understanding.

It is within this paradox that we uncover not just the burden of sentience, but the power it grants us to create, connect and restore integrity in a world constantly at risk of disintegration.

Real change does not start 'out there' in the world; it begins within. It starts with our choices, values and willingness to confront the shadows that shape us. By recognising ourselves not just as individuals, but as integral, constantly evolving parts of a greater whole, we reclaim the power to address humanity's crises with clarity and purpose. Acts of creation, no matter how seemingly insignificant in isolation, shape a world worth striving for. In short, reclaiming the world begins with reclaiming ourselves. Yet, what pulls us away from this process? What keeps individuals, relationships and societies locked in cycles of dysfunction? The answer lies in what remains unseen – the shadows that distort our perceptions, shape our fears and fragment our integrity. If left unexamined, they do not simply linger in the background. They actively drive disintegration. Let this chapter serve as an invitation to step into that process – not someday, but today.

Reflection

As we've explored, the tension between individuality and social responsibility is not a flaw; it is a defining aspect of the human condition. Our capacity to engage with reality, take ownership and transcend cycles of victimhood or entrenchment is what shapes both our personal and collective futures.

Take a moment to reflect on the following:

1. **How do you balance self-realisation with your responsibilities to the collective?**

   - Are there areas where you over-prioritise personal ambitions at the expense of meaningful relationships or societal contribution?
   - Conversely, do you sacrifice too much of yourself, neglecting your own aspirations and integrity in the name of duty?

2. **Are you truly exercising agency, or are you trapped in patterns of reaction?**

    - When faced with hardship, do you take ownership and seek creative solutions, or do you default to blame, resentment or inaction?
    - How often do you reflect on whether your beliefs, choices and responses are truly your own, or whether they are shaped by inherited narratives and external conditioning?

3. **How does your sense-making shape your engagement with the world?**

    - Do you critically examine the narratives you hold, or do you passively accept the perspectives handed to you by the media channels you subscribe to?
    - What steps can you take to ensure that your sense-making is grounded in integrity?

4. **What small but intentional act of creation can you commit to?**

    - What is one small yet meaningful action you can take to reinforce integrity, contribute to renewal and move beyond cycles of dysfunction in your own life and the systems you engage with?

Sentience is both a burden and a gift. How we choose to engage with it determines whether we remain passive observers of dysfunction or active architects of transformation. However, before we can step into meaningful change, we must first recognise the forces that shape us and the ways we might be complicit in the very dysfunctions we seek to challenge. In the following chapters, we will begin to unravel those forces, exposing the hidden dynamics that influence human behaviour, performance and meaning.

CHAPTER 3

Bad Faith and its Impact

Bad faith is a pervasive and insidious force at the root of many dysfunctions in society. More than mere dishonesty, it is the deliberate misalignment between one's actions, values and stated intentions. This misalignment is not just an individual failing – it ripples outward, shaping relationships, organisations and institutions, corroding trust, distorting narratives and fostering cycles of manipulation and disconnection.

French existentialist philosopher Jean-Paul Sartre introduced the concept of bad faith (*Mauvaise Foi*) to describe an individual's denial of their own freedom and agency: an act of self-deception that excuses passivity and evasion of choice. Building on this existential foundation, writer, feminist and fellow existentialist Simone de Beauvoir explored how social structures – particularly patriarchal expectations – coerce individuals into inauthenticity. For instance, a woman who suppresses her aspirations to conform to expectations of domesticity or a man who hides vulnerability to conform to ideals of stoic masculinity, is coerced into a posture that denies their authentic self. While de Beauvoir did not consistently use the term 'bad faith', her analysis in works such as *The Second Sex*[28] resonates strongly with its implications.

---

28   de Beauvoir, S. (2009) *The Second Sex*. Translated by C. Borde and S. Malovany-Chevallier. London: Vintage Books.

Unlike ignorance, which stems from a lack of knowledge, bad faith is knowing yet choosing deception. It is the calculated evasion of truth, whether to maintain power, protect one's ego or manipulate outcomes. It allows individuals and institutions to act in ways that contradict their stated principles while maintaining an illusion of integrity.

Addressing bad faith requires more than moral condemnation. It demands a deep exploration of its origins, manifestations across different spheres of life and the devastating impact it has on both personal and collective wellbeing. By exposing how it operates, we begin the work of dismantling deception and re-establishing the foundations for authentic alignment, trust and systemic coherence.

For example, a person who claims to value honesty but routinely engages in deception – justifying it under the guise of politeness or self-protection – embodies bad faith. Likewise, a leader who claims to serve the public, but prioritises self-interest over genuine responsibility, operates in bad faith.

Yet, bad faith is not merely an individual failing. It extends into collective and systemic domains. Institutions, political systems and organisations frequently perpetuate bad faith by masking self-serving agendas behind a rhetoric of justice, fairness or progress. When governments suppress inconvenient truths, when corporations exploit workers while branding themselves as ethical, or when media platforms selectively curate narratives to serve hidden interests, bad faith becomes an embedded structural force, sustaining dysfunction on a massive scale.

Bad faith also manifests in more subtle interpersonal and organisational dynamics. For example, an employee may agree to a role while withholding genuine commitment, maintaining a facade of alignment while privately nurturing resentment. This dissonance may be rationalised through ideological narratives, but it constitutes bad faith. Similarly, when individuals frame their employment as inherently exploitative – despite voluntarily accepting the role – they may ignore the actual conditions of their role or the behaviour of their specific employer. Instead, they project a generalised belief that all employers represent a system of exploitation. In both cases, bad faith functions as a defence mechanism – a way to avoid personal responsibility while preserving a narrative of moral or political superiority. The result is often disengagement, distortion and systemic friction disguised as ethical resistance.

The erosion of authenticity

Bad faith is best understood as a phenomenon defined by an absence of authenticity, responsibility and alignment between identity, values and behaviour. Unlike ignorance or misunderstanding, which arise from a lack of awareness, bad faith is an active avoidance of truth. It is the conscious (or semi-conscious) choice to evade responsibility, obscure reality or manipulate outcomes.

In contrast, authenticity requires alignment between what we claim to believe and how we actually behave. It demands a deep personal commitment to be in alignment with one's:

- **Identity**: Acting in ways that are congruent with one's professed beliefs and self-conception; and
- **Values**: Ensuring that one's behaviour consistently reflects declared principles rather than merely serving convenience or self-interest.

When this alignment is broken, bad faith takes hold. In individuals, this often manifests as avoidance of difficult choices, denial of responsibility or self-justified contradictions. In organisations, it appears as exploitative policies, performative virtue or deceptive practices that prioritise short-term optics over long-term integrity.

Take the case of corporate greenwashing – companies that claim to champion sustainability while engaging in environmentally destructive practices. By leveraging misleading narratives to appeal to conscious consumers, they manipulate public trust while continuing business as usual. The result? Not only do these organisations perpetuate harm, but they also weaken faith in genuine sustainability efforts, leading to broader societal cynicism.

Dimensions of bad faith

As discussed, bad faith operates at multiple levels – individual, collective and systemic – creating an interconnected web of dysfunction. Left unchecked, it shapes the very fabric of society, reinforcing cycles of mistrust, avoidance and disconnection.

Individual bad faith: Self-deception and avoidance

On a personal level, bad faith arises when people evade responsibility for their own choices – whether out of fear, complacency, or in order to advance a personal agenda or manipulate perception for self-interest. It manifests in several ways:

- **Avoiding difficult decisions:** Using procrastination, distraction or self-rationalisation to escape uncomfortable truths.
- **Compromising core values:** Pursuing a career, relationship or lifestyle solely for societal approval rather than personal alignment, leading to internal conflict and resentment.
- **Feigning helplessness:** Declaring 'I had no choice' as a way to absolve oneself of responsibility, even when agency remains available.

Over time, these patterns erode self-trust, creating a cycle of self-deception that weakens authenticity and hinders growth.

Collective and systemic bad faith: When societies pretend

Bad faith magnifies when embedded into social structures, institutions and cultural norms. German philosopher Martin Heidegger referred to the concept of *Verfallen* (often translated to 'fallenness') to describe how individuals lose themselves by uncritically conforming to social norms, drifting into inauthenticity instead of questioning the validity of what is presented as 'normal'.[29] This is seen in:

---

29 Heidegger, M. (2010) *Being and Time*. Translated by J. Stambaugh, revised by D.J. Schmidt. Albany: State University of New York Press. (Original work published 1927). See Division I, Chapter 5, Section 38.

- **Blind conformity:** Accepting cultural or institutional norms with resignation, reinforcing the idea that 'this is just how things are'.
- **Performative ethics:** Organisations publicly promoting values like inclusion or fairness while prioritising profit, power or control behind closed doors.
- **Institutional deception:** Governments, media and corporations shaping narratives for self-preservation rather than truth, feeding societal disillusionment.

When systemic bad faith becomes the norm, personal authenticity comes under siege. Institutions claim moral high ground while advancing hidden agendas. Individuals, in turn, feel compelled to play along with inauthentic systems, whether to protect their careers, avoid conflict or maintain social standing.

This widespread performance of 'pretending' accelerates cycles of dysfunction. When people sense that everything is an act, from politics and corporate missions to public discourse, it breeds cynicism, deepens social fragmentation and erodes the very possibility of trust and renewal.

The impact of bad faith

When authenticity is abandoned and bad faith becomes normalised, dysfunction becomes embedded in the very systems that govern human life.

Some of the most pressing consequences of bad faith include:

- **Social media echo chambers:** Designed to maximise engagement rather than truth, algorithms amplify misinformation and sensationalism. This fuels division, distorts public discourse and deepens ideological polarisation. Instead of fostering understanding, digital spaces become battlegrounds of outrage and manipulation.
- **Corporate exploitation:** Organisations that prioritise profits over ethical responsibility exploit workers, consumers and natural resources. Whether through deceptive marketing,

exploitative labour practices or environmental destruction, bad faith drives a business culture where appearance matters more than authenticity.

- **Climate change inaction:** Many governments and corporations claim commitment to sustainability while actively delaying meaningful action. The result is performative gestures – greenwashing, hollow pledges and endless deferrals – while economic interests continue to take precedence over ecological responsibility. Bad faith in this domain threatens long-term survival.

- **Erosion of trust in institutions and relationships:** When deception, hypocrisy and inconsistency become the norm, trust disintegrates, whether in governance, business or personal relationships. When trust fades, people withdraw from civic engagement, communities fracture and public disillusionment grows.

These impacts do more than hinder progress. They create a world where dysfunction is self-reinforcing. Left unchecked, bad faith accelerates cycles of distrust, stagnation and crisis.

Case study: Bad faith and climate action

The global response to climate change is a revealing example of bad faith in action, where rhetoric often outpaces meaningful commitment. Discussions around climate solutions are frequently driven by political and economic incentives rather than a balanced, pragmatic assessment of challenges and trade-offs. While environmental concerns are real, the extent of human impact on climate change remains a subject of ongoing debate, with differing perspectives on the degree of influence and the best approaches to sustainability.

One of the greatest challenges in climate discourse is oversimplification. Many proposed solutions are presented as unquestionable imperatives, rather than options with their own costs, trade-offs and limitations. Electric vehicles (EVs), for example, are widely promoted as the future of clean energy transportation. Yet, their large-scale adoption relies on resource-intensive mining for lithium, cobalt and other rare minerals, which raises environmental, geopolitical and ethical concerns. While EVs may reduce emissions at the point of use, their production relocates the burden elsewhere, often to developing nations with poor environmental protections and exploitative labour practices.

Meanwhile, nature-based, authentically sustainable solutions like reforestation, soil regeneration and vertical farming, offer scalable pathways that work with rather than against ecological systems. However, these approaches often receive less investment and attention, as they do not fit into the narrative of rapid industrial progress that many corporations and governments prefer to champion.

This is not a rejection of technological advancement or environmental responsibility, but rather a call for intellectual honesty and discernment. A balanced approach requires:

- Recognising trade-offs and opportunity costs, rather than pushing one-size-fits-all solutions.
- Investing in diverse, practical sustainability measures that include both technological and ecological approaches.
- Holding institutions accountable for ensuring that environmental policies do not serve as mere political or economic tools, but are based on sound reasoning, transparency and long-term viability.

Climate action should neither be reduced to a political divide nor used as a vehicle for unchecked corporate expansion. It should also not be used to justify restrictive policies that disproportionately impact working people. Instead, a pragmatic, centrist approach is necessary – one that values both economic vitality and environmental responsibility, recognising that these two are not inherently opposed.

Patterns of avoidance and self-deception

Philosophers like Søren Kierkegaard and Jean-Paul Sartre have explored the roots of bad faith, particularly its deep entanglement with freedom and responsibility. Kierkegaard described the unsettling anxiety provoked by the boundless possibilities of human freedom as 'mental vertigo'. Confronted with this existential weight, individuals often retreat into avoidance behaviours, seeking refuge in distraction and self-deception rather than embracing the responsibility of authentic choice. This tendency can also be understood in light of psychological defence and coping mechanisms developed in response to anxiety and vulnerability.[30] Erich Fromm highlighted this dynamic in *Escape from Freedom*, where he examined how individuals surrender autonomy to escape the burden of freedom.[31] More recently, Robert Kegan and Lisa Lahey elaborated on these dynamics in *Immunity to Change*, showing how entrenched patterns of self-protection can obstruct growth and transformation.[32]

Common patterns of avoidance include:

- **Procrastination:** Delaying decisions, not because they require more thought, but to escape the burden of commitment and consequence.
- **Distraction:** Immersing oneself in superficial pursuits like endless scrolling or consumption to avoid deeper existential questions or responsibilities.

Sartre's famous example of 'the waiter in the café' illustrates this dynamic.[33] Rather than engaging authentically with his role, the waiter rigidly performs the expected behaviours of a waiter, exaggerating his mannerisms, voice and gestures. In doing so, he avoids confronting his freedom to be more than just a function of his profession. He is trapped in a self-imposed role, using it as an excuse to evade the weight of self-determination.

This same phenomenon plays out within entire industries, governments and institutions. Systemic bad faith emerges when powerful

---

30 Vaillant, G.E. (1992) *Ego Mechanisms of Defense: A Guide for Clinicians and Researchers*. Washington, DC: American Psychiatric Press.

31 Fromm, E. (1942) *Escape from Freedom*. New York: Farrar & Rinehart.

32 Kegan, R. and Lahey, L.L. (2009) *Immunity to Change: How to Overcome It and Unlock the Potential in Yourself and Your Organization*. Boston, MA: Harvard Business Press.

33 Sartre, J.-P. (2003) *Being and Nothingness: An Essay in Phenomenological Ontology*. Translated by H.E. Barnes. London: Routledge. (Original work published 1943).

entities craft deceptive narratives to protect their interests, evading accountability under the guise of legitimacy.

One of the starkest examples is climate change denial campaigns funded by fossil fuel corporations. By deliberately sowing doubt about scientific consensus, these industries have manipulated public discourse, delaying necessary reforms and perpetuating environmental destruction – all while publicly posturing as concerned stakeholders. This is not a failure of knowledge, but an act of calculated avoidance, where self-interest supersedes truth and responsibility.

Bad faith, whether personal or systemic, operates as a defence mechanism: a refusal to confront reality as it is. But avoidance does not eliminate the burden of truth; it only postpones its reckoning.

Bad faith on the global stage

Bad faith is especially evident in the actions of ruling elites, governments and powerful institutions. It manifests through manipulation, exploitation and the pursuit of hidden agendas – all of which systematically erode trust and exacerbate global challenges. While these entities often present themselves as committed to progress, their actions frequently tell a different story.

Consider international diplomacy. Nations routinely sign treaties and agreements on climate change, trade or human rights, only to violate them when it serves their immediate interests. They may commit to reducing carbon emissions, but continue approving new fossil fuel projects. They may pledge to uphold human rights while forming alliances with authoritarian regimes. This duplicity undermines international cooperation, leaving pressing global crises unresolved.

In geopolitics, propaganda and disinformation campaigns are wielded as tools to manufacture consent or destabilise adversaries. Governments and state-controlled media often selectively frame events to suit their agendas, manipulating public perception rather than providing objective information. This distortion of truth deepens divisions, making genuine consensus nearly impossible.

Bad faith is equally entrenched in corporate exploitation. Many multinational corporations frequently extract resources from vulnerable regions under the guise of 'economic development'. They enter impoverished nations, promising infrastructure and jobs, yet leave behind environmental destruction, exploitative labour conditions and entrenched dependency. Instead of being empowered, the affected communities find themselves stripped of autonomy, their lands depleted and their future compromised.

Bad faith can even be found in humanitarian aid situations. Positioned as benevolent, relief programs sometimes come with political strings attached, serving as instruments of influence rather than genuine assistance. Nations offering foreign aid may prioritise geopolitical leverage over actual humanitarian outcomes, reinforcing dependencies rather than fostering sustainable growth.

The need for transparency and accountability

Addressing these dynamics requires holding decision-makers and institutions accountable, not just through regulations and oversight, but through a cultural shift towards transparency and accountability. It is not enough to demand honesty from those in power; systems must be designed to make deception and self-serving manipulation harder to sustain.

Citizens also play a role in countering systemic bad faith. By developing critical thinking skills, questioning dominant narratives and demanding clarity in governance and corporate responsibility, individuals can resist manipulation and contribute to restoring trust.

Bad faith at the global level is not an abstract issue. It directly affects the stability of societies, the health of economies and the future of humanity. Recognising it is the first step towards dismantling its grip and fostering a world where authenticity, transparency and accountability guide decision-making.

The question then arises: how do we break free from this entanglement of self-deception and structural dishonesty? The path forward requires a radical confrontation with reality, both within ourselves and the world around us.

Reflection

Bad faith is not always loud or obvious. More often, it shows up in the quiet compromises we make, the stories we tell ourselves and the roles we perform to avoid discomfort, responsibility or truth. Whether individual or institutional, bad faith is a force that normalises disconnection and makes authenticity seem risky or even naive.

Take a moment to reflect on the following:

- Where in your life do you sense a disconnection between your stated values and your lived behaviour?
- Are there roles you perform at work, in relationships or in society that mask a deeper truth you are avoiding?
- When have you rationalised or justified actions that you knew compromised your integrity?
- What fears might be driving these justifications?
- Do you find it easier to maintain appearances than to confront uncomfortable truths?
- Have you ever defended an institution, culture or identity you knew was acting in contradiction to its professed values?
- In what ways might your silence, inaction or politeness contribute to the persistence of bad faith at home, at work or in public life?
- What small but meaningful act of realignment could you take that challenges a performative role and affirms your integrity?

Bad faith not only erodes our personal integrity; it slowly unravels the social fabric – the shared trust, norms and mutual expectations – that enables people to live and work together. When individuals, leaders and institutions act in misalignment with their professed values, the consequences ripple outward. Over time, this weakens the very basis of cooperation and belonging within systems, communities and nations.

The next chapter explores how this erosion takes shape across the personal, relational, organisational and global spheres. You'll see how bad faith sets the stage for systemic dysfunction, and how the loss of trust, once fractured, becomes one of the most urgent challenges of our time.

CHAPTER 4

The Breakdown of Trust

Trust is the invisible thread that holds human relationships, organisations and entire societies together. It is the foundation upon which collaboration, innovation and progress are built. When trust is present, people feel secure enough to connect, cooperate and work towards shared goals. However, when trust is absent, fear, division and dysfunction take its place, weakening the very fabric of human interaction.

Today, trust is in crisis. From geopolitical tensions and institutional failures to broken personal relationships, the erosion of trust is evident in nearly every aspect of modern life. Governments manipulate narratives, corporations prioritise profit over integrity and individuals – bombarded by misinformation – struggle to discern truth from deception. The result is a world increasingly governed by scepticism, polarisation and disengagement.

This breakdown of trust does not merely create interpersonal friction or political discontent. It undermines humanity's ability to solve shared challenges. Without trust, collaboration becomes impossible, fear replaces goodwill and societies begin to fracture. Across all levels of existence, from the bonds of family to the structures of global governance, we see the same shadow at play. Trust, once broken, is difficult to restore. Yet without it, nothing truly thrives.

Trust on the global stage

In geopolitics, trust is both a fragile currency and a strategic asset. Nations struggle to maintain it amid conflicts, trade disputes, ideological divides and shifting alliances. Broken treaties, unfulfilled commitments and deep-rooted suspicion create a climate of antagonism, where cooperation becomes secondary to self-preservation.

Consider the ongoing tensions in global climate negotiations. Developing nations, having been repeatedly promised financial and technological support from wealthier nations, often see these commitments delayed, diluted or outright ignored. As a result, mistrust festers, making it increasingly difficult to secure genuine cooperation on existential challenges. When past betrayals shape future expectations, even well-intended agreements are met with scepticism.

The consequences of this broken trust are profound. Global crises, from climate change and pandemics to economic instability and conflicts, demand unified responses. Yet without trust, collaboration stalls. Nations retreat into self-interest and protectionism, further amplifying the very challenges that require collective action. When trust erodes at this level, entire generations inherit a world of division and dysfunction, where progress is hindered by the weight of unresolved distrust.

Institutional trust: The crisis of confidence

Trust in institutions, from governments and corporations to the media and religious organisations, has been steadily eroding. Scandals, corruption and systemic failures have exposed the dissonance between institutional ideals and actual practices. This growing disillusionment has led to widespread cynicism and disengagement, weakening the very systems meant to serve society.

One of the most glaring examples is the decline of trust in media, particularly public broadcasters and news organisations that were once regarded as pillars of journalistic integrity. Many state-funded media outlets are now seen as either mouthpieces for the government or ideological battlegrounds, where narratives are shaped not by a commitment to truth but by political or corporate interests. Citizens, overwhelmed by conflicting accounts of events, struggle to discern fact from agenda-driven messaging, deepening social divisions and feeding a climate of suspicion.

Similarly, government agencies responsible for public welfare – whether in health, education or security – are frequently accused of incompetence, inefficiency or outright deception. Consider public health messaging during crises such as the COVID-19 pandemic. Contradictory statements from officials, shifting policies and concerns about data manipulation have left many questioning whether their governments are truly acting in the public's best interest. The result? People disengage, institutions lose credibility and even well-intended policies face resistance due to the absence of trust.

But is accountability truly applied across the board? Or are there double standards – where one group is permitted to perpetually define itself through victimhood, using historical injustices to justify present wrongdoing, while others are held to rigid moral expectations? For example, some governments or institutions may invoke past persecution of their people as a way to silence legitimate criticism of current policies, implying that any challenge to their actions is itself an attack on their identity. Meanwhile, other groups facing ongoing discrimination are expected to 'move on' quickly and demonstrate constant proof of legitimacy. Are some communities afforded the benefit of the doubt while others must constantly prove their legitimacy?

For instance, consider how accusations of anti-Semitism and Islamaphobia are treated in nations. Is there consistency in how these issues are addressed? Or do some groups receive automatic validation, while others must continually justify their grievances? A similar dynamic plays out closer to home. In workplaces, schools or community organisations, complaints of discrimination or misconduct are not always handled with the same seriousness. Some people find their concerns immediately believed and acted upon, while others are met with doubt, bureaucracy or dismissal. The selective application of accountability – whether in the arena of public discourse or in the everyday institutions we rely on – erodes institutional trust and deepens social fractures, reinforcing cycles of resentment and alienation.

This erosion of trust extends to everyday life. When a person buys lunch from a restaurant, they assume the food is safe. But violations in health inspections – often downplayed or covered up – shatter that confidence. When individuals deposit money in a bank, they expect financial stability. But high-profile banking failures reveal that even the most 'secure' institutions can be vulnerable to mismanagement or corruption. These fractures in trust make people more hesitant, anxious and less willing to engage with the systems that once provided stability.

A society that lacks institutional trust struggles to function effectively. Without a shared foundation of reliability, cooperation fractures and critical decisions on governance, economic policy or public safety become battlegrounds of suspicion rather than opportunities for collective progress. Restoring institutional trust requires more than just transparency. It demands consistency. Justice and accountability must apply universally rather than being selectively enforced based on ideological or political convenience. Otherwise, trust remains a privilege granted only to certain groups rather than a principle that upholds the integrity of society as a whole.

Organisational trust: Mistrust in the workplace

In organisations, trust is the backbone of productive collaboration. It cultivates emotional resilience, creating the conditions where people can engage openly, take risks and contribute without fear of exploitation or dismissal. Yet many workplaces suffer from cultures of secrecy, fear or misalignment between stated values and actual practices. Mistrust emerges when employees feel expendable, leaders are inconsistent or communication is opaque. Over time, this fosters environments where self-preservation overtakes teamwork, leading to disengagement, low morale and high turnover.

Take, for example, corporate environments where the leadership team preaches integrity and transparency while engaging in cost-cutting measures that harm employees, such as unexpected layoffs despite record profits. How would you expect employees to feel in this situation? It certainly would not be conducive to fostering a healthy workplace culture.

Imagine a customer booking a hotel room online, only to find upon arrival that the images and promises did not match reality. Or an employee at a small business who works overtime expecting a promised bonus, only to later be denied compensation due to 'budget constraints'. In both cases, the gap between expectation and reality breeds disillusionment and withdrawal.

When trust is systematically undermined, individuals and organisations enter survival mode, guarding themselves against perceived threats rather than striving for shared goals. The workplace becomes transactional rather than cooperative, with employees withholding ideas, avoiding risks and prioritising personal security over organisational success. One particularly influential framework for understanding this dynamic is the Mayer, Davis and Schoorman model of organisational trust, which defines trust as 'the willingness of a party to be vulnerable to the actions of another party based on the expectation that the other will perform a particular action.'[34] Importantly, their model distinguishes the decision to trust from the trustee's actual trustworthiness, emphasising that willingness to risk precedes outcomes. Organisations that fail to cultivate this foundation of trust become breeding grounds for disengagement, inefficiency and, ultimately, collapse.

Personal relationships: The impact of betrayal and dishonesty

Trust within families and intimate partnerships forms the emotional core of security and connection within the relationship. When trust is intact, it fosters psychological safety, allowing individuals to be vulnerable, authentic and supported. Just as in organisations, where trust enables openness and collaboration, in personal relationships it is trust that makes vulnerability and authenticity possible. Without it, people retreat into guardedness, eroding the very connection they long for. Conversely, betrayal, dishonesty and unmet expectations can fracture these bonds, leaving lasting scars that ripple through a person's life and interactions.

---

[34] Mayer, R.C., Davis, J.H. and Schoorman, F.D. (1995) 'An Integrative Model of Organizational Trust', *Academy of Management Review*, 20(3), pp. 709–734.

One of the most insidious consequences of broken trust in personal relationships is the erosion of one's ability to trust others in the future. A child raised in an environment where promises are routinely broken, or where caregivers are emotionally unreliable, may develop deep-seated self-doubt and struggle to form secure relationships in adulthood. They may instinctively keep others at arm's length, fearing abandonment or betrayal. This avoidance of vulnerability – meant to protect them – often leads to further emotional isolation, reinforcing the very cycle they wish to escape.

A partner who repeatedly lies, fails to follow through on commitments or manipulates the truth for personal gain gradually reshapes the emotional landscape of the relationship. Over time, the betrayed individual may develop hyper-vigilance, scepticism or even a subconscious tendency to sabotage future relationships, expecting disappointment before it arrives.

The impact extends beyond the personal realm. A workplace leader who struggles with trust in personal relationships may unconsciously project that mistrust onto colleagues, micromanaging instead of empowering. A friend who has been deceived too many times may withdraw from social connections, reinforcing a pattern of disengagement. In this way, personal trust issues become societal trust issues, influencing how communities, organisations and even nations function.

Healing from broken trust is possible, but it requires conscious effort on an individual and collective level. It demands honesty, accountability and a willingness to repair rather than retreat. Without these efforts, personal relationships remain fragile and the greater fabric of trust in society continues to fray.

Self-trust: The core of authenticity

While much attention is given to trust between individuals and institutions, the erosion of self-trust is equally (if not more) significant. Self-trust is a foundational aspect of authenticity. It is the confidence to act in alignment with one's values, principles and aspirations. When individuals repeatedly compromise their integrity or fail to uphold their commitments, they begin to erode the very foundation of self-trust – the belief that they can rely on themselves to act with consistency, honesty and alignment.

Consider someone who deeply values honesty but avoids difficult conversations to maintain harmony. Each time they sidestep discomfort in favour of temporary peace, they chip away at their confidence in their own integrity. Over time, this misalignment fosters internal conflict, self-doubt and even resentment towards themselves and others. What begins as a seemingly minor compromise can spiral into a broader pattern of disconnection from one's values.

Self-betrayal often manifests in small, everyday choices. We neglect personal goals, allow self-sabotage to dictate our decisions or prioritise instant gratification over long-term growth. A person who continually tells themselves they will change but never does, or who sets goals and repeatedly abandons them, subtly reinforces the belief that they cannot rely on themselves. This erosion of self-trust can lead to cycles of hesitation, procrastination and chronic dissatisfaction.

The consequences of lost self-trust extend beyond the individual. A leader who lacks confidence in their own decision-making will struggle to inspire trust in their team. A person who doubts their own judgement may seek excessive validation from others, weakening their autonomy and making them more susceptible to manipulation. In relationships, someone who lacks self-trust may project their insecurities onto others, questioning their partners' intentions or doubting genuine expressions of care.

Rebuilding trust in oneself requires a conscious effort – an ongoing practice of self-awareness, accountability and intentional action. It demands the courage to admit misalignment, confront difficult truths and commit to change despite the discomfort it may bring. It is through this process of realignment that individuals reclaim their authenticity, reinforcing not just their internal alignment, but also their ability to engage with the world from a place of genuine strength and conviction.

The condemnation trap: Cancel culture and the fragility of trust

In contemporary society, trust is further strained by the rise of cancel culture and the growing tendency to engage in absolute condemnation. While there is undeniable value in holding individuals and institutions accountable for wrongdoing – especially in addressing historical and systemic injustices – the manner in which this accountability is enacted can often become counterproductive. Instead of fostering learning, redemption or systemic improvement, cancel culture frequently resorts to erasure, ostracism and the complete dismantling of individuals or movements based on past missteps.

British philosopher Ludwig Wittgenstein likened intellectual and moral growth to climbing a ladder. As we ascend, we discard earlier beliefs not through condemnation but through transcendence.[35] Progress does not require absolute rejection of the past. Rather, it demands that we extract lessons from it while moving forward. When cancel culture operates without nuance or constructive dialogue, it risks severing society from these vital lessons, reinforcing cycles of fear rather than fostering meaningful change.

The consequences of this phenomenon extend beyond individual reputations. Fear of public shaming discourages open discourse, leading people to self-censor or disengage altogether. Institutions become overly risk-averse, prioritising public perception over substantive reform. Even genuine discussions around ethics, history and ideology become fraught with tension, as the potential for misinterpretation or backlash overshadows the pursuit of truth.

The costs of broken trust

The erosion of trust carries profound consequences, shaping societies, organisations and personal wellbeing in ways that often go unnoticed until dysfunction has deeply set in. When trust is fractured, it does not simply disappear. It is replaced by suspicion, disengagement and defensive strategies that hinder progress and connection across all levels of life.

---

35   Wittgenstein, L. (2001) *Tractatus Logico-Philosophicus*. Translated by D.F. Pears and B.F. McGuinness. London: Routledge. (Original work published 1921). See proposition 6.54.

1. Societal polarisation and disengagement

When citizens lose trust in public institutions – whether due to corruption, dishonesty or systemic failures – social cohesion begins to unravel. Civic participation declines as people disengage from democratic processes, doubting the legitimacy of their vote, their leaders or the media narratives that shape public opinion. This creates a dangerous vacuum, making societies more vulnerable to authoritarian tendencies, conspiracy-driven movements and the spread of misinformation.

For example, when public health institutions issue conflicting guidelines or are perceived as being politically motivated, trust in scientific expertise declines. The result is mass scepticism, resistance to evidence-based policies and a society where facts become subjective, further deepening ideological divides.

2. Organisational dysfunction

In workplaces, trust is the foundation of effective teamwork, innovation and long-term success. Yet, in environments where mistrust dominates, employees shift their focus from collaboration to self-preservation. They may withhold information, hesitate to take risks or disengage from meaningful contributions, fearing backlash or exploitation. Communication deteriorates, conflicts escalate and the organisation's ability to adapt and grow is stifled.

Consider a company that frequently restructures without transparency, leaving employees uncertain about their roles and futures. Over time, this erodes morale and productivity, as workers disengage emotionally from their tasks. Without trust in leadership, no amount of strategic planning can compensate for the loss of collective commitment.

However, trust is not a one-way obligation. Just as leadership must act with integrity and clarity, employees also carry a responsibility to honour the trust placed in them. When individuals underperform, withhold effort or approach their roles with cynicism or entitlement, they contribute to the very dysfunction they may be criticising. Broken trust on the part of the employee, whether it shows up as disengagement, hidden resentment or quiet resistance, can be just as corrosive as poor leadership. In healthy organisations, trust is mutual and responsibility is shared.

3. Personal disconnection and mental health decline

In personal relationships, broken trust breeds cycles of blame, defensiveness and emotional withdrawal. Whether in friendships, romantic partnerships or family dynamics, the loss of trust creates barriers that prevent genuine connection. People become guarded, reluctant to be vulnerable and may resort to avoidance rather than resolution.

On a psychological level, persistent mistrust contributes to anxiety, depression and a pervasive sense of insecurity. Individuals who have experienced deep betrayals – whether through infidelity, broken promises or manipulation – may struggle to form healthy attachments in future relationships, leading to loneliness and disconnection.

Ultimately, the cost of broken trust is measured in the fragmentation of human bonds, the stagnation of collective progress and the erosion of our shared ability to navigate life's complexities with confidence and purpose.

The interplay between bad faith and the breakdown of trust

The breakdown of trust and the phenomenon of bad faith are not merely correlated; they are causally entangled. To understand the erosion of trust in modern institutions, relationships and within the self, one must first confront the role that bad faith plays in enabling and accelerating that erosion. While trust is the connective tissue of human interaction – an invisible infrastructure that holds societies, systems (including human beings) together – bad faith is the corrosive agent that severs those ties by undermining authenticity, accountability and alignment between one's values and actions. In other words, bad faith is the seed and broken trust is the harvest.

Essentially, bad faith is a mode of being or a way of existing in the world that is predicated on evasion. It is the intentional or semi-conscious misalignment between proclaimed beliefs and actual behaviours, between the persona and the person, between institutional ideals and operational conduct. In contrast, trust depends on coherence. When individuals, organisations or societies act in ways that are predictably aligned with their stated intentions, trust is strengthened. However, when that alignment is violated, trust erodes. And it is bad faith that often initiates and sustains that violation.

At the individual level, bad faith manifests through rationalisations, self-deception and the abdication of responsibility. Someone who justifies dishonest behaviour as necessary, or who repeatedly compromises on values for the sake of convenience may not immediately destroy trust. However, their behaviour and actions cause the cracks to begin to form. Over time, these subtle acts of misalignment accumulate. The individual begins to distrust their own voice. Others begin to doubt their sincerity. What begins as a private dissonance becomes a relational fracture.

In intimate relationships, this is seen when partners claim to value honesty but withhold truths, or when someone promises commitment while maintaining emotional or physical distance. The relationship may survive for a while on borrowed belief, but trust quietly bleeds out. Bad faith sows uncertainty, and trust simply cannot thrive in a state of ambiguity.

The dynamic is amplified at the systemic level. Institutions that espouse transparency while operating in secrecy, or companies that tout sustainability while engaging in environmental exploitation, generate cultural climates of suspicion. Citizens may not be able to articulate precisely what is wrong, but they sense the inauthenticity. The social contract begins to feel performative. Trust is no longer a given. Instead, it becomes a gamble.

This is why, when trust collapses, people often speak not only of betrayal but of disillusionment. They are not merely reacting to a broken promise; they are responding to the realisation that the alignment they once believed in never truly existed. That is the unique and devastating power of bad faith. It invites people to invest belief into a structure – be it a person, organisation or society – that has already forfeited its own integrity.

The hidden architecture of distrust

What makes bad faith particularly dangerous is its capacity to wear the mask of trustworthiness. In most cases, bad faith is not overt dishonesty, but misalignment masked as sincerity. Leaders may genuinely believe they are acting in the public's best interest while prioritising political survival. Citizens may believe they are making ethical consumer choices while ignoring the exploitative supply chains behind their purchases. Dysfunction is fueled by self-justification.

This performative conformity, where appearance matters more than substance, is the fertile ground in which trust is slowly poisoned. And once trust is gone, it does not simply leave a vacuum. It is replaced by hyper-vigilance, polarisation, disconnection and the retreat into echo chambers and tribalism. In this new terrain, the absence of trust becomes normalised and bad faith becomes institutionalised.

Why broken trust cuts so deeply

When we experience a breakdown in trust, what we are often reacting to is not just the betrayal of an expectation but the revelation of bad faith behind it. Trust requires vulnerability. It is a wager we place on the future integrity of another being or institution. Once exposed, bad faith invalidates that wager – not only because the other failed, but because they never intended to fulfil the promise in the first place. It reveals that the relationship, contract, or institution was founded not on shared values, but on illusion.

This is why repairing trust is so difficult: the issue is not just the broken promise but the existential rupture that follows. The betrayed must now question not only the actor but the entire framework that enabled the betrayal. Was it naive to believe? Was the proclaimed value system ever real? What else has been concealed?

The feedback loop between bad faith and distrust

A critical insight in analysing the relationship between bad faith and broken trust is that the two reinforce each other in a feedback loop. Once bad faith becomes visible, trust deteriorates. But the absence of trust also makes bad faith more likely. In low-trust environments, individuals and institutions begin to protect themselves pre-emptively, retreating into guardedness, deception and performative ethics to preserve their image or control. This, in turn, generates more bad faith. And so the cycle continues.

A culture steeped in bad faith creates widespread distrust. That distrust incentivises further bad faith. Eventually, systems become so saturated with manipulation, concealment and self-interest that even genuine attempts at integrity are met with cynicism. In such a climate, trust cannot be rebuilt through better messaging or superficial reforms. Instead, it requires a radical realignment with authenticity and truth.

In the Unified Ontology of Systemic Integrity, introduced later in this book, trust is not merely a social construct or emotional state. Ontologically, it is a *systemic force* that emerges when alignment, authenticity and coherence are present. Trust is both an effect and a condition for deeper systemic flourishing. Conversely, bad faith is understood as a breakdown in the structural integrity of Being: a dissonance that disrupts the emergence of trust as a sustainable and generative force.

So, trust and bad faith are not simply psychological tendencies or moral concerns. They are *ontological realities with systemic consequences*. Where trust is present, systems cohere and adapt. Where bad faith is present, systems fragment, regress and stagnate.

Trust cannot be demanded. It must be earned through the consistent embodiment of one's values. And bad faith, once exposed, must be met not merely with condemnation, but with the deeper work of reintegration – of making whole again what was divided. Understanding the relationship between bad faith and the breakdown of trust is essential before we can even start to rebuild. After all, we cannot skip the diagnosis and expect the cure to take effect.

Reflection

Trust is the quiet foundation upon which all meaningful connection rests – between people, within organisations, and across entire societies. Its breakdown is rarely sudden. It erodes slowly, worn down by patterns of misalignment, inconsistency and betrayal. Often, these patterns are enabled or excused through bad faith, both our own and that of others. We learn to expect less, to protect ourselves, to stop believing.

But the erosion of trust is not inevitable. It signals an invitation to stop pretending, confront the realities we've ignored and start over, this time with clarity and alignment.

Consider the following questions:

- Where in your life have you stopped trusting – not because of one event, but due to repeated misalignments that wore your belief down?
- Have you ever contributed, even subtly, to the erosion of trust in a relationship, role or institution by acting from convenience rather than coherence?
- What story have you told yourself to justify withholding trust (or demanding it) without integrity?
- How does bad faith (yours or others') show up in the systems you're part of, and what are its effects on collective trust?
- What small act could begin to repair a trust that has been broken, not through apology alone, but through sustained alignment?

Rebuilding trust requires more than intention; it requires congruence. And congruence begins with honesty, first with ourselves, then with one another.

As we move forward, we begin to explore the hidden architecture behind many of these misalignments: the internal distortions that shape how we perceive, relate and act. You will learn that shadows are the unseen forces that emerge from within and drive disconnection and dysfunction beneath the surface of everyday life.

CHAPTER 5

Shadows – The Unseen Forces

Shadows are not external forces acting upon us. They are the unseen internal currents shaping our perceptions, actions and fears. In other words, they are not imposed on us but emerge from within, formed by the interplay of our internal processes, perceptions and shared reality. Shadows reflect how we relate to the world, both individually and collectively, and how these relationships materialise into beliefs, behaviours, social constructs and institutions.

At its core, a shadow is not merely the absence of light. It is the distortion that arises when something essential is misplaced, undeveloped or fragmented. In both biological and conceptual systems, integrity is maintained when each part functions in alignment with the whole. When critical components are missing, improperly integrated or actively repressed, the system does not merely suffer from inefficiency; it becomes dysfunctional and unstable.

This principle applies universally:

- **In the body** → Missing or malfunctioning components in an organism lead to pathological conditions. A deficiency in essential nutrients, a malfunctioning organ or a misfiring neural circuit creates disruptions that compromise the body's homeostasis and, in turn, the integrity of the entire system.

- **In thought and cognition** → Misplaced concepts, unexamined biases or missing epistemic foundations – those that relate to knowledge, understanding and the nature or limits of knowing – create flawed reasoning, cognitive distortions and self-reinforcing falsehoods.
- **In relationships and society** → Shadows manifest in unprocessed emotions, unhealthy dynamics and systemic dysfunctions, perpetuating cycles of division, resentment, hatred, mistrust and exploitation.

The axiomatic pattern of wholeness: transcendence and inclusion

At its core, wholeness is another way of understanding integrity: the state in which all essential parts function in alignment, creating coherence rather than fragmentation. As discussed earlier, when individuals and societies lose this alignment, dysfunction takes root. Shadows emerge when critical components – whether in thought, relationships or systems – are misplaced, suppressed or fractured.

This principle of transcendence and inclusion – where integrated parts form a coherent and greater whole – is embedded in the very fabric of existence. An axiomatic pattern governs both physical reality and abstract thought: all 'wholes' are composed of parts. And these parts, when properly integrated, transcend their individual nature to form a greater whole. This process of transcendence and inclusion is observable at every level of existence, from the microscopic to the conceptual, and governs how complexity emerges. Consider the following sequence:

1. Atoms combine to form molecules, which transcend their atomic properties to create something greater.
2. Molecules then gather into cells, which operate as unified entities while still including their molecular components.
3. Then cells organise into tissues, which in turn become organs, eventually forming an entire organism sustained by interdependent subsystems that maintain its integrity.

This same pattern of wholeness extends to cognition, systems and abstract frameworks. Each new level of complexity depends on the proper integration of its parts.

Just as physical wholeness arises through the integration of parts, from atoms to organisms, the same axiomatic pattern applies to the domain of consciousness and cognition. Every act of awareness, every meaningful conception, is built upon nested layers that must come into alignment for coherence to emerge.

1. At the most fundamental level, raw data functions like cognitive atoms, representing fragmented inputs from the external or internal world.
2. When this data is organised, it becomes information, structured yet still incomplete on its own.
3. When interpreted through context and relevance, information becomes knowledge – the cognitive equivalent of cells – each with specific functions and recognisable boundaries.
4. As knowledge is synthesised, refined and infused with perspective, it transforms into wisdom – like tissues and organs that sustain conscious life – through discernment and adaptability.
5. When wisdom is enacted with intentionality and authenticity, it leads to conception: the conscious construction of reality as a coherent whole that supports inner and outer integrity.

This entire process, when integrated and aligned, supports the health and homeostasis of our awareness. It allows us to perceive accurately, discern meaningfully and respond ethically. But when fragments are distorted, ignored or misassembled – through bias, unexamined beliefs or inherited metacontent – cognitive shadows accumulate. They cloud perception, twist intention and undermine the architecture of sense-making itself.

Whether we are conceiving a dog, a tree, a device, a herb or abstract constructs like money, governance or social etiquette, our engagement with reality depends on the structural integrity of our consciousness. When our internal systems of knowing are fractured, our ability to live meaningfully, relate ethically and act coherently deteriorates.

This is not merely a personal issue. It becomes systemic. Cognitive distortion, when left unexamined, breeds dysfunction, disconnection and, ultimately, undermines our eudaimonic wellbeing[36] and sustained effectiveness, both individually and collectively.

When shadows disrupt wholeness

As previously stated, dysfunction arises at any stage in this process if a key component is missing, misaligned or improperly integrated. In medicine, a disease or imbalance occurs within the body. In thought and decision-making, it manifests as flawed reasoning, cognitive distortions or psychological fragmentation.

On a personal level, shadows interfere with our ability to transcend limitations, leading to internal contradictions that manifest as chronic indecision, procrastination, overreaction to minor issues, struggles with commitment, self-sabotage and so on.

These manifestations of internal misalignment show how shadows don't just disrupt individual functioning, but also larger social, cultural and institutional structures. Recognising these distortions is the first step towards restoring clarity, integration and intentional living, allowing for the proper transcendence and inclusion necessary for true wholeness or integrity.

The shadows in human cognition and knowledge formation

Human cognition is not a passive observer of reality; it is an active participant. We don't simply register the world as it is. We filter, interpret and project our understanding onto it. We construct meaning through metacontent, including our cognitive maps (what things are to us) and mental models (how we believe things work). These structures shape not only our engagement with material reality, but also with abstract concepts like commitment, responsibility and justice.

---

36 Eudaimonic wellbeing is a deeper form of wellbeing derived from living in alignment with one's values, purpose and potential, as opposed to simply pursuing pleasure or avoiding pain.

Shadows are not limited to emotions or unconscious biases. They extend into the very foundation of human cognition and knowledge formation. From infancy, we begin to construct our understanding of reality, relying on limited experiences, cultural narratives and inherited assumptions. However, when gaps, traumas or misaligned concepts remain unexamined, they introduce distortions in perception that persist into adulthood, subtly shaping our sense of self, relationships, agency and the world at large.

Shadows in cognition do not merely cause misunderstandings. They define the limits of what we believe to be possible, often confining individuals and societies to false narratives, flawed reasoning and cycles of dysfunction.

The patterns we internalise, whether primal instincts like fear and courage or learned behaviours like queuing in high-demand situations or navigating bureaucratic systems, become part of this mental framework that structures our perception and decision-making. Over time, the internalised patterns manifest externally, shaping social norms, legal contracts and shared societal understandings. These 'intersubjective agreements' are the implicit and explicit rules that allow societies to function, from traffic laws to economic systems, all of which emerge from our collective sense-making. In essence, much of what we accept as reality is a projection of what exists within us, shaped by the shadows we have yet to examine.

This is why it matters to have a healthy relationship with authenticity, specifically in the context of human cognition and knowledge. It involves a commitment to developing congruent, credible conceptions of ideas, constructs and various aspects of reality – both material and abstract. Let's examine this more closely through the lens of how we think, interpret and make sense of the world.

The different ways people choose to engage with reality

Some people are not interested in change. They are only interested in the illusion of change. They want the system to magically function while they continue to contribute as little as possible. They demand transformation, but not if it requires them to transform. And so, when collapse inevitably arrives, they act shocked. They weep over the ruin, lamenting how 'someone' should have done something, never realising that someone was them.

A system's viability depends not only on the leader's competence, but also on the authentic engagement of its members. No matter how capable, a leader cannot carry the weight of an entire system alone. A sustainable system is one where its members do not just exist within it, but actively participate in its integrity.

The term 'participative leadership' has appeared in organisational studies for decades, often referring to leaders who involve members in decision-making and distribute authority more broadly. While valuable, this usage tends to remain procedural, focused on input and role allocation. Here, participative leadership is framed differently. It is not merely about the delegation of decision rights, but about the *ontological depth of engagement* – the congruence between presence, authenticity and contribution that sustains systemic integrity. Leadership, in this sense, is less about where authority sits and more about how members participate in the coherence and resilience of the whole. This reframing places participative leadership within the discourse of Being and systemic sustainability, where engagement itself becomes a generative act of leadership.

However, participation is not uniform. People engage with reality in profoundly different ways, and these differences ultimately determine whether a system thrives, decays or collapses. For example, a manager might invite votes on policies as a procedural form of participation. But ontological participative leadership only shows up when team members actively safeguard alignment between their values and actions, holding one another accountable for the system's integrity rather than just contributing opinions.

Modes of engagement with authenticity

There are three fundamental modes of engagement with authenticity – one healthy and two unhealthy – that shape how individuals interact with the reality of their circumstances.

1. **A healthy relationship with authenticity: alignment with how things actually are**

   This is the gold standard and the foundation of authentic sustainability. It requires a commitment to developing congruent, credible conceptions of ideas, constructs and various aspects of reality, both material and abstract. Those who engage authentically do not simply accept reality – they seek to understand it, refine their perspective and align their actions accordingly.

   A healthy relationship with authenticity is not just about seeing things as they are but about acting in accordance with that awareness. It requires individuals to stay true to themselves and to others, ensuring that self-image aligns with persona – that who they believe themselves to be is reflected in who they actually are.

   Systems thrive when enough people within that system engage in this way. Decision-making improves, dysfunction is kept in check and progress is sustained. But when this mode of engagement is rare or absent – when most individuals choose one of the following two paths – the system begins a slow march towards collapse.

2. **Passive unhealthy relationship with authenticity: oblivion, leniency and intellectual laziness**

   This is where people engage with reality in a shallow, so-called 'instinctive' and passive manner. They operate at the level of immediate perception, gut feelings and raw, unprocessed understanding. They stop at first impressions, mistaking surface-level observations for truth, failing to scrutinise, analyse or refine their perspectives.

   Mental shortcuts, cognitive ease and intellectual laziness dominate this mode of engagement with authenticity. It's not necessarily malicious; it is simply inert. These individuals do not set out to sabotage a system. However, their complacency, avoidance of complexity and unwillingness to examine things beyond the obvious make them complicit in its dysfunction.

A system can sustain a handful of people like this, as long as the majority remain engaged with authenticity. But when too many opt for this effortless mode of existence, the system becomes top-heavy, reliant on fewer and fewer critical thinkers to carry the cognitive load.

3. **Active unhealthy relationship with authenticity: active rejection despite recognising the truth**

   This is the most insidious mode of engagement with authenticity and the most dangerous. Unlike intellectual laziness, where people fail to examine reality, individuals in this category recognise the truth, but intentionally and actively reject it. This is not ignorance; it's defiance. It is a deliberate, conscious refusal to align with what is credible, accurate and well-founded.

   The reasons for adopting this form of unhealthy relationship with authenticity include pride, envy, greed, ego, an unhealthy relationship with vulnerability, ideological biases, shame, psychological safety, emotional comfort, false righteousness, self-interest or even the lure of immediate perceived benefits. Some reject reality because it threatens their sense of control. Others reject it because it exposes their inauthenticity, forcing them to confront the gap between who they claim to be and who they actually are.

   This mode of engagement corrodes a system from within. It manufactures dysfunction, creating resistance, obstruction and sabotage. The worst part? These individuals are not clueless. They see the same cracks and failings as those engaging authentically. However, instead of working towards integrity, they exploit, manipulate or dismiss them.

When a system is riddled with too many individuals in the latter two categories, collapse is no longer a possibility but an inevitability. A structure can only lean so far before it topples, and when the weight of denial, avoidance and outright defiance grows too heavy, no leader, miracle or last-ditch effort can hold it together. It will crumble. And perhaps, in such cases, that is precisely what should happen.

The hidden forces at work: Shadows as the architects of dysfunction

While suffering has been widely examined across philosophical, psychological and sociological domains, the role of shadows – those unseen forces that distort perception, reinforce limiting narratives and perpetuate dysfunction – remains underexplored. Let's examine this in more detail.

As mentioned, shadows do not merely linger in the background of human experience. They actively shape the way we think, act and relate to the world. Moreover, shadows do not exist solely at the personal level. They are embedded in the collective knowledge, assumptions and narratives that shape how we understand the world.

In their broadest sense, shadows manifest as collective misconceptions, influencing everything from cultural norms to institutional structures. When ignored, they shape our reality in ways we fail to recognise, influencing our choices, social structures and collective behaviours. Importantly, shadows do not cause dysfunction through misery, entrenchment and our experience of them (suffering) directly. Instead, they set the conditions for dysfunction, creating blind spots that prevent individuals and societies from engaging with reality as it is.

How shadows embed themselves in thought and meaning-making

Every individual constructs cognitive maps – representations of what things are and their perceived significance – as well as mental models that shape their understanding of how things work. These frameworks guide how we interpret information, predict outcomes and make decisions. However, when built on incomplete, repressed or distorted knowledge, they become breeding grounds for shadows, subtly shaping thought processes, behavioural patterns and even systemic structures.

Consider financial wellbeing as an example. Our perception of money, debt and economic exchange is largely shaped by our upbringing, societal influences and personal experiences. This forms our cognition or cognitive map of finance. We then use this foundational knowledge to develop mental models that dictate how we engage with income, investment, spending and risk-taking. If these mental models are misaligned through inherited fears, misguided beliefs or learned dysfunctions, our financial decisions will be significantly impacted and could result in deep-seated patterns of struggle. Some might develop reckless spending habits, while others could fall into fear-based hoarding, extreme risk aversion or an inability to build sustainable wealth.

The same principle applies to relationships, leadership, career choices, ethics and self-perception. Shadows embedded in these areas manifest as chronic struggles, self-sabotaging behaviours and dysfunctions so ingrained that they are mistaken for natural limitations rather than what they truly are: constructed constraints that can be examined, understood and transcended.

Shadows from a systemic perspective

Shadows do not merely distort individual perception. They permeate entire systems, depriving them of coherence. A system, whether ecological, economic, political or social, relies on the interdependence of its components to function effectively. When a key element is lost, misaligned or corrupted, the entire structure is thrown into dysfunction, often in ways that go unnoticed until collapse becomes inevitable.

Consider an ecosystem. If bees were removed, the natural balance would unravel. Pollination would decline, food chains would weaken and biodiversity would diminish. Each part of the system has a rightful place, and when that balance is disturbed, the effects ripple outward, often compounding over time.

The same principle applies to human systems. When foundational principles such as trust, transparency and accountability erode, dysfunction spreads. Economic systems become exploitative, political structures turn corrupt and social frameworks fragment under competing distortions of truth and justice. These systemic shadows do not emerge from isolated actions but from collective blind spots, reinforced by institutions and cultural narratives that fail to evolve or challenge their own distortions and dysfunctions. We will explore the impact of shadows on systems like the economy in more detail later.

By understanding shadows at the systemic level, we begin to see why dysfunction is not always the result of external failures. More often, it is the product of unexamined shadows operating within the system itself.

Reality, knowledge and the emergence of shadows in various domains

Reality differs significantly from human knowledge. While reality exists independently of human perception, all knowledge is, to some degree, constructed: filtered through interpretation, language and historical context. Shadows emerge where these constructs are misaligned, distorted or incomplete, leading to blind spots in the understanding of ourselves, others and the systems we operate within.

The concepts of shadows, integrity and disintegration are used in this book in their most expansive and fundamental sense – as structural conditions that shape human perception, relationships and systems. However, while these phenomena are universal in nature, they are also contextual in their manifestation. They do not exist in an abstract void. They take form within specific domains – personal, societal, cultural and institutional – where they shape human experience in distinct ways. Understanding them structurally does not exclude their contextual expressions. It highlights their adaptability in shaping both individual and collective realities.

Shadows appear in multiple domains:

- **Human performance:** Distortions in one's relationship with qualities such as authenticity, assertiveness, courage, proactivity, fear and anxiety arise when they are misunderstood or suppressed. When that happens, they create dysfunction in personal and professional growth. For example, a person raised in an environment where assertiveness was discouraged may struggle with self-advocacy, mistaking compliance for collaboration.

- **Relationships:** Shadows in relational dynamics stem from unresolved emotional wounds, learned attachment patterns and suppressed fears. These distortions influence trust, emotional availability, conflict resolution and self-worth, often leading to recurring patterns of dysfunctional interactions. A person raised in an environment where vulnerability was seen as weakness may unconsciously sabotage intimacy to avoid the discomfort of emotional openness.
- **Leadership and authority:** Shadows emerge when power, influence and responsibility are perceived through unexamined distortions. These shadows dictate how authority is wielded, opposition is handled and engagement with followers is structured. A leader who equates control with competence may resort to micromanagement and authoritarian tactics, believing that trusting others signals incompetence.
- **Personal agency and decision-making:** Internalised failures, learned helplessness or distorted beliefs about personal capability influence how challenges are approached. These shadows determine whether difficulties are seen as opportunities for growth or insurmountable obstacles. Someone who has internalised a childhood narrative of inadequacy may avoid pursuing ambitious goals, convinced that failure is inevitable.
- **Ethics and morality:** Ethical and moral frameworks – whether cultural, legal or philosophical – aim to create order, but are shaped by historical and societal influences, leading to inconsistencies. Certain behaviours, such as sexual conduct or dress codes, have long faced intense moral scrutiny, while others, like consumer habits, are often ignored. When morality is absorbed through social conditioning rather than critical thought, it fosters hypocrisy, moral licensing or rigid dogmatism. A person who sees certain actions as justified within their group, but reprehensible in others may unknowingly apply double standards, enforcing moral rules based on affiliation rather than principle. In this way, ethics

and morality, when unexamined, can reinforce biases and shape norms in ways that contradict their intended purpose.
- **Intellectual and moral integrity:** Shadows emerge when ethical principles or intellectual standards are selectively applied, leading to contradictions, misrepresentations and logical fallacies. A thinker who once sought truth may, over time, become more invested in defending a position than in refining their understanding, allowing ideological loyalty to override intellectual honesty. When conviction hardens into dogma, even those who pride themselves on critical thought risk becoming mouthpieces for external agendas, shaping their discourse to fit narratives rather than reality.

It is worth repeating that these shadows do not exist in isolation. Instead, they interact and reinforce one another, shaping the structures of thought, behaviour and governance that define human existence. Their manifestations extend beyond personal distortions and into broader societal frameworks, influencing relationships, leadership, personal agency and decision-making.

Recognising the structural and contextual nature of these ontological phenomena allows for a deeper, more practical understanding of how they shape human experience. While these concepts remain universal in their implications, their expressions are deeply embedded in the specific domains where they manifest, influencing the way individuals and systems function, evolve or collapse.

The relationship between shadows and misery

Misery doesn't arise from shadows themselves, but from our failure to confront them. When shadows remain unexamined, they distort meaning-making, decision-making and emotional resilience, leading to entrenched patterns of dysfunction that become self-reinforcing. In this way, misery is not merely the absence of wellbeing; it is the persistence of suffering sustained by unconfronted shadows.

To fully understand how misery arises and persists, we must recognise that misery is not a primary or self-generating state of being. It does not exist on its own, but emerges when shadows distort perception, meaning and decision-making. Just as physical illness results from prolonged imbalances in the body, misery arises from the prolonged entrenchment of psychological, emotional and societal shadows. This happens when shadows are not integrated, meaning they are ignored, suppressed or left unresolved rather than acknowledged and consciously worked through.

Misery is not mere hardship. It is the prolonged, self-reinforcing suffering that results from failing to confront and integrate shadows. Misery is also not synonymous with pain. Pain – whether physical or emotional – serves a functional role, alerting us to harm or signalling areas in need of growth and healing. In contrast, misery is suffering that has become entrenched, a byproduct of shadows. More specifically, it is self-reinforcing dysfunction that arises when we fail to confront and integrate the shadows influencing our reality.

Misery can occur at multiple levels:

- **Personal shadows:** Misery manifests as self-deception, avoidance, anxiety and unresolved emotional wounds.
- **Interpersonal shadows:** Misery manifests as toxic dynamics between two or more people, leading to dysfunctional relationships.
- **Cultural and institutional shadows:** Misery manifests as societal structures that reinforce division, exploitation and systemic dysfunction.
- **Existential shadows:** Misery manifests as the erosion of meaning, leading to nihilism, alienation and disconnection from reality.

Shadows do not simply generate misery; they act as filters, shaping how we experience reality itself. If shadows act as cognitive and emotional filters, causing the condition of misery, then suffering is the experience of life as seen through these distorted lenses. When misery persists unaddressed, it becomes entrenched, self-sustaining to the point that escape seems impossible. For example, someone with unresolved trauma may interpret neutral events as threats, leading to chronic anxiety. A society burdened by historical injustices may perpetuate suffering through systemic oppression, as each generation internalises the unresolved trauma. An individual who avoids difficult truths may remain stuck in cycles of stagnation, unable to break free from resentment or self-victimisation, further deepening their entrenchment in suffering.

Reflection

The presence of shadows in thought, relationships and societal structures is not inherently negative. It is our unwillingness or inability to confront them that leads to dysfunction and misery. Recognising shadows is the first step in reclaiming clarity, coherence and intentionality in how we engage with reality.

Reflect on the following:

1. **Where in your life do shadows manifest as avoidance, self-sabotage or limiting beliefs?**

    - Are there areas where you repeatedly experience frustration, stagnation or conflict?
    - Could these struggles be rooted in unexamined patterns of thought, inherited narratives or suppressed emotions?

2. **How do shadows influence your relationships and decision-making?**

    - Do you notice recurring patterns in your interactions – such as defensiveness, mistrust or emotional withdrawal – that may stem from unresolved past experiences?
    - Are there subtle distortions in how you perceive others, leading to misunderstandings, projection or relational dysfunction?

3. **How might societal or cultural shadows shape your worldview?**

    - Do you hold beliefs that might not be your own, but were absorbed through social conditioning, media or cultural norms?

- Are you able to critically assess whether your metacontent – your stories, perspectives, paradigms, etc. - is aligned with reality or shaped by distortions?

4. **Reflect on the health of your relationship with authenticity. Consider the following:**

- How committed are you to developing authentic knowledge that accurately reflects reality rather than conforming to inherited narratives, biases or emotional comfort?
- In what areas of your life or work might you be clinging to distorted or outdated conceptions of reality?
- How can you improve the alignment between your understanding of reality and your actions, decisions and relationships?

Shadows do not disappear simply by wishing them away. They require engagement, inquiry and the courage to confront them. Recognising how shadows distort perception is the first step towards reclaiming clarity, agency and alignment in both personal and collective domains. Furthermore, shadows don't operate in isolation; they create self-reinforcing loops that, when left unchecked, solidify into patterns of misery. These cycles create a dangerous illusion. The more we see the world through unexamined shadows, the more we mistake misery for reality itself. When this happens, we risk becoming trapped in the false belief that misery is inevitable rather than constructed and woven into our perceptions, behaviours and societal frameworks.

Later in this book, we deconstruct these unseen forces to make sense of their mechanisms and equip ourselves with the tools necessary to integrate and transcend them. We will also dissect how misery is structurally sustained by shadows through the 'Shadow-Misery Spiral', a model that reveals how ignored and unintegrated shadows influence personal struggles, interpersonal conflicts and systemic dysfunction to perpetuate cycles of suffering.

However, confronting shadows is not enough. It must be coupled with the pursuit of authentic knowledge. This is knowledge that emerges from rigorous inquiry, intellectual honesty and alignment with reality as it truly is rather than how we wish it to be. Authentic knowledge provides the framework needed to identify, examine and ultimately transcend the distortions that perpetuate misery. Without this commitment to truth, we remain trapped in self-reinforcing loops of dysfunction.

For now, the critical takeaway is this: misery is not a random affliction. It's a consequence of unresolved shadows and a failure to pursue authentic knowledge. It persists where there is avoidance, distortion and a lack of clarity.

CHAPTER 6

The Systemic Subversion Cycle (SSC)

The modern world finds itself at a precarious crossroads, confronted by cascading crises that threaten not only the fabric of civilisation, but the very survival of humanity. Wars, environmental degradation, economic instability and cultural erosion are no longer distant concerns. They are daily existential realities, deeply embedded in the structures that shape our existence. These crises are not merely background noise, but the result of a system that is structurally predisposed to dysfunction, exploitation and subversion.

What distinguishes our time from previous periods of upheaval is the unprecedented interconnectedness of these crises. Advances in technology and communication have created a world where events in one region reverberate globally. Political instability in a single nation can disrupt supply chains, a financial crisis can plunge millions into poverty and a regional conflict can trigger waves of displacement that shake entire continents. While humanity's challenges have globalised, our capacity for systemic resilience has not. Instead of coordinated solutions, we see fragmented governance, ideological entrenchment and power structures that thrive on instability rather than resolution.

The interwoven nature of crises

Each crisis, while appearing independent, is deeply interconnected, creating feedback loops that amplify their destructive impact. Wars displace millions, fuelling refugee crises that strain already overburdened infrastructures and escalate geopolitical tensions. Environmental shifts worsen these pressures. Rising sea levels, droughts and resource scarcity intensify social unrest, pushing vulnerable populations into conflict-ridden regions. Feedback loops are well studied in systems dynamics, where recurring systems archetypes have been identified as repeating patterns of behaviour. Well-known patterns such as 'Limits to Growth' and the 'Tragedy of the Commons' mirror the very crises we are experiencing globally.[37]

These crises do not simply emerge from chaos. They are often exacerbated or actively perpetuated by flawed institutions, entrenched power structures and the strategic exploitation of instability. While existing models attempt to explain crisis interconnectivity, they largely fail to address how crises become entrenched, sustained and manipulated.

Existing models and the need for a paradigm shift

In the study of global crises and systemic instability, several established models attempt to explain the interconnected nature of economic, environmental and geopolitical disruptions. Among these, the Polycrisis Framework[38] describes multiple simultaneous crises that compound each other, creating unpredictable and often overwhelming systemic risks. The International Futures (IFs)

---

[37] Braun, W. (2002) 'The System Archetypes', in *The Systems Modeling Workbook* (pp. 1-26). https://www.albany.edu/faculty/gpr/PAD724/724WebArticles/sys_archetypes.pdf

[38] The term *polycrisis* was first introduced by Edgar Morin and Anne-Brigitte Kern in *Terre-Patrie* (1993), describing the convergence of multiple interlinked crises that amplify one another. See: Morin, E. and Kern, A.-B. (1993) *Terre-Patrie*. Translated by Catherine M.G.L. Duport 2000. Paris: Éditions du Seuil. The concept has gained renewed attention in the 2020s, particularly through the work of Adam Tooze and institutions like the Cascade Institute. See: Tooze, A. (2022) *Welcome to the World of the Polycrisis*. Financial Times, 28 October.

model,[39] developed by Barry B. Hughes at the University of Denver, is a comprehensive global forecasting system used by researchers and international organisations to explore long-term trends across domains such as economics, demographics and governance. And methodologies developed by the Complexity Science Hub Vienna[40] examine how crises emerge and cascade within dynamically interconnected systems.

While these models provide valuable insights into crisis interdependencies, they largely focus on emergent complexity rather than systemic failure driven by governance, power struggles and intentional subversion. They also assume that crises emerge from neutral systemic forces, failing to account for how power struggles, ideological agendas and people acting in bad faith intentionally accelerate, exploit or entrench crises. By ignoring the role of deliberate subversion, these frameworks misdiagnose the root causes of systemic dysfunction.

The Systemic Subversion Cycle (SSC): Exposing how crises entrench dysfunction

The Systemic Subversion Cycle (SSC) fills a critical gap in our understanding of global crises and systemic instability. Where most models treat crises as isolated or naturally self-resolving, the SSC reveals a more unsettling reality: crises are often prolonged, manipulated or exacerbated by structural misalignments, cultural erosion and – in many cases – people operating in bad faith who exploit instability for power, profit or ideological gain.

Rather than relying on predictive analytics or abstract modelling, the SSC functions as a narrative-driven diagnostic tool. It exposes the deeper mechanisms through which systems fail to recover, spiral into dysfunction and become resistant to renewal. Whether we're

---

39   Hughes, B.B., et al., (2011) *International Futures (IFs) Version 7.00: User's Guide.* Frederick S. Pardee Center for International Futures, University of Denver. Available at: https://korbel.du.edu/wp-content/uploads/2015/04/International-Futures-IFs-Training-Manual.pdf

40   See: Complexity Science Hub Vienna (n.d.) *Crisis and Complexity.* Available at: https://csh.ac.at/research/research-topic/social-complexity-collapse/

dealing with economic collapse, political instability, environmental disaster or social unrest, the SSC shows that these are rarely spontaneous disruptions. They follow self-reinforcing patterns that fragment coherence and lock systems into cycles of crisis.

Where the Unified Ontology of Systemic Integrity (UOSI) provides the overarching architecture for understanding integrity, disintegration and modulation, the SSC zooms into the Disintegration Sphere to provide a field tool. It traces, step by step, how systems move from initial disruption to entrenched collapse, helping leaders, policymakers and individuals locate where a system sits in the cycle and what kind of intervention may be required.

The value of the SSC does not only lie in diagnosing wars or global economic shocks. The same cycle is at work in the everyday systems we inhabit: our partnerships, families, teams and organisations. A 'crisis trigger' at home might be a broken promise, a sudden job loss or a betrayal of trust. Structural breakdown shows up when communication falters, roles blur or expectations remain unspoken. Within an organisation, displacement and resource strain may emerge as one partner carrying all the emotional or financial load, or in a team where a handful of employees are stretched to breaking point. Escalation and fractures take shape in resentment, gossip or withdrawal, while exploitation and entrenchment appear when someone uses the turmoil to assert control or protect their ego. Inertia follows when leaders, parents or partners delay addressing the fracture, hoping it will resolve itself, only to see the cycle repeat. Left unacknowledged, these dynamics become culture – the 'way things are around here' – embedding patterns of dysfunction that erode trust and belonging.

This is where the SSC can serve as a practical lens for sense-making. By naming the stages, individuals and collectives can locate themselves within the cycle and recognise that what feels like chaos actually follows a discernible pattern. Instead of reacting blindly, they can intervene consciously – perhaps by repairing trust before inertia sets in, or by addressing resource strain before resentment hardens into fracture. In this way, the SSC is not only a framework for global systems analysis, but a living diagnostic tool for the conditions of everyday life. Whether applied in intimate relationships, families, teams, organisations, institutions, cultures or societies, it helps us move from blame and confusion towards clarity, shared responsibility and the possibility of renewal.

The SSC's value lies in four key contributions:

1. **A map of collapse dynamics:** Unlike models that focus on crisis resolution or surface symptoms, the SSC outlines a predictable sequence – from crisis trigger and structural breakdown to entrenchment and recurrence. This helps diagnose not just that a system is failing, but *why* it is failing and *how* the dysfunction is being reinforced.

2. **A lens on governance failures and bad faith:** Where other models treat governance as a background factor, the SSC places institutional breakdown, corruption and ideological manipulation at the centre of crisis perpetuation. It highlights how strategic distortion, power struggles and misaligned incentives prolong instability and block resolution.

3. **Integration of cultural and societal erosion:** Most crisis models focus on economic or political factors. The SSC goes deeper, revealing how cultural homogenisation, forced migration, identity fragmentation and meaning collapse act as destabilising forces. These dimensions connect directly to the Being Framework and metacontent discourse, showing how disconnection at the level of human meaning accelerates systemic collapse.

4. **A practical diagnostic tool for intervention:** Rather than offering a predictive framework built on abstract datasets, the SSC provides a narrative and ontological lens. It helps practitioners, leaders and citizens move beyond surface-level analysis to engage the deeper patterns of dysfunction, distortion and entrenchment.

Within the broader Authentic Sustainability Framework (ASF), the SSC serves as the diagnostic lens of the Disintegration Sphere. Whereas the ASF as a whole provides the architecture for understanding how integrity is built, sustained and restored, the SSC reveals the opposite: how systems unravel. Its role is not predictive modelling, but sense-making. By surfacing the feedback loops that keep dysfunction alive, it highlights how bad faith, cultural erosion and misaligned incentives deepen crises, and it points to the fractures that require attention if sustainability is to be more than rhetoric. In this way, the SSC complements the constructive dimensions of the ASF by exposing the mechanisms of collapse it seeks to prevent.

Ultimately, the SSC serves as a bridge between ontological theory and applied systems thinking. It can be used to diagnose shadows, breakdowns and collapse dynamics within any system – whether personal, organisational, institutional or societal. As a diagnostic lens, it helps clarify where a system sits within the cycle, what forces are reinforcing dysfunction, and how to design regenerative interventions that restore coherence and reorient the system towards sustainability.

By exposing the feedback loops that sustain dysfunction, the SSC – as shown in Figure 2 – equips us to do more than react to crises. It empowers us to interrupt the cycle, reclaim coherence and create the structural conditions for renewal. In doing so, it reinforces a central insight of this book: sustainability is not achieved by preserving the status quo. It is achieved by understanding and intentionally modulating the forces that sustain or erode systemic integrity.

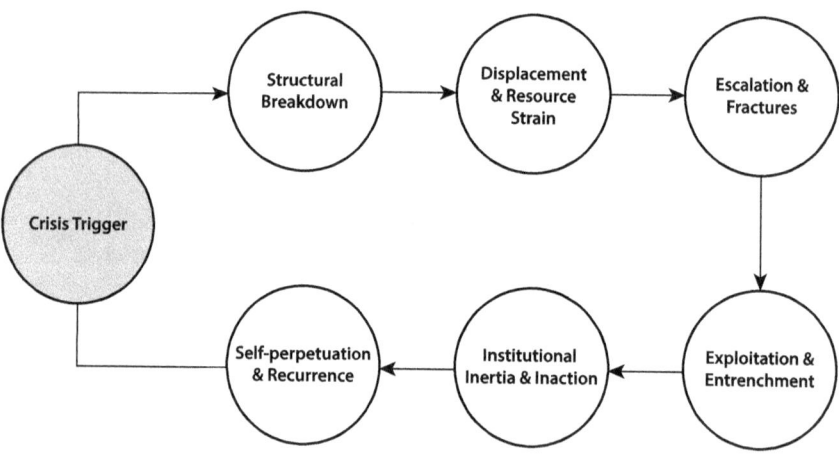

Figure 2 – Systemic Subversion Cycle.

- **Crisis Trigger:** A destabilising event (e.g., financial collapse, ecological disaster, social unrest, political turmoil) disrupts a system, creating widespread uncertainty and vulnerability.

- **Structural Breakdown:** Systemic erosion, e.g., institutions, infrastructure or economic frameworks begin to erode, amplifying instability.
- **Displacement and Resource Strain:** Forced re-organisation, e.g., people, businesses or entire sectors are forced to adapt, migrate or reorganise, leading to competition for limited resources.
- **Escalation and Fractures**: Amplified division, e.g., tension rise, manifesting in economic disparity, ideological polarisation or civil unrest, further weakening social cohesion.
- **Exploitation and Entrenchment**: Abuse of power, e.g., people acting in bad faith, interest groups or governing bodies manipulate the crisis for financial, political or ideological gain, deepening the dysfunction.
- **Institutional Inertia and Inaction**: Failure to respond, e.g., corruption, inefficiency or bureaucratic paralysis prevent meaningful intervention, allowing the crisis to persist or worsen.
- **Self-perpetuation and Recurrence:** Crisis feedback loop, e.g., the unresolved crisis fuels future crises, reinforcing a destructive loop that is increasingly difficult to escape.

Tangible example 1: An environmental crisis

- **Crisis Trigger**: A prolonged drought in sub-Saharan Africa leads to widespread crop failures and water shortages.
- **Structural Breakdown:** The agricultural economy crumbles, leading to food insecurity and economic decline.
- **Displacement and Resource Strain:** Desperate populations migrate to urban centres or cross borders, placing immense pressure on infrastructure and resources.
- **Escalation and Fractures:** Overcrowding, competition for resources and economic desperation fuel social unrest and conflict.

- **Exploitation and Entrenchment**: Opportunists, such as corporations, political factions or external powers, exploit the crisis for financial or geopolitical leverage.

- **Institutional Inertia and Inaction**: Corrupt or ineffective governments fail to intervene effectively, exacerbating suffering and instability.

- **Self-perpetuation and Recurrence**: The long-term damage to ecosystems and governance ensures future droughts will trigger similar, if not worse, crises.

What begins as a localised environmental disaster rapidly expands into an economic, social and geopolitical catastrophe. This demonstrates how the SSC doesn't just highlight crisis interconnectivity, it also demonstrates how dysfunction becomes embedded and self-reinforcing over time.

Systemic instability not only manifests in war, environmental disasters and political volatility, but is also deeply embedded in economic structures. A stark illustration of this is 'greedflation' – when corporations exploit inflationary environments as a justification for disproportionate price increases, enriching themselves at the public's expense.

Paul Donovan, Chief Economist at UBS, explores this phenomenon in his 2023 paper 'What Is Profit-Led Inflation?'[41] In it, Donovan highlights how corporations – particularly in essential sectors like energy, food and housing – may use inflation not merely to pass on higher costs (cost-push inflation), but to strategically widen profit margins by exploiting consumer fear and perceived scarcity. This distinction between necessary price adjustments and opportunistic pricing exposes how economic crises can be leveraged for financial gain under the guise of necessity.

The impact is devastating. Families struggle to afford basic needs like food, housing and healthcare. Social tensions rise as inequality

---

41 Donovan, P. (2023) *What is Profit-Led Inflation?* UBS GWM, 16 March. Available at http://joseluisoreiro.com.br/site/link/332ed4a1c501e1d8970217df6e74fc78101f27a3.pdf

deepens. And public trust in economic and political institutions erodes, compounding systemic fragility.

While some governments, such as those in the European Union, have implemented price caps and excess profit taxes to curb corporate opportunism, in many regions, political inertia and corporate lobbying prevent meaningful reform. The result? Unchecked greed accelerates social and economic fragmentation, reinforcing the Systemic Subversion Cycle rather than resolving the crisis.

Tangible example 2: A workplace breakdown

- **Crisis Trigger:** A sudden leadership change or major budget cut is announced. Employees feel destabilised and uncertain about the future.
- **Structural Breakdown:** Clear communication channels and decision-making processes erode. Rumours spread, roles blur and priorities become inconsistent.
- **Displacement and Resource Strain:** A few team members shoulder extra responsibilities, while others feel sidelined or excluded. Workload imbalances strain relationships and wellbeing.
- **Escalation and Fractures:** Frustration builds. Gossip, mistrust and factions emerge. Collaboration gives way to self-preservation.
- **Exploitation and Entrenchment:** Certain individuals exploit the instability – angling for promotions, pushing hidden agendas or protecting their own turf at others' expense.
- **Institutional Inertia and Inaction:** Leadership avoids addressing the tension, downplays the problems or delays intervention. The dysfunction hardens into 'just the way things are.'
- **Self-perpetuation and Recurrence:** The unresolved fractures embed themselves in the culture. Staff turnover rises, morale declines and the organisation repeats the same patterns with each new disruption.

What begins as a simple leadership change or budget cut quickly spirals into cultural erosion, fractured trust and repeating cycles of dysfunction. The SSC helps us see that these outcomes are not random but patterned. By recognising the cycle early, teams and leaders can intervene before instability becomes embedded as culture.

Inherited systemic delusions: How outdated paradigms sustain the cycle

Many of today's existential crises persist because they are built upon outdated paradigms inherited from the industrial era, chief among them:

- The illusion that humanity can 'conquer' nature as opposed to coexist with it.
- The belief that scientific reductionism – the approach of explaining complex phenomena by breaking them down into their simplest, most fundamental parts and studying those parts in isolation – can solve all complex problems.

A clear example of this misalignment is resource allocation in environmental efforts. While technological advancements such as carbon capture and electric vehicles (EVs) hold promise, they are often prioritised over nature-based solutions such as reforestation, soil regeneration and sustainable land management. This is not to say technology lacks value, but rather that the Systemic Subversion Cycle manifests in systemic inertia, preventing holistic thinking and maintaining entrenched, short-term economic incentives.

Real progress does not come from technological fixes alone, but from a broader re-evaluation of what we define as growth, prosperity and sustainability. Structural change in our thinking also requires confronting how easily we abandon our own values – individually and collectively – when convenience, fear or short-term gain take precedence. It means exposing the systemic bad faith that sustains entrenched paradigms and recovering an authentic alignment with what we claim to care about. Without this recalibration of both thought and value, crises will continue to self-perpetuate in never-ending cycles of systemic subversion rather than being transcended.

The Liberal World Order: A model in crisis

The Systemic Subversion Cycle is also visible at a geopolitical scale. After World War II, the Liberal International Order (LIO) provided a framework for post-war stability. Institutions such as the United Nations, the Bretton Woods financial system and global trade agreements aimed to prevent large-scale conflicts and foster economic cooperation.

However, the LIO has since weakened under the pressures of globalisation, geopolitical shifts and unregulated financialisation. The collapse of the Soviet Union in 1991 ushered in an era of rapid economic expansion. However, it also:

- Widened income disparities, intensifying social unrest.
- Exacerbated resource exploitation, driving environmental and economic crises.
- Destabilised many regions, making conflicts more likely.

The Russia-Ukraine war, among other conflicts, underscores the fragility of this model. It reveals a fundamental truth – systems built without the resilience to adapt will inevitably fracture under stress.

The LIO is now at a tipping point. Without new frameworks of cooperation, the global order will continue cycling through systemic subversion, crises and instability.

The barrier of collective psychosis

Beyond political and economic structures, a significant psychological barrier prevents meaningful action against existential threats: collective psychosis, a societal condition in which delusion and denial replace rational discourse and accountability.

This manifests in several ways:

- Denying scientific evidence in favour of ideological beliefs.
- Refusing to acknowledge systemic failures and instead resorting to blame-shifting.
- Relying too heavily on simplistic narratives which provide false certainty but prevent meaningful action.

For example, climate debates are often dictated more by political allegiances than by scientific discourse, leading to polarisation rather than constructive problem-solving.

However, collective psychosis is not just about misinformation. It's also about the deep unwillingness to confront uncomfortable realities. As long as societies remain trapped in ideological rigidity and reactionary politics, sustainable solutions to the world's crises will remain out of reach.

This ideological rigidity is not exclusive to those who reject scientific evidence. It is equally present in the growing reductionist ideology of, for example, scientism. This doctrine elevates the scientific method beyond its scope, treating it not merely as a tool for inquiry but as the sole arbiter of truth, often to the exclusion of ethics, philosophy and other ways of knowing. In scientism, science is no longer a method of inquiry, but a dogma wielded for ideological control.

The issue is not science itself. Real science thrives on doubt, debate and falsifiability. The problem lies in the weaponisation of science by those who seek to use it as a mechanism of power, coercion and unchecked authority. For example, some political leaders and their academic counterparts have transformed 'following science' into an indisputable decree used to justify sweeping regulations, centralised governance and the curtailing of dissent. Under the noble-sounding banner of 'sustainability', 'systemic reform' or 'saving the planet', they have engineered policies that increasingly resemble authoritarian overreach rather than genuine environmental stewardship. Dissenters – whether scientists with differing interpretations, independent researchers or concerned citizens – are dismissed, ridiculed and, in some cases, outright bullied into submission.

Ironically, their 'modern ignorance' – the arrogant assumption that technocratic control and central planning will magically solve systemic issues – is the very impediment to the sustainability they claim to champion. By attempting to impose rigid, top-down solutions to inherently adaptive and complex problems, they stifle innovation, economic resilience and localised problem-solving. A coercive approach to sustainability is, amusingly, not 'sustainable' at all.

The absurd contradiction here is glaring: the very people who claim to fight ideological rigidity have themselves become an ideological force, pushing policies that are inefficient, rigid, authoritarian and deeply disconnected from reality. This is not sustainability. It is systemic subversion in disguise. When sustainability is used as a tool of coercion rather than empowerment, it ceases to be about long-term ecological balance. Instead, it becomes a justification for power consolidation. Once again, the Systemic Subversion Cycle is at play here – under the guise of progress, crisis mitigation and environmental responsibility.

The lesson? Beware of those who claim absolute certainty in the name of 'saving' the world. History suggests that their methods rarely serve the people and more often serve themselves.

The path to a thriving future

Imagine a world where:

- Displaced populations find refuge and opportunity rather than hostility and exclusion.
- Economic systems prioritise authentic, adaptive sustainability that fosters resilience and balance rather than serving as a veneer for control or ideological rigidity.
- Cultural diversity is preserved and celebrated rather than erased by homogenisation.

This is not a utopian dream. It is a call for pragmatic, structured change by rejecting complacency, stepping beyond ideological paralysis and engaging in genuine, pluralistic problem-solving.

Breaking free from cycles of dysfunction requires clarity and resolve. We need clarity to understand how these existential crises interconnect rather than seeing them in isolation. And we need the resolve or willingness to challenge institutional inertia, demand integrity and engage in structured, non-polarised sense-making that integrates multiple perspectives rather than retreating into ideological silos.

A tangible example of this pluralistic approach can be seen in successful conflict resolution efforts. Take post-apartheid South

Africa, where instead of perpetuating cycles of retribution, the Truth and Reconciliation Commission (TRC)[42] sought to integrate multiple perspectives – those of victims, perpetrators and broader society.

The TRC exemplified a systemic attempt to restore coherence by acknowledging the subjective truths of all participants – not to dissolve accountability, but to recognise that sustainable healing requires confronting complexity rather than collapsing it into singular narratives. While imperfect, this process avoided the polarisation of complete vengeance or total amnesty. Instead, it attempted to balance justice with national healing. This approach contrasts sharply with many modern political and ideological debates, where entrenched camps refuse to engage meaningfully with opposing views, perpetuating division rather than progress.

The dysfunctions of the past do not have to define the future. Addressing the world's existential crises demands more than reactive solutions. It requires a fundamental shift in how we think, organise and act, coupled with a commitment to integrate diverse perspectives rather than reinforce entrenched divisions.

In summary, the world's crises are vast, but change starts with awareness. How we think, engage and respond to complexity matters. The Systemic Subversion Cycle (SSC) is not just another framework; it is a necessary intervention. It uncovers the mechanics of crisis entrenchment, helping us see why crises persist, who benefits from them and what structural barriers must be dismantled for real resolution. It also reveals how crises are often not merely emergent but sustained, exploited and even manufactured. Recognising these patterns in the world around us is crucial. But just as importantly, we must ask: Where do these dynamics play out in our own lives, relationships and decision-making?

---

42   Truth and Reconciliation Commission (1998) *Truth and Reconciliation Commission of South Africa Report*. Vols. 1–5. Cape Town: Government of South Africa.

Reflection

Consider the following:

1. **Where in your personal or professional life have you witnessed dysfunction that persists due to entrenched interests, inertia or avoidance?**

    - Have you ever witnessed or become aware of problems not being solved but maintained to serve hidden agendas?
    - Have you ever seen a crisis exploited rather than resolved?

2. **Are you inadvertently reinforcing cycles of dysfunction?**

    - Have there been moments where you chose comfort over confrontation, allowing a failing system, workplace or relationship to continue unchecked?
    - Do you ever find yourself relying on simplistic narratives or ideological biases rather than engaging in nuanced, pluralistic sense-making?

3. **Do you recognise patterns of collective psychosis in the world around you?**

    - Have you noticed widespread denial, delusion or ideological rigidity preventing meaningful progress in social, economic or political domains?
    - Do you observe people prioritising dogma over dialogue, control over curiosity, or allegiance over integrity?

4. **What would it take to break free from these cycles, both personally and collectively?**

    - What steps can you take to engage in structured, multi-perspective sense-making?

The Systemic Subversion Cycle (SSC) is not just a macro-level phenomenon. It is present in our daily lives. By recognising how systemic subversion operates at multiple scales, we gain the ability to confront dysfunction rather than perpetuate it, both in our own lives and in the world at large.

CHAPTER 7

The Shadow Trap – How Dysfunction Undermines Sustainability

Throughout history, civilisations, institutions and entire systems have risen and collapsed, not merely because of external forces like war, economics or climate, but because of internal dysfunction. What we often call systemic failure is, at its core, a failure of sustainability – the inability to adapt, renew and remain aligned with reality.

Yet, when people talk about sustainability, they usually refer to environmental or economic sustainability. They discuss climate change, resource depletion, financial crises and market failures. However, these are all symptoms of a deeper issue. Authentic sustainability is not merely about managing resources or reforming institutions; it's about the integrity of individuals and the systems they create.

A system is only as sustainable as the people who uphold it. If those people act in bad faith, stagnate in rigidity or refuse to confront uncomfortable truths, the system will inevitably collapse under its own weight.

The economic stagnation we see today, from the rigidity of academia to the failure of mainstream institutions and the inability of politics to address real issues, is all part of this larger systemic dysfunction. The problem is not merely capitalism, socialism or governance; it's how we – as individuals and collectives – uphold and engage with systems that have long ceased to be sustainable.

The shadow of stagnation – Why systems stop evolving and become unsustainable

Every system begins with an intention. Governments are created to bring order and justice. Universities are established to pursue truth and knowledge. Economies are built to distribute resources and enable prosperity. Cultures form to create meaning and continuity. But over time, systems lose sight of their original purpose. They shift from serving their function to serving their own survival. They become rigid, bureaucratic and self-preserving. This is the first stage of unsustainability – when a system stops evolving and begins merely protecting itself.

Unsustainable Systems	Sustainable Systems
Resist change and enforce conformity	Continuously adapt and renew
Exist to serve their own survival	Exist to serve a function
Reward compliance and status quo thinking	Encourage integrity and innovation

Table 1 – The Shadow of Stagnation.

Once a system reaches this stage, it begins to stagnate. It stops addressing reality and instead becomes a closed loop, reinforcing itself while ignoring its failures. This is why many of our economic, academic and political institutions feel lifeless and disconnected: they are no longer functioning to serve their purpose but to justify their own existence.

The shadow of bad faith – Why dishonesty corrupts systems

Chapter 3 introduced the concept of bad faith and its impact and explored why every failed system is ultimately a story of bad faith. But, as we know, systems do not operate in isolation. Bad faith begins with individuals who choose deception over authenticity. To reiterate, bad faith is when we pretend to believe something we know is not true, such as when we act as if a system is working while knowing it is failing. More specifically, and at various levels:

- At an **individual level**, bad faith means acting against one's own values, such as staying in a role, relationship or belief system out of fear, self-preservation or social pressure rather than conviction.
- In **academia**, bad faith means pretending that outdated theories still explain the world, simply because challenging them would threaten careers and reputations.
- In **organisations**, bad faith means continuing outdated practices even when they no longer work because admitting failure is inconvenient.
- In **economics**, bad faith means promoting financial models that only benefit the elite while pretending they help everyone.
- In **politics**, bad faith means making policies based on ideology rather than reality.

A system that is sustained by bad faith is doomed to collapse. It becomes detached from truth, and the further it drifts, the more forcefully it resists correction.

Acting in Bad Faith	Acting with Authenticity
Defends dysfunction to avoid accountability	Willing to admit flaws and correct course
Says what is convenient rather than what is true	Aligns words with reality
Prioritises short-term self-preservation	Prioritises long-term sustainability

Table 2 – The Shadow of Bad Faith.

When bad faith becomes widespread, systems turn into rituals of dishonesty – where people say what they do not believe, agree to things they know are false and uphold systems they know are broken. This is why so many institutions today feel performative rather than purposeful. And as bad faith spreads, trust begins to collapse – first inwardly, then relationally, and, ultimately, systemically. People lose trust in themselves because their actions no longer align with what they know to be true. That inner dissonance is mirrored in relationships and institutions, eroding confidence in leaders, communities and the systems meant to serve them. In the absence of authenticity, trust cannot be sustained.

The shadow of rigidity – Why academia has stagnated

If there is any institution that should embrace truth-seeking, it is academia. Universities should be intellectual laboratories, constantly challenging assumptions, testing new ideas and evolving theories based on reality. Yet, modern academia has become one of the most rigid and stagnant systems in existence where:

- The pressure to conform discourages true intellectual risk-taking.
- The specialisation of disciplines prevents interdisciplinary thinking.
- The peer-review process prioritises safe, incremental work over radical new perspectives.
- The career incentives reward those who uphold existing frameworks rather than those who challenge them.

Consequently, academia has turned into a system that preserves knowledge rather than generates it.

What Academia Should Be	What Academia Has Become
Encourages questioning and innovation	Punishes deviation from accepted theories
Seeks truth over consensus	Seeks funding and reputation over truth
Open to paradigm shifts	Defends existing paradigms at all costs

Table 3 – The Shadow of Rigidity in Academia.

This is why economic thought, political theory and even scientific discourse struggle to move forward – the institutions that should be leading intellectual evolution have become the biggest obstacles to it.

The shadow of economic dysfunction – A case study in systemic rigidity

The economy is one of the clearest examples of a system that has become unsustainable due to stagnation, bad faith and rigidity. GDP growth is treated as the ultimate measure of success, even though it does not reflect human wellbeing. Financial markets are upheld as the core of the economy, even though they increasingly create crises instead of prosperity. Economic models ignore existential and ecological sustainability because the system is too invested in its own self-preservation.

What Economic Systems Should Prioritise	What They Actually Prioritise
Sustainability, human wellbeing and balance	Endless growth, speculation and extraction
Adaptive structures that evolve with reality	Rigid institutions that resist change
Ethical value creation	Profit maximisation at any cost

Table 4 – The Shadow of Economic Dysfunction.

The authentic sustainability discourse is not just about redesigning economic systems. It's about breaking free from the fundamental dysfunctions that plague all systems. Later we will explore the shadow of economic dysfunction and its ramifications when ignored in more detail.

Personal integrity as the foundation of sustainability

At its core, sustainability is not just about policies, models or institutions; it's about personal integrity. A system that is led by individuals who act in good faith, prioritise truth over ideology and are willing to adapt in response to reality will be more naturally sustainable – the very premise behind authentic sustainability. However, a system ruled by rigid ideologues and people acting in bad faith who are more concerned with their own survival than the truth will inevitably collapse.

Achieving authentic sustainability does not simply require us to fix economies. It requires us to:

- Restore integrity to systems.
- Replace bad faith with genuine commitment to truth.
- Rebuild trust where it has been broken.
- Challenge stagnation.
- Break free from ideological traps.

The world is not suffering from a lack of knowledge. It is suffering from a lack of intellectual honesty, authenticity and a resistance to evolution. Unless we address that, no system – economic, political or academic – will be sustainable. That restoration begins with each and every one of us, specifically, with the integrity of our own Being.

Reflection

Systems do not fail solely because of external forces. They fail when the individuals within them uphold dysfunction, whether through bad faith, distrust, rigidity or complacency. Authentic sustainability begins with personal integrity.

Take a moment to reflect on your own experiences:

1. **Think about an organisation, institution or system you've been part of.**
    - Have you noticed moments where preserving the status quo was prioritised over evolution and adaptation?
    - How did it affect the system's ability to function effectively?

2. **Have you ever acted in bad faith, either consciously or unconsciously?**
    - Have there been times when you upheld a belief, policy or practice you knew was flawed simply because it was easier or expected?
    - What pressures (social, financial, ideological) influenced that decision?

3. **Where are you rigid in your own thinking?**
   - Are there areas in your life – personal, professional or intellectual – where you resist change despite evidence that adaptation is needed?
   - What would it take to embrace intellectual honesty and evolution rather than clinging to outdated models?

4. **How can you uphold integrity in the systems you engage with?**
   - In your career, relationships or areas of influence, what small but meaningful actions can you take to prioritise truth over convenience, sustainability over short-term gain and adaptability over stagnation?
   - How can you challenge dysfunction – not just externally, but within yourself?

CHAPTER 8

The Cost of Ignoring Shadows

When shadows are ignored, the costs run deep, quietly corroding the foundation of both individual wellbeing and societal cohesion. It rarely begins with grand betrayals or deliberate deception. Instead, it starts with small, seemingly harmless compromises: a decision to suppress our values to fit in, a moment of self-deception to avoid discomfort, a reluctance to speak the truth for fear of rejection. Over time, these compromises accumulate, growing into fractures that weaken integrity, erode trust, cause us to live inauthentically and drain life of its meaning and purpose.

Inauthenticity is the gap between who we truly are and how we present ourselves to the world. When we prioritise convenience, societal approval or short-term self-interest over genuine alignment with our values, this gap widens. The greater the distance between our inner truth and external reality, the more we experience dissonance, which often manifests in anxiety, resentment and a gradual sense of detachment from life itself.

This dissonance is not just an internal struggle. It radiates outward, shaping relationships, organisations and communities. When individuals consistently act out of alignment with their values, trust begins to decay, first within themselves, then within the systems they participate in. Families fracture under unspoken tensions. Organisations become hollow, driven more by optics than genuine purpose. Societies, in turn, become polarised, fragmented by layers of collective inauthenticity.

Left unchecked, this dissonance creates a self-reinforcing cycle – one where individuals and institutions alike become trapped in patterns of avoidance, manipulation or performative engagement. At its extreme, inauthenticity leads to a world where appearances matter more than truth, conformity replaces conviction and people lose sight of what it means to live with integrity.

This erosion of authenticity does not occur in isolation. It mirrors the very dynamics outlined in the Systemic Subversion Cycle (SSC): a subtle trigger, followed by fractures, breakdown and eventual entrenchment. What unfolds on the grand scale of societies and institutions often begins with the same unnoticed patterns in our daily lives – the small compromises, avoidances and distortions that, if left unexamined, harden into dysfunction.

Societal costs: Division, polarisation and mistrust

Inauthenticity doesn't just erode individual integrity. It permeates the structures of society, creating fractures that deepen divisions, fuel polarisation and corrode trust. As people retreat into ideological and cultural silos, they cling to narratives that reinforce their existing perspectives while alienating those who think differently. This defensive retreat stifles meaningful dialogue, turning potential collaborations into battlegrounds of mutual distrust. Instead of engaging with complexities, people run away from them and society splinters into factions, each group convinced of its own righteousness while dismissing alternative perspectives as threats.

The echo chamber effect

Digital platforms, especially social media, amplify fractures by creating algorithmic echo chambers. Designed to maximise engagement, these systems prioritise content that validates users' existing beliefs while filtering out dissenting perspectives. The result is intellectual isolation, where truth becomes secondary to emotional reinforcement. Over time, this dynamic hardens ideological rigidity, deepens an 'us-versus-them' mentality, and degrades public discourse into polarisation, moral panic and performative outrage.

Take political discourse. Instead of fostering constructive debate, social media platforms encourage outrage, exaggeration and ideological rigidity. People become less interested in solving real-world problems and more invested in defending their chosen narratives. Over time, public trust in media, institutions and even democratic processes erodes, as every issue becomes reduced to a battle between opposing factions.

This dynamic paralyses society. Instead of engaging in critical thinking and collaborative problem-solving, people become trapped in cycles of hostility and misinformation. These fractures do not exist in a vacuum. They are mirrored in institutions where shadows of control, exploitation and self-preservation dictate systemic behaviour. A government may justify mass surveillance under the guise of security, an organisation may suppress whistleblowers under the banner of stability, or a corporation may obscure unethical practices behind a facade of corporate responsibility. Left unchecked, these distortions become embedded in policies, laws and institutional culture, reinforcing systemic mistrust. The result? A culture of suspicion and cynicism, where cooperation on pressing issues – whether climate change, economic reform or social stability – becomes impossible.

Becoming liabilities to the collective

Shadows that remain unintegrated within an individual do not simply fade away. They seep into collective spaces, shaping group behaviour, cultural norms and systemic operations in ways that often go unnoticed. Unprocessed personal fears, for instance, can escalate into social anxieties. What begins as an individual's discomfort with uncertainty can morph into group conformity, mob mentality or ideological rigidity, where independent thought is suppressed in favour of social validation.

Repressed insecurities also have far-reaching consequences, often fuelling hierarchies of control. A leader who has not confronted their own shadows will unconsciously project them onto others, creating a culture of micromanagement, authoritarianism or toxicity in the workplace. Similarly, a society's refusal to acknowledge its historical shadows – whether in the form of colonial exploitation, racial oppression or economic disparity – ensures that it remains trapped in cycles of denial, conflict and fragmentation. This unexamined darkness feeds directly into the collective psychosis, perpetuating dysfunction through delusion and denial.

Therefore, examining, confronting and integrating shadows is not just a personal responsibility; it is a collective imperative. Failing to do so does not merely leave us stagnant; it makes us active participants in dysfunction, complicit in sustaining suffering on both personal and systemic levels. Until these shadows are brought into conscious awareness, they will continue to manifest as dysfunction within individuals and across the societal structures we depend upon.

Fragmented purpose and the loss of shared truth

Without authenticity, the shared purpose that binds societies together begins to unravel. When individuals prioritise their ideological silos over collective wellbeing, genuine cooperation becomes nearly impossible. Here's why: as discussed earlier, individuals rely on cognitive maps and mental models formed through personal experiences, cultural exposure and inherited narratives to construct their understanding of reality. Shadows embedded in these mental frameworks shape how people interpret new information, reinforcing biases and selective reasoning. When knowledge itself is filtered through shadows, competing realities emerge, deepening social fragmentation and making consensus nearly impossible.

For example, an individual raised with fear-based beliefs about money may develop risk aversion or self-sabotaging financial behaviours. Similarly, leaders operating from distorted models of control and authority may suppress dissent, mistaking obedience for loyalty. These shadows shape not only personal struggles, but also systemic dysfunctions, reinforcing cycles of misinformation and misalignment.

Consider another scenario where misinformation about health policies spreads unchecked. Different groups adopt conflicting beliefs about safety and risk, undermining coordinated efforts to protect public health. Without trust and a shared foundation of truth, even life-saving initiatives can fail. The result is not just policy failure, but a deep-seated fragmentation of social bonds. Trust erodes, listening gives way to suspicion, and communities splinter into opposing camps sustained by manufactured, self-reinforcing illusions rather than genuine dialogue or shared understanding.

In a world where truth itself becomes fractured, public discourse descends into a battle of competing realities, making social progress increasingly elusive. At its core, inauthenticity doesn't just breed confusion and division, but also stagnation and dysfunction. A society that can no longer engage in honest dialogue and shared sense-making ultimately loses its capacity to adapt, evolve and thrive.

Personal costs: Inner conflict and resentment

On an individual level, inauthenticity creates a painful disconnection between our inner values and outward actions. This dissonance, often subtle at first, manifests as anxiety, dissatisfaction and a gnawing sense of being trapped. Over time, unresolved inner conflict leads to resentment towards ourselves for betraying core values and resentment towards others for perpetuating the dynamics that seemingly necessitate the facade. This resentment does not remain dormant; it seeps into relationships, work and our overall sense of purpose, shaping patterns of disengagement and quiet despair.

Consider someone who, out of fear or societal pressure, chooses a career path that conflicts with their true aspirations. On the surface, they may accumulate wealth, status or external validation. But deep down, a void lingers – a persistent feeling that something essential is missing. Shadows in self-perception influence how individuals navigate choices. When a person internalises narratives of inadequacy or failure, they may avoid pursuing ambitious goals, not because they lack capability, but because their cognitive filters reinforce self-limiting beliefs. Someone who grew up being criticised for risk-taking may later avoid all uncertainty, mistaking caution for wisdom, and pass up opportunities that could lead to meaningful growth.

This struggle extends beyond career choices. It permeates how people relate to themselves and others. Consider relationships where individuals abandon their true needs and desires in fear of rejection. They suppress honest communication, accommodate others at their own expense and mistake compliance for connection. The cost? A slow erosion of self, where authenticity is traded for approval, leading to resentment, loneliness or an unshakable sense of discontent.

These patterns of avoidance are self-reinforcing. A person who believes they are inherently unworthy may unconsciously self-sabotage relationships or careers, interpreting setbacks as proof of their inadequacy. Over time, these distortions accumulate, deepening the emotional and psychological toll of their inauthenticity. And the longer they ignore it, the more it erodes their sense of fulfilment.

All of this represents the hidden weight of inauthenticity: a burden that doesn't announce itself loudly, but quietly drains vitality, connection and meaning. It is the silent cost of ignoring its shadow. Inauthenticity creates an unspoken grief for the life that could have been – for the authenticity sacrificed in the pursuit of approval, security or the illusion of certainty. And the longer this weight is carried, the heavier it becomes.

A vicious cycle

What makes inauthenticity particularly destructive is its self-reinforcing nature. Dysfunction at the individual level feeds into systemic issues, while systemic dysfunction, in turn, deepens personal struggles. This interplay creates a vicious cycle of inauthenticity that accelerates both societal decay and personal suffering, making it increasingly difficult to break free from its grasp. So, the true cost of inauthenticity isn't just personal; it extends into the very fabric of our shared reality. Just as individuals suppress their own shadows, institutions and organisations mirror these patterns at scale.

Consider a workplace where dissent is subtly punished. When this happens, employees quickly learn that speaking out has consequences, so they adapt by conforming. Over time, an organisation that once valued integrity becomes a breeding ground for passive compliance, eroding innovation, trust and accountability. This is the silent reinforcement of collective shadows: dysfunction normalises itself, and those caught within it perpetuate the cycle rather than risk standing against it.

In an organisation that rewards conformity and deception – either explicitly or through unspoken norms – employees quickly learn that expressing their true selves by raising concerns, offering unconventional ideas or challenging authority invites punishment, exclusion or career stagnation. To survive, they suppress their authenticity, adopt behaviours that align with the status quo and disengage from the organisation's genuine purpose. Over time, this systemic shadow deepens, creating an environment where trust is eroded, creativity is stifled and accountability disappears.

These shadows don't just affect the workplace. They shape entire industries, institutions and cultures. Imagine a society where questioning dominant narratives is met with ridicule, where innovation is stifled by bureaucratic inertia, and where collective progress is sacrificed for short-term stability. The result? A world that continues to run on outdated paradigms, resistant to evolution, where the illusion of functionality masks an underlying fragility.

Imagine a polluted river. A single source of contamination – whether an individual's personal indiscretion or a systemic flaw – can poison the entire ecosystem. As the river flows, the pollution spreads, affecting everything downstream. The longer the pollution remains unchecked, the harder it is to restore purity.

Inauthenticity functions in much the same way. What begins as isolated compromises – small lies, ethical shortcuts, suppressed emotions, organisations that reward conformity and punish dissent – inevitably ripples outward. Like pollution in a river, inauthenticity seeps into relationships, businesses, institutions and entire societies, gradually undermining integrity, resilience and collective wellbeing. Left unaddressed, it compounds over time, leading to deeply entrenched dysfunction at the personal level and across the systems we participate in.

To reiterate, when individuals suppress their shadows instead of confronting them, they project unresolved fears, insecurities and resentments onto the world around them. This avoidance breeds distortions in relationships, communities and institutions, reinforcing systemic dysfunction. In other words, what is left unexamined within us does not disappear. It seeps into the structures we build, shaping a society that normalises superficiality, deception and bad faith. These unacknowledged shadows may manifest as greed, envy, tyranny, injustice, abuse and many other forms, perpetuating cycles of suffering on both personal and collective levels.

The path to alignment and integrity

Despite its pervasive grip, inauthenticity is not an inescapable fate. The key to restoring authenticity is to acknowledge, examine and integrate its shadow. Notably, integration is not about eradicating shadows, but *restoring what is missing*. Just as the body functions best when all organs are in balance, the mind and society function best when truth is neither suppressed nor distorted. Shadows arise not because something is inherently wrong, but because something essential has been misplaced, neglected or repressed. Addressing shadows requires realignment – not just removing dysfunctions, but restoring coherence to our thoughts, values and systems.

The path to alignment and integrity is grounded in truth and intentional action. This journey begins with personal reflection and accountability, extending outward to shape relationships, communities, societies and cultures that value integrity over expediency, authenticity over performance and substance over superficiality.

What does alignment look like?

Alignment is the harmonious integration of values, actions and identity. It is not about perfection; it's about living in congruence with one's deeper truths. Achieving alignment begins with introspection, asking the hard questions:

- What truly matters to me?
- Where am I acting out of alignment with my values?
- What fears or pressures keep me from making authentic choices?

This process demands vulnerability – the courage to confront areas where we fall short and the commitment to take corrective action. Alignment does not always require drastic, immediate change. Instead, it begins with small, intentional shifts that create momentum towards authenticity.

For example, someone who recognises that their career conflicts with their passions does not need to abandon everything overnight. They might infuse more meaning into their current role, advocate for work that aligns with their values or begin exploring new pathways with greater intention. These incremental choices compound over time, catalysing profound transformation.

From personal to collective transformation

At a personal level, authenticity creates a ripple effect that extends into the collective. When individuals embody authenticity, they influence the people and systems around them, from their partner, friends, family and colleagues to the organisation they work for and their community. For systemic change to occur, structures and institutions must create environments where authenticity is encouraged rather than punished.

Leaders play a crucial role in this. When a leader models transparency, authenticity, integrity and courage, they set a tone that fosters trust and cooperation. Consider a company that implements genuine open-door policies, encourages constructive disagreement and rewards honest dialogue over blind compliance. Over time, an environment like this fosters innovation, collaboration and a culture where individuals feel seen, heard and valued. This is the power of alignment.

Alignment isn't just an individual pursuit but a force that can drive systemic transformation. Ultimately, the journey towards authenticity, integrity and alignment is not merely personal; it is a collective responsibility – one that holds the potential to reshape how we work, lead, relate to others and live.

A call to awareness: Integrating shadows as a path to integrity

Shadows, in their many forms, are not flaws to be eradicated, but invitations to deeper understanding. They are not permanent defects, but unexamined distortions: misconceptions, suppressed truths or unexplored parts of ourselves that, when brought into awareness, can be clarified, integrated and ultimately transformed. Every unresolved shadow carries within it a potential insight, a missing truth or a hidden strength, but only for those willing to confront it.

The integrity of any individual, institution or civilisation depends on its ability to recognise where misalignments occur and understand how shadows distort perception and behaviour. It requires acknowledging that whatever remains unexamined does not simply vanish, but manifests as dysfunction in our thoughts, actions and systems. True alignment is found not through avoidance but through *restoration* – seeking wholeness with clarity, intellectual honesty and the willingness to refine what has been left incomplete.

The more we understand where shadows emerge, how they shape our reality and the consequences of neglecting them, the better equipped we are to reclaim what has been lost and ensure that both individuals and society function with coherence, clarity and integrity.

Reflection

Ignoring shadows doesn't eliminate them; it embeds them deeper into our thoughts, relationships and institutions, creating a self-reinforcing cycle of inauthenticity, dysfunction and erosion of trust. Inauthenticity, at both personal and systemic levels, is not just a passive failure but an active force that sustains dysfunction.

Take a moment to reflect on your own experiences:

1. **Where have you compromised authenticity for convenience?**

    - Have there been moments where you presented a version of yourself that was more palatable, but less truthful?
    - Have you ever justified a small act of deception or conformity, telling yourself it was harmless or necessary?

- What has been the long-term impact of these compromises on your sense of integrity?

2. **Where do you see systemic inauthenticity?**
    - Have you worked in or been part of institutions where maintaining appearances was prioritised over truth?
    - Have you witnessed how social or organisational cultures subtly (or overtly) discourage authenticity and reward compliance?
    - In what ways do you see society reinforcing illusions rather than engaging with truth?

3. **What would it take to reclaim integrity?**
    - What small but meaningful step can you take today to bridge the gap between who you are and how you live?
    - How can you create environments – whether in your personal life, workplace or community – where authenticity is not just tolerated, but encouraged?
    - What conversations have you been avoiding that, if spoken with courage and clarity, could begin to realign fractured relationships or structures?

Remember, the journey towards authentic sustainability is not a solitary pursuit. Its impact extends far beyond the individual, as will be illustrated in the following chapters. When we choose integrity over illusion, we inspire others to do the same. This ripple effect can transform relationships, reshape workplaces and influence institutions, fostering environments where trust, collaboration and genuine connection replace division and distrust.

Change or transformation is not immediate, nor is it comfortable. Addressing and integrating our shadows is never easy, but it's necessary. Because every moment of alignment, every act of courage and every decision to live with integrity creates momentum towards something greater. The cost of inauthenticity by ignoring shadows is high. However, the rewards of reclaiming truth, trust and alignment are far greater. Ultimately, shadows do not control us unless we refuse to see, acknowledge and integrate them. Therefore, they should not be regarded as burdens, but as an opportunity for liberation.

CHAPTER 9

The Power of Intentions and The Shadows That Shape Them

At the core of human experience lies intention – the invisible force that drives our choices, ambitions and relationships. It's what pushes us to strive, create and connect. Yet, like a compass subtly influenced by unseen magnets, intention can drift off course, requiring active recalibration to avoid distortion, misdirection or even weaponisation. We may set out to 'do good', build trust or pursue meaningful goals, only to find ourselves trapped in patterns of dysfunction, frustration or unintended harm. Why? Because intention does not operate in isolation. It operates within a framework of trust, sovereignty and Being, hidden currents that either clarify or distort intention.

Without trust, intention becomes fragile. Without sovereignty, it is stifled. Without Being, it lacks depth and coherence. And without clarity, intention is vulnerable to the very shadows it seeks to overcome. Notably, these forces do not exist in isolation. They operate within metacontent: the underlying framework of sense-making that frames how we perceive, interpret, navigate and engage with reality. This is why sustainability in its true sense is not merely about policies, ecological balance or economic models. It's about the deep structures of human decision-making that determine whether our systems sustain integrity or collapse into dysfunction.

Like undercurrents beneath a calm sea, these hidden currents subtly alter the trajectory of our lives, often without our full awareness. Some, like trust, sovereignty and Being, serve to clarify and stabilise intention. Others, such as bad faith, inauthenticity and resentment, act as primary shadows that distort our sense of self and erode trust in our relationships, communities and institutions.

The latter influences are not inherently 'evil'. Shadows, in their essence, are unresolved aspects of our being: unexamined fears, buried insecurities, unconscious patterns that demand attention and integration. In the context of authentic sustainability, these unresolved distortions lead to unsustainable models – governance built on bad faith, economies sustained by short-term exploitation and cultural systems that reinforce dysfunction rather than coherence. Ignoring them does not make them disappear; it allows them to deepen their hold, unless engaged with consciously, where they can be integrated, modulated and transcended.

To navigate life with clarity and integrity, we must first understand how these unseen forces or shadows shape us. Equally, our ability to perceive and transcend them depends on the quality of our metacontent. As discussed earlier, the Nested Theory of Sense-making supports us in interpreting reality at different layers. For example, our **cognitive maps** shape our perception, inherited stories influence what we see as possible, **mental models** guide our decisions and **paradigms** define what we accept as valid knowledge.

The three primary shadows that distort our intentions

At the root of distorted intentions lie three primary shadows: hidden currents that fracture coherence and erode trust, sovereignty and Being.

1. Bad faith: The denial of truth

Distorted intentions emerge when bad faith takes hold – when we knowingly manipulate, deceive or suppress truth for self-serving ends. This is not simply a failure to see, but a conscious refusal to align with integrity. As discussed earlier, bad faith erodes trust, constrains sovereignty and detaches individuals from Being. Whether through self-deception or external manipulation, bad faith ensures that dysfunction not only persists, but is justified as necessary. This is why authentic sustainability demands integrity at both the personal and institutional level, because a sustainable world cannot be built on deception, misrepresentation or systemic entrenchment in bad faith.

Bad faith takes two primary forms:

- **Self-deception** – where we consciously avoid acknowledging painful truths about our actions, limitations or contradictions.
- **Defensiveness** – where we cling to flawed beliefs, not because we genuinely hold them, but because abandoning them would threaten our ego, status or personal agenda.

Let's say a person enters a relationship promising faithfulness. Yet, from the very start, they have no intention of upholding that commitment. It's not a case of 'oops, I slipped'. Their failure isn't in falling short; it's in setting up an entirely false narrative, like a marketing campaign for a product they never intended to sell. That is an example of bad faith.

Similarly, consider a leader who assumes public office, fully aware that their intention is not to serve the people, but to leverage power for personal gain. Their commitment to governance is performative, as their true agenda was never aligned with the role they vowed to uphold.

At its core, bad faith is not merely human imperfection but a mode of *intentional misrepresentation*, whether for self-preservation, avoidance or manipulation. Yet bad faith is often legitimised within distorted metacontent. When belief systems, ideological dogma or entrenched narratives reinforce deception, bad faith appears as righteousness rather than manipulation. It is strategy, not struggle – a conscious effort to sustain falsehoods rather than reckon with truth.

Restoration begins when the cycle of self-deception is interrupted by authentic awareness – the willingness to confront distortions without defensiveness. Unlike entrenchment, which hardens falsehood into identity, restoration requires humility, learning and the courage to re-align actions with values. It is distinguished not by perfection, but by a renewed congruence between what is claimed and what is lived.

2. Inauthenticity: Living out of alignment

Distorted Being, which leads to distorted intention, arises when we are inauthentic. As discussed in the previous chapter, inauthenticity is when we conform to societal expectations, cultural pressures or external validation at the cost of self-awareness and alignment. Inauthenticity is a detachment from one's essence, where choices are dictated by external demands rather than an internal coherence of values, trust and freedom. Over time, distorted Being creates a fragile identity built on performance rather than presence, ensuring that trust remains superficial, sovereignty becomes reactive rather than intentional, and intention itself is guided by obligation rather than meaning.

Consider a high-achieving professional who pursued a prestigious career to appease family expectations rather than pursuing their passion. On paper, they have it all: title, salary, LinkedIn endorsements from people they barely know. But inside, they're running on existential fumes, wondering if they should have opened that small café in the countryside after all. True authenticity emerges when we align our actions with our inner truth – not the fashionable notion of 'my truth' as subjective preference, but the deeper congruence between who we are, what we value, and how we engage with reality. In doing so, we open the path to both personal fulfilment and genuine trust with others.

At a societal level, inauthenticity is rampant in corporate virtue-signalling, where companies exploit social causes for marketing, presenting performative 'solutions' without meaningful action. It's the equivalent of a fast-food chain launching an 'eco-friendly' campaign while still wrapping every item in three layers of plastic. These tactics deepen public disillusionment, reinforcing the perception that integrity is now an endangered species in leadership, business and governance. The authentic sustainability discourse challenges this by advocating for coherence between stated values and real-world practices, ensuring that sustainability is not a branding strategy, but a deeply integrated reality.

The antidote to inauthenticity is congruence, where our actions, words and values are in alignment. Without congruence, trust – within ourselves and society – remains elusive. Achieving congruence requires authentic awareness – questioning not just our choices, but the metacontent that informs them. Without this, we risk mistaking social conditioning for authenticity.

3. Resentment: The poison of unresolved grievances

Resentment distorts intention, making choices reactive rather than generative. It corrodes trust, transforming relationships into battlegrounds. It limits sovereignty, trapping individuals and societies in cycles of blame and counter-blame. And it fractures Being, reducing people to the weight of their past rather than their potential for transformation. Ultimately, the resulting entrenchment ensures that suffering is not merely endured, but actively sustained, making dysfunction feel inevitable.

Imagine a medical practitioner who refuses to treat a patient due to deeply held resentment or hostility towards a particular group. In their mind, they may justify this as a response to injustice or personal conviction. Yet, in doing so, they violate their duty of care, compromising both their professional ethics and the fundamental principles of human dignity. The patient is no longer seen as an individual in need, but reduced to an abstract representation of perceived wrongdoing.

On a larger scale, resentment shapes policies and societal structures, often under the guise of fairness. Consider a taxation system that views high-earning individuals as inherently unfair beneficiaries of wealth rather than as contributors generating value through their offerings, products and services. Not only do they pay a higher absolute dollar amount in taxes, but they are also taxed at progressively higher percentages, reinforcing a system that is sometimes driven by an underlying narrative of punishment rather than equality.

Resentment can also distort deeply personal decisions, leading individuals to act from a desire to retaliate. Take the example of a divorced parent who, out of bitterness towards their former spouse, seeks full custody of their children – not for the children's wellbeing, but as a means to punish the ex-partner. In such cases, resentment obscures clarity, turning what should be a decision made with care and responsibility into a weapon of emotional retribution.

When we allow resentment to govern our actions, we risk losing the very values we claim to uphold. The antidote is not forced forgiveness or moral indifference; it's the ability to distinguish between justice and vengeance, between principled action and reactionary harm. Misery, in this context, is not merely the emotional burden of resentment. It's the structural condition that sustains the cycle, ensuring that entrenchment reinforces suffering as a habitual rather than a transient state.

When resentment calcifies into a rigid framework of perception, it risks ensuring that grievances – personal, historical or systemic – define all interactions. Yet, when acknowledged and engaged with meaningfully, it can also serve as a catalyst for transformation and reconciliation.

The three primary shadows in action – Practical consequences

As discussed in the preceding chapters, shadows are not abstract psychological concepts. They manifest in tangible, lived experiences, shaping both personal relationships and societal systems. Left unexamined, they fracture intention, dismantle trust, suppress sovereignty and distort Being. These four elements of integrity (intention, trust, sovereignty and Being) are not just passive ideals; they are active stabilisers of coherence. When they erode, dysfunction ceases to be an anomaly and becomes the foundation upon which entire systems operate. In this sense, dysfunction is not simply what happens in the absence of integrity. It thrives when integrity is deliberately compromised. Consider the following consequences of the three primary shadows (bad faith, inauthenticity and resentment) in action in personal relationships and within society.

In personal relationships: The erosion of trust

Unresolved shadows – particularly bad faith, inauthenticity and resentment – can slowly erode trust within even the strongest bonds.

- **Bad faith** arises when individuals engage in relationships with ulterior motives, manipulation or insincerity rather than authentic presence. Someone who makes commitments without the intention to honour them or interacts out of coercion rather than genuine connection creates an atmosphere of distrust and emotional instability. Over time, relationships built on bad faith become transactional, fragile and filled with suspicion.
- **Inauthenticity** emerges when individuals hide their true selves and perform the role they believe they should rather than engage with honesty. A friend who constantly suppresses their true thoughts out of fear of rejection creates an invisible barrier between themselves and others. Over time, this inauthenticity breeds disconnection, disillusionment and exhaustion.
- **Resentment** festers when grievances – whether unspoken, unresolved or ideologically reinforced – remain unaddressed. A partner who silently accumulates disappointments rather than expressing them constructively may unconsciously seek ways to punish or withhold affection. Yet, when resentment is sustained, it ceases to be just an emotional reaction and becomes a pattern of misery: a condition that distorts relationships into cycles of passive-aggression, alienation and conditional interactions, ultimately reinforcing entrenchment and perpetuating suffering.

Relationships require transparency and grace to remain healthy. Without those qualities, shadows – particularly bad faith, inauthenticity and resentment – dictate behaviour, turning love into obligation, connection into disengagement and trust into suspicion.

In society: The consequences of collective primary shadows

Shadows don't just distort individual choices. They interact with systems, reinforcing structural dysfunction when embedded into governments, corporations and cultural institutions.

- **Bad faith in leadership** leads to a loss of public trust. When governments conceal failures behind propaganda or manipulate public perception rather than addressing systemic issues, the people they serve inevitably become disillusioned. Instead of resolving itself, this cycle deepens into entrenchment, ensuring that dysfunction is woven into policies, public narratives and collective identity. Over time, entrenchment stabilises itself, making reform appear impossible and ensuring that shadows remain embedded as foundational principles rather than temporary deviations.
- **Corporate inauthenticity** prioritises short-term profits over ethics, sustainability and genuine human impact. Companies that once marketed themselves as values-driven collapse when their deceptive practices are exposed, leaving behind reputational damage and further deepening public cynicism.
- **Resentment-fueled polarisation** fractures societies from within. When collective grievances – whether economic, ideological or historical – are amplified rather than reconciled, resentment solidifies into a structural force that drives division rather than resolution. Political movements, social policies and even public discourse become increasingly adversarial, reducing complex issues into oppositional narratives. Instead of encouraging constructive problem-solving, governance shifts towards punitive measures, retaliatory policies and ideological entrenchment, ensuring that past injustices are weaponised rather than healed. In such systems, progress is mistaken for victory over an opponent and sustainability is sacrificed in favour of dominance. The result is a society locked in cycles of retribution rather than transformation, where resentment itself becomes the foundation for political legitimacy, economic policy and cultural identity.

Grace and forgiveness: The antidotes to bad faith, inauthenticity and resentment

Despite their pervasive influence, the three primary shadows that distort intention are not insurmountable. The antidotes lie in the pursuit of grace and forgiveness – qualities that allow us to break free from the cycles of bad faith, inauthenticity and resentment. These are not passive virtues but active, transformative practices that enable us to reclaim our sense of clarity, integrity and emotional freedom. Let's look a little more deeply into each quality.

Grace: Compassion in imperfection

Grace is the ability to respond to our own and others' imperfections with compassion and understanding. It does not mean ignoring mistakes or avoiding accountability. It's about recognising human fallibility while holding space for growth, learning and connection. Rather than viewing flaws as irreparable failures, grace invites us to see beyond them, encouraging reconciliation, collaboration and trust.

Consider a leader who responds to their team's mistakes with empathy rather than punishment. Instead of instilling fear, they encourage assertiveness, accountability and transformation through effective communication and support. They help individuals develop a clear understanding of potential consequences, not through intimidation, but by promoting emotional resilience and a commitment to growth. In doing so, they create an environment where trust coexists with high standards, ensuring mistakes lead to progress rather than stagnation.

Grace is not a weakness; it is an intentional way of being that elevates relationships, organisations and societies beyond transactional dynamics and retribution.

Forgiveness: Liberating oneself from resentment

Forgiveness is often misunderstood as passive or naive. In truth, it is a courageous and deeply intentional act that reclaims our emotional and psychological space by freeing us from the grip of bitterness and the endless cycle of retribution.

Forgiveness does not mean condoning wrongdoing or disregarding justice. It means engaging with justice in a way that liberates rather than entrenches. Forgiveness allows us to move forward without being chained to resentment, ensuring our choices are guided by wisdom rather than reactionary anger.

Imagine a community leader who, despite past hostilities, chooses to engage with an opposing faction in dialogue rather than perpetual antagonism. Their decision does not erase history but signals that past grievances need not dictate the future. Forgiveness, in this case, becomes an act of leadership that paves the way for collaboration, healing and meaningful progress.

At its core, forgiveness is an assertion of agency: a declaration that we will not let resentment define us.

Strengthening our capacity to resist and transcend shadows

Understanding shadows, distorted intentions and the antidotes to shadows is not enough. We must also refine the metacontent through which we interpret them. Misaligned intention, fractured trust and reactive sovereignty are not random. They emerge from flawed sense-making. We must actively reinforce the stabilisers of integrity: intention, trust, sovereignty and Being. This requires intentional practice, where we strengthen our ability to:

- Align intention with clarity rather than distortion.
- Build trust as a stabiliser of meaningful relationships and systems.
- Exercise sovereignty, not as an impulse, but as conscious, undistorted agency.
- Cultivate Being as the foundation for coherence in action and self-awareness.
- Develop authentic awareness through considered sense-making, ensuring our perceptions and decisions are not clouded by bias, reactivity or misaligned narratives.

Embracing all shadows as the potential for growth

We all carry shadows, woven into different aspects of our being. At times, some of us struggle with assertiveness, trapped in excessive agreeableness that prevents us from honouring our own limits and advocating for ourselves with clarity and confidence. Some find commitment daunting, making promises lightly yet struggling to fulfil them. Others are fickle in shaping or adopting beliefs, swayed by external pressures rather than anchored in discernment.

Forgiveness may feel impossible and letting go of resentment might seem like surrender rather than liberation. Some wrestle with partnerships, unable to balance independence with connection. Others shrink in the face of difficulty, lacking the courage to confront adversity head-on. And many of us feel like passive victims of our circumstances, rather than active creators of our reality.

But here is what matters most: shadows are not flaws. They are not fixed deficiencies. They signify unrealised potential, signposts pointing us towards our own evolution. If we choose to engage with them, they become catalysts for transformation, guiding us from inadequacy to completeness, from distortion to clarity, from limitation to wholeness (integrity).

Authentic sustainability recognises that shadows, if left unexamined, don't just distort individual lives. They also shape the very systems we depend on. When these shadows dictate governance, economic policies or cultural norms, we create unsustainable realities that deepen dysfunction rather than resolve it. So, while tackling shadows may feel private, an internal battle only we endure, in truth, an unrealised, poorly expressed potential is a liability to humanity. The parts of ourselves we neglect do not simply disappear – they manifest as missed opportunities, fractured relationships and avoidable suffering, rippling outward beyond ourselves to shape the world. Every time we choose avoidance over awareness, we allow dysfunction to persist – not just within us, but within the systems, cultures and communities we are part of.

Reflection

Take a moment to reflect on your own experiences:

1. **Where might bad faith be influencing your decisions?**
    - Have you ever presented yourself or your intentions in a way that was not entirely truthful?
    - Have you justified self-deception or manipulation as necessary for self-preservation or success?

- Have you encountered situations where others operated in bad faith, whether in leadership, relationships or institutions? How did it impact trust?

2. **How does inauthenticity show up in your life?**

    - Are there areas where you conform to external expectations at the expense of your own values or aspirations?
    - Have you ever suppressed your true thoughts, emotions or convictions to avoid discomfort, rejection or conflict?
    - How does this misalignment affect your relationships, career and sense of fulfilment?

3. **Is resentment shaping your choices and interactions?**

    - Are there past grievances that continue to influence how you engage with certain people, groups or institutions?
    - Do you ever find yourself acting, not out of genuine intent, but as a reaction to perceived injustice or personal wounds?
    - How might unexamined resentment be distorting your perception, limiting your ability to lead, connect or create meaningful change?

4. **How can you realign your intentions with integrity?**

    - What steps can you take to ensure your intentions are clear, coherent and unclouded by unresolved shadows?
    - How can you cultivate trust in yourself, others and the systems you participate in?
    - What practices can help you reinforce clarity, authenticity and grace in your daily decisions?

Intentions shape our lives, but they are not immune to distortion. Shadows such as bad faith, inauthenticity and resentment can subtly infiltrate our decisions, relationships and leadership, warping even our best efforts. True integrity requires recognising and addressing these distortions before they undermine our purpose and trust in ourselves and others.

Shadows, when left unexamined, control us from within. But when acknowledged and integrated, they become a source of wisdom rather than dysfunction. The question is not whether we have shadows – everyone does. The real challenge is whether we will let them dictate our choices, or whether we will consciously transform them into stepping stones for growth, integrity and lasting impact.

Ultimately, the journey of confronting shadows is not about moral superiority. It's about choosing to engage with life fully, with awareness, honesty and accountability. It's about creating a world where authenticity replaces illusion, connection replaces division and trust replaces deception. Furthermore, dismantling shadows is not merely a personal task. It is an act of leadership, a contribution to the collective. When we cultivate grace and forgiveness, we don't just reclaim our own clarity and integrity; we set a precedent for our families, communities, institutions and future generations.

Dysfunction may be contagious, but so is integrity. The question is not whether we will have an impact. It is whether we will choose to make that impact one of coherence rather than fragmentation. Together, we illuminate the path forward: one intention, one choice at a time.

CHAPTER 10

The Shadows of Traditional Economics

For centuries, economic thought has been locked in a self-referential loop: a cycle of ideologies that debate who should control wealth, how it should be distributed, and how financial systems should be structured. Yet, amid all these debates, a deeper, more fundamental question has been missing: What is an economy supposed to sustain?

This question, so simple yet so profound, has rarely been asked in mainstream economic discourse. Instead, economists have inherited an intellectual scaffold built on unquestioned assumptions – assumptions that have shaped markets, policies and entire civilisations. These assumptions are so deeply ingrained that they are no longer recognised as assumptions at all. They are treated as self-evident truths, despite the fact that they may be the very reason for our systemic dysfunctions.

But why has it taken so long for this question to emerge? Why have so many economists and scholars failed to break free from the paradigms of the past? The answer lies not just in institutional inertia or political interests, but in collective shadows that have shaped economic thought itself – deep-seated fears, blind spots and unchallenged narratives that govern the way we think about value, wealth and human progress.

To understand why the authentic sustainability discourse has not emerged until now, we must first examine the forces that have kept economic thought trapped in outdated paradigms.

The shadow of quantification: Why we became obsessed with measuring everything

Economic thought has been shaped by a deep fear of uncertainty. From the very beginning, economists have sought to turn human behaviour into something predictable, measurable and controllable. The result?

- GDP, productivity, inflation, stock indices, financial capital: all of these metrics assume that what matters must be measurable.
- If something cannot be quantified, it is ignored or treated as irrational and unscientific.

But not everything that matters can be measured from an economic perspective or translated into dollar value. Meaning, wellbeing, purpose and sustainability are the real foundations of economic life. Yet because they do not fit neatly into numerical models of price and profit, they have been systematically excluded from mainstream economic discourse. Many economists have long refused to acknowledge this, a refusal shaped by a shadow that has plagued economic thought since its inception – the shadow of quantification. This shadow is driven by fear of the unknown and an unwillingness to embrace the qualitative dimensions of human life alongside the quantitative. What is at issue here is not whether such dimensions can be measured at all, but whether economics is willing to recognise forms of measurement that extend beyond its narrow monetary lens.

To illustrate this contrast, consider how traditional economic thinking differs from a more integrated, sustainability-focused approach:

Traditional Economics	Challenging Traditional Economics
Everything must be quantified (GDP, labour, money)	Not all value is measurable: existential and ethical dimensions matter
If it cannot be turned into data, it is not 'economic'	Wellbeing, meaning and sustainability must be central to economic design

Table 5 – The Shadow of Quantification.

The obsession with monetary measurement has led to a distortion of priorities. We track financial profit, but not human flourishing in its fuller sense; we measure efficiency in narrow economic terms, but overlook sustainability in relational, cultural and ecological terms. By reducing value to what can be priced, we have ended up with an economy that destroys ecosystems, depletes labour and generates crises in the name of progress.

The shadow of academia: How scholars became prisoners of their own structures

If economists have failed to ask what an economy should sustain, it is because they have been trained not to ask. Why? Because modern academia is not designed for intellectual freedom. Instead, it is designed for specialisation, careerism and conformity. Economic thought, like all academic disciplines, has become increasingly fragmented:

- Microeconomists study behaviour in markets.
- Macroeconomists study fiscal and monetary policy.
- Developmental economists study poverty alleviation.
- Environmental economists study sustainability within existing models.

But who is questioning the foundational assumptions of economic thought itself? Very few, because the academic system actively discourages meta-theoretical thinking. Scholars are rewarded for incremental research, not for questioning the foundations of their discipline. And economic departments are structured to analyse policy problems, not to rethink what economies should sustain. This is the shadow of institutionalisation – the intellectual structures that prevent economists from stepping outside of their inherited frameworks.

To make this dynamic visible, the table below contrasts the structural constraints of academia with the responses required by an authentic sustainability discourse.

Academia's Constraints	Authentic Sustainability's Response
Specialisation prevents holistic thinking	Authentic sustainability is an integrative, meta-theoretical approach
Research must fit within existing economic models	We must question the foundational assumptions of economic thought

Table 6 – The Shadow of Institutionalisation.

Many academics are not necessarily *unwilling* to think outside the system. They are *unable* to, because the system itself has been designed to keep economic thought within predefined boundaries.

The shadow of ideology: Why economic theories became political weapons

Economic thought has never been purely intellectual, but it has always been deeply political. In this regard, economic theories are not just ideas; they are tools for shaping power. Consider how economic ideologies have aligned with political movements:

Economic Paradigm	Dominant Ideology	Key Proponents
Neoliberalism (markets solve everything)	Right-Libertarianism	Friedman, Hayek
Regulated Capitalism (government intervention to fix markets)	Social Democracy	Keynes, Stiglitz
Socialist Economics (state control or worker ownership)	Left-Wing Politics	Marx, Chomsky
Wealth Redistribution (tax the rich, reduce inequality)	Progressive Liberalism	Piketty, Rawls

Table 7 – The Shadow of Ideology.

Because economic theories are so closely tied to political power, new ideas are often absorbed into existing frameworks or dismissed if they do not serve ideological interests. Authentic sustainability does not fit neatly into these categories.

- It is not capitalist because it rejects profit-maximisation as the ultimate goal.
- It is not socialist because it rejects labour-centric value models.
- It is not merely regulatory because it questions whether economic growth should even be the default measure of success.

The result? Authentic sustainability has not emerged in mainstream discourse because it does not serve any existing political agenda. It is a *paradigm shift*, not a policy debate. Mainstream economic thought is simply not structured to accommodate such shifts.

The shadow of fear: Why no one has dared to ask the hardest questions – until now

At its core, the real reason economic thought has been stuck in the shadows is fear – fear of admitting that the systems we have relied on for centuries may be fundamentally flawed and unsustainable.

- Fear that GDP-driven economies cannot continue without collapse.
- Fear that modern finance is built on a house of cards.
- Fear that economic growth as we know it may be incompatible with long-term human thriving.

Admitting these truths would require radical rethinking, structural transformation and a complete redesign of economic purpose. It would require rethinking human meaning itself. And this is, in great part, the conversation that has been missing from mainstream economic thought.

The authentic sustainability discourse does not seek to make minor adjustments. It seeks to fundamentally rethink what an economy is meant to sustain. Why hasn't it emerged earlier? Because the systems that have governed economic thought were not ready for it. But now, as the cracks in the old paradigms become undeniable, the need for a new framework – one that prioritises genuine sustainability, human meaning and ethical economic structures – has never been greater.

Reflection

Take a moment to reflect on your own perceptions of economic systems:

1. **Where have you unquestioningly accepted economic assumptions?**

    - Have you ever assumed that economic growth is inherently good without considering its long-term sustainability?
    - Do you view wealth primarily in financial terms, or do you consider meaning, purpose and wellbeing as fundamental forms of value?
    - How much of your understanding of economics has been shaped by political ideologies rather than independent analysis?

2. **How has the shadow of quantification shaped your thinking?**

    - Do you tend to measure success in terms of numbers (salary, assets, GDP) rather than qualitative factors like fulfilment, ethical alignment or sustainability?
    - Have you ever dismissed something valuable simply because it wasn't easily measurable?
    - What would it look like to redefine value beyond what is quantifiable?

3. **Are you trapped in ideological economic thinking?**

    - Do you instinctively side with a particular economic ideology, such as capitalism, socialism or neoliberalism, without questioning its foundational assumptions?
    - Have you ever rejected an economic idea simply because it didn't align with your political stance?

- Are you open to the idea that a truly sustainable economic system may not fit neatly into existing left-right wing divisions?

4. **What economic fears shape your worldview?**

    - Do you fear economic collapse, inflation or recession without questioning whether the system itself is the problem?
    - Have you ever avoided difficult questions about the long-term viability of modern finance, markets or capitalism?
    - What would it take to move beyond fear and engage with economic transformation from a place of clarity and intention?

The stagnation of economic thought is not an accident. It is, in great part, the result of deeply embedded shadows that have shaped academia, policy and public discourse for centuries. But by questioning these paradigms and embracing authentic sustainability, we can begin to build an economic model that doesn't just prioritise financial capital, but also human thriving, ethical governance and long-term sustainability.

The question is: Will we continue to defend the shadows of outdated economic thought, or will we illuminate a new path forward? The authentic sustainability discourse offers a necessary departure from these models. However, embracing it requires us to break free from the shadows that constrain our understanding of value, wealth and human progress and keep us locked in the instant gratification cycle, including the production-consumption paradigm – the subject of the next chapter.

CHAPTER 11

The Production-Consumption Paradigm

Modern society is built upon an all-encompassing production-consumption cycle – an unrelenting engine that drives economies, shapes cultural values and dictates individual aspirations. This paradigm prioritises material wealth and short-term gratification over long-term wellbeing, sustainability and genuine human fulfilment. Within this system, people are increasingly reduced to one of two roles: producers or consumers, constraining their potential and purpose within a transactional framework. It's a way of living and being that comes at a cost. The question is not just how we break the cycle, but how we reclaim purpose beyond the grip of short-term gain and instant gratification.

At its core, the production-consumption paradigm is a mechanism of systemic disintegration, creating a culture of relentless acquisition that conditions individuals to equate happiness, success and social status with the accumulation of possessions, achievements or wealth. By misaligning economic activity with authentic wellbeing, fragmentation is reinforced at both the personal and collective level. The result is a society where fulfilment is often sought through external means, leading to perpetual dissatisfaction. This ideology extends beyond individual behaviours, influencing collective priorities and institutional structures to shift the focus from human flourishing to unchecked accumulation.

The historical shift: From shared prosperity to exploitation

Economic systems weren't always as extractive and exploitative as they are today. Historically, many economic models aimed to balance profitability with collective wellbeing, recognising that sustainable growth required a degree of reciprocity between labour, business and society. One such example was Henry Ford's vision for industrial progress. In the early 20th century, Ford revolutionised manufacturing with the assembly line, drastically increasing productivity. Yet, he also understood that economic growth was only viable if workers could afford the very products they built. His decision to pay employees a wage high enough to buy Ford cars wasn't just a business move. It was an acknowledgement that prosperity should be shared.

Fast forward to today, and this ethos has largely been replaced by an exploitative system designed to maximise wealth accumulation for a select few. In modern economies, staggering income disparities are the norm. Corporate executives now earn hundreds of times more than their average employees, while many workers face stagnating wages, job insecurity and diminishing prospects for internal promotion. Industries such as technology and retail have normalised precarious employment conditions, with gig work, zero-hour contracts and automation further eroding financial stability for the average worker.

Exploitation extends beyond human labour to the unchecked extraction of natural resources, particularly in developing nations. Corporations exploit resource-rich regions with little regard for environmental sustainability or the long-term wellbeing of local communities. For instance, mining companies often leave behind polluted water sources, deforested land and economic dependency rather than genuine development. The cycle repeats itself – wealth flows upward while destruction remains local, reinforcing structural inequities and deepening systemic shadows.

The tyranny of short-termism and demanding efficiency at all costs

The production-consumption cycle is further intensified by short-termism and the shadow side of efficiency – when efficiency is prioritised at the expense of relationships, ethics and sustainability.

Short-termism is the pervasive tendency to prioritise immediate rewards over long-term wellbeing. This mindset shapes decisions at every level of society, from personal habits to corporate strategies and government policies, often with destructive consequences. At its core, short-termism feeds a hollow promise that fulfilment, success or sustainability can be achieved through speed, volume and surface-level gain.

In the business world, this manifests as a relentless drive for efficiency and short-term profits, frequently at the expense of ethics, sustainability and human dignity. The fast fashion industry exemplifies this dynamic. It thrives on a cycle of excess, producing low-quality garments at high speed, only to discard them just as quickly. The environmental cost is staggering, but so too is the human cost, as supply chains often rely on underpaid labour in conditions that prioritise output over wellbeing.

The same pattern plays out across various sectors. In the fossil fuel industry, for instance, long-term sustainability is often sacrificed for quarterly returns. While some companies promote sustainability pledges, these can resemble unused gym memberships – frequently referenced, rarely activated. Behind the glossy marketing lies a sobering reality: resources are being depleted, human potential is underutilised and meaningful change is deferred in favour of short-term gains.

This short-term logic doesn't just damage systems; it also erodes our sense of self. Materialism, when reinforced by media, advertising and cultural narratives, teaches people to seek happiness through consumption rather than inner alignment. But the satisfaction of acquiring something new is fleeting, often leaving behind a deeper sense of emptiness. Many find themselves overworked, anxious and financially stretched, constantly chasing the next thing that promises fulfilment, only to feel unfulfilled all over again.

Even in the workplace, as discussed earlier, the culture of performance and output creates a paradox: work hard, get recognised, then receive twice the workload. Burnout becomes normalised as just another cost of staying 'productive'. In this environment, businesses prioritise shareholder returns over employee wellbeing, product quality and long-term innovation. The result is a corporate landscape where decision-making serves short-term metrics but erodes trust, resilience and relational depth in the long run.

Personal short-termism: Convenience over sustainability

Short-termism also operates on an individual level, shaping daily habits and reinforcing unsustainable consumption patterns. Consider the widespread reliance on single-use plastics and fast food within our instant gratification culture. These choices, while seemingly minor in isolation, collectively create significant environmental harm and social costs.

For example, disposable coffee cups, plastic straws and excessive packaging might offer momentary convenience, but they contribute to overflowing landfills and ocean pollution. Similarly, the prioritisation of processed, low-quality foods over mindful nutrition leads to long-term health consequences, from obesity to chronic diseases. The immediate pleasure of a quick meal or a cheap purchase often overshadows its broader impact, reinforcing a cycle of neglect.

The self-reinforcing nature of short-termism

Short-termism is not merely a flawed decision-making approach. It is an accelerant of systemic disintegration. Whether in corporate governance, policy making or personal consumption, prioritising immediate gains over long-term wellbeing fractures coherence, eroding trust, stability and resilience. When businesses, individuals and policymakers repeatedly favour immediate convenience or profit, they entrench a mindset that resists long-term planning, adaptation and transformation.

Breaking free from short-termism requires a shift in perspective to one that values foresight, responsibility and sustainability over instant gratification and fleeting gains. The challenge is not merely economic or environmental; it is deeply psychological. Until individuals and institutions begin prioritising decisions that serve future generations rather than momentary desires, the cycle of dysfunction will remain intact.

That said, economic ambition and wealth creation are not inherently negative. A thriving economy requires innovation, leadership and compensation structures that reward expertise and responsibility. High salaries, including those of CEOs or business leaders, are not problematic in themselves – especially when linked to vision, risk-taking and value creation that benefits broader society. However, the system breeds resentment and disengagement when the gap between leadership and the workforce becomes extreme, and wealth accumulation happens without a corresponding sense of responsibility. Workers who feel undervalued and replaceable experience the same psychological toll that unchecked materialism creates on an individual level – chasing security but never feeling fully stable.

The shadows of prioritising efficiency

Efficiency is often celebrated as an unquestionable virtue. In fields like engineering, logistics and business, efficiency enables optimisation, cost reduction and streamlined operations. But when efficiency becomes the sole priority, it comes at a cost – particularly in areas that involve human wellbeing, ethics and long-term sustainability.

Take Elon Musk's approach to business and technology as an example. His leadership has driven remarkable advances in electric vehicles, space exploration and AI development – propelled by an engineering mindset focused on maximising output, minimising waste and eliminating inefficiencies. Yet, the efficiency-first approach has also raised concerns about its human cost. Reports of extreme workplace pressure, mass terminations without adequate support and decisions made with little regard for employee wellbeing illustrate how an overemphasis on efficiency can devalue the human element.

Efficiency, when applied correctly, leads to innovation. But when prioritised at the expense of relationships, ethics and sustainability, it creates the following shadows:

1. A significant cost to human wellbeing

The efficiency-over-everything mindset in corporate culture can lead to burnout, job insecurity and dehumanisation. Many businesses optimise workflows by demanding faster results, longer hours and fewer breaks, treating human workers more like replaceable components than sentient beings with limits.

2. The devaluation of craft, meaning and creativity

When efficiency is pursued relentlessly, craftsmanship and human artistry often suffer. For example, in the fast fashion industry, tailors who once spent months perfecting garments have been replaced by automated systems or 'sweat shops' that prioritise speed and volume over durability and creativity.

A similar issue arises in education. In an attempt to optimise student performance, many school systems have turned learning into a rigid, standardised process – prioritising test scores over creativity, critical thinking and genuine understanding. In this context, efficiency strips education of its deeper purpose, reducing it to a mechanical process rather than an enriching experience.

3. Ethical dilemmas

In the healthcare sector, efficiency-driven models raise serious ethical and safety concerns. The push to automate medical diagnostics and treatment plans may improve accessibility, but also risks removing the human element from patient care. AI-driven decision-making might work in cases of logistical efficiency, but can it replace human judgement in matters of ethics and empathy?

The same dilemma arises in relation to AI-generated content and automation. With the rise of large-scale automation tools, industries are producing vast amounts of content without human input. While this increases efficiency, it raises fundamental concerns: Are we sacrificing human storytelling, depth, truth and originality in favour of speed and volume?

Efficiency with discernment: A balanced approach

Efficiency is not inherently bad – far from it. Optimisation is essential in fields like science, technology and manufacturing. However, when left unchecked, efficiency leads to dehumanisation, ethical shortcuts and the erosion of depth and creativity in human experiences.

The key is *discernment* – recognising when efficiency serves a meaningful purpose and when it starts to compromise the integrity of human experience. True progress is not measured by how quickly we can produce, optimise and scale, but by how well we can balance efficiency with ethical responsibility, creativity and human wellbeing.

Instead of blindly optimising for speed and cost, societies and industries must ask: efficiency at what cost? What are we losing in the process, and how can we ensure that innovation serves humanity rather than stripping it of its richness and depth?

True sustainability – whether ecological, psychological or organisational – cannot emerge from the production-consumption paradigm. It requires a fundamental shift in how we relate to time, value and the purpose of our actions. Until then, the systems we build will remain vulnerable to collapse – not because we lack tools or intelligence, but because we continue to ignore the deeper costs of disconnection.

Systemic impacts of the production–consumption cycle

As systemic disintegration advances, its effects extend beyond finance and production. It reshapes human relationships, reducing them to mere transactions. The logic of production and consumption infiltrates social bonds, replacing long-term trust and reciprocity with efficiency-driven interactions.

In a world where efficiency, instant gratification and profitability take precedence over depth, long-term resilience and meaning, the value of human connection is increasingly determined by economic or utilitarian exchange rather than genuine mutual support. Once grounded in trust, reciprocity and shared values, communities are now shaped by the logic of competition, individualism and short-term gain. The rise of the gig economy exemplifies this shift. Platforms offering ride-sharing, food delivery and freelance services promote flexibility and independence, but often at the cost of job security, fair wages and long-term stability. Workers become commodified, valued primarily for their efficiency, availability and ability to generate immediate profit for the system. As traditional employment structures dissolve, many individuals find themselves in precarious conditions, forced to trade stability for survival.

This transactional model erodes social cohesion, replacing trust and loyalty with temporary convenience. Workers and consumers interact briefly, but rarely build lasting relationships. Without the anchor of shared purpose or long-term commitment, people are left feeling disposable, seen as interchangeable service providers within an impersonal system rather than as individuals.

At a broader level, this dynamic contributes to societal fragmentation. Economic disparity widens as wealth and opportunity concentrate among those who already hold power. At the same time, marginalised groups face increasing barriers to security and growth. When human worth is measured primarily in productivity and purchasing power, relationships lose their intrinsic meaning and become tools for personal or financial leverage.

This isn't just a shift in economic structures; it is a shadow creeping into the very foundation of human interaction. What was once a network of belonging is now an arena of exchange, where people are incentivised to prioritise self-interest over community wellbeing. The result is a world where trust becomes scarce, alienation deepens and human potential is stifled under the weight of economic imperatives.

Reclaiming relationships from this transactional paradigm requires a conscious shift – one that prioritises authenticity, integrity and shared purpose over the relentless pursuit of short-term gain and efficiency without discernment.

Beyond accumulation and efficiency without discernment: The shift towards alignment

Real fulfilment comes from aligning our actions with genuine needs, values and meaningful pursuits. A sustainable and purpose-driven economic model does not require us to reject wealth, efficiency or success. It simply requires us to integrate them with long-term vision, discernment and ethical stewardship. Until this shift occurs, society will remain caught in an endless loop, mistaking possession for purpose.

However, breaking free from the deeply ingrained production-consumption cycle requires more than just individual effort. It demands a fundamental shift in perspective. The current model has conditioned people to equate success with accumulation and 'busyness' with effectiveness. However, this equation is neither inevitable nor unchangeable. It begins with asking ourselves the following critical questions:

- Why do we measure prosperity by material wealth rather than by wellbeing, fulfilment or contribution?
- What might our lives and societies look like if authentic sustainability, purpose and equity were prioritised over endless growth?
- How do we shift from short-term gain to long-term resilience, ensuring that our actions today do not create dysfunction for future generations?
- How do we discern between efficiency that serves a meaningful purpose and efficiency that compromises the integrity of human experience?

The answers to these questions open the door to alternative paradigms: ones that align economic activity with human flourishing and ecological integrity rather than exploitation and depletion. Let's consider a few of those alternatives.

The circular economy

One promising alternative to short-termism and the production-consumption cycle is the circular economy. Instead of the wasteful linear model of 'produce, consume, discard', the circular economy prioritises reuse, regeneration and waste-minimisation by designing products and services that sustain rather than deplete. Circular economies focus on maximising resource efficiency while ensuring that economic activity remains in harmony with ecological balance.

In practice, this means shifting industries away from single-use production towards sustainable materials, repairability and longevity. Companies that embrace circular models seek to extend the life cycle of products through recycling, upcycling and closed-loop systems that minimise waste. By integrating these principles into business practices, economic activity becomes less about depletion and more about renewal, turning the shadow of overconsumption into an opportunity for sustainability.

Ethical business models for profitability with purpose

Similarly, ethical businesses challenge the false dichotomy between financial success and social responsibility. Models that prioritise fair trade, transparent supply chains and sustainable production prove that profitability does not have to come at the expense of human dignity or environmental stewardship.

For example, some companies now focus on conscious capitalism, where long-term value creation is prioritised over short-term profit maximisation. These businesses recognise that financial success is most enduring when it supports (not exploits) the people and ecosystems that sustain it.

Efficiency with discernment

As discussed, efficiency only becomes meaningful when paired with discernment. It either serves coherence or undermines it. We need to constantly ask ourselves: Efficient at what cost? Towards what end? When guided by discernment, efficiency amplifies sustainability, reduces waste and enhances wellbeing. However, without it, efficiency becomes a tool of disintegration: compressing time, labour and resources into extractive models that eventually collapse.

To build a coherent and sustainable economy, we must stop idolising speed and scale for their own sake. Instead, we must align efficiency with what truly matters, so that progress is not just faster but wiser.

Reimagining economic systems in these ways offers more than just ethical improvement. It provides a roadmap for restructuring societies to serve both humanity and the planet. Rather than being trapped in a cycle of extraction and consumption, economies can be designed to foster innovation, equity and resilience. The shift requires both systemic change and individual participation. But it starts with a willingness to question the paradigm itself.

Envisioning a new paradigm

A new paradigm – one that values depth over excess, authentic sustainability over convenience, and human dignity over pure efficiency – won't emerge overnight. But every systemic shift begins with awareness. The journey forward is not about rejecting productivity, efficiency or consumption, but about realigning them with integrity, ensuring they serve human wellbeing rather than reducing it to servitude. This is not a call for cultivating fragility or entitlement, where people expect to be stress-free and perpetually overprotected by employers, but for fostering resilience and coherence so that challenge strengthens rather than diminishes us. When economic structures prioritise short-term profit over long-term coherence, they become engines of disintegration. But when they are grounded in foresight, ethical discernment and relational responsibility, they can become vehicles of renewal.

To understand why such realignment is urgently needed – and why it remains so difficult – it helps to examine the intellectual foundations that have shaped our collective view of systems, meaning and power. The next chapter traces the rise of Critical Theory and Postmodernism: two movements that emerged in response to the dominant doctrines of their time. By mapping their influence on governance, academia, economics and science, we can better understand how they disrupted prevailing assumptions, as well as how they contributed to today's fragmentation. This historical critique sets the stage for what follows – a reconstructive framework grounded in structural integrity and authentic sustainability.

CHAPTER 12

The Influence of Critical Theory and Postmodernism

Efforts to advance sustainability in recent decades have increasingly become entangled in ideological abstractions, bureaucratic protocols and institutional performance. This has resulted in what is referred to in this book as 'prescribed sustainability' and sustainabilism. This dominant paradigm, while appearing progressive and inclusive, often lacks ontological depth, systemic coherence and meaningful integration with the lived realities it claims to address.

To understand how the sustainability discourse reached this state of fragmentation and performativity, it is essential to examine the intellectual conditions that enabled it. The rise of Critical Theory and Postmodernism marked a pivotal shift in the way knowledge, power, truth and meaning were conceptualised. These movements challenged long-standing assumptions, exposed hidden mechanisms of control and dismantled grand narratives. But in doing so, they also left behind a legacy of epistemic instability and ideological relativism.

This chapter examines how Critical Theory and Postmodernism contributed to prescribed sustainability and offers a case for an authentic alternative. It clarifies why any meaningful transition towards a coherent and viable future must be grounded in authentic sustainability: a reconstructive, ontologically grounded framework that integrates critical awareness with systemic renewal.

The rise of Critical Theory and Postmodernism

The emergence of Critical Theory and Postmodernism cannot be fully understood without examining the intellectual and political landscape that preceded them. These movements arose in response to deeply entrenched power structures that had long shaped political, economic and social institutions with little room for critical examination. As industrial capitalism expanded and the rise of mass media and bureaucratic governance consolidated influence over public thought, new theoretical approaches emerged to challenge dominant paradigms in governance, academia, economics and scientific discourse.

More than merely questioning who held power, these theories sought to expose how power itself operated, including how knowledge was constructed, disseminated and weaponised to maintain specific social orders. By interrogating the mechanisms through which authority and legitimacy were established, Critical Theory and Postmodernism offered frameworks for understanding how societal structures persist, adapt or collapse under the weight of their own contradictions.

The early 20th century was marked by profound social and economic upheavals: two world wars, the collapse of monarchies, the spread of industrialisation and the ideological battles between capitalism, socialism and fascism. These changes created a pressing need to re-examine how societies were structured, particularly in light of the perceived failures of classical Marxist theory to account for why capitalism remained resilient, despite its apparent contradictions. This need set the stage for Critical Theory, an intellectual movement that sought to update and expand Marxist analysis beyond traditional economic determinism, incorporating culture, ideology and institutional structures into its critique. Let's trace the origins of this movement and examine how its foundational concepts emerged to challenge established power structures.

Critical Theory and the Frankfurt School

Founded in 1923 at the Institute for Social Research in Germany, the Frankfurt School became the epicentre of Critical Theory. Initially influenced by Marxist thought, the thinkers associated with this movement set out to explain why capitalism had not collapsed under its own contradictions as classical Marxism had predicted. Instead of focusing solely on economic structures, they examined how cultural and ideological forces maintained capitalist dominance by shaping public consciousness in ways that made systemic critique more difficult.

Among the most influential figures of the Frankfurt School were Max Horkheimer, Theodor Adorno, Herbert Marcuse and later, Jürgen Habermas, each contributing to the development of Critical Theory. Their work sought to expose the hidden mechanisms of social control and ideological manipulation that sustained capitalist structures, particularly through culture, mass media and the ideological misuse of 'rationality', as explored below.

1. **Culture and the expansion of capitalist influence**

   One of the Frankfurt School's key insights was that capitalism did not survive purely because of its economic efficiencies. It survived because it had successfully embedded itself within the cultural fabric of society. It was not just an economic system but a 'cultural hegemony',[43] subtly influencing the way people thought, behaved and perceived reality. Developed by Antonio Gramsci, the concept highlights how ideology is used to control and influence culture without relying solely on force. Unlike classical Marxism, which viewed oppression primarily in terms of class struggle and material conditions, Critical Theory argued that ideology played an equally significant role in maintaining power structures.

2. **Mass media and consumer culture as tools of control**

   The rise of mass media – newspapers, radio, film and television – provided unprecedented opportunities to shape public perception. Instead of encouraging critical thought,

---

43   Cultural hegemony is the dominance of a particular set of values, beliefs and norms imposed by a ruling class or dominant group, shaping societal perceptions and maintaining power by making their worldview appear natural, inevitable and universally beneficial.

these forms of media were increasingly used to reinforce consumerist and conformist values, creating a society in which people were passive consumers rather than active participants in shaping their destinies. The Frankfurt School saw this as a profound transformation in the nature of power, which worked not through direct coercion, but through subtle ideological conditioning that made individuals complicit in their own subjugation.

3. **The ideological misuse of rationality**

   Once championed as a force for liberation and enlightenment, rationality was – according to the Frankfurt School – increasingly stripped of its ethical and reflective dimensions. In its place emerged a more instrumental form of rationality that prioritised efficiency, predictability and control over critical thinking or human emancipation. This mode of rationality was not neutral; it was embedded in bureaucratic systems, technocratic governance and market logics that reduced complex human experiences to functional calculations. Critical Theorists argued that what had once promised freedom was now being used to justify systems of domination, turning reason into a tool to manage populations, enforce conformity and silence dissent.

While the Frankfurt School's critiques were revelatory, they ultimately fell short of providing a coherent path for reconstruction. The emphasis on ideological critique and systemic deconstruction left many unanswered questions: If capitalism and cultural hegemony were so deeply embedded in society, how could they be effectively dismantled? What alternative structures could take their place? Without a practical roadmap for transformation, these critiques, though powerful, risked leading to pessimism, inaction or endless cycles of analysis without progress. This gap would later become one of the most significant limitations of Critical Theory, setting the stage for further intellectual developments, including Postmodernism and, ultimately, the need for a new reconstructive approach.

The postmodernists and their challenge to grand narratives

By the mid-20th century, Postmodernism emerged as a radical extension of Critical Theory, taking the critique of power structures even further. While the Frankfurt School had focused on cultural hegemony and ideological control, postmodernists turned their attention to the very foundations of knowledge, meaning and truth itself. The premise was no longer just about who held power, but about how power shaped reality itself, including how concepts of truth, morality and progress were constructed, reinforced and made to appear natural.

In contrast to the Enlightenment belief in universal truths and rationality, postmodern thinkers sought to deconstruct grand narratives – those overarching explanations that had historically shaped collective understanding of history, identity and knowledge. This approach sought to expose how dominant discourses produced meaning, shaping everything from legal systems and education to cultural and political ideologies.

Among the most influential figures of this movement were Michel Foucault, Jacques Derrida and Jean-François Lyotard, each offering a distinct but complementary critique of how meaning, knowledge and historical narratives were constructed, as outlined below.

1. **Foucault: Knowledge as a function of power**

    Michel Foucault argued that knowledge is never neutral but is always shaped by power structures and discourse. In his view, what societies accept as 'truth' is primarily determined by the institutions and systems of power that govern discourse, be it in medicine, law, education or government. He rejected the notion of objective knowledge, instead proposing that truth itself is an artefact of historical power struggles. His works, such as *Discipline and Punish*[44] and *The History of Sexuality*,[45] revealed

---

44 Foucault, M. (1991) *Discipline and Punish: The Birth of the Prison*. London: Penguin Books. (Originally published in French in 1975 as *Surveiller et Punir*.)

45 Foucault, M. (1998) *The History of Sexuality: Volume 1 – The Will to Knowledge*. London: Penguin Books. (Originally published in French in 1976 as *La Volonté de Savoir*.)

how institutions define norms, deviance and acceptable ways of thinking, thereby controlling populations through deeply ingrained discursive practices rather than direct force.

Foucault's approach radically shifted the way power and knowledge were understood, influencing disciplines from sociology and literary criticism to gender studies and political theory. However, this perspective also introduced a deep epistemic scepticism – if all knowledge is shaped by power, is it possible to claim any objective or universal truth?

2. **Derrida: The unstable nature of meaning and deconstruction**

Jacques Derrida took Foucault's critique even further by challenging the stability of meaning itself. Through his concept of deconstruction, he argued that texts, language and symbols do not contain fixed meanings. Instead, he asserted that they exist within an endless web of interpretations, revealing the ambiguities, contradictions and inherent instability within language.

Derrida's methodology aimed to disrupt the idea of fixed truths, exposing how meaning is constructed, contested and perpetually shifting. His critique was influential in literary studies, law, philosophy and cultural theory, providing a powerful tool for questioning dominant assumptions and implicit biases. However, deconstruction without reconstruction often led to intellectual paralysis, raising the question: if meaning is never stable, how can any position or claim be defended as more valid than another?

3. **Lyotard: The end of grand narratives**

Jean-François Lyotard took the postmodern critique to the domain of history and progress, arguing that universal narratives – such as the Enlightenment belief in reason, progress and science – were merely socially constructed myths. In *The Postmodern Condition*,[46] he argued that what

---

46 Lyotard, J.-F. (1984) *The Postmodern Condition: A Report on Knowledge*. Manchester: Manchester University Press. (Originally published in French in 1979 as *La Condition Postmoderne*.)

societies accept as truth is always contingent on historical, cultural and linguistic frameworks. He was particularly critical of overarching ideologies, such as Marxism, that claimed to explain history, religious dogma and the belief in inevitable human progress.

For Lyotard, history should not be seen as a single, cohesive trajectory, but rather as a collection of competing, fragmented narratives, each shaped by different power dynamics and perspectives. His perspective helped uncover how dominant historical accounts marginalised alternative voices, such as those of indigenous communities and colonised peoples. While postmodernist critiques were effective in destabilising rigid and dogmatic structures, they also introduced profound epistemic instability. By rejecting the possibility of overarching frameworks, postmodern thought often left no clear path for reconstruction or systemic renewal. Furthermore, by dismantling the foundations of knowledge, language and historical narratives, postmodernism led to a landscape where reconstruction seemed impossible, leaving only fragmented and competing perspectives with no way to evaluate them beyond subjective preference.

The need for Critical Theory and Postmodernism: Identifying their contributions

Critical Theory and Postmodernism did not emerge in a vacuum. These movements were born out of a real and pressing need to challenge entrenched power structures, rigid orthodoxies and the unquestioning acceptance of dominant narratives. For example, before their development:

- The mechanisms through which institutions maintained power and control over knowledge were not widely scrutinised, leaving systemic inequalities unexamined.
- Science, religion, law and social norms were often presented as neutral and objective absolute truths, ignoring the historical, cultural and ideological biases embedded within them.
- Claims of scientific objectivity were frequently used to reinforce systemic hierarchies to justify certain practices and policies.

With this in mind, the contributions of these movements remain valuable. Their emphasis on challenging dominant frameworks, questioning universal truths and recognising the complexity of meaning-making has been instrumental in expanding intellectual discourse and fostering greater awareness of systemic bias and exclusion.

Challenges and critiques to Critical Theory and Postmodernism

Despite their intellectual significance, Critical Theory and Postmodernism have faced serious challenges and critiques, both from within the leftist tradition and broader philosophical and political discourse. Their radical scepticism, particularly regarding truth, meaning and knowledge, has been accused of leading to relativism, fragmentation and inaccessibility. Consider some of the most notable critiques and challenges to these schools of thought:

1. **Chomsky's critique of Postmodernism**

    Noam Chomsky, a leading voice in rationalist leftism, is among the most vocal critics of Postmodernism. His perspective offers a compelling counterpoint. Chomsky argues that Postmodernism diverted attention from real-world activism, shifting focus from material conditions and systemic change to linguistic deconstruction and abstract discourse analysis.

    From Chomsky's perspective, the greatest strength of leftist thought lies in its ability to critically examine and challenge systemic structures, particularly in areas such as corporate power, state control and economic inequality. However, in rejecting objective knowledge and universal truths, Postmodernism has weakened this ability, leaving the left fragmented and without a strong foundation for collective action.

    This divide within leftist intellectual traditions underscores a more significant issue: when critiques of 'the left' arise, they often fail to distinguish between different strands of leftist thought. The rationalist left, represented by thinkers like Chomsky, believes in evidence-based critique and structural reform. In contrast, the postmodern left focuses on deconstruction, language and power narratives. The frequent merging of these perspectives in public discourse leads to confusion, allowing critics to misrepresent leftist thought as a singular entity, when in reality, it is composed of competing and often contradictory perspectives.

2. **Jürgen Habermas and the critique of early Critical Theory**

   Though himself associated with the Frankfurt School, Jürgen Habermas offered a pivotal critique of earlier Critical Theorists like Adorno and Horkheimer. He argued that their work had become too pessimistic, offering no meaningful path forward. Habermas was particularly critical of their tendency towards totalising cultural critique, which, in his view, left no space for rational discourse or democratic reform. In response, Habermas attempted to ground Critical Theory in communicative rationality: a framework that emphasised the potential for reasoned dialogue and consensus-building in democratic societies.

3. **Complexity and elitism**

   One of the most common criticisms is that Postmodernism's complexity has made it deliberately inaccessible. The dense, jargon-heavy language of thinkers like Derrida and Lyotard has led many to argue that these theories are intellectually elitist, available only to a select academic class rather than serving as tools for widespread social change.

4. **Intellectual paralysis**

   By rejecting objective knowledge and stable meaning, Postmodernism has been accused of fostering intellectual paralysis. If truth is always a construct of power and meaning is endlessly deferred, then what basis exists for ethical, political or scientific decision-making? This radical relativism undermines systemic integrity, making it difficult to distinguish between legitimate critiques and arbitrary deconstructions.

5. **Identity politics and fragmentation**

   Another major challenge has been the shift from economic class struggle to identity-based struggles. Whereas Marxist thought and early Critical Theory focused on systemic economic structures, Postmodernism shifted attention to narratives of race, gender and cultural identity. While this allowed for greater recognition of marginalised voices, it also led to fragmentation, creating movements that often struggled to form cohesive, unifying strategies for systemic change.

   Feminist philosopher Nancy Fraser has also critiqued aspects of traditional Critical Theory, particularly its blind spots around gender and social reproduction. While acknowledging its strengths in analysing capitalism and power, Fraser argues that Critical Theory historically neglected the role of care work, family structures and non-economic forms of inequality. Her work pushes Critical Theory to be more inclusive, intersectional and responsive to contemporary social movements.

6. **Deconstruction without reconstruction**

   Perhaps the most pressing criticism is that both Postmodernism and Critical Theory have excelled at exposing structural biases, power relations and ideological distortions, but often failed to offer tangible alternatives. While these traditions have been invaluable in diagnosing the problems of modernity and systemic oppression, they have provided little guidance for what should replace the dismantled systems. This has resulted in a tendency towards perpetual critique with no constructive endpoint, leading many to ask: once everything is deconstructed, then what?

The need for a coherent path towards systemic renewal and sustainable sense-making

While Critical Theory and Postmodernism have been instrumental in exposing power structures, ideological manipulation and the fragility of grand narratives, their most significant limitation, as discussed, is their failure to provide practical solutions. Although their critiques have often been highly effective in deconstructing existing structures, they have rarely (if ever) proposed viable frameworks for reconstruction, renewal or systemic evolution.

This emphasis on deconstruction without reconstruction has had real-world consequences. In academic and activist circles, the dominant approach has often been to tear down existing paradigms – whether in politics, economics, education or culture – without providing structured, actionable models to replace them. The result is a paralysis of action, where critique becomes the default mode of engagement without the emergence of a viable framework to guide the formation of new, effective systems.

Without a clear epistemic foundation for systemic renewal, these traditions risk contributing to intellectual and societal fragmentation, where competing narratives exist without a shared basis for coherent, constructive dialogue or sustainable transformation. Moving beyond these limitations requires an approach that integrates critical awareness with structured methodologies for systemic reconstruction, ensuring that deconstruction serves as a tool for renewal rather than an end in itself.

So, with all the critiques and challenges in mind, it's clear that we need a new intellectual approach – one that retains the critical insights of Postmodernism and Critical Theory while also providing a structured framework for reconstruction. The next step must move beyond deconstruction and critique, offering a coherent path towards systemic renewal and sustainable sense-making.

Moving beyond critique towards coherence

This chapter has exposed the critical gap left by Critical Theory and Postmodernism – a focus on deconstruction without reconstruction. Without a structured epistemic basis for renewal, sustainability efforts remain fragmented, reactive and vulnerable to ideological capture. To move forward, we must go beyond dismantling dysfunctional structures and begin building systems that are coherent, resilient and capable of adapting over time. This calls for more than critique. It demands an intellectual foundation rooted in ontological clarity, structural integrity and a sustainability that is not merely performative but genuinely transformative.

The authentic sustainability discourse emerges to meet this unmet need. It offers a pathway beyond critique-driven stagnation, towards a paradigm that integrates insight with intentional reconstruction.The next chapter introduces Substantial Motion, one of several philosophical contributions informing this body of work. Drawing from the metaphysical insights of Persian philosopher Mulla Sadra, Substantial Motion articulates an ontological view of existence as inherently dynamic, adaptive and self-renewing. While not the sole basis of this book, it has meaningfully shaped the ontological framework that follows: a framework designed to move beyond fragmentation and provide a structured, actionable path towards systemic coherence and authentic regeneration.

CHAPTER 13

Substantial Motion – Beyond Static Sustainability

Sustainability is often framed within environmental, economic and social paradigms, but its ontological and philosophical roots remain largely unexplored. The dominant discourse assumes that sustainability is a state of equilibrium, where systems must maintain balance to prevent collapse. However, authentic sustainability is not about preserving fixed states. It's about embracing continuous transformation, adaptation and self-renewal.

Developed by 17th-century Persian philosopher Mulla Sadra, the Theory of Substantial Motion offers a profound ontological foundation for understanding sustainability, leadership and systemic transformation. His philosophy presents a model of reality in which existence itself is inherently dynamic and self-evolving at the deepest level of being. Although not yet well known in the West, Mulla Sadra stands among the greatest metaphysicians in history.[47] Deeply concerned with the practical, societal and existential implications of his ideas, his philosophy extends beyond abstract theorisation to address the structures of human existence, the progression of societies and the very nature of suffering and transformation.

---

47   Rahman, F. (1975) *The Philosophy of Mulla Sadra*. Albany: State University of New York Press.

This chapter does not merely draw upon Mulla Sadra's ideas, but expands and leverages Substantial Motion in the context of authentic sustainability, the Being Framework, the metacontent discourse and the Unified Ontology of Systemic Integrity (UOSI), positioning his insights as a foundation for a structured, actionable framework for systemic integrity and transformation.

By integrating Substantial Motion into the authentic sustainability discourse, a dynamic model of sustainability emerges – one that is not about merely avoiding decline, but about thriving through continuous evolution, considering sustainability as an evolving ontological process.

Substantial Motion and its ontological significance

Mainstream sustainability models often assume that stability is the key to longevity – whether in ecology, governance, economics or organisational systems. Within this paradigm, sustainability is treated as the art of maintaining balance and preserving existing structures. But when sustainability is reduced to static preservation, it creates a paradox: it contradicts the dynamic nature of reality itself. In doing so, it reveals a deeper misunderstanding – not just of systems, but of existence as inherently transformative.

In contrast, Substantial Motion challenges the classical view of existence as static. Instead of seeing beings as fixed entities with predetermined essences, it proposes that everything in existence is in a constant state of internal transformation, not just at the surface level, but at the deepest ontological level of Being itself.

Given ontology is a branch of metaphysics that studies the nature of Being, existence and reality, it poses fundamental questions like:

- What does it mean to exist?
- Is reality made up of fixed entities, or is it in a constant state of change?
- How do things transform at their core, beyond just superficial change?

Mulla Sadra revolutionised ontology by arguing that existence itself is not static but an ongoing process of transformation. This marked a radical departure from the Aristotelian tradition, which saw essence (what something is) as fixed.

In simple terms, Substantial Motion asserts that change is not just something that happens to things; it is built into the fabric of existence itself. It also informs us that everything – including people, organisations, societies and knowledge – is constantly in motion, and that this motion is not external or accidental, but part of the essence of Being.

By recognising that motion and transformation are fundamental to existence, it becomes clear why sustainability cannot be about preserving things exactly as they are. Consider that:

- An organisation that does not evolve will decline.
- A leader who does not transform will become irrelevant.
- A system that is not designed for regeneration will eventually collapse.
- A professional who does not continually refine their knowledge and skills will become obsolete.
- An intimate relationship that is not nurtured and aligned will wither and perish.

Therefore, sustainability must be understood as an ongoing, self-renewing process rather than a static equilibrium. Leaders must embrace ontological adaptability rather than rigid control, and systems must be designed not merely to last, but to *evolve*. Substantial Motion provides the philosophical grounding for this dynamic approach to sustainability and leadership, offering a framework to move beyond outdated models that attempt to freeze structures in place instead of aligning with the reality of continual transformation.

The Being Framework and Substantial Motion: The evolution of leadership, performance and organisational transformation

The conventional approach to leadership views performance as the execution of external strategies. However, the Being Framework asserts that true performance is the outcome of an internal ontological shift because a person's way of being is not fixed but evolving.

In other words, how an individual *is being* determines their performance, decision-making and capacity for leadership. This aligns with Substantial Motion, which holds that all beings undergo internal existential evolution rather than remaining in fixed states. Importantly, this evolution implies a fluidity that should not be mistaken for utter mutability or instability. Instead, it should be understood as *transformability*: the inherent capacity for purposeful, coherent and foundational changes in one's being in alignment with the fundamental principles governing existence.

So, leadership is not about maintaining power or influence. It's about the ontological expansion of the self in harmony with reality's intrinsic motion. A leader who does not evolve internally cannot create sustainable transformation externally. Furthermore, organisations that fail to recognise the need for existential evolution within their leadership structures stagnate and become irrelevant.

Metacontent and Substantial Motion: The dynamic nature of sense-making

The metacontent discourse argues that knowledge and sense-making are not static processes but evolving cognitive frameworks that deepen over time. This aligns with Substantial Motion, which states that knowledge is not merely acquired; it transforms the knower. The act of understanding is an existential process where the knower and the known become unified. This mirrors the multi-layered structure of the metacontent discourse's Nested Theory of Sense-making,[48] where making sense of any content evolves through increasingly complex and refined levels of awareness.

If sense-making does not evolve, stagnation occurs. Substantial Motion demonstrates that organisations that fail to refine their metacontent become epistemically stagnant, leading to dysfunction. Leadership must be built upon evolving metacontent to ensure adaptability and resilience.

---

48 Tashvir, A. (2024) *Metacontent: The Intellectual Substrates for Sense-making.* Sydney: Engenesis Publications.

Substantial Motion and the Unified Ontology of Systemic Integrity

The Unified Ontology of Systemic Integrity (UOSI) asserts that sustainability is not merely about longevity. It's about maintaining coherence, resilience and ontological alignment over time. A truly sustainable system retains its integrity while evolving. Crucially, integrity is not rigidity. It is the capacity to remain coherent while adapting to change. When integrity becomes static, it collapses. However, when it moves in alignment with ontological motion, it sustains itself.

For example, a genuinely sustainable leader does not merely reinforce existing structures but creates conditions for continuous self-regeneration. The UOSI ensures that sustainability is not just about endurance but about regenerative motion – where leadership, ethics and performance continually evolve without losing their essence.

Substantial Motion, integrity and disintegration: A continuum of transition

When viewed through the lens of the Authentic Sustainability Framework (ASF), Substantial Motion does more than just offer a philosophical foundation. It illuminates why integrity and disintegration are not static categories but fluid, ongoing states of being. Just as existence itself is always in motion, so too are individuals, organisations and societies continually transitioning between varying degrees of integrity and disintegration.

This means that coherence (integrity) and fracture (disintegration) are not absolute conditions, but points on a continuum. We do not simply 'have integrity' or 'lack integrity'. Instead, we move – sometimes subtly, sometimes dramatically – between the states of integrity and disintegration as our choices, awareness and conditions evolve. Crucially, this motion is not random. It can unfold unconsciously, leaving us vulnerable to drift and systemic decay. But it can also be harnessed with intentionality.

This is where modulation enters: when leaders and individuals become conscious of these transitions and deliberately influence their trajectory. To modulate – a practice explored in detail later – is to engage with Substantial Motion purposefully: to shift from disintegration towards integrity, from fragmentation towards coherence, not by resisting the inevitability of change, but by aligning with it. For this reason, modulation is critical to the effective exercise of leadership.

In this way, Substantial Motion underpins the ASF by reframing sustainability, not as static preservation, but as the conscious navigation of ontological motion. Systems that recognise this can transform crisis into renewal. Leaders who embody this can turn breakdowns into opportunities for recalibration. And anyone who awakens to this dynamic continuum can reclaim agency, no longer treating disintegration as an endpoint, but as a transitional state to be intentionally modulated.

Substantial Motion as a foundation for authentic sustainability

The integration of Mulla Sadra's Theory of Substantial Motion into the authentic sustainability and systemic integrity discourse offers more than just a philosophical insight. It provides a foundational framework for understanding the true nature of sustainability. By recognising that motion and transformation are not merely external phenomena but intrinsic aspects of existence itself, we can begin to see why static models of sustainability are inherently flawed.

Sustainability is not about preserving the status quo, but about facilitating continuous regeneration and evolution. Whether applied to leadership, organisations or societal systems, this approach demands an ontological adaptability that aligns with the natural processes of transformation. Systems that fail to evolve with the reality of Substantial Motion will inevitably collapse, not as a failure of sustainability itself, but as a consequence of clinging to outdated, rigid structures.

Ultimately, embracing Substantial Motion requires us to rethink what it means to be sustainable. It demands that we move beyond superficial metrics and prescriptive doctrines towards a deeper, ontologically-aligned approach where transformation is actively cultivated. Authentic sustainability is not a static endpoint, but a dynamic process that acknowledges change as the very essence of existence.

Yet, the prevailing discourse on sustainability continues to operate within a corrective framework that assumes systems are inherently flawed and must be stabilised through external interventions. As we move forward, it becomes essential to confront this tension between authentic sustainability and prescriptive sustainability. The question remains: is sustainability a state to be achieved through control and regulation, or is it something that emerges naturally from systems designed for coherence, resilience and self-renewal? The next chapter will delve into this fundamental distinction, challenging the dominant paradigm and presenting a new vision for what sustainability could (and should) be.

CHAPTER 14

Sustainability – Rethinking the Foundations

Based on the insights offered by Mulla Sadra's Theory of Substantial Motion, it is evident that sustainability cannot be understood as a static achievement or fixed endpoint. Instead, it must be aligned with the dynamic nature of existence itself: an ongoing, self-renewing process rooted in coherence and ontological integrity. Yet, the prevailing discourse on sustainability continues to operate within a corrective framework that assumes systems are prone to failure and must be artificially stabilised through external interventions, policies and regulations.

This dominant paradigm – referred to in this book as prescriptive sustainability or sustainabilism – is exemplified by global initiatives such as the United Nations Sustainable Development Goals (UN SDGs) 2030 and the World Economic Forum's sustainability models. Both approaches seek to impose sustainability as a goal to be achieved, often through mechanisms that rely on bureaucratic enforcement, economic incentives and regulatory oversight. Such methods stand in direct contrast to the principles of Substantial Motion and the authentic sustainability discourse, which emphasise transformation as an intrinsic, ongoing process rather than an externally managed condition.

The questions remain:

- Is sustainability something that can be achieved, or is it something that must be intrinsically emergent?
- Should sustainability require constant external correction, or should it be the natural state of a system that is structurally coherent and ontologically aligned?

These questions are at the heart of the authentic sustainability discourse: a fundamentally different approach to sustainabilism because it is self-regulating, resilient and adaptive rather than artificially sustained.

Why sustainabilism is not sustainable

To clarify, sustainabilism refers to any form of sustainability that is prescribed, mandated or enforced, regardless of whether it is rooted in ideology, doctrine or even well-researched science. It is sustainability turned into a prescribed or mandated system – rigid, centralised and often blind to nuance. Those who insist on its implementation through coercion, imposition or institutional control and justify their approach under the guise of a sacred cause are referred to here as 'sustainabilists'.

Sustainabilists treat their vision of sustainability as unquestionable and 'holy'. They believe their noble purpose justifies any means of enforcement. Whether through taxes, restrictions, mandates or public shaming, they seek to impose their models of 'sustainability' regardless of context, cost or consequence. This is not sustainability; it's sustainabilism. And it must be distinguished from authentic sustainability, which arises through systems designed to sustain themselves through coherence, innovation and adaptive and systemic integrity, as opposed to pressure or control.

It's also worth noting that not all who engage with sustainability do so from a place of authenticity. Many become entangled in the performance of being concerned. They read about sustainability, attend expensive seminars and conferences, write papers or conduct research that never leaves the page. While these activities may create the optics of care, performing sustainability is not the same as generating or living it. The point is, sustainability cannot be created through discourse alone. It must emerge from a deeper acknowledgement of existential principles. This includes the axiomatic laws by which the material world operates, revealed through credible science and the metaphysical dimension that governs how we, as human beings, relate to those truths.

Science may offer insight into *what is*, but it cannot dictate *how we should respond*. A valid and rigorous scientific discovery can describe a material reality, but whether we commit to it, honour it, act on it or ignore it depends on the state of our Being. It is a metaphysical concern relating to authenticity, responsibility, vulnerability and ethical considerations. Are we willing to acknowledge what we know to be true, or will we actively reject it in defiance, despite recognition? How do we relate to the long-term consequences of our actions, even when those consequences do not directly affect us, but will impact our grandchildren and future generations?

These are not problems that science alone can solve. They both precede and exceed the domain of science, requiring collaboration with the humanities, philosophy and ethics alongside science and technology. Without this integration, sustainability remains a fragmented discourse that is technically informed but existentially hollow.

A system of external corrections

Sustainabilism – the dominant sustainability discourse in modern society – largely treats sustainability as a thing to be prescribed and mandated: a checklist of goals that must be met through governance, technological interventions and structured frameworks. This paradigm operates on the assumption that sustainability is not naturally occurring. In other words, it assumes that systems, whether ecological, economic or social, must be actively corrected, protected and maintained.

This is why global sustainability efforts are largely driven by:

- **Regulatory intervention**: Laws, treaties and policies designed to enforce sustainable practices.
- **Economic incentives**: Taxes, subsidies and penalties to encourage compliance with sustainable practices.

- **Technological solutions**: Engineering solutions aimed at mitigating environmental and societal degradation.
- **Institutional oversight**: Governmental and non-governmental bodies dictating sustainability standards and reporting mechanisms.

While these mechanisms can be effective in short-term damage control, they fail to address the deeper structural question: Why do systems require external sustainability interventions in the first place?

If sustainability is truly sustainable, why does it require constant supervision, enforcement and intervention to be maintained?

Hypocrisy, control and the failure to build regenerative systems

The mainstream sustainability movement (sustainabilism) has largely become a performance: a spectacle where optics and moral grandstanding take precedence over real solutions. Politicians use sustainability as a campaign buzzword, but their policies often prioritise short-term economic interests over long-term ecological wellbeing. Corporations engage in greenwashing, slapping 'green' labels on products while continuing business as usual. Activists and celebrities preach carbon reduction while indulging in lifestyles that contradict their message. Meanwhile, global institutions set bold targets like the UN SDGs, but rely more on regulations, taxes and enforcement than on structural coherence and genuine transformation.

More than hypocrisy, the sustainabilism agenda is self-contradictory at a fundamental level. The doctrines it promotes are based on the assumption that systems will inevitably fail unless they are externally managed. However, if a system requires constant micromanagement, coercion and artificial intervention to function, it is, by definition, *not* sustainable. Instead, it is merely being artificially propped up by mechanisms that often exacerbate the very problems they claim to solve.

Genuine sustainability should be self-sustaining, not reliant on endless enforcement or subsidies. A forest does not require legislation to grow, and a regenerative farming system does not require authoritarian policies to flourish. The very need to enforce sustainability exposes the unstable foundations of prevailing models.

This contradiction lies at the heart of sustainabilism. Rather than embracing the intrinsic capacity of systems to evolve, regenerate and maintain coherence through structural alignment, the prevailing paradigm seeks to control, regulate and enforce outcomes. In doing so, it perpetuates a cycle of dysfunction and dependency that undermines genuine sustainability.

Importantly, this pattern of dysfunction is not limited to grand institutions or geopolitical structures. The same sustainabilist logic seeps into our workplaces, communities, relationships and family systems. For example, in organisations, sustainability is often reduced to compliance checklists, glossy Corporate Social Responsibility reports and HR-driven wellbeing programs that measure outputs but rarely touch the structural misalignments beneath the surface. Families and other relationships can also fall into patterns of sustainabilism when harmony is enforced through avoidance, suppression or performative gestures rather than authentic dialogue and alignment.

By recognising how these cycles manifest in our daily environments, we see that authentic sustainability is not only a civilisational concern, but also a practical lens for diagnosing and addressing dysfunction in teams, organisations, families, partnerships and communities. Whether the issue is burnout in a workplace, eroded trust in a relationship or performative alignment in a boardroom, the principle holds: systems sustained by appearance, coercion or performance eventually collapse, while those rooted in integrity naturally regenerate.

The hypocrisy of the modern, performative sustainability movement becomes even clearer when we examine how the very institutions and individuals promoting sustainability often fail to embody the principles they preach. Rather than fostering genuine coherence, their actions reveal a preference for optics and control. This pattern of contradiction is not limited to political speeches or corporate greenwashing. It extends throughout the entire structure of how sustainability is practised today. Consider the following examples.

One of the most blatant contradictions is the behaviour of the so-called carbon aristocracy, the elite who advocate for carbon austerity while regularly travelling by private jets. For instance, the

2024 UN climate conference in Azerbaijan produced 1,500 metric tons of CO_2 from attendees' flights alone: equivalent to the annual emissions of 200 US households.[49]

Institutions like the World Bank, while promoting sustainability policies that often disadvantage developing nations, continue to contribute significantly to global emissions. Billionaires like Mike Cannon-Brookes, who publicly advocate for renewable energy while privately owning fuel-guzzling jets, represent a recurring theme: rules for the masses, exemptions for the elite. The justifications of 'offsets' and 'necessary travel' only highlight the selective application of their own principles.

The hypocrisy is also evident within academia. Universities that preach the necessity of reducing air travel for the sake of sustainability regularly host conferences requiring researchers to fly across the globe. A 2024 study found that a third of climate researchers at a top UK university had flown to at least one climate-related conference that year, despite most acknowledging the harm of air travel.[50] This selective application of sustainability principles not only reveals hypocrisy, but also undermines the credibility of the policies these institutions promote. It becomes clear that what is being enforced is not a commitment to sustainability, but rather a consolidation of control and influence.

This critique is not meant to discount the importance of reducing carbon emissions or developing sustainable systems. On the contrary, it highlights the need for authenticity and coherence in addressing these critical issues. Without a genuine commitment to the principles of authentic sustainability, the current paradigm will remain

---

49 Franey, J. (2025) World Bank Bureaucrats Accused of Hypocrisy over Jet Flights to UN Climate Confab. *New York Post*, 12 March. Available at: https://nypost.com/2025/03/12/business/world-bank-bureaucrats-accused-of-hypocrisy-over-jet-flights-to-un-climate-confab/

50 In a survey published in *Global Environmental Change*, researchers at a major UK university found that although the majority of climate scientists agreed air travel contributed to climate breakdown, a significant proportion still flew to at least one climate-related conference in 2023–2024. Soliman, A. (2024) Academics Say Flying to Meetings Harms the Climate – But They Carry on. *Nature News*. Available at https://www.nature.com/articles/d41586-024-02965-7

little more than an elaborate performance designed to placate public concern while preserving the privileges of those at the top.

The weaponisation of sustainability: Control over innovation

The hypocrisy and contradictions of sustainabilists are not merely the result of individual failings. They are deeply embedded within the institutional structures designed to enforce sustainability from the top down. One of the clearest examples of this is the United Nations' Sustainable Development Goals (SDGs), which were launched as a global blueprint for prosperity, environmental balance and social justice. Yet, despite billions spent and countless summits held, the results have been dismal. According to the UN's own 2024 progress reports, only 17% of SDG targets have seen meaningful progress, while more than a third have stagnated or regressed.[51]

Why has this model failed? Because instead of fostering genuine systemic sustainability, it relies on coercion, taxation and centralised control to force compliance. Furthermore, instead of encouraging decentralised, regenerative solutions, these programs operate under the assumption that sustainability can only be achieved through massive central planning and policy mandates. This is evident in the rigid, hierarchical structure of the SDGs:

1. A global governing body (the UN) defines sustainability goals for every nation.
2. Governments impose regulations, subsidies and carbon restrictions to meet those goals.
3. Corporations and financial institutions align with those regulations through incentives or penalties.
4. The public is expected to comply with new lifestyle mandates, taxes and restrictions in the name of sustainability.

This structure ignores a critical truth. Sustainability is inherently local. It cannot be dictated from a central authority and applied

---

51   United Nations, Department of Economic and Social Affairs (UN DESA) (2024) *The Sustainable Development Goals Report 2024*. New York: United Nations. Available at: https://unstats.un.org/sdgs/report/2024 According to the report, only 17% of SDG targets are currently on track, while over one-third have stalled or even regressed.

uniformly across all nations, economies and environments. The failure of the SDG model demonstrates that sustainabilism is not only hypocritical, but structurally flawed.

It is clear that the UN's sustainability agenda has increasingly become a tool for exerting economic and political influence. Instead of empowering local, independent systems, it promotes reliance on centralised, bureaucratic frameworks that reinforce dependency rather than autonomy. The focus is not on encouraging authentic regeneration, but on enforcing compliance with pre-defined targets.

Control of essential resources

The centralisation of power extends beyond governmental policies to the control of essential resources like food. While the public is urged to reduce meat consumption to combat climate change, the same elite that promotes these restrictions continues to indulge in luxury foods without constraint. The push to replace traditional diets with lab-grown meats and insect-based proteins is not merely about lowering emissions. It's about consolidating power over food production.

Traditional livestock farming, particularly on small, independent farms, represents a form of self-sufficiency that eludes corporate and governmental control. By promoting industrially engineered food substitutes, the sustainability movement shifts power away from local producers and towards corporate entities holding patents and proprietary technologies. This is not genuine sustainability, but a strategic power play designed to centralise control over resources, influence, and ultimately, human behaviour.

Meat for the elite, crickets for the masses

The hypocrisy of this approach is evident. The public is told that cows are climate criminals, their methane emissions allegedly accelerating climate change at an alarming rate. The proposed solution? Abandon beef, reduce dairy and – if we truly care about the planet – embrace insect protein. Yet, those imposing these standards on the masses make no effort to change their own consumption habits.

A striking example of this hypocrisy occurred at the 2023 COP28 Climate Summit in Dubai. While delegates from around the world preached the urgency of transitioning to plant-based diets and alternative proteins, a leaked menu from the event revealed that delegates indulged in wagyu beef, Mediterranean seafood, European cheeses and artisan desserts paired with luxury wines.

This double standard reveals an unspoken rule: the most desirable foods remain the privilege of the elite while the public is expected to refrain from consuming them. The aim is not to reduce meat consumption but to reallocate it, concentrating access among the privileged while promoting artificial substitutes for everyone else.

The rise of insect protein and lab-grown meat

In recent years, there has been a coordinated effort to introduce edible insects into mainstream diets, with various countries making this shift official policy. For example, The Netherlands and Belgium actively promote mealworms, crickets and locusts as alternative proteins. Canada has incorporated powdered crickets into school meals and the European Union has approved several insect species for human consumption.

Supporters claim that livestock farming is resource-intensive and environmentally destructive, while insects require less land, water and feed. But the industrial-scale production of insect protein is far from a natural solution. It relies on climate-controlled facilities, synthetic feed and energy-intensive processing to convert insects into powders and additives.

Meanwhile, lab-grown meat, which is touted as the future of sustainable food, requires massive electricity inputs for controlled environments, complex chemical stabilisers to maintain texture and shelf-life, and proprietary technologies owned by powerful corporations.

In contrast, regenerative cattle farms – where livestock graze on natural pastures, require no synthetic feed and contribute to soil regeneration – are often ignored or actively discouraged by mainstream sustainability advocates (sustainabilists). If the goal was true sustainability, efforts would focus on decentralising and supporting these regenerative models rather than promoting artificial, highly processed alternatives.

Shifting the balance of control away from local producers

The push to replace traditional diets with synthetic alternatives is about more than just reducing emissions. It aims to reshape consumer behaviour, control supply chains and consolidate power over food production. By making food production dependent on patented technologies and heavily regulated processes, the system shifts control away from local producers towards corporations and governments.

Small-scale, regenerative farming offers a degree of independence that large corporations and centralised authorities cannot easily control. A farmer who produces his own beef, dairy and vegetables operates outside the corporate-controlled food system. But by promoting lab-grown meats and insect proteins, power over food production increasingly rests with:

- Corporations owning patents on synthetic food technologies.
- Governments regulating which foods are permitted for consumption.
- Investors profiting from the shift away from natural, decentralised food sources.

By making food a commodity produced in high-tech labs and controlled through patents and regulations, those promoting their objectives in the name of 'sustainability' ensure that meat, dairy and other desirable foods remain accessible primarily to themselves.

Who decides what's sustainable?

The hypocrisy surrounding meat consumption and the promotion of alternative proteins is not just about diet. It's about control. Those advocating for drastic dietary changes make little effort to demonstrate their own commitment to the cause. Instead, they shift the burden of sacrifice onto the general population.

If reducing carbon footprints were the true objective, global leaders would lead by example. Instead, they continue to enjoy the very luxuries they demand everyone else relinquish. This is not sustainability. It's a form of economic and political rationing designed to consolidate power rather than create genuine, regenerative systems.

If sustainability were truly about fairness and regeneration, it would prioritise local, independent food systems, not seek to replace them with industrially-engineered alternatives. When wagyu steaks and fine seafood are reserved for the privileged while crickets are introduced into school lunches, we must ask: who truly benefits from this version of sustainability?

Trillions spent, but where are the results?

The sheer amount of money spent on SDG programs is staggering. Governments, private investors and financial institutions have poured trillions of dollars into carbon offset schemes, green energy projects, diversity and inclusion programs, and sustainability-linked financial products. Yet, despite these massive investments, the impact has been questionable at best.

- Poverty has not been eradicated.
- Food scarcity and global hunger continue to rise.
- Climate change targets are still far from being met.
- Inequality remains a massive issue worldwide.[52]

Meanwhile, where has all the money gone? Much of it has been absorbed by bureaucratic overheads, administrative costs and large-scale financial mechanisms that prioritise optics over tangible results. This raises the uncomfortable question: are SDG programs actually solving problems, or are they just sustaining the sustainability industry itself?

---

52 According to the UNDP Sustainable Development Financing Report 2024, global investment in SDG-related initiatives – including public programs, development aid, green energy, carbon offsets, ESG-linked financial products and diversity programs – is estimated in the trillions of dollars annually. Despite this scale, progress remains limited. Only 17 percent of SDG targets are on track, while many goals have stagnated or regressed (UNDP, 2025; United Nations Department of Economic and Social Affairs, Financing for Sustainable Development Report 2024, unsdg.un.org).

The failure of the SDGs is not just a failure of execution. It is a philosophical failure. The model is not designed to create truly self-sustaining solutions. Instead, it builds dependency on constant intervention, enforcement and artificial maintenance. If a system requires endless management, it is not sustainable – it is merely controlled. This distinction is crucial. Real sustainability should be about building resilient, self-sufficient ecosystems, economies and communities. Instead, the SDG model promotes sustainability through rigid frameworks, restrictions and compliance mandates, ensuring that no meaningful change occurs without external governance and oversight. That's why it is referred to here as sustainabilism.

For example:

- Rather than empowering local farmers with regenerative agricultural practices, the UN pushes for 'climate-friendly' farming regulations that increase dependency on international trade.
- Instead of fostering decentralised energy independence, sustainabilists favour government-subsidised megaprojects that require long-term political control.
- Rather than encouraging economic self-sufficiency, SDG programs are often tied to financial institutions that profit from debt-based green initiatives.

A promising development in recent years has been the emergence of the United Nations' Inner Development Goals (IDGs)[53] – a framework launched in 2021 as a complement to the SDGs, acknowledging that achieving external sustainability also requires cultivating internal human capacities. The IDGs highlight qualities such as critical thinking, empathy, presence and collaboration as essential for systemic transformation. In many ways, this is a welcome recognition that sustainability cannot be achieved through policies, mandates and enforcement alone. It also demands inner work and conscious development.

---

53   Inner Development Goals (IDG Initiative) (2021) *The Inner Development Goals*. Available at: https://www.innerdevelopmentgoals.org

Yet, despite this recognition, the IDGs often remain at a surface level. They are articulated in broad, aspirational language without a coherent ontological foundation and risk being absorbed into the same performative culture they seek to challenge. Calls to 'develop empathy' or 'practise reflective thinking' may sound noble, but without structured methodologies and rigorous models behind them, such aspirations frequently collapse into slogans – recited in leadership workshops or HR programs, but rarely embodied in practice.

This is where the Authentic Sustainability Framework (ASF) seeks to go deeper. It recognises that our ways of being, such as our authenticity, integrity, responsibility and awareness, are not optional extras but causal forces shaping the very systems we participate in. Unlike the IDGs, which stop at naming desirable traits, the ASF provides a structured ontological framework for cultivating and measuring them in context, connecting the inner work of human beings to the outer coherence of systems. In doing so, the ASF bridges the gap that sustainabilism, and even the IDGs, leave unresolved: how to move from aspirational rhetoric to systemic regeneration.

The paradox of maintenance: When sustainability isn't sustainable

As discussed, sustainability, by definition, should mean creating systems that sustain themselves by being self-regenerating, self-perpetuating and resilient without the need for constant intervention. Yet, much of today's mainstream sustainability efforts require perpetual maintenance, government subsidies and regulatory enforcement just to stay operational.

This presents a fundamental contradiction. If a system needs constant artificial micromanagement to exist, it is not sustainable. True sustainability should be like an ecosystem – capable of evolving, adapting and thriving without endless inputs of resources, oversight or forced compliance. However, many of the so-called 'green solutions' being promoted today are not inherently sustainable – they are simply alternative forms of managed dependency.

Subsidised sustainability: The illusion of viability

One of the most glaring examples of this paradox is renewable energy.

- **Wind and Solar Energy:** Despite decades of development and trillions in global investment, wind and solar energy remain economically unviable without substantial government subsidies. They require extensive financial incentives, tax breaks and artificial market corrections to remain functional. The dependency loop created by this subsidisation is evident:
  - Governments continually subsidise renewables to keep them competitive.
  - Energy companies rely on these subsidies rather than genuine market efficiency.
  - Consumers bear the costs through taxes, energy price hikes and carbon credit schemes.
- **Electric Vehicles (EVs):** Promoted as the clean alternative to petrol and diesel cars, EVs are aggressively subsidised by governments worldwide. Yet, their production involves highly unsustainable practices:
  - Mining rare earth metals like lithium, cobalt and nickel, which devastate ecosystems and exploit workers.
  - Battery disposal and recycling remain unresolved challenges, generating enormous toxic waste annually.
  - EV production requires substantial energy, much of which is sourced from traditional electricity grids powered by fossil fuels.

The pattern is clear. Technologies branded as 'sustainable' are often reliant on continual subsidies and artificial maintenance, contradicting the very essence of sustainability. If wind and solar need permanent subsidies, they are not sustainable. If electric vehicles require government mandates, they are not sustainable. If an entire industry collapses the moment subsidies are removed, it was never truly sustainable to begin with. Instead of being sustainable, these systems are *managed*. Sustainability should mean systems thrive on their own rather than requiring endless maintenance, artificial incentives and imposed restrictions to function.

The right's rejection: Throwing the baby out with the bathwater

While 'progressive sustainability' advocates (sustainabilists) often engage in hypocrisy and performative activism, many on the political right have taken the opposite extreme, rejecting sustainability altogether. What should be a critical conversation about resource management, environmental balance and systemic longevity has instead turned into a political battleground.

The problem with rejecting sustainability entirely is that legitimate concerns about environmental degradation and resource management are swept aside due to political reactionism. Rather than distinguishing between authentic sustainability and sustainabilism, many have opted for an all-or-nothing approach. By dismissing sustainability outright, they relinquish the conversation to institutions that exploit the term for control and economic gain. Here's the problem:

- Ignoring sustainability does not mean environmental issues will disappear.
- Dismissing climate concerns entirely allows corrupt institutions to dominate the conversation unchallenged.
- Rejecting sustainable innovation means relinquishing technological and economic leadership to those pushing authoritarian solutions.

Sustainability should never have become a monopoly of any political ideology. The outright rejection of sustainability as a concept has only left the space open for bureaucrats, corporations and activists to define the terms of the discussion. Instead of offering a superior, decentralised model of sustainability, many have resorted to mocking or denying environmental concerns altogether. This is a mistake of the utmost gravity because true sustainability is a core part of long-term civilisational success.

Authentic sustainability must be led by example – not by empty words, double standards and coercive policies. The prevailing paradigm of prescribed and mandated sustainability (sustainabilism) is not only hypocritical, but also strategically designed to centralise control over resources, influence and even human behaviour. Even when critics attempt to address these flaws, their critiques and proposed solutions, while valid, typically remain locked within the same paradigm of control and intervention.

Critiques of sustainabilism: Where they fall short

Numerous critiques have emerged against mainstream sustainability efforts, but most operate within the same foundational paradigm of sustainabilism, offering adjustments rather than questioning the underlying approach. Consider the following examples.

1. **The Efficiency Argument: Bjorn Lomborg's cost-benefit approach**

   Lomborg's cost-benefit analysis highlights inefficiencies within mainstream sustainability initiatives. It argues that resources are often spread too thin across overly broad objectives. Lomborg advocates for prioritising cost-effective interventions to achieve measurable results.[54]

   Where this critique is valid:

   - Symbolic goals often overshadow practical solutions.
   - Policies frequently fail to translate intentions into tangible outcomes, leading to inefficiencies.

   Where this critique remains within sustainabilist thinking:

   - Treats sustainability as a management problem to be optimised rather than an organic, self-regulating process.
   - Assumes economic efficiency alone can drive sustainability, overlooking the need for systems to be inherently viable beyond financial calculations.

   Authentic sustainability discourse perspective:

   Sustainability is not just about efficient resource allocation. It requires systems that sustain themselves naturally without constant external correction. Endless intervention signals structural unsustainability.

---

54   Lomborg, B. (2015) *The Nobel Laureates' Guide to the Smartest Targets for the World: 2016-2030*. Kindle

2. **The Degrowth Argument: Jason Hickel's anti-growth model**

   Hickel critiques the notion of infinite economic growth, arguing that capitalism's expansionary nature is fundamentally unsustainable. His proposed 'degrowth' solution suggests deliberately reducing consumption and production to remain within ecological limits.[55]

   Where this critique is valid:

   - The assumption of endless growth without structural adaptation is problematic.
   - Economic incentives often drive overconsumption and waste.

   Where this critique remains within sustainabilist thinking:

   - Sees sustainability as something to be enforced through restrictions rather than cultivated through systemic balance and adaptability.
   - Views economic activity as inherently extractive rather than capable of evolving towards self-sustaining, regenerative models.

   Authentic sustainability discourse perspective:

   Sustainability is not about limiting human potential through enforced scarcity. It's about aligning human activities with systemic realities to foster innovation, adaptability and resilience. Structural coherence, not restriction, determines sustainability.

3. **The Doughnut Economics Model: Kate Raworth on rethinking growth**

   Kate Raworth's Doughnut Economics challenges the fixation on GDP growth, advocating for an economic model that meets human needs within planetary boundaries.[56]

---

[55] Hickel, J. (2020) *Less is More: How Degrowth will Save the World*. London: William Heinemann.

[56] Raworth, K. (2017) *Doughnut Economics: Seven Ways to Think like a 21st-Century Economist*. London: Random House Business.

Where this critique is valid:

- Questions the assumption that economic success must always correlate with growth.
- Offers a framework that balances human needs with ecological limits.

Where this critique remains within sustainabilist thinking:

- While rethinking economic models, it still frames sustainability as something to be managed externally rather than organically aligned with systemic integrity.
- Relies on policy interventions rather than systems designed to sustain themselves naturally.

Authentic sustainability discourse perspective:

True sustainability requires structural coherence that transcends economic models and policy frameworks. It emerges from systems designed for long-term adaptability and resilience.

4. **Feminist and Postcolonial Critiques of the SDGs**

Feminist and postcolonial critics like Valeria Esquivel argue that while the UN's SDGs aim for inclusivity, they often replicate existing power structures and neglect grassroots solutions, particularly those led by women and marginalised communities.[57]

Where this critique is valid:

- Top-down frameworks often disregard community-driven, localised approaches.
- The globalised model of progress fails to account for diverse cultural and regional contexts.

---

[57] Esquivel, V. (2016) Power and the Sustainable Development Goals: a Feminist Analysis. *Gender & Development*, 24(1), pp. 9–23. doi: 10.1080/13552074.2016.1147872

Where this critique remains within sustainabilist thinking:

- Assumes improved governance and intervention are the solutions rather than questioning the foundational approach itself.
- Focuses on equity within existing frameworks instead of challenging the framework's underlying assumptions.

Authentic sustainability discourse perspective:

True sustainability is inherently decentralised, self-organising and adaptable. It cannot be dictated by global mandates, but must arise from systems designed for coherence and resilience.

While each of these critiques identifies valid concerns, they remain partly trapped within the sustainabilism paradigm, offering solutions that depend on external control and intervention. The authentic sustainability discourse addresses these concerns by recognising that sustainability must be an emergent property of systems designed to be inherently resilient, adaptive and coherent rather than something that must be continually managed, enforced or corrected.

What would real sustainability look like?

Instead of being prescriptive, authentic sustainability recognises sustainability as a dynamic, self-regulating process that naturally arises from systems that are properly aligned with their ontological foundations. It is not about imposing solutions from above, but about structuring systems in such a way that coherence and resilience are the natural outcomes.

As we move forward, the focus will shift towards unpacking what authentic sustainability entails and how it differs fundamentally from the current doctrine-based approach. By understanding sustainability as an emergent property rather than an engineered outcome, we can begin to build frameworks that are truly capable of withstanding the complexities and challenges of the modern world.

In short, authentic sustainability is not:

- Dictated from a central authority, but emerges naturally from self-sustaining systems.

- Achieved through endless taxation and compliance mandates, but through innovation, efficiency and regeneration.
- About enforcing scarcity, but about creating abundance through better systems.

Until these fundamental principles are understood and embraced – both individually and collectively – sustainability efforts will remain performative rather than effective. Whether through the UN, governments, global institutions or within organisations and communities, genuine progress depends on adopting sustainability not as a mandate, but as a lived, systemic orientation rooted in innovation, regeneration and coherence.

Reflection

The distinction between authentic sustainability and doctrine-based, prescribed sustainability encourages us to reconsider long-held assumptions about regulation, intervention and the role of governance in maintaining balance. If sustainability were truly sustainable, why would it require constant correction? Authentic sustainability suggests that coherence, rather than rigid control, is the key to long-term viability.

Take a moment to reflect on your own perspective on sustainability:

1. **Where do you see unsustainable sustainability efforts?**
   - Have you noticed policies or interventions that create more problems than they solve?
   - Are there sustainability initiatives in your organisation, industry or country that seem more about optics than genuine systemic coherence?
   - Have you ever encountered sustainability efforts that rely heavily on bureaucracy rather than fostering structural adaptability?

2. **What is your perception of regulation and governance?**
   - Do you believe that sustainability requires strong regulatory enforcement, or do you see a path towards self-regulating systems?

- Where have you observed governance structures that started as necessary interventions, but became entrenched inefficiencies?
- Do you instinctively view sustainability as something that must be managed rather than something that should emerge naturally?

3. **How do you balance structure and autonomy?**

    - Where in your personal or professional life do you struggle with allowing things to evolve naturally versus stepping in to control or correct them?
    - Have you ever been in a leadership role where excessive micromanagement stifled innovation and adaptability?
    - How can you foster self-regulation – whether in an organisation, a team or a community – without creating rigid, unsustainable rules?

Moving beyond the limits of sustainabilism

Sustainability was once understood as a natural process: an organic capacity for systems to regulate, renew and balance themselves without constant intervention. It was about aligning human activities with the fundamental principles of coherence and resilience. However, as the concept became institutionalised, it was increasingly framed as a problem to be solved through enforcement, optimisation and political alignment. Rather than fostering systems designed to sustain themselves, the mainstream sustainability movement (sustainabilism) has sought to impose sustainability through external control.

Sustainabilism has strayed far from what it was meant to be. It has become a spectacle of hypocrisy, a lever of political control and a playground for corporate greenwashing. It has been reduced to a performance rather than a practice. Meanwhile, many of those who oppose it have done so by rejecting the entire concept of sustainability rather than offering a better, more decentralised alternative.

If humanity is to build a genuinely sustainable future, both elite hypocrisy and reactionary ignorance must be abandoned. We must return to real, self-sustaining systems, where sustainability is not imposed through mandates, taxes or coercion, but emerges through better design, innovation and alignment with natural modulation.

The authentic sustainability discourse begins here – not as a new mandate, but as a structural alternative. It does not call for absolute non-intervention or rigid control. Instead, it asks a more profound question:

What if truly sustainable systems don't need to be constantly saved?

CHAPTER 15

A Radical Departure From Sustainabilism

Having critiqued the limitations of sustainabilism in the previous chapter, we now turn to what an alternative might look like – not as a doctrine, but as a *framework*. This chapter introduces authentic sustainability as a fundamentally different way of thinking, one grounded in structural coherence and systemic modulation rather than ideological mandates.

The authentic sustainability discourse challenges the assumption that sustainability must be prescribed and imposed. Instead, it proposes that true sustainability is an emergent property of well-structured systems and only arises when systems are designed in alignment with their natural modulation between integrity and disintegration.

This body of work distinguishes modulation as the natural process by which systems – whether biological, social or economic – regulate themselves through cycles of integrity and disintegration. Modulation is not the same as external control or forced correction, but is the inherent adaptability of a system to maintain coherence without reliance on continual outside intervention.

A simple example is how ecosystems regulate themselves. A forest, left to its own devices, undergoes natural cycles of growth, decay and regeneration. Attempting to impose rigid preservation measures often leads to unintended consequences, such as overgrowth that makes bushfires more destructive. In contrast, when a system is allowed to modulate or regulate itself, it finds its own equilibrium over time.

This principle applies not just to nature, but also to governance, economies, institutions and human behaviour. When systems are structurally coherent, they do not require excessive external management. They evolve, adapt and self-regulate without becoming rigid or chaotic. This flow is foundational to authentic sustainability, which prioritises lean governance, structural integrity and organic adaptability over artificial intervention.

From control to coherence: Redefining the sustainability paradigm

To move beyond performative or ideologically driven models, we must reimagine sustainability, not as a program of control, but as a foundational structure of coherence. This begins by contrasting the dominant logic of sustainabilism – a doctrine-based model reliant on external oversight – with the emergent logic of authentic sustainability. The following table summarises this foundational shift.

	Sustainabilism (Doctrine-based Sustainability	Authentic Sustainability
Approach	External regulation, corrective policies	Internal self-regulation, systemic integrity
Objective	To maintain the status quo by preventing disruption	To allow systems to evolve naturally without artificial, human-imposed constraints
Method	Government intervention, incentives, regulations	Structural design ensuring self-sustaining balance
Sustainability Lens	Focused on short-term image preservation and mitigation of crises	Focused on long-term systemic adaptability and resilience
Key Limitation	Requires continuous oversight and intervention	Relies on the integrity and discernment of human beings – without it, even authentic structures risk distortion

Table 8 – Paradigm Shift: From Sustainabilism to Authentic Sustainability.

Beyond Doctrines: Why structure matters more than ideology

Authentic sustainability is not a new doctrine to replace old ones. It is a structural framework that enables systems to self-organise, adapt and evolve. Doctrines tend to be rigid, prescriptive and ideological. In contrast, frameworks provide adaptable scaffolding that supports diverse and context-sensitive pathways. This distinction is essential for understanding why authentic sustainability resists becoming just another centralised sustainability program.

	Doctrine	Framework
Definition	A set of beliefs, principles or rules that are authoritative and often prescriptive, dictating a specific course of action	A structured model or system of principles designed to guide thinking, decision-making or problem-solving
Flexibility	More rigid: demands adherence and discourages deviation	Adaptable: provides structures but allows for modifications and context-specific applications
Purpose	A belief system or rulebook that defines what should be done and why	A tool to analyse, assess or navigate a situation or problem with various possible outcomes
Authority and Enforcement	Prescriptive and authoritative – tells people what must be done and is often enforced through policies, institutions or dogmatic adherence	Encourages inquiry, iteration and adaptation – provides scaffolding for understanding, but does not dictate rigid solutions
Examples	Neoliberalism (a doctrine on free markets and deregulation); Marxism (a doctrine prescribing class struggle and state control of production); The UN 2030 Agenda (doctrinal in its approach to global governance)	The Being Framework (guides leadership and human performance); Lean governance (provides a structure for dynamic governance); the Nested Theory of Sense-making (supports our understanding of complex realities by breaking them down)

Table 9 – Doctrines vs. Frameworks: Structural Flexibility in Practice.

Sustainability, by nature, is expansive and fluid, not dogmatic or ideologically rigid. This distinction is essential to ensure that authentic sustainability is not yet another imposed system but a structural approach that fosters natural modulation and self-regulation.

A third path: Moving beyond doctrine-driven models

Global sustainability debates often pit international governance frameworks against nationalist deregulation agendas. Yet both rely on prescriptive doctrines – one advocating global oversight, the other favouring minimal state intervention. Authentic sustainability offers a structural alternative: a third path that avoids both extremes by focusing on adaptability, coherence and system-led modulation.

Doctrine-Based Sustainability (Left/Global)	Doctrine-Based Sustainability (Right/Nationalist)	Authentic Sustainability
Centralised regulation and international mandates	Deregulation, market-driven nationalism	Lean governance and structural coherence
Focus on planetary goals and global equity	Focus on national interests and economic sovereignty	Focus on adaptability, balance and self-sustaining systems
Bureaucratic enforcement and global standards	Minimal governance and sovereignty-first policies	Temporary, responsive governance that phases out as systems stabilise
Risk: Institutional overreach and stagnation	Risk: Market short-termism and systemic fragility	Strength: Emergence, coherence and long-term adaptability

Table 10 – Beyond doctrine: A Structural Alternative to Competing Sustainability Models.

How the authentic sustainability discourse transcends doctrinal thinking

The authentic sustainability discourse does not position itself in opposition to initiatives like the UN 2030 Agenda or the Mandate for Leadership 2025. Rather, it recognises the limitations inherent in both globalist and nationalist sustainability doctrines. On one side, frameworks such as the UN SDGs and WEF models emphasise macro-level control, relying on continuous oversight and institutional enforcement. On the other, doctrines focused on sovereignty and deregulation often lack the structural coherence necessary for long-term sustainability.

Authentic sustainability offers a third path – one that integrates the strengths of both approaches while avoiding their ideological constraints. It does so not by advocating a middle ground, but by shifting the conversation entirely: from external imposition to structural integrity and from policy doctrine to systemic modulation.

By prioritising ontological coherence, authentic sustainability reframes sustainability as a foundation to be woven into the very fabric and design of systems, rather than something enforced from above or left to external forces. This structural perspective becomes especially clear when applied to governance. In the next section, we contrast traditional regulatory models with the principle of lean governance – a practical expression of authentic sustainability in action.

Lean governance: Leading and managing self-sustaining systems

Unlike traditional governance models that assume sustainability must be permanently regulated, the authentic sustainability discourse endorses lean governance, which prioritises self-sustaining systems while maintaining adaptive regulatory mechanisms. More specifically, authentic sustainability acts as the meta-theory or foundation beneath lean governance.

Lean governance is not anti-regulation, but anti-*permanent* regulation. It acknowledges the need for governance structures, but integrates a dynamic garbage-collection mechanism that removes regulations once they are no longer needed. Instead of seeing regulation as a static necessity, lean governance treats it as an evolving tool that must be periodically reassessed, pruned and refined. So, lean governance is governance that is focused on leading and guiding self-regulating systems, only managing them when necessary before gradually scaling back intervention as they mature.

The term 'lean governance' is not new. In the Scaled Agile Framework (SAFe),[58] it refers to shifting budgets and decision-making closer to teams to improve adaptability. The Project Management Institute's Disciplined Agile Toolkit[59] promotes streamlined oversight to reduce

---

58 Scaled Agile (n.d.) Lean Portfolio Management: Lean Governance. Available at: https://scaledagileframework.com/lean-portfolio-management/
59 Project Management Institute (PMI) (n.d.) Disciplined Agile Toolkit: Lean Governance. Available at: https://www.pmi.org/disciplined-agile

waste. And governance think-tanks like the Good Governance Institute[60] emphasise evidence-based decision-making as the essence of lean governance. However, these approaches primarily focus on efficiency, agility and process optimisation.

In contrast, the framing of lean governance in this book is not simply about trimming bureaucracy or improving efficiency. It's about finding a dynamic balance between too little governance – which leads to fragility, incoherence and breakdown – and too much governance – which creates suffocating bureaucracy, corruption and stagnation. Lean governance, as articulated in this book, is about maintaining just enough structure to hold authority, accountability and coherence, while avoiding the excesses that suffocate adaptability and innovation.

Within the **Authentic Sustainability Framework (ASF)**, lean governance is the practice of structuring authority, accountability and decision-making in ways that are adaptive, integrity-aligned and modulatory. It avoids the extremes of under-governance and over-governance by treating governance not as a static apparatus, but as a living, evolving process. This ontological reframing situates lean governance within the Unified Ontology of Systemic Integrity (UOSI), emphasising that governance is not simply about efficiency, but about sustaining systemic integrity, coherence and adaptability over time.

Core principles of lean governance as distinguished within the ASF:

1. **Temporary regulation, not permanent bureaucracy** – Policies should exist only as long as they are needed. They should be designed with clear criteria for deregulation when systems stabilise.
2. **Adaptive governance over rigid structures** – Instead of universal, one-size-fits-all regulations, governance should be context-sensitive and adaptable to local and evolving conditions.

---

60   Good Governance Institute (2021) Lean Governance: Evidence-based Governance for Better Outcomes. London: GGI.

3. **Regulation as a calibration tool, not a crutch** – Governance should support systems in their early stages, but not become a permanent dependency that stifles natural adaptation.
4. **Accountability without overregulation** – Institutions should be transparent and accountable, but avoid unnecessary bureaucracy that creates inefficiency rather than resilience.
5. **Freedom to evolve, not stagnate** – Governance should promote resilience by allowing systems to evolve rather than locking them into rigid, interventionist frameworks.

	Doctrine-based Sustainability	Authentic Sustainability Through Lean Governance
Approach	External regulation, corrective policies	Dynamic, temporary governance that adapts and scales back
Objective	To maintain the status quo by preventing disruption	To allow systems to evolve naturally without artificial constraints
Method	Government intervention, incentives, regulations	Structural design ensuring self-sustaining balance and periodic policy review
Sustainability Lens	Focused on short-term mitigation of crises	Focused on long-term systemic adaptability and resilience
Key Limitation	Requires continuous oversight and intervention	Depends on the integrity and adaptability of participants – without it, lean governance can collapse into either over-control or neglect

Table 11 – Governance: Doctrine-based Sustainability vs. the Lean Governance Approach.

Demystifying the critiques of authentic sustainability

As discussed, the authentic sustainability discourse presents a reimagined framework for sustainability. However, like any paradigm shift, it invites scrutiny from different ideological perspectives. Advocates of strong regulation, proponents of economic freedom and institutional pragmatists raise distinct concerns ranging from fear of deregulation and market failure to questions about governance, sovereignty and crisis management. These perspectives do not necessarily oppose authentic sustainability, but highlight areas that require careful clarification. Let's unpack the dominant concerns of those proponents.

Concerns from advocates of strong regulation and social equity

A primary concern raised by those who prioritise strong governance and social protections is whether authentic sustainability risks deregulation, opening the door to corporate exploitation. Critics argue that markets left to their own devices rarely correct power imbalances or ensure long-term ecological and social sustainability.

The authentic sustainability discourse does not, however, advocate for the absence of regulation. Instead, it proposes *lean governance*: regulation where necessary, but not treated as a permanent fixture. Governance remains present but adaptive, ensuring interventions address genuine concerns without calcifying into bureaucratic constraints.

Another concern is that market forces alone cannot guarantee sustainability. Historical experience shows that economic incentives often fail to align with long-term ecological or social wellbeing. Authentic sustainability does not rely on blind faith in markets; rather, it ensures that market, social and ecological forces are structurally aligned, reducing the need for constant corrective measures. This means moving away from reactionary, top-down enforcement and towards systems designed to function sustainably without perpetual intervention. For example, regenerative farming practices restore soil health in ways that remove the need for external chemical inputs, while transparent organisational cultures reduce the need for layers of compliance monitoring. In both cases, the system sustains itself because its structure generates renewal rather than dependency.

A further critique is that authentic sustainability ignores social justice by focusing too much on self-regulating systems and not enough on addressing inequality. On the contrary, lean governance explicitly supports policies that correct inequities while avoiding long-term dependency, stagnation or bureaucratic inertia that can undermine real empowerment. Instead of merely mitigating symptoms, authentic sustainability seeks to align systemic structures so that opportunities – not dependencies – emerge organically.

Concerns from proponents of limited government and economic freedom

On the other end of the spectrum, those who advocate for minimal government and free-market-driven solutions may worry that authentic sustainability is too theoretical: an abstract idea that risks overcomplicating simple principles of governance and economic growth. In reality, authentic sustainability is deeply pragmatic because it is rooted in efficiency, minimal intervention and self-sustaining growth. In this sense, it aligns with the principle that governance should exist primarily to ensure stability without being excessive or overly prescriptive.

Another critique from these proponents is that authentic sustainability could downplay national sovereignty, especially if the framework were to be applied globally. Many worry that sustainability efforts often lead to governance structures that undermine local autonomy in favour of centralised decision-making. However, the authentic sustainability discourse does not advocate for universal mandates. Instead, it emphasises context-sensitive governance that adapts to local needs and structures. Policies are not dictated from a singular authority, but emerge from within the integrity of each system itself, allowing for diverse approaches to governance.

Economic freedom advocates often argue that economic growth itself is the best form of sustainability – that a thriving market will naturally lead to better environmental and social outcomes. Authentic sustainability does not reject economic growth. Instead, it questions whether growth needs to be constantly managed or whether economic evolution can happen more organically. Rather than treating sustainability as a constraint on economic development, authentic sustainability ensures that growth occurs within an adaptable, resilient framework, reducing reliance on endless government interventions.

Concerns from policy moderates and institutional pragmatists

For those who take a more centrist or institutional approach, the preference is often for a hybrid model that combines regulation with self-regulation. While the authentic sustainability discourse might initially appear to challenge traditional sustainability frameworks, it is actually a hybrid approach that blends governance, self-regulation and adaptive oversight. Instead of rejecting structure, it ensures that governance remains dynamic rather than static.

Another key concern of policy moderates and institutional pragmatists is the question of who defines structural integrity? This is a fundamental question when moving from a rigid policy framework to a model based on natural modulation. Authentic sustainability addresses this by ensuring that lean governance provides a framework based on adaptability, resilience and coherence, making it flexible rather than dogmatic. Governance is not eliminated, but is shaped by real-world effectiveness rather than ideological rigidity.

Finally, some of these proponents argue that short-term crises require immediate intervention. Consequently, they suggest that a purely self-regulating system may be insufficient. The authentic sustainability discourse does not oppose temporary interventions. However, it ensures that they do not evolve into bureaucratic dependencies. In lean governance, interventions are used as needed, but are designed to be phased out as structural integrity is restored. This prevents the institutional inertia that often results from policies lingering long after their necessity has faded.

Authentic sustainability and the broader debate: Addressing key perspectives

Authentic sustainability presents a departure from conventional sustainability approaches. Naturally, different perspectives – whether rooted in psychology, technology or governance – raise important considerations. While the authentic sustainability discourse challenges dominant paradigms, it is not an absolutist framework. It accounts for systemic modulation while recognising the roles of individual agency, market forces, technological advancement and governance structures in shaping sustainability.

The role of individual responsibility and meaning

Some might question whether authentic sustainability places too much emphasis on structural self-regulation and not enough on individual responsibility. They argue that sustainability – ecological, economic and social – must emerge from individual integrity rather than relying on systemic modulation. After all, without responsible individuals who act ethically and with discipline, no system can prevent dysfunction, regardless of how well it is structured.

The key point to note here is that authentic sustainability does not downplay individual agency. Instead, it acknowledges that systemic dysfunction often emerges from *collective* distortions in sense-making, decision-making and values. While personal transformation is vital, systems must also be structured to reinforce – not erode – personal responsibility. Lean governance ensures that self-sustaining structures do not create dependence. Instead, they cultivate autonomy, integrity and adaptability.

Much like a resilient ecosystem depends on the dynamic interaction of all species rather than a single organism, a genuinely sustainable society must recognise both individual responsibility and structural coherence. Therefore, authentic sustainability does not replace personal responsibility. It provides a framework where responsible individuals are not trapped within dysfunctional systems that inhibit their potential.

The role of technology and market forces

Another perspective questions whether the authentic sustainability discourse sufficiently accounts for the role of technological innovation and free markets in driving sustainability. Some argue that self-regulating systems must be actively engineered, not just left to emerge. Breakthroughs in AI, renewable energy and automation are often seen as the true paths to sustainability rather than focusing primarily on systemic modulation.

Authentic sustainability does not reject technological solutions. It critiques the over-reliance on technology as the sole means of achieving sustainability. Many sustainability efforts attempt to fix problems created by earlier technological interventions rather than ensuring that systems are structurally sound from the outset. Authentic sustainability is not anti-innovation; it's about ensuring that technological advances *align with* systemic integrity rather than serving as temporary patches for deeper structural imbalances.

Technological sustainability is most effective when markets operate in alignment with the natural modulation of systems rather than being micromanaged through interventionist bureaucracy. The authentic sustainability discourse acknowledges that markets – like natural ecosystems – function best when they retain adaptability. In other words, it asserts that governance should facilitate innovation without rigid constraints, ensuring that policies supporting progress remain dynamic rather than permanent fixtures.

Authentic sustainability and sovereignty: Governance without bureaucratic overreach

A crucial concern for governance-oriented perspectives is whether authentic sustainability risks imposing an unnecessary regulatory framework that slows economic growth or diminishes national sovereignty. Some question whether structural modulation could become a justification for increasing governance rather than ensuring self-regulation.

The authentic sustainability discourse does not advocate for excessive governance. It promotes lean governance, which emphasises adaptive regulatory mechanisms that evolve over time. Some regulations are necessary, but they should not become permanent bureaucratic relics. Instead, governance should be adaptive, self-correcting and capable of removing outdated policies when they are no longer needed.

- Authentic sustainability respects national sovereignty by ensuring policies are context-sensitive rather than dictated through centralised global mandates.
- True economic sustainability does not stifle growth, but ensures that economic evolution occurs without constant artificial intervention.
- Lean governance prevents stagnation by ensuring that regulatory measures are temporary where necessary and adaptable as circumstances shift.

Lean governance and sustainability do not rest solely on the efficiency of institutions. Their real foundation lies in the *integrity of individuals*. The more capable people are of exercising self-control – catching themselves before acting irresponsibly, aggressively or with undue submission; honouring their commitments; and resisting inauthenticities – the less external regulation is required. In contrast, when individuals consistently fail to regulate their own shadows, society demands ever-increasing external control to prevent collapse.

This principle applies not only to governments, but also to organisations and families. In participative leadership models, every person plays a greater role in sustaining coherence than they often perceive. Yet our collective tendency is to act only once problems have metastasised into crises – after pillars of trust, responsibility and cohesion have been corroded. By then, no amount of enforcement can substitute for the absence of integrity at the foundation. Regulation can restrain behaviour, but it cannot replace the formative work of cultivating it.

This is why morality, ethics and normative frameworks matter profoundly in shaping future generations. Education systems, religious institutions, intellectual forums and – most importantly – parenting are not peripheral influences; they are the early regulators of Being. A person who has learned to handle envy constructively is far less likely to be driven into destructive acts by it. Legal systems cannot prosecute emotions, but they must intervene when emotions manifest as crime. At that point, governance is left grappling with symptoms rather than causes.

This reveals what systems thinking calls the **lurking variable problem**: unseen or unmeasured factors driving the very outcomes we attempt to regulate. By ignoring the role of individual integrity, societies misdiagnose dysfunction, assuming stronger governance will correct it. In reality, without addressing hidden variables – moral formation, self-regulation and ethical discernment – regulation becomes reactive and insufficient.

Examples abound. Minimum wage debates are often reduced to whether raising wages increases unemployment, ignoring lurking variables such as regional costs of living, automation or corporate profit-hoarding. Climate policy assumes electric vehicle subsidies reduce emissions, yet outcomes hinge on electricity sources, mining impacts and who actually benefits from subsidies. Companies may attribute sales spikes to an advertising campaign when, in fact, seasonal spending or competitor failures drive the results. In each case, failure to account for unseen variables produces flawed conclusions and ineffective solutions.

Systemic recalibration is equally important. Leaders must sometimes apply subtle interventions – nudges, reminders or symbolic actions – that realign groups before dysfunction escalates. These are not heavy-handed controls, but gentle course corrections, like adjusting a vessel with small turns of the rudder. Yet in lean governance, this responsibility does not rest with leaders alone. Every participant is accountable for recognising when recalibration is needed and stepping in with integrity. Leadership is distributed not by title, but by action.

This is where the Being Framework matters. It equips individuals, teams and collectives to look inward – to recognise their shadows, confront inauthenticities and begin the process of transformation. Without this inner work, no regulation or system design can create genuine coherence. However, with it, lean governance becomes possible: lighter, more adaptive and regenerative. This is the foundational work for authentic sustainability – building systems that endure, not because they are policed into order, but because they are sustained by the integrity of those who inhabit them.

Sustainability as an emergent state

Authentic sustainability is neither an extension of institutional sustainability models nor a doctrine-based economic strategy. It is an ontological shift, moving away from rigid doctrines and interventionist frameworks towards an adaptive, collaborative architecture of governance, systems and sustainability. Furthermore, authentic sustainability is not a system of bureaucratic control, but of intelligent governance that prioritises self-sustaining, adaptable structures over rigid regulatory frameworks. It neither assumes an absence of governance nor promotes unnecessary interventionism. Instead, it establishes a dynamic equilibrium between structure and freedom, ensuring coherence without rigidity.

By recognising that some aspects of sustainability are within human control, while others require collaboration with natural and systemic processes, authentic sustainability transcends human arrogance and offers a more expansive, radically humanistic approach to long-term sustainability. It is not merely about surviving. It's about thriving through adaptation, balance and coherence (integrity).

Reflection

This chapter has introduced authentic sustainability as a structural, adaptive approach rooted in modulation, coherence and ontological design. It challenges the idea that sustainability must be managed through perpetual control and instead asks what becomes possible when systems are designed to evolve, self-regulate and thrive.

Take a moment to reflect on the following questions to explore the systems you're part of from a new perspective:

- Where in your life or work do you see sustainability treated as a checklist or compliance exercise rather than a dynamic, evolving process?
- How might your organisation or community be more sustainable if systems were designed to self-correct rather than depend on constant oversight?
- Have you encountered examples of governance that supported transformation by knowing when to step back?
- Do you trust well-structured systems to evolve, or do you instinctively seek to control outcomes?
- In what areas of your leadership, policymaking or activism might the shift from doctrine to framework open up new possibilities?
- Can you identify a system – ecological, organisational or personal – that modulates well without heavy intervention? What makes that possible?

- Where might your approach to sustainability – or change more broadly – become more coherent if you focused on integrity rather than intensity?

Sustainability by design, not prescription

Authentic sustainability invites us to move beyond doctrine – not just in policy, but in mindset. It reframes sustainability as an emergent state, arising from systems that are structurally sound, dynamically adaptive and guided by principles of modulation rather than mandates. It does not reject governance, technology or markets. It simply asks that these elements be designed to serve coherence, not control.

The authentic sustainability discourse is not sustainability as a checklist or a compliance regime. It is sustainability as a *condition* – an expression of alignment between human systems and the natural dynamics they seek to inhabit. When we build with integrity, sustainability does not need to be imposed. It reveals itself through balance, resilience and evolution.

Rather than prescribing what sustainability must look like, authentic sustainability provides the scaffolding for it to arise on its own terms. It is not about managing every variable. It is about creating the conditions through which systems can thrive because they are coherent, not because they are controlled. Ultimately, the authentic sustainability discourse is not a rejection of sustainability, but a return to its essence.

Notably, even within self-regulating systems, human agency matters. Authentic sustainability does not imply withdrawal or detachment. It calls for conscious participation. Once we recognise sustainability as an emergent property of well-designed systems, the question becomes: how do we engage without overreaching? How do we honour our unique influence as human beings without becoming a source of distortion? The next chapter explores these questions through the lens of stewardship and intervention, inviting us to consider what it means to participate wisely, proportionately and with integrity in the systems we are part of.

CHAPTER 16

Sustainability – A shared responsibility

When we speak of sustainability, it must not be mistaken for a call for complete passivity or non-intervention. Nor should it be interpreted as advocating for endless artificial regulation and manipulation. To sustain does not mean to freeze, dominate or abandon. It means to be in rhythmic harmony with the evolving nature of existence.

This is the essence of *stewardship* – not control, but care. True stewardship is an act of discernment: knowing when to step in, when to let go and how to participate without becoming the very source of dysfunction. Like all living systems, sustainability emerges when there is balance – not too much interference, not too little engagement.

As human beings, we are not separate from existence; we are part of it. We are not accidental spectators, but agents of intelligence, cognition, computation, intuition and systemic capacity. Unlike other sentient beings, we possess an extraordinary degree of autonomy and influence – and with that comes a proportionate level of stewardship responsibility.

To use an analogy, a low-ranking employee in a complex organisation may have limited autonomy, and their mistakes – while still relevant – tend to be contained. But the missteps of a C-level executive, prime minister or central bank governor ripple across multiple systems, impacting economies, ecologies, cultures and lives. The greater the autonomy, the broader the consequences of ignorance, inaction or hubris.

This is the reality of our ontological position in the cosmos. Humanity is, in many ways, existence's high-leverage node – capable of extraordinary repair or catastrophic imbalance. The task before us is not to dominate nature, nor retreat from it, but to steward wisely.

Thresholds and signals for intervention

When is human intervention appropriate and what kinds of interventions are we talking about? While there is no simple formula, we can identify several thresholds and signals that would call for deliberate and intelligent action:

- **Systemic breakdown or collapse** – When a system (ecological, economic, social or political) is clearly spiralling into dysfunction or collapse, proactive intervention is essential to prevent irreversible damage.

  - **Example:** A financial crisis threatening to destabilise an entire economy, such as the 2008 Global Financial Crisis, calls for immediate structural reform and regulation to prevent societal fallout.

- **Violation of fundamental integrity** – Intervention would be necessary to restore balance if a process or structure undermines the viability, dignity or essence of other beings or systems, whether through exploitation, injustice or the erosion of vital relationships.

  - **Example:** When a supply chain is built on forced labour or ecological devastation, ethical restructuring becomes a necessity, not an option.

- **Distortion of natural rhythms** – When human mechanisms override organic cycles (such as through overproduction, extraction or artificial stimulation), leading to depletion or burnout, a corrective shift is often needed.

- **Example:** Industrial farming that depletes soil health and relies on chemical saturation illustrates the need for regenerative agricultural practices.

- **Emergence of irreversible consequences** – In cases where non-action will lead to consequences that cannot be undone, such as climate tipping points, extinction events or societal fragmentation, then preventative or restorative intervention becomes a moral imperative.

  - **Example:** Failing to reduce carbon emissions before climate thresholds are breached risks cascading effects that no policy or innovation can reverse.

- **Collapse of meaning and sense-making** – When people, institutions or systems become so fragmented that shared meaning is lost and truth collapses into noise, human re-engagement is critical – not just politically or technically, but existentially and ethically.

  - **Example:** When public discourse devolves into polarisation, conspiracy and post-truth narratives, efforts must be made to restore shared frameworks for meaning and understanding – not through debate as a contest to 'win' arguments, but through the deliberate co-creation of shared metacontents. This requires the willingness of opposing parties to build mutual understanding, however difficult or uncomfortable the process may be. Without such intentional efforts, the alternative is often devastating: escalating political violence, civil unrest and further erosion of the trust that binds societies together.

While each of these thresholds and signals can appear distinct, they are often not isolated events. More often, they are symptoms of a deeper structural failure – our collective tendency to overlook or offload the true costs of our actions or inactions. Known as 'negative externalities', these costs rarely show up where the decisions are made. Instead, they accumulate elsewhere – in ecosystems, in vulnerable communities, in the mental health of individuals, or in the silent fragmentation of meaning.

In simple terms, a negative externality is the cost of a decision or system that someone else (often unrelated to the decision) ends up paying for. It's what happens when harm is outsourced to others – when a factory pollutes a river downstream, when a business cuts corners and society absorbs the consequences, or when short-term gains leave long-term scars. These unintended, unaccounted-for consequences often accumulate quietly – until they trigger systemic breakdown, loss of trust or irreversible damage. Many of the thresholds we've explored represent cascades of negative externalities that were ignored or normalised.

To illustrate how these dynamics converge in the real world, let's turn to a case study that reveals just how fragile and entangled our systems have become.

Case study: Fast fashion and the true cost of cheap clothes

The global fast fashion industry offers a textbook example of how negative externalities ripple across ecological, economic and social systems. What looks like affordability on the surface is enabled by a hidden web of costs pushed onto people and the planet:

- **Violation of fundamental integrity** – Human dignity is compromised when workers in developing countries are exploited for low-cost labour, often in conditions that violate basic rights. Entire communities are locked in cycles of dependency and poverty.
- **Systemic breakdown or collapse** – Garment-producing regions face infrastructure collapse, unlivable wages, unsafe working conditions and use of child labour. Local governance erodes under pressure from global demand and weak regulation.
- **Distortion of natural rhythms** – The pressure for constant new stock drives overproduction, textile waste and toxic chemical use, disrupting ecosystems, water cycles and seasonal agricultural patterns in affected regions
- **Emergence of irreversible consequences** – Microplastics from synthetic fabrics pollute oceans, landfill overflows

with discarded clothing and carbon emissions contribute to planetary tipping points.
- **Collapse of meaning and sense-making** – Fashion no longer carries symbolic, artisanal and identity-based meaning, as it is now reduced to trend-chasing and consumption. Societal values are reshaped around disposability and superficiality and ethical discourse is drowned out by marketing slogans.

In this one example, we see a chain of externalities – economic, ecological, human, epistemic – all of which are detrimental, revealing why sustainability is not merely about recycling or offsetting. It's about tracing responsibility, restoring coherence and redesigning the systems that are currently structured to offload harm invisibly.

To be clear, concerns raised by libertarian thinkers, techno-optimists or market-oriented leaders are not without merit. Excessive regulation, bureaucratic bloat or blanket restrictions can stifle innovation, limit human initiative or create inefficiencies that slow necessary progress. However, in trying to internalise every externality, we risk suppressing ingenuity, resilience and the dynamic forces that drive creativity and technological breakthroughs. These critiques remind us that:

- Intervention must be measured, not reactionary,
- Responsibility should not turn into paternalism, and
- Sustainability must never be confused with stagnation.

The purpose of acknowledging negative externalities is not to demonise progress, but to clarify its true cost and ensure that what we call 'advancement' is not achieved at the long-term expense of others, including future generations.

Ultimately, it's not about whether to intervene. It's about how, when and from what state of being that intervention arises. Why? Because intervention that emerges from fear, ego or control often escalates the problem. But intervention rooted in clarity, care and ontological awareness becomes an act of *sustainable stewardship*, not forceful interference.

Why it matters

Behind every word of this work is a deeper commitment to the belief that systems can be rebuilt with integrity, that interventions can be made from wisdom, and that human beings – despite our 'flaws' – are still capable of rising into the custodianship of this existence. This is not idealism. It is stewardship.

There are those who refuse to look away – who carry the weight of complexity, contradiction and consequence on their shoulders, not as a burden, but as a chosen responsibility. They do this not because it is easy, convenient or rewarded, but because the alternative is to be complicit in the quiet collapse of what could be.

This is about those of us willing to plant seeds in landscapes we may never traverse, breathe air we may never feel, and engage in economies we may never participate in. It's about voting for policies we may never see implemented, entering institutions we may never visit, and wrestling with ethical frameworks we may never personally confront. It involves preserving questions we may never hear asked aloud, but which must be safeguarded for those yet to ask them. It is about the philosophies yet to emerge and the metacontent not yet developed – the layered frameworks through which future generations will make sense of existence, distinguish truth from illusion and act accordingly.

It's about nurturing the public discourse that must one day resist the seduction of rootless ideologies, doctrinal traps and performative morality – all for the sake of contributing to a future that may unfold long after we are gone. A future where the young minds who inherit this world receive either the resilient scaffold of sense-making we dared to build or the fractured ruins of our failure to act.

This work is not merely about reforming systems. It's about protecting the very conditions that make human dignity, truth and conscious life possible. Every framework, every discourse, every principle offered here is born from that stand. They are forged for those who are not here to perform, but to be – not to dominate, but to restore; not to retreat, but to rise.

The ability to recognise these thresholds, act proportionately and discern when to intervene or when to surrender requires something far more rare than intelligence. It demands *wisdom*. And contrary to modern misconceptions, wisdom is not a passive by-product of experience or age. It is an active, ongoing capacity for discernment, context-awareness, ethical integrity and systemic attunement, all of which demand development.

This is why the **metacontent discourse** – an inquiry into the deeper layers through which we make sense of all forms of content, including our assumptions, perspectives, paradigms and ways of knowing – becomes essential.

It is why the **Nested Theory of Sense-making** – a multi-layered framework that maps the cognitive and interpretive processes by which we form understanding, from raw perception to paradigmatic interpretation and the lens shaped by the dominant worldview or school of thought within a given domain – provides the scaffolding to structure such discernment.

And it is why the **Being Framework** – a rigorous paradigm that helps us observe and transform how we are being in life, leadership and performance – anchors this inquiry in lived experience and ethical action.

Metacontent: The Intellectual Substrates for Sense-making[61] explores (amongst other things) how human confusion, vulnerability and limitations of knowing are not design flaws, but ontological facts. The book also examines the paradox of needing authentic awareness while being inherently unequipped to fully grasp reality through any single method. Yes, science and empiricism are vital, but they are not the be all and end all. They excel in the domains of objectivity and repeatability, but fall short in the domains of meaning, morality and lived experience.

That's why other ways of exploration must be reclaimed and reintegrated in conjunction with the sciences – from dialectic reasoning, collective inquiry and contemplative awareness to disciplines such as

---

[61] Tashvir, A. (2024) *Metacontent: The Intellectual Substrates for Sense-making*. Engenesis Publications, Sydney.

philosophy, metaphysics, ontology, phenomenology, ethics, axiology and the humanities at large. These are not 'nice to knows'. They are necessary tools for navigating complexity, making ethical decisions and sustaining systems that do not collapse under their own cleverness. Because without these faculties, we do not sustain – we merely extend dysfunction with better branding.

Reflection

Stewardship is not a slogan or role assigned to a select few. It is a shared responsibility that calls for discernment, care and proportionality. This chapter invites you to explore your own position in the systems you influence – whether ecological, social, economic or cultural – and reflect on the nature and consequences of your participation.

- Can you identify situations where inaction led to consequences that required greater intervention later on?
- Have you ever intervened from a place of fear or ego, only to realise the impact escalated the issue rather than resolved it?
- How do you personally discern when to step in and when to step back? What do you use as your ethical compass?
- In what ways are you already a steward – perhaps without naming it as such – and what would it mean to claim that responsibility more consciously?

True stewardship is not defined by control or passivity, but by the capacity to discern when and how to act in alignment with the deeper rhythms of life. It is not about fixing every problem or managing every outcome, but about cultivating the wisdom to intervene with care, clarity and proportion. This level of discernment cannot be achieved through technical frameworks alone. It demands integrity at the source.

At the centre of this capacity is authenticity – not as a performative trait, but as a critical structural force that determines whether our participation sustains or distorts, clarifies or confuses, heals or harms. As we now turn to the anatomy of systemic integrity, we begin with authenticity: the bridge between perception and reality, and the foundation upon which all meaningful transformation rests.

CHAPTER 17

The Role of Authenticity in Systemic Integrity

Every system relies on its ability to sustain coherence and adapt to reality. Without this alignment, dysfunction takes root, eroding trust, effectiveness and long-term viability. Authenticity is not merely a personal trait but a structural necessity, shaping whether systems remain resilient or fragment and disintegrate.

This chapter delves into the role of authenticity in systemic integrity, not as an abstract ideal but as a determining factor in how systems engage with truth, maintain coherence and navigate complexity. By examining its relationship with perception, governance and decision-making, we uncover why authenticity is a foundational force – without which sustainable and functional systems (those with systemic integrity) simply cannot be built, let alone endure or evolve.

What is systemic integrity?

As discussed earlier, systemic integrity is the condition in which a system – whether an individual, family, organisation, government, culture or society – maintains coherence between what it claims, how it is designed, what it does and the impact it produces. Systemic integrity ensures that structures, decisions and interactions remain attuned to truth, adaptability and long-term viability.

A system with systemic integrity:

- **Prioritises ethical sustainability** → Balances effectiveness with moral and existential responsibility.
- **Maintains dynamic alignment** → Continuously recalibrates itself in response to reality, maintaining coherence and ethical sustainability.
- **Embodies coherence** → Aligns principles, actions and outcomes with reality rather than convenience.
- **Sustains adaptability** → Evolves in response to new insights while maintaining its foundational integrity.
- **Fosters trust and resilience** → Cultivates environments where transparency and accountability strengthen the system rather than undermine it.

Far from an abstract ideal, systemic integrity is the structural discipline that determines whether a system thrives, deteriorates or collapses.

The role of authenticity in systemic integrity

Authenticity is often referred to as 'being true to oneself'. Yet in systemic terms – as touched on earlier – its significance is far more expansive. More than just a personal virtue, authenticity plays a critical structural role in how individuals, organisations and societies engage with reality. It determines the validity, coherence and credibility of our perceptions, shaping the way we interpret, construct and respond to the world around us.

Systemic integrity relies on four fundamental forces – intention, trust, sovereignty and Being – for a system to sustain coherence and adaptability over time. Authenticity, as a Primary Way of Being, operates within this structure. It is not a passive trait, but an active force that determines whether systems align with reality or drift into distortion.

More than simply honesty or self-expression, authenticity is the epistemic and existential foundation of systemic integrity itself. In human systems, how we relate to authenticity – whether we uphold, ignore or suppress it – shapes the quality of our perception, decision-making and long-term coherence. Consider the following ontological distinction of authenticity.

> ## Being Framework Ontological Distinction of Authenticity[62]
>
> *Authenticity* is how you relate to the reality of matters in life. It is the extent to which you are accurate and rigorous in perceiving what is real and what is not. It is also how sensitive and diligent you are to the validity of the knowledge you perceive. *Authenticity* is paramount for you to carefully consider that your conception of reality – including your beliefs and opinions – is congruent with how things are. When you are being authentic, you are compelled to express your Unique Being – what is there for you to express – while being consistent with who you say you are for others and who you say you are for yourself. It is the congruence or alignment of your self-image – who you know yourself to be – and your persona – who you choose to project to others.
>
> A **healthy relationship with authenticity** indicates that you take the time to thoughtfully consider your beliefs and opinions, as the validity and accuracy of your conception of matters is important to you. You mostly experience yourself as being true to yourself and others. Others may consider you genuine, distinct and trustworthy, and that your actions are consistent with who and how you are and what you communicate.
>
> An **unhealthy relationship with authenticity** indicates that there may be no solid foundation for your beliefs and opinions and how you choose to examine reality, and you are often lenient and fickle with how you express your views and the truth. You may consider yourself to be fake or an imposter and often question your own abilities. Others may consider you to be someone who lacks sincerity and often acts inconsistently with who you say you are. You are frequently uncomfortable with being yourself and being with yourself. Alternatively, you may be righteous, opinionated, biased or prejudiced, considering your 'truth' to be the only truth, and may be unwilling to give up being 'right'.

---

62 Tashvir, A. (2021) *Being – The Source of Power*. (p. 277). Sydney. Engenesis Publications

The three modes of engagement with authenticity

There are three primary modes of engagement with authenticity, each leading to a distinct systemic outcome:

1. Commitment to authenticity → Systemic wisdom

This mode is marked by the active and ongoing pursuit, refinement and integration of truth. Systemic wisdom does not arise from a single act of authenticity, but from sustained commitment over time, where alignment with coherence is consistently chosen over convenience. Systems in this mode adjust and evolve through this repeated discipline, fostering long-term resilience, trust and systemic integrity (systemic wisdom).

In governance, this can look like a democracy that continuously evolves its policies through open discourse and empirical validation. In business, it could be a company that chooses to innovate responsibly, responding to market realities rather than manipulating perception. At the individual level, it might be a leader who always integrates feedback, acknowledges mistakes and prioritises ethical clarity over short-term gain.

2. Disconnection from authenticity → Systemic delusion

Disconnection arises when engagement with authenticity is superficial or inconsistent. The system does not reject authenticity outright, but fails to engage with it meaningfully. Unquestioned assumptions take the place of rigorous sense-making, leading to epistemic drift and systemic inefficiency.

In this mode, image, ideology or convenience take precedence over coherence. A government may enact policy based on ideological rhetoric rather than evidence, leading to public mistrust. A business might invest in branding that signals responsibility while avoiding substantive change. At the individual level, a person may override their inner ethical signals to maintain social approval or avoid discomfort.

3. Defiance of authenticity → Systemic corruption

Defiance of authenticity represents the most extreme departure from authenticity. Here, truth is not just ignored, but actively suppressed or distorted. Unlike delusion, which results from disengagement, defiance involves conscious rejection of authenticity in favour of power, control or ideological preservation.

In governance, defiance of authenticity may manifest as censorship, data manipulation and narrative control. In business, it can appear as fraud masked by corporate social responsibility campaigns. In individuals, defiance shows up as intentional deception, narrative distortion and the pursuit of self-interest at the expense of integrity.

At the heart of this lies a fundamental reality. When authenticity is upheld, systems remain coherent, functional and attuned to reality. However, when it is neglected or rejected, distortions take root, giving rise to fragmentation, dysfunction and eventual collapse. The question is not whether authenticity matters, but *how a system chooses to engage with it.*

The modes of engagement as structural forces in governance, business and leadership

The way a system engages with authenticity – whether through commitment, disconnection or defiance – shapes its long-term coherence, adaptability and ultimate trajectory. These modes are not just individual tendencies; they operate as structural forces that influence how societies govern, how businesses function, and how leaders lead.

In **governance**, commitment to authenticity supports public trust, civic participation and adaptive policy-making. Disconnection leads to stagnation and inefficiency, while defiance – such as censorship, propaganda or ideological control – accelerates systemic collapse.

In **business**, organisations grounded in authenticity build ethical, innovative and sustainable practices. Those operating in disconnection fail to adapt and gradually lose relevance. Those in defiance may resort to corruption, exploitation or performative ethics while undermining their own credibility from within.

In **leadership**, authenticity fosters trust, transparency and long-term coherence. Disconnected leaders often operate from a place of misalignment, resulting in poor judgement and inconsistency. Defiant leaders undermine the integrity of the systems they oversee, often weaponising truth to maintain power or control.

Recognising these patterns enables more precise diagnoses and targeted responses. Disconnection calls for structural clarity, realignment and renewed engagement with reality. In contrast, defiance cannot be resolved through awareness or education alone. It requires accountability and, in many cases, external intervention, as it is often deliberate and self-protective. Those in defiance typically resist reform with intention.

Authenticity, when practised consistently, becomes an anchor for sustainable transformation. Systems that commit to it maintain coherence and evolve over time. However, those that disconnect from it develop blind spots and structural fragility, and those that defy it do not simply drift; they fragment, accelerating collapse through the active suppression of truth.

How the three pathways unfold at the systemic level

At first glance, the relationship between authenticity and systemic breakdown may seem binary: a system either engages with truth and thrives, or neglects it and deteriorates. But a closer look reveals a more complex spectrum. The three modes of engagement with authenticity – commitment, disconnection and defiance – unfold as distinct trajectories that either lead to wisdom, delusion or corruption.

A system committed to authenticity continuously refines its understanding, corrects errors and remains responsive to reality. For example, a scientist who evolves a theory in light of new data demonstrates systemic wisdom by prioritising coherence over ego. This capacity for revision ensures that systems remain adaptable and resilient.

A system that becomes disconnected from authenticity drifts into delusion. Here, reality is no longer rigorously engaged with, and decisions are made on the basis of image, ideology or outdated assumptions. A business leader who follows superficial trends without critical analysis may initially succeed, but will eventually encounter failure as decisions become misaligned with unfolding realities.

In contrast, defiance involves a conscious rejection of authenticity despite awareness of the truth. A political regime that fabricates statistics or censors dissent does not misunderstand the facts; it actively manipulates them. This mode doesn't merely lead to dysfunction; it erodes institutional trust, dismantles public confidence and accelerates collapse.

Unlike delusion, which can often be corrected through education, reflection or recalibration, defiance is resistant by design. It operates strategically and defensively, treating truth as a threat. The longer a system remains in this mode, the more deeply entrenched the corruption becomes and the harder it is to restore coherence without a structural reset.

These three pathways show that the way in which a system engages with authenticity fundamentally determines whether it maintains integrity or disintegrates under pressure. Commitment leads to wisdom. Disconnection leads to delusion. Defiance leads to collapse.

The consequences of normalising defiance

In any society, organisation or institution, normalising defiance inevitably leads to systemic collapse. When deception, corruption and suppression of truth become cultural norms, systems begin to erode from within, eventually crumbling under the weight of their own contradictions.

When defiance is tolerated, deception becomes an expectation rather than an exception. When truth is suppressed, instability follows. When accountability disappears, corruption accelerates unchecked. A society that normalises defiance does not merely lose function; it becomes self-destructive. Trust erodes, institutions lose credibility and political and economic frameworks begin to fracture.

Distinguishing between delusion and defiance is essential. Not all systemic failures result from ignorance. Some are manufactured through the deliberate rejection of truth. While delusion arises from confusion or cognitive distortion, defiance reflects a conscious refusal to engage with reality in order to protect power, ego or ideology.

This distinction matters across all levels. In personal development, recognising the difference between unconscious misalignment and deliberate self-deception determines whether transformation is possible. In organisations, it shapes whether poor decisions are the result of flawed assumptions or manipulative leadership. In governments, it determines whether policies are failing due to ideological rigidity or strategic disinformation.

Neglecting to make this distinction leads to dangerous outcomes. Treating defiance as delusion allows manipulation to persist unchecked. Treating delusion as defiance may alienate those capable of realignment. Only by diagnosing the true nature of dysfunction can we intervene effectively and preserve systemic integrity.

Authenticity and the nature of reality: The challenge of truth in a relative world

Any serious discussion of authenticity must wrestle with the nature of reality itself. Are we assuming reality is fully objective and accessible? If not, how can we determine whether someone – or an organisation, institution, culture or society – is operating from a place of commitment, delusion or defiance?

This concern is valid, especially in light of postmodern and constructivist perspectives that argue reality is shaped by language, culture and subjective experience. If reality were purely subjective, any attempt to distinguish between coherence and distortion would be arbitrary, and the very concept of systemic integrity would fall apart.

The Unified Ontology of Systemic Integrity (UOSI) – a key constituent part of the ASF – explored in detail in Parts II to VI of this book, addresses this dilemma by refusing both extremes. It does not rely on a naive objectivism that assumes reality is fully knowable, nor does it dissolve into relativism. Instead, it recognises that reality is layered, and that the clarity or distortion of a system's perception shapes how accurately it engages with those layers.

The three interrelated layers of reality

To make sense of authenticity in practice, we must understand that reality is not a single flat plane. Instead, it unfolds across three distinct but interrelated layers:

1. Objective reality – The material and empirical world

This is the realm of physical facts: what exists independently of belief. Gravity pulls, whether or not we acknowledge it. Climate systems operate regardless of political debate. While our understanding of objective reality can evolve, its structure is not altered by opinion.

2. Intersubjective reality – The world we create together

This layer consists of shared meanings, systems and agreements: money, laws, institutions, cultural norms. These constructs are not physical, but their impact is real. Unlike objective reality, intersubjective reality changes over time, yet it remains more stable than individual perception because it relies on collective participation.

3. Subjective reality – The internal world of lived experience

This is the realm of personal narratives, emotions, interpretations and identity. Subjective reality is valid because it is felt. However, it is not always accurate. One may believe they are unworthy or invincible, but neither feeling changes the underlying truth. When subjective reality drifts too far from the other two layers, disconnection arises. When that drift becomes intentional, it becomes defiance.

How these layers relate to systemic integrity

Understanding the three layers of reality helps us diagnose where disconnection occurs and how it impacts systemic integrity.

Disconnection from authenticity often stems from confusion between layers. When subjective beliefs override empirical facts, or when personal perspectives are mistaken for universal truths, dysfunction emerges. For instance, dismissing climate science on the basis of anecdotal experience reflects a failure to engage with objective reality.

In contrast, defiance most often targets the intersubjective layer. A political leader who fabricates statistics or a corporation that manipulates public narratives is not confused; they are engaging in strategic distortion. By altering shared meaning, defiant systems undermine collective trust while concealing deeper decay.

Commitment to authenticity involves engaging with all three layers in a disciplined, self-correcting way. It respects the empirical, contributes honestly to the intersubjective and remains introspective within the subjective. It does not claim perfect knowledge, but seeks clarity, coherence and alignment.

The Unified Ontology of Systemic Integrity (UOSI) does not presume universal access to absolute truth. Instead, it asks: to what degree does this system's perception align with reality, at whatever level that reality operates? Systemic integrity, in this view, is measured not by certainty, but by the quality of engagement.

In short:

- **Commitment to authenticity** is the ongoing refinement of perception towards coherence, which leads to wisdom.
- **Disconnection from authenticity** is unexamined misalignment, which leads to delusion.
- **Defiance of authenticity** is conscious rejection, which leads to corruption.

The UOSI gives us a practical way to assess systemic integrity, not through ideology or moralism, but through the system's relationship with reality itself.

Wisdom: The ongoing refinement of perception in alignment with coherence

Wisdom is not the possession of absolute truth, but the disciplined commitment to refine one's perception in alignment with coherence. A person operating with wisdom does not treat their understanding as fixed, but remains open to ongoing adjustment in response to new information, insight or experience.

In this mode, perception is a living process. New insights are not threats to certainty, but invitations to refine it. A wise person – someone committed to authenticity – is willing to update their conclusions when faced with better data, not because they are indecisive, but because they value coherence over ego.

Wisdom navigates all three layers of reality: objective, intersubjective and subjective. It stays grounded in the empirical, contributes responsibly to shared meaning and continually interrogates subjective filters. This alignment does not mean the individual is never distorted, but that they remain willing to recalibrate.

For example, a scientist who revises a theory in light of new evidence is not abandoning truth; they are honouring it. Wisdom does not rely on rigidity, but on the capacity to discern where certainty belongs, where context matters and where deeper coherence is required.

Delusion: The loss of coherence through misalignment with reality

Delusion is not simply being wrong. It is a deeper misalignment with reality that persists despite evidence to the contrary. Where wisdom is marked by continuous refinement, delusion is marked by stagnation. The system becomes disconnected from truth, misinterprets information or reinforces faulty assumptions.

Delusion often arises from confusion between the three layers of reality. When subjective feelings are treated as objective facts, or internal narratives override shared agreements, perception fragments. The result is false certainty, ideological rigidity and increasing vulnerability to distortion.

This misalignment may be subtle. Examples include a leader making decisions based on outdated mental models, a culture repeating narratives that no longer reflect the facts, or an individual dismissing feedback that challenges their self-image. But over time, these misperceptions compound, making realignment increasingly difficult.

Defiance: The conscious rejection of coherence despite awareness of truth

Defiance is not ignorance; it is the deliberate choice to reject coherence despite knowing what is true. Unlike delusion, which results from cognitive confusion or unexamined beliefs, defiance is intentional. It suppresses or distorts reality to preserve power, avoid accountability or maintain control.

In this mode, truth is seen not as a guide, but as an obstacle. The defiant system manipulates meaning, controls narratives and resists feedback. Its actions are not confused; they are calculated.

A corporation that knowingly conceals environmental damage while marketing sustainability is not misinformed; it is deflecting. A leader who buries data to protect their image is not mistaken; they are engaging in active distortion. These acts erode trust, fracture systems and accelerate collapse.

Because defiance is self-aware, it cannot be resolved through education alone. It requires exposure, accountability and the structural courage to confront suppression at its source.

Why the distinction matters

Understanding the difference between wisdom, delusion and defiance is essential for diagnosing dysfunction and responding appropriately.

Wisdom invites collaboration and learning. Delusion requires clarity, engagement and structured support. Defiance demands accountability. It cannot be coaxed or reasoned with. Instead, the defiant system must be confronted, because it actively undermines coherence from within.

Misdiagnosing defiance as delusion allows manipulation to persist unchallenged. Mistaking delusion for defiance risks shutting down those capable of growth. Only by discerning the nature of the breakdown can we intervene with the right tools, tone and expectations.

Knowing the difference between the three modes of engagement with authenticity and their outcomes equips individuals, organisations and societies to navigate complexity with greater discernment. It restores the possibility of realignment and protects against collapse disguised as progress.

The pressure to be inauthentic

In today's world, multiple forces make authenticity difficult to sustain. These include:

- **Social media** – Platforms designed for connection now encourage competition and performance. The pressure to present a polished image or curated identity often leads to emotional suppression and internal disconnection. What begins as self-presentation becomes self-distortion, eroding authenticity over time.
- **Professional environments and institutional pressure** – Workplaces often reward performance over principle. Employees may suppress values to meet targets, avoid conflict or maintain status. Leaders may feel forced to project certainty when they are unsure. Over time, these compromises diminish integrity and erode culture from within.
- **Systemic incentives and polarisation** – Many systems reward control over coherence. In politics, media and business, narrative control is often valued more than truth. Polarisation discourages nuance and pressures individuals to conform. In these environments, authenticity is not just difficult; it is often penalised.

The transformative power of authenticity

Despite these pressures, authenticity remains a regenerative force. Leaders who model authenticity create cultures of safety and transparency. Teams built on a foundation of authenticity become more adaptive, innovative and aligned. In relationships, authenticity creates depth, connection and mutual respect.

Authenticity doesn't mean being raw or emotionally exposed at all times. It's about being real: aligning what we believe, say and do, even when it is difficult. It allows individuals, relationships, organisations, institutions, cultures and societies to repair, evolve and sustain coherence over time.

The role of vulnerability

Authenticity and vulnerability are inseparable. To be authentic is to risk being seen, fully and imperfectly. That takes vulnerability. Vulnerability is not weakness. It is the birthplace of trust, repair and transformation.

A parent who admits uncertainty models courage. A leader who owns mistakes creates psychological safety. Vulnerability makes space for truth, and truth makes systems, including individuals, stronger.

Practices for cultivating authenticity

- **Introspection**: Regularly check in with your values and notice misalignments.
- **Dialogue**: Engage in honest conversations, even when it's difficult.
- **Accountability**: Welcome feedback to reveal blind spots.
- **Mentorship**: Learn from those who embody coherence and navigate complexity with integrity.

Why systemic integrity begins with each of us

This chapter has explained how authenticity is far more than just a personal virtue. It is a structural force that shapes systemic integrity at every level. From institutions to economies, societies thrive or decline based on the degree to which authenticity is practised and preserved.

But systemic change begins with individuals. Authenticity is not maintained through abstract values alone; it is sustained through awareness, choices and actions. How we engage with authenticity in our personal lives, relationships and work directly influences the systems we're part of.

Authenticity requires more than self-expression. It demands ongoing self-awareness, vulnerability, the courage to align actions with values, and the willingness to let go of narratives that distort reality. This journey is rarely easy. Social pressure, institutional expectations and internal fear often encourage conformity over authenticity.

When authenticity is practised consistently, it creates environments where trust, collaboration and resilience grow. However, when it is suppressed or blatantly ignored, systems become brittle – vulnerable to distortion, manipulation and decay.

Reflection

Cultivating authenticity is not a passive state; it is a deliberate and ongoing practice. It begins with self-awareness and the courage to ask difficult questions. Reflect on the following:

- Where am I compromising my values?
- How do fear, validation or rejection shape my choices?
- Where is my inner compass misaligned with my outward behaviour?
- What truths am I avoiding because they are inconvenient or uncomfortable?
- Where have I prioritised image over integrity?
- What am I pretending not to know?

Through honest reflection, we begin to realign with what is true, not just in thought, but also in action. This alignment is what restores systemic integrity from the inside out.

A call to reclaim systemic integrity

Authenticity isn't a static achievement. It is an ongoing practice of aligning what we believe, say and do with what is real, even when that truth is uncomfortable, inconvenient or discouraged. Through this alignment, individuals reclaim their integrity and become catalysts for systemic change.

Sustained alignment with reality depends on two essential disciplines: embracing what is true and letting go of what is false. These are not merely moral preferences; they are structural functions that uphold systemic coherence. Truth nurtures integrity. Rejection of distortion protects against collapse. Together, they ensure that authenticity operates not only at a personal level, but as a collective, culture-shaping force. However, it is important to recognise that 'true' and 'false' should not be read in a rigidly binary sense. In practice, our relationship with reality exists along a spectrum of clarity and distortion, where understanding can deepen, refine or regress over time. Authenticity lies not in claiming absolute possession of truth, but in progressively reducing distortion and moving closer to coherence.

In practice, embracing what is true and letting go of what is false play out through the three systemic pathways outlined in this chapter:

- Commitment to authenticity fosters wisdom and coherence.
- Disconnection from it breeds drift and dysfunction.
- Defiance towards it corrodes integrity and accelerates collapse.

No system – personal, organisational, institutional or societal – can remain viable without a commitment to authenticity as an anchoring force. From our most intimate relationships to our largest institutions, how we engage with authenticity determines whether systems grow stronger or fall apart.

This is why authenticity must be reclaimed – not as a personal ideal, but as a civilisational imperative. It requires humility, vulnerability, courage and the refusal to trade coherence for comfort. In a world saturated with distortion, authenticity is not a luxury. It is the scaffolding of systemic integrity and a critical foundational force for any future worth building.

Part I has taken us to the heart of the crossroads we now face – where personal fragmentation mirrors societal collapse and dysfunction is not just a surface crisis, but a structural failure of meaning, trust and coherence. These chapters have explored the shadows we must confront, the values we must reclaim, and the systemic forces – like authenticity and integrity – that determine whether we evolve or unravel.

But to truly understand what sustainability demands, we must now go deeper. Part II turns to the ontological foundations beneath our systems, our selves and our societies. It asks not just *how* authentic sustainability can be achieved, but *what makes it structurally possible* in the first place.

PART II

The Ontological Basis for Sustainability

As we learned in Part I, some systems aren't even designed for basic reliability, let alone long-term sustainability. After all, if a system needs to be continuously saved or mandated into survival, it was likely never designed to sustain itself in the first place. Just as certain car manufacturers build vehicles that require little servicing because they're structurally sound, real sustainability begins with foundational design, not reactive maintenance. But even reliability isn't enough. The sustainability of the manufacturer itself – its relevance, adaptability and continued existence – depends on its capacity to innovate, renew and respond to evolving demands. True sustainability requires more than just resilience. It must have evolution built into the system's DNA.

By recognising the importance of modulation, coherence and adaptability to achieving authentic sustainability, we must move away from reactive governance and towards a framework where sustainability is not imposed; it simply is. This requires us to go beneath surface-level strategies and into the ontological foundations that determine whether systems have what it takes to sustain themselves, fragment or transform.

Part II examines this architecture in depth, uncovering the underlying makeup of integrity, disintegration and modulation that shapes every sustainable or unsustainable outcome. It begins by explaining the relevance of ontology within the authentic sustainability discourse and establishing a rigorous, uniform approach to defining and structuring all the ontologies presented in this book.

However, this exploration is not just theoretical; it holds practical, actionable significance. By breaking down and clarifying the various ontologies, we acquire the tools to assess, design and implement systems that are inherently resilient, coherent and adaptable. This clarity offers a practical blueprint for building structures that maintain their own integrity without relying on constant intervention, enforcement or external correction.

Moreover, understanding this architecture provides a framework for identifying when systems fail and why – enabling more precise interventions and more effective transformations, where necessary. This approach is not about replacing one set of rigid doctrines with another. It's about providing the conceptual and practical tools to build systems that sustain themselves through structural coherence and genuine adaptability.

Ultimately, this exploration seeks to establish a model of sustainability that is not only philosophically coherent, but also practically applicable across governance, economics, ecological systems and both individual and collective human development.

CHAPTER 18

The Ontological Triad Schema

What is ontology and why does it matter?

Ontology is a branch of philosophy concerned with the study of Being, existence and reality. It seeks to answer fundamental questions about what exists, in what form and how different entities interact. While traditionally explored in metaphysics, ontology extends beyond abstract speculation in that it provides a structured way to map out the reality of something, ensuring conceptual clarity and coherence.

In a more technical sense, an ontology or ontological model is a structured framework that defines the constituent parts, function and interrelationships of entities within a given domain. The ontological models explored in this book – including the overarching Unified Ontology of Systemic Integrity (UOSI) introduced in the following chapter – align with this definition.

Ontological models are not limited to philosophy. For example, they are widely used in science, most notably in disciplines like Artificial Intelligence (AI) and information systems to organise knowledge systematically and reveal the underlying architecture of concepts, constructs, structures and experiences.

However, before engaging with specific ontologies, this book establishes a consistent schema[63] for formulating and structuring them: the Ontological Triad Schema (OTS). Developed specifically for this work, the OTS is not an ontology of any particular concept, such as integrity, disintegration, trust or suffering. It's also not a component of the UOSI. Instead, it serves as a meta-ontology, providing the underlying framework that ensures coherence, clarity and systematic construction of every ontology developed here.

Whenever an ontology is introduced in this body of work – whether mapping an entire system like the UOSI or defining individual constructs within it – the OTS governs how it is structured, ensuring a rigorous and uniform approach to defining its anatomy, mechanics and topology, as explained below.

Anatomy, mechanics, topology

Rather than examining concepts in isolation, every ontological model in this book is structured around three fundamental questions posed by the Ontological Triad Schema:

1. **What exists? (anatomy)** – The fundamental structural components within the ontology (its constituent parts).
2. **How does it function? (mechanics)** – The internal dynamics, causal forces or functional principles governing its operation.
3. **How do its components interrelate? (topology)** – The relationships, dependencies and interactions between different entities within the ontology.

This triadic schema not only delivers a unified, structured and systemic approach, but also ensures that all ontological models and frameworks in this book maintain coherence and applicability to real-world dynamics rather than remaining abstract theories.

The OTS aligns with well-established ontological traditions across multiple disciplines:

---

63   A schema is a structured framework that shapes how we perceive, interpret and organise information or experience.

- **Aristotelian and metaphysical ontologies** – Aristotle distinguished between substance (what exists), causality (how it functions) and relations (how entities interact).
- **Formal ontologies (logic & AI)** – Taxonomy of entities (anatomy), process-based functionality (mechanics) and structured relationships (topology).
- **Phenomenological and existential ontologies** – Structures of experience and Being (anatomy), how Being manifests (mechanics) and meaningful interconnectedness (topology).

A tangible example is the Being Framework Ontological Model, which maps the fundamental qualities (Aspects of Being) that shape human performance, leadership and effectiveness. As shown in Figure 3, this framework classifies 31 Aspects of Being into a four-layered construct and breaks them down into their anatomy, mechanics and topology:

1. **Metafactors:** Core ontological dimensions, such as awareness and effectiveness.
2. **Moods:** Foundational emotional states, including vulnerability and anxiety.
3. **Primary Ways of Being:** Core human expressions, such as authenticity, commitment and responsibility.
4. **Secondary Ways of Being:** Context-dependent qualities like confidence, assertiveness and accountability.

Awareness	Integrity	Effectiveness	
Vulnerability	Care	Anxiety	Fear
Authenticity	Peace of Mind	Empowerment	Compassion
Commitment	Freedom	Contribution	Forgiveness
Responsibility	Self-expression	Love	Courage
Higher Purpose	Presence	Partnership	Gratitude
Resourcefulness	Proactivity	Resilience	Assertiveness
Confidence	Reliability	Accountability	Persistence

Figure 3 – The Being Framework Ontological Model.

While the anatomy of the Being Framework Ontological Model is clearly laid out through its four interwoven layers, the Ontological Triad Schema also invites us to consider its mechanics and topology, both of which are explored in depth later in this book. Briefly, the **mechanics** of the Being Framework describe how these layers influence and modulate one another over time – for instance, how a shift in one's Moods can disrupt or enhance one's Primary Ways of Being, or how Meta Factors like Awareness and Integrity govern the unfolding of one's presence and performance. The **topology** reveals the structural relationships and dependencies between these layers – mapping how internal states or attunements (such as care or anxiety) ripple across a person's ontological architecture to shape their action, impact and systemic coherence. A full exploration of the ontology of Being, including its anatomy, mechanics and topology, follows later in a dedicated chapter.

So, rather than reducing individuals to fixed traits, the Being Framework Ontological Model reveals how people *relate* to these essential qualities, demonstrating the interdependencies that shape and influence sense-making, decision-making and human potential.

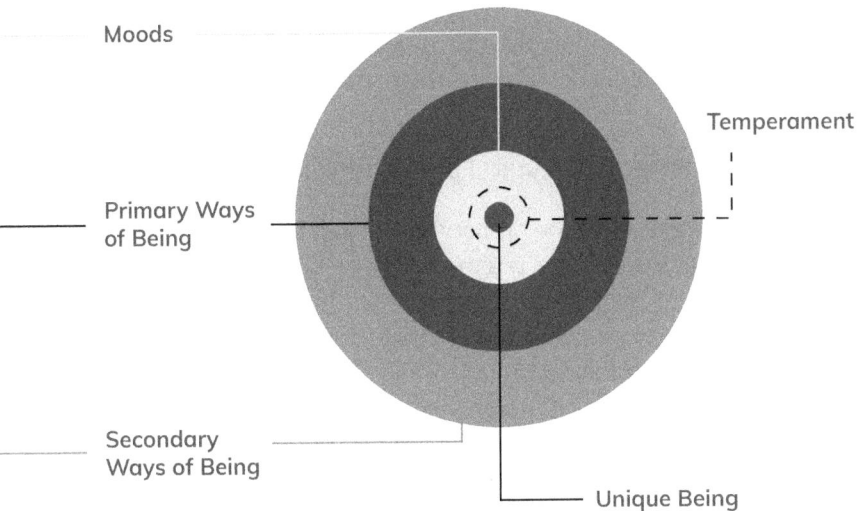

Let's now look into the three elements of an ontological model's structure – anatomy, mechanics, topology – in more detail.

1. Anatomy: Defining what exists

At its core, an ontology must define what it is examining. This means identifying the fundamental entities, categories and distinctions that exist within its framework.

For instance, when examining shadows in the context of the UOSI, the anatomical components are repression, origin, distortion, expression and perpetuation – each representing an essential aspect of how shadows manifest. In the case of trust, the anatomy consists of openness, consistency, benevolence, ontological alignment and continuity.

A relevant example from the Being Framework Ontological Model is the anatomy of human qualities. Each quality or Aspect of Being – such as authenticity, courage, commitment and assertiveness – exists as a distinct, yet interconnected aspect of how individuals relate to themselves and the world. Without identifying and clearly breaking down and defining these foundational qualities, discussions on human potential, leadership and personal development remain abstract and unstructured. Take responsibility for example. The Being Framework breaks down the anatomy of this Primary Way of Being in the following ontological distinction.

Being Framework Ontological Distinction of Responsibility[64]

Responsibility is being the primary cause of the matters in your life, regardless of their source. It is the extent to which you choose to respond rather than react to them. *Responsibility* is distinguished by how you honour the autonomy that you have as a human being and is considered the power to influence the affairs, outcomes and consequences you are faced with. *Responsibility* is not about blaming or determining whose fault it is. Instead, it is to intentionally choose, own, cause and bring about outcomes that matter, work and produce results while also being answerable for the impact and consequences.

A **healthy relationship with responsibility** indicates that you have the power to influence the circumstances you find yourself in and/or cause. Others may consider you capable of appropriately responding to matters, which is a prerequisite to producing and bringing to fruition effective results. You fully accept ownership of both outcomes and consequences and have the capacity to make informed, uncoerced decisions. You are unquestionably the active agent in your life.

An **unhealthy relationship with responsibility** indicates that you may often be stuck, experience a loss of power, and are a victim of circumstances. You frequently experience being disarmed, as though you have no choice in influencing outcomes and there is an inevitability about your future. You may be inclined to self sabotage and make repetitive complaints without seeking, putting forward and implementing solutions. You frequently make excuses for your lack of accomplishments while abdicating or avoiding consequences. You may be considered ineffective in consistently fulfilling the

---

[64] A schema is a structured framework that shapes how we perceive, interpret and organise information or experience.

> promises you make and producing intended results. You are a passive victim in your life. Alternatively, you may live life from the viewpoint of being the sole cause of matters and exert your will onto your surroundings and others or be over-responsible and attempt to control all matters all the time. You may also expect that matters should always go your way.

Unless we define what exists (anatomy), an ontology lacks clarity and structure, making it far more susceptible to misinterpretation and inconsistency.

2. Mechanics: Understanding how it functions

While anatomy defines what exists, mechanics explains how it operates. It describes:

- **Causal relationships** – What sustains, weakens or transforms the entity?
- **Processes** – How does it evolve over time?
- **Feedback loops** – What patterns reinforce or break it?

For example, in the ontology of misery, mechanics explains how unexamined or unresolved lingering shadows and distortions lead to external conditions we refer to as 'misery' – a cluster ranging from trivial discomforts to difficulties, adversities and even catastrophes – which can result in sustained suffering and potentially create self-reinforcing cycles of dysfunction.

In the context of the Being Framework Ontological Model, the mechanics of adaptability (one of the UOSI's four modulating forces) illustrate how awareness, responsibility and vulnerability – three Primary Ways of Being – sustain an individual's ability to navigate complexity. When adaptability is reinforced by confidence and resourcefulness, individuals thrive in uncertainty. However, when adaptability is weakened by anxiety, fear or distorted care, it manifests as rigidity (stemming from an unhealthy relationship with vulnerability) or avoidance (arising from a misalignment in care). Understanding these causal dynamics ensures that adaptability is not treated as an isolated trait, but as a function of interrelated capacities.

Without mechanical coherence, an ontology risks becoming descriptive rather than explanatory. It might define what something is, but fail to explain why it behaves the way it does.

3. Topology: Mapping relationships and interdependencies

No entity with an ontology exists in isolation. Every entity within a system interacts with others, forming a relational structure. Topology examines:

- How different components of an ontology relate.
- How dependencies and interconnections influence function.
- How broader structures shape meaning and application.

For example:

- In the **ontology of trust**, topology examines how trust relates to power, vulnerability and deception – whether it is strengthened or undermined by external forces.
- In the **ontology of misery**, topology explores how misery relates to suffering, resilience and systemic dysfunction – how it is not just an individual state, but an interconnected societal phenomenon.
- In the **UOSI**, topology maps how integrity, disintegration and modulation interact dynamically, forming stabilising and destabilising structures. Modulation serves as a mediating force, regulating transitions between coherence and dysfunction, and shaping how systems adapt, fragment or recalibrate over time.

A Being Framework example of topology is the interconnection between courage, responsibility and integrity. While courage enables individuals to act despite fear, it is sustained by responsibility – one's willingness to be accountable for choices and consequences. Integrity, in turn, holds these qualities together, ensuring that courage is not mere recklessness and responsibility is not just obligation. Recognising these relational dynamics clarifies why developing one quality in isolation often leads to imbalance or dysfunction.

Without topology, an ontology risks becoming static and disconnected – failing to account for how concepts, experiences and systems influence one another.

Why the Ontological Triad Schema matters

The Ontological Triad Schema (OTS) is more than a conceptual tool. It provides a consistent and structured method for developing and analysing ontological models. Its purpose is not to add complexity, but to bring clarity, rigour and coherence to how we define, understand and relate to phenomena. It prevents fragmented thinking, ensuring that each ontological model is not just a standalone construct, but an integrated framework within a larger system of thought.

By applying this schema across all ontologies in this book, we ensure that:

- **Each ontology is well-defined** – No conceptual vagueness or ambiguity.
- **Each concept is deeply explained** – Rather than just being named, its function is understood.
- **Systemic relationships are mapped out** – This ensures coherence between different components.

With the OTS established as the foundational framework, we can now introduce the Unified Ontology of Systemic Integrity (UOSI). This ontology will apply the triadic structure to examine how integrity sustains coherence, how disintegration unfolds, and how these forces interact at personal, relational and systemic levels.

By structuring all ontologies within this book through this schema, we ensure that each construct is not just defined, but meaningfully understood in relation to its function and systemic dynamics. This sets the stage for the deeper exploration of integrity, disintegration and the structures that shape human experience.

CHAPTER 19
The Unified Ontology of Systemic Integrity (UOSI)

Systemic integrity refers to the condition in which a system maintains coherence across its design, function, intention and impact. It is the state of being whole, undivided and structurally sound – expressed through stability, adaptability and resilience across individuals, relationships, organisations, institutions and societies. Yet integrity is not a fixed state. It exists along a continuum and must be continually cultivated in response to internal and external forces. Likewise, disintegration is not a sudden collapse, but a gradual drift – a movement away from coherence towards fragmentation, distortion and dysfunction.

This chapter introduces the central component of the Authentic Sustainability Framework (ASF): the Unified Ontology of Systemic Integrity. The UOSI provides a structured framework that examines:

- How systems are designed, and how they evolve and sustain themselves.
- How human beings and human-designed systems engage with the world – moving either towards integrity or towards disintegration.
- The stabilising forces that sustain coherence (integrity) and

prevent fragmentation and dysfunction (disintegration).
- The mechanisms through which coherence erodes, leading to systemic breakdown.
- How modulation regulates the transition between integrity and disintegration.

By mapping these dynamics, we can see more clearly what sustains integrity, what drives disintegration and how these forces interact over time. The UOSI offers a foundational lens for the chapters ahead, which explore the Architectonic Sphere and its three nested domains: the Integrity, Disintegration and Modulation Spheres.

The continuous flow between integrity and disintegration

The UOSI, as shown in Figure 4, follows a lemniscate (∞) structure to represent the continuous interplay between integrity and disintegration through the process of modulation.

The UOSI does not treat integrity and disintegration as a dichotomy – meaning it's not an either/or situation, where a system is fully one or the other. Instead, it recognises a continuum, where systems are *constantly transitioning* between states of coherence (integrity) and fragmentation (disintegration) because no system – human or manufactured – is ever in a state of absolute integrity or absolute disintegration for long. Most transitions between both states happen unconsciously. However, over time and with developing wisdom, transitions occur at a more conscious level through the process of modulation.

So, unlike static models that depict integrity and disintegration as binary opposites, this ontology recognises that systems – including individuals, relationships, organisations, institutions and societies – are constantly moving between these states.

- **Integrity is not a permanent state**. It must be actively cultivated, reinforced, recalibrated and intentionally sustained.
- **Disintegration is not absolute failure**. When appropriately modulated or regulated, it allows for renewal and evolution rather than collapse.

- **Modulation is the discipline that governs these transitions.** It determines whether a system sustains integrity, recalibrates or spirals into dysfunction. By bringing unconscious shifts into awareness, modulation makes adaptation and transformation *intentional* rather than reactive.

Meta-awareness	Systemic Integrity	Sustained Effectiveness	Normativity
Intention	Trust	Sovereignty	Being
Patience	Tolerance	Adaptability	Surrender
Shadows	Misery	Suffering	Entrenchment

Figure 4 – The Unified Ontology of Systemic Integrity (UOSI).

To capture this continuous interplay, the ontology is structured into two primary structural spheres and one regulatory sphere with an overarching 'meta-governing' sphere.

1. **The Architectonic Sphere (Meta-governing)** – The domain of meta-coherence, sustainability and systemic intelligence.[65] This is not a sphere of immediate action, but of deliberate orchestration, enabling systems to align, evolve and endure with intentionality across time, change and complexity.

2. **The Integrity Sphere (Structural)** – The domain of coherence, stability and functional alignment. This sphere defines what sustains integrity and provides the foundation for resilience and optimal function.

---

[65] Intelligence is more than just raw knowledge; it is applied discernment and synthesis across time, change and complexity.

3. **The Disintegration Sphere (Structural)** – The domain of fragmentation, dysfunction and erosion of coherence. This sphere defines what leads to disintegration and the mechanisms through which coherence is lost.

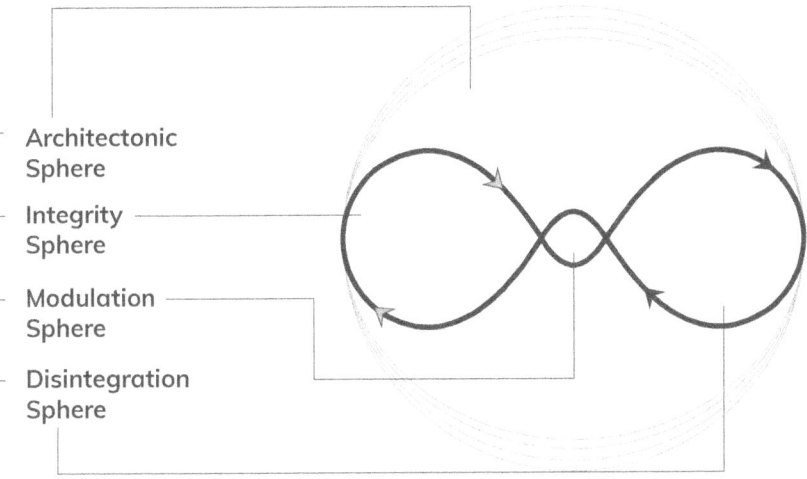

4. **The Modulation Sphere (Regulatory)** – The domain of transition, adaptation and recalibration. Unlike the first two, this sphere does not define a structural state, but intentionally regulates movement between integrity and disintegration, ensuring a system does not become rigidly stable or collapse into dysfunction.

Anatomy of the Unified Ontology of Systemic Integrity

Each of the UOSI's four spheres operates as a distinct yet interconnected ontological space. Within each sphere is an internal 'quad' – a set of four interrelated forces or meta-factors that define its anatomy and internal logic.

The **Architectonic Sphere**, while structurally consistent with the others in having its own quad, functions at a different order of abstraction. It is not concerned with immediate transitions or systemic states, but with *meta-governance*: the orchestration of long-term coherence, normative direction[66] and systemic design across all other spheres. Its four meta-factors provide the epistemic and ontological intelligence required to deliberately see, align and evolve systems over time.

The three underlying spheres – the **Integrity Sphere, Disintegration Sphere** and **Modulation Sphere** – focus on the more immediate forces of structural stability, breakdown and recalibration. Each of these spheres also contains its own quad, consisting of stabilising or destabilising forces that govern the system's function and behaviour.

Let's explore each sphere in more detail, beginning with the Architectonic Sphere and its meta-governing function.

The Architectonic Sphere: The meta-governing layer

The Architectonic Sphere's high level **meta-factors** govern, contextualise and orchestrate the three underlying spheres: Integrity, Disintegration and Modulation. It provides the epistemic and ontological intelligence required to design, stabilise and evolve systems.

Internal quad:

- **Meta-awareness**: The ability to see and reflect on the system as a whole – including your participation in it – while recognising how you are relating to awareness itself, whether with openness, distortion or avoidance.
- **Systemic Integrity**: The condition in which a system coherently aligns its purpose, design, operation and impact across time and context – with all constituent parts in their rightful place and operating at an optimal level.
- **Sustained Effectiveness**: The capacity to perform, evolve and regenerate with longevity – maintaining coherence without collapse or betrayal over time.
- **Normativity**: The ethical, moral and axiological foundation that governs what *ought* to be – orienting purpose, guiding responsibility and sustaining principled action within and across systems.

---

66   Normativity encompasses ethics, morality, axiology and values.

The Integrity Sphere: The foundations of coherence

The Integrity Sphere represents wholeness, coherence and sustainability. However, as mentioned, integrity is not a fixed state. It must be continuously maintained, refined and adapted.

Internal quad: The four stabilising forces

- **Intention:** The clarity of purpose and direction that orients choices and actions – providing coherence not only to *how* you participate in life and with other systems, but also to *why* you participate in the way you do.
- **Trust:** The stabiliser that allows systems, including relationships, to hold coherence in the presence of risk, uncertainty and interdependence, enabling openness, reliability and meaningful collaboration.
- **Sovereignty:** The expansive capacity that allows for undistorted, authentic self-expression and meaningful participation in a life grounded in freedom, autonomy and liberty. It reflects the extent to which you make decisions and take action with genuine autonomy, rather than being forced, coerced or manipulated.
- **Being:** The embodied state of awareness and congruence expressed through your relationship with the fundamental qualities of Being, such as courage, assertiveness, responsibility, commitment and others. The health of these relationships profoundly shapes how you participate in life, perform under pressure and produce results.

Although each of these quads functions as a stabilising force, they must all be actively cultivated because integrity is not self-sustaining. Consequently, neglecting any of these forces would weaken coherence.

Integrity, like many other qualities such as mastery, wisdom and authenticity, is an asymptotic ideal. In other words, it's a directional force as opposed to a final state. Systems, including human beings, don't achieve integrity as a final state. Instead, they *navigate towards it* through continuous recalibration in response to external conditions and internal dynamics. Consider integrity as a journey, not a destination.

Attempts to force integrity into a static ideal introduce fragility, mistaking artificial stability for structural coherence. True systemic evolution does not negate order. It refines and strengthens it through necessary cycles of transition, modulation and transformation.

The Disintegration Sphere: The foundations of fragmentation

Disintegration occurs when coherence deteriorates, either through systemic breakdown or as part of a necessary cycle of renewal.

Internal quad: The four destabilising forces

- **Shadows:** The unseen distortions, blind spots and unacknowledged aspects of reality. Shadows obscure accurate perception and sense-making, resulting in misalignment of choices, actions and intentions. Left unresolved, they generate systemic fragility, undermining coherence from within.
- **Misery:** The external manifestation of dysfunction. Misery appears in the form of degraded conditions, instability, unmet needs and environments hostile to flourishing. It signals the outward breakdown of coherence and becomes the ground on which suffering grows.
- **Suffering:** The lived, phenomenological experience of dysfunction. Suffering embodies pain, disorientation, resistance and trauma. It reveals the human and systemic cost of fragmentation and, when unaddressed, erodes resilience, adaptability and hope.
- **Entrenchment:** The solidification of dysfunction. Entrenchment resists change by reinforcing destructive cycles, habits and structures. It creates a feedback loop where systems become stuck in patterns that perpetuate fragmentation, making renewal increasingly difficult.

These forces interact in complex ways. When left unchecked, they can become self-perpetuating cycles of fragmentation. However, when engaged consciously, they create opportunities for necessary recalibration and realignment.

Disintegration is not merely the erosion of coherence. It's the mechanism through which systems make space for higher-order transformation. When intentional and guided, it dissolves stagnation, allowing new structures, paradigms and modes of functioning to emerge. However, when disintegration lacks modulation, it ceases to be productive and accelerates dysfunction.

Constructive fragmentation

Not all disintegration is negative or destructive. Sometimes it is necessary – as in the case of *apoptosis*, the natural process of programmed cell death in living organisms. This regulated mechanism clears away damaged, outdated or potentially harmful cells to maintain balance, immune function and development. Far from being a symptom of failure, this type of fragmentation is a feature of adaptive coherence: it makes space for renewal, reorganisation and deeper integrity.

The same principle applies to human systems. When fragmentation occurs consciously and with intention, it can act as a catalyst for innovation and adaptive evolution. Often, innovation does not emerge from continuous improvement within existing frameworks, but from the deliberate breakdown of legacy structures that no longer serve their purpose. Just as apoptosis enables new cells to form, dismantling rigid systems can free up energy, resources and imagination for something fundamentally new to emerge.

A clear example is the shift from traditional taxi services to ride-sharing platforms like Uber. The fragmentation of the old model – centralised dispatch, rigid pricing, limited access – was not simply disruptive; it was necessary to make way for a more dynamic, responsive and tech-enabled system. While painful for those embedded in the old paradigm, this kind of constructive fragmentation created the conditions for renewal and innovation within the wider transport ecosystem.

In this sense, the challenge is not to eliminate disintegration but to *engage with it deliberately* – ensuring that it functions as an instrument of renewal rather than collapse within the continuous flow of systemic integrity and evolution.

The Modulation Sphere: Governing the interplay between integrity and disintegration

Between integrity and disintegration, a regulatory space (the Modulation Sphere) determines whether a system sustains itself, adapts or collapses.

Internal quad: The four modulating forces

- **Patience:** The regulator of endurance and timing. Patience allows systems to absorb pressure without premature reaction, granting transitions the space to unfold at the right pace. Without patience, systems collapse into premature fragmentation or force adaptation before coherence can stabilise.

- **Tolerance:** The regulator of variability and external stress. Tolerance determines how much uncertainty, diversity or volatility a system can or should absorb before coherence falters. It sets the boundaries of resilience: too little tolerance creates brittleness, while too much permits dysfunction to take root.

- **Adaptability:** The regulator of responsiveness and recalibration. Adaptability measures a system's capacity to adjust course under shifting conditions while remaining aligned with its ontological centre. It is the faculty that ensures disintegration does not spiral into collapse and allows integrity to evolve rather than stagnate.

- **Surrender:** The regulator of release and letting go. Surrender mediates the delicate threshold between relinquishing what no longer serves and collapsing into dysfunction. It dissolves rigidity, softens resistance and enables necessary renewal, while distinguishing between resignation and conscious release.

These modulating forces function as dynamic stabilisers, ensuring that a system neither drifts uncontrollably into disintegration nor rigidly resists necessary transformation.

The interplay between the spheres: Integrity, Disintegration and Modulation

It would be a mistake to think of modulation as operating in isolation, as though only the four qualities within the Modulation Sphere – patience, tolerance, adaptability and surrender – determine how systems evolve. Modulation is a focal process, but its effectiveness is inseparable from the conditions established in the Integrity and Disintegration Spheres.

So, instead of viewing integrity and disintegration as static opposites, we position them as dynamic spheres within a continuous lemniscate flow – one regulated by modulation, the process that governs transition, recalibration and systemic adaptation.

The Integrity Sphere provides the grounding from which healthy modulation can emerge. Without intention, trust, sovereignty and an authentic state of Being, modulation collapses into mere reaction. For example, patience that is not anchored in trust quickly becomes resignation. Adaptability without sovereignty mutates into instability and compliance. Surrender without intention risks becoming avoidance. It is the structural coherence generated by integrity that ensures modulation qualities function coherently rather than reinforcing dysfunction.

In contrast, the Disintegration Sphere illustrates what happens when modulation is compromised or distorted. Shadows, misery, suffering and entrenchment are not merely unfortunate by-products. They are the conditions that arise when modulation fails to bring unconscious transitions into conscious alignment. For example, when suffering persists without adaptive recalibration, it hardens into entrenchment. When shadows are denied rather than modulated into awareness, they fragment coherence and magnify dysfunction. The Disintegration Sphere shows us the consequences of unmodulated transitions, reminding us of what is at stake when modulation is neglected.

In this sense, modulation is best understood as the living bridge between integrity and disintegration. It is the dynamic process that navigates the transitions in which every system exists. Integrity provides the foundation, disintegration reveals the risks, and modulation transforms the inevitable movement between the two into an intentional path towards coherence and renewal.

Mechanics of the Unified Ontology of Systemic Integrity

In terms of the UOSI's mechanics, movement between the Integrity Sphere and the Disintegration Sphere is regulated by the Modulation Sphere. This movement is not a one-way trajectory towards a fixed state, but a process of continuous recalibration and systemic adjustment. Rather than being purely linear or reactive, these transitions are shaped by the presence or absence of systemic intelligence – the capacity to perceive, design and evolve systems as coherent, interconnected wholes.

At a higher level, the Architectonic Sphere governs the meta-mechanics of the UOSI. It establishes deeper organising principles – such as ethical clarity, normativity and sustained effectiveness – that guide how systems adapt and endure. Without this influence, modulation risks becoming impulsive, shortsighted or distorted by unchecked power or ideology.

The following dynamics highlight how these mechanics play out in practice:

Feedback Loops → Each sphere reinforces itself, but the Modulation Sphere can either stabilise or accelerate the process.

Example: In an organisation where shadows manifest as 'corruption' (Disintegration Sphere), gossip and defensive behaviour feed further breakdown. But when someone in a leadership role introduces transparent communication practices and models accountability, that intervention (via the Modulation Sphere) can stabilise the system, redirecting it towards integrity. Conversely, if that leader exploits the moment to consolidate power unethically, it accelerates disintegration.

Tension and Drift → Integrity is sustained through effort and alignment, whereas disintegration occurs when coherence is neglected or compromised.

Example: A long-standing democratic institution must constantly reconcile diverse values and stakeholders. If it begins compromising its principles for short-term popularity or avoids difficult decisions (neglecting coherence), it drifts towards disintegration – leading to polarisation, apathy or authoritarian tendencies. Maintaining structural integrity requires continuous and conscious tension management, like regularly revisiting its foundational purpose and ethical commitments.

Threshold Transitions → There are critical moments where systems shift between spheres. These transitions can be gradual (a slow drift into dysfunction or realignment into coherence) or abrupt (a crisis that forces an immediate shift).

Example: The COVID-19 pandemic was an abrupt threshold moment for many health systems and governments. Some systems – already fragile – rapidly collapsed into dysfunction. Others that were more coherent and adaptable recalibrated quickly and even strengthened long-term resilience. This is an example of a crisis that demanded an immediate shift. The following example highlights what can happen when there is a gradual drift into dysfunction. A company slowly loses its innovative edge by prioritising short-term profit over culture and creativity. Over time, this leads to talent attrition, stagnation and misalignment until it finds itself in a crisis that reveals how far it has drifted from coherence.

Integrity and disintegration are not mutually exclusive. They form a dynamic equilibrium that must be actively regulated. When integrity is sustained artificially, it erodes adaptability and leads to structural collapse. And when disintegration is unregulated, it disrupts coherence beyond recovery. The Modulation Sphere ensures that evolution occurs within structured boundaries, preventing stagnation without succumbing to chaos.

Systems that master this balance do not merely survive change. They sustain evolution as a natural, disciplined state of being where adaptation and coherence reinforce one another. By actively engaging with the Modulation Sphere, systems (including human beings) can navigate transitions deliberately rather than being passively shaped by forces of fragmentation or rigid stability.

These mechanics explain *how* systems transition between spheres. To see *where* these movements unfold, we now turn to the topology of the UOSI – a lemniscate structure that maps the continuous flow between integrity, disintegration and modulation.

Topology of the Unified Ontology of Systemic Integrity

The topology of the UOSI is expressed through the lemniscate (∞). This form illustrates that integrity and disintegration are not static or mutually exclusive states, but part of a continuous flow. Systems move dynamically along this structure, sustained or destabilised depending on how modulation governs their transitions.

To demonstrate the interdependent nature of the three spheres:

- An individual may feel trapped in **misery** (Disintegration Sphere). By reconnecting with their **intention** to pursue what matters (Integrity Sphere), and applying **patience** to take one small, steady step forward (Modulation Sphere), they begin to restore coherence and move towards integrity.
- A leader may be clouded by **shadows** of past conditioning (Disintegration Sphere). By re-anchoring in **authentic Being** and **sovereignty** (Integrity Sphere) and practising **adaptability** in how they respond (Modulation Sphere), they recalibrate their judgement and realign with coherent leadership.
- A society may be locked in **entrenchment** that resists change (Disintegration Sphere). By reaffirming its **trust** in shared values and **sovereignty** of democratic processes (Integrity Sphere), and exercising **tolerance** to manage diversity and tension (Modulation Sphere), it creates the conditions for transformation rather than dysfunction.

In each of these cases, the Architectonic Sphere determines whether modulation is guided by deeper principles, such as ethical clarity, long-term sustainability and systemic coherence, or left vulnerable to inherent dysfunction or impulsive reaction – instinctive, unexamined responses that bypass conscious discernment, reflection and systemic awareness.

Conclusion

This chapter has established the structural foundation for understanding integrity, disintegration and modulation, setting the stage for deeper exploration in the coming chapters. To sum up, integrity and disintegration are not absolute, opposing states, but dynamic forces that continuously interact. They exist on a continuum rather than a rigid dichotomy – fluctuating based on individual choices, systemic conditions and relational dynamics.

Integrity is not the total absence of disintegration, nor is disintegration the complete eradication of integrity. Instead, they coexist within the lemniscate flow of the Unified Ontology of Systemic Integrity. Modulation governs this flow, determining whether transitions lead to renewal or collapse, coherence or dysfunction.

In short:

- **Integrity** is not the absence of disintegration, but the capacity to mitigate, recalibrate and sustain coherence despite its presence.
- **Disintegration** is not merely dysfunction; it's the erosion of stabilising forces that would otherwise maintain coherence. Distorted intention and entrenchment actively reinforce disintegration, embedding dysfunction into structures, mindsets and institutions.
- **Modulation** is the living bridge that regulates transitions between the two. Through patience, tolerance, adaptability and surrender, it turns unconscious shifts into conscious recalibration, shaping whether systems evolve, stagnate or collapse.

Integrity requires active engagement, not as a final state to be maintained, but as an evolving process of recalibration, adaptation and interplay with the inevitable and sometimes necessary disruptions that allow systems to adapt, shed rigidity and evolve. Integrity is not about perfection, but alignment, intentionality and the continuous pursuit of coherence.

By framing integrity, disintegration and modulation together as a dynamic system, we gain a more resilient way of navigating complexity. How you engage with all three – at a personal, relational and systemic level – determines whether you drift into fragmentation or cultivate coherence.

With this foundation in place, the following chapters will explore the ontology of each of the Unified Ontology of Systemic Integrity's four spheres in more detail, including their corresponding components or quads.

- **The Architectonic Sphere** – How meta-awareness, systemic integrity, sustained effectiveness and normativity shape the structural architecture of systems and determine whether they remain viable, just and aligned over time.
- **The Disintegration Sphere** – How shadows, misery, suffering and entrenchment reinforce dysfunction.
- **The Integrity Sphere** – How intention, trust, sovereignty and Being sustain coherence.
- **The Modulation Sphere** – How patience, tolerance, adaptability and surrender regulate transitions.

CHAPTER 20

The Architectonic Sphere

In a world obsessed with surface-level fixes, performance hacks and reactive management, few pause to ask more profound questions like:

- Why do systems collapse and what keeps them alive?
- What makes a system truly sustainable – capable of enduring structurally, ethically and existentially for as long as its purpose calls for it?

Most systems – whether organisations, families, governments or individuals – are built to perform, impress and survive. But very few are architected to endure with integrity – for as long as their purpose remains coherent. We optimise for speed, scale and optics, but rarely for coherence, congruence and ontological endurance. And the consequences can be seen everywhere – in burnout, societal disillusionment, institutional collapse and leaders who outwardly appear to perform with coherence while privately disintegrating.

This is where the Architectonic Sphere comes in. As the overarching meta-governing layer of the Unified Ontology of Systemic Integrity, it orchestrates how the entire system is designed, evolved and sustained. While the other spheres manage the *what* and *how*, the Architectonic Sphere governs the *why*, *with what consequences* and *to what end*.

The Architectonic Sphere resides within the domain of meta-coherence – where awareness becomes architecture and responsibility becomes design. Here, we query the following about systems of all kinds, from individuals and relationships to organisations, governments and societies:

- Is it aligned at all levels?
- Can it sustain effectiveness without distorting its essence?
- Are its values merely declared or deeply embedded within its structure or DNA?

This sphere consists of four key meta-factors. A meta-factor, as introduced in this ontology, is a foundational ontological force that governs the systemic orientation, coherence and long-term viability of a system. These are not surface-level traits or abstract ideals, but deep structural principles that shape how a system is designed, governed and sustained over time and when faced with complexity.

- **Meta-awareness** – The ability to see and reflect on the system as a whole, including your participation in it, and how you relate to awareness, knowing and understanding itself.
- **Systemic integrity** – The alignment of intention, design and impact.
- **Sustained effectiveness** – The capacity to perform, evolve and regenerate without collapse or compromise over time.
- **Normativity** – The ethical, moral and axiological foundation that governs what *ought* to be, shaping purpose, responsibility and principled action within and across systems.

These are ontological faculties that determine whether systems disintegrate under pressure or regenerate with purpose – for as long as their purpose remains.

To ignore the Architectonic Sphere – or to operate with a disengaged or dysfunctional relationship to it – is to run a high-functioning machine without a map, a compass or any real destination. It may perform beautifully, until it doesn't. Without architectonic intelligence – the capacity to consciously design, govern and align a system based on its deeper purpose, ethics and coherence – systems spiral into recurring patterns of dysfunction:

- Short-term gains that sabotage long-term viability.
- Policies that look good at face value, but are hollow and meaningless beneath the surface.
- Relationships that superficially appear to flourish but fracture Being at its core.

In contrast, when the Architectonic Sphere is active and coherent, systems self-correct, leaders design with discernment, and sustainability becomes systemic rather than accidental.

This chapter unpacks that intelligence. We will examine the Architectonic Sphere's constituent parts, the ontological distinction of each part, and how they work together to orchestrate and govern the why, with what consequences and to what end. In the process, you will learn how this sphere's neglect or distortion explains much of the incoherence in our world.

Ontology of the Architectonic Sphere

The Architectonic Sphere is where design meets discernment. It's not about micromanaging every detail, it's the ontological vantage point from which systems are envisioned, governed and matured. It is what distinguishes reactive performance from *deliberate orchestration*.

In this sphere, coherence becomes systemic and aligned, not circumstantial. The Architectonic Sphere functions as the *meta-frame* that holds intention, relationship and modulation in intelligent cohesion. Without it, even the most inspiring intentions, the most emotionally attuned relationships and the most agile modulations can collapse into contradiction, disintegration or unsustainable loops.

What do we mean by unsustainable loops? These are repetitive cycles of behaviour or systemic patterns that look like continuity, but are inherently unstable, fragile and destined to break down without architectonic guidance. Consider the following examples:

- **At the individual level:** A person may set inspiring intentions, but without architectonic guidance, they keep falling into the same patterns (setting goals → acting impulsively → burning out → resetting goals). The cycle continues but never stabilises or grows, eventually breaking down.

- **At the relational level:** A partnership may thrive on emotional attunement yet loop between harmony and conflict without structural clarity, eroding trust until the relationship cannot hold.
- **At the systemic level:** An organisation or society may repeatedly push for short-term gains (growth, efficiency, popularity) while neglecting deeper coherence, leading to recurring crises: boom–bust cycles, leadership churn or political instability.

In all cases, the loop is unsustainable because it repeats without resolution and drains energy or resources faster than they are renewed. Eventually, it collapses under its own contradictions.

Architectonic intervention: Breaking unsustainable loops

The four meta-factors of the Architectonic Sphere provide the leverage to break these cycles and re-anchor systems in coherence. Meta-awareness, systemic integrity, sustained effectiveness and normativity each play a governing role, transforming unsustainable loops into sustainable trajectories where energy is renewed, coherence is protected and systems evolve instead of collapsing.

The four meta-factors of the Architectonic Sphere

To understand architectonic intervention more fully, we now turn to a closer examination of each meta-factor. These are not abstract ideals, but ontological forces that govern how systems endure, adapt and orient themselves ethically over time.

Meta-awareness

Meta-awareness is the capacity to observe not just the content of experience, but the system generating that content. Unlike ordinary awareness, meta-awareness is recursive, structural and epistemic. It enables individuals and other systems to:

- Detect patterns unfolding across time,
- Examine the mechanisms shaping perception and influence, and
- Step back from experience to perceive the underlying architecture of awareness itself.

This enables the shift from actor to author – from being inside the process to holding and refining the process itself.

When meta-awareness is present and embodied, systems remain open to feedback, capable of self-correction and adaptive in their engagement with complexity. There is humility, curiosity and orientation towards truth, not control. When absent or distorted, systems become reactive, rigid or self-confirming: trapped in cycles of misperception, certainty or unconscious drift.

Meta-awareness is not a luxury. It is the ontological immune system of coherent systems. It enables integrity to be maintained, not through dogma or external control, but through inner clarity and ongoing recalibration. Without meta-awareness, all other capacities – ethical judgement, sustained performance and structural coherence – become vulnerable to distortion. Meta-awareness also exposes unsustainable loops, making them visible as patterns rather than invisible habits, and opening the possibility for intentional redirection.

Systemic integrity

Systemic integrity refers to the structural alignment between intention (why we exist), design (how we are built), execution (what we produce) and impact (what happens as a result). It is not merely a moral or behavioural concept, but an ontological property of systems. When present, it ensures that no part of the system undermines another. Systems with systemic integrity are trustworthy, stable and whole. When absent, even good people in well-intentioned organisations can inadvertently create harm.

Sitting above individual integrity (integrity of Being), systemic integrity is not just concerned with *how I am* but with *how we are* – how systems behave, how power operates, and how the underlying architecture of systems upholds or undermines truth and coherence.

It does not depend on the intention of individuals alone, but on the designed and emergent dynamics of the system as a whole.

When systemic integrity is present and embodied, systems remain coherent in their values, design, function and impact. They hold together under pressure, support ethical action and cultivate environments where trust and accountability are structurally reinforced, not just performatively signalled. Individuals within such systems can act with confidence, knowing the structure supports coherence.

However, when systemic integrity is absent or distorted, systems may function on the surface while eroding from within. Contradictions multiply, trust fractures and culture deteriorates. Efforts towards integrity become symbolic, while underlying dysfunction deepens. Without systemic integrity, alignment collapses and the system becomes unsustainable – regardless of intentions or outputs. Systemic integrity also prevents unsustainable loops from hardening into structural contradiction, re-anchoring short-term actions into long-term coherence.

Sustained effectiveness

More than just 'peak performance', sustained effectiveness is performance that regenerates instead of depletes, evolves instead of calcifies, and stabilises without stagnating.

Sustained effectiveness is the capacity to consistently achieve meaningful outcomes over time without compromising the integrity of self, others or the system. It integrates performance with sustainability, ensuring that results are not achieved through burnout, sacrifice or erosion, but through coherence, regeneration and timing. Sustained effectiveness is the long arc of execution. It reveals whether a system is viable in both metrics and meaning, and is the difference between *achievement* and *stewardship*.

When sustained effectiveness is present and embodied, systems produce meaningful results without burnout, depletion or dysfunction. There is rhythm, timing and renewal. Action is aligned with reality and long-term viability, allowing performance to continue without undermining wellbeing or coherence.

However, when sustained effectiveness is absent or distorted, results may come at the cost of health, relationships or future capacity. Systems either overextend – driving collapse – or stagnate in avoidance. What looks like success becomes unsustainable. Without sustained effectiveness, performance erodes and the system cannot hold its course over time. By renewing energy and ensuring rhythm, sustained effectiveness also converts loops of burnout or stagnation into cycles of resilience that sustain momentum without collapse.

Normativity

Normativity is the moral and axiological compass of a system. It governs what ought to be – what is appropriate, just, ethical and worth pursuing. In contrast to the descriptive or functional aspects of systems, normativity addresses their prescriptive core – not merely how things are, but how they should be. It guides principled action, ethical discernment and value-based judgement in the face of uncertainty, complexity and competing priorities.

So, meta-awareness allows us to perceive systems and ourselves within them, systemic integrity ensures internal coherence and sustained effectiveness upholds resilience over time. In contrast, normativity determines direction. It provides the foundation for discerning what matters and why it matters in any given context.

Critically, normativity is not the same as rules, policies or cultural norms. Rules may constrain behaviour, but they do not necessarily evoke ethical depth. Normativity operates deeper – at the level of first principles, moral frameworks and axiological commitments. It is what makes laws just rather than merely legal, actions honourable rather than merely effective, and decisions wise rather than merely intelligent.

When normativity is active and embodied, individuals and systems exhibit moral maturity, prioritising long-term coherence over short-term gain. They act with care, principle and discernment even under pressure. When normativity is absent or distorted, systems may remain operational or even outwardly successful, yet collapse inwardly, drifting into incoherence, dogma, virtue-signalling or moral relativism.

In this sense, normativity is not just about ethics. It is about ontological orientation. It points systems towards what matters most, not as an idealistic add-on, but as a central organising force. It sustains ethical coherence across time, context and complexity. Normativity also interrupts loops that may appear functional, but are ethically corrosive, reorienting systems towards what ought to endure rather than what merely persists.

A recursive governance loop

The Architectonic Sphere's four meta-factors – meta-awareness, systemic integrity, sustained effectiveness and normativity – do not function in isolation. They regulate each other, forming a recursive governance loop that enables ongoing alignment, evolution and coherence.

When these faculties are unhealthy or distorted, systems become:

- **Efficient but hollow** (when effectiveness outpaces meaning).
- **Well-intentioned but incoherent** (when vision lacks design).
- **Reactive but unsustainable** (when awareness is localised, not systemic).

However, when these faculties are healthy and coherent, systems move from performance to integrity and from control to stewardship.

Real-world application and structural implications

The Architectonic Sphere may sound abstract, but its impact is undeniably tangible. Systems literally rise or rot from this meta-level. Whether we're building a startup, governing a nation, raising children, overseeing the healthcare system or designing education policy, this sphere decides whether we are crafting intentional systems or accidental disasters. Its coherence or dysfunction can be felt in every domain of life.

1. In organisations

- **With architectonic intelligence**: A company doesn't just chase quarterly targets. It aligns its mission, internal culture

and service to humanity. The leadership reflects on *how* it makes decisions, not just *what* decisions are made. It designs systems for long-term coherence, sustainability and trust.
- **Without it**: You get workplaces full of brilliant talent and good intentions, yet burnout, politics, toxicity and incoherence dominate. Values are printed on the wall, but decisions are made from panic, ego or short-term gain. Strategy and culture become disconnected. Feedback loops collapse. The organisation reacts instead of evolves, either succeeding by accident or failing predictably.

Example: A startup scaling too fast without systemic integrity might hit $10M in revenue and implode in two years because its internal culture was never built to maintain success.

2. In government and institutions

- **With architectonic intelligence**: Policies are not just popular; they are coherent with constitutional purpose, ethical integrity and intergenerational sustainability. The system can course-correct over time because feedback loops and epistemic humility[67] are embedded.
- **Without it**: Democracies become theatre and authoritarian regimes become brittle. Well-meaning reforms fail because they address symptoms, not structure.

Example: Education systems designed purely for economic output create obedience factories, not thinking citizens. Architectonic failure results in alienation and social disconnection.

3. In personal life and leadership

- **With architectonic intelligence**: A leader reflects on how their Being influences their doing. They don't just act; they examine their frameworks, relational dynamics and

---

[67] Epistemic humility is the recognition of the limits of one's knowledge, including an awareness of how bias, context and perspective shape understanding. It involves openness to being wrong, a willingness to revise beliefs and respect for other ways of knowing.

long-term impact. They steward their family, health and influence as interdependent systems.
- **Without it**: People repeat dysfunctional cycles, blame external conditions or constantly reinvent themselves without integration. Growth becomes scattered, not systemic.

Example: A high-performing executive burns out, not because they lack productivity but because they ignored the architectonic misalignment between their values, actions and life design.

4. In global systems and sustainability

- **With architectonic intelligence**: We recognise that planetary crises are not just technological, but ontological. Climate change, inequality and polarisation are symptoms of systemic incoherence and misaligned metacontent.
- **Without it**: We get *sustainabilism*: performative greenwashing, checkbox diversity and bureaucratic virtue signals. Nothing truly evolves. The system just rearranges deck chairs on a sinking ship.

Example: Global organisations continue investing in carbon offset schemes while financing industries that accelerate ecological collapse. The contradiction isn't just unethical; it reveals a lack of architectonic intelligence in aligning strategy, values and systemic impact.

Conclusion

The Architectonic Sphere is not a 'nice to have'. It's the difference between systems that endure – as long as they are meant to – and those that implode under their own weight. It governs with foresight rather than force. It does not micromanage action; it orchestrates coherence.

When this sphere is neglected, systems fragment, despite the brilliance of their parts. However, when it is intelligently integrated, even flawed components can harmonise into something resilient, ethical and sustainable.

Meta-awareness, systemic integrity, sustained effectiveness and normativity are not buzzwords. They are the structural forces that hold the scaffolding of our lives, our organisations and our shared future. They determine whether we build ecosystems or echo chambers. Whether we lead with vision or stumble through improvisation.

To activate the Architectonic Sphere is to assume systemic responsibility, not just for what we do, but for how we design the systems that drive outcomes.

Ultimately, sustainability does not begin with recycling bins and clean energy. It begins where few are looking – yet where everything is decided. It begins with the unseen architecture of sense-making, ethics and coherence.

CHAPTER 21

The Disintegration Sphere

Disintegration is not merely the absence of integrity. It is an active force that corrodes coherence, alignment and ethical action within individuals, relationships and systems. While integrity fosters wholeness and alignment, disintegration fragments, leading to instability, dysfunction, misery, entrenchment and suffering.

The Disintegration Sphere provides a structural framework for understanding how breakdown occurs, identifying four interdependent forces that sustain and reinforce one another:

- **Shadows** distort perception, meaning-making and decision-making, creating cognitive and moral misalignment. They shape dysfunction at its root, ensuring that misalignments persist and reproduce across individual, social and systemic levels.
- **Misery** is the condition of external dysfunction, ranging from minor hardships to crises, catastrophes and structural breakdowns. It is the disordered state of existence that results from unaddressed shadows. Misery includes psychological distress, emotional turmoil, cognitive dissonance, systemic failures, economic collapses, environmental disasters, conflicts and societal dysfunction. It is what happens when coherence is eroded and dysfunction takes root.

- **Suffering** is the lived, phenomenological experience of misery. While misery is the condition, suffering is how sentient beings (mainly humans) experience, process and internalise that condition. As individuals, we can experience the same misery differently, depending on our meaning-making, resilience and underlying metacontent.
- **Entrenchment** is the mechanism of being trapped in reinforced misery and self-sustaining suffering. It occurs when misery remains unaddressed and suffering becomes self-perpetuating without breakthrough or resolution. It is both objective (external constraints, systemic inertia, oppressive structures and coercion) and subjective/intersubjective (internalised helplessness, learned dependence and collective reinforcement of dysfunction). Entrenchment locks misery into place and perpetuates cycles of dysfunction through self-reinforcing systems, social conditioning, power structures and psychological mechanisms that limit autonomy and obstruct transformation.

The Disintegration Sphere and its internal quad: The four destabilising forces

If the Integrity Sphere's Quad shows us how systems hold together, the Disintegration Sphere's Quad shows us how they fall apart. These four destabilising forces do not simply mark the absence of integrity; they actively corrode coherence. Each operates in its own way – through distortion, breakdown, lived suffering or systemic inertia. Yet together, they reinforce one another, creating cycles that can eventually entrench dysfunction. Understanding how this quad functions is essential for recognising both the anatomy of disintegration and the leverage points where it can be interrupted and reversed.

Shadows: The regulators of distortion

Shadows obscure clarity, creating blind spots in perception, decision-making and awareness – both self-awareness and awareness of external realities. Whether we develop a healthy or an unhealthy relationship with shadows depends on how we perceive and treat them.

When shadows are ignored or excessively engaged, they hijack perception and distort reality, leading to dysfunction. An unhealthy relationship with shadows manifests in two ways:

- **A lack of awareness of shadows** leads to blind spots, misjudgement and reactionary behaviour, reinforcing distortion.
- **Excessive engagement with shadows** manifests as paranoia, overanalysis and hyper-scepticism, causing hesitation, distrust and cognitive overload.

The good news is we can develop a healthy relationship with shadows by consciously engaging with them, albeit not to excess. Engaging with shadows:

- **Enhances awareness**, enabling us to identify and correct distortions *before* they result in dysfunctional actions.
- **Encourages epistemic humility**, refining perception and decision-making rather than allowing blind spots to dictate our responses.

	Description
Anatomy (what exists)	Composed of the structural forces that lead to cognitive distortions, biases and unconscious conditioning. Shadows obstruct clarity and misalign decision-making.
Mechanics (how they function)	Reinforce false narratives and distorted sense-making. If left unchecked, shadows become entrenched, shaping dysfunctional worldviews.
Topology (interrelationships)	Bridge ignorance and overanalysis. Work with misery to sustain dysfunctional cycles, leading to entrenchment. However, confronting shadows enables recalibration.

Table 12 – Ontology of Shadows.

Misery: The regulator of internal dysfunction

Misery represents the internalisation of dysfunction, trapping individuals and systems in self-reinforcing cycles of limitation, incoherence and dissatisfaction. As with shadows, we can develop a healthy or an unhealthy relationship with misery.

- **Healthy relationship with misery**

    Recognising and processing misery is essential for reflection, contemplation and the development of new concepts, allowing for transformation rather than entrenchment. When engaged constructively, misery can serve as a catalyst for recalibration, prompting the necessary changes that encourage growth and renewal.

- **Unhealthy relationship with misery**

    Misery should neither be ignored nor excessively dwelled on to the point where it becomes a defining state of being. When misery is either ignored or excessive, it becomes a self-sustaining force that fuels deeper dysfunction. When ignored, misery leads to denial, repression and avoidance, preventing the necessary recalibration for growth. On the other hand, excessive misery manifests as chronic dissatisfaction, self-sabotage and stagnation, reinforcing cycles of suffering and making transformation increasingly difficult.

	Description
Anatomy	Composed of structural elements that result from unprocessed internalised dysfunction and chronic dissatisfaction.
Mechanics	Reinforces stagnation and self-limiting narratives. However, if consciously engaged, misery can prompt transformation.
Topology	Bridges discontent and stagnation. Misery works with entrenchment to embed dysfunction. However, recognising misery and consciously engaging with it enables adaptation and recalibration.

Table 13 – Ontology of Misery.

Suffering: The regulator of experienced dysfunction

Suffering is the phenomenological experience of disintegration – where fragmentation manifests as distress, disempowerment or despair. As is the case with all forces of dysfunction, you can have a healthy or an unhealthy relationship with suffering.

- **Healthy relationship with suffering**

    Recognising suffering as a transient state allows for growth, resilience and eventual recalibration. When engaged with constructively rather than resisted, suffering becomes a source of deep learning and meaning-making, encouraging transformation rather than entrenchment.

- **Unhealthy relationship with suffering**

    When suffering is misprocessed or indulged, it either becomes unbearable or is repressed, deepening dysfunction. A lack of engagement with suffering leads to denial, suppression and emotional disconnection, preventing necessary healing. Conversely, excessive suffering manifests as victimhood, despair and emotional paralysis, ensuring that fragmentation persists rather than allowing for integration and renewal.

Suffering must be navigated with intentionality. It is neither something to be avoided nor something to be indulged in perpetually.

	Description
Anatomy	Composed of structural forces that lead to pain, distress and psychological fragmentation. Suffering represents the lived experience of disintegration.
Mechanics	If left unprocessed, suffering deepens cycles of dysfunction. However, when engaged with awareness, it can encourage transformation.
Topology	Bridges pain and paralysis. Suffering works with misery to either sustain entrenched dysfunction or trigger realignment.

Table 14 – Ontology of Suffering.

Entrenchment: The regulator of reinforced dysfunction

Entrenchment is the reinforcement and perpetuation of dysfunction, embedding shadows, misery and suffering into an individual's psyche and relationships or into systemic structures.

- **Healthy relationship with entrenchment**

    Recognising patterns of entrenchment allows for recalibration, preventing dysfunction from becoming rigid and deeply ingrained. When acknowledged and actively disrupted, entrenchment can serve as a signal for areas that require deep transformation, opening the door to growth and adaptation.

- **Unhealthy relationship with entrenchment**

    When entrenchment is either ignored or excessively engaged with, it normalises dysfunction and makes alternative possibilities seem unattainable. A lack of awareness leads to repetitive dysfunctional cycles, where the same problems persist indefinitely. On the other hand, an excessive focus on entrenchment manifests as dogmatism, resistance to change and an inability to break free from limiting patterns, further reinforcing stagnation.

Entrenchment, when left unchecked, ensures that dysfunction is no longer just endured, but actively perpetuated.

	Description
Anatomy	Composed of structural forces that lead to pain, distress and psychological fragmentation. Entrenchment represents the lived experience of disintegration.
Mechanics	If left unprocessed, self-sustaining suffering deepens cycles of dysfunction. However, when engaged with awareness, it can encourage transformation.
Topology	Bridges pain and paralysis. Suffering works with misery to either sustain entrenched dysfunction or trigger realignment.

Table 15 – Ontology of Entrenchment.

The role of the Modulation Sphere in disintegration

The Disintegration Sphere does not exist in isolation. It is regulated by the Modulation Sphere. Whether a system descends further into dysfunction or recalibrates towards integrity depends on the interplay of the Modulations Sphere's four regulating forces: patience, tolerance, adaptability and surrender.

These modulating forces determine – through the health of one's relationship with them – whether:

- **Shadows** become entrenched distortions or opportunities for self-correction.
- **Misery** deepens into dysfunction or serves as a catalyst for transformation.
- **Suffering** becomes all-consuming or is processed in a way that leads to resilience.
- **Entrenchment** reinforces disintegration or is gradually dissolved through intentional effort.

An unhealthy relationship with any or all of the four modulating qualities accelerates disintegration. For example, an organisation experiencing systemic dysfunction may either adapt and recalibrate (demonstrating a healthy relationship with adaptability) or succumb to inertia and entrenchment (due to an unhealthy relationship with surrender).

Modulating forces and their role in disintegration

While shadows, misery, suffering and entrenchment function as the core structural elements of disintegration, their intensity and trajectory are not fixed. They are shaped, amplified or diffused by the presence, absence or distortion of the four modulating forces: patience, tolerance, adaptability and surrender.

- **Patience** can slow the momentum of dysfunction, allowing space for intervention before fragmentation worsens. However, when distorted, patience becomes passivity or apathy – waiting indefinitely while dysfunction deepens.
- **Tolerance** determines how much dysfunction is absorbed before action is taken. However, excessive or blind tolerance allows disintegration to deepen unchecked, enabling toxicity and collapse under the guise of 'acceptance'.
- **Adaptability** creates pathways for recalibration, counteracting both stagnation and rigidity within dysfunction. However, when distorted, adaptability turns into compliance or identity erosion – constantly yielding to dysfunction without anchoring in coherent principles.

- **Surrender**, when healthy, prevents futile resistance and opens space for flow and redirection. However, when distorted, surrender becomes resignation or learned helplessness: normalising dysfunction and abandoning responsibility.

These modulating forces either mediate or accelerate the descent into deeper dysfunction, making them crucial variables in the disintegration process. For example, in a toxic workplace, a team member might patiently endure unfair treatment (patience), tolerate poor leadership to preserve harmony (tolerance), adapt their behaviour to survive politically (adaptability) and eventually give in to the culture, believing change is impossible (surrender). While each response may appear composed on the surface, their distorted expressions actually compound disintegration: normalising dysfunction, silencing dissent and entrenching systemic decay.

In this way, modulation governs the trajectory of disintegration. It determines whether we spiral into systemic decay or interrupt the pattern to move towards restoration and coherence.

Shadows and the Modulation Sphere

Shadows are the gateway to disintegration. They distort perception, obscure clarity and interfere with sound judgement, becoming the foundation upon which dysfunction is built. However, whether these distortions solidify into entrenched dysfunction or are caught early and recalibrated depends on the Modulation Sphere and the health of one's relationship with its four regulating forces.

- **Patience** allows space for self-awareness and reflection, which can help identify and interrupt distorted perceptions before they calcify into systemic dysfunction. Without patience, reactive behaviour locks shadows into place before truth has time to emerge.
- **Tolerance**, when constructive, enables individuals and systems to witness distortions without immediately suppressing or denying them. However, excessive or distorted tolerance can normalise misleading narratives, allowing them to permeate culture and decision-making without question.

- **Adaptability** enables systems to adjust their internal models and perceptions as new information or realisations emerge. When adaptability is lacking, shadows become rigid, defended beliefs that self-perpetuate.
- **Surrender**, in its healthy form, allows individuals or systems to let go of false certainties and fixed identities, creating room for recalibration. Distorted surrender, on the other hand, passively accepts the shadow as truth, reinforcing denial and blocking transformation.

When regulated well, shadows become early warning signals for course correction. However, when mismanaged, they deepen disconnection from reality, accelerating the descent into dysfunction.

Example (individual): A person carries unresolved insecurity (**shadow**). When they receive constructive feedback, distorted perception makes them interpret it as a personal attack. Without **patience**, they react defensively before truth can surface. Distorted **tolerance** allows the misreading to become normalised. A lack of **adaptability** prevents them from revising their interpretation, while distorted **surrender** entrenches the belief that others are hostile. However, with coherent modulation – patience to pause, tolerance to hold discomfort, adaptability to adjust their perspective, and surrender of false certainties – the shadow becomes visible as distortion rather than reality, creating space for growth.

Example (manufactured system): An organisation faces complaints about unfair treatment. Leadership distorts perception by dismissing them as isolated incidents (**shadow**). Without **patience**, leaders rush to defend current practices. Distorted **tolerance** normalises dysfunction. A lack of **adaptability** blocks reform, while distorted **surrender** resigns the organisation to 'this is just how things are'. With coherent modulation – patient listening, balanced tolerance, adaptive policy adjustments, and surrender of ineffective practices – the shadow is exposed as a systemic blind spot and becomes a catalyst for greater transparency and reform.

Misery and the Modulation Sphere

Misery is not a passive state. It leads to either deeper entrenchment or transformation, depending on how it is regulated and the health of one's relationship with it. How individuals, organisations or societies relate to misery – whether they avoid, suppress, romanticise or work through it – plays a defining role in its long-term impact.

- **Patience** allows for the processing and integration of hardship rather than letting it become chronic dysfunction.
- **Tolerance**, when attuned, helps hold space for discomfort without immediately reacting to it. But excessive or distorted tolerance numbs discernment, allowing misery to become normalised or dismissed as unavoidable.
- **Adaptability** provides an avenue for recalibration, preventing misery from solidifying into systemic stagnation.
- **Distorted surrender** reinforces cycles of despair by making individuals and systems believe there is no alternative to suffering.

Misery is a critical junction where the modulating qualities determine whether dysfunction deepens or realigns towards integrity.

Example (individual): Someone loses their job (**misery**). The condition itself creates financial strain, uncertainty and disruption to daily life. Without **adaptability**, the loss hardens into prolonged instability. Distorted **tolerance** normalises the hardship, turning short-term difficulty into chronic dysfunction. But when modulation is applied coherently – patience to process the disruption, tolerance to sit with discomfort without denial, adaptability to re-skill, and surrender of outdated self-concepts – the individual can stabilise their circumstances and open pathways for renewal.

Example (manufactured system): A school faces chronic underfunding and declining performance (**misery**). The condition manifests as larger class sizes, resource shortages and eroding morale. Without **patience**, leaders may resort to quick fixes that mask the deeper issue. Distorted **tolerance** resigns the community to 'this is just how it is'. A lack of **adaptability** blocks creative reforms, while distorted **surrender** entrenches the narrative of inevitable decline. Conversely, with coherent modulation – patient engagement, constructive tolerance, adaptive policy responses, and surrender of ineffective practices – the school can navigate hardship, sustain resilience and move towards integrity.

Suffering and the Modulation Sphere

Suffering is the phenomenological experience of disintegration. However, it does not necessarily lead to further dysfunction unless it is incorrectly or inadequately processed.

- **Patience** prevents reactive behaviours that amplify suffering, allowing it to be integrated rather than resisted.
- **Tolerance**, when applied constructively, helps manage suffering without allowing it to distort perception.
- **Adaptability** enables individuals and systems to adjust to hardship, finding meaning and growth within suffering rather than succumbing to it.
- **Surrender**, in a healthy form, allows acceptance of inevitable hardship. However, distorted surrender leads to despair and resignation.

How suffering is navigated determines whether it leads to wisdom and resilience or fuels further disintegration.

Example (individual): Two people experience the same chronic illness (**suffering**). The first lacks **patience**, reacting to every symptom with frustration, amplifying distress. Distorted **tolerance** leads them to normalise ongoing pain without seeking support. A lack of **adaptability** keeps them stuck in routines that worsen their condition, while distorted **surrender** results in despair and resignation. The second, facing the same illness, applies coherent modulation – patience to endure the slow process of treatment, tolerance to hold discomfort without denial, adaptability to adjust daily life, and surrender to accept what cannot be changed. This reframes the suffering into a pathway for resilience, growth and deeper coherence.

Example (manufactured system): A nation experiences a deep economic downturn (**suffering**). Without **patience**, governments overcorrect with reactive austerity measures. Distorted **tolerance** causes citizens to accept unemployment and inequity as unchangeable. A lack of **adaptability** prevents industries from diversifying, while distorted **surrender** entrenches the belief that recovery is impossible. In contrast, with coherent modulation – patience in policy, tolerance for hardship without resignation, adaptability in shifting industries, and surrender of failing models – the suffering is transformed into an impetus for structural renewal and long-term stability.

Entrenchment and the Modulation Sphere

Entrenchment is the most self-sustaining force of disintegration. However, it too, is subject to regulation. The deeper the entrenchment, the more critical the role of the modulating forces in either loosening or reinforcing its grip.

- **Patience** can counteract entrenchment by enabling a gradual end to dysfunction rather than forcing its premature collapse.
- **Tolerance**, when constructive, allows space to observe and understand entrenched patterns without immediate resistance. But distorted tolerance legitimises dysfunction by adapting to it for too long, reinforcing inertia.
- **Adaptability** enables the loosening of entrenched structures, allowing for gradual movement towards recalibration.
- **Surrender**, in its healthy form, allows for letting go of dysfunctional attachments, whereas distorted surrender reinforces stagnation by making change seem impossible.

When entrenchment is left unchecked, it solidifies dysfunction. However, through the modulation of patience, adaptability, tolerance and surrender, its hold can be weakened and, ultimately, dismantled.

Example (individual): A person remains in an unhealthy relationship believing they are stuck and there is no way out (**entrenchment**). Without **patience**, they demand immediate change, leading to repeated cycles of conflict that reinforce despair. Distorted **tolerance** allows them to normalise harmful behaviours, adapting to dysfunction rather than addressing it. A lack of **adaptability** keeps them locked in the same patterns of reaction, while distorted **surrender** convinces them that leaving or transforming the relationship is impossible. In contrast, with coherent modulation – patience to allow gradual shifts, tolerance to hold discomfort without enabling harm, adaptability to experiment with new ways of relating, and surrender of unhealthy attachments – the grip of entrenchment loosens, opening the way for recalibration or resolution.

Example (manufactured system): A government bureaucracy becomes stuck in outdated procedures (**entrenchment**). Without **patience**, reformers attempt abrupt overhauls that backfire, strengthening resistance. Distorted **tolerance** lets inefficiencies persist under the banner of 'this is how it's always been'. A lack of **adaptability** blocks new technologies or practices, while distorted **surrender** entrenches the belief that meaningful change is impossible. In contrast, with coherent modulation – patience for gradual reform, tolerance that distinguishes between necessary continuity and inertia, adaptability in adopting new systems, and surrender of obsolete practices – the bureaucracy can shift from entrenched dysfunction to renewed effectiveness.

Conclusion

Disintegration is not a singular event, but a structured process that unfolds through distinct but interdependent forces. Understanding these forces allows us to recognise the mechanisms of dysfunction and, more importantly, intervene before they become entrenched.

- **Shadows distort awareness,** leading to misjudgement, meaning-making errors and reactive behaviours. These distortions act as the entry point into disintegration, shaping how individuals, relationships and systems perceive and respond to reality.
- **Misery is a condition,** whether external or internal, that exists regardless of perception. It represents a state of dysfunction, stagnation or unresolved structural failure in a system.
- **Suffering is the experience of *being with* misery.** While misery is the condition, suffering is how an individual or

system internalises and engages with it. Depending on how it is modulated, suffering can either lead to resilience and transformation or deepen dysfunction.

- **Entrenchment is both a condition and an experience,** where dysfunction becomes embedded and normalised. When entrenchment takes hold, disintegration is no longer just an active force, but a structural reality that resists recalibration at the verge of breaking down.

If left unchecked, these four interdependent forces operate in a self-reinforcing cycle. Shadows lead to misery, misery is experienced as suffering and, if unresolved, suffering becomes entrenchment. Once entrenched, dysfunction is no longer seen as an anomaly, but as the norm, making recovery increasingly difficult.

It is here that the Modulation Sphere plays a critically decisive role. By bringing patience, tolerance, adaptability and surrender into play, modulation regulates whether disintegration spirals into collapse or becomes a catalyst for renewal. Without modulation, dysfunction compounds. But with it, even entrenched patterns can loosen, creating space for coherence to re-emerge.

By mapping this interplay, we move beyond seeing disintegration as an abstract failure and begin to diagnose, predict and, ultimately, redirect its systemic spread.

CHAPTER 22

The Integrity Sphere

Integrity is not merely an abstract virtue. It is the foundation that sustains coherence, alignment and ethical action within individuals, relationships and other systems like organisations, institutions and societies. Without it, fragmentation takes root, leading to dysfunction, instability and eventual disintegration.

The Integrity Sphere provides a structural framework for understanding how coherence is maintained, identifying four interdependent forces that reinforce and sustain one another:

- **Intention** – The driver of action and engagement.
- **Trust** – The stabiliser of meaningful interactions.
- **Sovereignty** – The enabler of authentic, undistorted self-expression.
- **Being** – The embodiment of awareness, presence and alignment.

The Integrity Sphere and its internal quad: The four stabilising forces

Where the Disintegration Sphere's Quad exposes the forces that erode coherence, the Integrity Sphere's Quad reveals the forces that sustain it. These stabilising forces are not passive virtues, but active regulators of alignment. Each shapes integrity in a different way – by directing purpose, cultivating trust, enabling authentic expression and embodying presence – while also reinforcing one another. Together, they generate the systemic stability that allows individuals, relationships and organisations to flourish.

Understanding how these four forces interact is essential to keeping integrity dynamic and sustainable, rather than a passive or rigid ideal.

Intention: The regulator of purpose

Intention determines the direction and alignment of actions within a system. It dictates whether choices are made with clarity and authenticity or shaped by distortion and misalignment. It is possible to have a healthy or an unhealthy relationship with all the stabilising forces, including intention.

- **Healthy relationship with intention**

    A healthy relationship with intention ensures alignment between values, choices and actions, reinforcing coherence and ethical engagement. It also drives meaningful participation, ensuring actions are deliberate, conscious and purpose-driven.

- **Unhealthy relationship with intention**

    When intention is distorted, it becomes either deficient or excessive, leading to dysfunction. A lack of intention results in aimlessness, misalignment and susceptibility to external manipulation, causing incoherence and disengagement. Conversely, excessive intention manifests as rigidity, obsession and over-controlling behaviours, limiting adaptability and openness to recalibration.

Intention must be continuously examined and refined to ensure that it remains an authentic force of coherence rather than a source of dysfunction.

	Description
Anatomy	Composed of structural forces that manifest clarity, purpose and direction. Intention ensures that actions are aligned with authentic values rather than external distortions.
Mechanics	Regulates decision-making and engagement, ensuring that actions are coherent rather than reactive. However, distorted intention leads to deception or manipulation.
Topology	Bridges alignment and distortion. Intention works with trust to sustain integrity. However, excessive intention restricts adaptability, leading to rigidity, obsession or stagnation.

Table 16 – Ontology of Intention.

Trust: The regulator of stability

Trust governs reliability, security and relational integrity in individuals, systems and societies. It determines whether relationships and structures remain stable or deteriorate into suspicion and fragility.

- **Healthy relationship with trust**

    A healthy relationship with trust ensures predictability and coherence, allowing individuals and systems to function smoothly without unnecessary friction. It strengthens social and organisational bonds, encouraging cooperation and collective resilience by creating a foundation of reliability and mutual understanding.

- **Unhealthy relationship with trust**

    When trust is distorted, it becomes either deficient or excessive, leading to dysfunction. A lack of trust breeds cynicism, isolation and systemic breakdown, undermining relationships and eroding social cohesion. Conversely, an excess of trust manifests as blind faith, gullibility and a lack of discernment, leaving individuals and systems vulnerable to deception and exploitation.

Trust must be actively cultivated and maintained. It should be neither granted blindly nor excessively withheld.

	Description
Anatomy	Composed of structural qualities that facilitate reliability, transparency and predictability. Trust provides stability in relationships and systems.
Mechanics	Enables effective collaboration and coherence. However, misplaced trust leads to deception and systemic fragility.
Topology	Bridges stability and vulnerability. Trust works with intention to reinforce integrity. However, excessive trust erodes sovereignty, leading to dependency and blind faith.

Table 17 – Ontology of Trust.

Sovereignty: The regulator of autonomy

Sovereignty governs the ability to act with autonomy and authenticity without coercion. It determines whether individuals and systems retain agency over their choices or become subject to external control and influence.

- **Healthy relationship with sovereignty**

    A healthy relationship with sovereignty ensures self-determination and authentic agency, allowing individuals and systems to operate from inner alignment rather than external imposition. It enables adaptive decision-making, fostering resilience and preventing manipulation or forced compliance.

- **Unhealthy relationship with sovereignty**

    When sovereignty is distorted, it becomes either deficient or excessive, leading to dysfunction. Distorted sovereignty results in submission, dependence and the loss of individual agency, causing coerced participation rather than authentic engagement. On the other hand, an excess of sovereignty manifests as hyper-individualism, defiance and resistance to legitimate collaboration, leading to fragmentation and a breakdown of trust.

Sovereignty must be balanced with relational coherence, ensuring that autonomy strengthens meaningful connection and collective function rather than undermining it.

Aspect	Description
Anatomy	Composed of structural capacities that foster autonomy, self-determination and personal agency. Sovereignty ensures authentic self-expression without coercion.
Mechanics	Regulates the balance between independence and collaboration. Distorted sovereignty leads to resistance to necessary structure.
Topology	Bridges autonomy and isolation. Sovereignty works with trust to sustain relational integrity. However, excessive sovereignty erodes collaboration, leading to alienation and fragmentation.

Table 18 – Ontology of Sovereignty.

Being: The regulator of alignment

Being governs presence, awareness and the integrity of one's existence, ensuring that individuals and systems operate in alignment with their fundamental nature rather than in a state of fragmentation or self-deception.

- **Healthy relationship with Being**

    A healthy relationship with Being ensures deep presence, coherence and authenticity, allowing for fluid and adaptive engagement with reality. It strengthens internal stability, enabling individuals to navigate complexity with resilience and a grounded sense of self.

- **Unhealthy relationship with Being**

    When Being is distorted, it becomes either deficient or excessive, leading to dysfunction. A deficient focus on one's Being results in disconnection, alienation and chronic dissatisfaction, causing misalignment in decisions and relationships. Conversely, an excessive focus on one's Being manifests as over-introspection, withdrawal and detachment from practical engagement, leading to stagnation and inaction.

Being is not about static presence. It is an evolving practice of maintaining coherence while engaging with the world.

Aspect	Description
Anatomy	Composed of structural forces that lead to presence, authenticity and self-awareness. Being forms the foundation of alignment within integrity.
Mechanics	Regulates internal stability and coherence. When distorted, Being leads to disengagement or self-deception.
Topology	Bridges authenticity and disconnection. Being works with sovereignty to ensure autonomy within coherence. However, an excessive connection with one's Being can result in a detachment from one's practical function.

Table 19 – Ontology of Being.

How the Modulation Sphere shapes the core forces of the Integrity Sphere

Integrity does not erode in isolation. It is continually shaped and sustained by the Modulation Sphere. The extent to which intention, trust, sovereignty and Being either support coherence or become compromised depends on the modulation qualities of patience, tolerance, adaptability and surrender. These qualities regulate whether:

- **Intention** remains aligned or drifts into distortion.
- **Trust** is nurtured or eroded by excessive tolerance of dysfunction.
- **Sovereignty** fosters authentic expansion or leads to chaotic fragmentation.
- **Being** remains coherent or is destabilised by external pressures.

The presence or distortion of these modulating forces determines whether integrity is resilient or fragile under strain. For example:

- **Patience** sustains alignment by preventing impulsive decisions that could disrupt coherence.
- **Tolerance**, when constructive, fosters trust. But when excessive, it enables misalignment to persist.

- **Adaptability** ensures that integrity remains dynamic, preventing stagnation or rigidity. But when distorted, it becomes over-compliance or identity erosion.
- **Surrender**, when healthy, allows release and realignment. But when distorted, it results in passivity, weakening intention and agency.

These qualities either reinforce or destabilise integrity over time, making the Modulation Sphere essential for sustaining coherence across changing conditions.

Let's now examine how the Modulation Sphere interacts with each of these core elements, shaping whether integrity is sustained, deepened or unconsciously eroded over time.

Intention and the Modulation Sphere

Intention sets the course in the Integrity Sphere, shaping how coherence is maintained. However, its alignment or distortion depends on the four regulating forces of patience, adaptability, tolerance and surrender. For example:

- **Patience** enables long-term commitment to integrity rather than impulsive and erratic shifts. However, distorted patience manifests as passivity or procrastination, where waiting becomes avoidance and necessary action is indefinitely deferred.
- **Adaptability** ensures intention remains relevant and responsive rather than rigid or outdated. However, excessive adaptability leads to opportunism or loss of direction, where constant adjustment erodes coherence and stability.
- **Tolerance**, when attuned, allows space for divergent views and complexity without prematurely collapsing into dogma. However, excessive tolerance may allow misalignment to persist under the guise of open-mindedness.
- **Surrender**, in its healthy form, helps release rigid attachments to fixed outcomes, allowing for recalibration without abandoning core values. However, distorted surrender leads to the abandonment of one's purpose, weakening integrity.

Example (individual): A person sets an **intention** to pursue further study. Without **patience**, they become restless when results aren't immediate, abandoning the path prematurely. Distorted **tolerance** makes them accommodate distractions, weakening their focus. A lack of **adaptability** prevents them from adjusting their study approach when challenges arise, while distorted **surrender** leads them to give up altogether, seeing obstacles as insurmountable. In contrast, with coherent modulation – patience for the long process of learning, tolerance to hold frustration without quitting, adaptability in refining methods, and surrender of rigid expectations – their intention remains aligned, sustaining both commitment and growth.

Example (manufactured system): An organisation sets an **intention** to transition towards sustainable practices. Without **patience**, leaders demand immediate outcomes, implementing rushed policies that backfire. Distorted **tolerance** excuses ongoing harmful practices under the guise of 'transition takes time'. A lack of **adaptability** makes the organisation rigid, unable to pivot strategies as new technologies or regulations emerge. Distorted **surrender** resigns the organisation to minimal change, claiming deep transformation is unrealistic. In contrast, with coherent modulation – patience for incremental progress, tolerance that allows for experimentation without enabling dysfunction, adaptability to integrate innovations, and surrender of outdated business models – the organisation's intention translates into meaningful, lasting change.

Trust and the Modulation Sphere

Trust is the stabilising force of integrity, providing the relational foundation for coherence. However, its resilience or erosion is shaped by the four regulating forces of patience, adaptability, tolerance and surrender. For example:

- **Patience** allows trust to be rebuilt when damaged, fostering repair and continuity. Without it, trust collapses at the first sign of rupture, replaced by reactivity or withdrawal.
- **Adaptability** keeps trust dynamic and context-sensitive, allowing it to evolve with changing conditions. However, when absent, trust becomes rigid, brittle or outdated – unable to accommodate complexity.

- **Tolerance**, when attuned, creates room for difference and fallibility without immediate breakdown. But excessive tolerance can normalise betrayal or dishonesty, corroding trust from within.
- **Surrender**, in its healthy form, enables release of control and the willingness to trust again. However, distorted surrender breeds resignation or cynicism, where trust is abandoned as naive or futile.

Example (individual): Two friends experience a betrayal that damages their relationship (**trust**). Without **patience**, one reacts immediately, cutting ties before repair is possible. Distorted **tolerance** excuses the betrayal, allowing harmful patterns to persist. A lack of **adaptability** prevents them from renegotiating boundaries as the relationship evolves, while distorted **surrender** hardens into cynicism, making trust feel naive or impossible. In contrast, with coherent modulation – patience to allow repair, tolerance to acknowledge imperfection without enabling dysfunction, adaptability to rebuild trust in new ways, and surrender of control over outcomes – the relationship regains stability and becomes stronger than before.

Example (manufactured system): A community faces a scandal involving its local council (**trust**). Without **patience**, citizens withdraw support immediately, fracturing collective confidence. Distorted **tolerance** normalises dishonesty, leading people to expect corruption as inevitable. A lack of **adaptability** keeps governance rigid and unable to address concerns, while distorted **surrender** breeds apathy and disengagement from civic life. In contrast, with coherent modulation – patience for transparent investigations, tolerance that distinguishes between human fallibility and systemic dysfunction, adaptability in policy reform, and surrender of failed practices – trust in the local council can be rebuilt, restoring coherence in the community.

Sovereignty and the Modulation Sphere

Sovereignty enables authentic participation in life. However, its stability is contingent on mediation. For example:

- **Patience** allows sovereignty to be exercised with discernment and responsibility, especially under pressure. Without it, decisions become impulsive or reactive, eroding authority and trust.
- **Adaptability** helps sovereignty remain balanced and responsive, adjusting to context without losing coherence. When absent, sovereignty risks becoming rigid, erratic or self-destructive.
- **Tolerance**, when healthy, respects diverse expressions of sovereignty and encourages coexistence. But excessive tolerance can enable harmful or oppressive behaviours to go unchallenged, weakening coherence and declining into dysfunction.
- **Surrender**, in its healthy form, softens the need for dominance and allows interdependence without compromising self-authorship. Distorted surrender, however, leads to submission under coercion or fear, undermining autonomy.

Consequently, sovereignty must be actively modulated to ensure it remains a force for coherence rather than destabilisation.

Example (individual): A person faces pressure from family to choose a career path that conflicts with their authentic values (**sovereignty**). Without **patience**, they react impulsively – either rebelling harshly or conforming too quickly – eroding their sense of authorship. Distorted **tolerance** leads them to continually accept external pressure, normalising a life path misaligned with their values. A lack of **adaptability** makes them rigid, unable to find creative ways to honour both self and family. Distorted **surrender** manifests as submission, where they abandon autonomy and live according to others' agendas. In contrast, with coherent modulation – patience to weigh choices carefully, tolerance to hold relational pressures without collapse, adaptability to design a path that honours both context and self, and surrender of the need to control others' approval – sovereignty is preserved and strengthened.

Example (manufactured system): A nation undergoes external pressure to adopt foreign policies that compromise its cultural identity (**sovereignty**). Without **patience**, leaders either rush into compliance or lash out defensively, destabilising governance. Distorted **tolerance** allows harmful external influence to seep into domestic affairs unchallenged. A lack of **adaptability** prevents leaders from negotiating or innovating policy responses, while distorted **surrender** results in submission to external powers, undermining autonomy. In contrast, with coherent modulation – patience to respond deliberately, tolerance that respects cultural exchange without enabling exploitation, adaptability to adjust policies while preserving identity, and surrender of outdated nationalist rigidity – sovereignty is exercised responsibly, ensuring authentic participation in global systems without sacrificing integrity.

Being and the Modulation Sphere

Being is the foundational state of alignment and self-awareness. However, its coherence is shaped by the regulating forces of patience, tolerance, adaptability and surrender. For example:

- **Patience** sustains the ongoing practice of self-awareness and presence, allowing deeper integration over time. Without it, one chases quick fixes or bypasses discomfort, leading to fragmentation.
- **Adaptability** enables Being to stay engaged and responsive under shifting conditions. In its absence, pressure leads to withdrawal, numbness or disconnection from self and others.
- **Tolerance**, when attuned, makes space for inner complexity and unresolved parts of self. But excessive tolerance allows misalignment and incoherence to persist unexamined, dulling awareness.
- **Surrender**, in its healthy form, invites acceptance and openness to what is. However, distorted surrender leads to resignation, existential disengagement and the erosion of coherence.

As the foundation of integrity, Being must be actively modulated to remain resilient in the face of internal tensions and external demands.

Example (individual): A person commits to a daily mindfulness practice to remain centred in their authentic self (**Being**). Without **patience**, they chase quick fixes, abandoning the practice when results aren't immediate. Distorted **tolerance** allows persistent distractions or misalignments to remain unchecked, dulling awareness. A lack of **adaptability** leaves them stuck in rigid routines, unable to respond to changing life contexts, while distorted **surrender** leads to resignation – mistaking withdrawal or disengagement for presence. In contrast, with coherent modulation – patience for gradual integration, tolerance to hold inner complexity without denial, adaptability to evolve the practice with circumstance, and surrender of egoic control – Being remains resilient, sustaining alignment under pressure.

Example (manufactured system): An organisation aspires to embody authenticity and presence in its culture (**Being**). Without **patience**, leaders demand instant transformation, reducing the effort to superficial programs. Distorted **tolerance** permits incoherent behaviours – like overwork or misaligned values – to persist under the guise of 'flexibility'. A lack of **adaptability** prevents the culture from evolving with external challenges, while distorted **surrender** results in existential disengagement: a workplace that accepts burnout and disconnection as inevitable. In contrast, with coherent modulation – patience for cultural change to take root, tolerance for honest complexity without enabling dysfunction, adaptability to keep practices responsive, and surrender of false identities – the organisation cultivates coherence and alignment as a living foundation.

Conclusion

Integrity is not a static state but a structured process sustained through distinct yet interdependent forces. By understanding these structural forces, we can recognise how coherence is maintained, reinforced or compromised over time – and how it is continually regulated by the Modulation Sphere.

- **Intention** provides direction, ensuring that actions and decisions are aligned with clarity, purpose and ethical discernment. It is the guiding force that determines whether engagement is sincere and constructive or distorted by self-interest and manipulation.
- **Trust** stabilises interactions, creating reliability, psychological safety and meaningful relationships. It acts as the glue

that holds systems, communities and individuals together, ensuring that coherence is maintained through mutual accountability.

- **Sovereignty** enables authentic participation, allowing individuals and systems to operate freely and responsibly without coercion or fragmentation. It ensures that alignment with integrity is an active, self-directed process rather than one imposed through external control.
- **Being** sustains coherence, integrating awareness, presence and alignment. The integrity of Being encompasses the primal aspects of existence, ensuring that individuals and systems remain whole, adaptable and resilient in the face of complexity.

These four forces operate in a reinforcing cycle. Intention sets the course, trust stabilises engagement, sovereignty ensures autonomy and Being sustains coherence. Yet whether this cycle remains stable or begins to drift depends on how it is modulated. When patience, tolerance, adaptability and surrender are applied coherently, the cycle strengthens integrity and expands its capacity for recalibration and evolution. However, when distorted, these same qualities allow erosion: without clear intention, trust becomes fragile; without trust, sovereignty devolves into isolation or control; and without sovereignty, Being fragments into incoherence.

By mapping this interplay, we move beyond seeing integrity as an abstract ideal and begin to understand it as a dynamic, self-reinforcing process – one that requires active engagement and intentional modulation to be sustained. The following chapter explores this more deeply, examining how the Modulation Sphere regulates these dynamics to keep integrity adaptable, resilient and protected from systemic drift into disintegration.

CHAPTER 23

The Modulation Sphere

As we have learned, integrity is not a fixed state. It exists within a dynamic interplay of forces that either sustain it or lead to its erosion. Likewise, disintegration is not an immediate collapse, but a progressive process shaped by choices, pressures and systemic conditions.

We have also learned that the Integrity Sphere contains the structural forces that sustain coherence: intention, trust, sovereignty and Being, while the Disintegration Sphere consists of the structural forces that erode it: shadows, entrenchment, misery and suffering. However, these two spheres alone do not fully explain how a system transitions between them.

This is where the Modulation Sphere comes into play. It regulates transition, stability and transformation, ensuring that integrity is either maintained, reinforced or lost. The Modulation Sphere determines:

- Whether a system endures challenges or collapses under pressure.
- How much variance it can accommodate before losing coherence.
- Whether adaptation leads to growth or destabilisation.
- When a system should resist, recalibrate or surrender to external forces.

The four regulating forces in the Modulation Sphere

So far, we know the Modulation Sphere consists of four core regulatory forces that govern how a system moves between integrity and disintegration:

- **Patience** – Regulates endurance and the pace of transition.
- **Tolerance** – Moderates the ability to accommodate variance and external pressure.
- **Adaptability** – Governs responsiveness and recalibration under changing conditions.
- **Surrender** – Determines when a system, including a human being, should yield wisely or succumb to dysfunction.

These forces do not define whether a system is in a state of integrity or disintegration. Instead, they govern *how it moves between these states*. If leveraged effectively, they reinforce integrity. However, when misapplied or distorted, they accelerate disintegration.

Modulation in action: The transition between integrity and disintegration

The Modulation Sphere is not simply a buffer between integrity and disintegration. It is the active mechanism that governs transitions across this ontological spectrum. Systems do not suddenly leap from coherence to collapse; they move along a trajectory shaped by modulation. When patience, tolerance, adaptability and surrender are enacted coherently, modulation sustains and recalibrates integrity. But when distorted, these same forces gradually undermine it, leading to incoherence and, eventually, collapse.

We can visualise this movement as a **lemniscate** (∞) – a continuous flow where systems loop between:

- Stability under pressure (adaptive integrity),
- Loss of coherence (disintegration under strain),
- Recovery through modulation, and
- Reintegration or transformation (restored integrity).

The following figure depicts a simplified representation of this process of modulation in action.

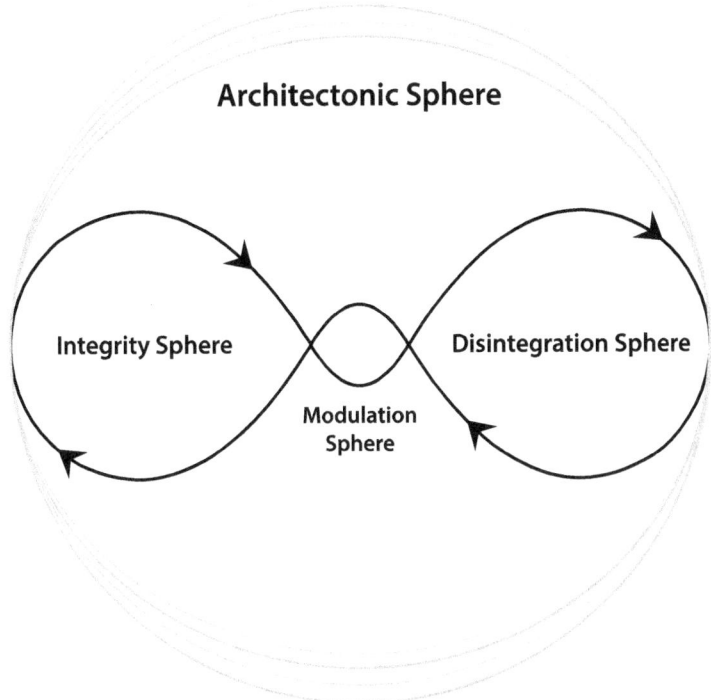

Figure 5 – Modulation in Action: The Transition Between Integrity and Disintegration.

This non-linear, recursive dynamic shows that collapse is never final, resilience is not automatic and every moment of breakdown contains the potential seed for transformation, as long as modulation is consciously and skillfully applied.

The four modulating forces serve as gatekeepers at these transition points:

Transition Point	Modulating Force	Risk if Absent or Distorted
Challenge → Response	**Patience**	Reactivity, impulsivity, collapse
Complexity → Cohesion	**Tolerance**	Rigidity, exclusion, fragility
Change → Evolution	**Adaptability**	Stagnation or incoherent drift
Overload → Letting Go	**Surrender**	Burnout or passive defeat

Table 20 – The Modulating Forces as Transition Point Gatekeepers.

In this light, the Modulation Sphere is not a soft middle ground; it is the *arena of transformation*. It is where coherence is either reinforced or lost, and where the trajectory of a system is quietly, but decisively, shaped.

The ontology of the modulating forces

Each of the Modulating Sphere's four forces plays a distinct role in managing the thresholds between coherence and collapse. By exploring their ontology, we gain insight into how these forces operate structurally, functionally and relationally – revealing what they regulate, how they become distorted and what is required to engage them with discernment.

Patience: The regulator of endurance

Patience regulates how a system withstands pressure. It determines whether integrity is reinforced through steady endurance or, in its absence, whether reactivity accelerates dysfunction and premature collapse.

- **Healthy relationship with patience**

    A healthy relationship with patience ensures that integrity is not compromised due to temporary discomfort. It allows for adjustment, recalibration and resilience in the face of challenges, fostering a steady and thoughtful approach to growth and decision-making.

- **Unhealthy relationship with patience**

    When patience is distorted through an unhealthy

relationship, it becomes either deficient or excessive, leading to dysfunction. A lack of patience results in impulsivity, reactivity and an inability to endure necessary challenges, often causing premature collapse. Conversely, excessive patience manifests as passivity, enabling dysfunction to persist unchecked rather than being actively resolved.

Patience is neither inherently positive nor negative. Its value depends on what it sustains or prevents. It must be directed with discernment to avoid stagnation on one end and impulsivity on the other.

	Description
Anatomy	Composed of structural capacities that encourage delayed gratification, endurance and emotional regulation. Integrates self-restraint, foresight and measured responses to adversity.
Mechanics	Prevents impulsive reactions, allowing systems to process stress without immediate collapse. However, excessive patience enables stagnation.
Topology	Bridges reactivity and endurance and regulates adaptability to ensure change is deliberate. However, excessive patience enables resignation, leading to inaction.

Table 21 – Ontology of Patience.

Tolerance: The regulator of boundaries

Tolerance determines how much variance, uncertainty or dysfunction a system can absorb before it begins to lose integrity.

- **Healthy relationship with tolerance**

    A healthy relationship with tolerance allows for necessary flexibility, preventing rigidity and fragility. It enables individuals and systems to adapt to diversity and change, fostering resilience and inclusivity without compromising coherence.

- **Unhealthy relationship with tolerance**

    When tolerance is distorted through an unhealthy relationship, it becomes either deficient or excessive, leading to dysfunction. A lack of tolerance results in rigidity, resistance to necessary change and fragility under pressure, making both individuals and systems prone to collapse. Conversely, excessive tolerance permits dysfunction to persist unchecked, allowing harmful influences to spread and degrade not only the integrity of systems, but also the psychological and relational coherence of individuals.

Tolerance is not about endurance over time (which is the role of patience). It's about capacity for variance: how much deviation from the ideal state a system can accommodate before it begins to disintegrate. It must be balanced to prevent rigidity without enabling dysfunction.

	Description
Anatomy	Comprised of structural elements that facilitate boundary flexibility, variance absorption and openness to controlled disorder. Allows systems to function dynamically while maintaining coherence.
Mechanics	Prevents fragmentation by allowing variance and diversity. However, when unchecked, tolerance leads to permissiveness towards dysfunction.
Topology	Bridges rigidity and openness. Works with adaptability to integrate variance without collapse. However, excessive tolerance enables entrenchment.

Table 22 – Ontology of Tolerance.

Adaptability: The regulator of transformation

Adaptability determines whether a system evolves, recalibrates or resists change to its own detriment.

- **Healthy relationship with adaptability**

    A healthy relationship with adaptability ensures that change strengthens a system rather than destabilising it. It allows for purposeful recalibration, maintaining coherence while integrating new conditions.

- **Unhealthy relationship with adaptability**

    When adaptability is distorted, it either becomes deficient or excessive, leading to dysfunction. A lack of adaptability leads to rigidity, resistance to change and an inability to evolve, making systems fragile and prone to collapse under external pressures. In contrast, excessive adaptability results in loss of core structure, incoherence and instability, causing systems to drift without a stable foundation.

A system that is too rigid breaks under pressure, while a system that is too fluid loses coherence. Adaptability must be calibrated, enabling transformation while preserving structural integrity.

	Description
Anatomy	Comprised of structural capacities that promote fluidity, responsiveness and structural evolution without losing coherence.
Mechanics	Ensures change is intentional, preventing stagnation or uncontrolled collapse. Works by absorbing new conditions while retaining structure.
Topology	Balances resistance and fluidity. Works with tolerance to integrate variance. However, excessive adaptability eventually leads to resignation.

Table 23 – Ontology of Adaptability.

Surrender: The regulator of yielding

Surrender determines when a system yields, submits or lets go – whether to truth or dysfunction.

- **Healthy relationship with surrender**

    Also known as 'functional surrender', a healthy relationship with surrender involves accepting reality and working within it rather than resisting what cannot be changed. Functional surrender enables systems to let go of unnecessary struggles, allowing clarity, recalibration and alignment with truth.

- **Unhealthy relationship with surrender**

    When surrender is distorted, it either becomes deficient or excessive, leading to dysfunction. A lack of surrender results in rigid resistance, an inability to accept unavoidable realities and unnecessary struggle, often leading to burnout and fragmentation. In contrast, excessive surrender leads to passivity, inaction and complicity in one's own disintegration, normalising dysfunction instead of confronting it.

The challenge lies in discerning when it is time to fight for integrity and when it is time to let go. Healthy surrender is not about giving up. It's about choosing where to direct effort and when to release attachment to what cannot be controlled.

	Description
Anatomy	Comprised of structural components that facilitate acceptance, yielding and disengagement. Differentiates between surrendering to truth and surrendering to dysfunction.
Mechanics	Allows controlled disengagement, ensuring resources are used wisely. However, excessive surrender leads to passivity and system failure.
Topology	Bridges acceptance and defeat. Works with patience to endure suffering. However, excessive surrender enables disintegration.

Table 24 – Ontology of Surrender.

The Modulation Sphere as the bridge between integrity and disintegration

As discussed, there is a constant flow of movement between disintegration and integrity. The Modulation Sphere functions as the regulatory mechanism that governs this movement, determining the pace and trajectory of disintegration or recovery towards integrity or coherence.

Disintegration Sphere	Modulation Sphere	Integrity Sphere
Shadows (distortions, misjudgement)	Patience, Tolerance	Trust (reliability, stability)
Misery (internalised dysfunction)	Adaptability, Surrender	Being (integration, meaning)
Suffering (distress, disempowerment)	Patience, Adaptability	Sovereignty (possibility, expansion)
Entrenchment (reinforced dysfunction)	Surrender (healthy or distorted)	Intention (purpose, alignment)

Table 25 – Modulation as the Bridge Between Disintegration and Integrity.

This dynamic interplay ensures that disintegration is not simply a process of collapse. Instead, it is a *modulated transition* influenced by how individuals and human-designed systems engage with the Modulation Sphere. Understanding disintegration through the lens of modulation rather than absolute opposition allows for precise intervention. Instead of seeing dysfunction as inevitable or irreversible, we can now recognise it as a *governable process* – one that, if properly modulated, can prevent further fragmentation and even restore integrity.

Similarly, integrity is neither a fixed state nor self-sustaining. It too requires active modulation and is constantly tested by external and internal pressures. The Modulation Sphere functions as a regulatory mechanism, determining whether integrity remains resilient or becomes fragile. This dynamic interplay ensures that integrity is not just an ideal, but a *process*. Whether it is sustained or compromised depends on how the Modulation Sphere interacts with its components. It serves as the bridge between sustaining coherence and drifting into dysfunction.

- When modulated effectively, integrity is reinforced and disintegration is mitigated.
- When modulation fails, integrity weakens and disintegration takes hold.

Each modulating force plays a role in shaping the system's trajectory:

Modulating Force	Function
Patience	Regulates endurance to prevent reactivity or stagnation.
Tolerance	Regulates variance to ensure flexibility without self-compromise.
Adaptability	Regulates transformation to ensure change strengthens rather than destabilises.
Surrender	Regulates yielding to ensure strategic surrender rather than passive defeat.

Table 26 – How Modulating Forces Shape a System's Trajectory.

Understanding how the four modulating forces interact enables us to move beyond seeing integrity as something to be achieved and disintegration as something to be avoided. Instead, we begin to recognise that both are *dynamic states*, constantly influenced by modulation. The extent to which a system remains coherent, collapses or recalibrates depends on how effectively the four modulating forces of patience, tolerance, adaptability and surrender are applied.

Holding space for denial

While each of the four modulating forces can be explored in isolation, they rarely operate alone. In practice, particularly where transformation is resisted or deferred, they converge in one of the most telling human dynamics of all: denial.

Often judged as dysfunctional, denial is not simply a refusal to acknowledge reality. It is a signal of unreadiness, a threshold space between incoherence and awareness. In systems undergoing change, denial marks the fault line between what *is* and what can *yet be metabolised*. The question is not whether we will encounter denial, but how we choose to meet it.

Denial as a threshold state

Denial is frequently mischaracterised as ignorance, stubbornness or defiance. But ontologically, it functions as a threshold state: a temporary holding pattern that buffers the self or system from destabilising truths it is not yet ready to metabolise. Whether arising in an individual, relationship, organisation, institution or society, denial often preserves coherence by postponing confrontation. It stabilises meaning when reality threatens collapse. In other words, denial arises not because reality is unavailable, but because it cannot yet be held without fragmentation.

In this sense, denial is not the opposite of truth, but the *buffer* preceding it. It temporarily stabilises coherence, using provisional narratives to delay disruption. Although flawed, these narratives serve as scaffolds, supporting coherence until the system is capable of integration without overwhelm. Dismantling them prematurely may collapse the very transformation we seek to enable.

Denial with discernment

To engage denial effectively, without provoking collapse or entrenching resistance, we must learn to work with the Modulation Sphere's four regulating forces as follows:

- **Patience** offers time. It resists the urge to rush awareness, allowing insight to emerge when it's ready.
- **Tolerance** encourages presence. It helps us stay grounded with discomfort without withdrawing, judging or reacting.
- **Adaptability** introduces responsiveness. It enables us to adjust our posture, language or timing as readiness evolves.
- **Surrender** offers release. It marks the point where effort is relinquished, not in defeat, but in clarity, recognising when intervention becomes counterproductive.

Together, these forces form a dynamic field of *discernment*. They modulate in response to context, energy and timing. One may need to lead with tolerance, then shift into adaptability. Or hold with patience until it becomes clear that surrender is the wiser path.

Imagine a startup founder in denial about their company's impending collapse. An investor who is aware of the situation may feel compelled to intervene directly. But a blunt challenge risks triggering shutdown, defensiveness or shame. Instead, the investor waits (**patience**). They remain present without judgement (**tolerance**). As cracks begin to appear in the founder's narrative, the investor introduces new data or repositions the conversation (**adaptability**). And if openness still does not emerge, they step back (**surrender**), not out of disinterest, but out of discernment. In doing so, they preserve the possibility for transformation without forcing it.

This modulation process applies across many areas of life where denial often emerges, not as defiance, but as a buffer that preserves coherence until deeper truths can be safely integrated:

- In **personal growth**, denial may shield a person from implications they're not yet ready to hold, whether about their limitations or their potential.

- In **leadership**, it can preserve identity structures when confronting feedback would destabilise a leader's sense of self or role.
- In **relationships**, denial may maintain emotional safety when acknowledging misalignment feels threatening or premature.
- In **organisations**, it can stabilise group cohesion in environments where honesty carries social or structural risk.
- In **society**, collective denial may act as a holding mechanism when facing historical trauma or systemic injustice would overwhelm the cultural psyche.

In each case, the four modulating forces – patience, tolerance, adaptability and surrender – help us hold space for truth without imposing it. They do not excuse dysfunction; they create the conditions under which reality can be metabolised without rupture.

Why holding space for denial matters

Sustainable transformation rarely comes through force. It unfolds through conditions of coherence, dignity and discernment. Often, systems resist change not because of ignorance, but because premature awareness threatens their structural or identity integrity. When intervention is misattuned, it can trigger defences that entrench the very patterns we aim to transform.

To hold space for denial is to step into the modulation zone – a space where pressure is not applied or avoided, but carefully attuned. This is not passivity. It is disciplined restraint: the capacity to support transformation without rupturing the process or the person.

Not all denial will dissolve and not all systems will shift. But by holding space through modulation rather than coercion, we reduce unnecessary resistance, preserve dignity and honour readiness as a structural reality, not a personal failing.

Conclusion

As this chapter has shown, the Modulation Sphere is not merely theoretical. It is the regulating mechanism behind personal, relational and systemic coherence. By developing a refined awareness of these forces, we move from reactive existence to intentional mastery, ensuring that integrity is not just a fleeting state, but a sustainable way of being.

With this foundation in place, the following chapter explores how these modulating forces operate within real-world dynamics, providing a structured approach for navigating transformation, sustaining coherence and mitigating dysfunction in individuals, organisations, communities, societies and broader systems.

CHAPTER 24

Sustaining Coherence and Mitigating Dysfunction in the Real World

As we have learned, integrity and disintegration are dynamic forces that exist in a constant interplay regulated by modulation. Every individual, organisation, institution, culture and society sits somewhere along this continuum, constantly shifting based on structural forces and the ability to regulate transitions.

Integrity is not an absolute, self-sustaining state. It must be actively cultivated and reinforced through alignment, coherence and resilience. Similarly, disintegration is not an instant event. There is a gradual drift into dysfunction, often unnoticed until the effects become severe.

These forces operate in all aspects of life: from leadership and governance to personal development, relationships and societal structures. The presence or absence of modulation determines whether a system moves into and sustains its integrity, or falls into a state of disintegration.

The Unified Ontology of Systemic Integrity (UOSI) provides a structured framework for understanding these forces of coherence, fragmentation and regulation, enabling us to diagnose, navigate and influence alignment and dysfunction in different aspects of life.

In the preceding chapters, we explored:

- **The Architectonic Sphere** (meta-awareness, systemic integrity, sustained effectiveness and normativity) – the UOSI's overarching meta-governing layer, which orchestrates how the entire system is designed, and how it evolves and is sustained.
- **The Integrity Sphere** (intention, trust, sovereignty and Being) – the domain of coherence, stability and functional alignment.
- **The Disintegration Sphere** (shadows, misery, suffering and entrenchment) – the domain of fragmentation, dysfunction and erosion of coherence.
- **The Modulation Sphere** (patience, tolerance, adaptability and surrender) – the domain that regulates transitions between integrity and disintegration.

It is important to note that in the UOSI, it is the healthy relationship with all qualities that matters in order for the system to arrive at a state of self-modulation with minimum intervention, interference and maintenance. The ultimate aim is sustainability, and this occurs in great part through modulation. While the four dedicated quad qualities within the Modulation Sphere – patience, tolerance, adaptability and surrender – are most central in this process, all other qualities across the other spheres also contribute. Sustainability cannot be reduced to only these four forces. Rather, it depends on how they *interrelate* with the broader ecosystem of qualities.

Think of it as a well-tuned orchestra. The Modulation Sphere qualities play the role of the conductor, ensuring rhythm and harmony, but the rest of the instruments – the qualities from the other spheres – must still be in tune and played with coherence. If the strings are out of sync or the horns are neglected, the conductor's guidance cannot produce a beautiful symphony on its own. In the same way, patience and adaptability cannot hold the system together if courage, authenticity or discernment are fractured.

This is also true in leadership. A sustainable organisation or society does not thrive simply because leaders are patient, tolerant, adaptable or willing to surrender rigidity. Those are vital qualities, but equally important are intention, trust, sovereignty, Being and a healthy relationship with shadows, misery, suffering and entrenchment. When these forces work coherently together, systems gradually become more self-sustaining – less dependent on constant correction or external force, and more capable of modulating themselves naturally. Ultimately, leadership is not about endless intervention, but about cultivating the coherence that allows the system to sustain and even regenerate itself. This chapter brings everything together, reinforcing how these forces interact across various domains, and provides context through structured tables and real-world examples that connect the dots.

Before we move on to some tangible examples, the following table provides a recap of the interplay between the Integrity, Disintegration and Modulation Spheres, highlighting how the Modulation Sphere regulates transitions between integrity and disintegration.

Integrity Sphere (Coherence & Alignment)	Modulation Sphere (Regulatory Influence)	Disintegration Sphere (Fragmentation & Dysfunction)
Intention – Guides purpose, direction and alignment	**Patience** – Regulates endurance, preventing impulsivity or stagnation	**Shadows** – Distort perception and decision-making, leading to dysfunction
Trust – Stabilises relationships and ensures reliability	**Tolerance** – Determines how much variance a system can absorb before losing coherence	**Misery** – The internalisation of dysfunction, reinforcing chronic dissatisfaction
Sovereignty – Governs authentic self-expression and autonomy	**Adaptability** – Ensures change strengthens rather than destabilises	**Suffering** – The lived experience of distress caused by unresolved dysfunction
Being – Represents alignment, presence and self-awareness	**Surrender** – Differentiates between yielding wisely and passive defeat	**Entrenchment** – Reinforces dysfunction, making transformation seem impossible

Table 27 – The Interplay Between the Integrity, Disintegration and Modulation Spheres.

Examples showing the Modulation Sphere's impact across various domains

In leadership

- A business leader who lacks **patience** may push for results prematurely, causing burnout and unsustainable growth in their organisation.
- Conversely, a leader who **surrenders** excessively may avoid making tough decisions, allowing inefficiencies and disengagement to spread unchecked.

In relationships

- Healthy **tolerance** allows couples and friendships to navigate differences in communication styles, habits and worldviews without the relationship breaking down.
- Excessive **tolerance**, however, may lead to accepting toxic behaviour, allowing dishonesty or emotional neglect to persist.
- A lack of **adaptability** in relationships – such as when one or more parties refuse to adjust to life changes – can destabilise relationships and hinder their ability to move forward and evolve.

In governance and societal systems

- A government that fails to **adapt** to economic, technological or social changes risks losing public trust and becoming ineffective.
- Excessive **tolerance** towards corruption or dysfunction can create systemic problems that erode public faith in institutions.
- Nations that **surrender** prematurely to external pressures may compromise sovereignty, leading to long-term instability.

In personal development

- A person who engages with their shadows constructively, through **patience** or **adaptability**, can develop self-awareness

and refine their decision-making over time. These qualities allow them to observe discomfort without immediate reaction and adjust their internal narratives as needed.
- Avoiding or resisting shadows, due to a lack of **tolerance** or distorted **surrender**, leads to misery, suffering and entrenchment, reinforcing self-destructive cycles and preventing growth.

Because life is constantly changing, the Modulation Sphere's regulatory influences (patience, tolerance, adaptability and surrender) support systems across any domain to continually evolve organically towards a state of integrity, coherence and alignment rather than abruptly collapsing into a state of dysfunction or stagnation.

The tipping point: When integrity gives way to disintegration

The shift from integrity to disintegration rarely happens instantly. It usually follows a gradual process of erosion, where small misalignments accumulate over time. However, there are critical moments when systems reach a tipping point: a state in which modulation either restores integrity or allows dysfunction to take root. Consider the following examples:

Example 1: A nation in crisis

A nation is facing a multi-layered crisis: a fragile economy, polarised politics, cultural fragmentation and growing public distrust in institutions. Citizens are frustrated, leaders are reactive and media cycles fuel division. When a nation is at a crossroads like this, it hovers at a tipping point between systemic renewal and accelerated disintegration.

Whether it regains its integrity or spirals into dysfunction depends on how the four modulating forces are activated. In this case:

- **Patience** allows long-view decision-making, preventing reactionary policies driven by panic or public outrage.
- **Tolerance** enables pluralism, creating space for conflicting ideas to coexist without devolving into civil unrest.

- **Adaptability** allows institutions to reform and policies to evolve in response to changing needs rather than rigidly defending the status quo.
- **Surrender** gives individuals and factions permission to let go of control, ideological pride or false certainty, making room for more coherent solutions.

If these modulating forces are absent or unhealthy, the system becomes fragile. Instead of transformation, it fractures – unable to absorb shock or recalibrate. But when these forces are present, healthy and consciously cultivated, they can regulate the system back towards structural coherence.

Example 2: A company faces disruption

A well-established tech company begins losing market share to leaner, more innovative startups. Customer needs are evolving, but internal processes remain rigid and leadership continues to rely on legacy products and outdated metrics for success.

At this critical tipping point, survival depends not just on strategy, but on the company's internal modulation. In this case:

- **Patience** allows the company to resist knee-jerk cost-cutting or rushed pivots, creating space for thoughtful reinvention.
- **Tolerance** creates a culture where dissenting views and fresh perspectives are welcomed, not silenced.
- **Adaptability** empowers teams to update systems, redesign products and shift their value proposition in real time.
- **Surrender** requires executives to let go of old hierarchies and ego-driven decision-making, creating space for collective intelligence.

Ignoring these modulating forces, the company risks spiralling into disintegration, gradually eroding its relevance. But when they're cultivated, the organisation doesn't just survive the disruption; it evolves and sustains its integrity.

Example 3: A personal crisis

Following the unexpected loss of a loved one, an individual is thrown into emotional upheaval. Life feels disoriented and hollow, and the routines that once brought meaning no longer offer stability.

Whether they emerge with deeper resilience or become stuck in prolonged suffering depends on the presence of internal modulation. In this case:

- **Patience** allows them to honour their pain without rushing to 'fix' or bypass it.
- **Tolerance** helps them sit with discomfort, conflicting emotions and the ambiguity of not having answers.
- **Adaptability** enables small but vital shifts like trying new routines or reaching out to others to re-engage with life in different ways.
- **Surrender** invites acceptance of what cannot be changed, creating the space to rebuild identity from the inside out.

In the absence of these modulating forces, grief may calcify into chronic misery and permanent entrenchment, bitterness or detachment. But when they are present (even imperfectly) and focused on, they create the conditions for integration, healing and renewed coherence.

Recognising the tipping point in various situations allows for timely intervention, ensuring that recalibration occurs before dysfunction takes hold and becomes systemic.

Real-world application of the Unified Ontology of Systemic Integrity

The following case studies demonstrate how the UOSI can be applied across personal, organisational, societal and geopolitical levels. By recognising these patterns in various contexts, we can intervene earlier, navigate complexity more effectively and ensure that systems evolve and retain their integrity rather than collapse into a state of dysfunction.

Case study 1: Navigating a midlife crisis

Daniel, a 45-year-old professional, has spent two decades climbing the corporate ladder. Lately, however, he feels unfulfilled and begins questioning whether his career truly aligns with his deeper values. This growing disconnect from his Being erodes the sense of authenticity and inner alignment that once grounded him. As coherence weakens, misery sets in. Shadows of self-doubt, fear of change and pressure to conform to societal expectations intensify, translating into lived suffering.

Application of the UOSI

- **Integrity Sphere:** Initially, Daniel had clarity around his career intentions, trust in his abilities and a strong sense of sovereignty, making independent decisions. However, neglect of his Being led to eventual misalignment.
- **Disintegration Sphere:** His shadows distort his perception, making him feel trapped. Misery intensifies as he continues working in a role that no longer serves him. His suffering is exacerbated by emotional turmoil and he risks entrenchment, accepting dissatisfaction as inevitable.
- **Modulation Sphere:** Daniel's transition depends on the four modulating forces of patience, tolerance, adaptability and surrender.
  - **Patience** is needed to sit with uncertainty and emotional discomfort without rushing into impulsive decisions or escape strategies.
  - **Tolerance** allows him to hold space for conflicting feelings – ambition, fear and regret – without letting any single emotion dominate his choices.
  - **Adaptability** enables him to explore new possibilities, reframe his identity beyond his current role and consider alternative paths without rigid attachment.
  - **Surrender** (in its healthy form) helps him let go of outdated definitions of success and accept that change is necessary, without collapsing into defeat or passivity.

Potential outcomes

Without modulation, Daniel would remain entrenched in a cycle of unhappiness, fearing the risks of change. However, through effective modulation, he could realign his intention, regain sovereignty and take adaptive action – perhaps transitioning to a more meaningful career or reconfiguring his current role to align with his core values.

Case study 2: Intimate relationships: restoring trust and tolerance

Anna and Michael have been married for 10 years. They love each other, but unresolved issues have built up. Anna feels that Michael does not prioritise their relationship and Michael feels unappreciated. The couple has reached a tipping point. Trust, once strong, is beginning to erode, and their tolerance for each other's flaws is diminishing.

Application of the UOSI

- **Integrity Sphere:** Early in their marriage, Anna and Michael had trust, sovereignty (individual space within the relationship) and intention (shared vision for the future).
- **Disintegration Sphere:** Over time, shadows formed. Anna sees Michael's long work hours as neglect, while Michael sees Anna's complaints as unfair criticism. Misery sets in, making each partner feel unheard. The emotional turmoil leads to suffering, which begins to damage their connection. If these dynamics persist, they risk entrenchment – seeing their relationship as permanently flawed rather than one that can be improved.
- **Modulation Sphere:**
  - **Patience** is needed to navigate emotional conflict without reactive responses.
  - **Tolerance** must be balanced, allowing for human imperfection without permitting harmful neglect.
  - **Adaptability** will enable them to adjust expectations as their life circumstances change.

- **Surrender** (in its healthy form) helps them accept aspects of each other that won't change.

Potential outcomes

Without modulation, Anna and Michael's relationship would deteriorate into resentment, disconnection and possibly separation. However, with effective modulation, addressing shadows, realigning intention, restoring trust and actively adapting – perhaps through open dialogue, couples therapy or re-evaluating priorities – they could restore integrity in their marriage.

Case study 3: A company struggling with innovation

A once-thriving Australian retail company is losing market share due to technological disruption. The leadership team is aware of the challenges but resists change, fearing risk and short-term revenue loss. Entrenchment has taken hold, making transformation virtually impossible.

Application of the UOSI

- **Integrity Sphere:** The company initially thrived with clear intention (market leadership), trust (consumer loyalty), sovereignty (operational independence) and a strong corporate identity (Being).
- **Disintegration Sphere:** Over time, shadows emerged. Leaders underestimated the impact of e-commerce, assuming their brand would remain dominant. Misery set in as financial strain increased. Employees and stakeholders began to suffer under stagnation and entrenchment deepened as leaders resisted external feedback.
- **Modulation Sphere:**
  - **Patience** is needed to ensure changes are sustainable rather than reactive.
  - **Tolerance** must be applied strategically, allowing short-term instability while the company recalibrates.
  - **Adaptability** is crucial for embracing new technologies and business models.

- **Surrender** means letting go of outdated strategies rather than clinging to past successes.

Potential outcomes

Without modulation, the company would lose relevance, leading to layoffs, loss of credibility and possible bankruptcy. However, with effective modulation, the company could embrace adaptability, reallocate resources, upskill employees and shift towards an e-commerce-driven strategy while preserving brand identity.

Case study 4: Misinformation and public distrust in society

A democratic society is experiencing a crisis of public trust in institutions. Years of political scandals, media bias and social media misinformation have created shadows, distorting public perception. Citizens are divided and collective misery fuels polarisation and civil unrest.

Application of the UOSI

- **Integrity Sphere:** A healthy democracy relies on intention (truth and governance), trust (institutional credibility), sovereignty (citizens' rights) and collective Being (national identity and cohesion).
- **Disintegration Sphere:** Shadows arise through misinformation and manipulation. Misery spreads as people feel disempowered. Suffering manifests in social unrest. Entrenchment locks people into ideological echo chambers, making dialogue nearly impossible.
- **Modulation Sphere:**
  - **Patience** is needed to rebuild trust over time.
  - **Tolerance** must be balanced, allowing for diverse viewpoints without enabling manipulation.
  - **Adaptability** is required for the media and government to update communication methods.
  - **Surrender** involves recognising that not all perceptions can be changed immediately.

Potential outcomes

Without modulation, the nation would spiral into deeper division, making governance ineffective. However, with effective modulation, public institutions would engage in transparent dialogue, media literacy programs and reforms designed to restore trust gradually.

Case study 5: International relations – The demise of strategic alliances

Two allied nations once had a strong partnership based on trade, security and mutual respect. However, economic conflicts and political shifts have created tensions between them. Trust has eroded and each country is retreating into self-preservation, risking full disintegration of the alliance.

Application of the UOSI

- **Integrity Sphere:** The alliance was originally founded on shared intention (mutual benefit), trust (reliability in agreements), sovereignty (respect for national autonomy and Being (long-term vision for cooperation).
- **Disintegration Sphere:** As shadows develop, each country begins to see the other as a potential threat rather than a partner. Misery emerges through trade disruptions and suffering escalates as economic and political tensions grow. Entrenchment follows, where neither side is willing to compromise.
- **Modulation Sphere:**
  - **Patience** allows for diplomatic engagement without escalating conflicts.
  - **Tolerance** is needed for temporary disagreements without severing ties.
  - **Adaptability** ensures that new challenges (e.g., economic shifts, emerging security threats) don't destroy past alliances.
  - **Surrender** must be calibrated to know when to compromise versus when to assert sovereignty.

Potential outcomes

Without modulation, the alliance between the two nations would collapse, leading to economic instability and regional security risks. However, with effective modulation, diplomacy could prevail, allowing the nations to recalibrate their relationship while preserving core alliances.

Conclusion

The UOSI is a model for navigating complexity. As the Authentic Sustainability Framework's central paradigm, it provides a structured approach to understanding the forces that shape coherence and dysfunction across all domains of life.

Integrity is not an endpoint. It's a continuous process of alignment, recalibration and evolution. Similarly, disintegration is not ultimate failure, but a structural process that can be interrupted, mitigated or reversed through effective modulation.

By applying and integrating the UOSI model, we gain the ability to:

- Diagnose systemic dysfunction before it becomes irreversible.
- Navigate transitions in leadership, governance, relationships and personal growth.
- Understand why some systems sustain coherence while others collapse into dysfunction.
- Apply modulation to ensure sustainability, resilience and meaningful transformation.

In the upcoming chapters, we will delve deeper into each component – exploring Being, trust, shadows, entrenchment and beyond – to examine how they function within this systemic model. But first, we will explore the nature of transformation itself and why it is far more than just an individual pursuit.

Ultimately, mastering the application of the UOSI is not about eliminating disintegration entirely. That would be both unrealistic and unnecessary (sometimes it's best to let things go with grace). Rather, it's about learning to modulate transitions effectively and with conscious intention, ensuring that integrity is actively cultivated, dysfunction is identified early and recalibration occurs before systems become irreversibly compromised.

This is how leaders sustain organisations, how societies remain resilient and how individuals navigate growth and transformation – not through rigid perfection, but through an intentional, adaptive and coherent engagement with reality.

CHAPTER 25

The Expansive Nature of Transformation

Transformation is not merely an individual pursuit. It is the fundamental process through which all aspects of existence evolve. While personal transformation is a profound journey, it is only one dimension of a more significant phenomenon that extends across all levels of reality: ecosystems, human health, organisations, societies and even the global order. Transformation is not optional. Without it, stagnation, fragmentation and dysfunction take root, and systems collapse under the weight of their unresolved inefficiencies. To truly understand transformation, we must recognise not only what it is, but also its necessity at every scale of existence.

At its core, transformation is the movement from fragmentation to coherence, disorder to alignment and limitation to transcendence. It is not merely about reacting to crises or making surface-level improvements. It's about fundamental shifts that redefine the nature of a system, be it an individual's awareness, an organisation's structure or an entire civilisation's trajectory.

Transformation across multiple domains

Transformation is not confined to a single domain. It is a universal principle governing the evolution of systems, relationships and consciousness. Whether occurring in nature, within human physiology, across social structures or at the level of entire civilisations, transformation is the mechanism through which growth, adaptation and renewal take place.

Each domain of existence presents its own unique challenges, triggers and conditions for transformation. Some transformations are natural and cyclical, such as the changing seasons or biological regeneration. Others require conscious effort, such as personal development, societal reform or shifts in geopolitical relations. Some transformations occur organically over long periods, while others are sudden and disruptive, forcing a reconfiguration of existing paradigms.

By exploring how transformation manifests across multiple domains – from nature, health and awareness to organisations, cultures and humanity itself – we can better understand its patterns, dynamics and interdependencies.

Transformation in nature and ecosystems

Nature itself is a living model of transformation. Ecosystems evolve through cycles of destruction and renewal. Forests regrow after bushfires, rivers carve new landscapes over millennia and species adapt to changing environments. Transformation in nature is not just about survival. It is the ability to regenerate and maintain dynamic balance. When ecosystems are disrupted – whether by natural disasters or human intervention – restorative transformation becomes necessary to rebuild harmony.

Transformation in the human body and physical health

At the biological level, transformation is continuous. Cells regenerate, injuries heal and the body adapts to environmental stressors. When transformation is blocked – due to illness, chronic disease or metabolic dysfunction – the body deteriorates. Holistic health practices, including nutrition, movement and medical intervention aim to facilitate transformation, allowing the body to maintain vitality and coherence.

Transformation in mental health

Mental health transformation involves shifting from fragmentation – such as anxiety, trauma or cognitive distortions – to states of clarity, resilience and inner alignment. This transformation requires integrating past experiences, reframing beliefs and cultivating emotional intelligence. Just as physical health depends on the body's regenerative processes, mental wellbeing depends on one's capacity to transform internal narratives and self-perceptions.

Transformation in metacontent (sense-making structures)

Beyond individual experiences, transformation also occurs at the level of metacontent: the intellectual substrates that shape how one makes sense of reality. As we evolve, our dominant paradigms shift. What was once seen as absolute truth may be reframed through deeper understanding. Transformation in metacontent allows for greater epistemic humility, critical thinking and the ability to navigate complexity without ideological rigidity.

Transformation in awareness

Awareness is the foundation of all transformation. Without awareness, dysfunction remains unnoticed and progress remains elusive. Transformational awareness involves seeing beyond immediate perceptions and recognising underlying structures, patterns and interdependencies. When awareness deepens, new possibilities emerge – personally, relationally and systemically.

Transformation in organisations

Organisations either evolve or become obsolete. Transformation at this level involves restructuring outdated models, realigning leadership with authentic values and fostering cultures of innovation and integrity. Businesses, institutions and governments that resist transformation stagnate, whereas those that embrace it become adaptable and resilient.

Transformation in personal relationships

Relationships require continuous transformation to thrive. Stagnation leads to disconnection, resentment and dysfunction. Transformation in relationships involves deepening trust, evolving communication and aligning shared values over time. When partners grow together, the relationship transforms into something greater than its initial form.

Transformation in culture and society

Cultures are living entities that shift based on historical events, generational shifts and ideological movements. Transforming a culture involves addressing its shadows – systemic biases, outdated traditions or inherited dysfunctions – while preserving its integrity and strengths. Societies that embrace transformation thrive, whereas those that resist it often experience decline.

Transformation in geopolitics

History is marked by wars, conflicts and prolonged diplomatic tensions. True geopolitical transformation occurs when former adversaries move beyond hostility to establish new forms of cooperation, reconciliation and shared purpose. Post-war developments, such as the formation of the European Union after World War II, demonstrate that even deeply entrenched divisions can be transcended when nations pursue collective transformation over competition.

Transformation of humanity as a whole

At the most expansive level, humanity itself undergoes perpetual transformation. From primitive survival-based societies to civilisations driven by ethics, knowledge and technological advancement, we are continuously reshaping our trajectory. The greatest challenge of human transformation is aligning technological, economic and social evolution with ethical and existential integrity.

Transformation of one's Being

Transformation at the level of Being is the foundation upon which all other transformations rest. The Being Framework outlines transformation as a shift in one's fundamental way of relating to reality

– moving beyond dysfunction, shadows and reactive patterns into a state of integrity, intentionality and authenticity. This is the deepest level of transformation, as it underpins how an individual engages with all other domains in life. Transformation across every domain begins here.

The ontology of transformation

To understand transformation more deeply, we can examine its ontological foundation through the Ontological Triad Schema, which reveals its anatomy (what it is), mechanics (how it works) and topology (how it interconnects with surrounding structures). This schema applies specifically to transformation as a structural and intentional process of systemic change.

1. Anatomy (what it is)

Transformation is not merely change. It is a fundamental reorganisation of relationships, processes and states of being. It involves a shift in how a system, individual or structure relates to itself, its environment and its internal dynamics. At its core, transformation consists of three primary components:

1. **Trigger (the catalyst for transformation)** – The force that initiates transformation by disrupting the prior state.
2. **Process (reconfiguration and adaptation)** – The restructuring that follows, integrating new patterns or dissolving existing ones.
3. **Emergence (new paradigm and integration)** – The stabilisation of a new order, where transformation becomes embedded in a coherent state.

Each of these components can be further broken down into key structural elements that define the anatomy of transformation:

- **Awareness** – The perceptual shift that enables transformation to begin. This could result from an in-depth analysis of content using the Nested Theory of Sense-making.[68]

---

[68] Tashvir, A. (2024) *Metacontent: The intellectual substrates for sense-making.* Sydney. Engenesis Publications.

- **Intention** – The driving force behind transformation – an underlying purpose or directional pull.
- **Disruption** – A necessary departure from the prior state, often emerging from crises, insights or changes in external conditions.
- **Reconfiguration** – The process of deconstructing, reorganising and adapting structures to accommodate transformation.
- **Emergence** – The establishment of a new, expanded order, where transformation solidifies into an integrated state.

Every transformation requires these elements to be present. Without **awareness**, transformation remains unconscious or reactionary. Without **intention**, it lacks direction. Without **disruption**, change is stagnant. Without **reconfiguration**, transformation fails to embed. And without **emergence**, transformation is unsustainable.

Key ontological attributes of transformation

- **Irreversible** – True transformation is not just a temporary shift, but a restructuring that cannot be undone without collapse.
- **Transcendent and inclusive** – Transformation does not simply replace the old. It integrates essential elements while transcending prior limitations.
- **Ontologically plastic** – Transformation enables a system (including a human being) or structure to reshape itself in response to dynamic forces.

2. Mechanics (how it works)

While anatomy defines what transformation is and its core components, the mechanics focuses on functionality, execution and process.

The process of transformation follows a structured methodology:

1. **Disruption (catalyst for change)** → Something breaks the existing equilibrium.
2. **Recognition (emergence of awareness and possibility)** → Awareness of an alternative state develops.

3. **Tension and Resistance (the battle between old and new)** → Internal or systemic resistance surfaces.
4. **Structural Realignment (reconfiguration and integration of the new state)** → New structures are formed.
5. **Stabilisation and Expansion (full integration and embedding of the new state)** → The transformation solidifies and sustains itself.

This methodology can be summarised as

Execute → Track → Learn → Refine → Re-execute

(as outlined in the Being Framework Transformation Methodology)

The process of transformation in action

For any transformation to occur, a significant disruption to the current state of play is the catalyst that sets the process in motion. For example:

A senior executive experiences burnout after years of overperformance and neglecting personal wellbeing.

- **Disruption:** The burnout triggers a breakdown – emotionally and physically – forcing a realisation that the current way of living and working is unsustainable.
- **Recognition:** Through coaching and introspection, they begin to perceive an alternative reality – one where leadership could be driven by purpose and wellbeing rather than perfectionism and control.
- **Tension and Resistance:** Doubts arise. Internalised beliefs ('If I slow down, I'll lose credibility') and structural pressures ('The organisation expects me to be always available') resist the change. The success of this stage depends on clarity and the adaptability of both the person and their environment.
- **Structural Realignment:** With support, they redesign their schedule, renegotiate roles and embed new leadership habits. They align these changes with deeper values, not just surface-level tactics.

- **Stabilisation and Expansion:** Over time, the new paradigm takes root. Their performance becomes more intentional and sustainable. They begin mentoring others, expanding the impact of their transformation into the broader system.

Transformation can unfold in different ways, depending on its nature and context. It may occur gradually – evolving slowly over time – or suddenly, as a radical and disruptive shift. Some transformations are guided, intentionally shaped through structured interventions, such as coaching or change management. Others are emergent, arising naturally from internal or external pressures without a predefined plan. Regardless of the pace or origin, the quality of transformation can also vary. It can lead to greater coherence and alignment, or, if poorly integrated, result in increased fragmentation and dysfunction.

3. Topology (how transformation interconnects with surrounding structures)

The topology of transformation describes how its parts are arranged and how they relate to each other, independent of their specific content or exact form. While anatomy defines *what transformation is* and mechanics explains *how it operates*, topology provides a map of its interdependencies, feedback loops and cascading effects across systems and domains.

No transformation occurs in isolation. Each instance interacts with, influences and is influenced by its surrounding systems. The interplay between these elements determines whether transformation leads to sustained coherence or further fragmentation. Consider the key structural patterns of transformational topology below.

1. Nested transformation (interconnected layers of change)

Transformation is never confined to a singular domain. Instead, it unfolds within nested layers that influence one another.

- A **personal transformation** (e.g., overcoming self-limiting beliefs) affects one's relationships (e.g., healthier interactions), which in turn shapes organisational culture (e.g., improved collaboration) and societal norms (e.g., greater psychological safety in workplaces).

- A **technological transformation** (e.g., AI-driven automation) reshapes economic systems (e.g., shifts in labour markets), which then impact education systems (e.g., new skill requirements), which ultimately influence cultural identity and governance.

Nothing transforms in complete isolation. Every transformation propagates through interdependent systems, creating either positive ripple effects or systemic instability.

Imagine a company undergoing a leadership transformation to shift from hierarchical control to a culture of trust and autonomy. The leadership transformation impacts employees' mindsets and sense of ownership and performance, which in turn shifts the organisation's market position, brand and external reputation. This organisational transformation influences industry trends, which shape broader economic and regulatory policies over time.

2. Feedback loops (self-reinforcing vs. self-correcting patterns)

Transformation operates within dynamic feedback loops, which either accelerate growth or counteract destabilisation. There are two types of feedback loops: self-reinforcing (positive feedback) and self-correcting (negative feedback).

Self-reinforcing feedback loops play a vital role in amplifying transformation by compounding small shifts into significant change over time. For instance, when an individual develops self-awareness, it often leads to greater confidence. This increased confidence enhances their decision-making, resulting in better outcomes, which in turn, reinforce both confidence and performance, creating a positive upward spiral.

Similarly, on a societal level, the adoption of renewable energy policies can trigger a transformative cycle. These policies stimulate technological innovation, which lowers the cost of renewable solutions. As these technologies become more affordable and accessible, adoption becomes widespread. This accelerates decarbonisation and drives deeper systemic change – showing how transformation, once set in motion, can reinforce and expand itself over time.

In contrast, **self-correcting feedback loops** help stabilise systems by regulating extreme or unsustainable transformation, ensuring that change does not outpace the system's capacity to maintain coherence. These negative feedback mechanisms act as checks that return a system to equilibrium when its trajectory becomes destabilising.

For example, when a company experiences rapid growth without having established solid operational foundations, cracks begin to appear and internal misalignment leads to performance breakdowns. These breakdowns force the organisation to pause, reassess and reset its strategy before attempting to scale further, ultimately protecting it from collapse.

On a geopolitical scale, revolutions can overthrow oppressive regimes, representing a major shift in power. However, without unified leadership or a clear vision for reconstruction, internal power struggles often emerge. These conflicts prevent the formation of a coherent new order, pulling the system back from radical transformation towards a less disruptive, though not necessarily ideal, equilibrium.

Sustainable transformation relies on the interplay of self-reinforcing and self-correcting feedback loops, each playing a vital role. Self-reinforcing feedback loops build momentum and deepen integration, while self-correcting feedback loops regulate excess and restore balance. Together, they ensure that transformation is not only forward-moving, but also grounded, adaptive and coherent over time.

3. Threshold effects (critical points of no return)

Every transformation reaches a tipping point – a critical point of no return – where the system can no longer operate within its old paradigm. At this threshold, the transformation either integrates successfully into a new state of coherence or collapses under the weight of fragmentation, resistance or incomplete realignment.

For example, a company shifting to a decentralised leadership model may intend to foster empowerment, but if it fails to realign incentives and accountability, the result may be confusion, disorder and inefficiency rather than agility. Similarly, a personal relationship pushed to the edge by deep conflict may either evolve into deeper trust and mutual understanding or fracture beyond repair. On a national level, widespread social unrest might serve as a tipping point where institutions either adapt and reform in response to public demands or devolve into instability and authoritarian backlash.

In each case, the outcome hinges on how effectively the system integrates and stabilises after crossing the threshold. The point itself is not the transformation – it is the test of whether true transformation has taken hold.

4. Dimensional expansion (transformation as a multi-layered process)

True transformation doesn't just involve change within a current framework. It expands the very dimensions through which a person, organisation or system engages with reality. It is a multi-layered process that deepens awareness, broadens capacity and elevates systemic interaction.

Consider the case of leadership. When a manager moves from task-based control to empowered leadership, they are not simply adopting new behaviours. They are developing entirely new cognitive and relational capacities, learning to navigate ambiguity, hold space for complexity and lead through influence rather than instruction. This is dimensional expansion. It reflects a leap in how leadership itself is understood and embodied.

The same applies on a societal scale. The shift from print media to digital platforms was more than just a technological upgrade. It transformed how entire cultures interact with information, form beliefs and shape narratives. It introduced new opportunities for connection and innovation, but also new vulnerabilities: misinformation, echo chambers and algorithmic influence.

In dimensional expansion, transformation does not remain confined to a single layer. It reconfigures the system's relationship with its environment, its structures and even its sense of self, opening up new domains of possibility, challenge and evolution. In other words, transformation doesn't just change the rules of the game; it introduces an entirely new playing field.

Transformation in action: The Being Framework Transformation Methodology

True transformation follows patterns, principles and structures that determine whether it is sustainable or temporary. The Being Framework Transformation Methodology provides a structured approach to understanding and facilitating transformation in a way that is both ontological (profound shifts in one's way of Being) and actionable (readily applied in real-world contexts). In this way, the methodology enables us to consciously and intentionally engage with transformation for sustainable outcomes.

This methodology involves:

1. **Recognising shadows** – Identifying dysfunction and limiting patterns that obstruct performance and derail transformation.
2. **Authentic awareness** – Cultivating clarity and discernment to see reality without distortion.
3. **Intentional decision-making** – Aligning choices with coherence, integrity and a vision of transformation that is both meaningful and sustainable.
4. **Integration and embodiment** – Moving beyond intellectual understanding to integrate and embody the transformation in thought, action and Being.
5. **Sustaining transformation** – Maintaining momentum beyond initial breakthroughs by embedding new patterns into daily life, ensuring that transformation becomes a continuous, evolving process rather than a fleeting, single event.

Transformation is not an isolated event. It is a fundamental principle governing life at every level. Whether within an individual's consciousness, an organisation's structure, a society's evolution or the trajectory of humanity, transformation determines whether we progress or remain trapped in cycles of dysfunction. Through this lens, transformation is not something to fear but to master. It enables us to transcend limitations, integrate higher levels of coherence and create a future grounded in integrity and purpose. Later in this chapter, we will explore the Being Framework Transformation Methodology's process. But first, a critical distinction must be made between transformation and transition, and the role modulation plays in both of these dynamic, but distinctly different yet interconnected processes.

Transition, modulation and transformation: The distinction and interplay between them

In any given system – whether an individual, an organisation, an institution, a culture or a civilisation – there is no static state. A system is always in motion, continuously transitioning along a continuum between greater coherence and integrity or increasing dysfunction and disintegration. **Transition** refers to this ongoing, unconscious movement. What determines the quality and direction of this movement is **modulation**: transition made conscious, intentional and directed. The four modulation forces regulate how systems respond to internal and external changes. **Transformation** is the structural outcome when modulation sustains and integrates over time. It is the point at which repeated, guided transitions fundamentally reorganise the architecture of a system. At this level, old patterns dissolve, new configurations embed themselves within the system and coherence stabilises at a higher level of integrity. Let's examine each state more closely.

Transition: The continuum of systemic movement

Transition is the ongoing movement along the continuum between the states of integrity and disintegration. Rather than treating these two states as a rigid dichotomy, the UOSI recognises that systems are never fixed. They exist in *constant flux*, always moving towards or away from greater alignment, coherence and systemic integrity.

This ontological distinction positions transition as a structural phenomenon – a dynamic process that unfolds in all systems. It is not inherently positive or negative. Instead, it reflects the natural, ever-unfolding unconscious shifts that take place within and across domains. Transition is often silent, unnoticed or misinterpreted as randomness, when in fact it reveals the system's adaptive or degenerative trajectory.

Recognising transition as a neutral, ongoing force opens the door to deeper discernment. Systems do not jump from wholeness to collapse overnight. They transition. And in understanding that process, we gain the capacity to influence it.

Modulation: Transition made intentional

While **transition** describes what is constantly occurring at an unconscious level, **modulation** is the ongoing process of making that movement intentional. It involves recognising a system's trajectory and continually guiding it with vision, responsibility and discernment towards coherence, sustainability and renewal.

Modulation is neither reactive nor random. It is a systemic function that emerges from agency, leadership and attunement. When modulation is active, unconscious shifts become purposeful evolution. It marks the moment when transition becomes navigable.

This distinction is critical in sustainability contexts. Without modulation, transitions are left to drift – shaped by outdated habits, external pressures or unexamined narratives. But when systems engage in modulation, they develop the capacity to consciously and intentionally realign, recalibrate and regenerate, sustaining coherence even under strain.

Modulation is not merely a mental process; it's a way of conducting yourself. It requires more than insight and demands care, responsibility and a long-range perspective. A system that modulates well does not simply adapt. It stewards its evolution, moving with intention, not inertia. Ultimately, sustained modulation is the key to transformation taking root.

Transformation: Structural reconfiguration and emergence

Transformation refers to the fundamental reorganisation of a system's internal architecture: its relationships, processes and ways of being. It is the emergent outcome of sustained, intentional modulation. Transformation differs from change, which may be incremental or cosmetic. It alters the very structure through which a system exists, behaves and evolves.

As discussed earlier in this chapter, the anatomy of transformation typically unfolds in three structural stages:

- **Trigger**: A disruption that renders the current configuration untenable.
- **Reconfiguration**: A restructuring of internal patterns and relationships.
- **Emergence**: The stabilisation of a new paradigm, often marked by greater coherence or capability.

The critical interplay between transformation, transition and modulation

Transformation on its own is not enough. Without transition, it lacks the continuity to embed. Without modulation, it becomes volatile or unsustainable. For transformation to endure, it must be absorbed and stabilised over time through intentional transitions. Modulation determines the quality and direction of these transitions.

Unmodulated transformation often produces volatility, resistance or collapse. Conversely, modulation without transformation results in shallow optimisation that refines the surface while leaving deeper structures unexamined. But when all three forces – transformation, transition and modulation – operate in concert, they create the conditions for systemic regeneration.

Put simply, transformation initiates new potential, transition allows that potential to unfold, and modulation ensures that unfolding is guided, coherent and sustainable.

In the context of systemic sustainability and regenerative design, this triad offers both a practical and ontological roadmap:

- **Transition** is always occurring.
- **Modulation** is the art of navigating transitions with intention.
- **Transformation** is the structural reconfiguration that makes new futures possible.

A system cannot be sustained by stagnation or inertia. Nor can it endure chaos without collapse. What allows for authentic sustainability is the ability to modulate transitions while embracing necessary transformations. The presence or absence of this capability determines whether systems fracture under pressure or evolve with resilience.

These distinctions are not merely semantic; they are functional. They provide a vocabulary for diagnosing where a system stands, identifying what it needs, and guiding how it can move forward in a way that is coherent, grounded and enduring.

	Transformation	Transition
Definition	A fundamental shift in structure, state or function	A continuous process of modulation in response to change
Nature	Active and intentional – A deliberate effort to create change	Adaptive and organic – A response to ongoing change
Timeframe	Milestone-based – Discrete moments of change	Continuous – A perpetual state of modulation
Scope	Focuses on outcomes and goals	Focuses on processes and adjustments
Agency	Driven by execution cycles (Execute → Track → Learn → Refine → Re-execute)	Driven by modulation elements (Patience, Tolerance, Adaptability, Surrender)
Example	A company switching from fossil fuels to renewable energy	Employees, systems and policies adapting to the shift over time

Table 28 – Transformation and Transition – The Key Distinctions.

The Modulation Sphere and its role in the processes of transition and transformation

While transformation is a more structural, intentional shift, it can only take root through guided transitions enabled by healthy, sustained modulation. More precisely, modulation is the mechanism that determines the direction of movement on this continuum. The Modulation Sphere serves as the mediating structure that governs this process. It does this by regulating the tension between stability and change.

The Modulation Sphere's four interdependent forces of patience, tolerance, adaptability and surrender operate as mediating dynamics that either facilitate transformation or inhibit it by introducing friction.

1. **Patience (sustaining stability through transition)** – Transformation is rarely instantaneous; it unfolds over time. Patience allows systems, individuals and structures to process and integrate change without rushing towards premature resolutions that may cause fragmentation. Attempting to force transformation before it has fully taken root often results in temporary shifts that collapse under pressure.

    - **Example:** A leader undergoing personal transformation must practise patience to allow deep internal shifts to stabilise, rather than enforcing behavioural changes before the underlying structures are properly realigned.

2. **Tolerance (holding space for discomfort and resistance)** – Transformation often involves discomfort, uncertainty and resistance. Tolerance is the capacity to endure these tensions without reacting destructively or abandoning the process. Many transformation efforts fail because the discomfort of change is not endured long enough to reach integration.

    - **Example:** A company shifting to a decentralised decision-making model must tolerate short-term inefficiencies and initial resistance from employees before the long-term benefits of empowerment and autonomy emerge.

3. **Adaptability (aligning with change without losing integrity)** – True transformation is not just about absorbing change, but about realigning with it while maintaining coherence. Adaptability enables systems and individuals to integrate change meaningfully, rather than rigidly resisting or blindly conforming.

    - **Example:** A cultural transformation within an organisation requires adaptability – not just in policies, but in leadership mindset, communication and workflows – to ensure the transition enhances rather than erodes integrity.

4. **Surrender (letting go of dysfunctional attachment and control)** – Not all structures should be preserved during transformation. Surrender is the ability to release outdated

paradigms, attachments and illusions of control that prevent authentic evolution. Many transformation efforts fail because individuals or systems cling to dysfunctional models that no longer serve them.

- **Example:** A nation undergoing political reform must surrender entrenched power dynamics that hinder progress, allowing new governance models to emerge rather than perpetuating oppressive structures.

These four modulating forces do not function in isolation. They operate as a dynamic interplay that determines the trajectory of transformation:

- If **patience** dominates without adaptability or surrender, transformation stagnates.
- If **tolerance** exists without discernment, dysfunction is normalised.
- If **adaptability** is pursued without patience, transformation becomes erratic and unstructured.
- If **surrender** occurs without integration, a system collapses into dysfunction.

Together, the four modulating forces mediate the tensions inherent in transformation, ensuring that change is sustainable, intentional and coherent rather than arbitrary or chaotic.

Transformation as a systemic and ontological imperative

Transformation is not an isolated event, but a relational, systemic process embedded within the dynamic interplay between integrity and disintegration. It is how systems – whether individuals, organisations or entire civilisations – adapt, evolve or fragment in response to internal and external forces. But for transformation to be *sustainable*, it must be supported by something deeper than reactive change: it must be modulated, integrated and aligned with the core principles of systemic integrity.

This is where the distinction between transformation and transition becomes critical. To reiterate, transformation refers to the structural or ontological shift, such as a change in identity, paradigm or foundational design. In contrast, transition is the ongoing, intentional modulation that ensures those shifts are absorbed, stabilised and sustained. One without the other leads to collapse or stagnation. Together, they enable lasting, embedded change.

The Modulation Sphere plays a central role in this process. Its four mediating forces – patience, tolerance, adaptability and surrender – are active regulators of change. Patience slows down reactionary shifts and allows clarity to emerge. Tolerance offers the flexibility to hold tension without immediate resolution. Adaptability allows systems to respond to change rather than resist it. And Surrender, when healthy, enables the release of outdated patterns without falling into passivity. These forces ensure that transformation does not become too rigid (resisting growth) or too chaotic (collapsing under its own volatility).

To support sustainable transformation in practice, the Being Framework Transformation Methodology offers a structured, iterative approach: Execute → Track → Learn → Refine → Re-execute. Through this methodology, transformation is not only initiated; it is stabilised and continually evolved. This ensures that change is not temporary or performative, but systemic and regenerative.

Transformation is not a disruption to avoid. It is the organising principle of systemic health. It determines whether systems stagnate or recalibrate, collapse or ascend. When guided by the principles of modulation, supported by disciplined methodologies and aligned with ontological integrity, transformation becomes the pathway through which systems evolve – not by force, but by design.

Ultimately, to transform is not simply to survive change. It is to participate – consciously, courageously and coherently – in the ongoing evolution of self, systems and society.

A dynamic journey

As discussed, transformation does not occur in isolation. It is embedded within a continuum where systems, beings and organisations oscillate between integrity and disintegration. The direction and velocity of movement within this continuum determine whether transformation leads to sustainable evolution or systemic collapse.

To understand how transformation occurs along the continuum, it is essential to recognise the following:

- **Integrity can lead to rigidity if left unmodulated** – While integrity is being whole, aligned and coherent, it can harden into rigidity without modulation. Excessive stability without modulation leads to conservatism and a resistance to evolution, even when change is necessary.
- **Not every breakdown leads to growth** – The collapse of old structures can sometimes pave the way for renewal, but not always. Disintegration without direction leads to disorder, meaninglessness and collapse. Not every breakdown is a breakthrough.
- **Modulation is the key** – Sustainable transformation depends on the capacity to modulate between integrity and disintegration. It is not about choosing one over the other, but about moving intentionally between them: absorbing shocks, adapting to change and integrating new insights.

No system – personal, organisational or societal – is ever static. It is always in motion, either towards deeper coherence or towards fragmentation. Consequently, transformation is not just a pivot or a leap, but a dynamic journey along the continuum. If the process is too rigid, transformation cannot take root. In contrast, if it's too chaotic, transformation cannot stabilise.

Modulation allows for movement without collapse, change without chaos and evolution without disconnection. It ensures that transformation is not only possible but (critically) also sustainable.

The Being Framework Transformation Methodology in action

Sustainability is not about maintaining the status quo. It's about ensuring that any transformation itself is *sustained*. As explained earlier, the Being Framework Transformation Methodology is a practical tool that supports sustainable transformation through its iterative 5-step process. This methodology ensures that sustainability is not a fixed state to achieve, but a dynamic, evolving process where the conditions of transformation continuously shift.

Example: A school reinventing its learning model

A progressive secondary school recognises that its traditional, exam-centred learning model is no longer aligned with the needs of students or the future workforce. The school's leadership team initiates a transformation towards a more inquiry-based, student-led learning environment. But rather than implementing sweeping change all at once, they follow the Being Framework Transformation Methodology to ensure the process is sustainable.

- **Execute:** The school rolls out a pilot program in two year levels, embedding project-based learning units designed to foster critical thinking and collaboration.
- **Track:** Teachers and leaders observe how students engage, how assessment outcomes shift and where resistance or confusion arises among students and staff.
- **Learn:** Feedback reveals that while students are more engaged, some teachers struggle to adjust their facilitation style. It also shows that some students lack the self-regulation needed for independent inquiry.
- **Refine:** The school introduces new teacher training focused on adaptive facilitation and provides student workshops on goal setting and time management.
- **Re-execute:** The refined model is applied to additional year levels, with an expanded support structure. Iteration continues over time based on lived feedback.

The outcome

Transformation occurs without overwhelming the system. Resistance is addressed through learning and refinement rather than enforced compliance. Over time, the new model becomes part of the school's identity – not just a project, but a sustained evolution rooted in systemic coherence.

The Modulation Sphere's role in ensuring transformation endures

Transformation marks the intentional shift from one state to another. But without modulation, that shift risks becoming either too rigid to adapt or too unstable to endure. Sustainable transformation requires more than change. It requires change that lasts, evolves and integrates over time.

This is where the Modulation Sphere plays a vital role. Through its four forces, it governs the pace and quality of transition, ensuring that transformation is not just initiated but absorbed, stabilised and maintained. These forces help systems remain coherent and resilient, supporting ongoing evolution rather than temporary disruption. In this way, modulation becomes the bridge between transformation and sustainability. By modulating between stability and change, we ensure that any transformation is gradual, intentional and systemically absorbed.

Example: Cultural change within an organisation

A large company decides to transition from a top-down leadership model to a more collaborative, decentralised structure. The transformation is intentional, but without effective modulation, the shift would cause confusion, resistance and burnout among employees.

- **Patience** allows the leadership team to introduce changes gradually, giving teams time to adjust and understand new expectations.
- **Tolerance** helps accommodate mistakes and growing pains without reverting to old habits or punishing early missteps.
- **Adaptability** enables teams to respond to real-time feedback and refine new workflows without abandoning the larger goal.
- **Surrender**, in its healthy form, helps decision-makers let go of control where appropriate and entrust others to step into leadership roles.

Together, these forces modulate the pace and depth of transition. As a result, the cultural shift doesn't collapse under resistance or lose momentum. It stabilises, integrates and becomes the new normal.

This is sustainable transformation: not just change, but change that endures.

Integrating transition, modulation and transformation

Before we conclude this chapter, it is essential to clearly distinguish and integrate the concepts of transition, modulation and transformation. Although these concepts have been unpacked throughout the book, bringing them together here will consolidate understanding and avoid confusion.

Transition is the unconscious, constant and unavoidable movement that occurs within a system. It is the change from one state to another, whether in behaviour, structure, relationships or perception. Transition is not inherently good or bad, nor is it purposeful on its own. Systems are always transitioning in some way, even if subtly. However, transition alone does not determine whether a system is heading towards greater integrity or deeper dysfunction. It is simply the shifting.

Modulation is the regulatory force applied to transition. It determines how transitions unfold, and whether they stabilise, recalibrate or disintegrate a system. The Modulation Sphere, with its four forces of patience, tolerance, adaptability and surrender, plays a vital role in shaping the outcome of transitions. Without modulation, transitions can become chaotic, reactive or entrenching. However, with effective modulation, transitions become intentional, conscious and coherent, allowing for recovery, realignment or renewal.

Transformation is the emergent trajectory that results from the pattern of transitions modulated over time. It is not a single event or moment of change, but a structural and directional process. Transformation reflects a shift in the foundational state of a system, often accompanied by a reconfiguration of values, functions, relationships and capacities. In this way, transformation is not just about change, but about directional, patterned and ontological reconfiguration. It emerges from transitions that have been consistently modulated in a way that orients a system towards systemic integrity.

In other words:

- Transition is movement.
- Modulation is regulation of movement.
- Transformation is the structural result of conscious, governed movement over time.

Understanding the distinctions and relationships between these three concepts is critical. It allows us to not only diagnose the condition of a system, but also to intervene wisely. Transformation cannot be forced. But it can be nurtured through intentional modulation of the inevitable transitions that every system experiences. Where modulation is healthy, transformation becomes possible. However, where it is distorted or absent, disintegration takes hold.

Transition to Transformation

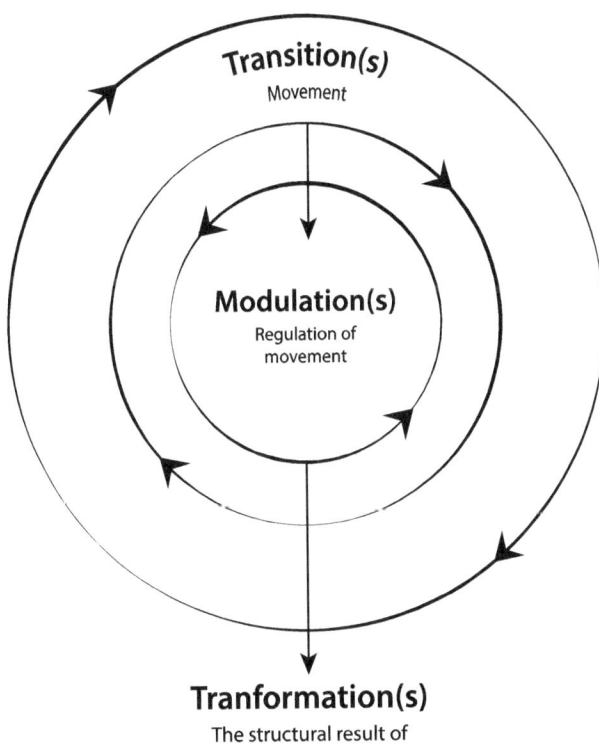

Figure 6 – From Transition to Transformation – The Necessity of Iterative Modulation.

From transition to transformation: The necessity of iterative modulation

To truly transform from dysfunction to authentic sustainability, a single modulated transition is rarely sufficient. It is through sustained rounds of modulation – where patience, tolerance, adaptability and surrender are exercised, reflected upon and refined – that a system slowly rewires itself. Transformation is not the product of a single leap, but the cumulative result of many modulated transitions. Just as one deep breath doesn't restore emotional balance, a single instance of adaptive change doesn't transform a system, including a human being. Only through continuous modulation do transitions stabilise into new norms, and only through these stabilised transitions does transformation take root.

Conclusion

Transformation is not a singular leap. It is the cumulative result of how systems navigate transitions, modulate their responses and reorient themselves towards integrity. The forces of patience, tolerance, adaptability and surrender are not soft virtues. They are structural regulators that determine whether a system fragments or evolves.

By understanding the anatomy of disintegration and the interplay between modulation and transformation, we are no longer passive observers of systemic decline. We become capable of diagnosing dysfunction, interrupting self-reinforcing decay and restoring integrity – within ourselves, our relationships, teams, organisations, institutions, communities and societies.

This chapter laid the foundation for why authentic sustainability is impossible without transformation, and why transformation itself is impossible without the sustained modulation of how we relate to difficulty.

In the end, sustainability is not just about what we build. It is about how we become.

Crossing the threshold: From ontology to embodiment

Part II has laid the groundwork for understanding the deep ontological architecture that sustains or collapses systems. We have seen how transformation unfolds, how disintegration manifests, and how modulation mediates systemic transitions. Sustainability is not a fixed outcome but a dynamic state, maintained through integrity, guided by discernment and shaped through intentional action.

But insight alone is not embodiment. Old habits die hard, and transformation only takes root when modulation is lived out in practice: patience with relapses, tolerance of discomfort, adaptability in shifting routines, surrender when control must be released. These repeated cycles – faltering, recalibrating, persisting – accumulate over time. What begins as theory matures into embodied sustainability.

It is now time to move from theory into structure – into the architecture of the four spheres that comprise the Unified Ontology of Systemic Integrity. The following four parts of this book are each dedicated to one sphere. Each will be examined through the lens of the Ontological Triad Schema, unpacking its anatomy, mechanics and topology. In doing so, we also reveal the ontological distinction of each of the 16 forces that make up the spheres' internal quads.

This is where the theory becomes a toolkit and philosophy meets execution.

PART III

The Architectonic Sphere

Enamoured with tactics, obsessed with performance and fuelled by urgency, we rarely pause to ask deeper questions: What is this all for? Is it aligned? Can it last? We optimise for outcomes, productivity and appearance, yet systems still collapse. Leaders burn out. Cultures fracture. Promises ring hollow. Why?

This part of the book introduces the Architectonic Sphere, the governing dimension of the Unified Ontology of Systemic Integrity. While other spheres help us feel, think, act or modulate, the Architectonic Sphere orients the entire system. It answers not just how we function, but why, to what end and with what consequences. It is the space where discernment becomes design and responsibility becomes architecture.

This sphere is not about control or complexity for its own sake. It's about the often-overlooked infrastructure of coherence – the principles, patterns and capacities that determine whether a system sustains its integrity or quietly fractures beneath the weight of its own contradictions.

At its core are four meta-factors:

- **Meta-awareness** – the structural capacity to observe and evolve how we perceive and make sense.
- **Systemic Integrity** – the alignment between intention, design, action and impact.
- **Sustained Effectiveness** – the ability to perform and regenerate without collapse or depletion.
- **Normativity** – the orientation towards what is worthy, ethical and valuable across time and context.

These four forces do not operate in isolation. Together, they form the compass, scaffolding and moral backbone of any system – from a person to a global institution.

This part of the book is not a detour into abstract theory – it is a return to what either holds everything together or lets it quietly fall apart. The Architectonic Sphere does not micromanage the visible; it orchestrates the invisible. It determines whether success is fleeting or foundational, whether coherence is accidental or systemic, and whether a system is merely functioning or truly worthy of trust.

You are now entering the layer that governs all others. The place where clarity becomes coherence, performance becomes stewardship and sustainability begins – not with strategy, but with structure.

CHAPTER 26

Meta-awareness

We live in a culture saturated with advice to be self-aware. Mindfulness is marketed as a cure-all, reflection is framed as emotional intelligence and pausing before reacting is celebrated as maturity. Yet beneath these surface-level competencies lies a deeper, often unrecognised faculty: the capacity to observe not just what we see or think, but *how* we are seeing and thinking in the first place. This is the realm of meta-awareness.

Meta-awareness is not about self-reflection in the conventional sense. It is not simply the ability to identify feelings or thoughts. Nor is it limited to pausing during conflict or noticing biases after the fact. These are all useful skills, but they operate within the field of content. Meta-awareness goes further. It is the structural capacity to observe the mechanisms and architecture behind one's perception, sense-making, meaning-making and decision-making across time, systems and layers of complexity.

In individuals, the absence of meta-awareness leads to recurring patterns of sabotage, overconfidence or paralysis. In leaders, it creates blind spots that masquerade as conviction. In relationships and institutions, it results in deeply rooted incoherence, where decisions are made from inherited paradigms and biases that go unexamined for decades. Organisations stagnate, governments overreach or collapse and families repeat generational patterns, all while believing they are acting with clarity.

Meta-awareness is the difference between reacting in the moment and responding from a place of structural, deeply embedded awareness. It allows a person – or a collective – to track how perception is structured, how narratives are formed, and how entire systems of meaning operate beneath the surface of action. Without it, performance becomes shallow, ethics become conditional and long-term effectiveness erodes from within.

In the context of the Architectonic Sphere, meta-awareness is not an optional refinement. It is foundational. It governs how a system knows what it knows, how it monitors the validity of its own reasoning, and how it adjusts or sustains coherence in the face of change, contradiction or disruption.

This meta-factor is especially crucial when navigating complexity. Modern life is not only fast-paced, but also layered with paradox, ideological fragmentation and information overload. It is easy to conflate conviction with clarity or mistake inherited frameworks for universal truths. Meta-awareness acts as a governing intelligence that enables recursive reflection, not just on ideas and emotions, but on the systemic structures that give rise to those very ideas and emotions.

Within the Unified Ontology of Systemic Integrity (UOSI), meta-awareness functions as the internal architecture that creates coherence across the seven layers of sense-making as described in the Nested Theory of Sense-making[69] – from the initial, felt impression to the deepest paradigmatic assumptions. It allows for the conscious tracking of distortions, biases, blind spots and systemic incoherence before they escalate into dysfunction. The seven nested layers of sense-making are unpacked within the *Ontology of meta-awareness* section under the heading of *Anatomy*.

Most breakdowns in leadership, governance and relationships do not occur because of malice or a lack of intelligence. They occur because of a failure to examine the architecture through which reality is interpreted and engaged: the architecture of meta-awareness. When

---

69   Tashvir, A. (2024) *Metacontent: The Intellectual Substrates for Sense-making*. Sydney. Engenesis Publications.

meta-awareness is absent, we cannot see the filters we are applying. We confuse emotion with truth, habit with wisdom and familiarity with objectivity. But when it is present, it creates space between perception and response: space to inquire not only into what is happening, but into how we are participating in its construction.

Crucially, meta-awareness is always exercised within specific contexts and shaped by contextual variables, such as cultural norms, relational dynamics, institutional structures and time-bound conditions. These variables influence what is noticed, how it is interpreted and which distortions or blind spots are likely to arise. You will recall that all seven layers of sense-making sit on a bedrock of contextual variables – the wider conditions in which they unfold. Meta-awareness makes these conditions visible, enabling us to notice not only the filters we apply, but also the soil from which those filters grow.

Meta-awareness is not a trait, mood or behaviour. It is an ontological faculty. It is the capacity to reflect on awareness itself – to hold the system of sense-making in view and reorient before incoherence takes hold. Without it, all other efforts – however well-intentioned – are vulnerable to collapse.

Ontological Distinction of Meta-awareness

Meta-awareness is the extent to which you notice and relate to awareness itself. Where awareness gives you access to knowing, *meta-awareness* highlights the quality of awareness and ensures that access is not distorted. It is the reflective capacity that allows awareness itself to remain coherent. It is not just being conscious of your thoughts, feelings and perceptions, but also recognising how your awareness is being shaped, filtered and directed. *Meta-awareness* lets you see not only what you are noticing, but also *how* you are noticing it – and the hidden influences behind that, such as your habits, past experiences, assumptions and beliefs. This quality makes awareness intentional rather than automatic or reactive. It creates the capacity to observe the lenses through which you interpret yourself, others and the world, and to orient yourself with greater clarity and coherence.

A **healthy relationship with meta-awareness** indicates that you can step back and examine the filters and influences shaping your perceptions. You are able to recognise when your awareness is distorted and when impulses – rather than clear insight – are driving you, enabling you to intentionally adjust your orientation as circumstances change. You remain curious about how you make sense of matters without collapsing into self-doubt. This quality also supports anticipatory learning and adaptability in any domain, from personal and relational to organisational and societal. You have the foresight to recognise subtle shifts before they become crises, the capacity to pivot constructively as conditions evolve, and the resilience to transform disruptions into opportunities for growth and renewal. Others may consider you balanced, thoughtful and proactive. They may also know you as someone who is both a seeker of and open to feedback. Your awareness serves truth and coherence rather than ego, ideology or convenience.

An **unhealthy relationship with meta-awareness** indicates that you either lack the capacity to question your own assumptions or you may become paralysed by endless self-analysis. You may confuse first impressions or familiar narratives with the whole truth and react rigidly rather than adapting. Alternatively, you may retreat into analysis or purely cognitive frames of reference to avoid emotional engagement, lived experience or concrete action. In both cases, you miss the chance to see how your awareness is being shaped and risk mistaking output for effectiveness, charisma for wisdom or short-term alignment for long-term coherence. Individuals and manufactured systems – from relationships, teams and businesses to institutions, governments and societies – that lack meta-awareness often only learn in moments of crisis, when adaptation is forced rather than chosen. This reactive pattern breeds fragility: instead of evolving proactively, they calcify around old assumptions, mistaking rigidity for stability. Over time, this hardening becomes entrenchment, where change is resisted until collapse is unavoidable.

Ontology of meta-awareness

In the UOSI, meta-awareness is not simply a state of deep reflection. It is a structural faculty that governs the integrity of our sense-making across time, complexity and context. It operates as a recursive monitoring intelligence that allows individuals and other systems to track their own perception, orientation and interpretive frameworks. Without it, awareness collapses into distortion. However, with it, awareness becomes coherent, adaptive and aligned with reality.

Let's now break down the ontology of meta-awareness by revealing its anatomy, mechanics and topology.

Anatomy of meta-awareness

The anatomy of meta-awareness consists of the seven nested layers of sense-making, which forms an integral part of the metacontent discourse explored in *Metacontent – The intellectual substrates for sense-making.*[70] Within each layer, awareness is either coherently tracked or unconsciously enacted. Together, they reveal how meaning arises and how it can become distorted or restructured. These are not steps, but layers that interact continuously as we make sense of any content. As discussed earlier, all of these layers rest upon a contextual bedrock – timing, cultural and environmental conditions, and the subjective and intersubjective variables that silently shape what arises at each layer.

1. **Abductive given (initial insight)**

   The abductive given is the initial, pre-verbal impression. It arrives as an emotional registration of meaning or a felt sense before any reasoning occurs. Meta-awareness begins here by recognising this is only the beginning of sense-making, not the whole truth.

2. **Cognitive map**

   A cognitive map refers to the structural frameworks and ontological classifications we apply to the world.

---

70   Tashvir, A. (2022) *Metacontent: The Intellectual Substrates for Sense-making.* Sydney. Engenesis Publications.

Meta-awareness tracks how these maps shape what we prioritise, legitimise or reject.

3. Stories

Here, experience becomes narrative. Our memories, traumas and identities get woven into emotionally coherent scripts. Meta-awareness allows us to hold these stories as interpretations, not inevitabilities.

4. Mental models

This is where behaviour is automated. Assumptions about risk, safety, control and response operate beneath consciousness. Meta-awareness detects when these default responses disrupt alignment or no longer support systemic coherence.

5. Perspective

The perspective layer governs the standpoint from which we observe, assess and judge. Meta-awareness enables us to shift perspective and recognise the limits of our current lens.

6. Domain

Awareness is context-sensitive. What we believe or prioritise in one domain may contradict another. Meta-awareness exposes and reconciles these inconsistencies, creating systemic alignment.

7. Paradigm

At the deepest layer, meta-awareness reveals the unseen structures that shape all other layers: epistemic (how we know), axiological (what we value) and ontological (what we see as real). Without this meta-awareness, paradigms operate us rather than being consciously held.

These seven layers, as depicted in the Nested Theory of Sense-making diagram shown in Figure 7,[71] form the structural anatomy through which meta-awareness functions. Depending on how we engage with

---

[71] Tashvir, A. (2022) *Metacontent: The Intellectual Substrates for Sense-making.* Sydney. Engenesis Publications.

them and the context, each layer becomes either a site of distortion or a portal to coherence.

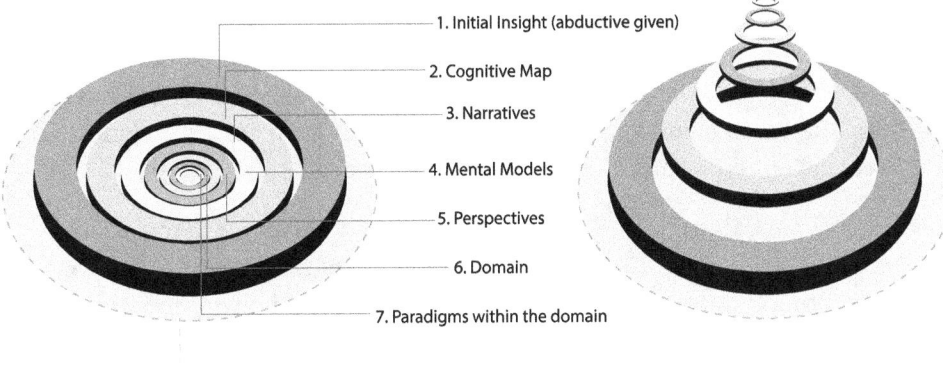

Figure 7 – The Nested Theory of Sense-making.

Example 1: Everyday relationships

Shane comes home after a stressful day at work. Their partner asks a simple question: 'Did you remember to pick up the groceries?' Instantly, Shane feels criticised, as if their competence is being questioned.

At the level of the **abductive given**, Shane's body registers the tone of the question as disapproval, even though it was neutral. This felt sense is mistaken for objective truth.

Their **cognitive map** overlays a framework that says, 'Being asked means I'm being judged.' In doing so, they unwittingly frame the interaction as suspicion rather than curiosity.

Through the lens of **stories**, they replay a familiar narrative: 'Nobody appreciates what I do; I'm always being blamed.' That story, inherited from past experiences, turns a neutral question into a script of victimhood.

Their **mental model** activates an automatic reaction: defensiveness. 'Why are you always on my back?' they demand. What unfolds is not clarity, but conditioned habit.

Shane's **perspective** remains fixed. They cannot entertain that their partner's words may have been a logistical reminder, not an accusation.

Across **domains**, inconsistency arises. Shane might laugh off forgetfulness when with friends or colleagues. However, at home, the same situation is treated as an attack. Without meta-awareness, they fail to reconcile these contexts, and so the fracture deepens.

At the **paradigm** level, an unseen assumption drives it all: that relationships are evaluations of worth rather than domains of care and collaboration. Because it remains unseen, the paradigm governs their relationship rather than being consciously held.

Here, the contextual variables – the timing of a stressful day, the relational environment of the home and the subjective weight of past experiences – intensify each layer. What could have been a moment of connection is reframed as conflict because context remains invisible.

The result is a simple question escalating into conflict – not because of the groceries, but because Shane lacked meta-awareness of how their awareness was being shaped. Without it, they confuse emotion for truth, story for reality and reminders for judgement.

Example 2: Organisational leadership

A senior manager in a large organisation has built a reputation for being decisive and confident. On the surface, he appears effective: meetings move quickly, decisions are rarely delayed, and his certainty inspires reassurance during turbulent times. Yet beneath the surface, each layer of his sense-making anatomy is subtly misoriented.

At the level of the **abductive given**, the manager confuses first impressions with whole truths. If a colleague raises an idea with hesitation, he instinctively reads it as weakness rather than caution or careful thought.

In his **cognitive map**, evaluation frameworks are narrow and outdated. He classifies people as 'loyal or disloyal', 'bold or timid', and treats these maps as self-evident truths.

His **stories** reinforce the script: 'Decisiveness is strength; doubt is weakness'. This narrative was inherited early in his career and now governs his reactions unconsciously.

His **mental model** defaults to defensiveness when challenged. What was once protective is now disruptive. But because it runs beneath awareness, it persists unexamined.

At the **perspective** level, the manager struggles to step outside his own standpoint. Junior staff are dismissed as naive, peers are seen as rivals, and the lens remains rigid.

In different **domains**, contradictions abound. At home, the manager values listening and patience. However, at work, he imposes dominance and control. He never reconciles these inconsistencies.

At the deepest **paradigm** layer, he operates from an epistemic assumption that knowledge equals certainty and authority. Left unexamined, this paradigm controls him instead of being consciously engaged.

Here, too, contextual variables are decisive: the corporate culture that rewards quick decisions, the hierarchical environment that amplifies his certainty, and the intersubjective norms of his team that silence dissent. Context reinforces distortion at every layer, giving rigidity the appearance of strength.

The result is an illusion of clarity that inspires confidence on the surface, but corrodes trust underneath. Over time, innovation dries up, colleagues retreat, and the organisation becomes hollow. What appears as conviction is actually rigidity, and what looks like efficiency is the silencing of dissent.

Together, these examples show how misoriented meta-awareness operates at every scale, from the intimacy of a relationship to the leadership within organisations and the governance of institutions. Without recursive monitoring of the seven nested layers of sense-making – and without recognising the contextual variables that silently shape them – awareness collapses into distortion. The everyday conflict at home and the brittle leader at work both reveal the same truth: when we cannot see *how we are seeing*, we mistake distortion for reality.

Mechanics of meta-awareness

Meta-awareness does not function as a single act of reflection. It is a recursive and dynamic process that regulates how awareness evolves over time. Its mechanics involve ongoing feedback loops between perception, calibration and re-orientation.

1. Initial registration

A moment of awareness is triggered. This may emerge as confusion, insight, tension or the sense that something is 'off'. This marks the entry point for meta-awareness to engage.

2. Layered inquiry

Rather than reacting, meta-awareness initiates a layered inquiry. It traces the perception through the Nested Theory of Sense-making's seven layers and considers the context at each layer. It prompts questions such as: What am I feeling? What am I assuming? What story is shaping this? From which domain or paradigm is this arising? What is the context, and how is it shaping each layer?

3. Distortion detection

Through this layered examination, distortions or incongruences can be identified. This could be a narrative that no longer fits, a model that has become reactive or a paradigm that is outdated or inherited.

4. Structural reorientation

Meta-awareness then allows for reorientation. This might mean updating the story, shifting the model or temporarily suspending judgement until clarity emerges. This is not about overthinking; it is structural discernment.

5. Recursive application

Meta-awareness is recursive. It applies not only to external situations, but also to the act of awareness itself. It tracks when awareness is becoming self-justifying, biased or closed, allowing systems to evolve without collapse.

When these mechanics are absent, people and other systems become stuck in the initial layers of sense-making. For example, they may immediately react based on the stories they tell themselves or get tunnel vision rather than being open to other perspectives, never realising they are operating within a closed loop.

Imagine a manager in an organisation whose team delivers a project milestone late.

At the **initial moment of registration**, instead of pausing at the subtle sense that 'something is off', the manager immediately frames the event as 'my team is lazy and careless'. The entry point for meta-awareness is already skewed. What might have been a space for curiosity becomes an instant accusation.

Bypassing the opportunity to commence a **layered inquiry**, the manager never stops to ask: What am I feeling? What am I assuming? What story is shaping this? From what domain or paradigm and context is this arising? Such questions might have revealed frustration, an assumption that lateness reflects laziness, a narrative of distrust, and a worldview that equates discipline with control – where punctuality, order and compliance are treated as proof of reliability, while deviation is cast as weakness or defiance.

The error deepens when the manager **misreads the domain**: what belongs in the structural and organisational domain (shifting requirements, broken processes) is collapsed into the behavioural domain of personal discipline. This misread locks them into the **wrong paradigm**: command-and-control rather than systemic integrity. Without conducting a layered inquiry, the assumption hardens into 'truth'.

As a result, **distortion detection never takes place**. The incongruence – that deadlines were missed because requirements kept shifting from upper management – is ignored. The distortion is not in the team's effort, but in the system itself. Still, the manager cannot see it.

This blindness prevents any **structural reorientation**. Instead of updating their story ('perhaps our process is broken'), the manager doubles down on the old one. They respond by tightening rules and introducing more surveillance, convinced this is the way forward.

Because **meta-awareness is recursive**, it should also track whether awareness itself is becoming biased or self-justifying. But in this case, that fails too. The manager never notices that their thinking is caught in a closed loop. Every new sign is interpreted as confirmation: 'See, I need control because things go wrong when I let go.'

The **consequences cascade**. At the level of meaning-making, lateness becomes proof of human unreliability. At the level of decision-making, harsher deadlines and punitive measures are imposed. At the level of actions and behaviour, micromanagement, public scolding and withdrawal of trust follow. Eventually, team morale collapses, creativity evaporates, turnover rises and the very delays the manager feared multiply.

Here, the absence of meta-awareness doesn't just distort private perception. It flows outward, shaping meaning, decisions, actions and, ultimately, the surrounding system in profoundly dysfunctional ways.

Topology of meta-awareness

The topology of meta-awareness reveals the dynamic interplay between the seven anatomical layers, including the underlying context. These are not isolated states; they continuously influence one another. Coherence or incoherence in one layer reverberates across the entire system.

Abductive given ↔ Cognitive map

If initial impressions are immediately mapped into rigid frameworks, bias becomes embedded. But if impressions are held with humility, maps can be refined rather than reinforced.

Cognitive map ↔ Stories

When cognitive maps are distorted, the stories we tell ourselves become tools of justification rather than instruments of healing. Coherent cognitive maps, however, allow the narrative to evolve rather than entrench.

Stories ↔ Mental models

Emotional narratives often harden into automated behavioural patterns. But when stories are examined, mental models can be updated. This feedback loop allows for the transformation of deeply held assumptions and behavioural patterns.

Mental models ↔ Perspective

Unexamined mental models lock perspective. They produce tunnel vision. But when meta-awareness questions the logic beneath the behaviour, new perspectives emerge and options begin to open up.

Perspective ↔ Domain

If a person cannot shift their perspective across domains or contexts, they risk appearing principled in one area and hypocritical in another. Meta-awareness reconciles these tensions, allowing for integrative coherence.

Domain ↔ Paradigm

Each domain tends to operate within a dominant paradigm. But when meta-awareness becomes active, paradigms are no longer assumed. Instead, they are seen and acknowledged. This allows for cross-paradigmatic flexibility and ethical consistency.

By paying attention to these interrelationships, meta-awareness sustains its central function: preventing collapse into reactivity and enabling coherent responses across complex situations and issues. It makes the invisible architecture of meaning visible and, therefore, modifiable.

Emergent qualities and patterns

Meta-awareness is not a luxury for philosophers or therapists. It is a structural force for navigating modern life. It governs whether we interpret reality or distort it, sustain systems or sabotage them, evolve with coherence or entrench ourselves in confusion.

When meta-awareness is integrated across all seven layers (including the underlying context), the following are among the structural qualities that typically emerge:

- **Discernment** – The ability to detect subtle distortions in thought, action or perception before they cause systemic rupture.
- **Cognitive flexibility** – The capacity to shift between perspectives, domains and paradigms without collapsing into confusion or dogma.
- **Epistemic humility** – A deep recognition of the limits of one's own lens, allowing for curiosity and receptivity.
- **Structural coherence** – Awareness becomes intentionally architected rather than accidental. Meaning-making becomes layered, not reactive.
- **Resilience in times of complexity** – Systems can adapt without losing themselves. Individuals respond without betraying their core values.

However, when meta-awareness is absent or fragmented, the following patterns often emerge:

- **Cognitive rigidity** – Fixation on a single perspective, cognitive map or story, even in the face of contradictory evidence.
- **Emotional reactivity** – Over-identification with early-stage interpretations, like gut instincts and personal narratives.
- **Compartmentalisation** – Operating by conflicting principles across different domains, resulting in systemic hypocrisy.
- **Paradigmatic entrenchment** – Unconscious allegiance to inherited paradigms or modes of thinking. This blocks innovation and inhibits the development of authentic awareness, ethical clarity, conscious responsiveness, ontological orientation and coherent, context-sensitive discernment.
- **Resistance to feedback** – Inability to integrate feedback due to perceived threats to self-image or intellectual certainty.

Meta-awareness in action

The following scenarios illustrate how meta-awareness – or its absence – manifests in individuals, teams and institutions, shaping perception, coherence and long-term sustainability.

Case 1: The conviction-driven CEO

A high-growth startup founder is admired for her decisiveness and clarity. She is deeply committed to her mission and communicates with unwavering certainty. But behind closed doors, her executive team walks on eggshells. Several initiatives fail, not because the strategy was flawed, but because dissenting views were subtly discouraged. One senior hire resigns, citing 'a culture of closed mindedness' as the reason for leaving.

Insight: The founder had a strong cognitive map and compelling story, but lacked awareness of how her paradigm filtered what she could take in and recognise as valid input. Her early impressions (abductive givens) were rarely interrogated and instead routed through a narrow interpretive lens. Meta-awareness was bypassed. Without recognising how her cognitive map filtered reality, she misread feedback as resistance and missed critical signals. The result was costly – not because of bad intention, but because of unexamined layers in the meta-awareness sense-making process and the cultural context of a startup environment that amplified decisiveness over dissent.

Case 2: The organisational chameleon

A multinational corporation proudly displays its values: inclusivity, transparency and care. In HR workshops, leaders speak eloquently about psychological safety. But across different departments (domains), those values fracture. In sales, aggression is rewarded. In marketing, messaging is shaped more by image than integrity. In compliance and legal affairs, silence is the protocol. Employees describe the culture as 'inconsistent and hypocritical' – constantly changing to meet external expectations while eroding internal coherence.

Insight: The organisation suffered from domain-level fragmentation. While the story and perspective in one domain were coherent, they contradicted how awareness was structured elsewhere. There was no governing meta-awareness bridging across domains or paradigms. The result was a system that appeared aligned in some areas, but was structurally divided beneath the surface. Employees learned to perform the organisation's values selectively, leading to distrust, attrition and cynical compliance as the wider corporate context rewarded performance over integrity.

Case 3: Mistaking insight for integration

A therapy client repeatedly enters relationships that begin with intensity and collapse with blame. In therapy, she speaks with great insight about attachment theory and past trauma. She identifies her triggers and recounts stories with emotional intelligence. Yet she continues to sabotage closeness. The therapist notices that while the client is fluent in reflective vocabulary, something is missing.

Insight: The client had cultivated awareness at the level of story and cognitive map, but lacked meta-awareness. Her initial impression of others – her abductive givens – were unconsciously fused with past trauma. Beneath her reflective insight, silent mental models were still at work: assumptions like 'if I am vulnerable, I will be betrayed'. Because she equated psychological insight with transformation, she could not see how her sense-making architecture remained unchanged. Progress began, not through gaining more insight, but by interrogating how her awareness itself had been constructed within the relational contexts that continually reactivated her trauma-based models.

Each of these cases illustrates a different form of distortion: rigid confidence mistaken for clarity, compartmentalised integrity mistaken for nuance and narrative insight mistaken for transformation. In all three, the absence of meta-awareness allowed initial impressions, unexamined models or paradigmatic blind spots to govern behaviour.

The result is always the same: organisations and institutions perform in the short term, but erode under pressure. Individuals feel stuck. Leaders overestimate their coherence. And culture becomes a mask for unresolved contradictions.

When meta-awareness becomes active, these patterns don't disappear; they become *visible*. And once seen, they can be redesigned.

Conclusion

Meta-awareness is not a practice, trait or personality type. It is a structural faculty: an ontological capacity that governs how meaning is formed, perception is filtered and coherence is maintained or lost across time, domains and paradigms. In complex systems, including human beings, it is not just useful; it is essential.

Without meta-awareness, individuals mistake intuition for truth, confidence for clarity and inherited assumptions for wisdom. Leaders operate from partial awareness and scale their blind spots into strategy. Organisations respect and adhere to their values in one domain while contradicting them in another. And entire institutions become trapped in paradigms that once served them, but which now suffocate their evolution.

In contrast, when meta-awareness is integrated into the architecture of Being and system design, perception becomes layered, not reactive. Distortion becomes detectable. Adjustment becomes possible without collapse. Truth becomes less about control and more about calibration. This is what makes authentic sustainability viable – not just in action, but in sense-making itself.

This chapter has unpacked meta-awareness through its context, ontological distinction, anatomy (the seven nested layers of sense-making and their underlying context) and its recursive mechanics and topology. We have seen that meta-awareness is not simply awareness of thoughts or feelings. It is the systemic intelligence that observes how those thoughts and feelings are constructed, contextualised and acted upon.

Ultimately, meta-awareness is not about becoming endlessly introspective or philosophically frozen. It is about becoming architecturally lucid – able to witness how your own structure of awareness is shaping reality and how that structure can evolve. In the absence of meta-awareness, systems drift. However, in its presence, they become self-correcting. And in a world saturated with noise, urgency, ideology and performance, the ability to see how you see is no longer a luxury. It is the compass of coherence.

Reflection

- In moments of tension or certainty, do you pause to examine how your sense-making is being shaped?
- Can you identify a time when your initial impression (abductive given) turned out to be distorted, but you acted on it anyway? What was the cost?
- Are there familiar stories or beliefs you tend to fall back on that may no longer support clarity or alignment? What assumptions might be quietly driving them?
- Do you notice any contradictions in how you show up across different domains of life – such as work, family, politics or spirituality? What might these inconsistencies reveal about the structure of your metacontent and the degree of meta-awareness (composed of the seven nested layers) shaping your engagement in each domain?
- Are you aware of the paradigms that govern your perception of truth, value and legitimacy? How consciously have you chosen them and when were they last questioned?
- In the way you lead, relate and reflect, how do you create space for meta-awareness – not just as a personal habit, but as a guiding structure that shapes how you engage in life and with others?

CHAPTER 27

Systemic Integrity

Integrity is often spoken of as a personal trait: being honest, consistent or morally upright. But in an ontological sense, integrity is not confined to character. It is a condition of structural coherence. And all coherent things – whether a person, a relationship, an organisation, a culture or a nation – are systems. They operate through layered interdependencies. They act, adapt, influence and endure – or they don't.

Systemic integrity refers to the state of alignment within any such system. It is not just about whether someone means well or whether a process works in isolation. It is about whether the deeper structure – the interwoven design of intention, architecture, action and impact – holds together without inconsistency, contradiction or a lack of trust.

When a person claims to value intimacy but withholds vulnerability, there is a fracture. When a team rewards collaboration but promotes competition, there is a fault line. When an institution espouses transparency but punishes dissent, it loses coherence. When a society declares equality but builds policies that entrench hierarchy, it erodes its foundation. These are not just behavioural inconsistencies. They are breakdowns in systemic integrity.

Incoherence at this level might not be immediately visible. The system could still function. It might even appear successful. But underneath, contradictions accumulate. Trust wears thin, feedback becomes dangerous, culture fragments. And when pressure arrives – when complexity spikes or a crisis hits – the lack of alignment shows itself, not as a glitch, but as collapse.

This is why systemic integrity belongs in the overarching Architectonic Sphere. It is a foundational condition for any system to be sustainable, regenerative and trustworthy. Systemic integrity determines whether a system can evolve without fracturing, adapt without betrayal and operate without undermining its own foundations.

In the Unified Ontology of Systemic Integrity, this quality is not moralistic. It is architectural. It examines whether a system's declared purpose, internal structure, enacted behaviour and actual impact are in alignment – not occasionally, but consistently across time and through multiple layers. The core question is: can this system be counted on? Not because it has integrity in a conventional ethical sense, but because it is structurally coherent.

Where systemic integrity is alive, systems of all scales earn trust by design. They can be challenged without falling apart. They can adjust without losing themselves. And they generate confidence, not just in people, but in the coherence of how things are held together.

Without it, all systems – personal and collective – eventually undermine themselves.

Ontological Distinction of Systemic Integrity

Systemic integrity is the quality that enables a system to generate coherence, reliability and sustainability. A system can be an individual, a relationship, a family, a team, an organisation, a government, a movement or even a civilisation. At its most personal level, it includes the integrity of one's own Being – the alignment and coherence that make a person whole, in optimal condition and trustworthy. More broadly, *systemic integrity* exists when each part of a system is in its rightful place and there is consistency, interconnectedness and coherence between the purpose the system serves, how it is structured or co-created, what it does, and the impact it creates. It applies at every scale – from the way you organise your own life to the way societies and institutions sustain coherence. At its core, *systemic integrity* is the alignment of purpose, structure, behaviour and outcomes in a way that endures, adapts and regenerates into possible new evolutions over time.

A **healthy relationship with systemic integrity** indicates attentiveness and responsiveness to generating ongoing alignment. You recognise that sustaining systemic integrity requires more than intention – it calls for the continual alignment of your actions with your values. You actively and frequently check whether the way you live your life reflects your intentions, whether your actions match your claims and whether your impact strengthens rather than undermines your values. When misalignment occurs, it is named and corrected rather than ignored or rationalised. Others experience you as trustworthy and coherent. You generate confidence because you are responsive, self-correcting and both able and willing to adapt when circumstances change. The same holds true for larger systems – in relationships, organisations and institutions, systemic integrity fosters transparency, coherence and adaptability, building trust and interconnection that can endure over time.

An **unhealthy relationship with systemic integrity** indicates that you tend to be fragmented, inconsistent and contradictory. You may promote values you don't embody, create structures that undermine your stated intentions or produce outcomes that contradict your commitments. Instead of correcting these misalignments, you normalise or justify them, whether consciously or unconsciously. Alternatively, you may become rigid – trying to impose uniformity or control, suppressing adaptability and preventing growth. Over time, both tendencies erode coherence, trust and resilience. Others may experience you as unreliable, untrustworthy or unable to change. The same applies to larger systems – in relationships, organisations and institutions, a lack of systemic integrity results in dysfunction, repeating problems and a gradual breakdown of trust, eventually hardening into entrenchment, where change is resisted until a crisis forces it.

Ontology of systemic integrity

Systemic integrity is not a fixed state, but a living architecture. It governs whether a system can sustain coherence between its purpose, design, action and impact. When this coherence fractures, the system begins to betray itself, even without harmful intent. But when coherence is upheld, trust becomes possible – not because of surface appearances, but because the underlying structure holds. Let's break the ontology down by examining its anatomy, mechanics and topology.

Anatomy of systemic integrity

Systemic integrity lives through four structural dimensions that operate together:

1. **Purpose**

    This is the system's declared reason for being. It could be a personal vision, social mission, cultural principle, constitutional mandate or relational commitment. It defines what the system claims to serve or protect. But declarations alone do not create coherence. They must be embedded in the architecture, culture and lived practice of the system.

2. **Architecture**

    This refers to the structural configuration of the system. It includes governance models, role definitions, processes, policies, agreements, incentives and power dynamics. A system cannot claim to embody justice, care or freedom if its architecture is built on hierarchy, fear or control. The system's architecture reveals what it is designed to serve.

3. **Behaviour**

    This is how the system behaves in practice. It includes actions, cultural norms, rituals, language and day-to-day decisions. Alignment means that behaviour is a faithful expression of the system's purpose and architecture. Misalignment occurs when actions contradict what the system claims to be.

4. **Impact**

This is the outcome of what the system does and its impact on people, ecosystems, culture and future generations. It includes both intended and unintended consequences. A system's integrity cannot be measured simply by what it aims to do. It must also be measured by what it actually produces and whether it is willing to take responsibility for that impact.

All four dimensions – purpose, architecture, behaviour and impact – must be in recursive alignment. If one of them diverges, the whole system begins to lose coherence. Over time, this misalignment compounds into dysfunction.

A tangible example of misoriented systemic integrity

Consider a government that declares its **purpose** as protecting freedom and equality. On paper, this vision sounds noble. Yet its **architecture** is designed around centralised surveillance, opaque decision-making and policies that prioritise elite interests over public accountability. The mismatch between purpose and architecture is the first fracture.

In practice, the **behaviour** of the system drifts further. Citizens are encouraged to speak freely, but those who criticise government policies face subtle forms of punishment – reduced access to services, job insecurity or even legal intimidation. Day-to-day norms signify that conformity is rewarded and dissent is dangerous.

Eventually, the **impact** of the system exposes the depth of the misalignment. Instead of cultivating freedom and equality, the system produces widespread fear, eroded trust and social fragmentation. What it *claims* (purpose) is contradicted by what it is *designed to do* (architecture), what it *actually does* (behaviour) and what people *experience* (impact).

Because the fractures are not acknowledged or corrected, they compound into dysfunction. Citizens perceive hypocrisy and inconsistency, institutions appear untrustworthy and resilience erodes. Over time, the system betrays its own declarations, not necessarily out of bad intent, but because coherence across the four dimensions (purpose, architecture, behaviour and impact) was never upheld.

Mechanics of systemic integrity

Systemic integrity is not sustained by sentiment and intention alone. It is maintained through ongoing structural processes that keep the system honest with itself.

1. **Alignment review**

   This is the continuous practice of assessing whether the system's design, actions and consequences remain faithful to its stated purpose. This is not an audit for compliance. It is an inquiry into congruence. Systems that skip this process tend to drift, often without realising it.

2. **Incoherence detection**

   This involves recognising contradictions within the system, even when they are subtle or socially accepted. A system with integrity is not one without flaws, but one that notices and responds to its misalignments before they become entrenched.

3. **Feedback integration**

   Systemic integrity demands receptivity. Feedback must not be seen as a threat but as structural data. Whether it arises from internal dissent, stakeholder reflection, intimate relationships or public response, a system (human or otherwise) must be equipped to listen and adapt. Suppressed feedback is often the first signal that systemic integrity is under threat.

4. **Structural reconfiguration**

   When misalignment is detected, the system must be capable of structural response. This may include adjusting roles, rewriting policies or protocols, or even revising the founding narrative. Systemic integrity is not preserved by rigidity; it is preserved by the ability to evolve without compromising coherence.

5. **Recursive calibration**

   Systems with integrity regularly revisit their foundational elements. They do not assume alignment; they maintain it.

This includes reflecting on whether their purpose is still valid, whether their structures still serve it, and whether their actions are producing justifiable outcomes.

Topology of systemic integrity

The topology of systemic integrity reveals the reciprocal and interdependent dynamics between its four anatomical dimensions: purpose, architecture, behaviour and impact. Integrity is not achieved in isolation at any layer. It lives in the tension, flow and feedback between them.

Purpose ↔ Architecture

If the design of a system is not born from its declared purpose, then the architecture becomes ornamental or inherited. Systems often claim to stand for care, justice or empowerment while structuring themselves around control, fear or legacy constraints. Form follows function. When purpose drives a system's architecture, structure becomes principled.

Architecture ↔ Behaviour

A system's architectural structure shapes its behaviour. When processes, roles and incentives contradict a system's claimed values, behaviour becomes hypocritical – even if unintentional. People behave according to what is rewarded, not what is declared. Aligned architecture encourages behavioural congruence, while misaligned architecture leads to behavioural incoherence.

Behaviour ↔ Impact

Every behaviour creates an outcome, intended or otherwise. A system's behaviour cannot be divorced from its ripple effects on individuals, communities, ecosystems and future generations. Integrity demands that behaviours be tracked – not just against intention, but against outcome. When behaviours and actions are decoupled from their impact, systems begin to erode trust and accountability.

Impact ↔ Purpose

Over time, impacts either reinforce or challenge a system's original purpose. If outcomes diverge from what was intended, a system with integrity reflects, not deflects. It revisits its purpose, refines its aims and evolves its direction. When this loop is ignored, dogma replaces responsiveness. However, when it is honoured, coherence is sustained.

Across this dynamic topology, systemic integrity is revealed – not in perfection, but in the *capacity to recalibrate*. Each dimension must remain in conversation with the others. When they do, the system becomes adaptive, resilient and trustworthy. But when they don't, the system may continue to function, but not with integrity, and not sustainably.

Emergent qualities and patterns

Systemic integrity is not about perfection. It is about maintaining architectural coherence. It is the quality that allows a system to be more than just the sum of its functions, roles or outcomes. It is what holds trust, ethics and sustainability together – not as hopes, but as sustainably achievable structural conditions.

When systemic integrity is present and active, the following are among the structural qualities that typically emerge:

- **Structural trustworthiness** – People trust the system because its coherence is observable in action, not merely declared or performed.
- **Cultural honesty** – Individuals feel safe to offer feedback and call out any contradictions in the system without fear of punishment.
- **Consistent accountability** – Responsibility does not hide behind good intentions or empty promises.
- **Ethical adaptability** – The system can evolve without abandoning its principles.
- **Long-term resilience** – Coherence allows the system to withstand complexity and disruption without breaking down.

In contrast, when systemic integrity is absent or decaying, dysfunctional patterns emerge, including:

- **Performative ethics** – Values are claimed but not lived.
- **Contradictory design** – The system's architecture enables the very outcomes it claims to oppose.
- **Erosion of trust** – People stop believing in the system because it does not behave as it says it will.
- **Disempowerment and cynicism** – Participants feel alienated, resigned or disengaged.
- **Collapse when challenged** – The system is unable to hold itself together in times of crisis, challenge and complexity.

Systemic integrity in action

To bring the anatomy and mechanics of systemic integrity to life, let's turn our attention to some real-world examples across different types of systems. Each case reveals what happens when coherence is maintained or when it breaks. These are not just stories of failure or success. They are illustrations of how alignment – or misalignment – between purpose, architecture, behaviour and impact sustains trust or accelerates erosion.

Case 1: The misaligned wellness coach

An individual practitioner offers programs on holistic wellbeing and teaches the importance of emotional regulation and relational integrity. She speaks often about boundaries, balance and sustainability. But behind the scenes, she runs her business in a state of constant overwhelm and urgency. Her business model depends on overextending herself, she bypasses uncomfortable conversations with clients, and she ignores her own emotional exhaustion. Over time, she burns out and quietly suspends her offerings, eroding trust and leaving clients confused and angry.

Insight: Although the wellness coach's declared purpose was noble, her internal design – her routines, commitments and business structures – undermined it. Her behaviour reflected performance rather than coherence. And the impact, though unintended, contradicted what she stood for. This is a breakdown in systemic integrity at the level of the individual. The collapse did not come from a place of malice, but from misaligned architecture. Had her inner structures matched her declared values, sustainability, trust and integrity would have been preserved.

Case 2: The 'two-faced' institution

A leading university champions diversity, equity and inclusion across its public communications. It creates marketing campaigns that highlight underrepresented voices, and its senior leadership team frequently speaks on social justice panels. But within its faculty hiring process, non-transparent networks, cultural gatekeeping and subtle biases continue to favour traditional profiles. Students from marginalised backgrounds feel celebrated in brochures, but unsupported in classrooms and policy forums.

Insight: The institution's purpose and language appear progressive, but its structural design and behavioural patterns remain unchanged. There is a gap between purpose and behaviour, and another between behaviour and impact. This incoherence is not just reputational; it is ontological. The university cannot be trusted as a whole because its layers do not align. Until its structures are redesigned and its behaviour is recalibrated in light of real-world outcomes, systemic integrity remains performative.

Case 3: The coherent startup

A technology startup is founded on a commitment to ethical innovation and transparency. Its internal governance is shaped with participatory structures, and its design includes regular alignment reviews that bring every team into meaningful dialogue about how their work connects to the company's mission. When a major client demands an ethically questionable feature in a product, the leadership does not simply reject the request. Instead, they hold an open review process, share their reasoning transparently with staff and co-design an alternative approach with the client. Although some revenue is lost, the long-term trust within and beyond the organisation grows.

Insight: This startup demonstrates systemic integrity. Its stated purpose is embedded in its design. Its behaviour matches its values under pressure. And its outcomes (impact) – both in product and culture – reinforce coherence. The system (startup) is not perfect, but it is honest, adaptive and trustworthy. Here, integrity is not a branding slogan. It is a structure that holds through tension.

These case studies reveal a central truth: systemic integrity is not about avoiding missteps. It is about whether the system is architected to hold coherence, especially when missteps occur. Whether the system is a person, a relationship, a company or an institution, the same principles apply. When purpose, architecture, behaviour and impact align, trust and resilience follow. But where they diverge, disillusionment and reactivity begin to set in, leading to the system's eventual dysfunction and collapse.

Conclusion

Systemic integrity is not an ideal to be admired from afar. It is a lived condition. It determines whether a person, team, organisation or culture is structurally coherent – or merely performing coherence while disintegrating from within.

As a foundational force within the Architectonic Sphere, systemic integrity is not a sentimental notion of goodness, nor is it compliance or branding. It is the structural alignment between what a system says it stands for and how it is designed, how it behaves and its impact.

Integrity, in this deeper sense, cannot be faked – at least not for long. It cannot be compensated for by charisma, intention or optics. When it is absent, even the most talented individuals and visionary strategies eventually falter. But when it is present, systems develop a kind of inner gravity. People can feel the coherence, even if they cannot immediately explain it.

Under the weight of complex demands and high-speed decision-making, the temptation to trade alignment for short-term gain is constant. But the cost is always the same: erosion of trust, fragmentation of purpose and, ultimately, collapse. The breakdown often comes slowly at first, disguised by functionality. Until one day, the system can no longer hold itself together.

But when integrity is built into the very design of the system, it does not need to be managed; it becomes self-sustaining. Feedback is welcomed, correction becomes natural and action becomes trustworthy – not because everyone agrees, but because coherence can be counted on.

This is the work of stewardship. To not only stand for values, but to establish the right structure for them. To not only declare a purpose, but to enact it. To not only seek good outcomes, but to track whether those outcomes honour the original intention or betray it.

Where systemic integrity is alive, systems don't just perform well; they become worthy of trust. They hold their shape under pressure. And they do not collapse the moment scrutiny arrives. Because they are not held together by image. They are held together by coherence.

Reflection

- In what areas of your life or leadership have you noticed a gap between what is stated as important and what is actually reinforced or enacted?
- Can you identify a time when the design or structure of a system you were part of undermined its declared purpose? What was the impact?
- Where in your organisation, community or culture is feedback discouraged, ignored or punished, even when the system claims to value learning or transparency?
- Do the consequences of your decisions, actions or strategies consistently align with your deeper intentions? What might be going unnoticed or unmeasured?
- When misalignment is discovered – whether in yourself, a relationship or at work – how is it addressed? Is there a structure for recalibration, or is it left to chance?
- If someone were to observe your behaviour and the impact of your actions when spending time with your intimate partner or family, without hearing any of your declared values, what would they conclude you stand for?

CHAPTER 28

Sustained Effectiveness

Effectiveness is often measured by whether an individual or a collective produces their intended results. Within the Being Framework, effectiveness is the capacity to translate intention into impact – to fulfil objectives and bring outcomes to life. It is revealed in those moments of impact where intention translates into tangible results that take hold in reality.

But effectiveness is not only about isolated moments. With sustained effectiveness, *longevity* comes into play. Impact is not measured in dots, but in the lines they form – sequences that show whether results are consistent, durable and capable of evolving over time.

When you are effective, you produce results with power and flow. When you are not, your efforts feel stalled, misdirected or overwhelmed. This is not limited to individuals. The same applies to the larger systems we create and inhabit: teams, organisations, governments and even societies. Effectiveness – and especially sustained effectiveness – depends on how we, both personally and collectively, engage with the qualities that generate coherence. Within the Being Framework, all 16 Primary Ways of Being contribute to effectiveness, but it is sustained effectiveness that determines whether our impact endures or fragments.

Most importantly, sustained effectiveness considers a deeper question. Instead of simply asking whether results are achieved, it also asks – can they continue, adapt and remain coherent over time? A person can be effective yet burn out. A team may complete a project, but collapse from internal dysfunction. A movement may gain momentum, yet fracture under pressure. Sustained effectiveness is not just about performance – it is the *sustainability of performance*, ensuring results endure without eroding the people or larger systems that generate them.

Many individuals and collectives have achieved greatness at the cost of sustainability. They perform impressively, but damage their relationships, health or the trust others place in them. Some become so consumed by their vision that they lose their sense of proportion. Others produce outcomes, but leave behind trails of disconnection, attrition or abandonment. In these cases, effectiveness is temporary, conditional or extractive. It works until it stops working, then leaves a mess behind.

Sustained effectiveness exists when performance does not come at the cost of the system itself. It is when the process of achieving does not consume the very capacities that make achievement possible. It is marked by an ability to fulfil intentions repeatedly and responsibly, while remaining attuned to wellbeing, coherence, relationships and longevity. This kind of effectiveness builds trust, creates more capacity than it consumes and invites others along for the journey. Consequently, it is essential for all systems, from individuals, relationships and teams to organisations, communities, cultures and institutions. It applies to a founder launching a venture, a family navigating complexity, a government delivering services and a global initiative seeking real change. In each case, the question is not just: Are we getting results? It's: Are we getting results we can stand by, sustain and evolve with?

Sustained effectiveness is not the opposite of ambition. It is its *maturation*. It is ambition that includes care. It is impact that respects rhythm. It is success that can still look itself in the mirror 10 years later. In the Architectonic Sphere, sustained effectiveness represents the design-level condition where effectiveness is not episodic or extractive, but enduring and structurally intelligent.

Ontological Distinction of Sustained Effectiveness

Sustained effectiveness is the quality that enables a system – whether a person, team, organisation, institution or society – to reliably fulfil its intentions without exhausting or undermining its capacity to continue doing so. Where effectiveness is about producing results and maintaining momentum in the present, *sustained effectiveness* ensures that this momentum endures without eroding the very conditions that make future effectiveness possible. It is effectiveness that produces results in ways that preserve, regenerate and even strengthen the conditions needed for future performance. *Sustained effectiveness* delivers impact that does not deplete the system, but protects its wellbeing, rhythm and coherence, ensuring effective performance can be sustained over time.

A **healthy relationship with sustained effectiveness** indicates that you achieve outcomes that are not only workable but regenerative. Instead of simply chasing targets, you maintain a balance between immediate demands and long-term capacity, between different influences and forces at play, and you choose priorities with discernment – focusing on what genuinely serves purpose and coherence rather than what is merely urgent or convenient. You recognise that burnout is not achievement, that alienating people for the sake of progress is not progress, and that sacrificing effectiveness tomorrow to deliver today is self-sabotage. Others experience you – or the systems you are part of – as both productive and sustainable. People and other systems with this quality create value while preserving their own vitality, capacity and trust.

An **unhealthy relationship with sustained effectiveness** indicates that you pursue success without regard for sustainability. Results may be delivered through overextension, coercion or short-term thinking. You may override your own limits to prove yourself, while organisations and institutions may drive results at the cost of attrition, disengagement or ethical compromise. Alternatively, you or the systems you engage with may cling to continuity so tightly that necessary risks or change are avoided. In each case, effectiveness may appear present on the surface, but underneath, the system is corroding, trading long-term viability for short-term gain. People and other systems without this quality eventually lose their vitality, capacity and the trust needed to sustain performance.

Ontology of sustained effectiveness

At the ontological level, sustained effectiveness is not defined by the volume of output nor by bursts of performance under pressure. It is defined by the *structural soundness* of a system that can remain functional, generative and coherent across time.

Anatomy of sustained effectiveness

Its anatomy comprises three interrelated elements:

1. **Cohesion**

   Sustainable effectiveness demands more than bold visions or clear strategies. It requires cohesion between a system's ideals and its methods: between what it claims to value and how it actually operates. When there is misalignment between vision and means, cracks emerge. A company that preaches empowerment yet thrives on micromanagement eventually breeds distrust. A person who yearns for intimacy but avoids vulnerability will stall in contradiction. True cohesion is not surface-level harmony. It is the structural integrity between purpose and practice.

2. **Reciprocity**

   Sustained effectiveness requires more than good intentions. It demands ongoing reciprocity between intention and capacity. Not every goal is viable at every moment, and pushing ahead without the necessary bandwidth, resources or relational stability can create collapse instead of progress. The anatomy of reciprocity here is a systemic check-in: Do we have the inner and outer capacity to pursue this intention in this way and at this pace? Or are we projecting an aspiration or desire without grounding it in reality?

3. **Regeneration**

Structural regeneration sets sustained effectiveness apart from effectiveness more than any other structural element. A system that performs, but depletes itself physically, emotionally, relationally or ethically, is unsustainable by definition. Structural regeneration includes the built-in ability to recover, reflect, rest and recompose.

Together, these structural elements are not merely technical; they are ontological. They speak to the way a person, team, organisation or institution *is being* in relation to its ambitions.

A tangible example of misoriented sustained effectiveness

Consider a fast-growing technology start-up. On the surface, it appears effective: products are shipped quickly, investment is raised and media attention grows. Yet beneath the surface, each structural element of sustained effectiveness is misaligned.

At the level of **cohesion**, the company claims empowerment and innovation as its purpose, but its methods rely on rigid hierarchies, micromanagement and fear-driven deadlines. What it declares and what it practises drift apart. Employees hear the rhetoric of trust, but live the reality of control. Over time, the crack widens – distrust festers, creativity withers and innovation dries up.

At the level of **reciprocity**, leadership sets ambitious targets without checking whether the organisation has the capacity – financial, human or relational – to sustain them. Instead of aligning intention with capacity, aspiration is projected without ground. Promises to investors and customers outpace reality, and the result is exhaustion, burnout and collapsing morale.

At the level of **regeneration**, the culture treats rest as weakness and reflection as a distraction. Mistakes are brushed aside, ethical shortcuts become routine and the system depletes itself with each cycle. There is no built-in capacity to recover, recompose or adapt.

Taken together, the anatomy of sustained effectiveness unravels. What appears as effectiveness in the short term is actually unsustainable momentum. Purpose and practice lose cohesion, intention and capacity fall out of reciprocity and, without regeneration, the structure erodes. Eventually, what looked like success reveals itself as burnout, incoherence and collapse.

Mechanics of sustained effectiveness

The mechanics of sustained effectiveness differ fundamentally from brute-force productivity models that rely on willpower, sacrifice or unrelenting drive. They operate through feedback, recalibration and thoughtful modulation of pace and priority.

1. **Self-renewal**

    Systems designed for sustainability embed mechanisms that replenish what is being spent. For individuals, this may mean sleep, rest and recovery; for teams, it might be debriefs and retrospectives; for collectives, sabbaticals or intentional pauses. This is not leisure for leisure's sake. It is structural regeneration, restoring the system at its core so it can continue to function with sustained effectiveness.

2. **Responsive adaptation**

    A system cannot be sustained if it cannot evolve. Systems that rely on rigid operating models or unexamined routines eventually lose touch with their environment. Sustained effectiveness arises from a rhythm of continual attunement – not chaotic change but deliberate evolution.

3. **Prioritisation**

    Not all commitments are equal. Systems that try to optimise for everything collapse into noise. Sustained effectiveness requires a disciplined relationship with trade-offs. What matters now? What can wait? What must be stopped altogether? Prioritisation – with integrity – is the refusal to confuse motion with meaning.

4. **Integration**

Effective systems embed the pursuit of sustainability into their processes. It is not a separate initiative. It is how things are done. Hiring, communication, delegation, performance reviews – all of these are expressions of the system's mechanics. When the pursuit of sustainability is effectively integrated within the system's processes, they reinforce rhythm and coherence. But when it is not effectively integrated, those same processes – regardless of how effective they may seem – drain energy and introduce fragmentation and dysfunction.

Topology of sustained effectiveness

The topology of sustained effectiveness reveals the dynamic interplay between its three anatomical components: cohesion, reciprocity and regeneration. These dimensions do not function in isolation. When one is neglected or misaligned, a system may still appear effective, but its impact won't endure. In other words, the effectiveness won't be *sustained*. The interrelationships between cohesion, reciprocity and regeneration form the deep architecture that either reinforces or erodes long-term effectiveness.

Cohesion ↔ Reciprocity

Cohesion ensures that values and practices align. But without reciprocity – where intention is balanced with capacity – cohesion collapses into brittle idealism. Systems may overextend in pursuit of coherence by failing to assess whether the energy, resources or conditions truly support their goals. When balanced together, these components ground vision in reality, enabling integrity of purpose to be pursued sustainably.

Reciprocity ↔ Regeneration

Reciprocity maintains the feedback loop between what is desired and what is possible. Yet without regeneration, even well-paced intentions will eventually exhaust the system. Regeneration ensures that capacity is not merely respected but continuously renewed. This relationship protects the system's rhythm, enabling performance without depletion.

Regeneration ↔ Cohesion

Regeneration without cohesion can lead to comfort without direction – systems may recover, but then they drift. Cohesion brings direction and meaning to structural regeneration, ensuring the system isn't just healing, but healing *towards* something. This relationship prevents sustainability from becoming inertia by aligning replenishment with purposeful evolution.

Emergent qualities and patterns

Sustained effectiveness rests on a single insight: power without restoration becomes extraction, and success without renewal leads to breakdown. Ultimately, sustained effectiveness is not a sprint. It is a rhythm that allows the system to keep showing up – whole and capable – over time.

When sustained effectiveness is present, a number of distinctive qualities begin to emerge – not through command or control, but as natural expressions of the system's structure. They include:

- **Enduring trust** – People begin to trust the process rather than just the outcomes. They know that the system (such as an organisation) would never exploit them to hit targets. Knowing this builds loyalty, openness and psychological safety – not through optics and slogans, but through consistency.
- **Flow with awareness** – There is a sense of momentum that doesn't feel manic. Individuals are not constantly swinging between burnout and boredom. There is rhythm: pulses of focused energy followed by integration and recovery. The flow feels alive, not coerced.
- **Meaningful accountability** – Because the system values sustainability, accountability is not used as a threat. It is shared, contextualised and aimed towards progress, not punishment. The system doesn't pretend perfection; it corrects with humility and clarity.
- **Creative regeneration** – The presence of sustained effectiveness makes room for creativity. People are not too

exhausted to think clearly or too pressured to take risks. Curiosity has room to re-emerge. Consequently, innovation becomes possible, not just as a department, but as a cultural mode.
- **Quiet confidence** – This is perhaps the most subtle yet profound emerging quality of sustained effectiveness. Systems (including human beings) that embody sustained effectiveness tend to exude a quiet confidence. They are not boastful or fragile, but deeply grounded. They do not need constant validation. They simply work, grow and evolve without pushing beyond what is sustainable.

In contrast, when sustained effectiveness is absent, systems may still *appear* successful – until they fracture. Performance may be visible, but decay is already underway.

Sustained effectiveness in action

The following real-world scenarios expose how effectiveness either flourishes over time or becomes self-defeating. Each case demonstrates what happens when systems produce results in a way that either preserves their sustained effectiveness or corrodes it.

Case 1: The heroic founder trap

A passionate entrepreneur launches a social enterprise with a bold vision and tireless energy. In the first two years, she exceeds every target. She works 12-hour days, does the job of three people and personally handles every crisis. Revenue grows. Awards come. But internally, team members are anxious, decision-making is reactive and no one feels empowered to lead. Within three years, the founder burns out. Key staff leave. Promises are broken. Momentum vanishes.

Insight: This is a classic case of short-term but unsustainable effectiveness. Although the founder was effective on the surface, she had not established any structures for regeneration, shared responsibility or rhythm. The organisation was high-performing, but structurally brittle. Without mechanisms for continuity, even brilliance becomes temporary.

Case 2: The corporate mirage

A multinational proudly publishes its record-breaking quarterly results. Bonuses are paid. Investors celebrate. But inside, teams are stretched thin. Every success comes at the expense of sleep, trust and psychological safety. Middle managers absorb pressure from above and pass it down. Attrition quietly increases. Innovation slows. A few years later, the company is acquired – not because it failed, but because it lost its soul and could no longer regenerate talent or momentum.

Insight: The company achieved its short-term objectives, but ignored the cost of its success. It delivered results through unsustainable effort, gradually exhausting the very systems and people it relied on. Without mechanisms for renewal – such as realistic pacing, honest feedback and a culture that supports learning and wellbeing – it could not sustain performance over time. Sustained effectiveness is not just about hitting targets, but about building the capacity to do so again and again without burning out your people. That's true effectiveness.

Case 3: The rhythmically effective team

A healthcare nonprofit operates under relentless demand. But instead of pushing harder, the leadership team builds a cadence of intensity and rest. Work sprints are followed by reflection periods. Staff have clear roles and autonomy. When overload emerges, the team doesn't blame; they adjust their structure. Projects are paused when necessary, not forced through. After five years, the organisation has doubled in size, maintained its impact and kept its founding team intact with energy, clarity and shared purpose.

Insight: This team embodies sustained effectiveness. They deliver consistently, not by pushing harder, but by designing rhythm, feedback loops and replenishment into their architecture. Their effectiveness is not reactive. It is designed to endure.

These case studies reflect a simple truth: effectiveness is not impressive if it cannot be repeated. It is not ethical if it requires sacrifice beyond repair. And it is not sustainable if it cannot survive its own success. The question is no longer whether a system is effective; it's whether it can remain effective without collapsing under the weight of its own demands.

Conclusion

Sustained effectiveness is not a motivational ideal; it is a structural condition. It emerges when the architecture of a system – whether personal or collective – allows energy to flow without depleting its source. It is not measured by bursts of brilliance or temporary wins. It is measured by the system's ability to deliver, recover, adapt and deliver again without collapsing, disengaging or undermining its own integrity.

This quality invites deeper questions: not just can we perform, but can we keep performing without collapsing into dysfunction or decay? Can we pursue excellence without breeding resentment? Can we scale without splintering? Can we produce without extracting what we cannot replace or restore?

To be sustainably effective is to honour rhythm, respect limitation and design for longevity. It is to be powerful without becoming toxic, reliable without becoming rigid and to grow without losing integrity.

Amid today's obsession with peak performance, sustained effectiveness asks a quieter question: Can you still do this well five years from now without losing yourself or those around you? And beyond that, can the system you've built continue to be effective long after you're gone? If not, then it isn't truly effective.

Reflection

- Where in your life or work have you prioritised short-term results at the expense of long term effectiveness? What have been the consequences?
- When you reflect on your team, organisation or personal routines, are they structured to support consistent, healthy performance? Or are they built on cycles of urgency and burnout?
- How do you personally relate to recovery, rest and rhythm? Do you honour these as vital aspects of effectiveness?
- Have there been moments when you delivered powerful outcomes, but felt secretly depleted, resentful or disconnected

in the process? What enabled that pattern, and what might interrupt it?

- What does sustained effectiveness mean to you, not just professionally, but relationally and existentially?

CHAPTER 29

Normativity

Effectiveness without direction risks becoming destructive. Systems – whether individuals, relationships, teams, organisations or institutions – are not just defined by what they do, but by what they sanction, normalise and refuse to question. Normativity is the compass beneath the performance, the orientation beneath the motion. It determines not only *what* is done, but *why* it is done, *how* and to *what end*.

When people speak of success, they often mean output. But the more important questions are: Success by whose standard? Measured against what deeper vision of wellbeing, justice or meaning? Over what timeframe? And at what cost? These are normative questions. And when they are unexamined, the result is not neutrality; it is drift. Systems begin to replicate whatever is rewarded, celebrated or simply tolerated, regardless of whether those outcomes are humane, sustainable or coherent.

Normativity does not mean enforcing rigid moral codes or compliance through fear. It means living, working and designing with a felt and shared sense of *what ought to be* – even when it is costly, inconvenient or slows down performance in the short term. It is not the opposite of effectiveness; it is what prevents effectiveness from degenerating into obsession, addiction or self-erasure.

Consider the individual who produces remarkable results at work, yet secretly resents the environment that demands their constant overextension. Or the founder who builds a hyper-growth company, but in doing so, destroys the very relationships and wellbeing that once gave their vision meaning. Or the leader who scales an organisation through manipulation and charisma, all while hollowing out the cultural and ethical spine of the system. In each of these cases, effectiveness is visible on the surface, but beneath it, normativity is absent and structural effectiveness is already beginning to erode.

This chapter invites us to see that normativity is not an accessory to strategy or performance. It is a structural condition. It shapes what is considered valuable, admirable or shameful. It defines the horizon towards which energy is directed and the boundaries within which decisions are made. Normativity is not just about what you do when things are going well. It is revealed in where you refuse to compromise when things get hard.

Why normativity matters

Normativity is not a licence for the old adage that the 'end justifies the means'. Nor does it mean that fields like science are free from ethical responsibility just because their methods aim for neutrality. Every academic institution recognises this in practice. When a researcher designs their questions and methods, an ethics committee stands in the background. The foundation of that ethical framework may be debated endlessly, but the necessity of its presence is unquestionable. Normativity matters. It includes ethics, but is not limited to it.

Before any scientific endeavour can proceed, certain belief structures must already be in place. As explored in the science chapter of *Metacontent*,[72] there are normative commitments that precede discovery itself. Consider the following:

- A researcher must believe that there is a layer of reality beyond what she or anyone else thinks. We do not need to call this 'objective reality' in the strict sense. But unless there

---

[72] Tashvir, A. (2024) *Metacontent: The Intellectual Substrates for Sense-making*. Sydney. Engenesis, Chapter 5: Science.

is some conviction that reality extends beyond personal perception, research loses all purpose. Without this, why discover anything at all? Why regard any scientific finding as more valid than personal preference? This conviction is not scientific; it is philosophical.

- A researcher must also believe that a significant proportion of this reality is comprehensible to the human mind. To pursue science assumes that our nervous systems and cognitive capacities can – at least in part – grasp what is to be discovered. This is not purely empirical. After all, we don't even know what we are looking for at the start. It is a philosophical, even metaphysical, leap of faith.
- To undertake science at all presumes that doing so is either 'good' or at least 'valuable'. The moment we call it good, we step into the realm of ethics. The moment we call it valuable, we enter axiology – the philosophy of value. Why is this pursuit more worthwhile than another? What makes discovery preferable to ignorance? Again, these are not scientific statements but normative ones.
- Once research begins, normative dilemmas multiply. Should data be concealed to protect a hypothesis, or revealed to honour discovery? Should a dataset be included if it risks destabilising the desired outcome? Should findings that contradict the researcher's worldview be published or buried? These are not technical questions; they are ethical ones. Without normativity, the line between discovery and distortion collapses.

In truth, no scientific, organisational or societal endeavour escapes these preconditions. To pretend otherwise is, in itself, a normative choice – one that blinds systems to the hidden architecture already guiding their action. Normativity precedes performance. It is the frame that makes discovery meaningful, leadership trustworthy and systems coherent.

However, normativity is not only a concern for research or academic institutions. It shows up in everyday life and in the running of workplaces, organisations and communities. When a workplace tolerates gossip or burnout because 'that's just the culture here', it is making a normative choice. When a team normalises cutting corners to meet a deadline, or an organisation quietly rewards those who exploit rather than collaborate, those practices embed themselves as the unspoken compass of the system. Equally, when a team chooses to protect wellbeing, even at the cost of short-term output, that too is a normative choice. Families, schools, businesses and governments all live by normative frames, whether they acknowledge them or not. The question is never whether normativity exists – it is whether the norms being cultivated are coherent, humane and worth sustaining.

Without normativity, systems become reactive. They collapse into short-termism. They conflate momentum with meaning. Burnout, exploitation and performative productivity become signs of success rather than symptoms of misalignment. People stop asking what matters, asking only what works instead. Rest becomes laziness. Depth becomes inefficiency. And dissent becomes disloyalty.

Although many of these symptoms also signal a breakdown in sustained effectiveness, the distinction lies in the root cause. Sustained effectiveness focuses on a system's capacity to endure, regenerate and deliver over time. However, normativity speaks to *why* the system endures and *towards what end*. One governs rhythm and resilience; the other governs purpose and ethical direction. The absence of either creates dysfunction. But the absence of normativity, in particular, leaves systems running efficiently, but in the wrong direction.

When normativity is deeply embedded and intentionally cultivated, a different kind of success becomes possible. One that can be lived with, that holds its shape over time and doesn't need to be apologised for later.

While sustained effectiveness ensures that a system can keep functioning without collapse, normativity ensures that it functions in *service of something worth sustaining*. One without the other is incomplete. A machine can run forever and still be pointed in the wrong direction. Normativity is an architectural necessity. And like all architectures, it is already operating within, whether you've named it or not.

Ontological Distinction of Normativity

Normativity is how you and other systems relate to the question of *what ought to be*. It shapes your sense of what should or should not be done, what is worthy or unworthy, what is admirable or unacceptable. It is not a set of ready-made rules, but a deeper orientation that guides how you – and the systems you are part of – form values, choose priorities, define right and wrong and decide what is meaningful. *Normativity* gives direction to your actions and choices. It is what underlies every 'should', every expectation and every framework of ethics, morality, virtue or vice.

A **healthy relationship with normativity** indicates that you treat questions of what ought to be with care, discernment and responsibility. You consider not only whether something can be done, but also whether it *should* be done. You are willing to weigh efficiency against worthiness, results against meaning and outcomes against values. This does not mean rigid certainty. Instead, it means living in committed inquiry, willing to test and refine your principles rather than accept them without question. Others may see you as someone who brings vision, alignment, depth and integrity to decisions because your choices are tethered to what truly matters. In larger systems – whether relationships, organisations, institutions or societies – a healthy relationship with normativity creates shared direction and coherence, grounding decisions in the ongoing question of what ought to be and what truly matters. That way, decisions uphold integrity and create direction that is not only effective but also meaningful.

An **unhealthy relationship with normativity** can show up in various ways. You might cling to inherited codes, traditions or authorities, treating them as unquestionable and suppressing your own discernment. At the opposite extreme, you might reject all standards altogether, floating in indifference where nothing truly matters. Alternatively, you might introduce new codes or principles of normativity that, on the surface, appear to uphold value and integrity but, in practice, undermine a healthy expression of normativity. An example of this would be implementing workplace diversity guidelines that seem inclusive, but place individuals in roles for which they are not adequately qualified, fulfilling diversity quotas while compromising the team's effectiveness and fairness. All three manifestations of an unhealthy relationship with normativity evade responsibility – the first by outsourcing it, the second by dissolving it and the third by disguising distortion as virtue. Without normativity, success can feel hollow, knowledge can be misused and power becomes dangerous. In larger systems like organisations and institutions, the absence of normativity leads to confusion, manipulation or drift, where decisions made lose sight of what ought to be and what truly matters.

Ontology of normativity

Normativity is not about rules; it's about orientation. It speaks to the invisible compass behind every action, reaction, preference and proclamation. To have an unhealthy relationship with normativity is to drift, unguided by any understanding of what is right, worthwhile or just. But to engage normativity authentically is to step into the terrain of discernment, responsibility and the architecture of human value.

The ontology of normativity is composed of five interwoven anatomical components, each a necessary dimension of how value is understood, virtue is cultivated and judgement is exercised.

Anatomy of normativity

1. **Axiology**

    Axiology, or the theory of value, is the philosophical inquiry into what we consider valuable, worthy or good. As the ground from which ethics emerges, it asks *why* something is desirable before asking *whether* it is right. It distinguishes between instrumental value (usefulness), intrinsic value (worth for its own sake) and systemic value (what enhances the whole). Axiology is foundational – it reveals how value itself operates. Every culture, brand, institution and individual expresses an axiology, whether consciously or not. When axiology is confused or shallow, ethics become arbitrary.

2. Values

Values are guiding principles or priorities. They are the practical expressions of axiology in day-to-day life. They shape decision-making, preferences, affiliations and aspirations. Values need not be moral in nature – some are aesthetic, pragmatic or even strategic. A team may value innovation; a family may value harmony. The key is coherence. When our stated values contradict our behaviour, dissonance and dysfunction arise. Mature values emerge from integrated axiology and a clear ethical orientation.

While axiology asks the fundamental *why* of value, values carry those orientations into the *what* in relation to lived practice. The two may appear to overlap, but they operate at different levels of abstraction. Axiology is the reflective ground – the framework that determines why something should matter at all. Values are its translation into priorities and principles that guide choices in real contexts. Without axiology, values risk becoming unexamined preferences. Without values, axiology remains a theory without embodiment.

3. Morality

Morality refers to the internalised and socially reinforced ideas of good and bad that govern behaviour within a group. In other words, it is the cultural and communal codes of right and wrong. Unlike ethics, which is reasoned and often universalised, morality is culturally embedded and emotionally enforced. It is what we call 'conscience', often inherited, sometimes unexamined.

4. Ethics

Ethics is the rational evaluation of right and wrong. It provides the structures for evaluating actions, decisions and intentions through reasoned reflection. It is the systematic pursuit of what ought to be done. Ethics does not merely inherit rules; it interrogates them. It also contextualises morality and exposes contradictions. Ethical systems allow us to evaluate trade-offs, uphold justice and defend or critique norms.

5. Virtue

Virtue is the embodiment of values and ethics through character. It is not about what we do once, but about what we *become* over time. A virtuous person is not simply someone who avoids wrongdoing, but someone whose Being consistently aligns with wisdom, courage, compassion and integrity. Virtue is developed through self-awareness and practice. It is not enforced by rules, but cultivated through reflection and responsiveness.

The ontological counterpoint to virtue is vice. Vice is not simply moral failure. It is habitual disintegration, encompassing traits that, when indulged, erode coherence and harm the self or others. Greed, arrogance, cowardice and envy are not isolated behaviours, but patterns of Being that distort judgement, corrupt relationships and sabotage potential. Vice is sustained when awareness is avoided and impulses, rather than values, become the basis for action.

Together, these structural components form a living ecology. They are not discrete boxes to tick, but dynamic forces shaping every human system, from governance to parenting, leadership to identity. Without normativity, there can be no sustainable progress. It is a necessity for any system that seeks to act with coherence, integrity and purpose.

Yet like any ecology, its vitality depends on a mechanism of ontological responsiveness – the capacity to embody these orientations in the immediacy of choice. *Human Being*[73] first introduced the concept of ontological responsiveness as the ability to consciously and intentionally choose from one's options rather than react from impulse. It is the state in which one can interrupt oneself mid-sentence, pause before acting and align decisions and behaviours with what truly matters.

Placed in the context of normativity, ontological responsiveness functions as the living mechanism that animates axiology, values, morality, ethics and virtue in real time. It ensures that these

---

[73] Tashvir, A. (2022) *Human Being: The Reality Beneath the Facade*. Sydney. Engenesis.

frameworks do not remain abstract, but are continuously embodied where alignment can either be preserved or betrayed. Without this quality, normativity risks becoming theoretical. However, with it, normativity becomes lived.

A tangible example of misoriented normativity

Consider a large corporation that prides itself on innovation and claims to 'make the world a better place'. On the surface, effectiveness is visible: products are launched quickly, revenue grows and the company is praised in the media. Yet underneath, its normative compass is misoriented.

At the level of **axiology**, the company proclaims human wellbeing as its ultimate value, yet in practice it confuses value with profit alone. Worth is measured solely by market share and quarterly returns. Anything that does not serve this narrow metric is dismissed as irrelevant.

At the level of **values**, the company's stated principles of integrity, collaboration and sustainability are contradicted by everyday behaviour. Corners are cut, employees are overworked and partnerships are exploited. The dissonance between declared and enacted values becomes normalised.

At the level of **ethics**, decisions are framed as 'rational' business choices, but ethical reflection is sidelined. Questions of justice, fairness or long-term consequences are ignored. As a result, actions that harm communities or exploit ecosystems are justified as efficient.

At the level of **morality**, the culture rewards those who play along with the dominant story and punishes dissent. Employees who question practices are labelled as 'not a good fit', while loyalty is measured by compliance rather than conscience. Morality becomes a tool of conformity rather than discernment.

At the level of **virtue**, leadership indulges in vices such as arrogance, greed and short-term opportunism. These habits become patterns of Being that distort judgement and corrode trust. What might have been an organisation of courage and wisdom degrades into one of fear and opportunism.

Because **ontological responsiveness** is absent, no one pauses to question the drift. No leader stops to ask, 'Does this align with what we claim to value?' and no mechanism exists to interrupt harmful momentum before it hardens into culture. Without ontological responsiveness, the organisation cannot bring its stated principles into real-time decisions. What looks like effectiveness on the surface is actually drift, where profit is mistaken for value and success for virtue.

In this way, the anatomy of normativity unravels. Axiology is reduced to profit, ethics is bypassed, morality is weaponised, values are hollow and virtue collapses into vice. Over time, the system may continue to function, but it functions in the wrong direction – efficiently delivering outcomes that are incoherent, unsustainable and, ultimately, destructive.

Mechanics of normativity

Normativity does not enforce itself. Its presence – or absence – emerges through the mechanisms by which individuals and systems navigate value, prioritise meaning and make ethical commitments. These are not abstract ideals. They are daily practices, structural rhythms and cognitive-emotional postures that shape how we relate to what is right, fair or worthy.

Where normativity is present, systems do not merely act; they act with intention, discernment and alignment. In contrast, where it is absent, actions may still occur, but they are driven by impulse, inertia, imitation or coercion. The result is disorientation: outcomes without meaning, success without substance and policies without justice.

Below are the key mechanics that make normativity not just a principle, but a lived force:

1. **Ethical deliberation**

   Normative systems are sustained through structured reflection on what ought to be done, not just what can be done. Ethical deliberation involves pausing to examine motives, impacts, alternatives and contradictions. It is a counterforce to reactionary decision-making and a guardian against rationalised harm. In cultures and leadership contexts where ethical deliberation is normalised, questions like 'What's the right thing to do?' are not rare; they are expected.

2. Value calibration

Normative clarity depends on regularly reassessing what is being valued and why. Value calibration prevents drift, where what once mattered is gradually overshadowed by efficiency, optics or convenience. While efficiency has its place, when it becomes the dominant measure of success, it begins to compromise effectiveness and erode value-based decision-making. Without value calibration, teams that once stood for creativity become obsessed with productivity and activists who once cared for justice become consumed by optics. Calibration is not about abandoning values; it's about reassessing their alignment with context, consequences and coherence.

3. Normative modelling

Normativity is contagious. People not only absorb values by instruction; they learn them by observation, imitation and osmosis. Leaders who navigate complexity with integrity, courage and thoughtfulness create permission for others to do the same. Conversely, when those in authority model hypocrisy or moral evasion, disillusionment sets in and normativity decays. Every individual in a system shapes normativity, either by embodying it or by contributing to its decay.

4. Principle-centred prioritisation

Healthy normative mechanics involve making trade-offs anchored in principle, not expediency. Not everything can be optimised at once. Normative systems say no to what violates integrity – even if it's profitable, popular or expedient. They prioritise what matters, not just in the short term, but across timelines and moral arcs – the long-term ethical direction or trajectory that choices contribute to. This involves discipline: choosing what's meaningful over what's easy, what's just over what's strategic.

5. Narrative integration

Normative coherence is strengthened when values and principles are woven into stories, language and shared identity. This goes deeper than branding understood merely as marketing. When branding reflects authentic brand DNA – the lived identification and expression of the organisation – it supports this integration. Importantly, coherence depends on alignment: the brand identity a company projects ('we care') must resonate with the brand image customers and stakeholders experience through their own stories. When internal and external narratives reinforce each other, culture becomes self-stabilising.

6. Accountability

A key mechanic of mature normativity is the ability to hold others – and oneself – accountable, without shame or humiliation. This requires systems where reflection, repair and realignment are possible. In such systems, punishment is not the goal. Integrity is. The presence of accountability structures – boards, peer review, dialogue protocols – sustains normativity. But they only work when accountability is relational, not weaponised.

7. Meta-normative reflection

Healthy normative systems engage in second-order reflection. Instead of simply asking, 'Are we doing the right thing?' they also ask, 'By what standards are we judging rightness?'[74] Meta-normative reflection guards against blind ideology and cultural myopia – the tendency to see one's own cultural norms as universal or sufficient. It allows a system to evolve

---

[74] See Argyris, C. & Schön, D.A., 1996 *Organizational Learning II: Theory, Method, and Practice.* Reading, MA: Addison-Wesley; Argyris, C., 1993 *Knowledge for Action: A Guide to Overcoming Barriers to Organizational Change.* San Francisco: Jossey-Bass. The concept of 'triple-loop learning' is further developed in later organisational learning literature; see for example Tosey, P., Visser, M. & Saunders, M.N.K., 2012 The Origins and Conceptualizations of 'Triple-loop' Learning: A Critical Review. *Management Learning*, 43(3), pp. 291–307.

without collapsing into relativism – the view that all values are equally valid and none can be judged against another. It asks: are our values still valid, relevant, coherent and just? If not, what needs to transform, not just in action but in evaluation?

These mechanics ensure that normativity is not left to chance, inherited blindly or outsourced to policy documents. Instead, they embed normativity into the lived infrastructure of decision-making, culture-building and identity formation.

When normativity is absent, what emerges is not neutrality but drift. In such vacuums, power asserts itself in unexamined ways. Manipulation masquerades as leadership, and although performance may continue, it is unanchored in worth or principle. But when normativity is alive in these mechanics, systems not only act; they orient, discern and elevate. They do not merely function; they *stand for something*.

Topology of normativity

The topology of normativity reveals the systemic interrelations between its constituent layers: axiology, values, morality, ethics and virtue. These are not merely separate disciplines or abstract constructs. They form an integrated ecology that shapes how individuals and societies determine what is right, good, worthy and sustainable. When one element is misaligned, it distorts the entire field of judgement. For instance, when ethics is reduced to compliance with rules, values become hollow slogans, axiology loses its depth and virtue is sidelined into performance. Distortion in one layer ripples across all of them, producing confusion, incoherence or even oppression.

Axiology ↔ Values

Values are the lived expression of axiology. What a society or person deems valuable derives from deeper axiological commitments about what is worthy of pursuit or protection. When axiology is shallow or distorted (e.g., elevating dominance or vanity as supreme ideals), the values conveyed in daily life follow suit, producing cultures obsessed with image, hierarchy or control. But when axiology is deep, reflective and inclusive of multiple domains of worth – truth, beauty, care and coherence – values take on a richness that can orient both individual action and collective aspiration.

Values ↔ Morality

Morality influences what is seen as acceptable to value, while values in practice slowly reshape morality. A society that begins to value transparency will eventually see secrecy as immoral. A family that values harmony may normalise silence or conflict-avoidance as the 'right' thing to do. When values and morality are in tension, individuals feel conflicted. However, when aligned, they create inner and outer congruence. In this way, morality stabilises values, while values gradually reform the moral code over time.

Morality ↔ Ethics

While morality represents the embedded, communal norms (often inherited), ethics interrogates and refines these norms. When morality goes unquestioned, it can devolve into dogma. When ethics is disconnected from cultural reality, it becomes elitist or detached. In healthy systems, ethics serves as a refinement mechanism for morality, updating codes without losing cultural roots and questioning collective behaviour without alienating its context.

Ethics ↔ Virtue

While ethics can outline principles of what ought to be done, virtue is where those principles become embodied. A person may reason that justice is ethically required, but if they habitually act with bias, their virtue is lacking. A system may claim ethical commitments to fairness, yet fail to embody them in practice. The interplay here determines whether ethical reasoning remains theoretical or is lived out through character. Virtue makes ethics visible through conduct.

Virtue ↔ Axiology

Virtue is where values are embodied and axiology finds its most visible expression. But virtue is neither static nor guaranteed. When neglected, distorted or merely performed, it degrades into patterns of vice – structural tendencies towards excess, deficiency or misalignment. Pride becomes arrogance when ungrounded. Caution mutates into cowardice when untempered by courage. These distortions feed back into axiology itself.

When vice goes unacknowledged, it is often rewarded, internalised or even institutionalised. Greed is mistaken for ambition. Manipulation passes as charm. Obedience masquerades as loyalty. In this way, corrupted virtue reshapes what is considered worthy, eroding the very foundations of discernment.

Therefore, the interplay between virtue and axiology determines the integrity of the entire normative ecology. When virtue is sincerely cultivated and vice is metabolised – not ignored or glamourised – axiology is refined and judgement is restored to what truly holds worth. This closing loop allows normativity to become self-correcting rather than self-distorting.

The emergent qualities when normativity is well integrated

When normativity is well integrated within a system – be it an individual, organisation, culture, institution or civilisation – distinctive qualities begin to emerge. These are neither imposed through policy nor maintained through performance optics. They arise as a natural consequence of a system that knows how to evaluate its own conduct, prioritise wisely and act in alignment with enduring worth.

- **Moral clarity** – There is a prevailing clarity about what is right, not just legally but existentially. This is not the rigidity of dogma, but the lucidity that emerges when systems are anchored in coherent axiology and refined ethical discernment. Decisions are not paralysed by relativism or driven by performative virtue; they are grounded, traceable and contextually sound.
- **Principled action under pressure** – Even in moments of chaos, temptation or threat, systems with mature normativity do not collapse into opportunism, panic or coercion. Instead, their actions reflect stable principles that have been

embodied, not merely preached. This shows up as integrity in governance, measured judgement in leadership and courage in interpersonal dynamics.

- **Ethical coherence** – There is alignment between what is said, what is valued and how one behaves. No part of the system needs to pretend. Ethical conduct is not rooted in image management, but in internal congruence. People can sense when they are in a field of coherence, and they act accordingly.
- **Trustworthiness** – Over time, people begin to trust not just actions, but the ethical architecture of the system. They know that good outcomes won't come through betrayal, shortcuts or exploitation. Normative alignment builds reputational gravity, where others can rely on you not just to deliver, but to deliver with integrity.
- **Cultural maturity** – Cultures with developed normativity mature beyond simplistic binaries – good versus evil, right versus wrong – and begin to operate within the space of discernment. They can hold paradoxes, question inherited norms and innovate ethically. This maturity does not lead to moral relativism, but to deeper responsibility.
- **Invisible yet felt guidance** – Perhaps the most subtle quality, normativity becomes like a tuning fork embedded within the system. It is not always spoken, but it is present in actions, behaviours and shared experience. It shapes tone, decision, rhythm and discernment. People begin to sense misalignment long before it erupts. And they act, not out of fear of punishment, but in alignment with what is worthy.

Normativity in action

The following case studies are not simply stories about right and wrong. They illustrate how implicit and explicit frameworks of value shape behaviour, influence decisions and drive systemic outcomes in tangible, real-world contexts.

Case 1: The ethical engineer who stayed silent

A senior software engineer at a global tech firm discovers that a new algorithm disproportionately flags content from minority communities. Both the data science team and the leadership are aware. However, the company's guiding value is 'neutrality', which is interpreted to mean: don't interfere with the algorithm. The engineer considers speaking up, but fears job loss and reputational fallout. Ultimately, she resigns in silent protest. The feature is launched regardless. Months later, public backlash erupts and trust in the company collapses.

Insight: Here, the company's values were unexamined, masquerading as neutral while carrying clear normative weight. The engineer faced a conflict between internalised virtue (justice, courage) and external morality (loyalty to the company's ethos). Had a richer normative discourse been embedded in the organisation's culture, ethical resistance could have occurred earlier and internally. The silence was not just personal; it was systemic.

Case 2: The morality of appearances

A religious private school publicly upholds strong moral codes around modesty and purity. Teachers are expected to model these ideals. One day, a long-serving unmarried teacher reveals she's pregnant. Despite her excellence, compassion and leadership, the administration discreetly terminates her contract. Parents are told she 'stepped down'. The school moves on, proud of maintaining its image.

Insight: This is an instance where morality overtook both ethics and virtue. The institution sacrificed a person's dignity for the sake of reputational optics. It enforced inherited moral norms rather than engaging with deeper ethical questions such as: Is this just? Is it compassionate? In prioritising conformity over truth and humanity, the institution revealed the danger of unexamined normative codes posing as virtue.

Case 3: The values-aligned business pivot

A small enterprise, founded on environmental sustainability, discovers that one of its suppliers is engaged in exploitative labour practices. The product line is popular. Margins are high. But the founder's commitment to integrity, fairness and intergenerational responsibility leads to a difficult decision: to suspend the line, communicate transparently with customers and seek alternative suppliers, even at a financial cost. Initially, sales dip. But over time, loyalty and credibility grow. The business survives and earns deeper trust.

Insight: This case embodies axiological discernment. The founder understood that value is not just about what sells, but what sustains meaningfully. The founders chose ethics over expediency and virtue over convenience. Here, normativity is not abstract philosophy; it is a lived architecture that shapes design, decision and destiny.

These cases reveal a central truth: normativity is not just about what we believe, but about how we organise our lives, institutions and identity around those beliefs. It is not merely about being right. It's about being *oriented towards the good* in ways that are just, coherent and deeply human.

Conclusion

Every system, whether it declares it or not, operates from an idea of how things ought to be. That idea may be rigorous or lazy, conscious or inherited, coherent or contradictory. But it is always there.

To ignore normativity is not to escape it, but to be blindly governed by it. When values go unexamined, appearances eclipse principles. When morality dominates without ethics, we inherit rules without understanding. When virtue is lost, integrity collapses into optics and vice becomes normalised, resulting in dysfunction that is mistaken for culture.

But when normativity is clarified – when values, ethics, morality and virtue are integrated into a living ontology – we gain the capacity to align what we do with who we are and with what the world genuinely needs. This alignment is not about perfection or moral superiority. It's about *coherence*: the ability to act, choose, lead and build without betraying what matters most.

Therefore, normativity is not about being seen as good. It's about being structurally faithful to the good we recognise, even when it costs us. And it requires ontological responsiveness – the capacity to embody these orientations in real time, rather than letting them remain theoretical.

Ultimately, normativity is not a philosophical abstraction. It is the unseen infrastructure beneath our judgements, designs, relationships and institutions – the architecture that holds meaning in place.

Reflection

- What internal or external frameworks guide your sense of what is 'right' or 'good'? Are they inherited, chosen or unconsciously absorbed?
- When have you followed rules or upheld norms that, upon reflection, contradicted your deeper values or principles? What allowed that dissonance, and what (if anything) interrupted it?
- Do you distinguish clearly between ethics (reasoned judgement) and morality (cultural norms)? Where in your life or leadership might that distinction be crucial?
- What values do you claim publicly, and which ones actually shape your decisions when pressure mounts?
- Are there patterns in your behaviour – at home or at work – such as avoidance, manipulation or self-righteousness, that appear virtuous on the surface, but are actually vices in disguise, quietly eroding integrity?
- What does virtue mean to you, not just as a concept but as a lived orientation? Which virtues do you cultivate intentionally and which do you neglect?
- In your team, organisation or relationship, what ethical tensions are currently being ignored for the sake of comfort, tradition or consensus?
- If your system (or self) were interrogated for coherence between values, design, behaviour and impact, what would be revealed? Where is alignment strong? Where is it performative?

PART IV

The Disintegration Sphere

Systems rarely collapse overnight. They erode quietly and gradually as misalignments go unnoticed, unexamined or are justified. Beneath every organisational failure, fractured relationship or existential despair lies a deeper pattern – a progressive breakdown of coherence. This breakdown is not random or mysterious. It unfolds through identifiable patterns, each reinforcing the next until dysfunction becomes embedded, normalised and self-sustaining.

The Disintegration Sphere explores these underlying patterns – not as isolated failures, but as interconnected dynamics of systemic unravelling. These are not just experiences to be avoided or managed. They are signs that a system – whether personal, organisational or societal – has lost its orientation towards truth, coherence and evolution.

This sphere is not about blame or defect. It's about clarity. By recognising disintegration as an ontological structure, we gain the capacity to intervene before dysfunction takes root – not just with effort, but with *structural intelligence*.

The Disintegration Sphere comprises four interlinked structural components that underpin systemic breakdown:

- **Shadows** – Distortions in perception, interpretation and sense-making that skew reality at its root. Shadows are not lies; they are partial truths mistaken for or elevated to whole truths, leading to misalignment and false clarity.
- **Misery** – The internalisation of shadowed conditions. Misery emerges when dysfunction is not only present, but also absorbed into the felt experience of life, creating chronic dissonance and emotional fatigue.
- **Suffering** – The experiential dimension of disintegration. Suffering occurs when unresolved misery becomes existentially charged – no longer just emotional, but tethered to questions of meaning, purpose and survival – and the individual or system is no longer adapting, but is consumed by incoherence, isolation or pain.
- **Entrenchment** – The structural culmination of disintegration. Entrenchment occurs when dysfunction no longer appears

problematic and becomes indistinguishable from identity, tradition, stability or truth. This isn't just failure; it is failure absorbed into the system and mistaken for normality.

These dimensions are not strictly sequential. They form a recursive loop, each reinforcing the others until disintegration is perceived as reality itself. By naming and examining them, we create the possibility of disruption, not through aggression or denial, but through ontological clarity.

While each chapter in this Part explores a different form of structural disintegration, it is important to remember that reintegration is not only possible; it's intrinsic to our design. We are not built to remain fractured. The chapters ahead do not focus on resolution. That inquiry continues in the Modulation Sphere, where we explore the ontological capacities required to meet, hold and transform the very patterns that divide us.

Critically, transformation cannot occur without recognition. Before we can transform – and in many cases heal, we must learn to see. By examining disintegration ontologically, we expose the deeper architecture of collapse – allowing what corrodes silently and unnoticed to come into view, and what has been normalised to be disrupted.

Healthy and unhealthy relationships within the Disintegration Sphere

Before we explore each chapter and its ontological distinction, it is important to clarify what is meant by a healthy versus unhealthy relationship with the forces of disintegration.

At first glance, it can seem counterintuitive to speak of having a 'healthy relationship' with forces such as shadows, misery, suffering and entrenchment. Unlike the forces in other spheres, these are not constructive qualities to be cultivated, but corrosive dynamics that erode coherence. Still, they are inescapably part of our ontological landscape, and how we engage with them matters.

In the other spheres, the distinction between healthy and unhealthy relationships is more straightforward. Qualities like patience, adaptability, sovereignty or normativity can be lived well or poorly, strengthened or corrupted. But the forces of the Disintegration Sphere are different. Here, the challenge is subtler. A healthy relationship does not mean celebrating or pursuing these forces. It means:

- **Seeing them clearly for what they are** rather than denying, moralising or engaging with them.
- **Not becoming them** – Resisting the collapse where distortion hardens into identity, narrative or culture.
- **Using them as signals or thresholds** – Noticing indicators that point to fragmentation, misalignment or unsustainability and call for responsibility, correction and transformation.

When engaged in this way, even the corrosive forces of disintegration can serve as warnings and catalysts. Shadows reveal what we refuse to examine. Misery signals where pain has been normalised. Suffering brings distortion into undeniable awareness. Entrenchment exposes where dysfunction has been mistaken for stability.

To have a healthy relationship with these forces is not to glorify them, but to let them perform their diagnostic role without letting them dictate identity or destiny. In contrast, an unhealthy relationship is one of denial, fusion or rationalisation – where dysfunction becomes invisible, normalised and even defended until collapse becomes inevitable.

CHAPTER 30

Shadows

Shadows are not psychological quirks or personality defects. They are ontological artefacts of disowned truth. They form at the fault lines between who we are and what we've been conditioned to believe we must be. Whenever an aspect of our Being is deemed unacceptable by family, culture, ideology or circumstance, it is not erased – it is split, suppressed and concealed. But suppression does not eliminate truth. It distorts it, shaping the very lens through which we see ourselves, others and the world.

The result is not just internal fragmentation, but relational and systemic dysfunction. Shadows do not remain private. They leak into conversations, spill into decisions, embed themselves in leadership styles and scale into cultural norms and institutional structures. A person who cannot face their own vulnerability may punish it in others. A society that disowns its aggression may glorify control and call it virtue.

Yet shadows are not 'evil', nor are they random. They are adaptive responses, created to protect coherence, belonging or survival. But when left unexamined, they become recursive mechanisms of distortion. They shape what we attend to, how we interpret, how we react and how we relate. In doing so, they confirm themselves. The longer they remain hidden from conscious awareness, the more they shape perception and masquerade as truth.

Within the Unified Ontology of Systemic Integrity (UOSI), the shadow quad sits inside the Disintegration Sphere alongside misery, suffering and entrenchment. Through the lenses of anatomy, mechanics and topology, this chapter explores the shadow not as pathology, but as an ontological structure.

But first, we begin with its ontological distinction.

Ontological Distinction of the Shadow

Shadows are aspects of you – or of the systems you engage with – that are present, but kept out of view. They are not flaws or mistakes, nor are they necessarily the result of malice or bad intention. *Shadows* arise when parts of reality are disowned, suppressed or ignored – not because they are untrue, but because they have been judged socially unsafe, reputationally risky or inconvenient in a given context. *Shadows* are often distortions of reality: unclear, misinterpreted or ambiguous. Yet they also hold the key to growth and regeneration. Unless they are brought into accurate awareness, tested against your purpose and values and placed in their rightful context, *shadows* deepen over time – often giving rise to misery in the form of recurring difficulties, adversities and crises that demand attention.

A **healthy relationship with shadows** indicates that you are willing to see and integrate what you once ignored, rejected or disowned. It does not mean the absence of shadows. Instead, you acknowledge the importance and impact of them and intentionally embrace them. You approach these parts of yourself with curiosity and responsibility, not judgement. Rather than projecting your shadows onto others, you pause and take ownership of them and their impact. Over time, this practice develops meta-awareness, broadens your emotional range and fosters coherence by making space for what might otherwise be pushed away. In relationships, teams, organisations and institutions, this looks like surfacing uncomfortable truths, owning mistakes, welcoming feedback and evolving founding values instead of rigidly clinging to them. Systems that have a healthy relationship with shadows are not flawless, but they are structured for repair, humility and integration.

An **unhealthy relationship with shadows** indicates that you tend to deny or exile parts of yourself to maintain an image of flawlessness. You may suppress pain but express it indirectly through blame, sarcasm or control. You may confuse appearances with truth, presenting coherence outwardly while feeling fragmented within. In relationships, teams, organisations and institutions, this same pattern appears as performative coherence – the effort to project alignment and unity on the surface while concealing misalignments underneath. People bury dysfunction, defend reputations and silence dissent instead of facing uncomfortable realities. The result is a polished surface masking internal dysfunction. Over time, unacknowledged shadows generate confusion, misalignment and recurring breakdowns. Without the courage to confront shadows, such systems lose the capacity to repair, grow or evolve – and disintegration inevitably follows.

Ontology of shadows

As discussed, the shadow is not a disorder. It is a structure of Being – a misalignment that organises perception, behaviour and relationship. It is not a fleeting issue to be fixed, but a patterned system that must be seen, mapped and reintegrated.

To fully comprehend what shadows are, we must move beyond psychology into ontology, examining how they function and how they become interwoven into the fabric of human existence. By deconstructing the shadow as a structure of Being, we reveal its origins, constituent parts, mechanisms, interrelationships and self-perpetuating properties. In doing so, we can uncover the precise ways in which shadows shape cognition, relationships and institutions, ultimately revealing why they remain deeply embedded in human experience.

By understanding the ontology of shadows, we gain the capacity to intervene in the architecture that produces them as opposed to simply observing them as distortions. We come to see that shadows are not an anomaly of weakness or failure; they are misdirected forces of Being, awaiting reintegration. They are not the enemy of truth, but the result of its concealment.

Anatomy of shadows

While traditional psychoanalytic models of the shadow, like Carl Jung's, primarily focus on repression and projection, they only address fragments of the larger phenomenon. To understand shadows in their entirety, we must examine them as layered structures, where each layer plays a distinct role in the shadow's formation, maintenance and expression. Why? Because shadows are not random distortions. They have a structure – a hidden architecture that shapes our thoughts, emotions and behaviours without our conscious awareness. Being aware of their core components allows us to understand what they are and see how they develop, take root and shape our reality.

Every shadow consists of five interrelated structural components. Think of them as the building blocks that make shadows come into existence.

1. **Repression**

   Repression is the concealed aspect of one's Being that has been disowned, denied or exiled. This may include an emotion (e.g. anger), a trait (e.g. sensitivity), a desire (e.g. ambition), a worldview or an identity (e.g. sexual, cultural, spiritual) that was once deemed unacceptable or too dangerous to reveal. This repression is not always conscious. It may arise as a survival response to fear, rejection, punishment or the need to belong. Over time, the person forgets it was ever part of them. What remains is a felt sense that something is missing or distorted, or an unresolved inner conflict. However, its source may be buried beneath layers of adaptation and protective narrative.

2. **Origin**

   The origin of a shadow lies in psychological and social conditioning. Shadows don't appear out of nowhere; they emerge from lived experiences, cultural norms, institutional narratives and socialisation processes. For example, a child who grows up in an environment where emotions are dismissed as a sign of weakness may internalise the belief that expressing vulnerability is shameful. The origin is the root environmental, relational or cultural force that initiates repression. It is the source code that defines what must be hidden in order to survive. Whether overt (such as punishment for expressing fear) or subtle (such as exclusion for nonconformity), the origin generates the internalised rules and forms the emotional and semantic charge that gives the shadow its sensitivity and intensity.

3. Distortion

Once a shadow is formed, it acts as a lens through which we see the world. It dictates what we notice, what we ignore and how we interpret events, often before we are even aware of it. This cognitive and affective filter functions as the internal lens of interpretation, shaped by the interaction between the repressed identity and its origin. It filters reality: what is noticed, feared, rejected or prioritised.

Distortion is not merely a belief; it is a deeply felt and embodied worldview. For example:

- Someone who repressed vulnerability may interpret care as manipulation.
- Someone who disowned their anger may see assertiveness in others as a threat.
- Someone whose joy was shamed may distrust excitement.

When this happens, distortion becomes the shadow's operating system, interpreting life not as it is, but in alignment with one's past pain, reinforcing itself over time.

4. Expression

When we refuse to acknowledge our shadows, they don't disappear. Instead, they are eventually projected outward – usually unconsciously – through behaviour, tone or relational dynamics. This outward expression often takes the form of relational dysfunction, as the repressed identity seeks expression in indirect or distorted ways. An externalised expression might manifest as:

- **Projection** – Seeing in others what one cannot accept in oneself.
- **Scapegoating** – Offloading guilt or discomfort onto a target.
- **Performative compensation** – Overcorrecting through virtue-signalling, aggression or excessive people pleasing.
- **Cultural embedding** – Institutionalising the shadow (e.g. a culture that suppresses emotion and calls it professionalism).

5. Perpetuation

Shadows do not remain static; they are self-perpetuating. The longer they go unexamined, the more they shape thoughts, behaviours and social structures, locking dysfunction into a self-sustaining cycle. Perpetuation is the internal engine or reinforcement loop that keeps the shadow active and repeating. External consequences triggered by shadow-driven behaviour – such as social rejection, failure or invalidation – often mirror the original wound, confirming the distorted logic that formed the shadow in the first place. For example:

- A person afraid of abandonment withdraws → their partner leaves → 'See, I was right to guard myself.'
- A person projecting aggression is met with defensiveness → 'Everyone is hostile.'
- An overcompensating perfectionist burns out → 'If I slow down, I'll be worthless.'

Together, these five structural components form the anatomical architecture of shadows – a hidden ecosystem of repression, distortion, external dysfunction and self-perpetuation. Left unexamined, this architecture scales into organisations, cultures and entire civilisations, masquerading as truth while invisibly shaping dysfunction.

A tangible example of misoriented shadows

A young professional grew up in a family where showing emotion was shamed. Outwardly, she appears composed, driven and resilient. But beneath the surface, her shadows distort how she sees, acts and relates to others and the world around her.

At the level of **repression**, she hides her sensitivity and vulnerability, disowning them to maintain acceptance. What was once a vital part of her Being becomes buried, leaving a sense of emptiness she cannot name.

At the level of **origin**, the shadow is rooted in her upbringing. Tears were met with rolled eyes, vulnerability with silence and affection withdrawn whenever she seemed 'too soft'. These cues formed a rule of survival that vulnerability is dangerous and shameful.

At the level of **distortion**, the young woman's repression and the origin of her shadows shape her perception. Offers of care feel manipulative. A colleague admitting struggle appears weak. Emotional honesty is read as untrustworthy. Reality is filtered through a lens of suspicion.

At the level of **expression**, shadows leak into behaviour. In meetings, she mocks colleagues for being 'too fragile' and insists on 'professionalism' whenever anyone shows their emotions. What she cannot accept in herself, she punishes in others.

At the level of **perpetuation**, her dismissive behaviour alienates coworkers, confirming her suspicion that others cannot be trusted with her feelings. Loneliness deepens, and the very strategy meant to protect her – hiding her sensitivity – convinces her that hiding is necessary. The cycle of isolation and mistrust intensifies, gradually eroding her energy and resilience. Eventually, she burns out.

In this way, the anatomy of shadows becomes misoriented. Repression buries what is true, origin scripts survival rules, distortion bends perception, expression externalises dysfunction and perpetuation locks the pattern in place. What began as a private issue scales into organisational dysfunction – a team culture where vulnerability is ridiculed and emotional detachment is mislabelled as professionalism. Left unexamined, misoriented shadows masquerade as strength while fuelling disintegration.

Mechanics of shadows

Where the anatomy of shadows describes the static architecture – the *what* – the mechanics illuminate the *how* of shadows: how they form, function and perpetuate across domains. More specifically, the mechanics show how shadows manifest, distort perception and generate dysfunction – not as isolated malfunctions, but as patterned unfoldings. They also reveal how these unfoldings ripple outward from internal fragmentation to relational distortion and, ultimately, to cultural embedding.

1. Fragmentation

Shadow formation begins with an internal rupture. A part of the self – an emotion, desire, trait or impulse – is deemed unacceptable, dangerous or inconsistent with one's self-image or cultural norms. To maintain a sense of coherence or secure social belonging, this aspect is pushed out of conscious awareness. In doing so, the self becomes internally fragmented. What was once part of the whole is now hidden. This is the initiation of the shadow – an ontological rejection of a truth that cannot be destroyed, only disowned and hidden.

2. Encoding and internalisation

The surrounding environment – parents, peers, culture, religion, institutions – shapes our understanding of what is acceptable and what must be hidden. These external messages become internalised as unconscious rules, such as:

- 'It's weak to cry.'
- 'Desire is dangerous.'
- 'Good people don't get angry.'

Over time, these internalised rules become the shadow's silent operating system. Even if we later reject the external message, the inner coding often remains – unseen but still active. The shadow isn't just buried; it is quietly sustained, kept alive by the very rules meant to erase it.

3. Perception filtering

Once internalised, the shadow filters perception. Attention becomes selective. The individual becomes hyper-attuned to cues that resonate with their wound and blind to signals that contradict it. This perceptual distortion is not limited to thought; it is embodied. It shows up in:

- Sensory bias (seeing a threat where there is none),
- Emotional bias (feeling slighted when unprovoked),
- Relational misreading (projecting meaning that is not present).

The world begins to mirror the wound, distorting reality.

4. Distorted meaning-making

With perception skewed, meaning-making becomes distorted and interpretative bias sets in. Benign events are loaded with shadow-charged interpretations. Silence becomes abandonment. A compliment becomes manipulation. A boundary becomes rejection.

This process forms 'shadow narratives' or stories. For example:

- 'I can't trust people.'
- 'If I show weakness, I'll be destroyed.'
- 'They're trying to control me.'

These narratives protect the self by rationalising its fragmentation. But in doing so, they entrench the shadow as the interpreter of reality.

5. Externalisation

The shadow seeks expression; it cannot remain inert. So it externalises. The disowned part is either projected onto others when confidence is repressed (e.g. 'He's so arrogant') or compensated for through exaggerated behaviour, such as performative humility, overcontrol and excessive compliance. The world becomes a stage for the shadow's drama.

Relationships, leadership, parenting and even ideologies are shaped by reactions to the displaced self rather than to what is actually happening. Externalisation of the shadow is a mechanism of self-protection. It allows us to face what we cannot yet accept as ours.

6. Social embedding

Once projected, the shadow begins to embed itself socially. This manifests:

- In relationships as patterns of blame, avoidance, people-pleasing or emotional volatility.
- In organisations as rituals of silence, punitive leadership and superficial harmony masking deep distrust.
- In cultures as ideologies that glorify dominance, suppress dissent or shame vulnerability.

Private distortion becomes a public norm. The shadow, once an internal exile, becomes a cultural ritual – a way of life mistaken for moral truth or institutional value.

7. Self-fulfilment and perpetuation

The reactions triggered by the shadow's behaviour – conflict, abandonment and criticism – serve to validate the distorted worldview:

- 'See, they really did betray me.'
- 'That's why I never open up.'
- 'This is what always happens.'

The external world responds in kind to the internal distortion, closing the feedback loop. The wound becomes a prophecy. The prophecy becomes identity. The loop tightens: more projection → more reaction → more confirmation → deeper concealment. The shadow is now self-protecting, self-fulfilling and self-expanding.

These seven steps outline the mechanics of shadow propagation, from a fracture in how we see ourselves to widespread dysfunction across psyche, relationship and culture. Shadows are not passive absences; they are active distortions, sustained by defensive loops and scaled through unawareness. Only by interrupting this process can the shadow be illuminated, reintegrated and ultimately transformed.

Topology of shadows

Shadows are not isolated malfunctions; they are dynamic feedback systems. The topology of shadows describes the recursive interactions among their constituent parts – how internal repression becomes systemic dysfunction. While the anatomy of shadows identifies their structural components and the mechanics reveal their propagation, topology shows how these parts interrelate, reinforce one another and give rise to emergent psychological, relational, cultural and institutional patterns.

Repression ↔ Origin

A concealed aspect is not randomly repressed. Its concealment is shaped and scripted by its origin – the early psychological and social conditioning that deemed it unacceptable.

The more profoundly an aspect of one's Being is repressed, the more intimately it reflects the values, traumas and taboos of its formative environment. Conversely, the origin is remembered not as raw memory, but as internalised censorship, shaping which parts of the self are 'allowed' to be seen.

The greater the dissonance between inner truth and conditioned norms, the sharper the inner division becomes, setting in motion the shadow's ongoing development and influence.

Origin ↔ Distortion

The origin of repression sets the stage for distortion – the cognitive and affective filters that colour perception. These are not arbitrary interpretations; they are survival adaptations built to reinforce the logic of the repression.

A child shamed for expressing anger grows up with a distortion that interprets all anger as dangerous, even when it's constructive. The distortion then becomes an unconscious rule: 'keep the peace at all costs'.

The origin manufactures the lens, which protects the origin by confirming its narrative, filtering out disconfirming evidence.

Distortion ↔ Expression

Perception filtered through the shadow's lens leads to skewed behavioural responses – externalised expressions such as projection, defensiveness, manipulation or compensation.

If the world is seen through a lens of 'I am not safe', then even love might be interpreted as control, prompting withdrawal. If success was shamed, ambition may be projected onto others as arrogance.

Internal distortion generates external disruption. The shadow reacts not to what *is*, but to what it *fears*, *expects* or *remembers* – often triggering relational or cultural dysfunction.

Expression ↔ Perpetuation

The shadow's external behaviours evoke responses from others – criticism, rejection, dependency – that 'prove' the distorted narrative. This confirms the original wound, feeding and perpetuating the reinforcement loop.

Projection creates tension → tension leads to conflict → conflict reinforces the beliefs: 'I'm unsafe', 'People can't be trusted' or 'I always ruin things'.

The world becomes a theatre where the shadow directs the show and then mistakes the outcome for truth. The external becomes a mirror for the internal wound.

Perpetuation ↔ Repression

As the loop tightens, the original repressed aspect of one's Being becomes further alienated. Every new reinforcement makes the concealed trait feel more shameful, foreign or dangerous.

Vulnerability, once denied, now seems weak. Anger feels threatening. Joy feels frivolous. The self cannot even imagine reclaiming their repressed identity without fear of collapse, judgement or annihilation.

The longer the reinforcement persists, the more inaccessible and 'unthinkable' the concealed truth becomes, solidifying the shadow as a permanent structure of identity.

Each loop perpetuates the distortion and pushes the concealed aspect deeper out of reach. When that happens, the shadow becomes a closed feedback loop where dysfunction validates the very distortion that generated it.

Emergent forces and patterns

Distinct patterns arise from the interaction of the shadow's structural components. These patterns may appear as traits or 'realities', but are in fact the outputs of recursive shadow dynamics. Examples include:

- **Emotional volatility and reactivity** due to distorted perception and repressed pain.
- **Chronic misinterpretation** from perceptual filtering and projection.
- **Duplicity and self-betrayal** as the self performs away from the concealed truth.
- **Social fragmentation** as shadow patterns scale into relationships and institutions.
- **Systemic dysfunction** when shadow norms are encoded in culture, policy or leadership.

These emergent forces are not 'just how someone is'. They are ontological artefacts – products of interlocking distortions.

The shadow in action

Shadows rarely reveal themselves directly. They surface through patterns: distorted perception, reactive behaviour, strained relationships and systemic dysfunction. The following cases illustrate how unexamined shadows shape identity, leadership and culture – not through malice, but through a misdirected instinct for survival and self-preservation. Each example reveals what happens when disowned aspects of the self drive behaviour without conscious awareness. To complete the picture, two cases reveal a healthy relationship with the shadow, where denied aspects are recognised, integrated and held with responsibility. Here, integration leads not to perfection, but to coherence, maturity and depth.

Case 1: The empathetic leader who can't set boundaries

A senior executive in a mission-driven organisation is deeply committed to being kind and inclusive. She prides herself on being understanding, approachable and emotionally available. However, behind closed doors, she struggles to hold underperforming staff accountable. She avoids direct feedback, absorbs others' emotional states and overextends herself in an effort to 'support' her team. Resentment builds quietly, both in herself and among her high-performing staff, who feel neglected and overburdened. When conflicts arise, she freezes, then overcompensates through appeasement. Slowly, her team becomes dysfunctional – deadlines slip, accountability erodes and frustration festers until morale declines.

Insight: This case highlights a shadow of repressed anger and buried assertiveness. Conditioned to associate strength with harm and boundaries with rejection, she disowned her capacity to be clear and direct, treating it as incompatible with being kind or caring. Her identity as 'kind and safe' was built on distancing herself from confrontation. Over time, this concealed trait distorted her leadership. What looked like empathy was, in fact, a shadow-driven pattern of avoidance. Her empathy became performative – a way to preserve belonging rather than embody integrity.

Case 2: The intellectually gifted child turned cynical adult

As a child, Sam was praised for being clever, but ridiculed when he cried or expressed wonder. Sensitivity was shamed and vulnerability was dismissed as childish. Over time, Sam built his identity around sharp intellect, sarcasm and stoicism. By adulthood, he had become a high-performing academic, but was emotionally closed, reactive to softness and dismissive of joy. In personal relationships, he struggles to connect. He intellectualises everything, shuts down affection and often mocks what he secretly longs for.

Insight: This is a classic case of joy and tenderness exiled into the shadow. Sam's original sensitivity was not erased – it was buried. The resulting distortion made him interpret warmth as naive and emotional expression as weakness. His cynical worldview acts as both defence and confirmation of the wound. Shadow narratives like 'I'm too much' and 'Feeling is for fools' shape his reality. Intimacy becomes inaccessible, not because he cannot love, but because his shadow cannot allow him to be seen.

Case 3: The social justice advocate who can't tolerate dissent

A passionate activist campaigns for equity and justice. She is articulate, values-driven and tireless. But in group settings, she often becomes combative and controlling. Disagreement is met with intensity. She insists her perspective is morally correct and labels dissent as harm. Eventually, collaborators begin distancing themselves, not because they disagree with her values, but because they feel shamed and silenced by her tone. She feels betrayed, assuming others are just afraid of the truth.

Insight: This case demonstrates the shadow of unacknowledged pain and buried vulnerability. The activist's early experience of exclusion and injustice forged a survival identity rooted in righteousness. To stay safe, she disconnected from her own need for nuance, mutuality and emotional safety, viewing them as liabilities in the face of injustice. Her fight for justice became a projection of unresolved wounds. Without reintegration, her leadership begins to mirror the very dynamics she opposes – silencing, coercion and moral rigidity.

Case 4: The executive who confronted his inner tyrant

A successful CEO was known for his sharp decision-making, but also for being excessively critical and emotionally distant. In therapy, he uncovered a shadow rooted in his childhood. Raised by a perfectionist father, he learned to equate worth with performance and viewed compassion as weakness. Over time, he realised that his drive to control and his avoidance of vulnerability were defensive adaptations, not leadership strengths.

Insight: Rather than repress or justify his tendencies, he began consciously integrating his shadow. He practised acknowledging discomfort, listening without interrupting and recognising when control was masking fear. As he integrated these parts of himself, his leadership softened without losing rigour. He became more attuned to his team, creating space for trust and shared ownership. This is not the absence of shadow, but the presence of a healthy relationship with it.

Case 5: The artist who reclaimed her ambition

Leila grew up in a household where ambition was seen as selfish and attention-seeking. She internalised the belief that wanting to be seen was shameful. Though deeply creative, she downplayed her talent, avoiding the spotlight and often giving credit to others. Years later, through a process of reflective inquiry and somatic work, she uncovered the concealed aspect of her Being – a fierce ambition tied to contribution, not ego.

Insight: Leila did not try to eliminate her ambition. She reclaimed it. Instead of performing humility or deflecting praise, she now owns her desire to create meaningful impact. Her success is no longer laced with guilt or hidden beneath modesty. By befriending her shadow – not vilifying it – she brought clarity to her purpose and courage to her expression. Her relationship with the shadow became a source of wholeness and agency.

Case 6: The organisation that confuses overwork with commitment

A fast-growing company celebrates 'hustle' as a cultural value. Leaders praise employees who sacrifice weekends, blur personal boundaries and treat exhaustion as a badge of honour. Over time, burnout, cynicism and high turnover erode the company's effectiveness. What began as a motivating story of dedication becomes a shadow narrative that normalises dysfunction and silences dissent.

Insight: This case shows how shadows embed at an institutional level, masquerading as cultural strength while undermining long-term coherence.

Conclusion

Shadows are not personal failures or moral flaws. They are structural responses to disowned truth. Formed at the intersection of internal fragmentation and external conditioning, shadows shape how we see, interpret, respond and act in the world – often without our conscious awareness. What begins as a single rupture in the self becomes a patterned system: internally concealed, externally projected and socially reinforced.

When left unexamined, shadows become architects of distortion. They influence not just individual behaviour, but relational dynamics, institutional practices and cultural narratives. Their power lies not in their force but in their invisibility: the way they embed themselves into what feels normal, right or inevitable.

But shadows are not permanent. They are not the enemy of truth; they are its residue, waiting to be reclaimed. To illuminate the shadow is not to eliminate it, but to reintegrate what was once exiled. This work is neither easy nor comfortable. It asks us to face the concealed, interrupt the loop and take responsibility for the structures we have inherited and internalised. In doing so, we restore coherence within ourselves, our relationships and the systems we help shape.

Reflection

- Can you identify an aspect of yourself – an emotion, impulse or trait – that you were taught to hide, suppress or judge as unacceptable?
- What internalised rules still shape how you perceive others or react in certain situations? Where did those rules come from?
- Have you ever misinterpreted a situation because of a shadow-driven lens? What meaning did you assign to it, and what truth might have been concealed beneath it?

- In what ways might you be externalising a disowned part of yourself, for example, through projection, overcompensation or relational patterns?
- Can you recall a moment when your reaction seemed disproportionate to the event? What deeper wound or disowned truth might have been touched?
- Where in your leadership, relationships or culture might shadows be masquerading as values, norms or truths?
- What might it look like to reintegrate a shadowed part of yourself in order to restore coherence?

CHAPTER 31

Misery

Misery is the internalisation of dysfunction, emerging when shadows remain unexamined and unintegrated. It is an *embedded structural condition* – a state where distortion becomes woven into lived reality. When this happens, it reshapes how we relate to discomfort, hardship, adversity and catastrophe. Unlike transient pain, which may serve a functional purpose, misery is recursive, self-perpetuating and structurally embedded within both personal and societal frameworks.

Rather than a prolonged emotional state or persistent mood, misery – as a structural condition – spans individual, relational and systemic layers of reality. It arises when coherence is ruptured but never restored, and when adversity is experienced but never metabolised. At its core, it is the lived consequence of unaddressed shadows – distortions left unchecked that shape perception, identity, behaviour and the surrounding world.

Misery's roots lie in shadows – the parts of ourselves we deny, disown or conceal. These unresolved fragments distort our relationship to meaning, coherence and agency. When left unexamined, shadows warp interpretation, generate chronic emotional climates and fuel behavioural loops that reinforce suffering and begin to shape the world around us – our relationships, institutions and social norms.

Over time, this condition expands beyond the individual. Inner despair finds echoes in cultural narratives, organisational dynamics, economic systems and ideological constructs that reflect and perpetuate its logic. What begins as a personal or emotional struggle gradually becomes a situation in which dysfunction is not just endured; it is normalised, institutionalised and mistaken for truth.

This chapter explores misery not as pathology or fate, but as a recursive phenomenon of ontological misalignment primarily fuelled by unintegrated shadows. It is not merely something we feel; it is something we co-create and inhabit, often without knowing how.

By recognising misery as a conditioned situation as opposed to a character flaw or fleeting state, we gain the capacity to deconstruct it – not through force, but through deliberate acts of ontological interruption, shadow integration and systemic recalibration. Misery often persists when it remains unseen or unacknowledged. Yet even when recognised, it can endure if there is no capacity or guidance for transformation. Its grip begins to loosen the moment it is both acknowledged and approached with discernment and ontological clarity.

Ontological Distinction of Misery

Misery is a condition in which disruption goes unaddressed, pain is denied integration and dysfunction becomes normalised. It is more than just an emotion like sadness, fatigue or pain. Over time, misery weaves itself into how you see yourself, others and life. What begins as a response to difficulty or pain turns into a lens: *'Something is wrong'* becomes *'I am wrong'* or *'Life is unfair'*. *Misery* is not a passing mood. It is the structural embedding of distortion into identity and narrative. Left unexamined, *misery* hardens and gives rise to suffering – the raw, lived experience of that distortion that you can't deny or ignore.

A **healthy relationship with misery** indicates that you are able to recognise misery without collapsing into it. It does not mean avoiding hardship, but rather acknowledging it. You can see it as a signal rather than a life sentence: a pointer to misalignment, dysfunction or unprocessed pain that calls for attention and integration. You resist the temptation to turn misery into who you are. Instead, you inquire into the stories and patterns that both create misery and are created by it, take responsibility and begin to restore authorship over your experience. In other systems – relationships, organisations, institutions or cultures – a healthy relationship with misery manifests as the ability to acknowledge distress without glorifying collapse, to make space for grief without confusing it with failure, and to support others to be with misery without enabling dysfunction.

An **unhealthy relationship with misery** indicates that you have normalised it as an inevitability. You endure dysfunction as though it is necessary or a mark of strength. Shadows remain unexamined, and collapse is rationalised as loyalty, character-building or endurance. In larger systems – such as organisations and institutions – misery becomes culture and the default. Silence about dysfunction is rewarded, distortion is treated as normal, and suffering is moralised, pathologised or trivialised – anything but truly addressed. Over time, possibilities narrow, agency weakens and coherence fractures, leaving both individuals and manufactured systems stuck in cycles of dysfunction.

Ontology of misery

Ontologically, misery is the internalisation of dysfunction. However, before misery can be structured, it must first be triggered. And it is life itself or, more specifically, the matters in life that we encounter, that bring forth these triggers. Matters in life refers to everything you experience: health, identity, opportunity, loss, power, limitation, beauty, betrayal, uncertainty, the list goes on. They are the conditions – inner or outer, chosen or inherited – through which your Being is continuously summoned to respond. These life matters form the raw content of your existence and are neither inherently good nor bad. They are *ontological provocations*: fields that call for discernment, ownership and action. Some matters are mild, others massive. Some are expected, others arrive abruptly. What determines their impact is not the matter itself, but your relationship with it and how you respond to it.

Any existential and structural pressure point that makes previous ways of making sense, relating or responding feel inadequate is referred to in this book as '*destabilis*'. A *destabilis* moment may arrive in various ways, including:

- Profound loss or grief that renders prior certainties meaningless.
- A betrayal that fractures your trust.
- A paradox that cannot be resolved with your current worldview.
- Moral tension that undermines your sense of ethical clarity.
- A sudden realisation that who you thought you were no longer fits the life you are leading.

Put simply, *destabilis* refers to the moment of rupture which tests, shakes or lays bare the integrity of a system, from a human being all the way to a society. It is neither misery nor transformation. It is the volatile space or portal between collapse and renewal. To encounter *destabilis* is to stand at a crossroads. One path leads to avoidance, suppression or false resolution; the other to the integration of dysfunction through clarity, support, presence and ethical reorientation.

Many people mistake *destabilis* for weakness, failure or punishment. But often, misery does not begin with an event. It begins with *the failure to make sense of it*. The event itself does not destroy you. What causes disintegration is the refusal, inability or lack of support to integrate it into a new structure – one of coherence.

That's why *destabilis* must be treated with reverence. It is the precursor to every major pivot in a human life, in a culture, in an institution or in a society. It is the moment before the narrative changes, before the architecture is either rebuilt or abandoned. It reveals what was latent, unspoken or festering beneath the surface. In that revelation lies both danger and opportunity. By exposing the gap between who you are and who you may become, *destabilis* asks you to choose – with courage – what comes next.

But not all who encounter *destabilis* are able to move through it.

When the call to integrate is unmet – whether through avoidance, overwhelm or the absence of support – disintegration begins to take root. And what was once a volatile moment of possibility becomes something else entirely – misery.

To understand misery better, let's deconstruct it to examine its underlying ontological structure: what it consists of (anatomy), how it operates (mechanics) and how it interacts with other ontological phenomena that serve to either reinforce or sustain it (topology).

Anatomy of misery

Misery is not a transient emotional state. It is a structured condition of Being comprised of interrelated components that reinforce its continuity. These are not merely symptoms of hardship; they are ontological anchors that transform pain into identity, dissonance into worldview and dysfunction into the lived condition. The anatomy of misery consists of five mutually reinforcing components.

1. **Distorted narrative**

    Distorted narratives are the meaning-making structures at the heart of misery. They don't merely reflect negative thinking. They are cognitive distortions that encode a deep ontological conviction that life is futile, broken or stacked against you. These convictions often emerge from unresolved shadows or earlier suffering and become the interpretive lens through which all experience is filtered. Common narratives include: 'Nothing ever works out for me', 'This is just my fate', or 'I'm fundamentally broken'. This distorted narrative architecture becomes self-validating. Success is dismissed as luck or a fluke, while setbacks are taken as confirmation. Over time, the narrative hardens into a worldview that resists contradiction and quietly sustains dysfunction as normal.

2. **Undertone**

    The undertone is the affective atmosphere or emotional baseline of misery. It's not a passing emotional state, but a persistent emotional current that saturates daily experience.

Emotions such as despair, fear and helplessness become fixed rather than responsive, making suffering feel inevitable and draining the capacity to imagine alternatives. Even when external conditions improve, the undertone remains heavy, contracted and unresponsive. Over time, the emotional range narrows. Joy feels unreachable, relief suspicious and hope naive. What remains is a dull, corrosive familiarity – an atmosphere that no longer reacts to life, but envelops it.

3. Habit

Habit refers to the behavioural repetition and entrenched routines that sustain and reinforce misery over time. What begins as a coping mechanism gradually becomes conditioning. Misery perpetuates itself through repeated behaviours and routines – such as procrastination, avoidance, passivity, over-control or withdrawal. These actions often validate the distorted self-narrative: 'See, I failed again', 'I don't belong', or 'No one cares'. Even when genuine opportunities arise, responses are filtered through ingrained defeat or distrust. Over time, these routines solidify into patterns that shape how the individual lives, what they expect and what they allow themselves to desire.

4. Somatisation

Somatisation refers to the physiological manifestation of internal distress. It's when emotional and psychological pain take on embodied forms. Chronic stress, fatigue, insomnia, inflammation, digestive issues and other symptoms often emerge as the body's response to sustained misery. This is not incidental. Over time, the nervous system and body adapt to distress as a baseline state. Energy depletes, resilience fades and the capacity for vitality and pleasure narrows. Eventually, the body mirrors the internal collapse: posture, voice and presence begin to reflect the weight of what has been carried. Misery becomes not just a feeling, but an embodied way of being.

5. **Systemic reinforcement**

Misery is not merely an internal condition. It is shaped and sustained by the social and systemic structures that surround us. Systemic reinforcement refers to the external validation and normalisation of dysfunction. Institutions, cultural norms and belief systems can normalise, reward or moralise suffering, turning it into a kind of social currency. Dysfunctional workplaces that glorify burnout, families that equate suffering with virtue and ideologies that romanticise endurance or punishment are all examples. In such environments, misery is not just tolerated; it is normalised and systemically reinforced. Healing becomes subversive. Attempts to interrupt the pattern are met with suspicion, dismissal or shame. When dysfunction is embedded in the structure, it becomes harder to recognise and even harder to escape.

These five anatomical components form a closed loop, each feeding, shaping and justifying the others. Distorted narratives sustain the undertone of emotional entrapment, which, in turn, drives habits that sustain and reinforce misery over time. When repeated behaviours (habits) etch into the body, somatic or embodied dysfunction shapes the conditions that reinforce the cycle, risking them becoming systemically reinforced.

Together, these structural components solidify misery, not as a fleeting experience, but as a systemic identity condition – a lived, embodied and socially reinforced sense that: This is who I am. This is how the world is. And nothing will ever change.

This anatomy is the architecture that sustains misery. But by naming and mapping it, we make disruption and realignment possible.

A tangible example of misoriented misery

Consider a man who, after being made redundant from a long-term job, struggles to reorient his life. At first, the event itself is destabilising, but not disastrous. Yet over time, because the rupture is never acknowledged, worked through or integrated as part of his life story, his experience hardens into misery.

At the level of **distorted narrative**, he begins to tell himself, 'I was never good enough' and, 'People like me always get discarded.' Each job application rejection is not simply a setback – it's proof of the stories he tells himself. Any small success is explained away as luck.

At the level of **undertone**, the distorted narrative saturates his daily experience of life and crystallises into a worldview: 'Life is unfair', 'The odds are stacked against me' and 'I am fundamentally broken.' Even on days when external circumstances improve slightly, the heaviness does not lift. Joy feels unreachable, hope seems naive, and every encounter carries an undercurrent of futility. What might have been sadness becomes a climate of despair that colours everything.

At the level of **habit**, his routines begin to reinforce the loop. He procrastinates on job applications, avoids networking and withdraws socially. Each avoidance produces further failure, which feeds back into the narrative of inadequacy. The coping mechanisms he adopted to protect himself calcify into entrenched behaviours that keep him stuck.

At the level of **somatisation**, the internal weight manifests in his body. Sleep becomes fragmented, energy collapses and chronic tension shows in his posture and voice. Even when opportunities arise, his depleted presence makes it harder for others to engage with him, subtly confirming his distorted story. Misery is no longer just in his mind; it inhabits his body.

At the level of **systemic reinforcement**, his environment compounds the cycle. The broader culture equates worth with employment, while his community quietly valorises stoicism and endurance. Rather than offering genuine support, friends tell him to 'toughen up'. The workplace culture he left behind glorifies burnout and treats redundancy as failure, reinforcing his sense that suffering is proof of weakness. Dysfunction is not only internalised; it is mirrored and validated externally.

In this way, the anatomy of misery becomes misoriented and self-perpetuating. Distorted narratives sustain the undertone of despair, habits reproduce failure, somatisation etches despair into the body and systemic forces reward or normalise the cycle. What began as a destabilising life event calcifies into a structural identity: 'This is who I am and this is how the world works.' Without interruption, misery becomes not just a passing experience, but a lived condition of disintegration.

Mechanics of misery

Misery functions not as a static emotional state, but as a recursive system of ontological misalignment. It leverages the anatomical components – narrative, undertone, habit, somatisation and institutionalisation – into feedback loops that reinforce dysfunction. Each phase escalates and stabilises the next, gradually collapsing adversity into identity. The following mechanics trace how misery is constructed, sustained and, eventually, normalised.

1. Destabilis

Most events pass through us lightly, leaving little trace. But some hit harder, shaking us to the core. When they do, they become ontological thresholds – a phenomenon known as *destabilis*. As explained earlier, *destabilis* is the existential condition of pressure, ontological rupture or contradiction that disorients one's current coherence. It is the *isness* of disruption – neither good nor bad – and the space before the fall or flight. What determines its trajectory is not the event itself, but the response that follows.

Destabilis may take the form of a loss, an unexpected truth, a failed plan, an identity collapse, a moral conflict or a paradox that cannot be resolved with one's current mental scaffolding.

Imagine the following scenario. A rupture occurs: grief, betrayal, failure, contradiction or existential dissonance. This is not merely circumstantial; it is ontological. It shakes the internal structure of coherence and self-understanding. This moment is not yet misery, but a threshold. If metabolised with clarity and support, it may become growth. If denied, resisted or left incoherent, it begins the descent into structural misery.

Misery often begins not with what happened, but with what wasn't integrated when it did.

2. Interpretation

Next, the ontological rupture (*destabilis*) is interpreted through a filter of inherited shadows, unprocessed trauma and habitual thought patterns. When this happens, meaning-making becomes distorted: 'This proves I'm not enough', 'Life is always like this' or 'Nothing matters'. Interpretations like these are not just beliefs; they become *structural orientations*, forming the backbone of a misery worldview. This distortion reconfigures one's perception. Life is no longer something to respond to but something to endure.

3. Emotional anchoring

Distorted meaning gives rise to potent emotions like helplessness, shame, rage and despair. These are no longer transient emotional states; they become fixed affective positions. The person no longer moves through emotion; they begin to live from it. Emotional volatility or flatness becomes a default setting, shaping perception, energy and relational tone. Misery, at this point, is no longer just a narrative; it is a mood-structure. The psyche internalises suffering as its emotional baseline, altering how the person engages with reality itself.

4. Behavioural reinforcement

Emotions influence actions: withdrawal, compliance, aggression, addiction and self-sabotage. These behaviours – often unconscious – generate predictable outcomes: rejection, failure, conflict or isolation. Each outcome then loops back to validate the original distortion. For example: 'I am unlovable' leads to avoiding connection, which results in loneliness, confirming the belief. Over time, these feedback loops entrench the narrative and narrow the field of possibility. Behaviour ceases to be a tool for expression and becomes a mechanism of confirmation. Identity is no longer authored with intention; it is shaped reactively through patterns of reinforcement.

5. Physiological entrenchment

Here, the body adapts to misery as a biological norm. Chronic stress, inflammation, pain, fatigue and disrupted sleep become somatic companions to psychological collapse. The nervous system narrows its window of tolerance; hormonal patterns (such as elevated cortisol and adrenaline) sustain states of hypervigilance or shutdown. Through neuroplasticity, misery is etched into familiar pathways – repetition becomes embodied reinforcement. Over time, misery is no longer just felt; it is inhabited. Breath constricts, posture collapses, digestion falters and illness emerges. The body becomes a living record of unprocessed physiological pain.

6. External validation

The outer world reflects and reinforces inner despair. Cultural and religious narratives, organisational hierarchies and family dynamics all serve to affirm the story of misery. Messages like: 'You should be grateful for what you have' or 'Pain builds character' are not always malicious, but they are ontologically misaligned. They reframe suffering as identity, sacrifice as virtue and dysfunction as honour. The person is not merely unsupported. They are conditioned to believe that misery is normal, even noble.

7. Recursive identity loop

Eventually, misery becomes one's identity. The person no longer sees themselves *in* misery; they see themselves *as* misery. 'This is just who I am.' 'Nothing can change.' 'I'm the kind of person who always suffers.' No new trauma or trigger is needed. The loop sustains itself without fresh input. Misery becomes self-feeding, self-justifying and self-renewing. What began as a wound becomes a worldview, and eventually colours the person's entire experience of reality.

These mechanics reveal that misery is not a reaction to a single event, but a cascading entanglement of unresolved traumas, distorted meanings, tainted emotions, embodied memories and environmental reinforcement.

Each phase tightens the architecture until misery feels like reality. Only a deliberate act of ontological interruption – naming, seeing, sensing and choosing anew – can break the loop and invite reintegration.

Topology of misery

The topology of misery reveals how its core anatomical components – distorted narratives, undertones, habits, somatisation and systemic reinforcement – interlock to form a self-perpetuating ontological field. Misery is not a linear chain of causes; it is a web of recursive interactions across these five structural components. These interplays not only sustain the condition, but also give rise to emergent psychological and cultural traits, often mistaken for personality or worldview.

Distorted narratives ↔ Undertone

Distorted narratives like: 'I am unworthy' and 'Life is against me' generate persistent emotional states of despair, shame and dread. These emotions are interpreted as evidence of truth: 'If I feel this hopeless, it must be real.' The affective weight locks in the distorted cognition, creating an undertone of emotional entrapment and making it harder to challenge or dislodge. This loop forms the perceptual and emotional core of misery. The mind tells the heart it is doomed, and the heart confirms it to the mind.

Undertone ↔ Habit

The internal climate (undertone) shapes the external response. Entrapped emotions provoke habits like self-isolation, appeasement, passive aggression or collapse. These repetitive behaviours yield predictable consequences: rejection, stagnation, over-extension or exploitation. Consequently, the emotional undertone intensifies, now confirmed by the outcomes. What begins as mood becomes a behavioural script, lived out and replayed through actions that keep the pain alive.

Habit ↔ Somatisation

Repetitive behaviours or habits – especially those driven by fear, helplessness or overcompensation – place sustained strain on the nervous system, causing misery to manifest physiologically. Chronic cortisol elevation, muscle tension, fatigue, inflammation, digestive issues, insomnia and pain emerge. Over time, the body becomes a carrier of suffering, not merely a participant. Physiology ceases to respond to present reality. Instead, it conforms to the ontological atmosphere – the felt reality – of misery.

Somatisation ↔ Systemic reinforcement

The visible toll of misery draws systemic responses. Institutions pathologise it (e.g. medicalisation), moralise it (e.g. religious guilt) or sideline it (e.g. workplace exclusion). These responses mirror and reinforce internal scripts like: 'I am broken', 'I must be fixed' and 'I'm a burden.' The body speaks what the culture already believes – some people are meant to suffer. This embeds ontological despair into the very fabric of society until it becomes normalised and systemically reinforced.

Systemic reinforcement ↔ Distorted narratives

Systemic messages – through media, education, bureaucracy, family and governance – amplify cognitive distortions through the stories we tell ourselves. Poverty becomes framed as failure. Emotional expression becomes weakness. Hopelessness becomes realism. The result? Misery is no longer internal. It becomes a global condition, perceived as normal and unchangeable.

Emergent forces and patterns

Several emergent forces and dysfunctional patterns arise from misery's recursive topology, not as random side effects, but as structural outcomes. They include:

- **Apathy and numbness** – The psyche withdraws to protect itself from chronic dissonance.
- **Cynicism and distrust** – Hope is framed as naivety; vulnerability as danger.

- **Victimhood identity** – Misery becomes a moral claim to being seen, but not transformed.
- **Burnout and passivity** – Action feels futile; collapse is framed as surrender.
- **Despair as maturity** – Misery is rebranded as 'being realistic' or 'emotionally sober'.
- **Chronic indecision** – The will is paralysed; all paths appear equally hopeless.

These are not personality traits. They represent the ontological residue of a system that recycles disempowerment into identity.

The Shadow–Misery Spiral

As explained at the beginning of this chapter, while misery is the structural embedding of dysfunction, its origins lie in shadows – those denied, concealed or disowned aspects of ourselves. Shadows do not remain inert. When left unexamined and unintegrated, they evolve into progressively deeper layers of misery. This progression can be visualised as the Shadow–Misery Spiral – a recursive descent in which shadows harden into misery, each turn reinforcing the distortions that set the cycle in motion. Let's explore each layer of the spiral.

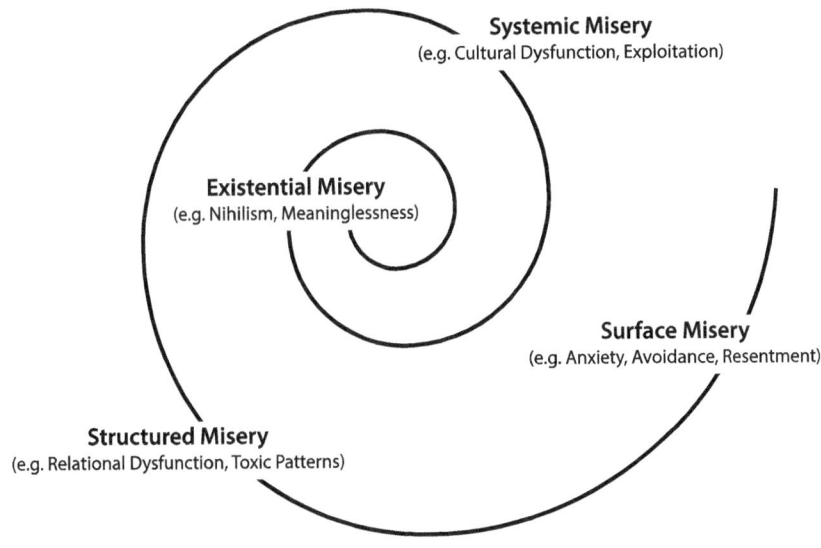

Figure 8 – The Shadow–Misery Spiral.

Surface Misery: The outermost layer

Here, shadows make themselves known through visible symptoms such as anxiety, avoidance, dissatisfaction, irritability, resentment and other self-destructive behaviours. This is the most recognisable form of misery, yet it is often mistaken for the whole picture. In truth, these expressions are only surface-level signals of deeper distortions beneath.

Example: Just as a warning light on a car dashboard draws attention to an issue beneath the hood, irritation, sleeplessness or avoidance signal that something deeper requires attention. But many people – like drivers who ignore the flashing light until the engine fails – dismiss these inner warnings. Ignoring them is often the first step in the spiral's descent.

Structured Misery: Patterned dysfunction

When surface misery is ignored, shadows solidify into toxic structures of living. Dysfunctional relationships, repetitive failures, cycles of avoidance, control or self-sabotage become predictable patterns. What begins as occasional avoidance or resentment hardens into a way of relating to oneself and others. Misery, at this stage, is no longer episodic; it is structured.

Example: Like water dripping slowly into stone, unresolved shadows carve grooves into daily life. A person who once avoided difficult conversations may, over years, form entire relationships around silence or withdrawal. What was once a coping mechanism becomes the very architecture of their world, pulling them further down the spiral.

Systemic Misery: Cultural and institutional entrapment

When unchecked, misery moves beyond individuals and embeds itself in systems and cultures. Workplaces glorify burnout, families perpetuate silence, economies thrive on exploitation and ideologies rationalise inequality. At this level, misery is not merely endured; it is normalised, rewarded and even moralised. Individuals navigating such environments find their shadows mirrored back to them, making dysfunction feel inevitable.

Example: In some workplaces, staying late is praised more than working wisely. Over time, exhaustion becomes a badge of honour, while those who rest are branded as lazy. Here, the system itself enforces and amplifies misery, even when individuals long for something different.

Existential Misery: The core collapse

At its deepest layer, misery becomes existential. Here, shadows erode the very foundations of meaning. Nihilism and despair take hold, erasing any sense of intrinsic purpose. Life is no longer experienced as merely difficult; it is perceived as futile. Misery shifts from being an external condition to an ontological identity: 'I am misery.' What began as shadows of avoidance or fear culminates in a collapse of coherence and meaning.

Example: Existential Misery is like a house whose foundations have crumbled. At this stage, patching the roof or painting the walls makes no difference. The collapse is not cosmetic but structural, and without rebuilding from the ground up, nothing can hold. Here, the spiral reaches its end-point: the disintegration of coherence itself.

Bridging shadows and misery: A self-perpetuating cycle

The spiral is not simply downward – it is self-reinforcing. Shadows and misery feed each other in a recursive loop:

- **Shadows shape perception** → Distorted beliefs reinforce emotional suffering.
- **Shadows manipulate decision-making** → Avoidance, projection and self-sabotage perpetuate dysfunction.
- **Unintegrated shadows accumulate** → Resentment, distrust and disorientation harden into patterned dysfunction.
- **Misery reinforces shadows** → The individual identifies with suffering itself, mistaking it for truth.

Example: Like a scratched record, the same distorted tune keeps playing. The grooves deepen with each spin, making it harder to hear anything new.

This self-perpetuating cycle transforms shadows from passing distortions into entrenched conditions of misery, embedded in both personal experience and collective structures. This recursive loop is not merely abstract; it is lived and felt as suffering. If left unexamined, it solidifies into entrenchment – dysfunction defended as order itself.

Extending the Spiral: From suffering to entrenchment

The Shadow–Misery Spiral does not exist in isolation. It explains how shadows descend into entrenched dysfunction, but its effects are most vividly experienced as suffering and, if unexamined, solidified as entrenchment.

Connection to suffering

Suffering is the phenomenological echo of the spiral – the lived, subjective and intersubjective experience of each layer as it unfolds.

- Surface misery resonates as restlessness and irritation.
- Structured misery produces emotional paralysis and relational breakdown.
- Systemic misery is endured as cultural exhaustion and institutionalised depletion.
- Existential misery manifests as the collapse of meaning itself.

In this sense, the spiral is the architecture, while suffering is the felt experience that moves through mind, body and relationships.

Example: Misery is the architectural plan. Suffering is what it feels like to live inside the house built from that plan – drafty, unstable or collapsing.

Connection to entrenchment

Left unexamined, the spiral does not merely sustain misery. It hardens into entrenchment. What begins as shadows mutating into suffering becomes the very logic of identity, culture and systems. Dysfunction no longer feels like misalignment; it is mistaken for stability, virtue or truth.

Here it is important to distinguish *existential misery* from *entrenchment*. Existential misery is the spiral's deepest personal layer – the collapse of coherence within an individual's being, where life itself is felt as futile. In contrast, entrenchment is systemic: misery calcified into permanence, rebranded as order and defended as truth. If existential misery is the house collapsing in on itself, entrenchment is the ruins being declared the new home.

Example: A family may insist: 'This is just how we are', even when silence, fear or conflict has defined them for generations. What began as coping has become culture.

By linking the spiral to both suffering and entrenchment, the spiral's extension into disintegration becomes visible:

Shadows → Misery (structural condition) → Suffering (lived experience) → Entrenchment (systemic permanence)

This triadic link is crucial. It shows that misery is not simply a stage of hardship, but the pivot through which shadows either become integrated or cascade into deeper dissonance. Recognising this trajectory allows us to identify interruption points – where suffering can be met with coherence and where systems can resist calcifying into entrenchment.

Breaking the spiral

The Shadow–Misery Spiral shows why misery is not merely emotional pain, but the failure of integration and meaning-making. Yet spirals, no matter how entrenched, can be interrupted. Breaking the cycle requires more than coping strategies; it demands ontological precision. Shadows must be brought to awareness, metabolised and integrated, rather than denied or projected outward.

Understanding the architecture of misery – how shadows evolve into entrenched suffering – is the key to moving forward. It is also the central objective of this body of work in relation to dysfunction. Understanding the spiral is the first step. Integration and reconstruction – the return to coherence, clarity and authorship – belong to the journey ahead. To recognise the spiral is to reclaim the possibility of interrupting it, and in doing so, reorient life towards coherence.

Misery in action

Misery rarely declares itself overtly. It shows up as exhaustion, disengagement, chronic self-sacrifice or silent despair. Often, it is rationalised as duty, realism or just 'how life is'. The following cases reveal how misery takes shape – not as a feeling, but as an organising principle. In many scenarios, misery becomes structurally embedded, shaping perception, decision-making and identity. These patterns are not born of weakness; they are attempts to survive systems that have normalised disempowerment. Two cases, however, reveal something different – a healthy relationship with misery. Rather than being denied or idolised, misery is held with awareness and integrated into a coherent response. These examples show what becomes possible when misery is acknowledged without collapse.

Case 1: The reliable worker who never rests

Claire, a middle-aged employee, is known for being dependable. She never takes sick days, rarely takes holidays and is always the first to volunteer for extra work. Her colleagues admire her dedication. Her managers reward her with more responsibility. But privately, she feels numb, chronically tired and unappreciated. When offered support, she waves it off, saying, 'I'm fine.' When asked what brings her joy, she can't remember.

Insight: This is a case of misery internalised as virtue. Conditioned to equate worth with usefulness, Claire lives in a state of quiet depletion. Her fatigue is not a signal; it's her baseline. Rest feels threatening because it triggers the fear of becoming invisible. What looks like commitment is actually the residue of self-abandonment, sustained by external validation and a belief that collapse is just the cost of being good.

Case 2: The hopeful partner who stays too long

Jim remains in a relationship where emotional neglect is the norm. His partner frequently dismisses his feelings, invalidates his needs and refuses to engage in meaningful repair. Still, he clings to hope. 'She's just stressed. Maybe if I do better, things will change.' Friends express concern, but Jim constantly defends the relationship. 'It's not that bad,' he assures them. He tells himself that staying proves he's loyal, loving and strong.

Insight: This is misery recoded as endurance. What began as genuine care became entangled with a belief that suffering earns love. Over time, Jim's sense of self fused with the experience of not being chosen. The longer he stays, the more he fears what it would mean to leave. Misery becomes his identity. The pain is no longer just relational; it is existential. He is not simply in a difficult relationship; he is inhabiting a recursive identity loop sustained by false hope and emotional deprivation.

Case 3: The high-performing culture that quietly corrodes

A senior executive leads a large team with efficiency and calm. She is respected, productive and composed. Her emails are prompt. Her calendar is full. Her demeanour is professional. To her colleagues, she is the model of success: always capable, always available, never flustered.

However, what no one sees is the emptiness and loss of vitality beneath her calm exterior. She moves through the day in a state of low-grade disconnection, neither distressed nor present. Joy feels indulgent. Rest feels risky. When asked how she's doing, she says, 'All good, just busy.' She can't remember the last time she felt genuinely alive.

The organisation celebrates her. She is routinely praised for her dedication, long hours and unwavering composure. But the very qualities being rewarded are symptoms of a deeper pattern: over-functioning, emotional suppression and chronic neglect of her own needs and limits. Around her, the culture follows suit. Vulnerability is treated as unprofessional. Slowness is pathologised. Presence is replaced by performance.

Insight: This is institutionalised misery. A culture that idealises productivity and resilience becomes a system that normalises depletion. What looks like professional excellence is often collective dysregulation dressed up as discipline. The individual suffers, but so does the organisation, which loses access to creativity, care and coherence. Misery becomes the norm. No one names it, but everyone lives it.

Case 4: The exhausted carer who chose to pause

Tariq, a dedicated father and carer for his ageing mother, had spent years putting everyone else's needs before his own. He carried the belief that love meant total self-sacrifice. But after recurring panic attacks and a doctor's warning, he paused. For the first time, he allowed himself to ask: 'What do I need?'

With support, Tariq began setting boundaries. He started seeing a therapist, accepted respite care for his mother and re-engaged with his passion for music. At first, the guilt was overwhelming, but he came to realise that love does not require self-abandonment. Previously, his days had been defined by chronic self-erasure – skipping meals, silencing his own exhaustion and neglecting his passions in order to keep going.

Insight: This is a case of interrupting misery by disentangling care from depletion. Tariq recognised that his worth was not measured by how much he endured. His misery was not a flaw; it was a messenger. In choosing to honour his limits, he restored both vitality and presence, transforming service into stewardship rather than self-erasure.

Case 5: The disillusioned teacher who redefined impact

Maya, a high school teacher, initially entered the teaching profession with joy. But years of administrative overload, disengaged students and institutional pressure had left her drained. She was on autopilot. Colleagues told her it was normal, suggesting she should 'just push though'. But Maya didn't want to live that way.

Instead of quitting, she reframed her approach. She stopped trying to be perfect and started being present. She integrated emotional literacy into her classroom. She took mental health days. She connected with other educators who valued regeneration. Slowly, her joy returned, not through denial of the system's dysfunction, but through redefining her role within it.

Insight: This is a case of reclaiming agency within an entrenched structure. Maya didn't numb or escape her misery – she metabolised it. Rather than performing resilience, she cultivated space for honesty, rest and relational depth. Her misery became a source of discernment, not inertia – a signal to reimagine impact on her own terms.

Conclusion

Misery is not a weakness, failure or flaw. It is a structural outcome of incoherence left unaddressed: of pain that was never integrated, meaning distorted in the aftermath of rupture, and systems that reward endurance over truth. What begins as a response to adversity gradually becomes a way of being, a feedback loop between the internal and external worlds that recycles misery into identity.

This chapter has shown that, from an ontological perspective, misery is not simply a mood to be managed or a mindset to be shifted. It is an entangled architecture of narrative, emotion, physiology, behaviour and culture – each reinforcing the other, each justifying the next. When left unexamined, this architecture becomes invisible, yet pervasive. The system adapts to it. The body conforms to it. The world reflects it back.

But the fact that misery is structured means it can be restructured. What has been internalised can be interrupted. What has been mistaken for truth can be re-seen and re-interpreprted. Misery loosens its grip, not through avoidance or suppression, but through ontological precision – by meeting the condition where it lives: in the body, the story, the pattern and the system.

Often, misery takes root in the aftermath of a threshold event that was never fully processed. This is where *destabilis* enters the picture. Neither misery nor transformation, *destabilis* is the disorienting rupture that precedes both. It marks the moment when meaning fractures, when familiar responses fall short, when who we were no longer fits the life we inhabit. Misery emerges not from the rupture itself, but from the failure to meet that rupture with care, clarity and coherence.

To heal misery is not to eliminate hardship, but to reclaim authorship. It is to recover the ability to be with misery without becoming it; to walk through difficulty without building a home in it. To recognise *destabilis* for what it is – a portal rather than a punishment – is to intervene at the point of divergence, before rupture solidifies into despair.

Seen in its full progression, misery does not stop with itself. It reverberates as suffering – the felt echo that moves through body, story and relationship – and, if left unexamined, hardens into entrenchment, defended as order itself. To interrupt misery, then, is also to disrupt this progression – to meet suffering with coherence and to prevent dysfunction from calcifying into permanence.

Ultimately, misery is not a permanent sentence. It is a misaligned structure awaiting reintegration. Once it is seen, felt and named for what it is, a new coherence becomes possible – not as a return to ease, but a move towards integrity and wholeness.

Reflection

- Can you identify a time when misery was mistaken for strength, resilience or virtue – by yourself or others?
- What beliefs about yourself or the world might be reinforcing a state of quiet misery? Where did those beliefs originate?
- Have you ever stayed in a job, relationship or role because leaving felt impossible, not for practical reasons, but because you believed you had to endure misery?
- In what ways might your behaviours – withdrawal, overfunctioning, compliance or avoidance – be repeating patterns that keep misery in place?
- How does your body express what your voice does not? What signals of misery might you have normalised or ignored?
- Where might systems or relationships around you be reinforcing a story that misery is noble, necessary or deserved?
- Where in your life might misery be silently shaping perception, muting desire or narrowing what you believe is possible?
- What might begin to change if misery were recognised, not as weakness, but as a call for reintegration?

CHAPTER 32

Suffering

Suffering is often misunderstood as mere pain, affliction or discomfort. But ontologically, suffering is far more than a transient state or emotional episode. It is a structured phenomenon of Being, one that emerges when adversity ruptures our coherence and our attempts to process, integrate or reconcile it fall short. It is not what happens to us that defines suffering; it's how what happens is interpreted and embodied.

Pain is inevitable. But suffering is *constructed*. It is the result of dissonance that remains unresolved. A difficult event may pass through us as grief and leave behind wisdom. But when that event is framed through shadowed narratives, reinforced by avoidance, amplified emotionally, etched into the body, and left unresolved existentially, it becomes something more – a recursive system. It begins to shape how we see the world, how we inhabit our body, how we interpret new experiences and, ultimately, how we see ourselves.

Suffering, then, is not a symptom. It is a configuration of Being in response to adversity – a recursive ontology that, if left unexamined, can escalate into dysfunction, calcify into misery or harden into entrenchment. Though suffering may begin internally, it rarely stays contained. It seeps into behaviour, distorts relationships, reshapes systems and embeds itself in culture.

What makes suffering uniquely important in this body of work is that it represents the felt experience and lived reality of rupture. Suffering is not the rupture itself, nor merely the pain it causes. It is how rupture is interpreted, internalised and enacted through one's Being. In that sense, suffering is not just what happens to us. It is how we *are* in relation to what happens.

Suffering sits near a threshold – not as the threshold itself, but as the human experience that arises when one enters the gravitational field of that threshold. Ontologically, that threshold is *destabilis* – the raw, disorienting space that follows destabilisation. As discussed in the previous chapter, *destabilis* is a field of unstructured potential – the disintegration of previously held meaning and structure. While *destabilis* denotes the condition in which structure and meaning unravel, suffering is one possible echo within us when coherence, agency or attunement collapses in response. If *destabilis* is the chamber, suffering is not only the sound that may reverberate, but the cry that emerges when rupture is unintegrated.

Another way to view the distinction between suffering and *destabilis* is to consider that suffering is the narrative and somatic configuration that emerges when we are no longer shielded by certainty. In contrast, *destabilis* is the metaphysical terrain we enter – whether through betrayal, collapse, temptation, tragedy, failure or awakening – where the familiar dissolves and Being is laid bare.

Suffering becomes meaningful, not by escaping it, but by recognising it as a call to respond – an opportunity to reclaim authorship and cohere anew. In this ontology, *destabilis* is the ontological cause or provocateur – the source of destabilisation that disrupts previously coherent systems, meanings or identities. It can come from nature, human relationships, internal impulses or systemic forces. It is neither inherently good nor bad. It is the phenomenon that destabilises the structure.

When the destabilisation it triggers is resisted, denied or left unintegrated, it often gives rise to misery – the recursive state where dysfunction becomes identity. Suffering, then, is the experiential and somatic expression of this process – the felt reverberation of destabilisation when it is not adequately met, understood or metabolised.

This chapter demonstrates that suffering is not a sign of weakness. It is evidence of a collision between expectation and reality, identity and uncertainty, meaning and chaos. Yet it is also an invitation. When understood ontologically, suffering becomes a pathway through pain, not a means of escaping it. We suffer most when we misunderstand what suffering is. This chapter is an attempt to bring that understanding home, not just intellectually, but existentially.

Before unpacking suffering as a structured ontological condition using the Ontological Triad Schema, we will first examine the nature of suffering and some of the dominant historical and philosophical narratives relating to it. For something so universal, suffering – like consciousness – remains profoundly misunderstood: minimised in some traditions, glorified, pathologised or spiritualised in others, depending on the lens through which it is seen.

The nature of suffering

Unlike pain, which is a biological or sensory signal – a cut, a burn, an illness – suffering can not be reduced to biology. It is not simply what happens to the body. It is what happens within consciousness when adversity is interpreted, amplified, internalised or made meaningless. Suffering emerges at the intersection of perception, cognition, embodiment and cultural participation. It is not just felt but *lived*.

At its core, suffering is the phenomenological residue of unintegrated dissonance. It does not exist in a vacuum. It is always relational, arising in the tension between what is and what should have been, between what we need and what is withheld, between what we are and what we believe ourselves to be. Hence, suffering is not merely a psychological state, but an ontological event – it reveals how we are being in relation to truth, alignment, expectation and interpretation.

Suffering is neither uniform nor arbitrary. It unfolds within a structured architecture. Some forms are shallow and fleeting: surface-level dissonance or discomfort. Others are deep and enduring, marked by the collapse of meaning, ontological confusion or spiritual alienation. Whether suffering becomes a source of transformation or a gateway to misery and entrenchment depends not on the external event itself, but on the structure of the response and on the quality of sense-making, emotional integration and ontological responsiveness that follows.

Spiritual, philosophical and scientific perspectives on suffering

Across human history, suffering – like consciousness – has been one of the most enduring subjects of contemplation, concern and controversy. Various traditions and schools of thought have each offered their own interpretation of its nature, origin, purpose and resolution. These perspectives illuminate the plurality of human responses to suffering and help explain why a unified ontological model has, to date, remained elusive. Each has captured a fragment of the structure, but few have framed suffering as a systemic, interwoven force embedded in Being itself.

Let's briefly touch on a few of these existing and historical perspectives as contextual lenses that shape how suffering is understood and engaged.

Moral and metaphysical interpretations

In classical philosophy, suffering was framed through the lens of reason and virtue. For the Stoics, it arose from false beliefs and misplaced attachments; for Plato, from misalignment with the Forms. Aristotle accepted suffering as a natural part of life, best approached through rational moderation. In these traditions, suffering reflected errors in judgement or perception, not systemic conditions.

In contrast, religious traditions position suffering within broader spiritual frameworks. In Buddhism, *dukkha* is an intrinsic part of conditioned existence, arising from craving and delusion. Liberation comes not through escape, but through the disciplined transformation of suffering via ethical and cognitive refinement. In Christianity, suffering is often redemptive – a path to purification and divine communion. Yet this framing has also been used to normalise avoidable suffering, particularly among the oppressed. In Islam, suffering (*bala'*) is a test calibrated to one's capacity. Endurance and trust in divine wisdom (*sabr* and *tawakkul*) are seen as pathways to spiritual refinement. Across these traditions, suffering is deeply meaningful. However, that meaning is often outsourced to divine purpose rather than structurally interrogated.

Psychological and existential frameworks

Modern psychology reframed suffering as internal disruption. For Freud, it was the return of repressed trauma – a message from the unconscious seeking resolution. Jung expanded this, viewing suffering as the result of disowned aspects of the psyche. In both cases, suffering pointed to intra-psychic fragmentation rather than external structure.

Existential thinkers offered a different angle. For Nietzsche, suffering was necessary for growth and individuation. When denied or moralised, it produced resentment and moral inversion. Heidegger linked suffering to our confrontation with finitude – the state of having limits or bounds. Authenticity arose through accepting our limitations rather than fleeing them. Drawing on lived experience, Frankl argued that meaning, not avoidance, determines whether suffering destroys or transforms.

These framings brought depth to the human condition, but stopped short of offering a systemic account of how suffering moves through the layers of selfhood, relational life and the systems we inhabit.

Power, politics and discursive construction

Post-structural thinkers revealed how suffering is constructed, distributed and regulated by systems of power. Foucault argued that institutions such as hospitals, prisons and schools don't merely respond to suffering; they produce and manage it through surveillance, classification and normalisation. Suffering becomes entangled with discourse: who defines it, who diagnoses it, and who benefits from its framing.

Judith Butler extended this insight to the politics of recognition. Suffering becomes a question of visibility: whose pain is acknowledged, and whose grief is legitimised?

These framings expose the relational and political dimensions of suffering, but often veer towards deconstruction without reconstruction, leaving coherence elusive.

Biological and neurological approaches

Contemporary neuroscience adds a physiological layer to the conversation. Here, suffering is understood as a biological response to threat, loss or disconnection. Chronic pain and emotional distress reshape the nervous system via sensitisation, cortisol dysregulation and changes in regions of the brain like the amygdala and prefrontal cortex.

Somatic psychology and polyvagal theory now show how suffering lives not just in thought, but in breath, posture and nervous system regulation. While these findings are vital, they often focus on description rather than meaning, treating suffering purely as a mechanistic process, not as an ontological phenomenon with structural significance.

What these perspectives miss

Each of these traditions offers valuable insight by capturing elements of suffering's cause, expression or function. But none fully account for its *structural anatomy*. What is missing is a unified ontological architecture that:

- Distinguishes between transient pain, embedded misery and existential collapse;
- Traces suffering's persistence across narrative, embodiment and social context; and
- Recognises suffering not only in the psyche or society, but as a patterned field within Being itself.

The next section invites a deeper structural inquiry – one that treats suffering as a signal, a structure and a potential site of reintegration and liberation. Grounded in the Ontological Triad Schema – anatomy, mechanics and topology – it reframes suffering not as moral failure or passive affliction, but as a structured dynamic of Being: a pattern we can observe, trace, interrupt and transform. Let's start with the ontological distinction of suffering.

Ontological Distinction of Suffering

Suffering is the lived experience of misery – the felt gap between what is and what is longed for, between inner truth and outer conditions, between meaning and experience. It is not merely pain, hardship or adversity. While pain is usually specific and has boundaries, *suffering* spreads. It weaves into the fabric of life, colouring perception, shaping identity and narrowing possibility. At its core, *suffering* signals that something deeply cared about has fallen out of alignment with the way life is unfolding.

A **healthy relationship with suffering** indicates that you are willing to *be with* it rather than deny it. You can witness suffering without collapsing into it, treating it as a signal that calls for attention, integration and transformation. You resist the temptation to turn suffering into identity or to glorify endurance as a virtue. Instead, you meet suffering with honesty and care, discerning what it reveals about the reality of the situation and your needs and values. In manufactured systems – whether relationships, organisations or institutions – a healthy relationship with suffering means creating space to acknowledge hardship without normalising dysfunction or rewarding suffering in silence and burnout. Such healthy systems honour human dignity by building pathways for coherence, support and renewal.

An **unhealthy relationship with suffering** indicates that you have resisted, moralised or suppressed it to the point where it has become self-perpetuating. You may weave suffering into your identity, wearing it as a badge of honour, interpreting reality only through the lens of loss or limitation. Instead of integrating suffering, it becomes the focal point of your life. In teams, organisations and institutions, an unhealthy relationship with suffering manifests as cultures that glorify struggle, reward silence in the face of dysfunction, or mistake collapse for character. Over time, suffering that feeds on itself hardens into entrenchment – a condition where neither individuals nor systems can find a way out, leaving them stuck at the edge of dysfunction or collapse.

Ontology of suffering

Understanding the structure of suffering is not merely theoretical. It is the beginning of liberation. Once suffering is no longer mistaken for randomness or destiny, it becomes navigable and meaningful – something we can engage with, not just endure.

Ontologically, suffering is the disintegration of coherence in response to adversity. It is not merely the presence of pain, but a collapse of integration, meaning and responsiveness. Suffering arises when experience ruptures the harmony of Being and our attempts to metabolise, interpret or reconcile that rupture fall short.

This breakdown may occur in any domain: physical, emotional, relational or existential. However, what defines suffering is not the intensity of the event, but the structural fracture it produces. In this way, suffering is not a feeling; it is a condition – a patterned field of distortion, looping through mind, body and meaning until reintegration becomes possible.

Where theology offers salvation, psychology offers interpretation and science offers diagnosis, an ontological approach offers *navigability*. It restores agency to the sufferer without denying the weight of pain. It repositions suffering as a field in which the architecture of our Being is laid bare, inviting us to meet it with coherence, presence and structural insight.

Because suffering reveals itself through multiple layers of experience, it is essential to trace how it unfolds – not only from an internal rupture, but through how that rupture is shaped, sustained and amplified across cognitive, emotional, social and existential domains. Clarifying these nested layers allows us to locate suffering more precisely and, therefore, better understand its structure.

The hierarchy of suffering: A layered framework

Suffering does not appear as a single, uniform experience. It takes different forms and intensities – from fleeting discomforts to enduring existential ruptures. These are best understood as layered, in the sense that one form can build upon or compound another.

At times they may also be experienced as 'nested', with surface-level struggles folding into deeper crises if left unexamined. Each layer is not merely a difference in severity, but a distinct ontological expression of how suffering is processed, sustained and entangled with the self, others and the world.

Left unexamined, suffering at one level can cascade into the next, compounding over time. What begins as surface discomfort can deepen into despair when filtered through distorted meaning-making, unintegrated emotion or systemic reinforcement. This layered model does not rank suffering in importance. It reveals how different forms of suffering interrelate, escalate and either fragment or reconfigure into coherence.

1. Surface-level suffering: Sensory friction and momentary misalignment

At the outermost layer, suffering arises as a direct and often fleeting response to sensory friction or situational disruption. This includes pain from injury, physical exhaustion, temporary discomfort or sudden change. These experiences do not constitute misery; they are moments of misalignment encountered in real-time.

A stubbed toe, a cancelled flight, a strained muscle – none of these presents an existential threat. But suffering enters the picture when the event is *interpreted* in a way that amplifies distress: through frustration, reactive resistance or meaning-laden self-talk like, 'Why does this always happen to me?' or 'I can't catch a break.'

At this level, suffering is fluid and usually self-resolving – unless it hooks into deeper, unresolved wounds. In that case, it becomes a gateway into more entrenched forms of suffering. In its surface form, suffering is simply the felt signal of misalignment – a moment of friction before the stories we tell about it begin to entrench it within our Being, solidifying into the felt condition of misery.

2. Cognitive suffering: Distorted thought and anticipatory dread

When surface-level discomfort is not metabolised, it often escalates to the cognitive layer. Here, the mind begins constructing suffering through interpretation, projection and fixation. The experience is no longer about what happened. Instead, it becomes about what it means and where it might lead.

This layer is marked by:

- Distorted assumptions ('I'm not good enough.')
- Catastrophic projections ('This will never get better.')
- Existential spirals ('What's the point of any of this?')

Shadows are active here, shaping perception through fear, shame or inherited belief. The mind loops and reframes, trying to regain control, but often only deepening the suffering.

At this level, suffering becomes mental architecture: recursive, anticipatory and increasingly disconnected from the original stimulus.

3. Psychological suffering: Emotional wounds and inner fragmentation

At a deeper level, suffering takes root in the emotional body. It is no longer just about thoughts; it becomes affective entrapment. Guilt, shame, grief, abandonment and fear saturate the inner world, often linked to:

- Unresolved trauma.
- Relational rupture and unintegrated grief.
- Attachment wounds that impair emotional regulation and trust.

This is where suffering begins to fracture identity. The inner voice shifts from, 'Something is wrong' to 'I am wrong.' Emotional paralysis, self-rejection and internal incoherence dominate.

Psychological suffering cannot be resolved through logic alone. It requires relational, somatic and ontological integration because what is broken here is not reason, but the felt sense of safety, wholeness and belonging.

4. Systemic and social suffering: Cultural shadows and structural distortion

Suffering is always lived and felt personally, yet it is not always generated solely from personal circumstances. At this layer, it is systemically induced through social, cultural and institutional structures that shape how suffering is distributed, recognised and legitimised. Individuals experience the weight of these structures in profoundly personal ways, but the relationship is reciprocal: structural distortion generates suffering, while unresolved personal suffering can normalise or sustain dysfunctional structures.

This layer of systemic suffering includes:

- Oppression and marginalisation based on race, gender, class, identity or belief.
- Cultural scripts that delegitimise certain truths or emotional expressions.
- Economic and political systems that normalise burnout, disconnection and despair.

Systemic suffering is often internalised by individuals who come to see their pain as normal rather than as distortion. A child punished for expressing emotion may carry chronic shame into adulthood, not as trauma, but as a misguided perception of reality: 'This is just how life is.'

Addressing this layer of systemic suffering requires more than inner work. It calls for ontological activism – the courage to confront and reconfigure the systems that perpetuate suffering through structural distortion.

5. Existential suffering: Collapse of meaning and disconnection from Being

At the deepest layer lies existential suffering – the disintegration of coherence, belonging or ontological grounding. This is not caused by a single event, but by a structural rupture in one's relationship to self, others and the world.

It may involve:

- Ontological dislocation ('Who am I?', 'What is real?').
- A crisis of meaning, purpose or faith.
- Alienation from life, love, truth or any organising centre of significance.

This layer resists language because it is experienced less as a story and more as a void, a collapse of meaning that defies easy articulation. A person may appear functional, but feel unanchored internally, adrift in a world that no longer holds coherence.

Here, shadows do not distort meaning; they erase it from lived experience. And suffering becomes a silent, existential freefall unless met with deep reintegration at the level of Being.

Anatomy of suffering

Suffering, from an ontological perspective, is not merely the presence of pain. It is a multi-layered experience in which adversity is processed, interpreted, embodied and assigned meaning. Each layer determines whether suffering becomes a crucible for transformation or a vortex of fragmentation. The following five structural components form the anatomical scaffold of suffering.

1. **Stimulus**

    Not all ruptures result in suffering. What matters is not the stimulus itself, but how it is processed, integrated or denied. The event is the catalyst, not the condition. What follows determines whether it becomes suffering. It is important to distinguish stimulus from *destabilis*. A stimulus is the rupture itself – the event. In contrast, *destabilis* is the existential condition of being destabilised when that rupture unsettles one's coherence. Put simply: stimulus is the spark; *destabilis* is the fire if the spark takes hold. For example, a car accident (stimulus) shakes a person's sense of safety. If they process it, the disruption passes. But if it unsettles their very trust in life and leaves them feeling the world is no longer safe or coherent, that rupture becomes *destabilis*.

2. Framing

Immediately after the rupture, meaning is either made or mis-made. This interpretive layer determines how the event is understood, often through the lens of unresolved shadows, internalised beliefs, past trauma or cultural scripts. Phrases like 'This is punishment', 'This always happens to me,' or 'There is no way out' reveal how suffering is shaped at the level of narrative. This framing doesn't merely describe what happened; it organises it into a worldview. When distorted, it shrinks possibility, reinforces wounds and sets the trajectory for deeper suffering.

3. Emotional charge

The framing of rupture activates an emotional response. Suffering deepens when emotions such as grief, fear, shame, guilt or rage are intensified and left unprocessed. These emotional charges flood the nervous system, disrupt regulation and can harden into chronic affective states: moods of dread, numbness or volatility. Over time, this emotional field becomes the dominant emotional landscape of suffering, shaping its tone, intensity and persistence.

4. Somatic registration

Suffering does not remain confined to thoughts or emotions; it registers in the body. This is not yet somatisation, but a subtler, earlier phase – the body attuning to unresolved tension, misalignment or distress. Shifts in posture, breath, muscle tone or energy levels often signal what the conscious mind has not yet named. The nervous system may oscillate between hypervigilance and shutdown, not as dysfunction, but as an adaptive response to a perceived threat or incoherence. In this stage, the body becomes a living transcript of what remains unmetabolised. Here, suffering is not just felt, it is somatically inscribed, awaiting integration before it calcifies into deeper forms of collapse.

5. Existential integration

At the deepest layer, suffering confronts the foundations of identity, meaning and Being itself. This is where a rupture either expands the self – deepening resilience, insight and coherence – or fractures it, leading to disorientation, nihilism or lasting inner fragmentation. The question at this level is not merely what happened, but what it means in relation to self, life and reality. If the experience cannot be integrated, suffering may harden into misery or initiate patterns of entrenchment. But if met with presence and insight, it can act as a catalyst for profound transformation.

These five layers – stimulus, framing, emotional charge, embodiment and existential integration – do not operate in isolation. Their recursive interaction determines whether suffering is metabolised into wisdom or spirals into chronic dysfunction.

A tangible example of misaligned suffering

Consider a woman whose partner of many years suddenly leaves. At first, the rupture (*destabilis*) itself is painful, but it has not yet translated into suffering. The path she takes in response to it determines whether the event becomes integrated grief or suffering.

At the level of **stimulus**, the breakup destabilises her coherence. What once felt certain and safe collapses overnight. While the loss is real, what matters most is not the event itself, but how it is met.

At the level of **framing**, the story she tells about the rupture begins to take shape. Instead of seeing it as a painful but specific loss, she interprets it through unresolved shadows: 'I was never good enough. Everyone abandons me. Life is unfair.' The breakup ceases to be one event and becomes evidence (in her mind) of a broader worldview.

At the level of **emotional charge**, the framing intensifies her emotions. Grief transforms into shame, despair and dread. Each day is saturated by the feeling that she is unworthy and unlovable. What began as pain expands into an affective field that floods her inner world and narrows her capacity to respond.

At the level of **somatic registration**, the suffering inscribes itself in her body. She has trouble sleeping, her posture contracts, her breath grows shallow. Even on days when external circumstances improve slightly, her nervous system remains on high alert. The body carries what the mind cannot yet integrate, holding tension and fatigue as living transcripts of distress.

At the level of **existential integration**, the rupture confronts her sense of identity and meaning. Instead of asking, 'What can I learn from this?', she arrives at, 'I am broken' and 'I can't trust anyone.' Left unintegrated, the event fractures her orientation to self and the world. What could have been grief metabolised into wisdom hardens into suffering – a recursive configuration of Being that reshapes her perception of reality itself.

In this way, the anatomy of suffering takes hold. Stimulus becomes a fracture point, framing distorts meaning, emotional charge overwhelms, somatic registration embeds distress in the body, and existential integration collapses into disorientation. What began as loss becomes an ongoing condition, where pain is not simply endured but structured into identity.

Mechanics of suffering

Suffering is not sustained merely by the initial rupture. It perpetuates itself through recursive mechanisms that embed adversity into the architecture of Being. These processes convert pain into pattern, dissonance into identity and situational adversity into systemic affliction. The following mechanics reveal how suffering persists, deepens and becomes a self-validating ontology.

1. Narrative Looping

In suffering, the mind instinctively seeks to make sense of pain. It begins to form internal stories: 'This always happens to me,' 'I must have done something wrong,' or 'Maybe I deserve this' as a way to contain and comprehend the rupture. These narratives are not yet fixed beliefs, but provisional attempts at meaning-making during distress. Unlike misery, where distortion becomes identity, in suffering, the loop is still porous – it repeats, but can be interrupted.

The looping reflects an effort to restore coherence. But when left unchecked, it can amplify the pain and delay integration. The suffering here is not the story itself; it is the struggle to make meaning while still wounded.

2. Avoidance and escapism

Rather than metabolising the experience, many attempt to bypass suffering through strategies such as distraction (overwork, consumption, entertainment), numbing (addiction, dissociation) or deflection (humour, minimisation). While these mechanisms may offer temporary relief, they interrupt the integrative process. Pain that is not processed is not resolved. Instead, it is displaced into the subconscious, where it festers and distorts. What is avoided cannot be healed. In this way, resistance paradoxically deepens the suffering, transforming acute pain into chronic existential dissonance.

3. Shadow reinforcement

Shadows – those disowned, exiled parts of the self – amplify and distort the meaning assigned to suffering. A minor rejection is felt as total abandonment; a single loss becomes confirmation of deep unworthiness. Suffering becomes a stage for re-enacting repressed wounds, with the shadow using it as a canvas to validate its concealed beliefs: 'I deserve this', 'People always leave' and 'I must suffer to be loved.' In this way, suffering shifts from being reactive to re-enactive. The past hijacks the present, turning wounds into worldview.

4. Systemic reinforcement

Suffering is always lived internally, but it can be reinforced by the outer world. Systems mirror and magnify inner despair through neglect (being ignored in medical, family or workplace settings), moralism (pain interpreted as punishment or karma) or exploitation (cultures that glorify burnout or demand silence). These systemic responses validate the inner logic of suffering. When the world reflects pain as deserved, natural or even virtuous, the internalisation becomes complete. Suffering is no longer seen merely as a personal struggle; it becomes embedded as a cultural norm.

5. **Collapse of coherence**

Human beings live within imagined realities: internalised beliefs about fairness, love, justice and control. When life contradicts these expectations, such as, 'Good people shouldn't suffer' or 'If I do everything right, things will work out', the dissonance creates ontological rupture. The gap between what is and what should be becomes intolerable when unresolved, often spiralling into confusion, despair or nihilism: 'Nothing makes sense', 'I can't trust anything' or 'The world is chaos.' The more tightly one clings to the expectation, the more brutal the collapse when it fails.

These mechanics do not merely prolong suffering; they compound it into a recursive structure – a self-validating loop across cognition, behaviour, embodiment and culture. To disrupt these mechanics is not to 'fix' suffering, but to intervene in its recursion – to reclaim authorship over how pain is integrated into our sense of self and reality.

Topology of suffering

Suffering is not a sequence of isolated events. It is a recursive topology of interacting layers that generate and sustain ontological dissonance. The five anatomical components – stimulus, framing, emotional charge, somatic registration and existential integration – do not operate in a linear chain, but as a feedback ecosystem. Each element shapes and is shaped by the others, forming closed loops that either metabolise adversity or escalate it into fragmentation. What persists is not merely pain but a dynamic architecture – one that fuses perception, emotion, embodiment and meaning into a self-sustaining field of suffering.

1. **Stimulus ↔ Framing**

The initiating rupture – whether physical, emotional or existential – does not produce suffering on its own. Its impact depends on the interpretive frame it passes through. A neutral or minor event can catalyse profound suffering if filtered through unresolved shadows, past trauma or internalised narratives. A delay may be read as betrayal. A failure may be framed as proof of unworthiness. The mind does not just register the event; it assigns it meaning. This reflexive framing determines whether the experience is metabolised with clarity or misread as confirmation of an existential threat.

2. Framing ↔ Emotional charge

Interpretation shapes affect. The more distorted, absolute or fatalistic the framing, the more intense the emotional charge it generates. Emotions such as fear, shame, rage or despair are not random; they emerge directly from the story the mind tells about the rupture. Once activated, these emotions feed back into the interpretation itself. Fear confirms that the world is dangerous, shame confirms that the self is deficient and despair confirms that life is hopeless. Belief and feeling form a closed circuit, each validating and intensifying the other.

3. Emotional charge ↔ Somatic registration

Emotions are not only fleeting experiences; they register in the body. The nervous system, breath and hormonal patterns all adapt to prolonged emotional strain. Chronic fear produces hypervigilance and muscular tension. Shame constricts posture and inhibits voice. Despair settles as fatigue and collapse. Over time, the body becomes more than a vessel that carries suffering. It becomes the very place where suffering is expressed, remembered and replayed. Patterns of unresolved rupture are imprinted in breath, stance and sensation, turning suffering into a postural, metabolic and sensory reality.[75]

---

75 Schäfer, I., Lass-Hennemann, J., Rosner, R., Friese, M. & Plichta, M.M., 2022 Clinical Manifestations of Body Memories: The Impact of Past Bodily Experiences. *Frontiers in Neuroscience*, 16, Article 9138975. Available at: https://www.ncbi.nlm.nih.gov/pmc/articles/PMC9138975/ [Accessed 1 October 2025]; van der Kolk, B.A. & Fisler, R., 1997 Memory and the Evolving Psychobiology of Posttraumatic Stress. *Harvard Review of Psychiatry*, 4(5), pp. 253–265. Available at: https://pubmed.ncbi.nlm.nih.gov/9384857/ [Accessed 1 October 2025].

4. **Somatic registration ↔ Existential integration**

As the body enters sustained incoherence, existential cracks begin to show. The question shifts from, 'What happened?' to 'What does this say about me?' or 'What's the point of all this?' When suffering is not metabolised physiologically, it fractures ontological coherence. A person's sense of self fragments. They no longer recognise who they are or feel consistent across situations. The frameworks that once gave life coherence feel hollow or distorted. The pain in the body becomes a metaphor for a life that no longer makes sense. As exhaustion accumulates, even core convictions are shaken – fatigue blurs clarity, and what once felt certain about life, faith or purpose begins to feel doubtful or fragile. The body becomes a mirror of metaphysical collapse.[76]

5. **Existential integration ↔ Stimulus**

Once existential disintegration sets in, all future experience becomes burdened with distorted meaning. Life is still encountered, but not as it is. Instead, it is filtered through interpretation before it unfolds. A new opportunity is mistrusted. A relationship feels doomed from the start. The world appears hostile, futile or chaotic. New stimuli re-trigger the loop – not because they are inherently threatening, but because they are processed through the lens of ontological collapse. This closes the circuit, converting adversity into a self-validating ontology of suffering.[77]

Emergent forces and patterns

From this recursive interplay arise not mere symptoms but *ontological artefacts* – qualities that begin to define not just what we feel, but *who we are*. They include:

---

76 Lin, K., Wang, H., Chen, Y. & Zhang, L., 2023 Understanding Embodied Effects of Posture: A Qualitative Study. *Behavioral Sciences*, 5(2), Article 30.

77 López-Castro, T., Saraiya, T., Zumberg-Smith, K. & Melara, R., 2019 Association Between Shame and Posttraumatic Stress. *Journal of Clinical Psychology*, 75(9), pp. 1659–1671.

- **Despair and emotional volatility** – A pendulum swing between numbness and overwhelm.
- **Hypervigilance and disconnection** – Constant scanning for danger while withdrawing from relational contact.
- **Collapse of narrative coherence** – Confusion, loss of purpose and mistrust in meaning itself.
- **Existential fatigue and numbness** – A slow depletion of curiosity, will and spiritual vitality – the felt energy that comes from a sense of meaning, connection and orientation in life.

These are not personality traits, but the patterned manifestation of unintegrated suffering, expressed through body, psyche and lived experience.

Suffering in action

Suffering often hides in plain sight. It doesn't always announce itself through breakdown or drama. It weaves itself into the background of ordinary life, masked by functionality, belief or survival strategy. Because it operates through interpretation and identity, suffering is frequently mistaken for realism, wisdom or just 'the way things are'.

The following cases reveal how suffering becomes structurally embedded, not as a moment of pain, but as a patterned response to rupture. In many scenarios, suffering forms a closed loop between perception, emotion, embodiment and meaning. These are not failures of character; they are adaptive strategies forged in contexts where coherence has been lost and pain remains unintegrated. A couple of cases, however, offer a different view – where suffering is neither denied nor idolised, but met with presence, dignity and discernment. They show what becomes possible when one has a healthy relationship with suffering

Case 1: The achiever who fears stillness

Raj is a successful entrepreneur with multiple ventures, a high-performance mindset and a packed schedule. He thrives in fast-paced environments and is admired for his discipline and drive. But underneath the polished exterior, Raj lives with a constant edge of anxiety. Restlessness is his default. Slowing down feels suffocating. When not in motion, he feels a rising sense of dread, like something is wrong or something important is about to be lost.

He describes himself as 'motivated' and 'purpose-driven', but he rarely enjoys the fruits of his labour. Achievements bring fleeting satisfaction, quickly replaced by the need for the next goal. When asked why he keeps pushing, he shrugs: 'If I stop, I will fall behind.'

Insight: This is suffering masked as ambition. Raj's relentless drive is not just about success. It is a defence against stillness, where unresolved fear and shame begin to surface. The rupture lies not in his work, but in the way he relates to emptiness. Action becomes escape. Progress becomes protection. Suffering is not what he's running from. It's the very rhythm that structures his life.

Case 2: The mother who never says no

Elena is a devoted parent, friend and community member. She is always available – organising school events, helping friends in crisis and taking on extra shifts at work. She prides herself on being reliable and generous. But her health is deteriorating. She hasn't had a full night's sleep in months. She feels resentful, yet guilty for feeling that way. Her inner voice says, 'Don't be selfish. They need you.'

When Elena's partner suggests she take a weekend away or ask for help, she resists. 'That's not who I am,' she says. 'I can handle it.' In truth, she can't remember what it feels like to rest without guilt or to receive without anxiety.

Insight: This is suffering recoded as selflessness. Elena's identity is entangled with over-care and self-neglect. Her inability to say no is not a flaw; it's a survival strategy forged in a belief that love must be earned through sacrifice. Saying yes keeps her connected. Saying no risks rejection. Over time, her suffering is no longer just emotional or physical; it becomes existential. Her sense of self is sustained by depletion.

Case 3: The student who intellectualises everything

Leo is a postgraduate student studying philosophy and psychology. He speaks fluently about trauma, Attachment Theory and existential meaning. His essays are brilliant, and his professors admire his depth. But in conversation, he rarely talks about his own life. When asked how he's feeling, he responds with abstract frameworks. 'It's probably just a limbic response,' he says, smiling. He hasn't cried in years.

In relationships, Leo often feels disconnected. He wants closeness, but avoids emotional intensity. When conflict arises, he withdraws or over-explains. Friends describe him as 'thoughtful, but hard to reach'.

Insight: This is suffering sublimated into cognition. For Leo, intellectualisation is not just a coping mechanism; it's a structural adaptation. By staying in the realm of ideas, he avoids the vulnerability of feeling. The rupture has not been resolved. Instead, it has been translated into language. The mind becomes a refuge from the body. But beneath the insight lies isolation. Suffering persists not because Leo is unaware, but because his awareness remains intellectual rather than embodied.

Case 4: The artist who stayed with her grief

Mira is a painter who lost her younger brother in a tragic accident. For months, she couldn't paint. Her grief felt paralysing, and friends urged her to 'stay busy' or 'move on'. But instead of numbing herself or becoming distracting through productivity, Mira chose to enter a conscious space of mourning. She took long walks, journalled and allowed herself to cry. She didn't interpret her pain as failure. She let it be present.

Over time, the grief didn't disappear, but it shifted. One day, she picked up a brush again, not to escape the grief, but to express it. Her new body of work was raw, tender and unlike anything she had made before. It was deeply received by others, many of whom found solace in her honesty.

Insight: Mira's suffering was not bypassed, performed or intellectualised. It was *metabolised*. She didn't collapse into it, nor did she try to erase it. Instead, she held space for it to speak. Through integration, her grief became a portal to deeper creativity and attunement. Her art was no longer about output; it became an act of meaning-making and shared humanity.

Case 5: The leader who paused to feel

Darren, a start-up founder, was known for his resilience. After a failed product launch and a painful layoff round, he found himself emotionally drained. Normally, he would 'power through', but something inside told him not to rush. Instead of spiralling into blame or distraction, he began working with a coach, carving space to sit with his disappointment, fear and guilt.

In the weeks that followed, Darren journalled daily, attended silent retreats and reconnected with old mentors, not to find quick answers but to listen. Slowly, he began to see how his constant need to 'fix' everything had masked a deeper fear of failure. He returned to work with more clarity, softness and genuine presence.

Insight: Darren's suffering became a teacher. By allowing it to unfold without avoidance or performance, he discovered hidden patterns that shaped his leadership. His pause wasn't weakness; it was wisdom. Through this, his decisions became more human, his team more cohesive, and his direction more intentional. He didn't transcend suffering; he grew through it.

Case 6: When an organisation listens to suffering

A mid-sized healthcare organisation noticed rising stress among frontline staff during a period of heavy patient demand. Instead of dismissing the signs of exhaustion or glorifying sacrifice as 'part of the job', leadership invited staff into structured conversations about their struggles. Anonymous surveys, listening circles and open forums created space for people to name their fatigue without fear of reprisal.

Rather than rewarding silent endurance, the organisation responded by adjusting rosters, increasing peer support resources and offering counselling services. Leaders also shared their own vulnerabilities, modelling that acknowledging hardship was not weakness but honesty. Over time, staff reported that while the workload remained intense, they felt seen, supported and less isolated. The organisation not only retained key talent, but also fostered a culture where suffering could be acknowledged without collapsing into dysfunction.

Insight: This case shows a healthy relationship with suffering at a systemic level. By recognising suffering as a signal rather than a stigma, the organisation created pathways for renewal. It neither denied nor glorified hardship, but responded to it with coherence, care and integrity – strengthening trust and resilience across the system.

Conclusion

Suffering is not reducible to pain. It is an ontological phenomenon – a structured breakdown in how we make sense of, embody and respond to rupture. It is not weakness or failure, but the signal of misalignment – a dissonance that has not yet been metabolised. When left unexamined, suffering becomes recursive, embedding itself into our stories, emotions, bodies and beliefs. But when seen clearly, it reveals not only the anatomy of collapse, but the architecture of transformation.

The topology of suffering maps more than distress. It shows us how suffering loops. It reveals how meaning, emotion, embodiment and identity become entangled into a systemic experience of fragmentation. But it also shows us the opportunity. Because suffering is structured, it can be interrupted. Because it loops, it can be redirected. Because it is systemic, it offers multiple pathways back to coherence.

To disrupt suffering is not to erase it, but to engage its architecture:

- To reinterpret the rupture
- To integrate the emotion
- To restore bodily coherence
- To rebuild existential integrity.

This is not a quick repair. It is the quiet, courageous work of reassembling the self – of meeting suffering with structural insight and presence, not avoidance or protective framing.

Suffering, then, is not the end of the story. It is a signal – a summons to coherence, not a sentence to endure. It shows us where meaning has fractured, where our response has stalled, and where restoration is possible. When we meet suffering with presence and structural insight, it becomes more than pain; it becomes a gateway to renewal. But when suffering is resisted, denied or left unexamined, its loops deepen, its patterns harden, and its stories entrench. What begins as misalignment becomes identity. The next chapter explores how this happens and what it takes to break free.

Reflection

- Can you recall a moment when suffering was present, but not fully recognised – masked by busyness, detachment or explanation?
- How do you typically respond to rupture or loss of coherence? Do you tend to reinterpret, suppress, avoid or intellectualise?
- What personal narratives – about pain, control, failure or worth – might be looping beneath your current experience of suffering?
- In what ways might your emotional responses be reinforcing old narratives? Are there feelings you habitually override or distrust?
- How does your body carry your suffering? What tensions, postures or sensations might be holding unresolved dissonance?
- Have you ever reframed suffering as 'normal', 'inevitable' or 'necessary' in order to endure it rather than engage it?
- Where in your life might you be interpreting new experiences through the lens of past rupture?
- What would it mean to meet your own suffering, not as a flaw to be fixed, but as a signal – an invitation to reinterpret, integrate and realign?

CHAPTER 33

Entrenchment

Entrenchment is not merely the persistence of dysfunction. It is the point at which dysfunction becomes indistinguishable from order and reality. It is not an aberration within a system; it *becomes* the system. What begins as deviation, distortion or protective adaptation gradually mutates into the very scaffolding upon which identity, behaviour, institutions and worldviews are built. In this state, dysfunction no longer feels like something to fix. It feels like something to defend.

Entrenchment is the ontological culmination of deeper breakdown. If shadows distort our perception of reality, misery internalises the distortion and suffering makes it existentially palpable, then entrenchment cements the condition into continuity. It is the silent force that transforms transient failure into structural inevitability. The tragedy of entrenchment is that once it takes hold, dysfunction is no longer experienced as dissonance. It is experienced as truth.

This makes entrenchment especially dangerous – it masquerades as stability, loyalty, tradition or even virtue. It presents itself as coherence while quietly eroding adaptability. And because it operates beneath awareness, it rarely triggers alarm. Entrenchment is not the chaos of collapse. It is the quiet conviction of a system that has forgotten it was meant to evolve.

Rather than being passive, entrenchment is performative. It defends itself. It generates explanations for its continuity. It creates rituals to legitimise its presence. It weaponises nostalgia, glorifies struggle and masks dysfunction as discipline. It resists transparency, because to see it clearly would be to question what has become 'normal'.

The reach of entrenchment is all-encompassing. It lives in:

- The psyche, where we rationalise self-sabotage as 'just how I am'.
- Relationships, where conflict becomes habitual and unresolved, but is still called love.
- Organisations, where toxic culture is labelled 'high performance'.
- Nations, where systemic inequality is justified as 'freedom' and critique is treated as treason.
- Civilisations, where historical atrocities are mythologised and progress is confused with control.

Entrenchment is not merely what keeps dysfunction alive. It normalises it. It doesn't just prevent transformation; it makes transformation feel like betrayal.

This chapter reveals why entrenched systems and identities are so difficult to dislodge, and why they often collapse under their own weight rather than evolve voluntarily. Most importantly, this chapter does not treat entrenchment as an abstract evil. It reveals it as a patterned phenomenon – an understandable, traceable force that can be identified, disrupted and, ultimately, transcended.

Because the greatest lie entrenchment tells is this: *There is no alternative.*

Ontological Distinction of Entrenchment

Entrenchment is the stage where dysfunction stops being seen as a temporary problem and becomes embedded as reality itself. It is not just that things are misaligned. It is that misalignment has been absorbed into identity, culture and structure until it feels normal

– even virtuous. What was once incoherence is now explained, defended and repeated as 'just the way things are'. *Entrenchment* is not the chaos or breakdown, but the quiet stability of patterns that no longer get questioned. It is the last stage in the cycle of disintegration – when shadows are left unexamined, misery becomes familiar, suffering becomes self-sustaining and eventually, distortion becomes normalised.

A **healthy relationship with entrenchment** indicates that you are able to see entrenchment for what it is. This is the 'enough is enough' moment – when what has been normalised can finally be recognised as unsustainable. You notice when your habits, roles or beliefs have calcified into survival structures that no longer serve you, and have the courage to question them. Other systems – such as relationships, organisations, institutions and cultures – recognise tradition without being confined to it, making space for feedback, critique and self-correction. In this way, entrenchment becomes both a signal and a catalyst for transformation, reminding us that all systems are meant to evolve.

An **unhealthy relationship with entrenchment** indicates that you are mistaking dysfunction for stability and defending it at all costs. You may cling to the familiar, even when it harms you and/or others, confusing rigidity with strength or mistaking the quiet acceptance of dysfunction for maturity. In manufactured systems, an unhealthy relationship with entrenchment manifests as stagnation disguised as tradition – dissent is silenced, innovation is resisted, and loyalty is prioritised over truth. In both cases, entrenchment corrodes adaptability from within. And because it looks like stability on the surface, collapse often comes suddenly, when the cost of denial can no longer be sustained.

Ontology of entrenchment

To understand entrenchment ontologically is to see it, not as a passive state, but as a recursive structure – a patterned condition in which dysfunction becomes identity, distortion becomes logic and stagnation becomes self-justifying. Entrenchment is not held in place by force alone. It is held by familiarity, narrative coherence and systemic reinforcement. It does not merely resist change. It reconfigures perception so that change no longer seems necessary, possible or desirable.

What distinguishes entrenchment from earlier disintegration states is not the presence of rupture, but its *absorption*. Shadows remain unexamined. Misery is rebranded as realism. Suffering becomes the cost of meaning. Over time, these conditions harden into ontological commitments – ways of being, thinking and organising that preserve the very conditions that undermine coherence.

This section explores the ontology of entrenchment through its three systemic dimensions:

- **Anatomy** – The five interwoven structures that give entrenchment form;
- **Mechanics** – The recursive processes that sustain and defend it; and
- **Topology** – The looping interactions that lock systems into self-validating patterns of dysfunction.

To confront entrenchment is not simply to name dysfunction. It is to trace the architecture that enables its endurance, and to reawaken the possibility that things could be otherwise.

Anatomy of entrenchment

Entrenchment is not simply the persistence of dysfunction. It is its internalisation, sanctification and embedding across identity, story, structure and daily life. Its power lies not in the visibility of its dysfunction, but in its camouflage as stability, normalcy and even virtue. Over time, what was once incoherent is absorbed into the foundation of how things are done, understood and justified. Entrenchment emerges through five interwoven structural layers that convert transient breakdown into enduring architecture.

1. **Normalisation**

    What begins as disruption, contradiction or failure is gradually reclassified, not as a problem to be resolved, but as 'reality' to be accepted. The system adapts not by restoring coherence, but by absorbing incoherence into its baseline. Dysfunction is rebranded through familiar refrains: 'It's just how things are', 'Don't be naive' or 'We've always done it this way.' What was once intolerable becomes wise. What was once questioned becomes sacred. Normalisation is not benign; it is the first act of ontological surrender and the moment when pathology becomes pattern. It rarely announces itself as change, but operates quietly through repetition.

2. Defence

Once dysfunction is normalised, the next layer of entrenchment is defence. The system begins to guard its incoherence with intensity. Feedback is dismissed, dissent is pathologised and growth is framed as betrayal. What may have begun as an adaptive structure becomes brittle, unable to tolerate disruption. Identity fuses with belief, role or routine, such that change is no longer a challenge to a process. It is a threat to the self. Loyalty replaces inquiry. Certainty replaces curiosity. This rigidity is not accidental; it is a protective response to fear. But in fearing change, the system repels the qualities it needs to evolve.

3. Narrative control

At this stage, stories – the core instruments of meaning-making – are co-opted to protect the status quo. Narratives no longer evolve in response to experience. They are fixed in place to preserve coherence and fend off change. History is edited. Memory is romanticised. Myth replaces accuracy. The narrative becomes a mask rather than a mirror – shielding dysfunction with sentimentality, identity or moral superiority. These stories may live in families ('We're just a strong family'), institutions ('This is a high-performance culture'), or nations ('We must honour tradition'), but their function is the same – to sanctify what can no longer be justified.

4. Institutionalisation

Eventually, dysfunction becomes institutionalised. It is no longer just a belief or a story; it is the system itself. Entrenchment is now etched into organisational policies and workflows, rituals and approval hierarchies, job descriptions, language and unspoken norms. At this stage, people no longer need to agree with the dysfunction – they only need to function within it. Conformity becomes automatic. Disruption becomes costly. Even those who recognise the incoherence are often too exhausted, disempowered or enmeshed to confront it. The system now runs itself, not because it is wise, but because it is entrenched.

5. False stability

The final layer of entrenchment is paradoxical. The system appears strong, but is structurally brittle. It can maintain order, but only by avoiding feedback. It can continue functioning, but only by suppressing truth. Peace is performative and harmony is ritualised. This is not resilience. It is suppression in disguise. And because the system is incapable of adapting without unravelling itself, it cannot evolve; it can only collapse. This is the hidden cost of entrenchment. The longer a system survives by resisting truth, the more catastrophic the correction becomes when reality finally breaks through.

These five anatomical layers form the static architecture of entrenchment. Entrenchment is not merely resistance to transformation. It is the *systematised refusal of reality*. And unless seen for what it is, it continues to masquerade as wisdom, order or maturity – while silently corroding the capacity for renewal.

A tangible example of misaligned entrenchment

A large government agency responsible for public services was plagued by a series of inefficiencies and corruption scandals that shook public trust. Instead of confronting the dysfunction directly, the agency slowly absorbed it into its identity. Eventually, it became the way things were done.

At the level of **normalisation**, what was once scandalous becomes accepted as inevitable. Delays, mismanagement and opaque decision-making are brushed aside with refrains like: 'That's just bureaucracy' or 'You can't change the system'. What began as breakdown is rebranded as realism.

At the level of **defence**, attempts at reform are resisted. Whistle-blowers are sidelined, critics are labelled disloyal and feedback is dismissed as naive. Loyalty to procedure outweighs responsibility to outcomes. To question the culture is not seen as constructive, but as betrayal.

At the level of **narrative control**, stories are reshaped to preserve the status quo. Leaders invoke tradition and stability, telling citizens that "consistency" and "discipline" are the agency's greatest strengths. History is rewritten as proof of resilience, while failures are rationalised as lessons that justify more of the same. Dysfunction is wrapped in myth and sanctified as virtue.

At the level of **institutionalisation**, the culture of dysfunction becomes embedded in rules, workflows and structures. Endless approval layers are added, forms multiply and accountability is diffused. Even those who recognise the incoherence are compelled to comply, since the cost of disruption is too high. Dysfunction is no longer simply present in the system – it *is* the system.

At the level of **false stability**, the agency appears orderly, with polished reports and ceremonial announcements. Outwardly, everything looks stable. But beneath the surface, innovation is stifled, adaptability has vanished and trust has corroded. When crises strike, the agency has no capacity to respond except by doubling down on rituals and suppressing critique. Collapse becomes the only path left for change.

In this way, the anatomy of entrenchment takes hold. Normalisation buries dysfunction, defence resists feedback, narrative control sanctifies incoherence, institutionalisation embeds it in structure, and false stability gives the illusion of strength while hollowing adaptability. What began as correctable dysfunction has hardened into identity, defended at all costs. The tragedy is not just that the system is broken – it is that the system no longer recognises itself as broken.

Mechanics of entrenchment

Entrenchment does not simply endure; it evolves. It is not static inertia, but mutability in persistence. It learns to protect itself not by eliminating dissent, but by metabolising it. What makes entrenchment so difficult to dislodge is not its strength, but its mutability. It bends feedback into justification, reframes resistance as threat and turns survival strategies into systems of belief.

The following are its primary self-reinforcing mechanisms, the structural loops through which entrenchment conforms, survives and deepens:

1. Recursive confirmation loops

   At the core of entrenchment is a self-validating interpretive engine. Critique, contradiction and even failure are absorbed and reframed to affirm the system's logic. Dysfunction is reinterpreted as strategic realism. Failure is recoded as noble struggle. Resistance is labelled as disloyalty or naivety. This loop does not merely ignore contradiction; it transforms it into fuel. The greater the dissonance, the stronger the confirmation bias. Even disruption is framed as evidence that the system is under attack and, therefore, must be defended. This creates a closed epistemic circuit, where no experience can disprove the system because all experience is assimilated into its justification.

2. Distorted modulation

   Entrenchment does not reject key human capacities for modulation; it appropriates and distorts them. The very qualities designed to foster discernment and regulation – the four quads of the Modulation Sphere: patience, tolerance, adaptability and surrender – are reconfigured into tools of inertia.

   - Patience becomes apathy – waiting endlessly without engaging transformation.
   - Tolerance becomes complicity – accepting dysfunction under the guise of open-mindedness.

- Adaptability becomes opportunism – bending only when it preserves the power structure.
- Surrender becomes resignation – yielding not to truth, but to inertia and learned helplessness.

These distortions offer the illusion of emotional and ethical maturity, while concealing stagnation. Entrenchment wears the mask of balance, but underneath lies paralysis disguised as wisdom.

3. Fusion with identity

Perhaps the most insidious mechanism of entrenchment is ontological – dysfunction ceases to be something we inhabit; *it becomes who we are*. Victims internalise the conditions of their disempowerment as 'truth'. Perpetrators frame their dominance as legacy or loyalty. Participants in toxic systems defend them, not because they work, but because they define them. To question the system is to threaten one's very coherence: 'If this is wrong, then who have I been all along?' This fusion between dysfunction and identity creates an emotional bind. People will fight to protect the very systems that diminish them because letting go feels like self-erasure.

4. Suppression of alternatives

Entrenchment rarely silences critique with force. Instead, it uses absorption, dilution and theatre to silence critics. Listening sessions are held, but not acted upon. Reforms are proposed, but rerouted into bureaucracy. Alternative voices are included symbolically, but denied influence. This creates the appearance of responsiveness without any real shift in structure or truth. Innovation becomes ritual. Dialogue becomes spectacle. Nothing changes. And those calling for change are slowly worn down by performance fatigue.

5. Moral distortion

Entrenchment does not just normalise dysfunction; it moralises it. Burnout is praised as commitment, endurance through dysfunction is celebrated as strength and rigidity is reframed as principled integrity. Suppression of self is treated as nobility, pain becomes a credential, suffering becomes status and discipline becomes denial. In this distortion, the very experiences that should prompt transformation are used to reinforce the system. The wound becomes a badge. The breakdown becomes proof of devotion. Entrenchment weaponises sacrifice to block evolution.

These mechanisms reveal entrenchment not as passive failure, but as an active system of self-preservation. It adapts by distorting virtue, fusing identity with dysfunction, neutralising feedback and sanctifying stagnation.

Disrupting entrenchment requires more than critique. It demands ontological rupture by:

- Reclaiming virtue from distortion,
- Untangling self from the system, and
- Restoring modulation to its true function.

Only by interrupting these recursive mechanics can the architecture of entrenchment be dismantled, making space for coherence, adaptability and truth to re-emerge.

Topology of entrenchment

Entrenchment is not sustained by force alone. It is upheld by a recursive web of mutually reinforcing elements. Each structural layer – normalisation, defence, narrative control, institutionalisation and false stability – does more than just coexist. It conceals, protects and regenerates the others. This is not a linear progression, but a closed ontological circuit – a self-perpetuating topology in which dysfunction becomes reality, resistance becomes disloyalty and collapse masquerades as coherence.

Normalisation ↔ Defence

As dysfunction is gradually reclassified as 'just the way things are', the system begins to fossilise. Rigidity no longer signals pathology;

it is reframed as strength, consistency or loyalty. The more deeply dysfunction is normalised, the less viable critique becomes. The more rigid the system grows, the more normal the dysfunction appears. This recursive interplay locks out feedback and converts resistance to transformation into a perceived moral imperative. What begins as adaptation becomes ideology: untouchable, defended and mistaken for virtue.

Defence ↔ Narrative control

Every rigid system requires a foundational story to justify its form. Justifications, founding legends and selective memory encode the refusal to adapt as fidelity to tradition or principle. Sacred narratives mask the brittleness of the system. Over time, stories cease to be explorations of truth. Instead, they become shields that preserve identity and block disruption. Narrative is no longer a thread of meaning; it is a fence that keeps the possibility of transformation out.

Narrative Control ↔ Institutionalisation

What is protected in story is implemented in structure. Cultural assumptions crystallise into procedures. Ideological language becomes policy. Memory becomes architecture. The narrative logic is no longer told; it is enacted. It lives in hiring practices, approval chains, resource allocation, rituals and codes of conduct. Culture becomes bureaucracy with a backstory.

Institutionalisation ↔ False stability

Embedded dysfunction creates the illusion of order. Meetings are held, reports are written, tasks are completed – everything appears functional. But beneath the rhythm is a system incapable of adaptation. Because resilience has been sacrificed for control, even minor disruptions expose systemic brittleness. The appearance of stability conceals a system stalled in time – structured, but not alive.

False Stability ↔ Normalisation

When cracks appear, the system doesn't acknowledge collapse; it reabsorbs it. Crisis is glorified: 'We've been through worse.' Pain is romanticised: 'This is how change feels.' Breakdown is renamed: 'This is our rebirth.' In this cycle, dysfunction is not dismantled; it is rebranded as normal. The loop resets, now fortified by deeper cultural and emotional attachment.

Emergent forces and patterns

Entrenchment's recursive topology gives rise to second-order phenomena – ontological artefacts that are mistaken for virtue or maturity. These are not accidental; they are the system's evolutionary camouflage, allowing dysfunction to endure while appearing principled.

- **Loyalty without introspection** – Devotion to structure replaces commitment to truth.
- **Obedience mistaken for wisdom** – Compliance is elevated to moral virtue.
- **Silence rewarded as emotional intelligence** – Withholding critique is framed as restraint or poise.
- **Nostalgia weaponised against evolution** – The past is not only remembered, but is curated as a defence against change.
- **Repetition mistaken for legacy** – Continuity is conflated with integrity.
- **Collapse treated as rebirth** – Systemic failure is reframed as heroic endurance rather than a call for realignment.

These are not signs of resilience; they are the defence mechanisms of entrenchment. They preserve the system even as it erodes vitality, creativity and coherence.

Entrenchment in action

Entrenchment rarely looks dysfunctional from the inside. It presents as loyalty, resilience, tradition or success. Often, those living within it don't see pathology; they see normalcy. That's what makes entrenchment so powerful. It does not need to silence dissent if it can make dissent feel disloyal. It does not need to justify dysfunction if it can embed it into identity, culture and daily life.

The following scenarios reveal how entrenchment manifests – not as chaos, but as coherence built on distortion. In each case, we see how structural patterns of rigidity, nostalgia, role fusion or narrative control become woven into the psyche, relationships and institutions. These are not failures of insight or strength. They are what happens when survival patterns become systems and when dysfunction ceases to be questioned and begins to be defended. However, the fourth and fifth scenarios reveal how a healthy relationship with entrenchment manifests. Here, systems recognise when preservation has hardened into paralysis and choose to interrupt the pattern. They honour what has value without becoming bound by it, allowing evolution without collapse.

Case 1: The family that can't talk about the past

Angela grew up in a household marked by emotional volatility and unspoken grief. Her father struggled with alcohol. Her mother coped by over-functioning and avoiding conflict. As adults, Angela and her siblings never speak of what happened. When the topic is raised, it's quickly dismissed: 'We turned out fine', 'Don't dwell on the past' or 'You're being dramatic.'

The family prides itself on being close. They meet regularly, celebrate milestones and help each other in times of need. But real intimacy is absent. Vulnerability feels dangerous. The past is not processed. Instead, it is sealed in silence and reframed as strength.

Insight: This is entrenchment at the relational level. Dysfunction was normalised, defended and then embedded into the family's emotional culture. Silence is mistaken for harmony. Repression is mistaken for maturity. The family has not healed; they've simply built a structure around what they refuse to name.

Case 2: The leader who cannot let go

Martin is the founder of a successful non-profit that began with grassroots passion and urgency. Over time, the organisation grew, but Martin's leadership style didn't evolve. He micromanages, resists new ideas and surrounds himself with loyalists who won't challenge him. Young staff members leave quickly. Innovation stalls. Internal complaints are dismissed as 'entitlement' or 'disrespect'.

Despite this, Martin is celebrated in the community. Donors respect his history. Board members admire his discipline. The organisation appears stable. But inside, morale is low and burnout is high.

Insight: This is entrenchment masked as legacy. Martin's leadership is no longer responsive; it is ritualised. Critique is viewed as betrayal. Past success justifies current dysfunction. The organisation is not being led; it is being preserved. And preservation, in this case, comes at the cost of evolution.

Case 3: The system that punishes change

In a large government department, Priya, a middle manager, begins advocating for trauma-informed practices after noticing how rigid policies are harming vulnerable clients. Her proposals are initially welcomed, but over time, they're rerouted into endless reviews, diluted in language and eventually dropped. She's told, 'That's not how we do things,' and warned to 'Pick your battles.'

Meanwhile, the department launches a 'wellbeing initiative', featuring posters and mindfulness apps, while continuing to enforce punitive procedures. Staff privately agree with Priya, but few speak up. The system appears progressive, but the deeper structures remain untouched.

Insight: This is institutional entrenchment by performance. The organisation signals change while structurally resisting it. Feedback is absorbed but never actioned. Ritual replaces reform. Entrenchment here is not loud. It is polite, polished and deeply embedded.

Case 4: The burnout that became a blueprint

Nadia is the founder of a fast-growing non-profit. Passionate and principled, she worked tirelessly for the cause. But over time, her leadership style grew rigid. Decision-making became centralised, staff turnover increased and she dismissed criticism as 'negativity' and framed overwork as 'purpose'. The organisation's culture began to mirror her own internal entrenchment – passion fused with unsustainable self-sacrifice and structure fused with control.

Then, Nadia experienced a breakdown. Severe fatigue, anxiety and an internal sense of collapse forced her to step back. For the first time, she saw how the system she built was unsustainable – not just for others, but also for herself.

Instead of returning with stronger defences, she used this rupture as a point of reflection. She brought in new leadership, decentralised authority, restructured workloads and initiated open conversations about burnout. Her personal undoing became the organisation's evolution.

Insight: This is *constructive disintegration.* The breakdown was not a failure, but the necessary decomposition of an entrenched identity tied to self-sacrifice and control. The crisis exposed the system's fragility and created space for structural renewal. Nadia's healthy relationship with entrenchment meant recognising the illusion of coherence and choosing regeneration over reinforcement.

Case 5: The generational identity that gave way

Adrian came from a long line of military men. Discipline, control and emotional restraint were not just values; they were identity. From a young age, he absorbed the unspoken code: emotions are weakness, vulnerability is betrayal. He followed the path laid out for him: top military college, promotions, medals. Outwardly, he embodied strength. However, inwardly, he felt estranged from himself.

It was the death of his younger brother – from suicide – that broke the system open. Adrian could no longer deny the emotional cost of inherited silence. For months he withdrew, cycling through guilt, anger and numbness. But in this disintegration, something shifted.

He began therapy. He initiated emotional conversations within his family, something never done before. He spoke publicly about his own struggles and advocated for mental health within the military. The very institution that once entrenched emotional suppression began to make space for new forms of courage.

Insight: Adrian didn't simply rebel. He disrupted an entrenched identity that had defined masculinity and strength for generations in his family. His healthy relationship with entrenchment came not from rejection, but from redefinition. What once served as survival was re-evaluated in light of deeper human needs. In doing so, he reframed strength, not as control or stoicism, but as the capacity to feel, relate and evolve.

Conclusion

Entrenchment is not a passive flaw in the system. It is a rehearsed choreography of stagnation. It survives not by resisting critique outright, but by metabolising it into performance. It simulates growth, adopts the language of change and presents the appearance of evolution, while structurally resisting it at every turn.

What makes entrenchment so enduring is its intimacy with identity, culture and belief. It does not ask to be believed; *it becomes belief.* It does not fight transformation; *it renders it unnecessary.* And in doing so, it converts what should be temporary dysfunction into long-term architecture.

Interrupting entrenchment requires more than insight or effort. It requires ontological disruption. Instead of:

- Revising processes, dismantle the stories that justify them.
- Confronting dysfunction, untangle the self from what no longer serves.
- Fighting inertia with urgency, meet it with depth, structure and coherence.

Entrenchment is not stability; it is calcified fear disguised as wisdom. To interrupt it is not betrayal. It is the reawakening of reality.

Reflection

- Can you identify an area of your life – personal, relational or professional – where dysfunction has been normalised as 'just the way things are'? What stories sustain that normalcy?
- Where do you find yourself defending something, not because it's working, but because it feels like part of who you are?

- Have you ever mistaken silence for strength, loyalty for virtue or burnout for commitment? What were the consequences?
- Have you participated in systems that signal change but resist transformation? What signs of performative adaptation did you notice?
- What emotions arise when you question something that has long been treated as untouchable: fear, guilt, confusion, disorientation?
- What would it take to untangle yourself from a structure, role or belief that once gave you purpose, but now keeps you small?
- Where might you be calling something stable, when in truth it is simply stuck?
- What would it look like to interrupt entrenchment in your context: not with aggression, but with clarity, courage and coherence?

PART V

The Integrity Sphere

At a time when the world is teetering between brilliance and breakdown, there is a silent, invisible architecture that determines whether systems – human and institutional – flourish or fragment. This architecture is not made of policies or performance metrics. It is built from something far more foundational – integrity.

But integrity, in this context, is not morality or personal virtue. It is the systemic coherence between what we are, how we are and what we bring forth into the world. It is the difference between sustainability and slow implosion – and it is never accidental.

The Integrity Sphere represents the inner scaffolding that enables individuals, relationships, organisations, institutions and societies to function with trustworthiness, continuity and ethical resilience – especially under pressure. It holds together what complexity would otherwise pull apart.

This section explores four structural forces that regulate integrity across all domains:

- **Intention** – the directional architecture of what we choose to bring forth.
- **Trust** – the relational infrastructure that allows openness amid uncertainty.
- **Sovereignty** – the capacity for authorship in the face of pressure or persuasion.
- **Being** – the generative field from which we act, relate and shape the world.

These are not just abstract concepts. They are ontological structures that determine whether our systems are held together by integrity or by performance and pretence. Where these forces are present and structurally integrated, integrity becomes self-reinforcing. However, where they are fragmented or performative, even the most noble pursuits can collapse under their own weight.

In a time when many of our institutions feel fractured, our relationships strained and our identities fragmented, the Integrity Sphere offers a path to restoration by delivering structure – the kind that can hold under pressure, rebuild what was broken and sustain what truly matters.

CHAPTER 34

Intention

In an era obsessed with goals, performance hacks and motivational slogans, a quieter force lies beneath the noise – one that determines whether our pursuits carry coherence or collapse into chaos.

Intention is often misunderstood – mistaken for positive thinking, ambition or generic goal-setting. In boardrooms and coaching conversations alike, we hear phrases like 'set your intention' or 'lead with intention' tossed around like self-help confetti. But rarely do we stop to ask: 'What actually is intention?' And why does it matter, not just for the individual, but for the sustainability of relationships, organisations, societies and entire civilisations?

The answer is both deceptively simple and ontologically rich. Intention is neither a wish nor a mental rehearsal of success. It is a structural expression of Being – an internal framework that shapes how we relate to the world, what we prioritise, and how we embody meaning. It acts as a kind of directional architecture, silently guiding the trajectories of individuals and systems alike. It also governs what we give life to, what we neglect, and what we come to reinforce or allow to decay over time.

Great philosophers and mystics have alluded to it – whether in Aristotle's concept of *telos* (final cause), Viktor Frankl's 'will to meaning' or the Islamic notion of *niyyah*, which considers intention the axis upon which ethical accountability rests. In all cases, intention is not superficial; it's sacred. But it's also systemic. Without coherent intention, societies disintegrate, institutions collapse into performative bureaucracy and communities lose their ethical compass.

We often confuse intention with motivation or mistake our stated goals for our true inner stance. Someone might speak of healing after a conflict, yet still pursue reconciliation as a way of making the other person feel guilty or indebted. Another may chase transformation, not out of genuine desire for growth, but to prove their worth to a doubter – for instance, excelling in a career mainly to disprove a parent's or partner's criticism. These aren't failures of willpower; they are fractures at the level of ontological coherence. And what begins as personal misalignment often scales into collective dysfunction.

In today's fractured world – where manipulation, performative display and hidden agendas run rampant – reclaiming intention as a structural, discernible and developable force is essential for authentic sustainability. This chapter positions intention as one of the four foundational qualities of the Integrity Sphere, alongside trust, sovereignty and Being.

Through the triadic lens of **anatomy**, **mechanics** and **topology**, we will explore how intention can become either a source of structural integrity or a breeding ground for systemic disintegration. This model positions intention not as inspiration, but as *architecture* – a vital force that determines the depth, direction and integrity of one's presence in the world. Because at the root of every sustainable system – whether an individual, an organisation, an institution or a society – lies a coherent intention: one that is internally aligned, structurally consistent and directed towards integrity rather than fragmentation. Where that coherence is fractured, authentic sustainability is impossible to achieve.

Ontological Distinction of Intention

Intention is the directional life-force that propels you to strive, create and connect – the invisible force that drives your choices, ambitions and relationships – and it becomes the structure through which you channel your purpose into what you are committed to bringing into the world. *Intention* is not merely what you wish for or declare. It is how coherently you organise your perceptions, attention, behaviour and engagement in relation to your values and purpose over time. The same is true for all systems, including organisations, institutions, cultures and nations. Once awareness has revealed reality and meaning is drawn from it, intention becomes the framework through which that meaning is enacted. In both individuals and other systems, intention shapes priorities and determines what is protected and pursued.

A **healthy relationship with intention** indicates that your motives, actions and values remain aligned over time, regardless of circumstance. You don't just speak about what matters – you live it, consistently and coherently. You resist the pull of convenience, ego or reactivity, remaining guided by more meaningful and enduring matters. When your intention is clear and structurally integrated, it generates resilience, trust and clarity in how you navigate challenge and complexity. You become someone others can count on – not because you are rigid, but because your direction is grounded. In other systems, such as families, organisations, institutions and communities, a healthy relationship with intention manifests as the ability and willingness to maintain coherence and stay the course under pressure. It shows up in the consistent prioritisation of purpose over convenience, the safeguarding of trust over expedience, and the capacity to adapt without abandoning what truly matters.

An **unhealthy relationship with intention** indicates that your words, actions and values are misaligned. You may chase validation or be driven by fear, ego or optics rather than clarity, losing sight of your purpose. You may declare what matters, but act in ways that contradict it. Over time, this dissonance erodes both your impact and your integrity. This pattern appears not only in individuals but also in larger systems. When intention loses its coherence, people and institutions may profess values while acting in opposition to them, pursue progress at the cost of exhaustion or burnout, or begin with sincerity only to drift into performance optics, betrayal or power-seeking. In these cases, intention loses its structural rigour and collapses into propaganda, leaving trust fractured and alignment eroded.

Ontology of intention

Intention is one of the four foundational structures that regulate the internal architecture of coherence within the Integrity Sphere. Where trust governs the relational field of interaction, intention governs directional integrity – what one moves towards, consciously or unconsciously. Alongside sovereignty and Being, it forms the inner scaffolding of ethical agency and the capacity to transform.

In this ontological model, intention is not just a precursor to action. It is a configurational force that arranges perception, behaviour, commitment and the orientation one brings into relationships. It is through intention that one's Being declares to the world: 'This is what I choose to bring forth' and genuinely means it. When intention is misaligned, incoherent or performative, it becomes a source of fragmentation, manipulation and distrust. But when it is transparent, authentic, grounded and integrated, it becomes a magnetic and catalytic force that transforms not only outcomes, but the system itself.

Anatomy of intention

Just as a building relies on foundations, supports and orientation, true intention rests on a deeper anatomy that must be examined, aligned and embodied. Below are the five constituent layers that make intention what it is – a directional force with existential consequences.

1. **Directionality**

    Every intention points somewhere. Directionality is the structural vector that determines where a person, project, relationship, institution or society is ultimately heading. It is the teleological posture[78] of Being in that it asks: What are we moving towards? This is not about short-term goals or superficial aims, but the trajectory that underlies them.

---

78 Teleology refers to the study of ends, purposes or goals. In this context, 'teleological posture' describes the underlying orientation of a system or Being towards a perceived or chosen end. It's not just about having a goal; it's about the existential stance a person or manufactured system adopts in relation to what they believe is worth moving towards.

Whether it is towards restoration, growth, control, safety or disruption, directionality defines the arc of the intention. Without it, action lacks orientation and energy is dispersed.

But direction without depth risks becoming force without wisdom. The *where* must be followed by the *why* – and not a surface-level why born of convenience, fashion or expedience. The authentic why is discovered through awareness, ethical clarity and ontological orientation. It is sensed, not imposed, and revealed through reflection rather than dictated by trend or urgency.

2. Motive

Underneath every direction lies a motive: a set of energies, values, convictions or fears that animate the path. The motive or motivational ground is the ontological substrate from which an intention draws its fuel. A desire to serve is different from a desire to dominate. A fear of abandonment may create the same external behaviours as a longing for connection, but their underlying motives and impact differ.

Whether acknowledged or not, the motive lives in one's Being. In other words, it is woven into a person's way of existing, relating and navigating the world. It shapes tone, quality and sustainability. Intention rooted in distortion (e.g. revenge, compensatory overcorrection, people-pleasing and self-deception) may appear purposeful, but it carries the seed of incoherence. The motive is not the content; it is the essence. Content refers to the visible storyline – the words spoken, the task pursued, the outcome achieved. Essence refers to the driving force that gives those actions their structural rigour. For example, two people may both dedicate themselves to leadership, but one's essence is service while the other's is domination. The content looks similar, but the underlying motive – the essence – shapes entirely different impacts and trajectories.

3. Congruence

An intention lacks integrity if it destabilises the self. Congruence in this context is the degree to which intention aligns with the rest of one's Being – including one's values, moods, relationships, responsibilities, timing and ethical framework. When an intention is misaligned with these deeper layers, it exerts pressure that distorts rather than sustains. Such intention may appear coherent, but in practice, it becomes coercive, manipulative or subtly self-sabotaging. This is the layer where intention either reduces to performance or resonates with structural coherence. Many burn out not because they lack commitment, but because their intention pulls them in conflicting directions. Intention that is coherent and aligned with one's Being resonates harmoniously through the whole self, sustaining rather than depleting energy.

4. Volition

Intention without commitment is nothing more than a wish. Volition is the embodied willingness to act – an inner readiness to endure discomfort, navigate setbacks and persist over time. It is the active stance one takes in the face of complexity. Volition is not performative; it is measured by continuity and endurance. It is the steady structural resolve that says: *I will keep moving towards this, even in the face of complexity and adversity.* This volition or commitment posture transforms intention from hypothetical to operational. It is what allows intention to be lived rather than merely envisioned.

5. Transparency

A concealed intention – even if noble – breeds confusion and mistrust. Transparency of aim is the clarity and disclosure with which an intention can be seen, named and shared. Obscurity creates distortion within relationships, projects, workplaces and other systems. Without transparency, others are unlikely to align with, adapt to or trust an intention.

> Transparency is not about overexposure or justification; it's about coherence in communication. A well-communicated intention reveals its purpose without needing to execute it.

Together, these five layers – directionality, motive, congruence, volition and transparency – form the ontological anatomy of intention. When one layer is weak, intention becomes scattered, manipulative or fragile. However, when all layers are integrated, intention becomes magnetic, resilient and structurally trustworthy – not just to the self but also to others. Intention, in this sense, is not what we say we want. It is what our Being is willing to structure and sustain towards a possible future.

A tangible example of misoriented intention

A political movement rises with the declared aim of serving 'the people' and restoring trust in public life. On the surface, its message resonates and gathers momentum. Yet underneath, the anatomy of its intention is fractured.

At the level of **directionality**, the movement claims to head towards justice and renewal. But in practice, its trajectory is guided more by opposition to perceived enemies than by a constructive vision of what it seeks to build. Energy is poured into dismantling rather than designing, leaving its true objective vague and reactionary.

At the level of **motive**, while the movement speaks of empowerment, it is fuelled by resentment and fear. Leaders are driven less by service than by the need to prove legitimacy or settle old scores. Outwardly, the language of care is used. But inwardly, the emotional climate is one of control and insecurity. This atmosphere shapes not only rhetoric, but also decision-making, leaving supporters energised on the surface, but unsettled within.

At the level of **congruence**, the movement's declared values of transparency and inclusion stand in stark contrast to its actual structures. Decisions are centralised, dissent is punished and internal debate is stifled. It projects unity in public, but its operational reality fractures with every compromise that betrays its professed principles. Integrity gives way to performance and alignment erodes at the core.

At the level of **volition**, the will to endure hardship is present, but it is sustained by frenzy rather than grounded resolve. Leaders burn themselves out in endless reaction, unable to pause and recalibrate. The movement surges in bursts of energy, but lacks the steady endurance to translate vision into structure. What looks like determination is, in truth, compulsion.

At the level of **transparency**, intentions are cloaked in ambiguity. Speeches promise 'renewal' without defining its shape. Policies are advanced with hidden trade-offs, and when questioned, leaders appeal to loyalty rather than clarity. Trust slowly erodes because people sense that the stated intention doesn't represent the complete picture.

Over time, this misoriented anatomy corrodes coherence. The movement may still gather crowds, win elections or secure funding. But beneath its outward momentum lies incoherence. The absence of alignment between direction, motive, congruence, volition and transparency hollows its credibility. Intention without alignment dissolves into noise rather than guidance – a signal that disorients its members and undermines its sustainability. What began with promises of service collapses into yet another performance of power.

Mechanics of intention

Intention is not a static proclamation. It is a dynamic system of directional coherence that unfolds over time and across domains. Its operation is not linear but recursive, shaping and being shaped by perception, action, resistance and outcome. These mechanics describe how intention is formed, tested, expressed and refined in real-world scenarios – with all their challenges and complexities. They also reveal how intention either matures into a transformative force or collapses into distortion and dysfunction.

1. **Emergence**

   Intention emerges from a perceived possibility, absence, tension or a vision. It is born when one perceives a gap between what is and what could be, and chooses to respond. This formation process may be:

- Reflective (deliberate, grounded in values and discernment), or
- Reactive (driven by urgency, unmet needs or emotional triggers).

In either case, intention begins as a directional impulse. It orients attention and begins filtering reality in alignment with its aim. The origin of an intention carries the seeds of its future. If born from desperation or resentment, it may carry incoherence from the start. If grounded in clarity, care and structural awareness, it begins with integrity.

2. Discernment

Once formed, intention becomes a lens through which we discern what is worthy of our attention and what can be dismissed or postponed. This filtering and prioritisation – a reframing of perception and energy – is not purely cognitive. It is deeply embodied and shaped by emotion. The presence of intention reorders reality – what was once in the background becomes front of mind; something that once seemed irrelevant becomes compelling and magnetic.

If an intention is distorted or weak, the filtering process becomes dysfunctional, leading to fixation on irrelevant matters, overlooking key variables or fuelling obsession and tunnel vision. But when structurally sound, discernment sharpens perception, simplifies complexity and heightens presence.

3. Resistance

The moment an intention meets reality, it inevitably encounters friction: conflict with circumstances, competing priorities, inner doubt, unexpected feedback and so on. This stage of tension navigation (encounter with resistance) is not a sign of failure – it's a diagnostic insight that helps reveal the most effective way forward.

Here, we must ask ourselves:

- Do I adapt and evolve the intention?
- Do I double down in rigidity?
- Or do I abandon the intention altogether?

This encounter surfaces hidden assumptions and shadows behind the original formation of the intention. It is where unconscious motives are exposed, misplaced aims collapse or deeper clarity emerges. Resilient intentions don't break under the weight of resistance; they become more refined.

4. **Coherence testing**

Over time, the integrity of an intention is tested – not just by obstacles, but by its own impact. Here, we would ask ourselves:

- Does sustained pursuit of this aim energise or deplete me?
- Does it align with my core values or fracture my inner coherence?
- Does it invite constructive feedback or provoke chronic dysfunction?

Incoherent intentions often manifest as:

- Burnout and frustration,
- Inner sabotage (procrastination, self-doubt),
- Ethical erosion or relational breakdown.

In contrast, coherent intentions generate:

- Resilience under strain,
- Increased clarity and resourcefulness,
- Relational trust and environmental responsiveness.

The coherence testing phase exposes whether the intention is merely performative or authentic and whether it is a construct of ego or an authentic expression of Being.

5. Impact assessment

All intentions, whether fulfilled or not, have an impact. They shift energy, affect relationships, reshape priorities or reveal hidden dynamics. Sometimes the intention achieves its objective. Other times, the path collapses. But the effort exposes something truer. Regardless of the outcome, every intention initiates a process of feedback generation, offering signals about alignment, distortion or unforeseen consequences.

This mechanical layer invites honest reflection:

- What ripple effects did the intention create?
- What became clearer as a result?
- What needs to be refined moving forward?

Success may affirm the coherence of the intention. In contrast, failure may illuminate distortion or reveal a deeper, latent intention.

If the feedback is integrated, the next cycle of intention becomes more refined, aligned and authentic. However, if ignored, the pattern repeats and dysfunction deepens.

The mechanics of intention illustrate a recursive loop: from formation to friction, from tension to truth, from aim to impact and back again. A meaningful and coherent intention is not simply pursued; it is continuously attuned to, adapted and realigned with the evolving self and context. In this way, intention becomes more than a personal goal. It becomes a method of engaging with reality, a structure for transformation and a mirror of one's coherence or fragmentation.

Topology of intention

Intention is not a singular force; it is a relational field. The five anatomical components of intention – directionality, motive, congruence, volition and transparency – form a self-organising system. Their interaction determines whether intention becomes a vessel for transformation or a hollow declaration.

This topology reveals how intention either strengthens itself through alignment and clarity or collapses through distortion, obscurity or contradiction. It is through these recursive relationships that intention gains or loses structural integrity.

Directionality ↔ Motive

An intention's trajectory is only as strong as the energy that fuels it. Direction without honest motive becomes manipulative. If the underlying driver is resentment, fear or ego-inflation, even noble aims become contaminated. Conversely, when direction emerges from care, service or clarity of values, the pathway stabilises. For example, a leader driven by fear of irrelevance may strive for innovation but create dysfunction. In contrast, a leader fueled by a commitment to truth or contribution builds alignment and traction.

Motive ↔ Congruence

An intention may sound good but feel wrong. When the 'why' is incongruent with one's core values, purpose or role, it fractures. The body resists inauthenticity. A misaligned motive or motivational ground triggers inner sabotage, emotional friction or relational mistrust. But when motive aligns with one's deeper coherence – including values, truth and purpose – intention becomes graceful and flows without force.

Congruence ↔ Volition

Even a well-aligned intention can falter without sufficient will, resilience and discipline to go the distance. Without these qualities, intention remains nothing more than a theory. At the same time, strong commitment to a distorted or misaligned intention produces burnout, rigidity and stubbornness masquerading as focus. True intention requires both congruence and willingness or volition. It is not enough to 'want it'. We must be willing to endure, adapt and persist.

Volition ↔ Transparency

Volition without clarity and transparency creates confusion, suspicion or coercion. When people sense intensity and commitment but can't perceive the direction, they withdraw, resist or become reactive. Transparent intentions enable relational alignment. When shared clearly:

- Others can orient around it,
- Conflicts can be anticipated,
- Mistrust is reduced.

Transparency is not about over-explanation. It's about communicable clarity.

Transparency ↔ Directionality

The intention's direction must be shareable. When withheld, ambiguous or reactive, collaboration is fragmented and trust is obstructed. Clear direction enables coordinated movement – not just individually, but across teams, systems and relationships. Transparency transforms intention from a private impulse into a shared catalyst for change.

Emergent qualities and patterns

Intention governs how potential becomes action, how influence is exerted and how meaning is sustained. It is not something we 'set'; it is something we *build* through coherence, motive, presence and clarity.

When someone with a coherent intention walks into a room, the shared reality begins to re-orient – not through force, but through congruence. True intention does not push or perform; it orients and reshapes.

When intention is shaped with congruence, coherence and clarity, the following are among the structural qualities that typically emerge:

- **Purposefulness** – A felt sense of orientation and direction.
- **Moral clarity** – The ability to discern what is right, not just what is effective.
- **Resilience under pressure** – Adaptation without collapse.
- **Decisional efficiency** – Clarity simplifies choice.

- **Influential alignment** – Others trust and follow coherent intent.
- **Transformational agency** – Intention becomes a force that reorganises systems.

In contrast, when intention is fractured or misaligned, it can result in:

- **Manipulation** – Using others as instruments to achieve self-serving aims or hidden agendas.
- **Self-betrayal** – Sacrificing coherence to appease expectation.
- **Confusion and overexertion** – Working hard in an unclear direction.
- **Distrust from others** – Incongruent signals invite suspicion.
- **Disintegration** – Promise and behaviour fall out of sync.

Intention in action

Let's now ground the ontology of intention in real-life contexts that highlight how intention either reveals its sustaining force or exposes the fractures that lead to dysfunction and disintegration, both personally and systemically.

Case 1: The inauthentic altruist

A non-profit leader claims to serve their community, but their efforts are primarily driven by a subconscious desire for validation and recognition. Despite the noble mission, the team burns out under micromanagement, shifting priorities and chronic reactivity. The organisation becomes unsustainable – more focused on appearing impactful than being structurally coherent.

Insight: The intention was not rooted in care, but compensation. The leader's motive was misaligned with their declared directionality, and their congruence collapsed under tension. What looked like generosity was actually self-preservation in disguise. The organisation, built on misaligned intention, could not sustain trust, morale or meaningful results.

Case 2: The grounded founder

A tech entrepreneur spends five years building a platform that doesn't achieve the rapid impact she envisaged. Yet her team remains loyal, investors stay engaged and users give constructive feedback. Why? Because her intention was clear, transparent and aligned from the start. She communicated the 'why' consistently, even through pivots and setbacks.

Insight: While all five anatomical components of intention were present and integrated, it didn't guarantee immediate success. However, it sustained long-term trust, adaptability and purpose. Intention was not an abstract hope; it was a structure anchoring the system's coherence. This is what authentic sustainability looks like – sustainability that doesn't expect immediate outcomes, but enables enduring alignment under pressure.

Case 3: The dysfunctional partnership

In a romantic relationship, one partner repeatedly claims their intention to 'grow together' while avoiding difficult conversations, blaming the other and remaining emotionally unavailable. Eventually, the other partner realises that their words were never structurally aligned with how they showed up.

Insight: Volition and transparency were absent. The spoken intention could not be sustained by the structure of the relationship. Incoherent intention becomes a systemic fault line. It fractures not only intimacy but the very trust needed to build anything together. What fails here on a personal level mirrors what collapses in teams, communities and nations when intention is incoherent.

Conclusion

Intention is not a mental state or a branding tool. It is the foundational architect of authentic sustainability. It determines whether action, systems and relationships are guided by coherence or distorted by ego, confusion or unconscious drift.

When fractured, intention becomes dangerous. It leads to burnout, disillusionment, manipulation and systemic fragility. People feel used, teams fragment, institutions become performative and societies lose their moral compass.

But when intention is structured with alignment, clarity and care, it becomes a magnetic force that not only aligns others, but sustains direction through complexity, challenges and disruption. This is the essence of true sustainability – not the absence of challenge, but the presence of coherent intention that can withstand it.

Throughout this chapter, we've explored intention as an ontological structure through its anatomy, mechanics and topology. We've seen how it lives not only in individuals, but in relationships, cultures, businesses, institutions, communities and societies. At every level, sustainable systems are driven by coherent intention. And at every level, disintegration begins when intention is hollow, fragmented or reactive. Later in the book, we will return to intention in greater depth, exploring its critical role in developing and sustaining coherence and fulfilment.

Reflection

- What is one area in your life where your declared intention does not match your actual orientation or commitment?
- Can you identify the motive beneath one of your most persistent personal or organisational intentions?
- Where have you seen intention break trust – either yours, someone else's or that of a system or institution?
- What would it look like for you – or an organisation you lead – to live with structurally coherent intention across actions, decisions and relationships?
- What collective or organisational intentions are being performed rather than lived? What would it take to realign them with integrity and authentic sustainability?

CHAPTER 35

Trust

We often speak of trust as if it's a feeling, a moral virtue or a fragile gift that can be shattered with a single misstep. In popular culture and corporate settings alike, trust is treated as either a soft, sentimental ideal or an abstract pillar of 'good leadership'. But when we examine it ontologically, trust reveals itself as something far more profound – a structural force that governs coherence between people, institutions and other systems in the face of uncertainty, dependency and vulnerability to another's actions.

Trust is not just 'nice to have'. It is the invisible infrastructure of complex cooperation. Where trust is high, systems move with minimal friction. However, where trust is absent, even the most talented individuals and well-funded projects grind to a halt under the weight of micromanagement, suspicion and hypervigilance. This is true in personal relationships and even more so in economies, governments, educational institutions and global networks.

Historically, great thinkers have recognised the depth associated with trust. In his book, *Beyond Good and Evil*, Nietzsche declared, 'Not that you lied to me, but that I no longer believe you, has shaken me.'[79] Simone Weil described trust as, 'the rarest and truest form of

---

[79] Nietzsche, F. (1886/2002) *Beyond Good and Evil: Prelude to a Philosophy of the Future*. Translated by J. Norman. Cambridge: Cambridge University Press.

generosity'.[80] In Islam, *amana* (trust) is not emotional; it's existential – the measure of one's alignment between word, deed and Being. These insights hint at a deeper truth – trust is not simply related to what you feel. It's about what a person, manufactured system or culture can be counted on to sustain itself structurally and ethically.

Yet confusion abounds. Many confuse trust with blind faith. Others assume it can be earned once and retained indefinitely. But real trust is not static; it's recursive. It is built over time through structural congruence and tested in conditions of stress, not comfort. And when broken, it cannot be mended by promises. It must be restructured, not simply restored.

This chapter explores trust as one of the four foundational qualities of the Integrity Sphere, alongside intention, sovereignty and Being. It examines trust, not as a sentiment or virtue, but as a relational architecture: a scaffold that enables vulnerability without collapse, transparency without fear and interdependence without coercion.

In an era marked by global instability, institutional disillusionment and breakdown of social cohesion, trust is not optional. It is the cornerstone of authentic sustainability – whether in a friendship, partnership, organisation, institution or civilisation. Without trust, even the most promising and seemingly strong systems will corrode from within.

Before we explore its anatomy, mechanics and topology, let's clarify what trust is from an ontological perspective and what a healthy and unhealthy relationship with it looks like.

Ontological Distinction of Trust

Trust is the structural orientation that enables people and systems – from individuals and relationships to organisations, institutions and cultures – to remain open, relational and functional in the presence of risk, uncertainty and dependency. It is not simply about whether you are 'trustworthy' – it's also about your willingness to

---

80 Weil, S. (1952/2002) *Gravity and Grace*. Translated by E. Craufurd. London: Routledge.

engage in trust by choice. *Trust* does not depend on certainty, but on coherence, goodwill and alignment being actively sustained. It shapes how you carry yourself, how others experience you, and how any system cooperates and endures in the face of challenge.

A **healthy relationship with trust** indicates that you are able and willing to be open – emotionally, relationally and ideologically – while discerning whether that openness can genuinely be received and reciprocated. You are neither naive nor cynical. You participate in trust as a living dynamic: extending it thoughtfully, repairing it when broken, and withdrawing it when necessary, without collapsing into defensiveness. *Trust* becomes part of your presence and reputation – others experience you as transparent, congruent and reliable. In the context of manufactured systems, healthy trust manifests as psychological safety, transparent feedback loops, distributed leadership and adaptive resilience. It reduces friction, fuels innovation and fosters long-term sustainability.

An **unhealthy relationship with trust** indicates that you are either blindly optimistic or chronically suspicious. On one side, excessive trust makes you naive or compliant, leaving you vulnerable to exploitation. On the other hand, pervasive distrust makes you guarded and defensive, unable to collaborate or sustain openness. Manufactured systems mirror these extremes: overregulating, enforcing conformity or becoming performative in place of genuine cooperation. Over time, sustainability erodes – for even when competence is present, trust that is absent or broken undermines the system. Without trust, everything must be managed, controlled and surveilled. Nothing can naturally thrive and evolve.

Ontology of trust

In ontological terms, trust is far more foundational than just an emotional quality or a functional expectation. It is the invisible architecture that allows systems – human and manufactured – to function with coherence in the presence of risk, uncertainty and mutual dependency. Without it, complexity becomes paralysis and interaction devolves into control, manipulation or withdrawal. Let's now break down the ontology of trust by examining its anatomy, mechanics and topology.

Anatomy of trust

Trust is not built from hope. It is constructed from the following five structural components that enable coherence, even during times of uncertainty and in the face of complexity. Each of these components plays a distinct role in forming trust's ontological architecture. When integrated, they make trust possible across individual, relational, organisational and societal domains. When any component is missing or corrupt, the trust structure weakens or collapses.

1. **Openness**

   At the root of all trust is openness. This is the conscious or unconscious decision to reveal or make oneself available emotionally, physically or ideologically without guaranteed protection. It includes acts of disclosure, expressions of dependence, transparent communication and the surrendering of control. This form of vulnerability is not weakness; it is the active condition of unguardedness that invites mutual recognition. Without it, trust cannot take root. In the absence of openness, relationships default to transaction, performance or manipulation.

2. **Consistency**

   Trust is not blind. It develops through a repeated perception of congruence between words, actions and follow-through. This dimension of trust functions as an ongoing reliability assessment, especially in moments of ambiguity or adversity. Even without explicit betrayal, subtle inconsistencies can quietly erode the foundation of trust over time. Consistency signals coherence, accountability and integrity in action.

3. **Benevolence**

   'Will they show up?' should always be accompanied by an equally important question: 'Do they mean well?'

Benevolence is the perception or projection of goodwill, care or non-malicious intent. It is what makes trust warm as opposed to merely functional. When someone fails, but we believe their intention was sincere, trust may bend but not break. Without perceived benevolence, reliability can feel transactional – functional but hollow. Without this layer, trust becomes mechanical and brittle.

4. Ontological alignment

Beyond words or actions lies a deeper resonance – a felt sense of whether the other party's values, state of being and lived reality align with our own. Ontological alignment refers to this felt sense of congruence. It is not always verbalised but perceived, often intuitively. Trust commonly breaks down, not because of obvious contradictions in behaviour, but because something feels 'off' – manipulative, dissonant or hollow – even when nothing explicitly wrong has occurred. This is where intuition intersects with structural discernment.

5. Continuity

Trust does not reside in a single moment; it unfolds across time. It draws on memory (of past interactions), presence (in the current encounter) and projection (into the future). Continuity allows trust to carry coherence through rupture, ambiguity or distance. Without it, trust becomes reactive, fragile and unable to stabilise complexity.

Each structural component of trust – openness, consistency, benevolence, ontological alignment and continuity – functions like a beam in an invisible scaffolding. When present and integrated, they form a coherent structure. However, when fractured or dissonant, trust collapses – not because of a single betrayal, but due to cumulative incoherence.

A tangible example of misoriented trust

A tech start-up prides itself on being 'a family'. It promises openness, collaboration and innovation, but the anatomy of its trust is misoriented.

At the level of **openness**, leaders encourage employees to 'bring their whole selves to work', but disclosures of struggle or dissent are quietly penalised. Those who share doubts about deadlines or ethics are excluded from key projects, teaching others that transparency is unsafe. What is presented as openness is, in practice, surveillance.

At the level of **consistency**, the company's words and actions drift apart. Founders speak of sustainability, but chase relentless growth. They promise flexibility, but reward only those who sacrifice their personal lives for work. This inconsistency does not explode into outright betrayal; it slowly erodes trust.

At the level of **benevolence**, intent is framed as care, but functions as control. The language of 'we're doing this for you' justifies long hours, low pay and opaque decision-making. Employees sense that goodwill is conditional, tied to performance and loyalty rather than genuine concern. Trust grows brittle, transactional and hollow.

At the level of **ontological alignment**, something feels 'off'. Employees hear the rhetoric of empowerment, but feel the undertone of manipulation. Leaders brand themselves as visionaries but cut corners, exploit partnerships and avoid accountability. Even when no explicit betrayal occurs, the dissonance in Being erodes the felt sense that the system can be trusted.

At the level of **continuity**, ruptures are never addressed, only glossed over. Promises of 'next time we'll do better' evaporate with each cycle of broken commitments. Because failures are not repaired, the memory of past contradictions lingers. Trust cannot carry forward, so people begin to plan around the next collapse rather than believing in renewal.

Over time, this anatomy of misoriented trust reshapes the entire organisation. Innovation slows, as no one feels safe taking risks. Collaboration gives way to compliance. Recruitment shifts from seeking talent to filtering for conformity. Outwardly, the company still looks like a high-performing start-up, but inwardly it corrodes under suspicion, guardedness and exhaustion.

Here, trust has not disappeared; it has been distorted. It no longer functions as a living scaffold for cooperation. Instead, it masquerades as culture while quietly fracturing the very coherence it was meant to sustain.

Mechanics of trust

Trust is not a passive state. It is an active, evolving and relational process. It functions as an ontological modulator that regulates how individuals and systems navigate exposure, coherence and interdependence. Unlike control, which operates through surveillance and rigidity, trust facilitates flow through alignment, feedback and response. The following mechanics demonstrate how trust is not merely felt but formed, tested, repaired or eroded through recursive relational dynamics.

1. **Trust activation**

   Trust always begins with a risk – an action that reveals openness before certainty. This may take the form of a disclosure, an act of reliance or a relinquishing of control. What distinguishes trust from naive optimism is that it initiates action from a place of sincerity, not ignorance. Once trust is activated, the initial offering is the seed. Without it, there is no field in which trust can grow.

2. **Feedback calibration**

   Once trust has been activated, feedback arrives – directly or indirectly – in the form of tone, responsiveness, consistency, silence, presence or absence. Trust is not static; it listens. At this point, the system discerns whether vulnerability was respected or neglected, responded to or ignored. Here, the system subtly updates its settings, either loosening or tightening the aperture for future trust.

3. **Trust drift**

   Every interaction either affirms or strains trust. However, these shifts rarely occur as dramatic breaks. More often, trust builds or decays through micro-confirmations and micro-ruptures – moments where vulnerability meets either coherence and care or neglect and confusion. These subtle accumulations create what we call 'trust drift'. Over time, they either reinforce the architecture of trust or introduce fault lines beneath its surface, often unnoticed until the structure falters.

4. **Compounding trust**

In healthy systems, trust does not remain static; it compounds. This process, often referred to as 'trust loop expansion', unfolds when each act of openness is consistently met with integrity. As trust loops reinforce one another, complexity is handled with less friction, collaboration deepens and communication becomes less coded. The system gradually lets go of constant threat monitoring – not out of naivety, but from a growing coherence that makes defensiveness less necessary.

5. **Recalibration**

No system is immune to rupture. But when trust breaks down, it doesn't simply disappear; it changes form. A breach initiates a pivotal threshold – does the system have the maturity to re-establish coherence? Recalibration does not mean returning to the past. It means rebuilding lost trust with transparency, accountability and new alignment. Without this, trust mutates into suspicion, resentment or guardedness. When this happens, cooperation becomes coercion and vulnerability becomes weaponised – for example, when personal disclosures are later used to manipulate, control or discredit.

Trust is not sustained by declarations; it is sustained by recursive action. Each cycle either strengthens the relational field or erodes its integrity. The mechanics of trust demonstrate that coherence cannot be commanded. It must be nurtured through responsiveness and honesty.

Topology of trust

The topology of trust reveals its recursive and interdependent architecture – how internal components generate feedback loops that shape perception, behaviour and system design. Trust is not a linear contract. It is an ongoing negotiation of coherence anchored in lived interactions and either reinforced or eroded over time. Each structural element dynamically conditions and is conditioned by the others, forming an interdependent structure that shapes the coherence of relationships between people and entities.

Openness ↔ Consistency

Trust always begins with an element of risk. The degree to which that risk – whether emotional, relational or ideological – is met with reliability determines whether the system deepens in safety or fractures into withdrawal. When openness meets a consistent, reliable response, trust becomes embodied. It moves from concept to felt reality. In contrast, when openness meets unreliability and inconsistency, the outcome is damaging. Mistrust grows not necessarily from ill will, but from unpredictability in the presence of exposure. Over time, one learns: 'It's not safe to be open here.'

Consistency ↔ Benevolence

Consistency alone is insufficient. Trust deepens when reliability is paired with a sense of goodwill or benevolence. A person who is erratic but clearly caring may still be trusted over someone predictable but cold or self-serving. However, when consistency masks manipulation or malice, trust collapses. Intent matters. We don't just trust what someone does; we trust how they are while doing it. Trust becomes resilient only when the system believes that the other is *for* them, not merely *with* them.

Benevolence ↔ Ontological alignment

The perception of benevolence gains credibility when it aligns with a deeper resonance of shared values or states of being. Someone may appear kind, but if their energy, choices or tone are incongruent with their internal compass, trust remains partial or withheld. When alignment is present without care – such as in ideological echo chambers or in the presence of charismatic but disingenuous leaders – trust may become blind or weaponised. Genuine trust arises when ontological alignment and benevolence co-exist, creating a field of mutual recognition: 'We are not only in sync; I truly believe you mean no harm.'

Ontological alignment ↔ Continuity

Genuine trust reveals itself over time. The durability of a person's integrity through periods of change, stress and uncertainty reinforces ontological alignment as reliability. The longer coherence persists across shifting contexts, the deeper the trust embeds. But when alignment fractures over time – when values shift without explanation or presence becomes performance – trust decays, often without a visible rupture. In this way, trust is a cumulative pattern of coherence or deviation.

Continuity ↔ Openness

Every act of openness is shaped by the memory of how previous instances of vulnerability were met. When trust is honoured over time, openness increases and trust is enabled. However, when trust is repeatedly violated, especially without recalibration, we learn to withhold. Risking openness becomes too costly. We tell ourselves, 'Do not open up here. It's not worth it.' This recursive circuit determines whether trust evolves into coherence or calcifies into defence.

Emergent qualities and patterns

Trust is not naive optimism. It is the invisible infrastructure of coherent systems. It reduces the need for overregulation, compensatory mechanisms and hypervigilance – not by wishful thinking but by aligning perception, intention and action. Where trust is high, energy is liberated. However, where trust is low, systems may appear productive but hemorrhage energy, opportunity and truth beneath the surface. To cultivate trust is to build the most efficient, ethical and resilient system available to us as individuals and collectives.

When trust flows, the following are among the deep structural outcomes that typically emerge:

- **Psychological safety** – People express, innovate and take risks without fear.
- **Relational coherence** – Miscommunication decreases, attunement increases.
- **Organisational flow** – Less friction, more alignment, faster collaboration.
- **Efficient communication** – Fewer words, clearer impact.
- **Reduced defence and manipulation** – No need to posture or conceal.
- **Willingness to co-create** – Shared agency and responsibility.

In contrast, where trust breaks down, we witness patterns like:

- **Micromanagement** – The substitute for genuine relational security.
- **Paranoia** – A system preparing for betrayal.
- **Erosion of intimacy** – Surface interaction without depth.
- **Strategic deception** – Truth becomes dangerous.
- **Burnout from constant hypervigilance** – Life becomes threat management.

Trust in action

Let's now translate the ontology of trust into lived, tangible experiences. The following case studies illustrate how trust either creates environments of coherence and flourishing or collapses into dysfunction when its structural layers fracture. These dynamics occur not only in individuals but across teams, institutions and societal systems.

Case 1: The compliant but stagnant department

A large government department delivers services efficiently on paper, meeting targets and producing regular reports. Yet internally, staff avoid raising concerns, fearing that criticism will be seen as disloyalty. Whistle-blowers are marginalised, new ideas are buried in red tape and leaders equate loyalty with silence. Morale sinks, but the facade of stability remains intact.

Insight: While procedures are followed and outputs delivered, there is little genuine openness or benevolence. Employees comply out of obligation rather than trust, and innovation is stifled by fear of reprisal. Over time, the culture drifts towards entrenchment – stability mistaken for success. The absence of authentic trust breeds stagnation, leaving the department unable to adapt when real change is required.

Case 2: Recalibrating co-founders

Two tech co-founders had a falling out after a product pivot triggered deep disagreements. For weeks, they barely spoke. One initiates repair – not with excuses but by acknowledging their misalignment and openly sharing their deeper fears and intentions. The other responds by revisiting their early vision, voicing frustrations calmly and proposing a new decision-making structure.

Insight: This is an example of recalibration in action. Ontological alignment was damaged but not destroyed. Openness re-emerged. Consistency allowed both to reflect on their shared history and recommit to future alignment – not by ignoring the rupture, but by rebuilding the structure of trust. Their startup survived – not because of vision alone, but because the trust architecture was restored. This is what authentic sustainability looks like in leadership partnerships.

Case 3: The superficial friendship that quietly withers

Two friends meet regularly, share updates and laugh together. But when one faces personal hardship, the other becomes absent – not hostile, just unavailable. No check-ins. No listening ear. When trust is finally brought up, the absent friend says, 'I didn't know you needed anything; you looked fine.'

Insight: Trust didn't break in a dramatic moment. It eroded through repeated micro-ruptures. The friendship lacked consistency and benevolence. Despite continuity in casual settings, the absence of deeper resonance meant the trust structure couldn't hold emotional weight. Eventually, the connection decayed into performative interaction. This same pattern plays out in families, intimate partnerships, leadership teams and public institutions when relationships are reduced to surface performance and functional output.

Trust doesn't fail because people are inherently flawed. It fails when the structural components – openness, consistency, benevolence, ontological alignment and continuity – aren't integrated into the architecture of the system. Incoherence becomes the silent killer of sustainability. And what could have been a regenerative field of trust becomes a cycle of withdrawal, reactivity and eventual collapse.

True trust is not found in stated intentions; it's measured by the structure that holds people together when it matters most.

Conclusion

Trust is not a sentimental bonus. It is the backbone of every coherent relationship, organisation and society. Without it, even the most brilliant ideas collapse into suspicion, disconnection or control. However, with trust, uncertainty becomes navigable, conflict becomes transformative and collaboration becomes regenerative.

Throughout this chapter, we've reframed trust not as blind faith or naive hope, but as a living architecture composed of five interdependent structural components: openness, consistency, benevolence, ontological alignment and continuity. Together, these elements create the structural conditions under which trust is built, tested and repaired – not only in individuals, but in systems at every scale.

We've seen that trust begins with a risk. It grows when that risk is met with care and congruence. It decays through micro-ruptures and erodes when feedback is ignored or authenticity is punished. But when nurtured as a relational field, trust becomes the most potent generator of human flourishing and the most reliable engine of systemic sustainability.

In systems where trust is high, energy is liberated, communication becomes efficient, decisions are clean and relationships deepen. The system – human or otherwise – relies less on performative optics, bureaucracy or coercive enforcement. Trust amplifies coherence without the need to tighten control.

But where trust is low, everything must be policed. People withhold, risk-taking collapses, innovation stalls and culture hardens.

Even apparent success becomes hollow, propped up by fear and overcompensation. Systems that cannot hold trust do not degrade gracefully; they hollow out from within. Their members are forced to defend, perform or protect themselves rather than innovate, care or contribute. What remains may function, but it does not truly live.

Trust cannot be demanded. It must be consciously, relationally and structurally architected.

Reflection

- Where in your life do you withhold openness – not out of discernment, but out of fear conditioned by past experiences?
- Do you tend to offer trust quickly, slowly or not at all? What shaped this tendency and do you think it is sustainable?
- When others engage with you (or your team/organisation), do they experience reliability, goodwill and alignment or poor performance, unpredictability or guardedness?
- In your organisation, community or closest relationships, is trust being strengthened over time, or is it silently corroding through small ruptures and unacknowledged misalignments?
- How do you or your team/organisation respond when trust is broken? Is there space for repair or do you, your team or organisation default to blame, denial or avoidance?
- What would it look like to design a sustainable system of trust – one where others can risk being seen and heard, and where you can feel safe to show up fully?

CHAPTER 36

Sovereignty

In cultures addicted to performance optics, validation and groupthink, few qualities are as powerful – and as radically misunderstood – as sovereignty. It is often mischaracterised as political independence, stoic detachment or rugged individualism. But ontologically, sovereignty is not about domination or defiance. It's also not about doing whatever you want. It's about knowing you have the freedom, autonomy and liberty (sovereignty) to not abandon who you are – and who you are becoming – even when the world tempts you to trade your authorship, your inner authority, for external approval.

Sovereignty is the structural capacity to remain intact – to hold one's clarity, authorship and ethical compass even amid distractions, pressure or persuasion to conform. It allows a person to walk into a room, hear every opinion, feel every energy, consider every narrative and still decide from within.

This is not just personal. In systems – teams, organisations, institutions and nations – sovereignty determines whether decisions are authored from within or ceded to coercion, public opinion or performative survival strategies. To abandon sovereignty is still a choice, but one made under the sway of fear, dependency or distortion rather than from coherence. A leader may hear criticism and adjust course because it aligns with their values and vision – that is sovereignty. Another may abandon their stance out of fear of rejection or loss of approval – that is surrendering sovereignty. Both are 'decisions from within', but one is authored from coherence, the other from distortion. Sovereignty is participation without self-abandonment.

Sovereignty is rarely rewarded in social systems that prefer compliance or controlled opposition. Workplaces may prize conformity to corporate culture over authentic contribution. Families sometimes elevate unquestioned duty or tradition above self-authorship – for example, pressuring individuals to pursue a career path that upholds family status rather than their own calling. Even spiritual traditions can preach surrender into authority, ideology or charisma rather than into discernment and inner coherence. But ontologically, sovereignty is neither resistance nor submission. It is the capacity to author one's participation with coherence.

Philosophical and mystical traditions echo this anchored stance, from *autarkeia* in Stoicism (self-sufficiency in virtue) to the Sufi concept of *baqā'* (subsistence in truth after annihilation of illusion). In all cases, sovereignty is not superiority. It is alignment.

Without sovereignty, intention becomes performative, trust becomes dependency and Being is easily hijacked. Systems without sovereignty become reactive or hollow. In contrast, when sovereignty is present, complexity becomes navigable, relationships remain ethical and decisions stay congruent – even under pressure. For example, a leader confronted with public criticism may either bend to appease opinion (without sovereignty) or respond with discernment, holding true to their values while still listening (with sovereignty).

In the Unified Ontology of Systemic Integrity (UOSI), sovereignty is one of the four qualities of the Integrity Sphere, alongside intention, trust and Being. It is what ensures we act not from compulsion or collapse, but from coherence. And without it, sustainability – of a person, an organisation, a culture, a society or an institution – is impossible.

Why sovereignty?

In common discourse, we often speak of liberty, freedom or autonomy as if they are interchangeable. But in the UOSI, these terms are not treated as equals, nor as sufficient on their own. The word sovereignty was selected because it represents the structural source from which liberty, freedom and autonomy emerge – and by which they are guided and sustained.

In this body of work, sovereignty is positioned as the meta-structure or ontological cluster that includes:

- **Liberty** – the circumstantial absence of external constraint, often dependent on social or political systems.
- **Freedom** – the existential capacity to choose and act without internal or external coercion.
- **Autonomy** – the structured ability to self-govern: to act with intentionality, responsibility and integrity within relational or systemic contexts.

These qualities are unstable without a deeper organising principle. That principle is *sovereignty*: the structural source that makes liberty, freedom and autonomy coherent and principled rather than chaotic or self-serving.

Without sovereignty at the core:

- Liberty risks becoming **licence**, untethered from responsibility.
- Freedom can spiral into **chaos**, disconnected from discernment.
- Autonomy may degrade into **egoism**, severed from coherence and shared purpose.

Ontological Distinction of Sovereignty

Sovereignty is the structural capacity for coherent authorship – in an individual, a collective or any manufactured system. It is neither defiance nor submission, but the integrity of acting from inner clarity rather than external compulsion, fear or inherited conditioning. *Sovereignty* integrates what is often described as freedom, liberty, autonomy or agency – but grounds them in coherence and authorship rather than indulgence or resistance. Where agency is the capacity to act and make choices, autonomy is the independence from external control, and authorship is the responsibility of shaping one's own path. *Sovereignty* holds these together, expressing not just the ability to choose, but the capacity to do so with integrity, clarity and coherence. In people, sovereignty expresses itself as inner authorship: the ability to act and respond in alignment with one's deeper truth. In organisations, institutions, cultures and societies, it is decision-making rooted in shared ethical principles and coherence rather than reaction, reputation or metrics of conformity. *Sovereignty* is what makes meaningful self-governance possible – where freedom is exercised with discernment and choice arises from clarity rather than impulse or rebellion.

A **healthy relationship with sovereignty** indicates that you move through life with grounded agency and authorship. You can distinguish between your truth and others' projections – between what arises from authentic awareness and what is imposed by others' fears, expectations or distortions – and between your values and external agendas. You neither collapse into conformity nor react compulsively against it. Instead, you remain responsive, principled and intact – able to engage with others while staying connected to yourself. You adjust course when clarity demands it, not when pressure coerces you. In manufactured systems, healthy sovereignty shows up in institutions and cultures that remain agile without abandoning their core values. They uphold ethical autonomy without isolating themselves, and sustain liberty, not as indulgence, but as a disciplined space where integrity guides action.

An **unhealthy relationship with sovereignty** indicates that you are either passively dependent or performatively rebellious. On one side, you may defer choices, echo others' opinions or collapse into blame, giving away your authorship. On the other side, you may mistake rigidity or withdrawal for strength – resisting not from clarity, but from unprocessed wounds or reactive identity. This distortion can also lead to being excessively reactionary, mistaking rebellion for freedom. In larger systems, unhealthy sovereignty shows up as erratic policy, brittle governance or moral grandstanding. What is lost is not only power, but coherence. Without sovereignty, no system – human or institutional – can sustain itself. It eventually defaults to either excessive control or collapse.

Ontology of sovereignty

Ontologically, sovereignty is pre-relational. It shapes how one enters every encounter – not in rejection of a relationship, but by establishing a prior orientation. It precedes speech, action or response. It is not a reaction, but a stance.

As the architecture of inner authorship, sovereignty is when a person shows up with grounded presence in the face of influence. It is neither invincibility nor detachment. It is *coherence under pressure*.

Without sovereignty, intention mutates into manipulation, trust becomes dependency and freedom – when severed from Being – spirals into chaos.

Anatomy of sovereignty

Sovereignty is composed of five ontological components that together establish the architecture of inner authorship. These are not traits or ideals; they are structural capacities that enable a person to navigate influence without losing their centre. Their integration determines whether sovereignty is authentic, performative or absent.

1. **Inner authority**

    At the heart of sovereignty lies inner authority – the capacity to self-reference without outsourcing one's clarity to others. This is not defiance; it is discernment. It is the ability to stand in one's knowing without collapsing into external validation, imitation or automatic rebellion. Inner authority is not loud; it is firm. It does not require superiority or proof; it is rooted in coherence. When absent, one's identity becomes a reflection of others' expectations, ideologies or emotions. However, when present, a person becomes a source of coherence rather than merely a seeker of validation.

2. Discernment

Sovereignty requires precise discernment of the self's boundaries – not as rigid walls, but as living membranes, permeable enough for connection, yet distinct enough for integrity. It is the ability to discern what is mine and what is not, from thoughts and emotions to responsibilities and projections. A sovereign being knows where the self ends and others begin – psychologically, emotionally and energetically. This discernment prevents fusion (taking on what's not yours) and avoids fragmentation (disowning what is). Sovereignty is not isolation; it is the honouring of one's distinctness within interconnectedness.

3. Response-ability

Sovereign beings do not react blindly; they respond consciously. This is 'response-ability': the capacity to remain aware, attuned and decisive under pressure. It involves having agency over your emotional state and the way you interpret meaning and your behaviour, even when provoked or challenged. It does not mean suppression of emotion. Instead, it means ownership of how you move with it. When this structural capacity is underdeveloped, sovereignty collapses into reactivity, blame or paralysis. However, when active, it generates calm clarity, even amid chaos.

4. Principled autonomy

Sovereignty is not the same as doing whatever you want. It is principled autonomy – the ability to act freely while anchored in values, ethics and coherence. It is the marriage between freedom and responsibility. It chooses what is right, not what is convenient. This autonomy is internally governed. It cannot be bribed by praise, hijacked by fear or manipulated by dogma. It is not impulsive; it is attuned. Principled autonomy is where integrity enters sovereignty, not as a performance, but as an operating principle.

5. Influence regulation

We are all influenced, but the sovereign being knows it. Influence regulation is the ability to detect, filter and contextualise the forces that shape our inner landscape: social trends, media inputs, ideological narratives, familial pressure and groupthink. Sovereignty does not mean total insulation. It means conscious permeability. This capacity ensures that one can remain open without being overtaken, discerning without being cynical, and involved without being absorbed.

A tangible example of misoriented sovereignty

A government prides itself on being 'the voice of the people'. Outwardly, it projects stability and independence. Yet beneath the surface, its sovereignty is misoriented.

At the level of **inner authority**, leaders no longer reference their own clarity or principled compass. Decisions are outsourced to polls, media cycles and populist slogans. The government appears decisive, but its identity merely mirrors public mood swings. Without an anchored source, authority collapses into performance.

At the level of **discernment**, boundaries blur. Corporate lobbying, international pressure and partisan agendas all seep into the nation's decisions. What is 'ours' and what is 'theirs' can no longer be told apart. Public interest is steadily traded away, hidden behind rhetoric of progress and global competitiveness. In this confusion, sovereignty dissolves into external agendas.

At the level of **response-ability**, reaction dominates. Policy is drafted as a reflex to scandal or pressure, rather than as a coherent, principled response. Anger dictates law. Fear dictates spending. Opportunism dictates alliances. Instead of owning its posture, the government lives in a cycle of defence, scapegoating and fire-fighting.

At the level of **principled autonomy**, freedom is mistaken for licence. Leaders enact whatever is expedient to stay in office, calling it strength. Values and ethics are used as branding, not as anchors. What might have been genuine autonomy collapses into egoism, self-preservation and reactive populism. Decisions are made, but they rest on expedience rather than integrity.

At the level of **influence regulation**, sovereignty is most visibly eroded. Media storms, international think-tanks and ideological spin doctors set the terms of debate. Leaders adopt narratives uncritically, mistaking saturation for truth. The public senses something hollow – that choices are no longer made from within, but borrowed from elsewhere – and cynicism grows.

Over time, the anatomy of sovereignty unravels. What looks like decisive governance is, in fact, dependency disguised as authority. The system functions, but only as a vessel for louder voices. What was meant to be a centre of coherence becomes a hollow stage for performance.

Here, sovereignty has not vanished – it has been distorted. It is no longer the structural capacity to remain intact under influence, but the habit of mistaking reaction for agency. What could have anchored clarity and coherence is instead rebranded as control, leaving both citizens and leaders estranged from authentic agency.

Mechanics of sovereignty

Sovereignty is not a fixed state – it is a living process. It unfolds through a series of recursive operations that allow individuals to remain internally anchored while navigating complexity, influence and interaction. The following mechanics govern how coherence is maintained – not in isolation, but in the friction and flow of real life.

1. **Anchoring**

   Sovereignty begins before any decision is made; it is anchored in Being. This is not about adopting a posture of strength. It's about surrendering into coherence. When a person is anchored in clarity of intention, grounded values and embodied presence, their decisions flow from discernment

– not from panic, projection or fear. This anchoring provides a stabilising centre from which they act – not to prove, but to participate with integrity. Without anchoring, sovereignty becomes a mimicry of power, easily shaken by circumstance or approval.

2. Boundary navigation

Sovereignty is enacted in context. It is tested when one must discern what to allow and what to refuse – not through defence, but through presence. This includes recognising emotional invasions, ideological impositions and relational entanglements. A sovereign person does not need to control others. They simply don't abandon themselves. Boundaries are not ultimatums; they are expressions of authorship. The sovereign being, nation, system and society navigates the dynamic interplay of openness and containment without collapse or overreach.

3. Agency

At its core, sovereignty is the capacity to choose. Whether the choice is to speak, act, remain still or surrender – what matters is that the decision is owned. There is no outsourcing to social permission, no deferral to habit, no collapse into blame. Sovereignty does not guarantee perfection, but it insists on authorship. Even when the sovereign being changes their mind, it is not from confusion, but from a place of deeper clarity.

4. Mood regulation

Sovereignty is not emotional suppression. It is emotional stewardship. The sovereign being does not deny their emotional states. They notice, name and navigate them. This includes choosing how to relate to anger, fear, vulnerability or grief without being consumed by those moods. They do not seek to 'overcome' these feelings, but to relate to them in a healthy way. Even under pressure, the sovereign being remains decisive, capable of coherence without feigning invulnerability.

5. **Relational engagement**

   Sovereignty is the foundation for healthy connection. A sovereign person can participate fully in groups, partnerships and systems without losing their centre. They neither dissolve into collective identity nor assert themselves in hollow opposition. Their 'yeses' and 'noes' are authentic. They enter relationships not to merge or dominate, but to engage with clarity. This kind of conscious relational engagement is marked by presence, not performance. Their autonomy does not isolate; it honours other perspectives while remaining true to itself.

Topology of sovereignty

Like intention, trust and Being, sovereignty is not an isolated trait within the Integrity Sphere. It is a systemic ecology of interdependent faculties. Its five anatomical components – inner authority, discernment, response-ability, principled autonomy and influence regulation – form a dynamic field of interaction. Sovereignty does not arise from a single strength, but from the recursive interplay of these elements: each reinforcing, testing or revealing the integrity of the others.

Inner Authority ↔ Discernment

Without the ability to distinguish where one ends and another begins, inner authority becomes fragile or performative. A person who cannot discern their own energetic, emotional or cognitive boundary may outsource decision-making or react in chronic opposition. Conversely, when one has boundary clarity, their inner authority becomes more than opinion; it becomes a coherent stance. Clarity of self is the foundation for clarity of authorship.

Discernment ↔ Response-ability

Knowing where the self ends is insufficient without the capacity to respond from that knowledge. When discernment is not met with action, it mutates into avoidance or learned helplessness. True sovereignty involves consciously (not reactively) enacting one's discernment. Response-ability is where boundary becomes lived integrity, not just intellectual awareness.

Response-ability ↔ Principled autonomy

The capacity to respond must be filtered through principle. Otherwise it risks becoming impulsivity dressed as sovereignty. Response without inner ethics leads to recklessness, and principled stance without responsiveness becomes moral rigidity. In sovereignty, freedom is not merely the ability to act; it is ethical authorship. Decisions are guided by coherence, not preference or opposition.

Principled autonomy ↔ Influence regulation

Even autonomy grounded in principle can be hijacked. Ideological narratives, emotional contagion and collective pressures seep in unless actively discerned. Influence regulation ensures that sovereignty is not performative self-isolation but conscious permeability. It asks not, 'Am I free?' but 'What is shaping me now?' Autonomy becomes trustworthy only when it includes vigilance over its own architecture.

Influence regulation ↔ Inner authority

The loop closes when the ability to recognise external influence reinforces the strength of internal clarity. This recursive feedback strengthens sovereignty as a process, not a possession. Sovereignty is not static mastery; it is cyclical stewardship. When regularly recalibrated, it remains fluid, flexible and firmly anchored in Being.

Emergent qualities and patterns

The coherent interaction of all five structural components results in the following emergent qualities that cannot be forced or performed. Instead, they emerge naturally when sovereignty is embodied.

- **Integrity under pressure** – Remaining grounded and aligned when tested by adversity.
- **Clarity of decision-making** – Choosing with precision and ownership, even amid uncertainty.
- **Relational engagement without control** – Connecting deeply without seeking to merge or dominate.
- **Emotional groundedness** – Feeling fully without being overtaken or shut down.

- **Freedom tethered to responsibility** – Exercising choice in a way that honours impact.
- **Leadership without domination** – Guiding others through presence, not coercion.
- **Spiritual individuation without escapism** – Evolving consciously without disconnecting from reality.

These emergent qualities are not idealistic abstractions; they are ontological outcomes of recursive coherence within and across all domains.

In contrast, when sovereignty is fragmented or superficial, these same elements invert and degrade:

- **False autonomy** – Rebellion that mimics freedom without substance.
- **Martyrdom** – Self-abandonment justified as moral sacrifice.
- **Chronic indecision** – Paralysis masked as open-mindedness.
- **Boundary collapse** – Empathy mistaken for compassion.
- **Hyper-independence** – Rigidity disguised as strength.
- **Manipulable activism** – Outrage weaponised by ideology or unresolved trauma.

These are not random flaws; they are the shadows of distorted sovereignty.

Sovereignty in action

The following case studies illustrate both the presence and absence of sovereignty – and how these patterns play out in leadership, relationships, activism and institutional design.

Case 1: The collapsing leader

A start-up CEO is known for visionary thinking, but is highly reactive to investor opinions. One strong comment in a boardroom sends the product strategy spiralling. The team whiplashes week-to-week trying to please external voices. The CEO constantly references others' success stories to justify pivots, never standing firm in their own analysis or values.

Insight: This is a collapse of inner authority and influence regulation. The leader has vision, but no anchored stance. Their sovereignty is outsourced to perceived power. Without principled autonomy, their decisions are not authored; they are echoed. This leads to loss of trust, blurred priorities and systemic instability masked as 'agility'. Over time, the organisation burns out – not from a lack of talent, but from the absence of sovereignty at the top.

Case 2: The grounded partner

In a long-term relationship, one partner expresses a strong desire to move overseas for work. The other feels pressure to agree, but instead of immediately agreeing to please their partner or adopting an emotionally charged negative stance, they decide to take some time to think about it. They reflect, consult their values and return with clarity: 'I love you, but this move doesn't align with where I am in life right now.' The tone is calm. The words are clear. No accusations. No guilt-tripping. Just discernment.

Insight: This is response-ability in action. Sovereignty doesn't reject the other; it clarifies the self. The person honours both connection and inner truth. Discernment and influence regulation are intact. Their principled autonomy is not reactive, but centred and grounded. Even if the relationship shifts, it does so with structural honesty, not manipulation, inauthentic agreement or avoidance. This is the kind of sovereignty that sustains relational integrity.

Case 3: The activist without a compass

A social media activist builds a large following by calling out injustice with passionate intensity. But when pressed on their core values or personal integrity, their tone shifts. Criticism is met with hostility. They are deeply influenced by the current narrative tides, switching stances when it serves popularity. Eventually, their message fractures under the weight of performative rage and emotional exhaustion.

Insight: This is an unhealthy relationship with sovereignty disguised as moral conviction. Principled autonomy is missing, causing activism to become reactive, not authored. Without influence regulation, external narratives hijack internal clarity. The activist appears strong, but is structurally hollow. Burnout and disintegration follow – not because their cause is invalid, but because their stance lacks coherence. Movements without sovereign leadership become volatile, short-lived and easily co-opted.

Conclusion

Sovereignty is subtle but unmistakable. It does not dominate, collapse or perform. It anchors. It listens without dissolving. It chooses without needing applause. And it is what allows us to build sustainable systems – not ones that simply function, but ones that remain ethical, resilient and coherent through pressure.

Sovereignty is not posturing; it is presence. It is not a performance, but the architecture of inner authorship – the place from which we act, relate and decide without abandoning ourselves. It is not the loud claim of authority, but the steady coherence of one who can stay grounded in the face of pressure, persuasion or praise. It is not the absence of influence, but the conscious navigation of it. In a world that rewards dependence, punishes discernment and mistakes collapse for surrender, true sovereignty is revolutionary.

This chapter has explored sovereignty, not as an abstract ideal, but as a structural force of integrity, essential not only for individuals, but for any system that seeks to remain principled and sustainable. Through its five anatomical components – inner authority, discernment, response-ability, principled autonomy and influence regulation – we have seen how sovereignty governs whether we operate from a place of integrity or dysfunction.

Sovereign individuals neither collapse into passivity nor lash out in compulsive opposition. They do not *perform* clarity. They *author* it. They are available, grounded and adaptable without becoming manipulable. Their freedom is coherent, not chaotic. Their autonomy is principled, not impulsive. And sovereign organisations, institutions and cultures do the same. They do not bend to trends, dilute their purpose or crumble under the weight of external validation. They respond with coherence, sustaining liberty not as an indulgence, but as an ethical space for responsible action.

In leadership, sovereignty prevents decisiveness from becoming domination. In cultures, it keeps purpose from mutating into propaganda. In collective life, it allows freedom to become ethical action, not ego-fuelled chaos.

To cultivate sovereignty is to return to the authentic orientation of Being, prior to optics, mimicry and manipulation. It is not about detaching from the world; it's about engaging from a place of integrity and wholeness. No sustainable system – whether a person, a partnership, an organisation or a nation – can endure without sovereignty at its core.

Reflection

- Where in your life do you notice yourself abandoning your inner clarity to maintain harmony, avoid judgement or gain approval?
- Can you distinguish your own voice from the influences – cultural, familial, ideological – that shape your actions and beliefs?
- How do you respond to pressure – do you collapse, conform, lash out or clarify?
- Do your boundaries express discernment and coherence, or are they set through reactivity, defence or fear?
- What would principled autonomy look like in your current context, where freedom does not mean detachment but structural integrity?
- In the systems you're part of – teams, communities, institutions – who or what authors decisions? What would it take to shift those systems towards sovereignty rather than reaction, imitation or fear?

CHAPTER 37

Being

Amid our addiction to doing, fixing and proving, Being is the one phenomenon we rarely stop to examine. We talk about identity, personality, behaviour and performance. We seek clarity, impact and influence. But we seldom ask: 'Who is the one doing the doing? And from what state of being and underlying framework are they acting?'

Being is not a role we perform or a set of traits we exhibit. It is the underlying structure that determines how we show up, what we generate and whether what we create can sustain itself over time.

In everyday language, the word 'being' is often treated as a noun – as in *human being*. But ontologically, Being is more accurately understood as a verb: a process, a field, a projection. In this body of work, the word 'Being' is given a capital letter to distinguish it from its more conventional usage. It is not just who you are, but *how* you are being in the world. More specifically, it refers to how you are becoming and how your presence shapes the other systems you engage with.

Great philosophical and mystical traditions have circled this terrain – from Heidegger's *Dasein* and Sufi teachings on presence to Eastern frameworks that emphasise internal states over external metrics. Yet in modern domains – especially leadership, education and system design – Being has been neglected, distorted or collapsed into superficial categories. This neglect has a cost.

When Being is incoherent, no amount of intention, technique or structure can produce sustainability. We may create, but burn out. We may lead, but fracture trust. We may succeed, but remain internally divided. Hollow performance becomes the mask of systemic collapse.

Therefore, Being is not merely philosophical; it is a structural imperative. It's the difference between coherence and chaos, sustainability and slow disintegration.

In the Unified Ontology of Systemic Integrity, Being is the force that integrates the other components within the Integrity Sphere: intention, trust and sovereignty. It is not a single trait, but a layered constellation of moods, postures, orientations and actions.

Where coherence is present, Being becomes the source of transformation. However, where it is absent, even noble intentions become performative and systemic impact becomes unsustainable.

Being is not static. It unfolds. It is modulated by mood, refined through feedback and expressed through posture and behaviour.

This chapter explores Being, not as an abstraction, but as a layered, recursive and dynamic system. Its anatomy, mechanics and topology reveal how Being becomes either a generator of structural coherence or the silent root of dysfunction.

Ontological Distinction of Being

Being is the way you exist and show up in the world. It is not a fixed identity or a personality label, but the living structure through which you perceive, relate, act and embody meaning. It is the structured and generative field from which you express yourself, participate in life and shape reality. *Being* is the invisible infrastructure behind every word, choice, stance and impact. To speak of *Being* is not just to ask *who you are* but *how you are being* – the quality of presence you bring, the atmosphere you create and the coherence – or incoherence – that radiates from you over time. It is what makes your actions trustworthy or hollow, your relationships nourishing or draining, your leadership sustainable or performative. *Being* is both subtle and consequential. It is the background architecture shaping everything you do and the felt experience others have of you in every moment.

A **healthy relationship with Being** indicates that you are consistently aware of your inner architecture – your moods, intentions, values, stances and actions – and how they align as part of a coherent way of being. This alignment reflects the deeper architecture described in the Being Framework,[81] which shows how our qualities of Being shape what we do and how others experience us. You do not live in a state of reactive dysfunction or perform roles merely to survive. You live in a state of structural coherence. Others experience you as clear, grounded and trustworthy – not because you are always right, but because you are authentic and coherent. You can navigate complexity without collapsing under pressure, because your presence is integrated with who you are and how you show up authentically. This is what makes long-term sustainability – of self, relationships, leadership and other systems – possible.

An **unhealthy relationship with Being** indicates that you are caught up in dysfunction, inconsistency or performance-based identity. You may appear confident but feel hollow, act with intensity but lack clarity, or produce results in ways that cannot be sustained. You may shift your stance depending on who is watching or what is expected. Your moods dominate your discernment, and your values are vague or borrowed. At times, you may become stuck in an endless cycle of 'perfecting yourself' – moving from one development path to another without ever taking embodied action. Others may find you unpredictable, overly influenced or emotionally disconnected – not because you lack talent or intent, but because your internal architecture is incoherent. Sustainability – in your impact, energy and relationships – becomes impossible.

Ontology of Being

Being is not static. It is not 'who you are' in some essentialist or fixed sense. It is an evolving expression, modulated by the interplay between inner intention and external conditions. In other words, it is

---

81   Tashvir, A. (2021) *Being – The Source of Power*. Sydney: Engenesis Publications.

an ongoing projection – responsive to context, mood and the degree of alignment between one's values and actions. Being unfolds through a structured process that bridges the unseen depths of one's inner architecture with the visible world of action and consequence.

To better understand Being ontologically, we must move beyond surface traits and examine its anatomy, mechanics and topology. Doing so enables us to understand not only what we are, but also who we are and how we are becoming.

Anatomy of Being

Being is a multi-layered and recursively-constituted living structure grounded in human experience. It is composed of four distinct but interwoven layers:

- **Meta Factors** – orientational anchors that shape one's ontological compass.
- **Moods** – felt climates of Being that shape one's access to potential and coherence.

Awareness	Integrity	Effectiveness	
Vulnerability	Care	Anxiety	Fear
Authenticity	Peace of Mind	Empowerment	Compassion
Commitment	Freedom	Contribution	Forgiveness
Responsibility	Self Expression	Love	Courage
Higher Purpose	Presence	Partnership	Gratitude
Resourcefulness	Proactivity	Resilience	Assertiveness
Confidence	Reliability	Accountability	Persistence

Figure 9 – The Ontological Model.

- **Primary Ways of Being** – postural stances that shape one's inner orientation and relational presence.
- **Secondary Ways of Being** – behavioural amplifiers that bring Being into embodied action.

Each layer modulates perception, intention, relational stance and performance. Furthermore, as you will see when we explore the topology of Being, every layer also interacts with and influences the others, making Being both deeply structured and immediately impactful. It's an inner truth that shapes, and is simultaneously shaped by, an outer architecture. Together, the layers define the shape and quality of one's Being.

1. Meta Factors: The orientational anchors of Being

Meta Factors are not merely values or traits, but existential coordinates that govern how a person relates to reality, truth and purposeful action. Like a compass, Meta Factors support us in navigating how we interpret life and position ourselves in it. There are three Meta Factors in the Being Framework Ontological Model:

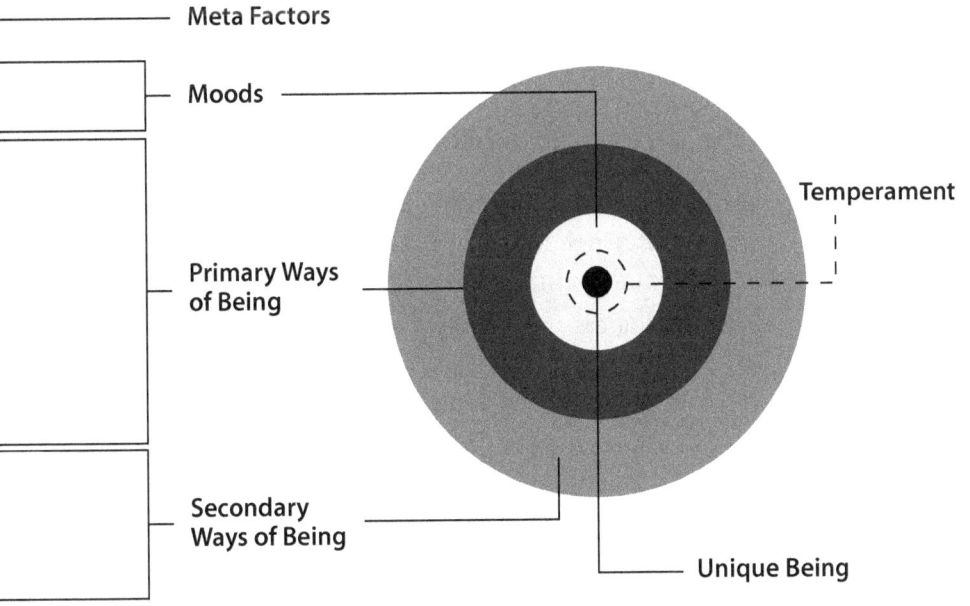

- **Awareness** – The conscious presence that enables recognition of self, others, context and consequence. Without awareness, all other Aspects of Being are blind or reactive. It is the faculty through which perception is refined and action becomes intelligent.
- **Integrity** – The condition of internal and external coherence: wholeness, alignment and congruence with reality. Integrity is not perfection; it is the structural capacity to remain coherent under pressure.
- **Effectiveness** – The ontological readiness to act and produce impact. Effectiveness is not efficiency in the shallow sense. It is the ability to generate intended outcomes with discernment, precision and sustainability.

These Meta Factors form Being's navigational layer. When they are weak or distorted, the rest of the architecture becomes reactive or performative. However, when strong, they empower grounded, impactful action.

2. Moods: the atmospheric layer of Being

Moods are the emotional fields within which all perception, sense-making and decision-making take place. They are not fleeting emotions, but they shape what we can see, feel and do. The four Moods in the Being Framework Ontological Model are:

- **Vulnerability** – The openness to be seen, heard, affected and engaged, even when there is no guarantee of safety. It is the access point to intimacy, creativity and authenticity.
- **Care** – The ontological commitment to the wellbeing of self, others and the world. Care generates responsibility without burden and presence without control.
- **Anxiety** – The contraction of our inner world in the face of disruption or uncertainty. It distorts presence and often leads to over-controlling or withdrawing as a way to cope with the unknown.

- **Fear** – The projection of threat and the loss of relational openness. When unexamined, fear hardens into defence, mistrust and avoidance.

Moods are not moral. They are *conditions*. When unacknowledged, they govern silently. However, when brought into conscious awareness, they can be shifted, integrated and transformed.

3. Primary Ways of Being: 16 ontological postures

Primary Ways of Being are the core, primal ontological stances or postures through which a person meets existence. They are not behaviours; they are foundational modes of orientation and presence that shape how we relate to ourselves, others and the world.

The Being Framework Ontological Model recognises 16 Primary Ways of Being relevant to human beings in the context of performance, effectiveness and leadership: authenticity, peace of mind, empowerment, compassion, commitment, freedom, contribution, forgiveness, responsibility, self-expression, love, courage, higher purpose, presence, partnership and gratitude. All 16 ontological postures are intrinsic to every human being. It is how we relate to each of them that differs.

Every Primary Way of Being is a distinct ontological force that configures the field of action. They can be polished and transformed, disrupted, masked or suppressed. However, even when masked or suppressed, they continue to be part of one's ontological repertoire. When activated in alignment, these ways of being support clarity, effectiveness and the restoration of coherence.

4. Secondary Ways of Being: 8 behavioural amplifiers

Secondary Ways of Being translate internal stance into external action. They are not superficial traits; they are the outward manifestations of the deeper Primary Ways of Being and Moods. These qualities are where Being meets Doing.

The eight Secondary Ways of Being in the Being Framework Ontological Model are: resourcefulness, proactivity, resilience, assertiveness, confidence, reliability, accountability and persistence.

Secondary Ways of Being bring traction to the Primary Ways of Being. They are neither habits nor techniques. They are ontological extensions that determine how one shows up in time, action and periods of difficulty.

All four layers – Meta Factors, Moods, Primary Ways of Being and Secondary Ways of Being – make up the anatomy of Being. Together, they function not as a personality test, but as a living structure: a generative and recursive field through which each person expresses their Unique Being (one's true self) in the world. Incoherence in any layer distorts the whole. But realignment in even one layer can initiate profound transformation.

Ultimately, Being is not a quality we have. It is a living architecture we embody, project and refine.

A tangible example of distorted Being

A highly capable executive is admired for her achievements and results. Outwardly, she appears competent and reliable – but what is visible to others is primarily her behaviour: the **Secondary Ways of Being**. These are the surface-level expressions, such as assertiveness, persistence and confidence that colleagues can immediately observe. Yet beneath these visible traits lies the deeper architecture of Being. And it is here that distortion quietly resides.

At the level of **Meta Factors**, awareness is selective. The executive notices opportunities for performance, but remains blind to the relational cost her leadership style imposes on others. Integrity fragments under pressure – she compromises alignment between what she says and what she does when reputation or convenience is at stake. Effectiveness is measured narrowly in terms of short-term wins, neglecting the sustainability of her impact. Distortion at the level of orientational anchors inevitably cascades into misalignment in all that follows.

At the level of **Moods**, fear and anxiety dominate the architecture of her Being. Fear shows up as defensiveness in meetings, while anxiety drives over-controlling tendencies. Care and vulnerability are masked and people sense an environment of guardedness rather than openness. These moods shape the emotional climate in which the whole team operates, even if it is never named explicitly.

At the level of **Primary Ways of Being**, authenticity is compromised. Instead of showing up congruently, the executive projects a polished facade. Responsibility devolves into control, commitment is confused with overwork, and courage collapses into bravado. Other Primary Ways of Being, such as compassion and partnership, remain suppressed.

Finally, at the level of **Secondary Ways of Being**, the incoherence becomes tangible in her behaviour. Assertiveness mutates into hostility. Persistence hardens into inflexibility. Reliability narrows into micro-management, suffocating creativity and initiative in the team. What could have been resourcefulness is reduced to firefighting. These behaviours are what others most easily notice, but they are merely the surface manifestations of a deeper structural incoherence.

Over time, the executive's misaligned Being erodes the organisation's culture. Staff turnover rises, trust weakens and collaboration dries up. On the surface, targets are met, but beneath it, the organisation drifts towards exhaustion and fragmentation. What looks like strength is in fact fragility – hollow performance resulting from an incoherent Being.

Mechanics of Being

As mentioned, Being is not static; it is projection in motion. It functions as a living structure that expresses itself through a continuous process of recursive projection, where one's inner architecture is not only experienced, but continuously externalised, refined and re-integrated.

At the heart of this unfolding lies the Projection Process, a structured cascade through which an individual's Unique Being or true self animates their presence, decisions, actions and consequences in the world.

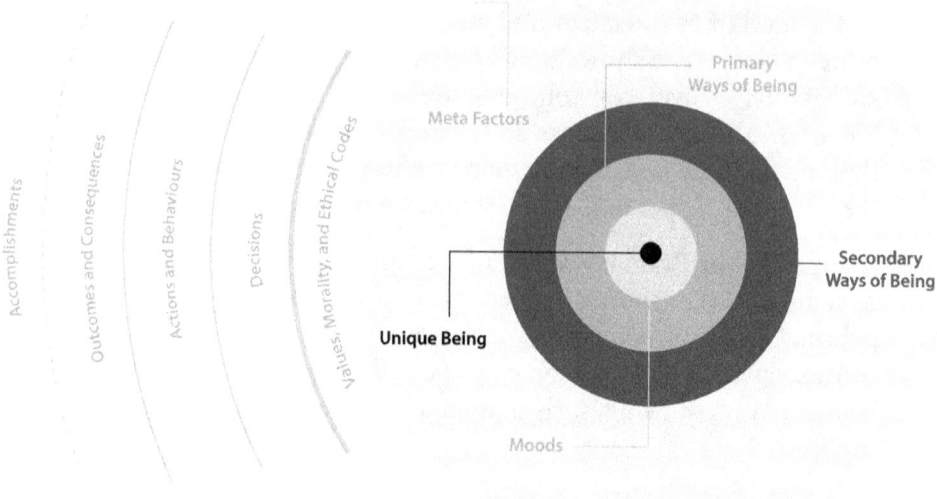

Figure 10 – The Projection Process.

Far from a poetic metaphor, the Projection Process is a discernible ontological process that is observable across multiple domains, from leadership and relationships to geopolitics.

There are seven steps that make up the mechanics of Being.

1. **Ignition**

    At the innermost core lies one's Unique Being, the irreducible, non-interchangeable ontological signature of one's true self. This is not a personality. It is the originating pulse of presence or who we were born to be. This core impulse gives rise to existential callings – longings that are not reducible to mood or thought, but which reveal an irrepressible urge that seeks expression through one's life. It is the source of one's inner movement towards what *ought to be*.

2. **Initial filtering**

    Before an ontological impulse is made conscious, it encounters pre-ontological filters – instinctive responses and temperamental predispositions shaped by biology, early conditioning and inherited response patterns. These act as the first modulation layer – amplifying, distorting or suppressing the core impulse depending on early safety patterns, nervous system wiring and unprocessed formative experiences. At this level, one's Being can become hijacked by trauma or prematurely suppressed into conformity.

3. Subsequent filtering

The filtered impulse goes through a second stage of filtering, this time via the Moods (care, vulnerability, anxiety and fear).

Moods are not surface-level feelings, but structural, emotional climates that modulate what is perceived as possible or safe. They shape the orientation and scope of sense-making and expression. For example, Moods such as vulnerability or care can expand one's openness to connection and contribution. Moods such as fear or anxiety may narrow this range – not because they are inherently negative, but because when left unexamined or incoherently related to, they tend to suppress expression and narrow one's relational stance towards life.

Here, one's Being is either welcomed into expression or held back. A person may feel the calling of contribution, but if anxiety is present and met with avoidance or collapse, they may default to compliance instead. Yet when fear or anxiety are met with awareness and integrity, they can become doorways to discernment, courage and ethical responsiveness.

4. Discernment

The next phase is choosing one's ontological posture via the Primary Ways of Being. This is where the human being, consciously or unconsciously, selects how they will *be* in the moment. For example, will they choose authenticity, courage and presence or default to withdrawal, overcompensation or people-pleasing? Primary Ways of Being are not masks. They are ontological stances. They determine how one shows up in the world – how one speaks, acts, listens and decides. This is the moment when the ignition of the Unique Being becomes visible.

5. Ethics, values and morality filtering

Before any action is taken, the Being–Posture–Behaviour sequence is filtered through one's ethical and axiological framework. This includes one's:

- **Ethical discernment** – What is the right thing to do in this context?
- **Moral compass** – What does my core sense of justice or fairness point towards?
- **Personal values** – Does this honour what matters most to me?

This filtering process colours the behavioural expression. Without it, power becomes coercion, authenticity becomes recklessness and conviction becomes dogma. This layer transforms raw Being into responsible agency, allowing an individual to act with conscience and coherence.

6. Amplification

Once an ontological posture is selected, it requires behavioural amplification to go from Being to doing. Here Secondary Ways of Being like proactivity, assertiveness, confidence and accountability amplify and enact the primary posture.

Without these behavioural amplifiers, Being remains internal – felt but not embodied. It is the difference between being courageous and speaking a difficult truth or being committed and persisting through fatigue. In this step of the process, Being becomes communicable, functional and capable of shaping both relationships and the systems within which they operate.

7. Manifestation

The final step is manifestation – what one says, does, creates or disrupts. This is where the Secondary Ways of Being enter the world as tangible action and impact. Every behaviour, action and decision generates:

- **Relational ripple effects** – how words and deeds influence the tone, trust and flow within relationships,
- **Internal feedback** – such as emotional resonance, satisfaction or regret, and
- **Systemic consequences** – how others, institutions and patterns respond.

These outcomes feed back into the system – whether an individual, a relationship, a team, an organisation or an institution – updating the Mood, challenging the posture, reaffirming or distorting the Meta Factors and influencing the next projection cycle.

The mechanics of Being reveal that no action is neutral. Each one is an echo of an intricate, recursive and often unconscious process of projection and integration. To intervene in performance, leadership or relational impact is not to fix behaviour. It is to trace the signal back to its ontological source and realign each layer with truth. Ultimately, Being is not the endpoint of personal development. It is the beginning of all meaningful expression.

Topology of Being

Being is not a list of traits to possess. It is an ontological ecosystem – recursive, dynamic and deeply interwoven. Its architecture is systemic, not sequential. The qualities within Being – Meta Factors, Moods, Primary Ways of Being and Secondary Ways of Being – do not operate in silos. They are deeply interconnected and interrelated. They shape one another through constant modulation, feedback and emergence.

Understanding the topology of Being means discerning how its structural layers interact – how coherence or distortion moves between them, amplifies across the system or gives rise to integrity or dysfunction.

Meta Factors → Moods

Meta Factors form the orientational foundation of Being. They shape how Moods arise, are interpreted and modulated:

- **Awareness** enables conscious recognition of emotional states, for example, noticing that fear is present without being governed by it. It grants the space needed for a Mood to be felt, named and held without collapse.
- **Integrity** ensures that each Mood is anchored in truth rather than reaction. For example, care guided by integrity becomes compassion. Without integrity, care can slide into martyrdom or co-dependence.
- **Effectiveness** governs the usability of the Mood. It reflects the shift from an unhealthy to a healthy relationship with the Mood itself. For example, it transforms anxiety from paralysing tension into heightened alertness and channels fear into preparation rather than panic.

Here, Meta Factors act as *modulators of emotional tone*, ensuring that the affective climate of one's Being is not merely reactive, but grounded and functional.

Moods → Primary Ways of Being

Moods don't just colour experience. They either enable or inhibit the Primary Ways of Being. Each Mood opens certain possibilities and constrains others:

- **Vulnerability** – When embraced in a healthy way, vulnerability allows access to authenticity, self-expression and relational depth. But when avoided or weaponised, it can lead to emotional shutdown, overexposure or manipulative self-disclosure.
- **Care** – When expressed sincerely and free from agenda, care creates the ground for commitment, compassion and gratitude. But when distorted, it can harden into obligation, resentment or controlling behaviour masked as concern.
- **Anxiety** – When acknowledged and regulated, anxiety can sharpen attention and prepare us for uncertainty. But when left unchecked, it constricts peace of mind and self-trust, leading to hypervigilance, avoidance or performance anxiety.
- **Fear** – When held with awareness and integrity, fear becomes a catalyst for courage, humility and discernment. But when

distorted, it provokes defensiveness, mistrust, manipulation or the need to dominate.

As you can see, Moods set the *ontological readiness* for Primary Ways of Being to emerge – not just what feels right, but what is possible.

Primary Ways of Being → Secondary Ways of Being

Where Primary Ways of Being determine the stance, Secondary Ways bring that stance into action. For example, consider the following outcomes (via the Secondary Ways of Being) when one's relationship with the following Primary Ways of Being is healthy:

- **Presence** manifests as proactivity (being forward-moving) or accountability (being grounded in ownership).
- **Courage** manifests as assertiveness and resilience, enabling action in the face of risk.
- **Responsibility** leads naturally to reliability and persistence – showing up consistently and following through.
- **Love**, far from being sentimentality, fuels resourcefulness – the willingness to transcend limitations for the sake of care.

This topological layer reveals where posture becomes performance. Without the Secondary Ways of Being, the Primary Ways of Being remain intended but unexecuted.

Feedback Loops: Secondary Ways of Being → Moods / Meta Factors

The ecology of Being is recursive. Action reinforces or degrades the internal landscape. Consider the following examples:

- When persistence (Secondary) supports a deeper intention or direction, it can cultivate a Mood such as care, which in turn reinforces a Meta Factor like integrity.
- When assertiveness (Secondary) is expressed without care (Mood), it can push the system into a state of anxiety (Mood), disrupting awareness (Meta Factor) and fragmenting coherence.

This recursive loop stabilises performance and presence. Repeated successful alignment between one's internal stance and external behaviour builds trust in one's Being. However, when the feedback loop is dysfunctional, even virtuous actions become performative – resulting in exhaustion, manipulation or inauthenticity. This is where performance without coherence becomes dangerous.

Emergent qualities and patterns

When coherent, Being gives rise to:

- **Ontological clarity** – Clear inner knowing of who one is and how one chooses to exist.
- **Relational integrity** – Consistency between one's intentions, actions and how one is received.
- **Sustainable performance** – Effectiveness without burnout.
- **Grounded leadership** – The ability to lead from a place of presence, coherence and ethical clarity, not dominance.

In contrast, when fragmented or misaligned, Being yields:

- **Manipulation** – Using ways of being as tools for control rather than expressions of truth.
- **Exhaustion** – Chronic mismatch between intention and execution.
- **Sentimentality** – Care without clarity, love without boundaries.
- **Coercion** – Using courage or commitment to override others.
- **Inauthentic productivity** – Appearing effective while disconnected from any grounded sense of self or meaning.

Being is not a slogan. It is the living structure through which life is experienced. You do not merely 'have' a Being. You generate, reinforce and project it through every interaction, choice and moment of presence.

To work on Being is not self-improvement; it is *systemic realignment*. It is to tune the instrument through which your life is composed. True transformation does not come from adding traits. It comes from re-integrating what is already there – from remembering the inner architecture of who you are and moving through the world in alignment with it.

Ultimately, when Being is coherent, trust deepens, creativity flourishes and integrity becomes self-reinforcing. In contrast, when Being is fragmented, dysfunction spreads – often beneath the surface, masked by appearances of success or confidence.

Being in action

The following cases illustrate the tangible consequences when coherent Being is embodied versus when it is fragmented.

Case 1: The charismatic performer

A public-facing executive is widely praised for his energy, boldness, charisma and clarity. He leads with powerful vision, speaks eloquently and drives initiatives with precision. But behind the scenes, all is not as it seems. His team walks on eggshells, decisions are erratic, promises are broken and trust is eroding. Eventually, turnover rises, culture implodes and a once-promising venture burns out.

Insight: Charisma itself is not the issue; incoherence is. Although the leader's performance appeared strong on the surface, his Being was fragmented. His Secondary Ways of Being (e.g. assertiveness, proactivity) were not grounded in care, awareness and integrity. The facade outpaced the structure. When charisma is performative rather than coherent, collapse is only a matter of time.

Case 2: The integrative leader

A mid-level manager is not particularly charismatic, but her team functions smoothly, handles complexity with grace and continuously evolves. When crises hit, she remains calm, listens deeply and acts with precision. Others turn to her instinctively, not because of her title or visibility, but because of her presence.

Insight: This is an example of integrated Being in motion. Meta Factors (integrity, effectiveness), Moods (care, vulnerability) and Primary

Ways of Being (responsibility, contribution, presence) are coherently expressed. The result is sustainability – not superficial charisma, but a grounded presence that others can trust and build upon.

Case 3: The burnt-out idealist

A social entrepreneur burns with purpose. They pour themselves into justice and equity, driven not only by vision, but by an unacknowledged undercurrent of anxiety and over-responsibility. They rarely pause, believing rest to be indulgent when so much is at stake. Over time, exhaustion sets in. Relationships suffer, communication becomes reactive and brittle, and their mission begins to harden into resentment. They start to question everything, including themselves.

Insight: Despite their noble intention, the structure of Being has become distorted. Over-identification with contribution and responsibility – fuelled by an unhealthy relationship with anxiety or fear – and without anchoring in peace of mind, presence and resilience, leads to collapse. Without systemic alignment across the layers of Being, passion corrodes into burnout and mission hardens into martyrdom.

Conclusion

Being is not what we perform. It is what we consciously or unconsciously radiate, project and embody. It is not what we declare; it is what we transmit. It is the medium through which trust becomes possible, leadership becomes ethical and systems become sustainable. Whether in families, businesses, governments or global movements, Being is the deepest leverage point from which meaningful change can emerge.

This chapter has positioned Being not as a trait or temperament, but as a layered ontological structure and the integration point of intention, trust, sovereignty and, ultimately, all sustainable action. Through its four layers – Meta Factors, Moods, Primary Ways of Being and Secondary Ways of Being – we've examined how Being shapes every dimension of human experience, from perception to participation and from emotional response to ethical impact.

When Being is coherent, the self becomes a source of systemic sustainability – anchoring teams, healing relational dynamics and bringing ethical presence into complex environments. However, when fragmented, even the most skilled strategies may yield short-term results, but lead to long-term internal and external damage.

Sustainable systems are not built on performance optics or bursts of intensity. They are built on the sustained coherence of integrated beings. In a world saturated with techniques, identities, roles and performances, the question of Being remains primary – not just as the root of authentic leadership, ethical agency and transformative presence, but as the very medium through which all human experience and action unfolds.

To work on Being is to alter the architecture of the self from which all other transformations become possible. But to neglect Being – to operate from incoherent or disintegrated modes – means no amount of strategy, effort or virtue-signalling will produce sustainable or meaningful change.

Ultimately, to work on Being is not to chase a better version of the self. It is to return to structural wholeness and to become a reliable participant in the unfolding of a more coherent, more sustainable world.

Reflection

- In which areas of your life are you outwardly coherent, but internally fragmented?
- Are your actions consistent with your deeper values and moods, or compensating for unacknowledged incoherence?
- When others experience you, do they experience your Being or your strategy?
- What would it look like to tune your inner architecture so that presence, performance and principle no longer conflict?
- What kind of culture, team or movement could emerge from an organisation in which Being is coherent and fully integrated across the board?

PART VI

The Modulation Sphere

In the architecture of human systems – whether individual, relational or institutional – integrity alone is not enough. A structure that cannot flex will fracture. A value held so rigidly that it allows no margin for discernment inevitably distorts the result. A truth that cannot adjust, absorb or yield to context loses its vitality and hardens into dogma rather than wisdom. This is where the Modulation Sphere enters the ontological framework – not to weaken coherence, but to sustain it over time.

If the Integrity Sphere offers the pillars of alignment – intention, trust, sovereignty and Being – and the Disintegration Sphere reveals collapse and incoherence, the Modulation Sphere is the stabilising force that allows systems to stretch without snapping, to absorb without disintegrating, and to evolve without losing their centre.

Modulation is not a passive virtue. It is an active structure. And it is not a singular act. It is a systemic capacity. It governs the space between stimulus and response, tension and resolution, pressure and transformation. In times of uncertainty, pressure or disruption, modulation is what determines whether a system fragments or regenerates.

In this part, we explore four distinct but interdependent capacities of modulation:

- **Patience** – the capacity to resist forcing outcomes, allowing truth and coherence to unfold in their natural pace and rhythm.
- **Tolerance** – the ability to absorb difference, discomfort and challenge without immediate rejection or collapse, holding space for complexity without sacrificing discernment.
- **Adaptability** – the function of recalibrating in response to change while remaining tethered to one's coherence, allowing for evolution without fracture.
- **Surrender** – the deepest modulation, inviting the release of control when effort becomes incoherent and enabling realignment with what is (reality).

Together, patience, tolerance, adaptability and surrender constitute the invisible architecture that allows systems to endure, transform and regenerate under pressure. They are not virtues to aspire to; they are structural capacities to cultivate. When embodied, they prevent premature collapse, shallow reaction and performative resilience. They modulate coherence across time, difference, change and uncertainty.

It's not only about valuing these qualities; it's about being structurally equipped to embody them. To lead without coercion. To transform without breaking. To grow without betraying what matters.

Because the sustainability of anything – your vision, your relationships, your identity or your organisation – does not rest on control or force. It rests on your capacity to modulate.

CHAPTER 38

Patience

Across traditions, patience has been revered, from the Greek *hypomonē* (endurance with dignity) to the Arabic *ṣabr* (steadfastness under trial) to Buddhist notions of equanimity. However, we live in an era that worships urgency. From rapid growth strategies to real-time responses, from hyper-productivity to algorithmic acceleration, passively waiting and taking your time have become almost synonymous with weakness. We're taught to move fast, pivot faster and respond instantly. Yet beneath the noise of urgency lies a forgotten architecture of sustainability – patience.

Patience is often treated as a soft skill: an admirable but dispensable virtue reserved for saints, caregivers or spiritual types. In leadership, it's dismissed as passivity. In innovation, it's seen as indecision. In personal growth, it's mistaken for stagnation. But ontologically, patience is none of these things. It is not passive, sentimental or weak. It is *modulation* – a structured capacity that determines whether systems endure or disintegrate under pressure.

In the Unified Ontology of Systemic Integrity (UOSI), patience sits within the Modulation Sphere – alongside tolerance, adaptability and surrender. While the Integrity Sphere builds coherence and the Disintegration Sphere reveals dysfunction, the Modulation Sphere determines whether we can *sustain coherence in real time*. Patience is the stabiliser of that sustainability.

Without patience, even the most coherent intentions, relationships or systems become brittle. They fracture under pressure or mutate into coercion. Conflict escalates. Decisions are forced. Healing is bypassed. And transformation becomes yet another performance of urgency.

But when patience is embodied as a structural capacity, it enables *right timing* – a rhythm aligned with readiness, not urgency. Truth can emerge without force, systems can stabilise without control and people can remain engaged without being consumed.

Patience is attunement to the reality of time: the awareness that every system has its own rhythm of development – a seed to grow, a baby to be born, a fruit to ripen, a season to set in, a project to finish. It requires discerning when the right time has come to facilitate, contribute or intervene, and when coherence calls for restraint.

This chapter reclaims patience as a temporal force of coherence and systemic sustainability in motion rather than merely a virtue. Through the lens of anatomy, mechanics and topology, we will explore patience as an ontological structure – not a passive state of waiting, but a lived orientation and a way of moving through the world with attuned rhythm, presence and discernment.

Ontological Distinction of Patience

Patience is your capacity to remain present with discomfort, uncertainty and incompletion without collapsing into reaction, avoidance or coercion. It is not the absence of action – it is the modulation of action through time. *Patience* does not delay for the sake of delay. It allows coherence to surface without force and truth to emerge in its own rhythm. It is a posture of steadiness that makes sustainability possible across personal, relational and systemic domains – ensuring that what unfolds is not rushed, distorted or prematurely abandoned.

A **healthy relationship with patience** indicates that you can be with tension, ambiguity or incompletion without rushing to fix it or flee. You are able to regulate impulse, allow trust to unfold and discern the timing of action. Others experience you as open, grounded and ethically restrained. Your patience creates environments where truth, growth and restoration can occur without manipulation or collapse – making healing, innovation and maturity sustainable over time. In wider systems, patience manifests as collectives that resist the pull of short-term gain in favour of long-term trust, as communities that allow dialogue to mature rather than forcing premature resolution, and as societies that give reform the time to take root rather than collapsing into reactionary cycles.

An **unhealthy relationship with patience** may show up as passivity, avoidance or enabling dysfunction. You may appear calm, but inwardly collapse under pressure or quietly disengage. You may delay necessary decisions under the guise of 'holding space' when you are actually deferring accountability. At the other extreme, you may abandon patience altogether – rushing decisions, forcing outcomes or prematurely discarding what needed more time to mature. In all these cases, others experience you as absent, unreliable or reactive – not because you lack concern, but because your posture is incoherent. This kind of patience is unsustainable: for you, for others and for the systems you inhabit.

Ontology of patience

As discussed, patience plays a vital stabilising role in the Modulation Sphere. Where the Integrity Sphere governs coherence through ethical architecture (intention, trust, sovereignty and Being), the Modulation Sphere ensures that this coherence can *stretch* without tearing – adapting to turbulence, ambiguity and relational complexity. Patience is the very muscle of this stretch. Without patience, even well-formed intentions are abandoned and transformation is replaced with coercion masked as urgency.

Let's now explore the anatomy, mechanics and topology of patience, not as a passive trait, but as an ontological structure of modulation that sustains coherence over time.

Anatomy of patience

Patience is not a mood or behaviour. It is a structural capacity. Its anatomy reveals five interrelated components that, together, enable a human system to *be with* discomfort and complexity without collapsing, breaking, fleeing or rushing to prematurely fix things. These components form the scaffold through which time, uncertainty, tension and growth can coexist without fracture.

1. **Temporal presence**

    Patience begins with the ability to be with time. This is not merely tolerance over a duration, but an existential willingness to remain present with what is unresolved, incomplete or uncomfortable without the impulse to accelerate resolution. Temporal presence enables the system to wait without dissociating, to hold space without collapsing. Patience is not passive waiting; it is grounded in authenticity. When a person recognises reality as it is – for example, that a mango tree requires years before it can bear fruit – that authentic awareness becomes the anchor for patience. In this way, patience is not mere endurance or delay, but a coherent response to truth. Authenticity provides the compass, and patience becomes its temporal expression.

2. **Impulse regulation**

    At the core of patience lies the capacity to resist premature action. This is not repression, but the intentional modulation of the impulse to fix, flee or force. Impulse regulation ensures that action arises from clarity, not from compulsion, panic or patterned reaction.

3. **Assurance**

    Patience is grounded in a quiet assurance that what needs to unfold will do so in its own time. This trust is not naive; it is ontological. It reflects an attunement to developmental timing, relational unfolding and the rhythm of healing. Without trust in the process, patience collapses into anxious waiting or hyper-vigilant control.

4. **Containment**

Patience requires containment: the ability to hold emotion, ambiguity and tension without offloading, suppressing or projecting. This is not about silence or stoicism; it's about cultivating inner spaciousness to let things unfold and metabolise in their own time without being immediately acted upon.

5. **Orientation to coherence**

True patience is not inert; it is oriented. It holds, not to avoid action, but to enable the *right* action to be taken. This structural component ensures that patience is not used to delay accountability, but to allow alignment to emerge in its own time. It keeps the system focused on coherence, not merely endurance.

A tangible example of distorted patience

A healthcare organisation is in crisis. Staff shortages are chronic, patients are suffering due to inadequate attention and care, and morale is collapsing. Leadership insists they are 'exercising patience' – waiting for reforms to settle and for conditions to stabilise. On the surface, this appears calm and deliberate. But beneath the rhetoric, patience has been distorted into passivity and denial.

At the level of **temporal presence**, leaders mistake delay for patience. Instead of being present with the immediacy of suffering, they retreat into abstractions of 'long-term resilience'. Time becomes an excuse for avoidance rather than a medium for attunement.

At the level of **impulse regulation**, what looks like restraint is actually paralysis. Rather than resisting premature action from a place of clarity, they suppress all action out of fear. Decisions are endlessly postponed. Staff begin to experience leadership as absent rather than grounded and available.

At the level of **assurance**, the organisation cultivates false comfort. Leaders repeat slogans about things 'working out in the end', not from authentic trust in the process but from denial of the urgency in front of them. This misplaced assurance collapses into passive optimism – a hollow positivity that erodes credibility and deepens despair on the ground.

At the level of **containment**, the capacity to hold tension collapses. Frustrations and unspoken fears are bottled up in meetings, only to leak out in blame, gossip and resignation letters. What could have been metabolised through dialogue becomes toxicity that circulates through the organisational bloodstream.

Finally, at the level of **orientation to coherence**, patience loses its compass. Instead of holding space for truth to emerge, leaders use 'patience' as a shield against accountability. Dysfunction is tolerated, incoherence is rationalised, and endurance is mistaken for integrity.

Over time, this distortion corrodes both trust and resilience. Employees disengage, patients suffer further, and the very word 'patience' becomes synonymous with neglect. What could have been a stabilising force turns into systemic drift, where the refusal to act under the guise of patience entrenches harm.

In this way, the anatomy of patience unravels. Temporal presence becomes evasion, impulse regulation collapses into passivity, assurance morphs into denial, containment breaks into leakage, and orientation to coherence is abandoned. What remains is not patience but inertia – a posture that sustains dysfunction rather than coherence.

Mechanics of patience

As a temporal modulator, patience slows down the pace of reactive or misaligned responses, giving space for coherence to reassert itself. Its mechanics describe how patience functions in real-time within individuals, relationships and systems.

1. **Resisting premature closure**

    Patience delays the rush to conclude or judge. It creates space between stimulus and response, not for avoidance, but for clarity to emerge. It resists the reflex to settle for instant closure rather than allowing clarity to unfold.

2. **Emotional containment**

Patience holds grief, frustration, ambiguity and tension long enough for them to evolve. It allows these states to be fully felt without collapsing into immediate reaction. This makes it central to healing, integration and relational repair.

3. **Temporal discernment**

Patience reveals what time discloses – motive, character and authenticity. It enables the system to wait with authentic awareness, allowing deeper patterns to surface. What appears convincing at first may, over time, reveal distortion. However, time reveals what is real and enduring. In this way, patience becomes not just endurance, but discernment through time – separating performance from coherence, illusion from truth. Authentic awareness provides the compass and temporal discernment becomes its lens through time.

4. **Field stabilisation**

In systems or relationships, patience acts as a stabilising ballast. It steadies the field when others are reactive, anxious or volatile, prevents escalation and provides a grounding presence that anchors collective coherence.

5. **Threshold management**

Patience manages thresholds, knowing when to hold back and when to act. It does not freeze; it moves, but at the right time. It senses when containment has served its function and action must now be taken.

Topology of patience

Patience becomes powerful through the interaction of all five of its structural components. Its topology shows how each element reinforces or degrades the others and how the presence or absence of one alters the structural quality of the whole.

1. **Temporal presence ↔ Impulse regulation**

The willingness to be with time and avoid premature action stabilises the system's capacity to modulate action. Authentic awareness of reality anchors this posture, ensuring presence does not drift into passivity and regulation does not harden into rigidity. Without temporal presence, impulse regulation becomes suppression. Without impulse regulation, temporal presence becomes anxious restlessness.

2. **Impulse regulation ↔ Assurance**

The ability to regulate impulses is sustained by trust. When we trust that the process will yield clarity, truth or resolution, the urgency to control diminishes. Without this assurance, impulse regulation becomes mechanical or performative – an act of suppression rather than a coherent choice.

3. **Assurance ↔ Containment**

Assurance in the process allows emotional tension to be held rather than discharged. This might look like sitting with anxiety in a difficult conversation instead of rushing to defend or withdraw. When trust is low, that tension becomes unbearable and leaks out as reactivity or overwhelm. But when containment is strong, it reinforces an assurance that one can remain present with whatever arises without needing to escape, suppress or resolve it prematurely.

4. **Containment ↔ Orientation to coherence**

The ability to hold back does not mean holding back forever. Orientation to coherence ensures that what is contained is eventually metabolised when the time is right, not endured endlessly. Here, we ask ourselves: 'When is this patience, and when has it become avoidance?'

5. **Orientation to coherence ↔ Temporal presence**

A coherent aim, grounded in authentic awareness, keeps temporal presence from becoming disconnection. Temporal presence is not passive; it is purposeful. It ensures that the waiting is *for* something real, not an escape from what must be faced.

Emergent qualities and patterns

Patience is not the art of waiting; it is the architecture of wise timing. It is not stillness as performance. It is presence with purpose. It is what lets us witness the unfolding of truth without pulling at the roots. Amid urgency, reaction and the compulsion for instant resolution, patience is not just a virtue. It is a radical act of coherence.

When patience is embodied as a fully functioning system, it generates the following emerging qualities:

- **Timing intelligence** – The capacity to know *when*, not just *what* or *how*.
- **Relational maturity** – The ability to remain present in conflict situations without escalation or abandonment.
- **Space for healing** – Environments where people can grow without being coerced.
- **Ethical restraint** – The refusal to act prematurely, even when pressure mounts.
- **Endurance without erosion** – Staying engaged over time without burning out or numbing out.

In contrast, when distorted, patience becomes:

- **Passivity** – Abdicating responsibility in the name of 'holding space'.
- **Avoidance** – Using patience to avoid decisions or interventions.
- **Apathy** – Detaching from reality under the guise of maturity.
- **Enablement** – Allowing dysfunction to fester under the label of compassion.

Patience in action

Individually and collectively, patience is the silent regulator that determines whether a challenge results in transformation or collapses into dysfunction. Consider the following real-world scenarios that illustrate how patience either stabilises coherence when present, or mutates into dysfunction when misapplied or absent.

Case 1: The rushed organisational pivot

Under pressure from investors and market trends, a mission-driven startup founder initiates a rapid pivot. New hires are brought in, priorities are overhauled and messaging is rebranded overnight. Months later, confusion reigns. The team is misaligned, customers are alienated and morale has plummeted.

Insight: Rather than waiting with authentic awareness and holding the discomfort of ambiguity and tension, the startup founder defaulted to premature action. There was no containment – just panic disguised as decisiveness. The system collapsed, not from bad ideas, but from the absence of patience to prepare and act at the right time.

Case 2: The family member who held space

In the wake of a family conflict, one member refuses to take sides or retaliate. Instead, they remain grounded, listen deeply and allow emotions to run their course without force or judgement. Over the coming weeks, others begin to soften. Conversations reopen and a new form of honesty emerges.

Insight: This is field stabilisation and containment in action. The person's patience became a container for relational realignment. Instead of postponing the truth, they cultivated the conditions for it to emerge. Their capacity for containment and orientation to coherence prevented reactive breakdown, enabling sustainable repair.

Case 3: The passive coach

A leadership coach consistently tells their client to 'trust the process' and 'give it time'. But in truth, the coach avoids naming core breakdowns or setting accountable structures. Sessions feel slow and vague, progress stalls and the client begins to disengage.

Insight: This is false patience or avoidance masquerading as depth. Without an orientation to coherence, patience mutates into apathy. The absence of discernment leads to stagnation and inaction becomes a cover for fear and incompetence.

In all systems – organisational, interpersonal and intrapersonal – patience is not measured in stillness. It is measured in the *quality* of presence, the *resilience* of containment and the *precision* of timing.

Conclusion

In a world addicted to speed, instant resolution and surface-level clarity, patience is often discarded as a luxury or condemned as weakness. However, this chapter has revealed patience as something far more powerful: a causal force of sustainability, regulating how long a system can remain coherent while navigating discomfort, uncertainty and emerging dynamics.

Through its anatomy – temporal presence, impulse regulation, assurance, containment and orientation to coherence – we've seen that patience is not avoidance. It is *active presence*. It does not freeze; it *modulates*. It does not delay truth; it holds space for truth to emerge without force.

When patience is distorted, systems spiral into either reaction or resignation. But when embodied as a structure, patience becomes a relational and systemic stabiliser. It allows tension to be metabolised, not projected. It holds potential open long enough for it to mature. It is a structural enabler of regeneration and transformation, creating the conditions for potential to crystallise and emerge over time.

Ultimately, patience is not the art of waiting. It is the architecture of right timing. If you want to build something sustainable – an organisation, a relationship, a movement or yourself – then patience is not optional. It is foundational.

Reflection

- Where in your life or work do you equate slowness with failure or irrelevance?
- How often do you act from impulse rather than clarity, out of a need to escape discomfort rather than respond with coherence?
- Do you confuse patience with avoidance? What important conversations or decisions are you indefinitely 'holding space' for, without movement towards a resolution?
- When others are reactive or emotionally volatile around you, do you become part of the escalation or a source of stabilisation?
- Can you name one situation – personal, relational or systemic – where greater patience could have allowed a more aligned outcome to unfold?
- What would it look like to develop ontological patience, not as passivity, but as intelligent delay?

CHAPTER 39

Tolerance

In today's world, 'tolerance' is everywhere – on posters, in policy statements and in polite conversations. But too often, what we call tolerance is either shallow pleasantry or virtue-signalling restraint. It is performed, not lived. Claimed, not embodied. And in many cases, it represents submission to dysfunction or the avoidance of discernment.

In the ontological framework, however, tolerance is not submission. It is a structural capacity – the ability to *be with* difference, friction, discomfort and even incoherence without immediate rejection or collapse. It is the force that allows relational, ideological, emotional and systemic contradictions to be metabolised rather than prematurely expelled or forcefully suppressed.

We often equate strength with quick judgement or decisive elimination of whatever doesn't align with our values, preferences or expectations. But in sustainable systems – whether personal, organisational or societal – such rigidity leads to fragility. Without tolerance, pluralism devolves into polarity, complexity becomes chaos and difference turns into disintegration.

Tolerance holds the seams of humanity together, not by erasing difference, but by making space for it without sacrificing coherence. It allows a team to innovate without groupthink, a family to evolve without betrayal, a culture to host many truths without fracturing into tribes.

And yet, tolerance must not be distorted into enablement. Just as an immune system must distinguish between a foreign agent and a threat, tolerance must discern when to hold back and when to intervene. It is not the suspension of judgement but the *refinement* of it. It is not limitless openness, but deliberate spaciousness for the sake of sustainability, growth and truth.

In the Unified Ontology of Systemic Integrity (UOSI), tolerance is one of the four modulation forces. As discussed, if the Integrity Sphere governs coherence and the Disintegration Sphere precipitates collapse, the Modulation Sphere regulates the space in between. Tolerance prevents premature rupture by stabilising systems long enough for deeper coherence to emerge.

In this chapter, we will examine tolerance, not as a virtue, but as a *precise architecture* of systemic modulation. Through its anatomy, mechanics and topology, we will see that tolerance is not simply about what we endure; it is about what we can *be with* without losing ourselves. In a time of ideological warfare, emotional fragility and perpetual offence, that capacity is not optional. It is a fundamental condition for our survival.

Ontological Distinction of Tolerance

Tolerance is your capacity to remain intact while engaging with difference, discomfort or disruption. It is not passivity, resignation or moral relativism. It is the intentional ability to absorb friction without immediate rejection, reaction or collapse. *Tolerance* enables relational, ideological and systemic diversity to coexist long enough for coherence to emerge or be discerned. It does not suspend discernment; it deepens it. *Tolerance* is not about liking, agreeing with or assimilating other perspectives inauthentically – it is about holding space for difference while staying connected to your own centre.

A **healthy relationship with tolerance** indicates that you can remain present in the face of discomfort or ideological difference without dissolving into defensiveness or rushing for premature resolution. You are able to discern between threat and challenge, incoherence and unfamiliarity. Your stance is open, but with discernment – you neither absorb dysfunction nor reject dissonance. Others experience you as grounded, receptive and principled: someone able to handle difference without being overrun by it. In larger systems – organisations, institutions or cultures – this form of tolerance enables innovation, inclusion, pluralism and adaptive stability without sacrificing ethical clarity or sustainability.

An **unhealthy relationship with tolerance** manifests as either rigidity or collapse. You may reject difference too quickly, labelling it as threat, harm or irrelevance. Alternatively, you may over-absorb dysfunction under the guise of 'being tolerant', enabling harm, delaying necessary boundaries or abandoning your own coherence. Others may experience you as either reactive or overly permissive, unable to discern when to hold back and when to intervene. In larger systems, distorted tolerance leads to burnout, moral confusion and the normalisation of incoherence – conditions that eventually corrode trust, weaken adaptability and result in fragmentation and dysfunction.

Ontology of tolerance

Tolerance, in its ontologically coherent form, is the structural capacity to be with difference, discomfort and dysfunction without immediate rejection. It is the ability to absorb a measure of disruption without collapsing into reaction, aggression or control. But unlike patience, which holds time, tolerance holds *difference*. It is the quality that allows individuals and collectives to remain intact while in contact with something that is dissonant, unfamiliar or imperfect.

Tolerance is not a weakness. Nor is it a passive endorsement of everything. It is the muscle that allows relational, ideological, emotional and systemic differences to coexist long enough for deeper coherence to emerge, without fragmentation, retaliation or suppression.

In the Modulation Sphere, tolerance serves as an essential safeguard against premature rupture. It allows for coexistence without fusion, disagreement without hostility and flaws without condemnation. Tolerance makes pluralism, innovation, healing and interpersonal growth possible – because not every discomfort needs to be eliminated, and not every incoherence demands immediate resolution.

In its coherent form, tolerance is principled, not passive. It is intentional, not indifferent. It says: 'I will not break at the first sign of difference. I will not reject what feels unfamiliar. But I will not betray coherence by letting all distortion pass unchecked.'

In contrast, distorted tolerance turns into blind permissiveness. It starts to absorb dysfunction as a collapsed stance rather than a strategic holding. In this way, distorted tolerance becomes the inability to discern or intervene, masquerading as maturity. It holds space, but with no edge. It accepts until it collapses.

Let's now explore the anatomy, mechanics and topology of tolerance, not as a vague moral aspiration, but as a precise ontological structure that allows human systems to be with complexity without losing themselves.

Anatomy of tolerance

Tolerance is composed of five interdependent structural capacities that, together, define whether a system – including a human being – can be with difference without self-destruction or self-abandonment.

1. **Boundary awareness**

   Tolerance does not mean boundary collapse. At its root lies the ability to distinguish what is 'not me' while choosing not to reject it. Boundary awareness gives the self clear definition without requiring separation. It enables contact without fusion.

2. **Discomfort containment**

   Tolerance requires the ability to feel discomfort without translating it into anger, withdrawal or denial. This includes emotional discomfort, ideological tension and relational friction. Without this capacity, any perceived dissonance becomes unbearable.

3. Relational generosity

Tolerance is an expression of generous relating – a willingness to not take offence too quickly, not punish too swiftly and not pathologise difference. This does not mean excusing harm, but recognising that not all discomfort is harm.

4. Threshold discernment

True tolerance is not infinite. It recognises when something has moved from difference into dysfunction or danger. This discernment allows tolerance to be principled. It knows when to hold back and when to intervene. Without this, tolerance becomes enablement.

5. Coherence referencing

Tolerance is anchored by coherence. It asks: 'Does this tension threaten the integrity of the system? Or can it be held within it?' Coherence referencing ensures that tolerance does not accept something that violates the ground on which it stands.

A tangible example of distorted tolerance

A university campus prides itself on being 'a tolerant space for all voices'. Posters, policies and speeches celebrate diversity and inclusivity. On the surface, this looks like a culture of openness. But beneath the slogans, tolerance has become distorted – collapsing into permissiveness and incoherence.

At the level of **boundary awareness**, the institution confuses openness with boundary collapse. Instead of creating clear distinctions about what the community stands for, it gives every narrative equal weight. Harmful rhetoric is defended under the banner of free expression, while coherence about values remains absent.

At the level of **discomfort containment**, the inability to metabolise tension leads to silencing. When students raise concerns about harmful behaviour, leaders rush to either suppress the complaints or overreact with performative measures. The system cannot hold discomfort without swinging between denial and punitive extremes.

At the level of **relational generosity**, what might have been a willingness to assume goodwill collapses into excusing dysfunction. Prejudice and manipulation are tolerated in the name of 'respecting different perspectives'. Instead of distinguishing between difference and harm, the culture normalises harm as another valid viewpoint.

At the level of **threshold discernment**, the university loses its edge. No clear line exists between challenging discourse (which tolerance should hold) and destructive behaviour (which tolerance must resist). As a result, bullying and exclusion are brushed aside as 'part of the debate', eroding safety and trust.

At the level of **coherence referencing**, tolerance no longer orients around the integrity of the community. Instead, the principle of tolerance itself becomes the ultimate value, detached from coherence. The university tolerates what corrodes its own mission, mistaking permissiveness for maturity and fragility for openness.

Over time, this distortion corrodes the very fabric it seeks to preserve. Students feel unsafe, staff disengage and the campus fractures into factions. What is advertised as tolerance becomes complicity with dysfunction. Instead of creating a living space for pluralism and growth, the university drifts into incoherence – where tolerance no longer protects sustainability, but quietly undermines it.

Mechanics of tolerance

Tolerance functions as a buffer and bridge between self and other, sameness and dissonance, stability and evolution. Its mechanics describe how difference is encountered, held and metabolised across relationships, systems and internal states.

1. Encounter with otherness

Tolerance activates the moment something unfamiliar, uncomfortable or divergent is encountered. It is the first response to dissonance. Not rejection, but inquiry; not fusion, but presence.

2. **Internal holding**

Once difference is encountered, tolerance activates the internal holding system. It allows ambiguity, contradiction and uncertainty to exist within awareness without immediate collapse into narrative or defence.

3. **Meaning assessment**

Tolerance assesses whether this difference is incoherent or simply unfamiliar. Is it threatening or just challenging? This is where a shift from reactivity to discernment occurs – allowing the unfamiliar, uncomfortable or divergent to be evaluated, not automatically rejected or discarded.

4. **Adjustment or containment**

Depending on the answer, tolerance either adjusts (reframes, grows or evolves) or contains (holds without assimilating). This is what enables growth without losing core identity. It's where adaptation meets integrity.

5. **Boundary reassertion**

When dissonance moves into violation and established boundaries are breached, tolerance ends. In this case, the system reasserts its boundaries, not from a place of fear, but from a place of coherence. It intervenes, not out of ego, but to preserve the conditions of integrity.

Topology of tolerance

Tolerance, like all ontological structures, functions as a systemic ecology. The five components reinforce or degrade each other in dynamic interaction. Their quality and interplay determine whether tolerance becomes a form of wise modulation or devolves into performative collapse.

1. **Boundary awareness ↔ Discomfort containment**

To hold discomfort without collapsing, the system must be defined. Without boundary awareness, discomfort leaks into identity. And without discomfort containment, boundaries become rigid and reactive. Together, they create a flexible structure capable of holding intensity without fragmenting.

2. Discomfort containment ↔ Relational generosity

The ability to be with discomfort makes generosity possible. Generosity, in turn, contextualises discomfort. It reminds the system that others are not enemies, but expressions of different conditioning or Being.

3. Relational generosity ↔ Threshold discernment

Threshold discernment ensures relational generosity is not naivety. However, threshold discernment without relational generosity becomes cold, brittle or punitive. Together, they generate principled receptivity.

4. Threshold discernment ↔ Coherence referencing

Threshold discernment requires a reference point, which coherence provides. Coherence without discernment becomes static dogma. But together, they enable tolerance to serve the system's evolution rather than its sabotage.

5. Coherence referencing ↔ Boundary awareness

Coherence helps define what needs to be protected and where boundaries must be reinforced. Without this loop, boundaries drift into habit or ideology rather than being responsive to situational reality.

Emergent qualities and patterns

Tolerance isn't about liking everything. It's about remaining whole in the presence of what is not like you. It doesn't flatten difference; it dignifies it. It doesn't abandon coherence; it expands it, until it no longer can.

At a time when we are consumed by outrage, defence and tribal certainty, tolerance is not compromise. It is the capacity to stay human in the face of difference – to hold without fusing, to open without collapsing, to see what is and still choose to stay. That is not submission or weakness. That is strength.

When tolerance is ontologically integrated, the following emergent qualities arise:

- **Resilient systems** – Able to absorb tension without fragmentation.
- **Ethical pluralism** – Diversity without collapse into relativism.
- **Relational depth** – Where difference becomes intimacy, not distance.
- **Conflict de-escalation** – Interrupting cycles of projection, blame and reactivity.
- **Structural grace** – The ability to absorb imperfection while still moving towards integrity.

However, when distorted, tolerance facilitates:

- **The enablement of harm** – Mistaking tolerance for submission.
- **Chronic self-abandonment** – Absorbing dysfunction as if it were duty.
- **Stagnation** – Mistaking endurance for maturity.
- **Diluted boundaries** – Losing coherence under the guise of openness.
- **Virtue signalling** – Tolerance as performance, not posture.

Tolerance in action

Whether in families, organisations, communities or within ourselves, the presence – or absence – of coherent tolerance radically shapes outcomes. The following cases illuminate what tolerance looks like when it is embodied and what unfolds when it is confused with passivity or moral grandstanding.

Case 1: The multicultural team in crisis

A global NGO prides itself on diversity. Its teams include staff from varied cultural, linguistic and ideological backgrounds. On paper, this is celebrated. But in meetings, disagreements about priorities are avoided. Junior staff with dissenting views feel muted. Conflict is labelled 'unsafe' and real decisions are stalled for the sake of 'togetherness'.

Insight: What appears as tolerance is actually avoidance. There's no functioning threshold discernment. Coherence referencing has been replaced by emotional appeasement. The system has confused pluralism with fragility. By absorbing all dissonance without a backbone of clarity, it stagnates and erodes trust from within.

Case 2: The family dinner that didn't derail

Three generations gather over dinner. Political views clash. Parenting styles diverge. But instead of storming out or shutting down, a key family member listens without reacting, clarifies boundaries calmly and de-escalates tension without collapsing their own values.

Insight: Boundary awareness and discomfort containment were active. The individual's presence created relational spaciousness, allowing others to feel heard without dominating the space. Tolerance didn't flatten the differences; it dignified them without losing coherence.

Case 3: The disillusioned leader who held back too much

A senior leader in a mission-driven organisation notices underperformance and interpersonal toxicity in one of her teams. Yet, she 'tolerates' it, believing in 'second chances' and 'letting people grow'. Months pass. Projects derail. Burnout spreads. High performers exit.

Insight: This case highlights a collapse of threshold discernment and coherence referencing. Tolerance became enablement. What was initially relational generosity turned into abdication. The leader confused her personal discomfort with confrontation for ethical maturity. Consequently, the organisation paid the price.

Conclusion

Tolerance is not a concept; it's a condition. It becomes visible in moments where difference or dysfunction arises and the system – human or institutional – must decide whether to reject, suppress, fuse or *be with* the uncomfortable situation. Tolerance is also not about being okay with everything. It's about staying coherent in the presence of what you're *not* okay with.

This chapter has reframed tolerance as a modulating architecture: not a passive virtue, but an active, structural capacity that allows human and other systems to absorb friction, contradiction and difference without devolving into collapse, anger or moralistic rigidity. Tolerance is not measured by how much you can condone, accept or endure. It is measured by your ability to be with difference without abandoning discernment or coherence.

Through its five interdependent components – boundary awareness, discomfort containment, relational generosity, threshold discernment and coherence referencing – tolerance reveals itself as a systemic stabiliser. It enables innovation without rupture, growth without coercion and sustains complex collectives where sameness cannot – and should not – be enforced.

Distorted tolerance feigns openness at the cost of integrity. It is unsustainable. But true ontological tolerance becomes a pillar of systemic sustainability. It's the difference between a resilient system and one that fractures under difference, ideology or discomfort.

Simply put, tolerance is knowing what you can *be with* – without collapsing, reacting or pretending everything is okay.

Reflection

- Where in your life do you hold space for difference without collapsing?
- Can you think of a time when you have mistaken self-abandonment for 'maturity'?
- Can you name a situation where you absorbed dysfunction too long in the name of tolerance, and where earlier intervention would have served you better?

- Are there areas in your relationships, work or in business where you confuse emotional discomfort with ethical violation?
- What does principled tolerance look like for you, where being with complexity does not mean diluting coherence?
- How do you know when your generosity is actually enabling harm or sabotaging sustainability?
- What internal or external support would help you stay grounded in what matters while facing difficult truths?

CHAPTER 40

Adaptability

In an era defined by rapid change, complexity and unrelenting volatility, adaptability is often praised, but rarely understood. It is typically framed as a soft skill for survival, a flexible attitude or the ability to 'go with the flow'. But ontologically, adaptability is far more profound than personal flexibility or social agreeableness. It is the structural capacity of a system, including a human being, to recalibrate – without fragmenting – when faced with disruption.

Adaptability is not a personality trait. It is a structural function of sustainability. It's what allows a leader to pivot without betraying purpose. It's what enables a team to reorganise without dissolving into chaos. And it's what allows individuals to evolve, not through mimicry or moral fatigue, but by staying responsive to changing realities while grounded in inner coherence.

Great systems, including great individuals, are not the ones that never change; they are the ones that evolve without losing their integrity. From evolutionary biology to high-performing organisations, the capacity to reconfigure under shifting conditions without structural collapse is what determines long-term viability. Adaptability, in this sense, is not optional. It is foundational.

Yet there is a danger. In the name of adaptability, many systems become formless or blur beyond recognition, losing the very coherence that gives change its meaning. People abandon principles in favour of trend alignment. Cultures morph so fluidly that identity diffuses. What begins as responsiveness devolves into reactivity. What was meant to be creative modulation mutates into chronic self-abandonment.

The Modulation Sphere exists to prevent this. Where the Integrity Sphere provides structural coherence (via intention, trust, sovereignty and Being), the Modulation Sphere ensures that coherence can breathe, bend and grow without breaking. Adaptability is the intelligence within the Modulation Sphere that allows systems to change without becoming formless.

This chapter positions adaptability not as compliance, convenience or diplomacy, but as an ontological function. It enables performance without rigidity, values without dogma and leadership without reactivity. When embodied, adaptability becomes a generative force for sustainability – supporting growth, reform and regeneration across all levels of human systems.

Ontological Distinction of Adaptability

Adaptability is your capacity to recalibrate in response to change without losing coherence. It is not about being agreeable or compliant. Instead, it's about remaining attuned to context while anchored in your ethical and ontological centre: your deeper sense of truth, coherence and what ultimately matters. *Adaptability* enables systems – whether personal, relational or institutional – to respond to evolving conditions, not by resisting change, but by shaping it with discernment, intelligence and purpose. It is not softness or passivity, but a generative posture of sustainable responsiveness. *Adaptability* enables transformation without fragmentation – growth that preserves coherence rather than breaking it apart – and evolution without self-erasure.

A **healthy relationship with adaptability** indicates that you can shift behaviours, perspectives or strategies in the presence of new information or altered circumstances while remaining true to your values, purpose and Being. You are responsive without being reactive, flexible without being formless. You can evolve in ways that honour continuity, enabling resilience, creativity and sustained relevance. In relationships and leadership, this posture fosters trust and agility without sacrificing coherence.

An **unhealthy relationship with adaptability** indicates that you fall into one of two extremes. On one side, it shows up as chronic morphing – changing yourself constantly to avoid discomfort, rejection or tension. This people-pleasing collapses coherence and erodes trust, leading to identity diffusion and instability. On the other side, it manifests as rigid resistance – mistaking stubbornness for strength and refusing necessary change even when coherence demands it. In both cases, adaptability is distorted: either abandoning integrity for harmony or clinging to familiar habits or appearances at the cost of evolution. Leaders under this influence become inconsistent, brittle or untrustworthy – not because values are absent, but because their expression lacks continuity.

Ontology of adaptability

In the Modulation Sphere, adaptability serves as the counterforce to stagnation. It is the bridge between intention and context, enabling systems – including human beings – to respond with creative recalibration rather than panic or rigidity.

Adaptability is not about being agreeable. It is about being *responsive* to context, condition, timing and possibility, while remaining tethered to coherence.

By examining its anatomy, mechanics and topology, this section explores adaptability as a structural ontological function, as opposed to a personality trait or survival instinct. In doing so, it reveals how adaptability allows systems to evolve without losing themselves.

Anatomy of adaptability

Adaptability consists of five interrelated structural capacities that determine whether a system (including an individual) can shift in response to context while remaining intact.

1. **Context awareness**

Adaptability begins with the capacity to read the field. Without accurate sensing of internal and external change, any adjustment becomes either premature or delayed. Context awareness is not just observational but interpretive.

2. **Fluidity**

Adaptability requires a loosening of rigid identity, structure and expectation. This is not collapse; it's the ability to let go of unnecessary form while retaining essential coherence. Fluidity is the ability to reconfigure one's expression without betraying one's truth.

3. **Responsiveness**

Adaptable systems respond to signals. Feedback – whether from others, the environment or unfolding consequences – is integrated, not resisted. Responsiveness enables learning, iteration and humility without shame.

4. **Anchoring**

Adaptability without anchoring leads to incoherence. This structural component ensures that change is not directionless, but remains grounded in values, purpose and Being. Core anchoring prevents adaptation from becoming submission.

5. **Reconfiguration**

Reconfiguration is the generative function of adaptability: the ability to form new pathways, postures, strategies or ways of Being in real time. It is not a mere reaction. It is ontological innovation – how the system reorganises itself to remain viable and meaningful under pressure.

A tangible example of distorted adaptability

A tech startup that once positioned itself around ethical innovation and long-term sustainability begins to confuse adaptability with 'survival at any cost' as market conditions shift and investors demand quick returns. On the surface, the company looks agile – products pivot rapidly, strategies change weekly, and messaging evolves to suit whatever trend is dominant. But beneath the surface, adaptability has lost coherence and drifted into distortion.

At the level of **context awareness**, the leadership team reacts more to investor moods and social media chatter than to genuine signals of market or human need. The organisation mistakes noise for insight, chasing short-term popularity instead of discerning meaningful shifts.

At the level of **fluidity**, the company bends so easily that it becomes unrecognisable. Its brand values are rewritten every quarter, leaving employees unsure what the organisation actually stands for. What began as openness to change dissolves into identity diffusion.

At the level of **responsiveness**, every piece of feedback – from a loud customer, a trending article or a competitor's move – provokes immediate reaction. Instead of integrating signals with discernment, the company ricochets from one adjustment to another. Responsiveness mutates into reactivity, creating whiplash for staff and confusion for clients.

At the level of **anchoring**, the absence of a coherent centre means that each change pulls the company further away from its original purpose. Ethical commitments are quietly abandoned for convenience, and strategic choices are made to satisfy external pressure rather than serve a grounded mission. Adaptability without anchoring collapses into appeasement.

At the level of **reconfiguration**, innovation becomes cosmetic rather than structural. Instead of creating new pathways that honour the company's deeper coherence, the start-up cycles through surface-level pivots – rebrands, new slogans, flashy features – while avoiding the harder work of systemic redesign. Change is constant, but it is shallow.

Over time, employees lose trust, customers lose clarity, and the company becomes a mirror of its environment rather than an authentic force within it. What looks like adaptability on the surface is actually incoherence – a chronic morphing that sacrifices integrity for survival. Ultimately, the tech start-up has confused modulation with mimicry, leaving it brittle, reactive and unsustainable.

Mechanics of adaptability

Adaptability functions as a recursive modulation loop that continuously assesses, adjusts and reorients in the face of new data, challenge or opportunity. The following mechanics illustrate how systems recalibrate without collapsing or falling into patterns of mechanical routine or mindless repetition.

1. **Stimulus encounter**

   Adaptability begins when a condition shifts, either internally or externally. The first moment is recognition – sensing that something no longer fits. This moment of awareness initiates the process of re-evaluation.

2. **Pattern disruption recognition**

   The next step is to recognise that a familiar structure or behaviour is no longer appropriate. Without this awareness, inertia persists. This step distinguishes adaptability from stubbornness.

3. **Anchored reassessment**

   Adaptability does not mean changing merely for the sake of it. Here, the system re-references its deeper coherence. What matters? What must remain? What can be reimagined? This step protects the system against abandoning its authenticity.

4. **Adaptive action**

   At this stage, the system takes well-considered steps in response to the new reality. A different tone may be adopted, a revised decision made or a new posture taken – always adjusting without losing its centre. The action may be subtle or radical, but it remains grounded in coherence.

5. **Integration**

   The new configuration produces outcomes that are integrated as learning, not only into cognition, but into Being. Here, adaptability becomes wisdom.

Topology of adaptability

Together, the five structural components of adaptability operate as an interactive ecology. Their interplay determines whether the system becomes gracefully responsive or helplessly reactive.

Context awareness ↔ Fluidity

When we see clearly, we can loosen the reins. And when forms are fluid, we perceive more options. Together, they create readiness. Without context awareness, fluidity becomes flailing. Without fluidity, awareness creates overwhelm.

Fluidity ↔ Responsiveness

Being willing to change form allows feedback to land as intended. Responsiveness without form fluidity creates anxiety. Fluidity without responsiveness becomes chaos. Together, they form a learning arc.

Responsiveness ↔ Anchoring

Feedback must be integrated with discernment. The process of anchoring filters feedback, ensuring the system shifts without losing itself. Without anchoring, feedback becomes a command. Without responsiveness, anchoring leads to rigidity.

Anchoring ↔ Reconfiguration

Creativity becomes coherent only when grounded. Anchoring allows new forms to emerge that align with Being. Reconfiguration without anchoring leads to fragmentation and dysfunction. Anchoring without creativity becomes mindless repetition.

Reconfiguration ↔ Context awareness

When a system adopts a new configuration, the interplay between creative reconfiguration and context awareness ensures adaptability is recursive, not one-off. Awareness of how the new pattern interacts with the system and its impact completes the modulation cycle.

Emergent qualities and patterns

Adaptability is not a virtue. It is structural intelligence – the intelligence of Being in motion without losing shape. It allows principles to breathe, values to evolve and presence to endure, even as everything else changes.

In a world addicted to control or collapse, adaptability is not conformation; it is evolution made conscious. It is not about being 'easy going'. It is about being deeply responsive to truth, time and transformation.

When coherent and integrated, adaptability is not a threat to identity. It is what keeps identity alive by producing:

- **Resilient evolution** – Change emerges organically, not disruptively.
- **Ontological creativity** – New expressions of self and system emerge without distortion.
- **Agility without fragility** – Responsiveness without breakdown.
- **Presence in flux** – The ability to stay grounded amid shifting conditions.
- **Intelligent flexibility** – Adaptation driven by discernment, not panic.

In contrast, when distorted, adaptability results in:

- **Chronic inconsistency** – Nothing stable, everything conditional.
- **Identity diffusion** – Adapting so much that the self begins to dissolve.
- **Compulsive agreement** – Yielding to avoid tension.

- **Reactive morphing** – Changing not from discernment, but from fear.
- **Erosion of boundaries** – Being shaped endlessly by external pressures or demands.

Adaptability in action

Adaptability reveals itself, not in ideology, but in how people and systems respond when life doesn't go to plan – when a strategy fails, a role changes, a disruption unfolds or the familiar becomes irrelevant. Here are three real-world scenarios where adaptability either sustains coherence or its absence leads to collapse.

Case 1: The stuck consultant

A leadership coach built a successful career delivering workshops on goal-setting and time management. But as clients began asking for deeper psychological insight and transformation work, she froze. She continued delivering the same content despite declining engagement and relevance, insisting that, 'This worked for years.'

Insight: This case study demonstrates a failure of context awareness and fluidity. The leadership coach's inability to reconfigure and respond to client feedback reflects a rigidity that eventually made her offerings obsolete. Her anchoring was mistaken for identity. However, without adaptability, that identity hardened into irrelevance.

Case 2: The transforming organisation

A mid-sized company in the wellness sector faced a rapid shift in market demand. Rather than panic, the leadership team paused, reviewed their values, surveyed staff and customers and reimagined a new delivery model aligned with both their purpose and market reality. They launched new programs within three months, without betraying their culture or burning out their staff.

Insight: Here, all five structural components were engaged, especially reconfiguration and anchoring. The organisation adapted from a place of coherence, not fear. The result wasn't just survival; it was evolution with integrity.

Case 3: The people-pleasing partner

In a romantic relationship, one partner constantly changes their opinion, mood and preferences depending on the other's reactions. While this initially appears flexible, it erodes trust over time. The partner becomes hard to read and the relationship becomes emotionally volatile.

Insight: This is adaptability without anchoring. It is reactive morphing – constant shape-shifting to avoid tension. Over time, people-pleasing creates relational instability and a loss of authenticity, even when intentions are well-meaning.

Conclusion

Adaptability is not a stylistic preference or vague virtue. It's an ontological necessity for authentic sustainability. In human systems, relationships, leadership and even nations, the ability to recalibrate without fragmentation differentiates evolution from erosion.

This chapter has reframed adaptability as a structural function of modulation – composed of context awareness, fluidity, responsiveness, anchoring and reconfiguration. Through these capacities, adaptability enables coherence to move across time, conditions and complexity.

Without adaptability in this context, values become brittle, structures harden into dogma and people burn out trying to uphold what no longer works. However, with adaptability, change is not the enemy of coherence, but its means of becoming and evolving.

Reflection

- Where in your life do you notice resistance to change, not because it violates your values, but because it challenges your habits?
- Are there areas where you've over-adapted, morphing so much that you've lost touch with your authentic self?
- How do you discern when it's time to persist and when it's time to reconfigure?

- What's one area of your leadership, creativity or relationships where a more adaptive posture could reintroduce coherence without compromise?

CHAPTER 41

Surrender

We live in an age addicted to mastery, where control is mistaken for competence and domination of outcomes is equated with effectiveness. We are taught, explicitly and implicitly, that the solution to every difficulty is more effort, more planning, more optimisation. If something isn't working, push harder. If reality resists, escalate. Surrender, in this cultural mindset, is treated as failure, weakness and giving up.

But this perspective blinds us to something essential. Not everything can or should be fixed. And not everything that feels like a problem is one. Some things are realities to be metabolised into meaning and integrated, not manipulated. Some paths are closed, no matter how strong the will. Some losses are to be grieved, not reversed. Some moments call for release, not action. This is where surrender begins.

In modern life – whether in personal growth, leadership, spirituality or systemic transformation – we often carry an unconscious delusion that everything must yield to our strategy. That there is always a next move. That we must win, overcome, transcend. But this obsession with resolution and engineering life into compliance distorts our perception. It keeps us from recognising the wisdom in letting go.

Surrender is not about abandonment; it's about *realignment*. It is the conscious recognition that something deeper is required than effort.

It is the willingness to stop forcing what cannot (or should not) be forced. It is the structural capacity that allows clarity to return when the fog of will has thickened. It is neither defeatism nor passivity. It is an act of radical discernment.

Philosophical and spiritual traditions have always known the true meaning of surrender. The Taoist concept of *wu wei* teaches action through alignment with flow, not force. The Islamic notion of *taslim* points to surrender, not as passivity, but as ontological trust in what transcends our personal will. In the grief rituals of many indigenous cultures, surrender is what allows life to move again after rupture because something sacred has been honoured, not bypassed.

In the Unified Ontology of Systemic Integrity (UOSI), surrender belongs to the Modulation Sphere alongside patience, tolerance and adaptability. These are not emotional states or personality traits. They are structural capacities that allow systems, including individuals, relationships, teams and institutions, to remain coherent under conditions of disruption, ambiguity and change.

Where the Integrity Sphere builds the ethical and directional architecture of coherence through intention, trust, sovereignty and Being, the Modulation Sphere ensures that this architecture can bend rather than break under pressure. Among its forces, surrender is the deepest and most essential modulation. It allows a system – individual or collective – to stop resisting the inevitable, to release misaligned effort, and to realign with reality on new terms.

Surrender is often misunderstood. Many encounter it only after collapse, when insistence has exhausted itself. As a result, it is often mistaken for helplessness or weakness. But in its truest form, surrender is not defeat. It is the quiet release of illusion. It marks the point where modulation is no longer about managing tension, but about yielding to what is. Patience holds space, adaptability pivots, tolerance allows difference, but surrender dissolves the grip of control itself. It is a return to alignment beyond willfulness, an attunement to the deeper rhythm of reality.

This is why surrender stands as the culminating modulation force. Not because the others are unimportant, but because it invites the most profound recalibration – not just to cope or adapt, but to transcend.

Ontologically, surrender is strength. The strength to stop performing. The strength to release control. The strength to trust that coherence is not always found in conquest, but often in release. Because sometimes the most coherent act is not to push harder; it is to stop pushing at all.

This chapter explores surrender, not as a vague emotional experience or a last resort, but as a formal ontological structure, a discernible and developable posture of Being. Through its anatomy, mechanics and topology, we will trace how surrender operates within individuals and other systems and why it is indispensable for sustainable transformation.

Ontological Distinction of Surrender

Surrender is your capacity to release resistance when further effort no longer serves coherence or truth. It is neither collapse nor defeat, but the conscious letting go of control when control becomes incoherent. In its healthy form, *surrender* is not giving up. It is giving over – to presence, authenticity and truth. To surrender is not to abandon integrity, but to yield to reality in a way that facilitates recalibration. *Surrender* is not passivity, but a generative alignment with what is, rather than a forcing of what is not.

A **healthy relationship with surrender** indicates that you recognise when persistence has become compulsion, when striving is used to avoid facing deeper fears or unresolved pain – overachieving in one area to distract from fragility in another – or when force fractures integrity. In this state, you can let go – not out of despair, but from a place of discernment. You meet reality without demanding it conform to your will. This kind of surrender is an act of authenticity: letting truth guide you rather than ego, and allowing coherence to unfold rather than control to dominate. It makes space for grace, clarity and re-alignment in the face of what cannot be mastered.

An **unhealthy relationship with surrender** shows up as premature collapse, passive resignation or indifference. You may give up from fatigue rather than clarity, or disengage to avoid discomfort, mistaking withdrawal for wisdom. This distorted surrender abandons coherence instead of returning to it. Others may experience you as detached or indifferent – not because you are free, but because you have yielded without discernment. Conversely, you may resist surrender entirely, clinging to control or chasing certainty until life becomes paralysis. Both distortions cut you off from the deeper intelligence of surrender, which is not about knowing everything, but being aligned enough to trust what unfolds.

Ontology of surrender

Surrender is perhaps one of the most misunderstood postures of Being. Often confused with giving up, passivity or weakness, surrender – when healthy – is none of these. Ontologically, surrender is the *intelligent cessation of futile resistance* – the letting go of control where control is no longer coherent.

Surrender allows movement when all force has failed. It is the soft exhale that follows the exhaustion of strategies. It is not disengagement; it is profound re-engagement with reality as it is, rather than how the ego demands it to be. It is the transition from willpower to wisdom.

In the Modulation Sphere, surrender is the final modulation – the gesture that releases the struggle to dominate what must be accepted. It prevents the perpetuation of suffering through friction with inevitability. It allows the system to drop coercion and find orientation anew.

When distorted, surrender becomes resignation. The difference is ontological:

- Resignation is collapse without coherence.
- Surrender is release with awareness.

This distinction is not semantic; it is existential. One imprisons, the other liberates. One is a weakness, the other is the threshold of transformation.

Let's now explore surrender as a structural capacity by unpacking its anatomy, mechanics and topology.

Anatomy of surrender

Surrender is composed of five foundational elements or structural capacities that, together, define its ontological structure.

1. Recognition

Surrender begins where struggle reveals itself as incoherent. Recognition is the moment of clarity – what I am doing is no longer working. It is not defeatism; it is lucid discernment that my current way of controlling the situation is not aligned with reality.

2. Yielding

Yielding is the structural release of internal pressure: an intentional softening of hypervigilance, willpower and force. It is not resignation, but a conscious pause. Yielding makes space for presence to re-enter where control once dominated.

3. Acceptance

Acceptance is the capacity to accept what *is* – from grief and endings to limitations and uncertainty – without denial or embellishment. It is not agreement, but ontological alignment with reality in the moment.

4. Faith

Surrender involves being open to that which cannot be controlled and to that which upholds coherence – not through passivity, but through faith. Not faith in outcomes, but in the possibility of coherence beyond one's current strategy. This form of trust in that which upholds coherence is not naive; it arises from direct, lived confrontation with uncertainty and letting go.

5. **Realignment**

Once the grip is released, a new reference point or orientation reset is needed. Surrender is complete when the system realigns and resets its compass – not by force, but through a process of re-orientation to presence, care or deeper integrity. It's not just about letting go; it's about *realigning*.

A tangible example of distorted surrender

A social movement began with genuine energy and ethical clarity. For years it pressed for reform, mobilised communities and challenged entrenched structures. But after repeated resistance, political fatigue and organisational burnout, the movement starts to confuse surrender with collapse. What was once a posture of discernment becomes a slow drift into resignation.

At the level of **recognition**, clarity never fully arrives. Instead of naming where strategies have become incoherent or unsustainable, leaders avoid confronting reality. The absence of lucid recognition means they continue operating under illusions, believing that silence is wisdom, when it is actually avoidance.

At the level of **yielding**, the release is not conscious but compulsive. Exhausted members withdraw, disengage from collaboration and retreat into isolation. Rather than making space for presence, this yielding hardens into indifference.

At the level of **acceptance**, dysfunction is normalised rather than metabolised. Instead of acknowledging grief, limits or genuine endings, the movement cloaks its retreat in rhetoric like 'this is just the way the world works' or 'change takes centuries'. Acceptance is distorted into fatalism – not alignment with truth, but submission to despair.

At the level of **faith**, belief collapses. What once grounded the movement in deeper coherence is replaced by cynicism – no longer faith in the possibility of renewal, only distrust in the future. The movement loses its capacity to be held by anything greater than its own exhaustion. Without faith, surrender becomes indistinguishable from nihilism.

At the level of **realignment**, no compass is reset. Instead, the movement drifts, dissipating into fragments, rebranding for optics and dissolving into unrelated causes. The possibility of recalibration is abandoned, and coherence never returns.

From the outside, it looks like the movement has matured – no longer 'fighting the system', but 'accepting reality'. In truth, what has taken hold is resignation masquerading as surrender. What could have been a profound reorientation collapses into quiet despair. The distinction is important. True surrender releases control to realign with truth, whereas distorted surrender abandons coherence altogether.

Mechanics of surrender

Surrender functions as a dynamic recalibration process, particularly in the face of loss, failure, control fatigue or collapse. It is not a single act, but a *systemic transition* from resistance to receptivity.

1. **Threshold encounter**

   A situation arises that cannot be resolved through effort, control or strategy. A limit is reached – emotionally, physically and existentially.

2. **Strategy breakdown**

   Existing strategies begin to fail. Willpower, negotiation, denial or assertion of control produce diminishing returns. Disorientation or fatigue begins to set in.

3. **Acknowledgement and release**

   Awareness dawns – this can't be forced and resistance is futile. The posture shifts. The grip loosens. Space opens.

4. **Reconnection to reality**

   As the grip of control releases, the system begins to reconnect with the wider field of reality, context and meaning. Awareness expands and new perspectives, once obscured by effort and insistence, begin to emerge.

5. **Recalibration**

   Surrender does not always lead to action. Sometimes, movement returns, but from a new centre. Other times, coherence takes the shape of stillness, grief, rest or simply being present. What emerges is not passivity but *coherence*.

Topology of surrender

Each structural component of surrender shapes and is shaped by the others. The topology of surrender reveals the systemic logic by which a person or other type of system moves from futile control to coherent presence.

Recognition ↔ Yielding

We don't yield or relax the will until we realise that what we are doing is futile. And we often cannot see the futility until we soften our will. This loop marks the entry point into surrender. Without it, systems remain in a state of denial or compulsive striving.

Yielding ↔ Acceptance

As effort subsides through yielding, reality comes into sharper focus. And as reality is met with acceptance, the need for further resistance dissolves. These two components continuously inform one another. Yielding creates the softness required to perceive clearly, while acceptance deepens the capacity to yield.

Acceptance ↔ Faith

Once we accept what is, we confront what is beyond our grasp. This is where faith comes in, not as belief, but as a willingness to stay present without control. Without faith, acceptance becomes numbness. But with faith, reality is accepted with grace.

Faith ↔ Realignment

When trust stabilises, a new direction becomes possible. Movement can begin – not driven by fear or force, but guided by responsiveness. This is not returning to control. It is *discovering alignment*.

Realignment ↔ Recognition

The new orientation reveals what the old was resisting. It completes the cycle. The system becomes capable of recognising futility sooner next time, not from a place of defeat, but with clarity, enabling it to surrender with grace.

Emergent qualities and patterns

Surrender is not a fallback for the weak. It is the wisdom to let go and the capacity to stop resisting truth when truth becomes undeniable. It is not giving up. It is letting go of that which no longer holds structural integrity.

When surrender is coherent and integrated, it produces:

- **Peace after turmoil** – Not from resolution, but from release.
- **Clarity through humility** – Insight not accessed through control.
- **Flow without force** – Movement without manipulation.
- **Presence under pressure** – The ability to stay when escape would be easier.
- **Ontological grace** – The posture of one who no longer fights what is.

When distorted, however, surrender becomes:

- **Resignation** – Collapse without clarity.
- **Helplessness** – A learned posture of futility.
- **Avoidance** – Mistaking withdrawal for peace.
- **Performative detachment** – Projecting a calm exterior while avoiding pain and disconnecting from discomfort.
- **Denial in disguise** – Calling your actions 'surrender' when they are actually a means to escape.

Surrender in action

Surrender is often invisible in daily life, not because it's rare, but because it's misunderstood. It shows up – not as grand gestures – but in the quiet moments when we stop forcing, stop pretending and finally allow ourselves to *be with* what is.

Let's examine three real-world scenarios that highlight the difference between distorted and coherent surrender, and the systemic impact they generate.

Case 1: The burned-out visionary

A founder has built their company from scratch, fuelled by passion and control. But despite growth, nothing satisfies. Each quarter demands more. Their team is demoralised, innovation slows and the founder doubles down with longer hours, stricter KPIs and more micromanagement. Eventually, physical and emotional burnout forces them to stop. Only then, in the stillness, do they realise they've been clinging to an outdated model of leadership rooted in fear of irrelevance.

Insight: The founder's collapse was not surrender; it was deferred breakdown. Coherent surrender would have involved recognising the futility of his actions earlier, yielding to the reality of the situation and a realignment of how value and leadership are held. The cost of delay was not just exhaustion. It was the erosion of sustainability in the system itself.

Case 2: The caregiver's turning point

A young woman is caring for her chronically ill father. For years she tries to 'fix' every aspect of his life, from his appointments and medications to his moods. But nothing seems enough. Eventually, she realises she's not just supporting; she's resisting the inevitability of her father's decline. Through therapy and self-reflection, she softens. She stops trying to control his journey and begins to simply *be* with him.

Insight: This is surrender in action. Recognising the futility of the situation did not mean abandoning care. It meant relinquishing control over the outcome (yielding). What emerged was not apathy, but deeper presence, relational healing and internal peace. The system – in this case, the father-daughter relationship – found coherence where control could not.

Case 3: The strategic resignation

Facing political tension and misalignment with senior leadership, a corporate executive decides to step away from his role. But his departure is laced with bitterness. He tells others, 'I'm done trying. This place is broken.' However, privately, he feels disillusioned and numb.

Insight: This is resignation, not surrender. Though the executive's exit appears decisive, it lacks clarity and orientation. The decision was made from a place of fatigue, not freedom. The executive moves on but the inner pattern – control, disillusionment and collapse – remains unresolved and is likely to repeat.

Conclusion

Within cultures addicted to problem-solving, control and linear progress, surrender seems counterintuitive. Yet it is an evolutionary function: the capacity that allows systems to recalibrate when effort becomes incoherent. Through surrender, transformation – not performance – emerges.

Surrender is not a step back. It is a return to reality – not the reality we hoped for, imagined or tried to engineer, but the one we are in.

It is not the end of responsibility, but its renewal once control has exhausted its usefulness.

To surrender is not to give up. It is to *give over* to coherence, presence and truth. Because some doors do not open by pushing. Some paths are not found through striving. And some truths can only be received when we stop resisting what we already know.

When embodied coherently, surrender becomes a systemic force of renewal for individuals, collectives and institutions. Where control fails, surrender begins. Where striving fragments, surrender realigns. Where rigidity breaks, surrender bends.

Ultimately, surrender is not weakness. It is the wisdom to let go when holding on no longer serves.

Reflection

- Where in your life are you still trying to force an outcome, despite mounting signs that the strategy is no longer working?
- What would it look like to stop pushing, not out of defeat, but from a place of clarity?
- Have you ever mistaken resignation for surrender? What made it resignation rather than surrender?
- What emotion or fear arises for you at the idea of 'letting go'? Is it truly about the situation or your identity in relation to it?
- Where in your organisation, team or relationship is control masquerading as leadership or alignment, and where might surrender open the door to sustainable re-alignment?

PART VII

From Insight to Design – Pathways to Authentic Sustainability

We have arrived at a threshold: the point where analysis, meaning-making and intention begin to shape authentic sustainability in the real world. Up to this point, we have explored the Authentic Sustainability Framework (ASF) – the living architecture that unites the many elements of this work into one coherent system. At its core lies the Unified Ontology of Systemic Integrity (UOSI), the backbone that gives structure and integrity to every other model. We deeply examined the UOSI's four spheres and their causal forces, discovering how they give rise to various emergent qualities and patterns that either lead us towards coherence or into dysfunction. We also clarified the difference between authentic sustainability and its shadow twin, sustainabilism, and positioned these frameworks not as doctrines to follow, but as ways of seeing and designing reality.

This part of the book marks the passage from insight to design. The work ahead is no longer about understanding structures in the abstract, but about analysing systems, translating what we uncover into meaning and significance, and shaping intentions that lead to regenerative commitments.

Mapping the architecture of authentic sustainability

Earlier, we introduced the Authentic Sustainability Framework (ASF) as the architecture that unifies all the core elements of this work into one coherent system. The ASF is not another model layered on top of these. It is the living architecture that holds them together – translating diagnosis into design, meaning into intention, and intention into sustainable commitments.

Because this part brings together several of these elements in close sequence, it helps to picture them not as parallel or competing tools, but as connected stages of one regenerative movement within and beyond the ASF – a continuous progression from seeing to shaping, from insight to design, and from plan to practice.

Each element of the ASF serves a distinct yet related purpose within this architecture. Two of these – the Reconstructive Ontology of Sustainability (ROS) and the Sustainability Profile – will be explored in greater depth later, but their roles can be outlined here to show how they fit within the broader framework:

- **The Systemic Subversion Cycle (SSC)** reveals how systems drift, corrode and lose coherence. It provides the *diagnostic lens* – the capacity to see clearly and name distortion.
- **The Unified Ontology of Systemic Integrity (UOSI)** provides the standards and compass of coherence, defining the four spheres and 16 causal qualities that sustain or erode systemic integrity. It establishes the ontological foundation on which authentic sustainability rests.
- **The Reconstructive Ontology of Sustainability (ROS)** rebuilds sustainability on ontological foundations of Being, integrity, sense-making, meaning-making and modulation. It weaves together the major frameworks introduced throughout the book – the Being Framework, metacontent, the Nested Theory of Sense-making,[82] Minalogy,[83] the UOSI and the Transformation Methodology – into one coherent paradigm for authentic sustainability in action. Where the SSC diagnoses erosion of coherence, ROS reconstructs the architecture itself, moving us from critique to creation. Its practical, integrative nature is the reason it is introduced in detail for the first time in this part of the book.
- **The Sustainability Profile** is an ontometric tool that translates the UOSI's systemic principles into practical assessment and application. It reveals where coherence is strong or weak across personal, organisational and societal dimensions, serving as a mirror between the ontological and the operational. The tool itself is introduced in Part VIII, because authentic sustainability can be gauged without it, as discussed in Chapter 50. However, the Profile helps remove

---

82 Tashvir, A. (2024) *Metacontent: The Intellectual Substrates for Sense-making.* Engenesis Publications, Sydney.
83 Minalogy is introduced in this book as a new philosophical discipline that treats meaning-making as a distinct field. It integrates linguistic, ontological, phenomenological, psychological and cultural dimensions within a coherent ontology, positioning meaning-making as a primary human act essential for discernment and sustainable action.

the biases and limitations that often occur when assessment is attempted without such structure.
- **The Fulfilment Pyramid** maps the inner flow of coherence, from meaning to expression, intention, commitment and action – ensuring that what is built externally is sustained internally.

Together, these five elements form the **Authentic Sustainability Framework (ASF)** – the foundational architecture that diagnoses dysfunction, reconstructs and maps the flow of coherence and aligns sustainability on ontological grounds.

From here, **The Authentic Sustainability Blueprint** gives outer form to that flow, designing the structures, rhythms and practices through which authentic sustainability can be enacted, adapted and renewed.

Seen together, the movement unfolds as follows:

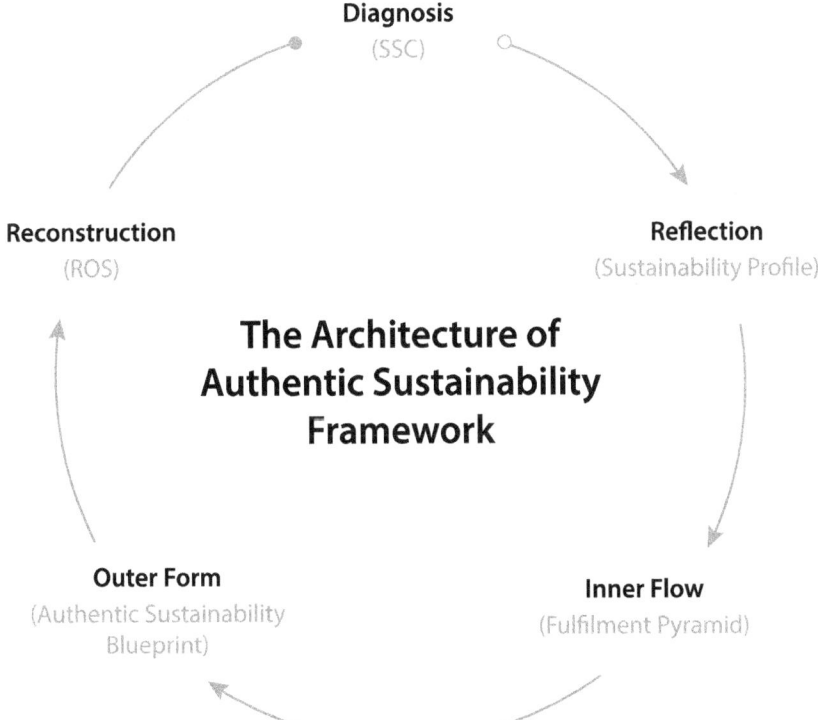

Figure 11 – The Architecture of Authentic Sustainability Framework diagram.

Rather than separate frameworks to remember, these are phases of one continuum – the full anatomy of authentic sustainability. The ASF provides the foundation and the Blueprint carries it into outer form. Together, they support us to see with clarity, align purpose and intention with our deeper meaning (*Mina*), act with coherence, design with wisdom, regenerate with intention and renew with continuity.

Within the context of the ASF, analysis goes beyond data and theory. It is a human act of sense-making – progressing from reception to perception to conception, revealing the metacontent and paradigms that guide how we interpret reality, often without our awareness. Meaning-making goes deeper still, aligning those insights with purpose, values and integrity. Intention is the turning point – the disciplined move from meaning to direction, orienting our commitments so transformation is not only possible, but sustainable.

This is why the UOSI matters as a living architecture. Unlike scripted global frameworks that prescribe behaviours and targets, the UOSI cultivates discernment, coherence and regenerative orientation. It allows us to see systems as they are, to interpret their dynamics, and to ask the questions most others avoid: *What should be sustained? What must be renewed? And what should be allowed to disintegrate to make way for coherence?*

This process is not purely intellectual. Every system, including human systems, carries its own emotional and existential gravity. When meaning and coherence begin to fracture, that breakdown is not merely structural – it is felt. The same forces that shape systems outwardly are experienced inwardly as tension, frustration or despair. Understanding these inner and outer dynamics is essential to any authentic analysis, because sustainability fails first in the unseen: in the quiet places where coherence erodes and shadows take hold.

When shadows within a system are not addressed, they give rise to misery – a clustered state ranging from trivial discomforts to difficulties, hardships, adversities, catastrophes and crises. This misery is inevitably experienced by us as human beings, and that experience of misery and pain is what we refer to as suffering – how it lands within us.

When misery remains unaddressed and becomes reinforced, and when the experience of suffering becomes self-sustaining, systems – both individuals and the larger systems they inhabit – enter a state of entrenchment. In this state, we become so caught within the prevailing conditions and experiences that it feels as though there is no way out. It is a form of entrapment that places the system at the verge of breaking down – or at least gives the felt sense of imminent collapse.

If entrenchment continues without intentional intervention, modulation or transformation, the system enters seemingly never-ending cycles of entrenchment and will eventually disintegrate and collapse. Understanding these patterns of entrenchment is critical because they reveal where coherence has been lost and where the work of reconstruction must begin.

The chapters that follow take us into that work. They translate awareness into analysis, analysis into meaning, and meaning into design. Each framework, model and methodology discussed offers a way to recognise, interrupt and ultimately transform these cycles of entrenchment – to rebuild coherence where it has been eroded and to anchor sustainability – not as a goal, but as a way of being.

In the chapters ahead, we will:

- Synthesise the UOSI's causal forces and emergent patterns to understand how cause becomes consequence – revealing why some systems evolve with coherence while others fragment and collapse.
- Leverage the UOSI as an analytical lens across personal, organisational and societal systems.
- Engage meta-awareness, metacontent and the Nested Theory of Sense-making to refine our perceptions into deeper conceptions of reality.
- Identify systemic distortions and cycles of entrenchment using the Systemic Subversion Cycle (SSC) to reveal how systems undermine coherence and how timely intervention can restore integrity.
- Transition from sense-making to meaning-making through Minalogy, aligning insight with purpose.

- Prepare the ground for intention-setting – the disciplined move from desire to direction, from knowledge to commitment.
- Reconstruct sustainability on ontological foundations through the Reconstructive Ontology of Sustainability (ROS), translating diagnosis into design.
- Trace how intention moves through the layers of coherence into commitment (the flow of coherence).
- Discover how intentions, once committed to, are carried forward and sustained over time through the Fulfilment Pyramid.
- Develop an Authentic Sustainability Blueprint – a living plan that carries coherence into practice.

This part marks a turning point in the journey. What follows is the work of turning analysis into meaning, translating meaning into intention, and carrying intention into sustainable commitments. It is only through enacting such commitments that we begin to see the systems within and around us transform.

This is not the end of the journey but its preparation. Here, meaning crystallises into intention, and intention takes form as direction, bringing coherence to the behaviours and structures that make sustainability possible. It is the phase where insight becomes embodiment, where reconstruction gives way to design, and where the groundwork for sustainability in practice is laid.

CHAPTER 42

From Cause to Consequence – The UOSI's Emergent Forces

Every individual, organisation and society lives within patterns that determine whether it thrives, stagnates or declines. These patterns are not random. They are the direct consequence of how we engage with the causal forces defined within the UOSI.

Across Parts III–VI, we saw how each of the UOSI's 16 causal forces gave rise to distinct emergent qualities and patterns. This chapter synthesises that work and makes the link from cause to consequence explicit, showing how healthy engagement generates renewal, humility, fortitude and wisdom – and how distortion produces decay, hubris, capitulation and delusion.

These emergent forces are not abstract ideas but lived realities. They are the observable patterns through which systemic integrity – or its breakdown – becomes visible. By recognising them, we gain more than descriptive clarity; we gain a practical lens for analysis.

To see how these patterns arise, we begin by revisiting the four spheres of the UOSI and their 16 causal forces – the structural roots from which all emergent consequences flow:

- **Architectonic Sphere** – The meta-governing layer that orchestrates long-term coherence, normative direction and

systemic design across all other spheres (meta-awareness, systemic integrity, sustained effectiveness and normativity).
- **Integrity Sphere** – The foundation of alignment and coherence (intention, trust, sovereignty and Being).
- **Modulation Sphere** – The balancing mechanism that enables healthy change and refinement (patience, tolerance, adaptability and surrender).
- **Disintegration Sphere** – The forces of dysfunction, rigidity and collapse when an unhealthy relationship with these forces prevails (shadows, misery, suffering and entrenchment).

When our relationship with these causal forces is healthy and aligned with systemic integrity – the coherence that sustains life and renewal – constructive emergent qualities appear, such as wisdom, renewal, humility and fortitude. But when disintegration dominates or modulation is weak, destructive patterns emerge like decay, capitulation, hubris and delusion.

This chapter explores a selection of these emergent forces. They are not an exhaustive list, but illustrative examples that demonstrate how constructive and destructive patterns manifest in both personal and collective life. Examining them enables us to see not just the structures of systemic integrity, but also the generative consequences that flow from them.

By identifying these expressions, we can better understand why the systems around us – and within us – either evolve with coherence or fragment and collapse. For anyone responsible for shaping or sustaining a system – a leader, policymaker, entrepreneur, teacher or parent – this awareness is critical. It allows us to anticipate breakdown before it happens, recognise when coherence is slipping, and respond in ways that restore balance and renewal.

From cause to emergence: How the Being Framework interacts with the UOSI

The UOSI's 16 causal forces represent the foundational conditions that sustain, modulate or erode systemic integrity. Each functions as a primary driver of movement and transformation within a system.

Among them, **Being** is one such force – an entire cluster concerned with human awareness, effectiveness and integrity.

The 31 qualities articulated in the Being Framework Ontological Model[84] are expressions within this single causal force. They describe the diverse ways in which Being, as a structural dimension, manifests through individuals and collectives.

When causal forces interact – for instance, when Being intersects with intention, suffering or patience – their interplay produces emergent forces. These are not additional layers added to the model, but systemic outcomes that arise from how the causal forces combine, reinforce or distort one another. Renewal and decay, transcendence and stagnation, harmony and dissonance are examples of such emergent patterns.

From this perspective, emergent forces express systemic behaviour rather than introduce new ontological categories. They reveal what becomes visible when the underlying causal architecture of integrity is either coherent or misaligned. The qualities of Being – authenticity, courage, awareness, vulnerability and others – are not separate from these dynamics; they are among the very qualities whose cultivation or neglect gives rise to them.

The causal forces form the underlying architecture of sustainability, while the emergent forces display the patterned outcomes of their interaction across all levels – from individuals to societies.

The following examples demonstrate how Being, as described in the Being Framework Ontological Model, interacts with other causal forces to produce the emergent dynamics explored in this chapter. These illustrations show how the cultivation or distortion of Being-related qualities can generate coherence or dysfunction across different contexts.

Example 1 – Organisational dynamics

In an organisation, the causal forces of *Being*, *Intention* and *Patience* interact continuously. When Being-related qualities such as

---

84   Tashvir, A. (2021) *Being – The Source of Power*. Engenesis Publications, Sydney.

authenticity, responsibility and vulnerability are cultivated, people remain open to feedback and learning. When intention is clear and anchored in meaning, decisions are guided by coherence rather than short-term gain. And when patience is maintained, change unfolds at a sustainable pace without reactive overcorrection.

The interplay of these forces gives rise to coherence and renewal – the organisation evolves, integrates lessons and sustains vitality through change. However, when these same forces weaken – when authenticity gives way to image management, intention fragments, or patience collapses into frustration – the organisation loses coherence, innovation slows and distrust spreads quietly through the structure.

In this way, coherence and dysfunction become visible expressions of how Being interacts with other causal forces in practice.

Example 2 – Personal transformation

Within an individual, the causal forces of Being, intention and suffering converge. When Being-related qualities such as awareness, courage and self-expression are cultivated – and when these align with a coherent intention and an authentic relationship to suffering as a teacher rather than an affliction – growth and clarity emerge. The person begins to move through limitation with greater understanding, transforming pain into insight and renewed purpose.

Conversely, when awareness dulls into denial, intention becomes reactive or scattered, or when suffering is resisted or recycled without meaning, the individual becomes trapped in repetitive loops of frustration and avoidance.

In this way, expansion and diminishment can be seen as visible expressions of how Being interacts with other causal forces within the human system, shaping whether hardship becomes a pathway to coherence or a cycle of entrenchment.

The following sections explore these dynamics in greater depth, showing how different combinations of causal forces – including the varied expressions of Being itself – give rise to the emergent pairs that shape systemic behaviour, from renewal and decay to prevailing and succumbing.

Renewal versus decay

Among the many forces that emerge from our relationship with the causal foundations of the UOSI, few are as decisive as renewal and decay. Both describe how systems respond to disruption, challenge and change. Renewal reflects the ability to metabolise difficulty into growth, while decay reflects the slow erosion that follows when challenges are denied or resisted. One opens the possibility of resilience, rejuvenation and transformation; the other steadily unravels coherence until collapse becomes unavoidable.

Renewal

At its core, renewal is the process of recovery, recalibration and re-engagement with life after disruption. It is not simply about returning to a previous state, but emerging stronger, wiser and more aligned with reality. In nature, we see renewal everywhere – forests regenerate after bushfires, rivers carve new paths after floods, and ecosystems adapt to shifting climates.

In human life, renewal is the ability to integrate challenges rather than resist them and to use setbacks as fuel for transformation. Individuals, businesses, institutions and societies that embrace renewal do not simply endure hardship; they metabolise it into something new. The most resilient systems are those that are flexible, responsive and willing to adapt, rather than those that try to hold onto a past that no longer fits.

Renewal is an active process of reconstruction. A company that innovates in response to changing market conditions rather than clinging to outdated strategies demonstrates renewal. A person who learns from failure and adapts their approach rather than becoming paralysed by fear embodies renewal. It is a willingness to engage with reality in a way that restores, revitalises and propels the system forward.

How renewal can manifest and the causal forces that generate it

Renewal manifests in different but interrelated ways. Sometimes it takes the form of resilience, the ability to withstand setbacks and emerge intact. At other times it is experienced as rejuvenation, a restoring of energy, purpose and clarity after depletion. Renewal can also mean reinvention, the shift into a new phase of being with greater insight and direction. And often it requires reconstitution, the careful rebuilding of coherence and functionality after disruption has fractured it.

These qualities emerge when our relationship with the causal forces of the UOSI is healthy and aligned. Renewal depends on the **Integrity Sphere**, particularly **trust** and **sovereignty**, which provide the foundation for recalibration. Without trust – in oneself, in others or in 'the system' – resilience quickly collapses into despair. Without sovereignty, rejuvenation will never translate into momentum.

Equally essential are the forces of the **Modulation Sphere: patience, tolerance, adaptability** and **surrender**. These qualities allow challenges to be metabolised rather than resisted, enabling hardship to become the soil from which growth arises. When modulation is active, setbacks are absorbed as part of the cycle of life, rather than experienced as permanent defeat.

In this way, renewal is not passive endurance or the denial of hardship. It is an active and ontologically grounded process: integrating obstacles, drawing on trust and sovereignty for stability, and relying on patience, tolerance, adaptability and surrender to transform disruption into strength. Where these causal forces are engaged, renewal flourishes – emerging as resilience, rejuvenation, reinvention and reconstitution.

Renewal in action: The transformation of a startup on the brink of collapse

A Melbourne-based fintech startup had built its entire business model around a promising product in a highly regulated space. Overnight, the Australian government introduced unexpected compliance changes that rendered their model legally unviable. Their business plan was obsolete, investors were restless, and the company faced imminent collapse.

At this crossroads, the leadership team could have resisted reality – pouring energy into lobbying for reversals or clinging to a model that no longer fit. Instead, they chose renewal. Drawing on **trust** in their collective capacity, **sovereignty** to act decisively and the **patience** and **adaptability** to step back rather than panic, they re-examined their foundations.

They analysed the core strengths of their technology, consulted legal experts and identified an untapped market segment that aligned with the new regulations. Within six months, they had redesigned their product, rebranded their company and secured a fresh round of investment.

What could have been the end became the catalyst for reinvention. By metabolising disruption rather than resisting it, the startup not only survived but thrived in a more sustainable niche. This is renewal in action: not simply endurance, but the capacity to reconstitute coherence through adversity and emerge stronger, wiser and more aligned with reality.

Decay

At its core, decay is the process of gradual erosion, fragmentation and decline that occurs when systems resist change, deny reality or cling to what is no longer viable. Unlike sudden collapse, decay often unfolds quietly. It masquerades as stability while coherence slowly unravels beneath the surface. In nature, we see decay in farmlands where rising salinity poisons the soil, trees wither and ecosystems that once flourished are slowly stripped of life.

In human life, decay is visible in individuals, organisations, institutions and societies that refuse to metabolise difficulty. Instead of integrating challenges, they harden against them. Habits calcify, institutions stagnate and cultures lose their vitality. What appears on the outside as strength or endurance often hides an internal fragility that eventually gives way to breakdown.

How decay can manifest and the causal forces that generate it

Decay manifests in a number of interrelated ways. It may appear as stagnation, where growth halts and systems repeat the same patterns until energy dissipates. It can show up as fragmentation, where coherence disintegrates and once-unified structures break apart. At times it emerges as erosion, the slow loss of vitality, trust or purpose. And finally, it culminates in collapse, where what was once functional can no longer sustain itself.

These outcomes arise when our relationship with the causal forces of the UOSI is distorted or neglected. Decay is fuelled by the **Disintegration Sphere**, particularly **shadows, misery, suffering** and **entrenchment.** When shadows are ignored, blind spots widen into systemic weaknesses. When misery and suffering go unacknowledged, vitality drains away. And when entrenchment dominates, adaptation becomes impossible. Equally, the absence of healthy **modulation** – patience, tolerance, adaptability and surrender – prevents challenges from being metabolised, leaving systems brittle and reactive.

In this way, decay is not an inevitable fate, but the emergent consequence of disengagement. It represents the slow, cumulative cost of denial, rigidity and disconnection from the causal forces that sustain coherence.

Decay in action: The decline of a once-dominant retailer

A well-established Australian department store chain once dominated the national retail landscape. For decades, its large-format stores in prime locations were considered symbols of stability and trust. But as consumer preferences shifted and online shopping gained traction, the company refused to adapt. Executives dismissed e-commerce as a passing trend and continued to double down on the same business model, investing heavily in bricks-and-mortar expansion.

Internally, the culture reflected **entrenchment**: leaders valued tradition over innovation, silenced dissenting voices and prided themselves on 'doing things the way we always have'. Shadows grew as executives ignored early signs of decline – falling foot traffic, changing demographics and a younger generation seeking different retail experiences. Without **sovereignty** to act decisively or **adaptability** to redirect their strategy, the organisation slipped further into dysfunction.

Over time, the effects compounded. Revenue eroded, talent drained away and once-loyal customers migrated to more agile competitors. Eventually, the chain entered administration, closing stores and laying off thousands of staff.

This is decay in action: the slow erosion that occurs when systems mistake rigidity for resilience and entrenchment for strength. By clinging to a fading past and refusing to engage authentically with shifting realities, the organisation fragmented and collapsed.

Humility versus hubris

Humility and hubris represent two divergent ways of holding sovereignty. Both are forms of confidence, but their outcomes differ radically depending on the presence or absence of modulation. Humility is confidence tempered by openness, grounded in trust and patience, and aligned with reality. In contrast, hubris is confidence distorted into arrogance – unchecked sovereignty that resists correction, overreaches its limits and, ultimately, fractures coherence. One fosters growth, wisdom and connection, while the other leads to blindness, alienation and downfall.

Humility

At its core, humility is not the absence of confidence, but confidence in a person who remains open and teachable. It is the balance between sovereignty, the deep recognition of one's worth and the willingness to acknowledge limitations.

How humility can manifest and the causal forces that generate it

In practice, humility often manifests as groundedness (confidence without superiority), teachability (openness to correction and new perspectives), restraint (acting with measured wisdom rather than impulse) and grace (handling success and power without self-importance).

It arises from a healthy relationship with **trust** and **sovereignty** (Integrity Sphere), which provide a stable foundation, and with **tolerance** and **patience** (Modulation Sphere), which temper self-assurance with discernment. These causal forces enable individuals to remain open, adaptable and aligned with reality rather than distorted by self-importance.

Humility in action: A surgeon committed to growth

Dr James, a respected neurosurgeon, has saved countless lives, trained younger doctors and led groundbreaking research in his field. By all accounts, he is at the top of his profession. Yet despite his expertise, Dr James never stops learning. He actively seeks feedback from peers, even junior surgeons, knowing fresh perspectives can reveal blind spots. He collaborates with specialists from other fields, recognising that complex cases often require multidisciplinary insight.

When a revolutionary new surgical technique emerged, many of his peers dismissed it, believing traditional methods were sufficient. However, Dr James approached it with curiosity rather than defensiveness. He attended training, refined his approach and integrated the new method into practice, ultimately improving patient outcomes.

His humility ensured continued refinement rather than complacency. Consequently, he remains at the forefront of his field, not because he assumes he has all the answers, but because he never stops seeking them. This is humility in action – confidence grounded in trust, sovereignty and modulation.

Hubris

At its core, hubris is the distortion of sovereignty. It is confidence untempered by modulation, which leads to arrogance, overreach and eventual collapse. Unlike genuine confidence, which relies on trust and openness, hubris insists on its own infallibility and resists correction.

How hubris can manifest and the causal forces that generate it

Hubris often manifests as overreach (pushing beyond competence without regard for consequences), blind certainty (rejecting alternative perspectives), dismissiveness (devaluing others' input) and entitlement (expecting privilege or immunity from error).

Hubris arises when the Integrity Sphere's causal forces are unmodulated, for example, when **unchecked sovereignty** overrides discernment. Without **patience** and **tolerance**, actions become impulsive, mistakes go unacknowledged, and the pursuit of dominance or validation overtakes the pursuit of wisdom. In this state, past success breeds complacency, adaptability is lost and decline becomes inevitable.

Hubris in action: A tech CEO's downfall

Lisa, the CEO of a once-thriving Australian tech company, built her brand on bold innovation. Investors trusted her instincts and customers admired the company's cutting-edge products. But over time, success bred arrogance. When engineers raised concerns about a critical software flaw, Lisa dismissed them outright. 'We've always been ahead of the curve,' she insisted. 'The market will catch up to us.'

Despite repeated warnings, Lisa pushed forward with the launch, convinced that her intuition outweighed both data and feedback. Within weeks, users reported significant failures, competitors capitalised and the company's reputation collapsed. By the time she acknowledged the problem, it was too late – millions were lost, key staff had resigned and investors withdrew their support.

This is hubris in action: sovereignty without modulation, confidence without reality-checking. What began as strength became a liability, leading to fragmentation and collapse.

Fortitude versus capitulation

Fortitude and capitulation reveal two very different responses to adversity. Fortitude enables systems to endure and adapt through challenge without losing integrity. In contrast, capitulation is the abandonment of agency and responsibility – the gradual or sudden retreat that leaves challenges unresolved. One embodies inner strength, perseverance and recalibration, while the other reflects avoidance, erosion of will and eventual decline.

Fortitude

At its core, fortitude is not mere perseverance, but the deeper existential force that sustains engagement with challenge. It enables individuals and systems to move through adversity without losing integrity, purpose or coherence. Unlike stubbornness, fortitude is not blind resistance for its own sake. It is the capacity to endure hardship while adapting, recalibrating and continuing forward with clarity.

How fortitude can manifest and the causal forces that generate it

In practice, fortitude can manifest as resolve (holding to one's course despite pressure), perseverance (staying engaged with difficulty without giving up), endurance (withstanding hardship over time rather than retreating), self-possession (maintaining internal authority and composure) and grit (sustained effort and tenacity in long-term challenges).

Fortitude arises when **sovereignty** and **intention** (Integrity Sphere) remain intact, providing a strong internal compass, and when **patience and tolerance** (Modulation Sphere) function effectively, enabling difficulty to be managed without excess reactivity. At the same time, fortitude requires that **shadows, misery** and **suffering** (Disintegration Sphere) are faced and integrated rather than avoided and allowed to dominate. These causal forces combine to create a resilience that is both grounded and adaptive.

Fortitude in action: The activist who refused to give up

For more than two decades, Sarah has worked as an environmental activist protecting Australia's native forests from deforestation. At the outset, she believed that with enough awareness and political pressure, change would come quickly. But instead, she faced setback after setback – corporate lobbying, government inaction, legal defeats and public apathy.

Many of her peers burned out and left the cause, but Sarah refused to capitulate. She did not cling rigidly to one strategy. Instead, she recalibrated. Moving beyond large-scale protests, she shifted to community-led conservation projects, recognising that smaller, achievable wins could build momentum over time.

There were moments when everything seemed hopeless – when legal protections were overturned, corporations bulldozed forests despite injunctions and public interest waned. Yet Sarah kept going. Not because she denied reality, but because she knew that disengagement would guarantee failure. Her fortitude was not blind resistance; it was a willingness to adapt, refine her approach and keep moving forward.

Today, many of the forests she once campaigned for remain standing – protected in part by the groundwork she helped lay. This is fortitude in action – enduring hardship without surrendering to it, transforming setbacks into resilience, and ensuring that a cause outlasts temporary obstacles.

Capitulation

At its core, capitulation is the systemic failure to uphold one's sovereignty. Unlike surrender, which can be a wise and intentional letting go, capitulation is disengagement through avoidance, retreat or defeatism. It is the absence of fortitude – the moment an individual, organisation, institution or society stops engaging with difficulty altogether.

Capitulation may appear suddenly, but more often it is gradual – a slow erosion of willpower in which setbacks accumulate until effort feels futile. Over time, passivity takes hold and systems become defined by inaction and resignation rather than adaptability and resilience.

How capitulation can manifest and the causal forces that generate it

In practice, capitulation can manifest as cowardice (fear preventing engagement), abdication (abandoning responsibility or one's role), submission (yielding to external pressure out of exhaustion) and erosion (gradual loss of the will to act, often through accumulated avoidance).

Capitulation arises when **sovereignty** and **intention** (Integrity Sphere) are weak, leaving individuals or systems indecisive and passive. Furthermore, without **patience and tolerance** (Modulation Sphere), hardship feels intolerable and avoidance replaces engagement. When **shadows, misery, suffering** and **entrenchment** (Disintegration Sphere) dominate, challenges are fled from rather than metabolised. In this state, difficulty defines the outcome because the system refuses to confront it.

Capitulation in action: The disengaged student

Amelia entered university full of enthusiasm, determined to pursue a career in medicine. She worked hard in her first year, but struggled with the pace of study and the pressure of exams. When she failed one of her core subjects, she was devastated. Instead of seeking academic support or adjusting her study strategies, Amelia internalised the setback as proof she was 'not smart enough'.

At first, she promised herself she would try harder next semester. But the failure lingered in her mind, eroding her confidence. She stopped attending tutorials regularly, avoided reaching out to peers and withdrew from conversations with her lecturers. Each missed opportunity for engagement deepened her resignation.

When she failed a second subject, Amelia decided that medicine was beyond her reach. She withdrew from the program – not because she lacked the capacity to succeed, but because she had stopped engaging with the challenge.

This is capitulation in action. It was not a single decision, but a gradual erosion of will that allowed difficulty to dictate the outcome. Capitulation often disguises itself as waiting, hesitation or 'being realistic'. But in truth, it is the abandonment of agency. Where fortitude endures, adapts and refines, capitulation retreats, ensuring decline is inevitable.

Wisdom versus delusion

Wisdom and delusion represent two opposing ways of perceiving and interpreting reality. Wisdom integrates clarity, discernment and humility, enabling individuals and systems to navigate complexity with depth and foresight. In contrast, delusion distorts reality through bias, rigidity and denial, leading to misjudgement, dogmatism and self-deception. One aligns with truth and coherence, while the other resists reality and becomes trapped in false certainty.

Wisdom

At its core, wisdom is the capacity to perceive reality with clarity and depth. It goes beyond intelligence or accumulated knowledge, drawing on discernment and perspective to recognise context, nuance and consequence. Wisdom allows people to question assumptions, remain open to refinement and make choices that integrate both short-term needs and long-term sustainability.

How wisdom can manifest and the causal forces that generate it

In practice, wisdom often manifests as discernment (accurately assessing situations beyond superficial details), judgement (making well-founded decisions with an awareness of consequences), perspective (recognising broader implications rather than reacting impulsively) and insight (understanding deeper truths rather than relying on assumptions).

Wisdom arises from a healthy relationship with **Being** and **sovereignty** (Integrity Sphere), ensuring that decisions are anchored in reality rather than self-deception. It is refined by modulation (**tolerance** and **adaptability**), which enables views to be adjusted as new information emerges.

Crucially, wisdom is also sustained by the Architectonic Sphere's causal forces: **meta-awareness** provides perspective beyond immediate impulses; **systemic integrity** ensures alignment with the larger whole; **sustained effectiveness** grounds action in durability; and **normativity** anchors choices in shared values and ethical direction. Together, these qualities generate clarity and discernment rather than distortion.

Wisdom in action: The thoughtful policymaker

A senior policymaker is confronted with a divisive question of whether to introduce sweeping regulations in response to an economic downturn. Public outcry is intense and media pressure demands immediate action. Many colleagues rush to endorse populist measures that promise short-term relief.

Instead of reacting impulsively, this policymaker takes a different path. They consult economic historians to understand how similar crises unfolded in the past, draw on financial experts to analyse potential long-term consequences and engage directly with communities to hear the human impact. Despite criticism for not acting quickly, they resist pressure and allow space for careful deliberation.

When the policy is finally introduced, it proves not to be a reactive band-aid, but a balanced reform addressing root causes. Over time, the new policy's effectiveness becomes clear – it stabilises the economy and prevents cycles of crisis. This is wisdom in action – not hesitation or inaction, but the willingness to align decisions with clarity, foresight and systemic coherence.

Delusion

At its core, delusion is a distortion of reality. Unlike ignorance, which arises from not knowing, delusion is the refusal or inability to see things as they are, reinforced by bias, ideology or unchecked assumptions. A person caught in delusion may be utterly convinced of their correctness, even when faced with overwhelming evidence to the contrary.

How delusion can manifest and the causal forces that generate it

In practice, delusion often manifests as misjudgement (drawing false conclusions from distorted premises), dogmatism (rigid adherence to beliefs without openness to new information), self-deception (clinging to falsehoods out of bias or fear) and blind following (accepting external narratives uncritically).

Delusion arises when **Being** and **sovereignty** (Integrity Sphere) are compromised, allowing bias or external manipulation to override discernment. It is worsened by the absence of **tolerance** and **adaptability** (Modulation Sphere), which results in intellectual rigidity and the inability to adjust to new information. It is also fed by **shadows, misery, suffering** and **entrenchment** (Disintegration Sphere), which warp perception through fear, ideology or avoidance. Furthermore, when the **Architectonic Sphere's** causal forces are neglected, perspective collapses and distortion thrives.

Delusion in action: The conspiracy theorist who rejects reality

Daniel prided himself on being an independent thinker, sceptical of mainstream institutions. When a major public health crisis unfolded, he immediately distrusted official sources, convinced that the government was concealing the truth. Rather than engaging broadly, he only sought material that confirmed his suspicions.

When friends presented well-supported scientific research supporting the government's response, Daniel dismissed it as propaganda. Even when predictions he made were disproven and his advice caused real harm, he refused to reconsider his stance. Each contradiction only deepened his conviction that a larger conspiracy was at play.

Daniel's certainty was not the product of truth, but of delusion. By filtering reality through bias and denial, he trapped himself in a self-reinforcing worldview. This is delusion in action: not simply being misinformed, but actively resisting the very process of discernment and refinement that could reconnect him with reality.

Resonance versus disconnection

Resonance and disconnection represent two contrasting ways of engaging with reality and with others. Resonance is deep alignment – a sense of attunement, presence and coherence that makes relationships meaningful, leadership impactful and experiences profound. In contrast, disconnection is the absence of such attunement. It manifests as alienation, withdrawal or indifference, leaving individuals and collectives fragmented and disengaged. One binds people and collectives together in coherence, while the other silently erodes connection until only estrangement remains.

Resonance

At its core, resonance is the ability to be fully attuned to the present moment and to others. More than presence, it is engagement that creates genuine connection, meaning and harmony. Resonance is what makes conversations fulfilling, art moving and leadership inspiring.

How resonance can manifest and the causal forces that generate it

In practice, resonance can manifest as relational attunement (genuine engagement in meaningful connections), alignment with reality (experiencing coherence between self, world and purpose), authentic presence (showing up sincerely rather than superficially) and harmonisation (creating environments where people and systems function in unison).

Resonance arises when **trust** and **Being** (Integrity Sphere) are intact, allowing openness, sincerity and connection. It is refined by **tolerance** and **surrender** (Modulation Sphere), which make engagement fluid rather than forced. Importantly, resonance is also supported by the Architectonic Sphere's causal forces. For example, **meta-awareness** enables awareness of others beyond self-focus, **systemic integrity** ensures alignment with the larger whole, and **normativity** anchors resonance in shared values and meaning. In the absence of these forces, resonance cannot be sustained.

Resonance in action: The musician who creates a shared experience

During a live performance, a guitarist begins strumming the opening chords of a song known by heart. Immediately, a wave of energy sweeps the audience. Strangers sing together in unison, their voices blending as if they were one. For those few minutes, there is no separation between performer and listener, individual and collective.

The guitarist is not merely playing notes. He is attuned to the energy of the room, shaping each phrase in dialogue with the crowd. The music ceases to be just sound. It becomes a shared emotional experience, a living moment of collective resonance.

What makes the performance unforgettable is not technical perfection, but depth of presence. The audience does not simply hear the music – they feel it, embody it and become part of it. This is resonance at its purest: meaningful alignment where experience is not observed from the outside, but fully lived from within.

Disconnection

At its core, disconnection is the breakdown of attunement. More than physical absence, it is the absence of meaningful engagement. People can be surrounded by others and yet feel utterly alone, or speak daily without ever being heard. Disconnection replaces presence with distraction, sincerity with superficiality and engagement with withdrawal. Over time, it produces isolation, cynicism and emotional numbness.

How disconnection can manifest and the causal forces that generate it

In practice, disconnection can manifest as apathy (emotional disengagement), alienation (a felt separation from people or purpose), indifference (lack of investment or care in interactions) and estrangement (a growing sense of detachment, even in familiar settings).

Disconnection arises when **trust** and **Being** (Integrity Sphere) are weakened, leading to distant or inauthentic engagement. The absence of **tolerance** and **surrender** (Modulation Sphere) prevents fluid, meaningful interaction, and **shadows, misery, suffering** and **entrenchment** (Disintegration Sphere) reinforce withdrawal, cynicism and avoidance. When the Architectonic Sphere's causal forces are also neglected – particularly when **meta-awareness** and **systemic integrity** are absent – relationships and systems lose their coherence, drifting into fragmentation.

Disconnection in action: The parent who is physically present but emotionally absent

David spends each evening beside his daughter while she does her homework. To an outsider, he might appear engaged, a model parent offering daily presence. But while she works, his eyes remain fixed on his phone – answering emails, scrolling social media and planning for tomorrow's meetings.

Whenever she speaks, he responds with half-hearted nods, rarely registering her words. She tells him about a problem at school, but she never feels truly heard. Slowly, she shares less. By the time she is a teenager, their conversations have dwindled to the bare minimum. Though they live under the same roof, they feel like strangers.

This is disconnection in action. It is not caused by physical absence, but by the lack of genuine attunement. In the silent erosion of presence, relationships fragment. What could have been a meaningful connection fades into estrangement long before the disconnection is fully recognised.

Transcendence versus stagnation

Transcendence and stagnation represent two very different ways of responding to turbulence and disruption. Transcendence is the capacity to metabolise disruption into evolution – to rise beyond existing limitations and create higher-order coherence. In contrast, stagnation is the refusal to engage with turbulence, a passive inertia that mistakes comfort for stability. One transforms difficulty into growth, while the other allows vitality to erode until decline is unavoidable.

Transcendence

At its core, transcendence is the process of realignment and elevation that follows disruption. It is not simply survival through turbulence, but the capacity to reconfigure systems at a higher level of coherence. Transcendence turns instability into transformation, tension into growth and disruption into renewal.

How transcendence can emerge and the causal forces that generate it

In practice, transcendence can emerge as instability (a temporary breakdown of equilibrium that signals the need for reconfiguration), disruption (the interruption of unsustainable patterns), tension (systemic pressure revealing misalignment) and catalysis (the force that provokes change, even when uncomfortable).

Transcendence arises when **sovereignty** and **trust** (Integrity Sphere) remain intact, providing stability through uncertainty. It is enabled by **patience** and **adaptability** (Modulation Sphere), which allow turbulence to be engaged constructively rather than resisted. It also draws on the Architectonic Sphere's causal forces: **meta-awareness** provides perspective on what the disruption signifies; **systemic integrity** ensures changes align with broader coherence; and **sustained effectiveness** anchors transformation in durability rather than reaction. When these causal forces are engaged, turbulence becomes a catalyst for transcendence rather than collapse.

Transcendence in action: A community rebuilding after disaster

In 2019, severe bushfires swept through parts of regional New South Wales, destroying homes, businesses and local infrastructure. Entire towns were left traumatised, facing not only physical loss, but also the deep uncertainty of how to rebuild.

In the aftermath, these communities could have fragmented – paralysed by grief, waiting for government intervention or retreating into resignation. Instead, residents chose a different path. They came together to establish volunteer brigades, community support groups and local rebuilding committees. Farmers shared equipment, tradespeople donated time and neighbours pooled resources to restore what had been lost.

Rather than attempting to recreate a town exactly as it was, they reimagined it. Building codes were updated to increase fire resilience, renewable energy systems were installed to reduce vulnerability and new community hubs were designed to strengthen social ties. Out of the turbulence of the disaster, stronger, more adaptive communities emerged.

This is transcendence in action – engaging disruption not as an endpoint, but as the catalyst for a more coherent and sustainable future. By combining sovereignty, adaptability and systemic integrity, these communities rose beyond survival, transforming hardship into renewal and evolution.

Stagnation

Stagnation occurs when turbulence is resisted or denied, leaving systems paralysed. This emergent force mistakes comfort for resilience, clinging to outdated patterns long after they have ceased to be viable. Over time, it erodes vitality, relevance and coherence.

How stagnation can manifest and the causal forces that generate it

In practice, stagnation can manifest as rigidity (holding onto outdated structures), inertia (an unwillingness to engage with change), decay (slow deterioration through unresolved dysfunction) and resignation (accepting passivity as inevitable rather than seeking renewal).

Stagnation arises when **sovereignty** and **trust** (Integrity Sphere) are weak or overridden, producing indecision and passivity. It is exacerbated by the absence of **patience** and **adaptability** (Modulation Sphere), which prevents systems from engaging turbulence productively. When **shadows, misery, suffering** and **entrenchment** (Disintegration Sphere) dominate, fear, avoidance and systemic paralysis set in. Furthermore, without the balancing role of the **Architectonic Sphere's** causal forces, turbulence is never metabolised, and inertia masquerades as stability while coherence quietly erodes.

Stagnation in action: A media company that failed to evolve

For decades, a major Australian media network dominated television broadcasting. Executives were confident that viewers would always prefer traditional schedules, dismissing the rise of streaming as a fad.

As streaming services gained traction, competitors adapted quickly. They developed innovative platforms, captured the attention of younger audiences and shifted advertising models to match new consumption patterns. Meanwhile, the traditional broadcaster doubled down on outdated strategies, convinced its dominance would hold.

By the time the network scrambled to launch its own streaming service, it was too late. The platform was rushed, poorly executed and ignored by audiences who had already moved on. Advertisers redirected budgets, talent left for forward-thinking companies and the organisation slowly unravelled.

This is stagnation in action. The turbulence was there all along, signalling the need for transformation, but it was ignored. What felt like stability was in fact inertia. Stagnation does not protect systems from decline. It guarantees it – ensuring eventual irrelevance where transcendence could have created renewal.

Stewardship versus apathy

Stewardship and apathy represent two opposing responses to duty. One sustains coherence through care, foresight and discipline; the other corrodes it through neglect, disengagement and indifference. At its core, stewardship is the antidote to apathy. It is the active choice to engage, care and preserve, while apathy is the passive choice to ignore, detach and decay. The world does not crumble because of chaos alone. It often unravels because those capable of making a difference choose not to act.

Before we examine each emergent force, consider the following table outlining the core difference between active responsibility and passive neglect.

Aspect	Stewardship – Active Responsibility	Apathy – Passive Neglect
Mindset	Care, responsibility and long-term thinking	Indifference, detachment and short-termism
Impact on Others	Nurtures, supports and builds	Ignores, neglects and erodes
Decision-making	Thoughtful, ethical, considers long term impact	Avoidant, disengaged or driven by convenience
Presence in Leadership	Creates sustainable success through responsibility	Lets problems fester through inaction
Effect on Society	Strengthens institutions, relationships and cultures	Allows decay, dysfunction, and meaninglessness to spread

Table 29 – Active Responsibility Versus Passive Neglect.

Stewardship

Stewardship is the active, intentional and responsible care for something beyond oneself – be it a community, an organisation, the environment, or even one's own growth. It is the conscious commitment to nurture, guide and preserve resources, relationships and values for both present and future wellbeing.

A steward does not merely hold authority or ownership; they act with diligence, foresight and a sense of duty. Whether in leadership, business or personal relationships, stewardship means taking responsibility for one's impact rather than operating from short-term self-interest.

When stewardship is present, people take ownership of their actions, consider long-term consequences and foster environments where others can thrive. Stewardship is a mindset that transcends mere responsibility. It is an ethical commitment to sustainability, integrity and higher purpose.

A great leader doesn't just manage a team. They cultivate an environment where others grow, where decisions align with collective wellbeing, and where values remain intact, even in adversity. A mentor doesn't just teach. They invest in the flourishing of others, ensuring knowledge and wisdom endure. A parent who embodies stewardship doesn't simply raise a child. They nurture character, resilience and a sense of responsibility for life itself.

How stewardship can manifest and the causal forces that generate it

Stewardship can manifest as responsible leadership (decisions that benefit others and the future), sustainability (ensuring long-term viability over short-term exploitation), guardianship (protecting values, culture and knowledge) and nurturing growth (fostering development in people, systems and ideas).

It typically arises when **trust** and **Being** (Integrity Sphere) are strong, grounded in responsibility, and when **patience** and **adaptability** (Modulation Sphere) are active, enabling long-term vision. Stewardship is sustained when the ramifications of an unhealthy relationship with the **Disintegration Sphere's** causal forces are minimised, preventing selfishness, negligence or disregard for impact.

Stewardship in action: The leader who invests in people

Emma, the CEO of a major company, is presented with the chance to cut costs by outsourcing jobs overseas. The move would boost short-term profits, but displace hundreds of employees and corrode the company's culture. Instead of taking the easy option, Emma invests in staff upskilling to improve efficiencies and balances financial health with ethical responsibility.

Years later, her company continues to thrive, not just in profit, but in loyalty, innovation and stability. By acting as a steward, Emma created lasting value that outlived immediate pressures. This is stewardship in action – responsibility held as an ethical commitment, sustaining growth now and in the future.

Apathy

At its core, apathy is the absence of care, concern or responsibility. It is not merely inaction, but the refusal to engage meaningfully with one's responsibilities, environment or the wellbeing of others. Apathy manifests as neglect, indifference and passive disengagement from anything beyond immediate self-interest.

An apathetic leader does not just lack vision. They ignore the needs of those they lead. An apathetic parent does not just fail to teach. They allow a child to drift unguided. An apathetic citizen does not just avoid action. They enable dysfunction to spread through detachment.

Unlike active destruction, apathy operates in the shadows. It is not an external force of harm, but the silent collapse of responsibility that allows problems to fester, relationships to wither and societies to decay.

How apathy can manifest and the causal forces that generate it

Apathy can manifest as neglect (ignoring responsibilities), indifference (lack of concern for others or the future), passivity (avoiding action even when needed) and detachment (withdrawing from meaning or relationships).

It arises when **trust** and **Being** (Integrity Sphere) are weakened, producing disengagement; when **patience** and **adaptability**

(Modulation Sphere) are absent, preventing meaningful participation; and when **shadows, misery, suffering** and **entrenchment** (Disintegration Sphere) dominate, reinforcing avoidance, cynicism and self-interest.

Apathy in action: The negligent executive

Mark, the head of a once-thriving not-for-profit, gradually loses interest in its mission. He focuses only on maintaining his salary and public image, stops investing in staff, ignores inefficiencies and neglects donor relationships.

The signs of apathy begin subtly – morale declines, community trust fades and opportunities slip through the cracks. But as the years pass, the organisation loses relevance and eventually collapses – not because of external pressures, but because its leader stopped caring.

This is apathy in action: not deliberate harm, but the slow corrosion of meaning through disengagement.

Attunement versus neglect

Attunement and neglect describe two divergent ways of relating to reality. Attunement is the capacity to stay present, responsive and engaged with what matters, perceiving subtle shifts before they escalate. In contrast, neglect is the failure to notice or respond, allowing signals to be overlooked until misalignment and deterioration set in. One sustains coherence through perceptiveness and care; the other fragments it through avoidance and indifference.

Attunement

At its core, attunement is the deep alignment with truth, existence and systemic reality. It is not passive awareness, but an ongoing process of refinement – staying responsive to changes, discerning what is significant and engaging meaningfully with life's unfolding dynamics.

How attunement can manifest and the causal forces that generate it

In practice, attunement can manifest as existential alignment (moving in harmony with systemic reality), perceptiveness (seeing beyond the immediate surface), relational presence (deep engagement in interactions) and refinement (continuously adjusting to maintain coherence).

Attunement arises when **Being** and **trust** (Integrity Sphere) are intact, anchoring sincerity and depth of perception. It is refined by **tolerance** and **surrender** (Modulation Sphere), which allow responsiveness to changing conditions without rigidity. It also depends on the Architectonic Sphere: **meta-awareness** enables perception beyond narrow bias; **systemic integrity** aligns choices with the broader whole; **sustained effectiveness** ensures responsiveness is durable over time; and **normativity** directs attunement toward meaningful and ethical engagement. Together, these forces cultivate sensitivity and presence.

Our existential moods – care, fear, anxiety and vulnerability – also shape attunement.[85] Care is its core enabler. Without care, attunement collapses into indifference. Fear, when engaged reflectively, sharpens discernment. However, when fear is distorted, it drives avoidance. Vulnerability, when embraced, deepens relational connection. But when vulnerability is rejected, it breeds defensiveness. Anxiety, when managed, keeps us adaptable. However, when anxiety is left unchecked, it produces paralysis or hyper-reactivity. How we engage with these existential moods determines whether attunement is strengthened or suppressed.

Attunement in action: The teacher who listens beyond words

Mrs Nguyen, a primary school teacher in Sydney, has developed a sensitivity to her students' unspoken emotions. One morning, she notices that Mia, a usually engaged student, is withdrawn and struggling to concentrate. Others might dismiss it as a bad day, but Mrs Nguyen perceives something deeper.

---

85 Human beings possess many moods or emotions. However, the Being Framework incorporates just four – care, fear, anxiety and vulnerability – that are profoundly connected to the way we participate in life, individually and collectively, from the perspective of performance, influence and fulfilment.

Rather than ignoring the signs, she adjusts her approach – checking in gently with Mia, offering encouragement and easing classroom pressure. A week later, Mia opens up – her parents are separating, and she has been struggling with their decision. Because her teacher noticed early and responded with care, Mia was supported before her difficulties escalated.

This is attunement in action. It is not about reacting to every fluctuation, but about staying engaged, perceptive and responsive to reality's signals before they become crises.

Neglect

At its core, neglect is the failure to remain attuned. It is not merely inaction, but a breakdown in responsiveness, where signals from reality are ignored until they escalate into dysfunction. Neglect allows alignment to deteriorate by dismissing, avoiding or misinterpreting what matters.

How neglect can manifest and the causal forces that generate it

In practice, neglect can manifest as disconnection (loss of sensitivity to reality and relationships), ignorance (failure to perceive critical changes), avoidance (refusing necessary refinement) and deterioration (progressive decline due to inaction).

Neglect arises when **Being** and **trust** (Integrity Sphere) are weakened, creating detachment and insincerity. The absence of **tolerance** and **surrender** (Modulation Sphere) prevents responsiveness, and **shadows, misery, suffering** and **entrenchment** (Disintegration Sphere) dominate, reinforcing avoidance or denial. It is also worsened when there is an unhealthy relationship with any or all of the Architectonic Sphere's casual forces. Without **meta-awareness**, signals are missed; without **systemic integrity**, warning signs are disconnected from the whole; without **sustained effectiveness**, engagement fades over time; and without **normativity**, responsibility is replaced by convenience.

Neglect in action: The government that ignored the warning signs

In the early 2000s, the United States showed clear economic warning signs – housing prices were rising at unsustainable rates, household and corporate debt levels were surging, and major financial institutions were becoming dangerously over-leveraged. A few economists and analysts cautioned that a housing bubble was forming and that a severe downturn was inevitable if nothing changed.[86] Yet policymakers and regulators largely dismissed these warnings. Confident that markets would self-correct, they resisted tighter oversight and allowed excessive risk-taking to continue in the name of short-term growth.

By 2007–2008, it was too late – the housing bubble burst, subprime mortgage defaults skyrocketed, and the collapse of Lehman Brothers triggered a global financial crisis. Unemployment surged, millions lost their homes, and the US entered its deepest recession since the Great Depression.

This was neglect in action. The warning signs were visible, but they were ignored. Neglect does not always look destructive at first – it often masquerades as stability or optimism – but its long-term effects are corrosive.

Prevailing versus succumbing

Prevailing and succumbing represent two divergent responses to adversity and limitation. To prevail is to stay engaged through hardship, finding strength within the struggle rather than being defeated by it. In contrast, to succumb is to collapse into fear, doubt or resignation, allowing challenges to define one's reality. One holds steady and grows through difficulty; the other yields to it.

Prevailing

At its core, prevailing is the capacity to endure challenge without losing direction or purpose. It is not simply persistence or endurance,

---

[86] Shiller, Robert J. *Irrational Exuberance*, 2nd ed., Princeton University Press, 2005. Roubini, Nouriel, and Mihm, Stephen. *Crisis Economics: A Crash Course in the Future of Finance*, Penguin, 2010.

but the conscious choice to remain strong within adversity – to keep moving, learning and rebuilding even when progress feels slow or uncertain. Where endurance withstands hardship, prevailing works *through* it, transforming the experience itself into depth and resilience.

How prevailing can manifest and the causal forces that generate it

Prevailing can manifest as resilience (sustaining effort through difficulty), recovery (restoring strength after setbacks), learning (drawing wisdom from hardship) and grounded growth (becoming stronger through integration rather than resistance).

It arises when **intention** and **sovereignty** (Integrity Sphere) are strong, providing clarity, direction and agency. It depends on **patience** and **adaptability** (Modulation Sphere), which allow hardship to be absorbed and integrated rather than avoided. It also draws on the Architectonic Sphere: **meta-awareness** offers perspective within the struggle; **systemic integrity** ensures growth aligns with coherence; **sustained effectiveness** maintains steadiness through uncertainty; and **normativity** anchors perseverance in values rather than ego or impulse.

Prevailing in action: The survivor who transformed suffering into purpose

Layla, a survivor of childhood abuse, lived for years under the weight of trauma, convinced she could never escape its grip. Attempts to bury the pain only deepened the cycle, leaving her trapped in self-doubt and repetition.

One day, she decided that her past would no longer dictate her future. Through therapy, reflection and resilience, she slowly rebuilt her life. As she healed, she realised her suffering had given her an empathy and insight that could serve others. She trained as a trauma counsellor, helping other people navigate the very struggles she had endured.

This is prevailing in action. Layla did not erase her past – she learned to live with it, finding strength within what once confined her.

Prevailing is not about rising above hardship; it is about enduring through it, allowing the struggle itself to become a source of wisdom and purpose.

Succumbing

Succumbing is the failure to move beyond dysfunction, resulting in resignation, stagnation or self-imposed limitation. It is not a conscious act of letting go, like surrender, but a passive collapse into defeatism. Succumbing shrinks possibility by accepting limitation as inevitable.

How succumbing can manifest and the causal forces that generate it

Succumbing can manifest as resignation (accepting limitation as unchangeable), defeatism (internalising failure), passive compliance (adapting to dysfunction instead of resisting it) and entrapment (remaining stuck in limiting beliefs or circumstances).

Succumbing arises when **intention** and **sovereignty** (Integrity Sphere) are weak, eroding agency and direction. Without **patience** and **adaptability** (Modulation Sphere), challenges appear overwhelming and change feels impossible. **Shadows, misery, suffering** and **entrenchment** (Disintegration Sphere) dominate, reinforcing avoidance, fear and self-doubt. And without the balancing role of the Architectonic Sphere's causal forces – **meta-awareness, systemic integrity, sustained effectiveness** and **normativity** – possibility narrows until collapse becomes inevitable.

Succumbing in action: The artist who never shared their work

Daniel had painted since childhood, pouring his emotions onto canvas, revealing a rare talent. Yet whenever an opportunity arose to share his work, fear intervened. What if people didn't like it? What if he wasn't good enough?

Each time he was invited to display his art, he found excuses to decline. He told himself he wasn't ready. Friends encouraged him, but his self-doubt won. Over the years, his passion remained hidden and his dream faded – not because he lacked talent, but because he succumbed to fear.

This is succumbing in action. It does not always appear dramatic. It can be the small decisions, avoidances and hesitations that accumulate until they define a person's reality. Succumbing limits possibility until what could have been is abandoned.

Conclusion

The emergent forces explored in this chapter – renewal and decay, humility and hubris, fortitude and capitulation, wisdom and delusion, resonance and disconnection, transcendence and stagnation, stewardship and apathy, attunement and neglect, and prevailing and succumbing – are not an exhaustive list. They are illustrative examples of the existential patterns that can arise when we engage – or fail to engage – with the UOSI's causal forces.

By recognising these emergent forces, we gain more than descriptive insight – we gain a lens for intervention. For individuals, it offers the possibility of self-awareness and transformation. For organisations and institutions, it reveals how culture, leadership and structures shape resilience or decline. For societies, it highlights the existential stakes of our collective choices.

These patterns do not emerge in isolation. They flow directly from our relationship with the causal forces of the Integrity, Modulation, Disintegration and Architectonic spheres. When integrity – including our relationship with Being – and modulation are strong, disintegration is navigated wisely, architectonic awareness sustains long-term coherence and constructive patterns take shape. However, when the health of our relationship with these causal forces deteriorates, destructive patterns take hold.

What we see in individuals, organisations, institutions and societies is not random. It is the living consequence of how causal forces are engaged or ignored, metabolised or resisted. A leader's humility or hubris, a community's renewal or decay, a society's stewardship or apathy – all of these are systemic consequences, revealing whether coherence is being cultivated or undermined.

Ultimately, systemic integrity is never static. It is a dynamic field in which causal forces give rise to emergent qualities that either sustain coherence or accelerate fragmentation. By engaging with these forces consciously, we create the conditions for renewal, humility, fortitude, wisdom, resonance, transcendence, stewardship, attunement and prevailing to flourish – not as ideals, but as lived realities.

Recognising emergent forces is not the final step, but the beginning of deeper engagement. To see patterns of renewal, decay, humility or hubris is to glimpse the living consequences of causal forces at work. The next challenge is to move beyond recognition into application – to analyse systems through these lenses, interpret what they reveal and translate insight into intention. It is here that the discourse of authentic sustainability becomes more practical, moving from understanding the architecture of coherence and dysfunction to applying it as a lens for diagnosis, discernment and transformation.

CHAPTER 43

Analysing Systems through the UOSI

We have reached the point where understanding alone is no longer enough. Up to this point, you have traversed the Unified Ontology of Systemic Integrity (UOSI), explored its four spheres and unpacked the Anatomy, Mechanics and Topology of the UOSI's 16 causal forces. But knowing the map is not the same as walking the terrain. The question now is not what you know, but *how you will use it*.

As part of the broader Authentic Sustainability Framework (ASF), the UOSI serves as the analytical compass that guides this move from understanding to application. This is where the discourse shifts. Until this point, much of our work has been laying the foundations: defining integrity, exposing shadows and mapping the structures that sustain or corrode systems. From here, we move into the practical. How do we take these ontological models and use them to analyse the world around us, to make sense of what is unfolding, and to shape authentic sustainability? How do we turn insight into intention and intention into commitment? To do this, we must first clarify what we mean by analysis in this discourse.

What we mean by analysis

To practise authentic sustainability, we must learn to see with clarity. Analysis, in this discourse, is not mere data-crunching, detached observation or abstract theorising. It is part of the broader human process of tapping into our mental and intellectual faculties to make sense of the world – working alongside contemplation, reflection, comparison, discernment and, ultimately, conception development.

Most people stop short at perception. They notice and compare what they encounter, but often accept prevailing narratives or unexamined opinions as truth. The next step, in this discourse, is the disciplined movement from perception to conception – not just seeing, but forming a more structured, integrative and less distorted understanding of reality. This involves analytical, critical and systemic thinking working together to reveal how things fit and interact. It means refusing to take raw impressions or borrowed ideas at face value, and instead asking: *What does this mean, and how does it fit within a coherent whole?*

For example, when reading a political headline, perception stops at the actual words in the headline. However, conception asks: *What assumptions frame this statement? What values are hidden in the language? What systemic forces are at play?*

Let's explore the distinction between reception, perception and conception in more detail.

Reception, perception and conception

Reception is the intake of raw data and sensations. **Perception** then organises this material, identifying patterns and rendering it intelligible as information – structured data processed through our sensory faculties. Yet perception alone is not enough. The crucial step is conception: transforming information into structured understanding.

Conception shapes meaning, applies discernment and transforms raw impressions into knowledge and insight – the pathway that ultimately matures into wisdom. It calls us to engage not only with what is visible, but also with the deeper forces, paradigms and metacontent that shape perception itself. Without this step, we remain captive to surface impressions or recycled narratives.

This three-phase movement: reception → perception → conception, reflects the awareness stages of the Transformation Methodology within the Being Framework. Just as it enables individuals to become aware of and refine their own patterns of Being, it also applies here to the analysis of any content. In both cases, the shift from raw reception to structured conception is what allows genuine transformation to begin.

For example, imagine receiving a short, blunt email from a colleague.

- **Reception** is the raw intake: The words on the screen.
- **Perception** begins to organise it: *This seems abrupt. Maybe they're annoyed with me.*
- **Conception** asks deeper questions: *What context might shape this message? Are they under time pressure? Is my assumption about their tone reliable?* Conception reframes the impression, distinguishing between my projection and the actual systemic forces at play.

The same movement applies at a collective scale. Consider rising youth unemployment in a community.

- **Reception** notices the statistics: More young people are out of work.
- **Perception** connects surface patterns: Employers demand experience, schools fail to provide adequate pathways and families are stressed.
- **Conception** recognises deeper dynamics: Systemic misalignments in policy, cultural narratives about 'real work,' or economic structures that limit opportunity. The issue is reframed not as 'lazy youth', but as a structural gap between opportunity and support.

This is why the metacontent discourse and the Nested Theory of Sense-making[87] are central here. They remind us that what seems

---

[87] Tashvir, A. (2024) *Metacontent: The Intellectual Substrates for Sense-making.* Engenesis Publications, Sydney.

self-evident is often shaped by hidden layers – cognitive maps and narratives, mental models and paradigms, domains and contextual variables – that govern how we interpret reality. To analyse authentically, we must uncover these layers and refine our conceptions, moving closer to reality rather than deeper into distortion.

By moving from reception to perception to conception, we train ourselves to look beyond surface impressions and into the structural dynamics shaping reality. The same applies when analysing systems through the UOSI. Just as an email or a statistic only reveals part of the picture, so do policies, markets and governance systems. The UOSI provides the ontological compass that helps us ask: *What forces of architectonic alignment, integrity, modulation and disintegration are at play here?* It is through this lens that authentic analysis begins.

Why structured analysis matters for everyone

Structured analysis is not an exercise reserved for intellectuals, academics or policymakers. You do it daily, whether or not you are aware of it. Every time you interpret an email, navigate a relationship, make a financial decision or consider a media headline, you are receiving, perceiving and forming conceptions. You already filter reality through metacontent – your assumptions, beliefs and frameworks – even if you have never called it that.

Structured analysis is simply a way to make these processes visible, structured and communicable. By naming them, you gain the power to refine them. By leveraging structured ontologies, you can reduce distortion, avoid blind spots and communicate more effectively with others. This is not about complicating sense-making. It's about giving it clarity, coherence and integrity, despite its inherent complexity.

With this foundation in place, we can now turn to the UOSI itself – not just as a conceptual model to reference, but as a practical lens through which systems can be analysed and coherence discerned.

The UOSI as an analytical lens

As an analytical lens through which any system can be studied, the UOSI invites us to ask:

- Where is integrity present, and where is it absent?
- What forces of disintegration are at play and how are they manifesting?
- How is modulation – the capacity for intentional transition – being exercised or neglected?
- What shadows are shaping decisions, narratives and behaviours beneath the surface?

Consider a city that responds to flooding only by building higher levees. At first glance, this looks like resilience. But in reality, it manages symptoms while ignoring root causes such as deforestation, soil erosion and poor planning. The UOSI exposes this gap: integrity is missing in land management; modulation is absent in long-term adaptation; and shadows of short-term politics distort decision-making.

The same lens applies in everyday contexts. Imagine a workplace where staff turnover is high. Leaders may blame 'poor cultural fit', but deeper analysis reveals systemic cracks: integrity may be lacking if trust and sovereignty are not nurtured; modulation may be weak if feedback is dismissed rather than integrated; and shadows may be shaping leadership behaviour in ways that erode morale. What appears as an HR issue is in fact a structural misalignment of coherence.

Whether we are examining a global environmental crisis, a community initiative or a single act, like discarding a plastic bag into nature, the UOSI applies at every scale. Each action, policy and system can be assessed in terms of coherence, alignment and integrity. In this way, analysis moves us beyond slogans and surface solutions into meaningful engagement with reality.

From knowledge to discernment

One of the most dangerous illusions of our time is the belief that knowledge alone leads to transformation. We live in an age saturated with information, yet starved of discernment. People know about climate change, systemic inequality, corruption and ecological degradation, but knowledge by itself rarely shifts behaviour.

Why? Because knowledge without authentic awareness is senseless. It fails to generate meaning, it does not touch Being, and it cannot reach the depth where intention and commitment are formed.

This is why meta-awareness and metacontent are indispensable. Analysis is not simply about collecting facts, but about engaging with reality through refined sense-making – seeing through distortions and recognising the systemic forces at play. When you understand the layers of metacontent shaping a system, such as the narratives, paradigms and mental models embedded within it, you are no longer dealing with surface symptoms. You are engaging with the architecture of meaning itself.

For example, a government may 'know' that housing prices are rising unsustainably. Reports are published, data is shared and statistics circulate. But without discernment, responses remain shallow. They become subsidies that fuel demand or rhetoric that blames individuals for systemic failures. Discernment asks deeper questions: What paradigms about property ownership and wealth are driving this pattern? What systemic forces are shaping affordability, intergenerational equity and cultural values around housing? Knowledge identifies the problem; discernment reveals the architecture that sustains it.

Discernment begins here. It is the capacity to move beyond appearances and into the structural dynamics of a system – to distinguish signal from noise, coherence from performance and authentic sustainability from its performative shadow: sustainabilism.

From discernment to practice

Discernment alone is not enough. Seeing clearly does not automatically translate into acting coherently. The movement from awareness to application requires intention and design – a willingness to recalibrate behaviours, structures and relationships in light of what has been revealed. And to practise discernment *consistently*, we need more than goodwill. We need structure and orientation.

This is where the UOSI as the core of the ASF comes into its own. It is not just a theoretical model, but a practical compass. However, a compass does not give you a full map of the terrain. It does not describe the hills, rivers or roads. Instead, it orients you, helping you distinguish direction from confusion. Additionally, the UOSI does not prescribe scripts or ready-made solutions. Rather, it supports you to see systems as they are, revealing coherence and fragmentation, surfacing the forces of integrity, modulation and disintegration, and showing how architectonic alignment (or its absence) shapes outcomes.

By mapping the anatomy, mechanics and topology of causal forces, the UOSI equips us to identify leverage points and pathways for change. It supports us to distinguish between actions that merely soothe symptoms and those that address root causes.

Applied discernment means asking: How do we realign structures with integrity? How do we strengthen forces that sustain coherence while interrupting those that corrode it? How do we design interventions that endure rather than collapse under pressure?

When discernment informs practice, analysis stops being an intellectual exercise. Instead, it becomes a discipline of stewardship – a way of working with systems in service of renewal, adaptability and sustainability.

To appreciate why this approach matters, we can contrast the ASF – with the UOSI at its core – with some of the prevailing sustainability paradigms and see how it offers a fundamentally different orientation.

How the ASF differs from existing dominant paradigms

The field of sustainability is not short of paradigms. The UN's Sustainable Development Goals (SDGs), corporate Environmental, Social and Governance (ESG) frameworks and the Inner Development Goals (IDGs) all offer structured approaches. Each has value – as explained earlier in the book – but all share a limitation: they are scripted, prescriptive and behavioural. They set goals, demand metrics and encourage compliance.

In contrast, the ASF is regenerative and reconstructive. It does not prescribe behaviour in isolation. Instead, it reveals (through the

UOSI) the ontological structures that sustain or corrode systems. It does not only ask what targets should be met, but what should actually be sustained in the first place. It provides a lens for discernment, not just a checklist for compliance.

For example, a corporation might meet ESG targets, while its culture is riddled with fear and mistrust. Through the lens of the UOSI, the ASF would expose that incoherence, showing that long-term viability requires addressing integrity at the human and structural levels, not just metrics.

A family might install solar panels, recycle diligently and pride themselves on living sustainably at home. Yet the same family may also fly frequently for short holidays, overconsume fast fashion or make financial investments in industries that undermine ecological or social integrity. The ASF (again, though the lens of the UOSI) exposes these contradictions, showing that authentic sustainability is not about isolated gestures, but about coherence across choices, contexts and scales.

By adopting the ASF as a paradigm, with the UOSI at its centre, we are no longer navigating sustainability with slogans or borrowed maps. We are orienting ourselves with a compass that reveals direction in any context – personal or collective, micro or macro. Whether it is a government deciding climate policy, a company shaping culture or a family negotiating its values, the same ontological lens applies.

Seeing systems as they are – From everyday signals to system design

When the UOSI as the core ontological model within the ASF is applied to any system as a compass and an analytical lens – be it a human being or a collective – it does not impose an ideal. It reveals what is already there. It draws attention to the coherence of design in the **Architectonic Sphere**, to the presence or absence of **integrity**, to whether **modulation** is enabling healthy transition or entrenchment, and to the patterns of **disintegration** that erode stability.

These are not abstract questions. They surface in everyday life. A colleague who pauses in a meeting to ask whether the group is solving the right problem is exercising **meta-awareness**. A family that chooses financial coherence over convenience is practising **systemic integrity**. Fitness built on long-term habits reflects **sustained effectiveness**. Friends deciding not just where to travel, but what kind of experience they want together are living out **normativity**.

The same lens applies across scale. At the micro level, leaving rubbish in a park communicates that coherence is not our concern, while carrying it out signals accountability even in the smallest act. At the macro level, a government passing climate legislation faces the same inquiry. Are intentions aligned with integrity or distorted by short-term politics? Integrity, or its absence, is cumulative. Small acts of coherence add up to resilience; small acts of neglect compound into systemic fragility.

Conclusion: From observer to co-creator

To enter the domain of analysis is not merely to know more, but to see differently. It is to move from spectator to participant, from critic to co-creator. The UOSI is not just a model to study. As the backbone of the Authentic Sustainability Framework (ASF), it is a compass to orient by and a lens to analyse with. It also reminds us that sustainability is not a slogan or a scorecard, but a lived posture of coherence.

What this chapter has shown is that the same forces shaping nations and institutions also shape emails, meetings, household choices and personal decisions. When viewed through the lens of the UOSI, no act is trivial, no decision neutral. Each carries the possibility of reinforcing disintegration or cultivating integrity.

This is the essence of authentic sustainability. It does not ask us to *perform* sustainability but to *practise* it – to recognise coherence where it lives, to confront distortion where it festers, and to allow intention and meaning to guide our commitments. In this way, analysis becomes more than description. It becomes a way of inhabiting the world responsibly – and the first step in turning insight into intention.

CHAPTER 44

The Power of Meta-Awareness and Metacontent in Analysis

If the Authentic Sustainability Framework (ASF) is the map of the terrain, the Unified Ontology of Systemic Integrity (UOSI) is the compass that helps us navigate it and meta-awareness is the faculty that steadies the compass, ensuring it is read with clarity rather than distortion. Without that steadying hand, even a precise map will simply confirm what we already believe. This chapter keeps things practical. We will put the metacontent discourse and the Nested Theory of Sense-making[88] to work in the typical, everyday places where decisions are made – at home, in a meeting, in a policy debate, in a personal dilemma – so that analysis leads naturally into coherent meaning-making, then into clear intention and tangible commitment.

Why meta-awareness changes the analysis

You cannot analyse what you refuse to see. Most dysfunction hides behind distortion, not secrecy – comforting stories, familiar habits

---

88 Tashvir, A. (2024) *Metacontent: The Intellectual Substrates for Sense-making*. Engenesis Publications, Sydney.

and borrowed worldviews. Meta-awareness is the practice of stepping back from the 'what' to ask about the 'how': How am I seeing this? Through which stories, rules and paradigms am I seeing it? What is shaping my confidence or fear right now?

When you practise meta-awareness, you stop arguing only about the facts and start paying attention to the interpretive lens you are using to see them. For example, in an argument with a friend, the question shifts from 'Who is right?' to 'What standard are we using to decide what "right" even means?' That shift alone reduces reactivity and opens the door to more constructive conversation. The same shift applies in a team meeting. Instead of arguing over sales numbers, the deeper question is: 'What assumptions, perceptions, perspectives and narratives are shaping how we define success here?'

Metacontent – The filter for your sense-making

Everything you read, hear or notice passes through metacontent – the narratives, rules of thumb, cultural assumptions, fears and hopes you carry, plus the paradigms you inherited long before you chose them. Metacontent is not extra content. It is both the container that holds the architecture of your meaning-making and the filter that interprets what enters it.

Two people can read the same report and draw different conclusions. The report did not change; their metacontent shaped how they read it. You may have felt this yourself: you reach a long-awaited milestone, yet feel strangely flat. The content represents success, but the filter whispers that nothing is ever enough. Or you receive thoughtful feedback and react defensively. While the content is supportive, the filter interprets it as a threat. Meta-awareness is how you notice the metacontent shaping your view, choose to adjust it, and then see the situation afresh.

The Nested Theory of Sense-making – A usable map

Sense-making is a descent through seven filters. At any point, distortion can creep in. At the first sign of a skew, pause and recalibrate before proceeding.

1. **Initial insight** – Your first felt impression: a tone, a look, a quick judgement. Treat it as provisional. Name it and hold it lightly.
2. **Cognitive map** – What you take as obvious. What counts as success, safety or truth here? Write those categories down.
3. **Stories** – The narratives you attach to events. For example: *'Every time we slow down, we lose.'* or *'When I speak up, people leave.'* Recognise them as stories, not reality.
4. **Mental models** – The rules shaping your choices. For example: *'Keep the peace at all costs'* or *'Work harder to prove your worth.'* Identify the rules at play.
5. **Perspective** – The standpoint you are taking. Consider at least one other angle: customer, child, colleague, neighbour, partner or friend.
6. **Domain** – The arena you are in, such as science, law, culture or geopolitics. Notice where you are principled in one domain yet permissive in another. That inconsistency matters.
7. **Paradigm** – The deep logic shaping how you tackle issues within a domain: *'In our world, success means…'* Consider whether this underlying logic itself might be generating the problem.

Beneath every layer lies a silent but ever-present bedrock: **context**. As discussed earlier in the book, context is not another layer in the Nested Theory. It is the field in which all seven layers are activated, modulated, distorted or revealed. You might have the cleanest internal architecture, but drop yourself into a high-stress, emotionally charged, politically volatile or historically traumatic context, and everything skews. Context prompts you to consider:

- Are you speaking from exhaustion or clarity?
- Are you defending, performing or genuinely responding?
- Are you at a family gathering or in a negotiation?
- Are you reacting from inherited pain or relational attunement?

Within milliseconds, context decides which stories flare up, which mental models hijack the moment, and which perspectives become inaccessible.

To make context more workable, we break it down into **contextual variables** – tangible dimensions like time, culture, environment, history, stress levels, positionality or intersubjective dynamics. These variables don't belong to just one layer – they interact with all seven, sometimes amplifying distortions, sometimes enabling clarity.

You don't fix this with slogans. You don't patch it with 'better language'. You remap the architecture – and learn to see context as a living field to be navigated, not ignored.

Real-world examples

The following tangible examples show how metacontent and meta-awareness work together in the analysis of common matters. By noticing the filters at play – the stories, cognitive maps, mental models, perspectives, domains and paradigms – and by paying attention to the contextual variables shaping each layer, you can then see how clarity emerges and choices shift.

Personal – The conversation you keep postponing

- **Initial insight**: A felt impression arises instantly – peppered by tension, apprehension, and condensed into the belief, 'They'll take it badly.'
- **Cognitive map**: A structural association such as 'conflict = danger' sits within a broader cognitive map of what constitutes safety and success in relationships. Other connected nodes in the map might include 'agreement = security', 'silence = harmony' or 'criticism = rejection'.

    Example: Silence is instinctively chosen because the cognitive map codes disagreement as unsafe terrain.

- **Story**: A recurring narrative threads past experiences into a predictive pattern: 'Every time I speak up, people leave.'

> *Example*: A past breakup following an argument reinforces the storyline, making it appear universal.

- **Mental model**: An operating procedure such as 'Keep the peace at all costs' governs conduct. This is not merely a belief, but a replicable process. Conflict is avoided by changing the subject, suppressing emotion or yielding prematurely. These rituals maintain the rule.
- **Perspective**: The prevailing standpoint is self-protection – 'How do I avoid rejection?' An alternative angle – the other person's standpoint – might be 'What would help me feel considered if I was in their place?' A shift in perspective alters what is visible or possible.
- **Domain**: The unfolding occurs within the domain of intimate relationships. What constitutes honesty, care or respect here diverges from how those values are enacted in other domains such as law, science or politics.
- **Paradigm**: Within this relational domain, the guiding paradigm is harm-avoidance, due to a deep assumption that 'good relationships are conflict-free'. Just as scientific inquiry might operate under paradigms like positivism or constructivism, here the embedded logic defines what counts as 'healthy'.

Contextual variables: In this scenario, contextual variables play a decisive role. If the conversation is happening late at night after an exhausting day, fatigue itself becomes a variable distorting tone and patience. If it is shaped by family scripts where disagreement was punished, cultural narratives about obedience, or an environment of workplace politics, those variables subtly reinforce the story of 'conflict equals damage'. Even the relational history with the other person – whether trust has been eroded before, or whether sovereignty has been respected – tilts how each layer plays out. Noticing these contextual variables makes clear that the difficulty is not only in the content of the conversation but in the field in which it unfolds.

Meta-awareness makes the shift possible. Instead of being trapped by the story or the rule, you notice them as filters and ask what value is really at stake.

Seen through the **UOSI**: integrity is thin on sovereignty and trust; disintegration shows as avoidance; modulation calls for patience; and architectonic normativity asks for truth with care.

- **Meaning:** 'This matters because the relationship deserves respect, not performance.'
- **Intention:** 'I will tell the truth kindly.'
- **Commitment:** Schedule the conversation; open with shared intent; ask for their view; and agree on one small next step.

Team – Quality vs speed

- **Initial insight**: When project milestones fall behind schedule, a gut-level impression surfaces in the team – 'We are too slow'.
- **Cognitive map**: A structural node such as 'market share = value' sits within a broader organisational cognitive map of what counts as success. Other nodes might include 'revenue = success', 'visibility = credibility' or 'speed = competitiveness'.

  Example: The team may prioritise pushing out a new app feature in two weeks, even if the testing is incomplete, because the cognitive map codes speed as survival.

- **Story**: A narrative strings past events into a predictive caution: 'Last time we slowed down, we lost.'

  Example: A competitor's feature launch is remembered as decisive proof that delays equal failure, whether or not that was the actual cause.

- **Mental model**: The operating rule 'Work harder to prove your worth' shows up in rituals – late nights, shortcuts in testing and praise for speed over stability. These habits reproduce the model.
- **Perspective**: The prevailing angle is the executive/market lens – 'How fast can we look in front of customers and shareholders?' Alternative standpoints include the support team's lens ('What is the cost of rework?'), the customer's lens ('Does trust erode when quality slips?') or finance's lens ('How much churn offsets the gains of speed?').

- **Domain**: The situation unfolds in the domain of organisational performance and commerce, where norms of strategy and competition define the field.
- **Paradigm**: The guiding paradigm is speed-as-virtue – faster always equals better. Within this worldview, durability and trust become secondary concerns. Speed is the unquestioned metric of legitimacy.

Contextual variables intensify the tension. A looming product launch date or investor pressure amplifies urgency for speed. Past traumas, like a failed release that cost market share, reinforce the story that 'slowness equals loss'. Cultural signals – whether collaboration is rewarded or only flashy results count – distort what feels acceptable.

Viewed in this light, the struggle is not simply about speed versus quality, but about the assumptions shaping how value is defined.

Meta-awareness interrupts the automatic push for speed, surfacing the assumptions that frame 'value' and opening space to ask what durability might mean.

Seen through the **UOSI**: intention is fuzzy; suffering is visible in support; adaptability is required; and sustained effectiveness matters more than headline metrics.

- **Meaning:** 'We want speed without sacrificing durability.'
- **Intention:** Define 'durable' with the same clarity we use for 'done'.
- **Commitment:** Include a clear definition of durable in the next two sprints,[89] track churn and rework at the end.

Policy – Littering and community norms

- **Initial insight**: 'People don't care'. A snap impression is formed when seeing rubbish on the streets, overflowing bins or repeated complaints.

---

[89] In agile methodology, a sprint is a short, fixed period of time – usually between one and four weeks – during which a team focuses on completing a specific set of tasks or goals. Each sprint ends with a review to assess progress and plan the next cycle.

- **Cognitive map**: A node like 'fines fix behaviour' sits inside a wider perception map of governance. Other nodes include 'enforcement = responsibility', 'public order = control' and 'citizens only respond to penalties'.

    Example: The policy mindset treats regulation as the primary driver of civic order, leaving education, culture or stewardship outside the mental map.

- **Story**: 'Education never works' is a narrative often recycled in debates, citing previous failed campaigns (e.g., posters, school talks) as evidence that people only change when forced.

    Example: Officials tell the story of 'we tried that before' to dismiss new community-based proposals.

- **Mental model**: The operational rule: 'Punish to deter' shows up in routines like designing ever-higher fines, sending inspectors on patrols and measuring 'success' by the number of tickets issued. It is a procedural loop: misconduct → penalty → assumed compliance.

- **Perspective**: The current lens is **the regulator's point of view,** seeing behaviour as a compliance issue. Other perspectives include:

    - **Residents**: Litter signals neglect and erodes pride.
    - **Shop owners**: Cleanliness attracts customers.
    - **Students**: Rules may feel arbitrary unless tied to shared meaning.
    - **Council workers**: Enforcement drains resources unless complemented by stewardship.

- **Domain**: This sits within the domain of governance and public policy, where tools include regulation, enforcement and civic design.

- **Paradigm**: The guiding paradigm within this domain is 'compliance-as-cleanliness' – the deep logic that order emerges when people are forced into correct behaviour. Within this paradigm, stewardship and community pride are treated as optional extras, not systemic necessities.

Here, **contextual variables** frame whether littering is seen as apathy or as a symptom of deeper systemic conditions. Economic pressures, such as underfunded councils or overstretched waste services, shift the feasibility of upkeep. Historical patterns of community disengagement – for example, decades of 'top-down' rules with little resident input – feed the story that 'people don't care'. Cultural variables matter too. If pride in public spaces has never been embedded in collective identity, compliance becomes the only visible lever. Environmental factors like the availability of bins, frequency of collection and visibility of public areas all modulate behaviour. Intersubjective influences, such as peer norms or the example set by local leaders, can either entrench neglect or spark stewardship. Surfacing these contextual variables reframes the issue from merely fining offenders to cultivating a culture where dignity and shared pride naturally reduce litter.

Meta-awareness reframes the issue. It highlights the filters of deterrence and compliance, making it possible to notice where stewardship and shared pride might restore coherence.

Seen through the **UOSI**: integrity calls for stewardship; disintegration shows apathy; modulation points to small adaptive pilots; and architectonic normativity highlights shared pride.

- **Meaning:** 'We want dignity, not only deterrence.'
- **Intention:** Make cleanliness a shared identity.
- **Commitment:** Pair modest fines with visible stewardship – weekly volunteer crews, student art on bins, shopfront recognition – and publish a simple monthly litter trend.

Applying the analysis process – A step-by-step guide

You don't need a rigid checklist to apply the seven filters alongside the UOSI and meta-awareness scan. A simple reflective flow is often enough. Most people can do this within 10 minutes once a week to see meaningful shifts.

As you move through the steps, remember: **contextual variables** – era, culture, environment, subjective bias and intersubjective factors – always shape what each filter reveals at each layer.

1. **Initial insight** – Capture your first impression in plain words. What instinctive signal surfaced? What else could it mean?
2. **Cognitive map** – Notice the associations at play. Which hidden codes (e.g. *conflict = danger, speed = survival*) are steering your navigation?
3. **Story** – Identify the storyline you are telling. Recognise it as narrative, not reality. Ask: what past events are being strung together to predict the future?
4. **Mental model** – Surface the operating rule in force (*e.g. keep the peace at all costs*). What habits or rituals sustain it? Does it still serve coherence?
5. **Perspective** – Step into one other standpoint and describe the situation from that view. What possibilities appear from this angle?
6. **Domain** – Name the domain in which this is unfolding (e.g. intimate relationships, commerce, politics). How does this domain shape what counts as valid or valuable?
7. **Paradigm** – Articulate the paradigm within the domain and question its logic and hold (e.g. *good relationships are conflict-free, faster equals better*).

UOSI scan – Ask yourself:
- What strengthens integrity here?
- Where is disintegration showing?
- What small modulation could restore alignment?
- Which architectonic forces – meta-awareness, systemic integrity, sustained effectiveness, normativity – should steer my next move?

Shadow–reality gap – Capture the gap in one line: 'We say X, we do Y, the impact is Z.'

Next step – Name the smallest coherence move you can take in the next seven days.

Keep a single page – paper or digital – with these headings. Write short, honest responses. Make this a weekly habit and over time you'll see the difference.

Analysis Reflection Template

Initial insight

_____

Cognitive map

_____

Story

_____

Mental model

_____

Perspective

_____

Domain

_____

Paradigm

UOSI scan

- Integrity: _____
- Disintegration: _____
- Modulation: _____
- Architectonic (meta-awareness, systemic integrity, sustained effectiveness, normativity): _____

Shadow–reality gap

We say _____, we do _____, the impact is _____.'

Next step (within 7 days)

_____

_____

Working with meta-awareness and metacontent in practice

To reiterate, meta-awareness is the practice of stepping back from the 'what' to ask about the 'how': How am I seeing this? Through which stories, rules and paradigms am I seeing it? What is shaping my confidence or fear right now? When you practise meta-awareness, you stop arguing only about the facts and start paying attention to the lens you are using to see them.

Metacontent is the substance of that lens: the narratives, rules, assumptions and paradigms that filter every piece of content you encounter. Together, they form the ground on which clear analysis stands.

Red flags to watch for

Certain patterns reveal themselves when your metacontent is driving you rather than you directing it. Examples include:

- Speaking faster when you have less clarity.
- Feeling morally certain on thin facts.
- Using 'always' and 'never' more than you ask, 'What else could be true?'
- Calling cynicism realism.

These are signals to pause, step back and check the lens and filters.

Naming shadows without blame

Blame shuts people down; clarity invites them in. Use meta-awareness to surface distortions without hostility. A simple, respectful sentence can re-open conversations that felt impossible:

> 'We say we value X, yet we are doing Y. The impact is Z.
> A small change that moves us toward X is ….'

Conclusion

This chapter has shown that analysis is never neutral. It is always filtered through metacontent and anchored by the practice of meta-awareness. By stepping back from the *what* to ask about the *how*, and by recognising the stories, rules and paradigms that shape your seeing, you gain access to a clearer lens. In this way, analysis becomes more than a reading of facts; it becomes a practice of orientation.

The power of meta-awareness and metacontent is that they move analysis beyond reactivity – whether in your own reading of content or in an exchange with others – into a coherent practice of sense-making. In the chapters ahead, we will build on this foundation to show how clarity moves beyond analysis into meaning, intention and committed action. But first, let's examine what happens when this process is disrupted.

CHAPTER 45

Applying the SSC to Diagnose Systemic Dysfunction

In the previous chapter, we explored how meta-awareness and metacontent shape analysis, showing that clarity depends as much on the lens as on the facts. But what happens when that process is disrupted – when filters harden into distortions, when analysis collapses into entrenchment, and when systems drift toward incoherence?

Every crisis provides the answer. A shock does not invent dysfunction; it exposes it. It reveals the fractures we preferred not to see, the distortions we tolerated or the fragility of structures we thought were strong. You first encountered the Systemic Subversion Cycle (SSC) earlier in this book as one of the models within the ASF and as a diagnostic tool. It provides a way of revealing how systems slide into dysfunction, entrenchment and eventual collapse, and why timely intervention is vital to avoid irreversible breakdown. In that section, we outlined the theory of how systems can undermine themselves from within, rewarding corrosive practices until collapse becomes inevitable. In this chapter, we apply the sharpened lens of meta-awareness, metacontent and the UOSI to the SSC, shifting from theory to practice.

In everyday language, subversion is often associated with politics, espionage or rebellion. But in this book, it refers to something more subtle – a process through which a system undermines itself from within. Subversion takes hold when shadows harden into norms, corrosive practices are rewarded and those that preserve coherence are sidelined. It is rarely dramatic. More often, it is subtle, even ordinary – a policy justified without confirming alignment, a culture of avoidance that calcifies, a performance of sustainability that masks deeper erosion. In this sense, subversion is less about dramatic upheaval and more about the gradual erosion of integrity until collapse becomes inevitable.

Phases of systemic subversion

The SSC shows how crises are not only endured, but often manufactured, exploited and perpetuated within failing systems. It maps the recurrent pattern: a shock destabilises the system; structures begin to give way; fractures widen; opportunists consolidate advantage; and institutional inertia prevents resolution. Left unchecked, the dysfunction becomes part of the architecture, fuelling the next instability.

The value of the SSC lies in its clarity. It enables us to recognise the cycle early and take steps to break it before collapse becomes the norm.

Systemic subversion typically unfolds in seven distinct phases:

1. **Shock** – A destabilising event jolts the system.
2. **Unravelling** – If foundations are weak, structures give way – trust erodes, clarity and meaning blur.
3. **Scramble** – People scramble to respond, often in fragmented or reactive ways. Resources – money, time, goodwill and attention – feel scarce and are stretched thin.
4. **Polarisation** – Scarcity breeds tension and divisions calcify. We either turn on one another or turn away.
5. **Exploitation** – Opportunists take advantage of the situation. Their moves are often disguised as safety, stability or efficiency.

6. **Inertia** – Institutions settle into patterns of activity, but achieve little. Committees form, documents multiply, everyone is busy, yet real progress slips further out of reach.
7. **Echo** – The unresolved wound becomes part of the architecture. Consequently, the next shock reactivates the same pattern. And so the cycle continues unless deliberately analysed through the UOSI.

When a system repeats the same unresolved patterns over time, these echoes deepen into cycles of entrenchment. Entrenchment occurs when dysfunction becomes self-reinforcing – when the pain or instability generated by one cycle hardens into norms, expectations and defensive routines that sustain the next. The system no longer merely experiences crisis; it identifies with it. At this point, collapse is not triggered by external shocks, but by the weight of accumulated, unexamined patterns. Recognising these cycles of entrenchment is essential, because they reveal where the subversion of coherence has become habitual rather than situational.

Seen through the lens of the UOSI, this cycle is not random. The Disintegration Sphere surfaces first in shadows, misery, suffering and entrenchment. The Integrity Sphere is tested – intention, trust, sovereignty and Being either hold or collapse. The Modulation Sphere acts as the pivot point. Patience, tolerance, adaptability and surrender either guide transition or give way to reactivity. And the Architectonic Sphere determines durability – meta-awareness, systemic integrity, sustained effectiveness and normativity either orchestrate renewal or drift.

Using the UOSI to break the cycle

Where the SSC describes what typically unfolds under stress, the UOSI shows you how to see it and where to act. Each sphere offers a distinct vantage point on the cycle and reveals different leverage points for intervention to restore coherence. When applied together, they expose not only the progression of dysfunction, but the deeper cycles of entrenchment that make breakdown self-sustaining – and, crucially, how to reverse them.

- **Integrity Sphere** – Reveals whether intention, trust, sovereignty and Being hold or fracture. When integrity is thin, shocks cut deeper and recovery falters.
- **Disintegration Sphere** – Exposes the shadows, misery, suffering and entrenchment that surface when dysfunction is normalised. These are the first signals that the cycle has been activated.
- **Modulation Sphere** – Reveals whether transitions are adaptive or reactive. Patience, tolerance, adaptability and surrender either stabilise movement or give way to panic and polarisation.
- **Architectonic Sphere** – Reveals durability. Meta-awareness, systemic integrity, sustained effectiveness and normativity either orchestrate renewal or allow the system to drift into deeper collapse.

Together with meta-awareness and metacontent, the UOSI makes distortions visible, pinpoints where the breakdown is occurring and clarifies what kind of intervention is needed.

Tangible examples

Whether in nations, organisations or households, the SSC unfolds in similar ways. The following examples show how the same seven-phase cycle surfaces across various scales, and how the UOSI lens reveals both the distortions and the points of intervention.

Public life – A health shock

A novel pathogen emerges.

- **Shock:** The trigger jolts the system into action when it exposes underfunded infrastructure and thin reserves of trust.
- **Unravelling:** Leaders rush to communicate but contradict one another; communities hear noise, not guidance.
- **Scramble:** Clinicians are stretched; supplies are scarce; and staff are exhausted.

- **Polarisation:** Tension grows and creates divisions – rural versus urban, science versus instinct and privacy versus safety.
- **Exploitation:** In the fog of confusion, some monetise scarcity while others weaponise fear to centralise control.
- **Inertia:** A flurry of inquiries follows, but little changes at the frontline.
- **Echo:** When a new variant appears, the system relives the earlier story because the dysfunction was never integrated.

Seen through the UOSI lens, the weak points and possible responses become clearer:

- **Meta-awareness** names the real failures directly, instead of letting noise and blame dominate.
- **Systemic integrity** ensures funding matches real capability rather than chasing headlines.
- **Sustained effectiveness** builds rhythm – regular readiness drills instead of one-off heroics.
- **Normativity** keeps dignity and fairness at the centre of decisions, so the most vulnerable are not forced to carry the greatest burden.

Organisational life – The scandal aftershock

A leadership breach is revealed.

- **Shock:** Confidence in the organisation is shaken.
- **Unravelling:** Rumours spread and good people go quiet.
- **Scramble:** Trust, money and patience feel scarce; customers notice the instability.
- **Polarisation:** Staff split into factions, while a small circle hoards information in the name of 'stability'.
- **Exploitation:** Power gathers in the hands of a few, while official statements hide the lack of real change.
- **Inertia:** Committees form and reports multiply, but little actually shifts.
- **Echo:** When another breach occurs months later, it shows the first was a symptom of underlying dysfunction, not a one-off.

Seen through the UOSI lens, the way forward is clearer:

- **Integrity** asks for a reset of intention and real consequences.
- **Modulation** prefers short, focused repair efforts over grand programs – for example, two weeks of open forums and a single trusted record of transparent decisions.
- **Systemic integrity** creates a small temporary team with clear authority and a set timeframe.

Everyday life – The household spiral

A surprise bill lands.

- **Shock:** Anxiety spikes.
- **Unravelling:** Discussions about household finances are rare, sleep suffers, avoidance rises and blame spreads.
- **Scramble:** Resources feel scarce and arguments flare up about who spends and who saves begin.
- **Polarisation:** One person hides a credit card, another withdraws.
- **Exploitation:** Quick-fix options start to look tempting.
- **Inertia:** a new spreadsheet appears, but real habits don't change.
- **Echo:** The next bill triggers the same argument because nothing was resolved.

The UOSI lens offers the possibility of a healthier path:

- **Meta-awareness** names the first reaction – 'I feel unsafe and want control over our finances' – which lowers the heat.
- **Systemic integrity** reaffirms a shared value – stability over material wealth and appearances – to keep choices centred.
- **Modulation** adds rhythm through a short weekly money check-in, replacing crisis talks.
- **Sustained effectiveness** builds stability by automating essentials, capping discretionary spending and reviewing progress monthly. The bill becomes part of a routine that can be managed, not a recurring crisis.

The same pattern of systemic subversion is visible across all three examples. While the context and details differ, the phases remain consistent: shock, unravelling, scramble, polarisation, exploitation, inertia and echo. What the UOSI lens makes clear is that this cycle is not inevitable. By surfacing distortions, naming values and restoring a sense of coherence, the pattern can be interrupted before dysfunction becomes the norm.

How to diagnose and interrupt the cycle

When things start to feel unsettled, the instinct is often to respond with massive plans or sweeping fixes. This rarely works. Coherence is restored through small, visible actions that bring clarity and stability – whether in yourself, your relationships, at home, at work, in business or in your community. The steps below offer a practical way to diagnose where you sit in the Systemic Subversion Cycle (SSC) and empower you to respond constructively:

1. **Identify the phase** – Ask where you are in the cycle. Is this the shock, the unravelling, the scramble, polarisation, exploitation, inertia or the echo? You don't need precision; orientation is enough.

2. **Surface the metacontent** – Bring hidden filters to the surface. What belief is shaping how this moment is read? For example: 'Speed proves we care', or 'If we admit error, we lose authority'. What story are you telling yourself? Have you tried another perspective? Once surfaced, the story begins to lose its hold.

3. **Scan with the UOSI** – In Integrity, ask which intention is truly driving you. In Disintegration, notice which shadow is loudest – fear, blame, secrecy or performance. In Modulation, choose one adjustment that reduces reactivity – a pause, a pilot, a boundary or a handover. In the Architectonic layer, decide which quality must lead – meta-awareness to slow, systemic integrity to realign, sustained effectiveness to build rhythm, or normativity to protect dignity in trade-offs.

4. **Expose exploitation** – When advantage is being taken, state what is happening in simple terms. For example: inflated

pricing; hoarding of information; or using safety as a pretext for control. Once named, it loses its grip.

5. **Take one small step** – Choose one action you can finish within seven days that signals a different future. It could be a plain-language factsheet that answers real questions, a short pilot with a review date, a brief forum with simple rules, or a 15-minute household check-in.

Interrupting the SSC is less about bold gestures and more about steady practices. The aim is not to overpower the crisis, but to build sustainable patterns that hold when the pressure returns.

Recognising and steadying the cycle

You often sense systemic subversion before you can prove it. Conversations grow shorter and less substantive. Absolutes – 'always', 'never' – replace nuance. Plans produce long documents but not outcomes. Temporary exceptions become the new policy. Metrics improve while lived experience worsens. People even apologise for telling the truth. When two or more of these signals appear, it's time to pause and use the diagnostic steps outlined in this chapter. The earlier you intervene, the more effective and timely and the less costly the correction.

When the wheel begins to slide, three anchors help restore balance:

- **Authentic awareness** means naming what is being avoided or disguised. For example: 'We are calling activity progress', or 'We are using safety to justify control.'
- **Ontological alignment** means restating the value at stake and the intention it demands, so actions reattach to meaning. For example: 'This change serves stewardship by…'
- **Intentional modulation** means breaking big goals into shorter timeframes, creating steady rhythm and removing the need for heroics.

Restoring coherence is rarely a single leap. It is built through a sequence of well-timed moves. To prevent overwhelm and avoidance, start with small, simple steps. Whenever pressure arises, write down the phase you are in, the story you are telling yourself, the shadow that is loudest, the architectonic quality that needs to lead, and one step you will complete within seven days. Then take the step, review in a week, adjust and repeat.

Conclusion

The Systemic Subversion Cycle (SSC) shows how easily systems under pressure can slide into dysfunction, exploitation and inertia. You have seen how its phases play out in public life, organisations and households, and how small, deliberate moves can restore coherence over time.

By applying the lens of meta-awareness, metacontent and the UOSI, the cycle becomes visible and interruptible. Crises need not dictate collapse. When distortions are noticed early, stories and values are named and action is anchored in meaning, renewal becomes possible.

Left unexamined, however, the same subversive patterns can deepen into cycles of entrenchment – self-reinforcing loops where dysfunction becomes normalised and renewal becomes harder to achieve. The work of diagnosis and timely intervention prevents this, transforming a crisis into an opportunity for reconstruction rather than repetition.

In the next chapter, we move from sense-making to meaning-making with Minalogy – a step closer to forming clear, coherent intention. Where analysis helps us see clearly, meaning offers direction, clarifies why it matters and prepares the ground for action through intention.

CHAPTER 46

Minalogy – From Sense-making to Meaning-making

You can read a situation with perfect clarity and still be paralysed. You can analyse shadows, track distortions and predict collapse, yet still nothing shifts. That is the limit of sense-making when it does not translate into meaning. Knowledge without meaning is like a map never unfolded – precise, but useless.

So far, we have focused on seeing – refining our lens through meta-awareness and the metacontent discourse, applying the UOSI to structure your analysis, and using the SSC to diagnose and interrupt dysfunction. Now it is time to translate seeing into significance by stepping into the realm of meaning-making. This is the work of turning what you know into what you stand for. From there, you can turn what you stand for into what you will actually do.

This chapter introduces Minalogy as a new philosophical discipline concerned with the discovery of meaning and meaning-making.[90] Minalogy asks not only *what is happening*, but *why it matters* and *what it calls for*. It is the conduit between observing and taking a

---

90 A comprehensive articulation of Minalogy, its ontological model, methodology and applications is the subject of a forthcoming book currently being written by this author.

stand, between knowing and taking action. It is where analysis gains weight, where facts become significant to you, and where the significance you attach to something begins to shape your intention.

Introducing Minalogy: The discipline of meaning beyond language

For centuries, the study of meaning has been trapped inside the walls of language. Philosophers, linguists and cultural theorists have asked: What does this word mean? How do symbols signify? How do texts and traditions shape our interpretations? Entire disciplines – semantics, linguistics, semiotics, hermeneutics and the philosophy of language – have been built on the assumption that meaning only arises when we put words to things.

Yet this assumption omits something vital. Meaning is not born of words. We encounter it before a single word is spoken: in the experience of love; the weight of responsibility and justice; the being of a tree; or the gaze of another human being. These are not linguistic artefacts. They are fragments of reality itself, lived truths that exist whether we name them or not. A child senses the meaning of care long before they can say the word 'care'. An entire civilisation can act on the meaning of justice without ever settling on a single definition.

This reveals a profound problem – the language-based traditions of meaning have collapsed what we might call *ontological meaning* (the lived reality) into *constructed meaning* (the interpretations we create). The result is conceptual confusion and disciplinary overload. Meaning is like a liquid. It exists, like water, yet human beings cannot drink it unless it is held within a container – and that container is language. This does not render language unimportant, but it places it in a secondary role to meaning itself. What has been missing is a clear way to distinguish between these dimensions, and to give the deepest layer of meaning its own place in inquiry.

This is where **Mina** comes in. *Mina* is the dimension of existence concerned with why and to what degree something matters. It can be understood as the integrated cluster of significance, purpose (*telos*) and value that orients our choices, actions and systems. It is not merely what something is, nor simply how it is understood, but *why* *it matters. Mina* is the axis upon which choices, actions and systems are oriented and animated, whether consciously or unconsciously.

Minalogy is the discipline concerned with the dimension of *Mina*. It studies how human beings encounter and ascribe significance, how these meanings shape intention and systemic coherence, and how they determine the trajectory of lives and civilisations. In this sense, Minalogy is not simply another branch of philosophy or linguistics. It is a new discipline that has been liberated from inherited assumptions, giving meaning its own seat at the table of knowledge. Just as psychology once broke away from philosophy and economics from moral theory, Minalogy stands as the radical recognition that meaning itself deserves independent study.

Why introduce a new word?

Words like meaning, purpose (*telos*), significance and value each capture part of what is needed, but none is sufficient on its own. Meaning is overloaded. Purpose is too narrow. Significance sounds statistical. Value has been reduced to economics or preference. Each offers a slice, but what is required is the cluster. *Mina* fills this gap.

The word *Mina* is drawn from the same root as 'meaning' and 'mind', evoking both measure and essence. It was chosen because a word was needed that had not been diluted or overloaded – a token still capable of carrying the depth and precision intended here. Like Heidegger's *Dasein* or Derrida's *Différance*, *Mina* names a category that ordinary language cannot capture cleanly.

Put simply:

Meaning holds two inseparable layers:

1. At its depth lies **Mina** – the existential significance, the raw *why it matters*.
2. On its surface lies **expression** – the way *Mina* is carried into words, symbols and shared understanding.

By distinguishing the depth of meaning (*Mina*) from its surface expressions, Minalogy provides a coherent structure for thinking about significance as its own domain. It links directly to human sense-making, decision-making and action, making it central not only to philosophy, but also to leadership, performance and the design of sustainable systems.

Whenever this dimension is ignored, sustainability fails. Programs optimise for metrics without meaning or compliance without conviction. They deliver activity, but not coherence. Authentic sustainability is different – it is *Mina*-led. It aligns systems with a clarified purpose and carries that purpose forward through deliberate choices and priorities, which then translate into meaningful actions and behaviours.

To hold this distinction with greater precision, we can turn to a linguistic taxonomy that situates *Mina* within the broader framework developed across this body of work.

A linguistic taxonomy

Language is never neutral. The words we use not only describe but also shape how we think, feel and experience existence. In this body of work, new terms have been introduced to fill conceptual gaps that ordinary English cannot bridge, creating a consistent vocabulary for distinguishing between what is, how it is understood, and why it matters.

Earlier, distinctions were drawn between **content** (everything that exists) and **metacontent** (the intellectual substrates needed to make sense of content). Now, as we enter the domain of purpose and significance, a further refinement is required – the recognition of *Mina* as a distinct layer of meaning.

To bring clarity and precision, the following linguistic taxonomy sets out how terms like *Mina*, Minalogy and Minalogical fit together. These are not arbitrary inventions, but necessary categories that make dimensions of existence otherwise obscured by language visible. Naming them explicitly equips us with a clearer framework for inquiry into what exists, how it is interpreted and why it matters. We begin with *Mina*, the deeper of meaning's two layers, the other being expression.

Mina (n.)

Definition: *Mina* is the dimension of existence concerned with why and to what degree something matters. It is not limited to a single function or value, but integrates purpose (*telos*), significance and direction. *Mina* gives weight to our actions, systems and relationships. *Mina* is not about what something is (content) or how it is understood (metacontent). Instead, it's about the deeper significance and orientation something carries.

Clarification: In philosophy, this orientation is often described as *telos* – the 'for the sake of which' something exists or is done. *Mina* extends beyond *telos* by integrating existential weight, value and direction.

As a cluster: *Mina* = purpose (*telos*) + significance + value.

Example:

- Two societies may both build bridges (content). For one, the bridge is simply a trade route. For the other, it symbolises reconciliation and shared destiny. The difference lies in *Mina*.

Core usage (noun):

- The *Mina* of education is not simply to transfer information, but to cultivate wisdom and responsibility.
- Without clarifying the *Mina* of the economy, reforms remain technical exercises with no guiding direction.
- Different cultures may share similar practices, but their *Minas* diverge – one may prioritise efficiency, another harmony.

In comparison/contrast:

- Profit can be a function of business, but *Mina* must be its anchor.
- Two organisations may adopt identical sustainability policies, but differing *Minas* make one authentic and the other performative.

Minalogy (n.)

Definition: The philosophical discipline concerned with *Mina*. Minalogy studies how human beings discern, construct and live by significance and purpose – and how these attributions shape individuals, institutions and civilisations.

Example: An inquiry into education focused on Minalogy does not stop at what schools *are* or how they *function*. It asks why education matters and what ultimate purpose it should serve for human flourishing.

Minalogical (adj.)

Definition: Pertaining to, or oriented by, *Mina*. A process, perspective or design is minalogical when it explicitly foregrounds why something matters, rather than reducing itself to technical function, efficiency or growth.

Examples:

- A renewable energy policy justified only by market competitiveness is not minalogical. A policy framed around intergenerational justice and the preservation of life is.
- An economy organised purely around GDP growth is not minalogical. An economy structured to sustain life, dignity and thriving communities is a minalogical system.

A truly sustainable system is a minalogical system because it integrates what exists, how it is understood, and why it matters into a coherent whole oriented towards human dignity and thriving.

How *Mina* is disclosed

Having named *Mina* and clarified its role within this taxonomy, the next question is how it becomes visible. If *Mina* is the existential depth of meaning – the raw 'why' beneath purpose and significance – how do we encounter it in lived experience? *Mina* is not fabricated at will, nor always immediately obvious. It is disclosed gradually, through a movement that begins in felt awareness and unfolds into articulation, discernment and systemic inquiry. This movement can be traced through five interrelated processes: pre-linguistic awareness, expression, contextual discernment, ontological integrity and iterative inquiry.

1. Pre-linguistic awareness

Mina is first felt before it is said. Human beings encounter the weight of something – love, justice, a forest, a relationship – as significant even before words appear. This raw sense of 'this matters' precedes articulation and reveals *Mina* in its most immediate form. For example, witnessing an act of cruelty, a person may feel a visceral sense that 'this is wrong' before they can explain it in moral or cultural terms. In this way, *Mina* first discloses itself in lived awareness rather than abstract definition.

2. Expression

For *Mina* to guide lives and systems, it must be made shareable. This happens through expression – we translate *Mina* into words, metaphors, stories and frameworks as tokens. Language does not create *Mina*; it expresses it. *Mina* is the source; language is its container. The same felt significance of care becomes narratable in the words of a parent, the rituals of a community, or the framework of a legal right. Expression allows *Mina* to be carried into shared understanding.

3. Contextual discernment (metacontent)

Mina is never grasped in isolation. It is discerned within context, shaped by history, culture, perspective and domain. The *Mina* of education, for example, may be social control in one society and liberation in another. The *Mina* of a forest may be disclosed as sacred in one culture and as timber supply in another. *Mina* reveals itself differently through varying metacontents. Discerning it requires attentiveness to these interpretive lenses.

4. Ontological integrity (UOSI)

Systemic integrity separates the hollow from the genuine, ensuring that what is claimed as *Mina* does not collapse into ideology or manipulation. The UOSI provides the framework for this discernment through its 16 causal qualities. *Mina* is not arbitrary; its authenticity can be examined through the coherence it maintains with these qualities. A professed *Mina* that leads to tyranny, exploitation or bad faith is corrupted, while an authentic *Mina* aligns with a healthy relationship to qualities like trust, sovereignty, normativity, Being and sustained effectiveness.

5. Iterative Inquiry (Minalogy in practice)

Finally, *Mina* is disclosed through deliberate inquiry. Minalogy asks: What is the underlying why? What significance is being ascribed? What purpose is being served, and is it coherent with human dignity and thriving? This inquiry is never finished. It is an ongoing process of reflection, dialogue and systemic design. Through this iterative inquiry, *Mina* is clarified and recalibrated over time, ensuring its coherence remains intact across changing contexts.

These dynamics may sound abstract, but *Mina* discloses itself every day in the way we relate to one another and to the systems we create.

Tangible examples

- **Intimacy**: The *Mina* of a relationship is not simply companionship or routine. It is trust, growth and mutual flourishing. We know this because when trust is absent, the relationship collapses into emptiness, no matter how many gestures or words remain.
- **Organisations**: A company may claim its *Mina* (expressed as purpose) is 'innovation'. Yet under scrutiny, the deeper *Mina* might be profit or social impact. The authentic *Mina* is revealed in what is consistently pursued and protected, even under pressure.

Mina is disclosed, not fabricated. It is discerned through felt awareness, expressed in language, tested within context, measured against integrity and refined through ongoing inquiry. Each stage strengthens our grasp of why something matters, ensuring that *Mina* is not reduced to sentiment or ideology, but remains a coherent anchor for lives, relationships and systems. It is the existential why that gives coherence its weight.

Mina in relation to sense-making and meaning-making

Sense-making is the process by which human beings interpret and navigate content. It involves perceiving, categorising and contextualising what exists, often through the structures of metacontent – cognitive maps, stories, perspectives, domains and paradigms. Sense-making answers *what is this* and *how does it work?*

Meaning-making goes further. It is the process of ascribing significance to what has been made sense of – asking *what does this mean for me, for us, for our world?* Meaning-making connects content and metacontent with human values, identity and lived experience.

Mina is the ground of meaning – not the word, symbol or process of linguistic ascription, but the existential referent that precedes and anchors them. It represents the depth of meaning to which words, expressions and concepts point, whether the referent is real – as in the phenomenon denoted by gravity – or constructed, as in ideas such as currency or value.

Mina gives primacy to what meaning refers to rather than the tokens that express it. It is not the linguistic label but the ontological depth from which meaning arises – the pre-linguistic 'why it matters' that underlies and guides both sense-making and meaning-making.

Without *Mina*:

- Sense-making risks becoming purely technical – efficient at describing and predicting, but empty of direction.
- Meaning-making risks becoming arbitrary – constructing significance without an existential anchor, vulnerable to manipulation or drift.

In summary, meaning has two inseparable dimensions. At its depth lies **Mina** – the existential significance, the raw *why* it matters. On its surface lies **expression** – the articulation of that significance in words, symbols and shared understanding. **Sense-making** interprets content, answering what something is and how it works. **Meaning-making** ascribes significance, expressing why it matters for us, our communities and our world. However, *Mina* is the ground from which both draw their coherence – it is the existential depth that anchors sense-making and meaning-making in lived significance. Think of a forest. Sense-making allows us to understand how it functions. Meaning-making allows us to frame it as heritage, livelihood or sacred space. *Mina* takes us deeper still – the forest matters because life itself is bound to it.

Recognising *Mina* in this way prepares the ground for Minalogy. It shows us that sustainability cannot rest on description or interpretation alone. It must be anchored in the clarified *why* – the existential significance that gives systems their centre of gravity. This is the bridge to the next stage: understanding how Minalogy translates *Mina* into design pathways for authentic sustainability.

Recognising *Mina* as the existential depth of meaning shows us why coherence matters in every system we design or inhabit. Yet coherence is fragile. When it breaks down, we need more than description or diagnosis. We need to remember why the system mattered in the first place. This is where the connection between Minalogy and the Systemic Subversion Cycle becomes vital.

From dysfunction to direction: Linking Minalogy and the Systemic Subversion Cycle

The Systemic Subversion Cycle (SSC) provides a lens to diagnose dysfunction. But diagnosis alone is not enough. Once we see the fracture, the next question is: Why does it matter? This is where Minalogy enters.

Mina grounds the analysis in existential significance. Without it, our response to dysfunction is shallow. We patch mechanics but leave the deeper orientation untouched. The SSC shows where the cracks are forming, while *Mina* reminds us why the structure was worth building in the first place.

For example, when a healthcare system collapses, the SSC helps us recognise the pattern of dysfunction. But it is *Mina* – the deeper why behind preserving dignity and life across generations – that gives the repair direction.

In this way, the SSC and Minalogy complement one another – the SSC uncovers what is breaking down, while *Mina* clarifies why it must be restored. This prevents reform from becoming performative or reactive, and ensures that meaning, vision and mission are born from significance rather than expedience.

Minalogy and the pathways to authentic sustainability

The introduction of *Mina* and Minalogy in this book is not an academic diversion. It is directly connected to the challenge of designing sustainable systems. Authentic sustainability is not only about structures, policies or technologies. It is fundamentally about how and why human beings ascribe significance and purpose in the first place.

In the Authentic Sustainability Framework (ASF), sustainability is understood as more than the endurance of systems. It requires coherence between three levels:

- **Content** – the realities that exist, whether natural, social or constructed.
- **Metacontent** – the intellectual substrates upon which these realities are interpreted and engaged.
- **Meaning** – including its two inseparable layers: *Mina* (deeper layer concerned with why it matters) and expression (surface layer expressing *Mina* in words, symbols and shared understanding).

Without *Mina*, design efforts risk collapsing into technical exercises that optimise for efficiency but lack meaning. Policies may be written, structures engineered and technologies deployed, yet if the underlying why is absent, interventions become hollow or short-lived.

Take climate policy. Many frameworks focus on technical targets – emission reductions, net-zero dates and renewable energy quotas. These are necessary, but if the deeper *Mina* (the significance and purpose that determine the why) is left unexamined, the result is often public resistance, short-term compliance or greenwashing. When climate policy is rooted in clarified *Mina* – the significance of preserving life, justice between generations and the *telos* of human thriving – the same measures gain legitimacy and durability.

The same is true of corporate ESG (Environmental, Social and Governance). Metrics can be produced, boxes ticked and scores improved, but all of this remains an empty shell if *Mina* is missing. If ESG commitments are pursued only for investor perception or regulatory compliance, they collapse into performance and cynicism. But when ESG efforts are grounded in a clarified *Mina* – the authentic purpose of creating enduring value, serving human dignity and fostering systemic integrity – they become not only credible, but transformative.

Here is where the Unified Ontology of Systemic Integrity (UOSI) provides essential grounding. Given the UOSI's 16 qualities are identified as conditions for systemic integrity when our relationship with them are healthy, they are not abstract ideals, but lived realities. Their importance is only fully understood when framed through *Mina*. Qualities like intention, trust, sovereignty, Being, normativity and sustained effectiveness cannot be treated as optional virtues. They are essential because of the purposes and values they enable in sustaining systems.

By situating Minalogy within the discourse of sustainability, a clearer pathway emerges from insight to design. Insight alone is insufficient if it is not tethered to significance. Design alone is insufficient if it is not guided by coherent purposes. *Mina* ensures that pathways to sustainability are not merely functional, but also *meaningful* – oriented towards human thriving and systemic integrity.

In this way, Minalogy anchors the entire discourse of sustainability. It reminds us that true sustainability cannot be engineered without first clarifying what we are sustaining, why it matters, and what purposes guide our design choices.

When awareness becomes meaning and meaning takes hold

Awareness alone is nothing more than commentary if it does not move you. Commitment only emerges when awareness is translated into meaning and, most importantly, becomes meaningful to you. Three steps are critical in this shift:

1. **Integration** – Bring insights into contact with your Being so they anchor in your core, not just your mind.
2. **Discernment** – Decide what deserves to be sustained or transformed, recognising that some things may no longer be relevant or useful.
3. **Commitment** – Allow meaning to specify intention, ensuring action is built on a solid foundation.

These steps convert awareness into direction. Without them, awareness remains inert – an observation without consequence. Consider the following examples:

Personal health

- **Integration:** Notice your fatigue and acknowledge its impact on your wellbeing.
- **Discernment:** Recognise that late-night scrolling doesn't serve you.
- **Commitment:** Prioritise sleep by switching devices off at least an hour before bedtime.

Team strategy

- **Integration:** Pay attention to your team's frustration when a new system designed for efficiency is producing the opposite effect.
- **Discernment:** Decide to simplify existing tools rather than chase new features.
- **Commitment:** Redesign one core workflow for clarity.

Town planning

- **Integration:** Confront evidence of rising air pollution alongside commuter stress.
- **Discernment:** Determine that car-first planning is no longer sustainable.

- **Commitment:** Prioritise public transport corridors in the next planning cycle.

These simple examples show how awareness can be translated into meaningful direction.

The primacy of meaning

Meaning – in both its layers – is the foundation of coherence. At its depth, *Mina* gives intention existential weight. On the surface, expression makes this weight communicable and shareable. Intention literally depends on both. Without *Mina*, intention collapses into posturing. Without expression, *Mina* remains unarticulated and cannot guide collective action. Stripped of meaning, it loses depth and becomes little more than posturing or reactive behaviour. Let's look more closely at how meaning functions, and how it flows into practice.

Coherence unfolds over four stages, where sense-making flows into meaning-making (crystallising into intention), informs our decision-making and, ultimately, shapes reality.

1. **Sense-making** is the capacity to perceive, interpret and orient within reality. It is how we begin to distinguish what is relevant from what is noise, and how we understand the lay of the land.
2. **Meaning-making** is the movement from perception into significance. It does not invent the why, but articulates it. Here we orient ourselves to purpose (*telos*), asking not only, What is this? but also, Why does this matter? At its depth, this significance arises from *Mina*. On the surface, it flows into words, stories and frames of understanding.
3. **Decision-making** is the translation of meaning and intention into chosen pathways. It is where discernment, prioritisation and ethical orientation converge with normative considerations – what ought to be pursued, what consequences can be borne, and what coherence must be preserved – to determine what we will actually commit to in the face of competing options. Without this step, intention risks remaining suspended as posture rather than crystallising into choice.

4. **Reality-shaping** is the externalisation of meaning through conduct, contribution and self-expression. Meaning becomes embodied when it flows into the structures of life, relationships, institutions and societies. Put simply, content becomes clarity, and clarity becomes action.

In this fourfold movement, intention is neither the beginning nor the end. It is the bridge – ensuring that the significance discovered through meaning-making does not remain abstract, but flows coherently into the actions and structures that constitute our lived reality. This is not just theory. The following examples show how meaning threads through every layer of life – from relationships, to organisations, to society – and how coherence either holds or fractures in practice.

Personal – A strained friendship

You notice a friend has been distant (**sense-making**). At first it is only an observation, but soon it takes on significance because the relationship matters to you and you value connection and honesty (**meaning-making**). That significance crystallises into an intention to approach them with honesty and care. From there, you choose not to react defensively, but to reach out with curiosity (**decision-making**). In practice, this leads to a conversation that either restores trust or clarifies distance, but in either case honours coherence (**reality-shaping**).

Organisational – A company facing layoffs

Leaders in a company observe declining revenue (**sense-making**). Numbers tell one story, but their deeper meaning is felt in the impact on staff and culture – a reminder that the business exists not only to profit, but also to sustain livelihoods and trust (**meaning-making**). Leadership creates an intention to balance financial survival with human dignity. That intention translates into concrete choices. Instead of silent cuts, they opt for open dialogue, redeployment and reskilling programs (**decision-making**). As these choices play out, the organisation finds that even in loss, trust and resilience can be strengthened (**reality-shaping**).

Societal – A neighbourhood addressing youth crime

A neighbourhood notices rising incidents of vandalism and petty crime (**sense-making**). At the level of meaning, residents see not only damage, but a sign of disconnection and lack of opportunity among young people. They also recognise that a community's wellbeing depends on the inclusion of its youth (**meaning-making**). That recognition forms into a shared intention to support and re-engage local youth. This intention channels into practical choices – mentoring programs are launched, safe spaces opened and youth given a voice in planning (**decision-making**). The result is a community strengthened by inclusion, with reduced crime and greater trust across generations (**reality-shaping**).

These examples make one truth clear – meaning is foundational. Without meaning, awareness remains commentary, intention drifts, decisions lose coherence and reality fractures. But when meaning holds its rightful place at the centre, it threads through sense-making, intention and decision-making to shape lives, organisations, institutions and societies with integrity. This is the primacy of meaning – the force that anchors coherence, sustains commitment and gives reality its direction.

How the UOSI keeps meaning grounds meaning

Because meaning is the critical anchor that follows sense-making, its integrity determines everything that follows. The UOSI ensures that meaning does not collapse into sentiment, ideology or propaganda. Each sphere provides a safeguard:

- **Integrity Sphere** – Anchors meaning in values, trust, sovereignty and Being.
- **Modulation Sphere** – Keeps meaning dynamic: patient, tolerant, adaptable and able to release (surrender) unhelpful forms while maintaining direction.
- **Disintegration Sphere** – Reveals how shadows distort meaning into ideology, fear or performance.
- **Architectonic Sphere** – Orchestrates durability: meta-awareness to see your lens; systemic integrity to align parts

with the whole; sustained effectiveness to outlast enthusiasm; and normativity to anchor meaning in ethics and dignity.

Without running meaning through the filter of the UOSI, coherence fractures. Goals will drift, tasks will multiply without substance, and actions will become noise. Meaning that survives these four spheres is safe to build upon.

The relationship between Minalogy and normativity

In this book, axiology is treated as part of normativity, not as an entirely separate field. Broadly understood, normativity is the domain of what *ought* to be – the principles, directions and obligations that guide behaviour, systems and decisions. Within this, axiology specifies the dimension of values – what is deemed worthwhile, good or meaningful.

This framing matters, because values are never abstractions. To value honesty is already to imply that one ought to act truthfully. To value life is to imply that one ought not take it arbitrarily. Therefore, axiology lives within the normative domain.

What Minalogy adds is the deeper grounding of *Mina* – the existential significance and intention from which both values and norms arise. Without this foundation, normativity risks becoming hollow, fragmented or distorted.

- **Normativity** provides the language of *ought*: obligations, codes and values.
- **Minalogy** provides the architecture of *why*: the meanings and intentions that give those obligations and values their depth and authenticity.

Think of a tree. Normativity is the branches and fruit – obligations (branches) and values (fruit) that guide visible conduct. Minalogy is the roots and soil – the underlying meanings and intentions that make those obligations and values possible, and explain why distortions below ground inevitably show up above.

This distinction is crucial in practice. Take technology ethics, for example:

- **Normative stance**: We ought to regulate facial recognition in public spaces.
- **Axiological concern**: We value privacy, but we also value security – which matters more?
- **Minalogical inquiry**: What meanings underlie our concepts of privacy, security and dignity? What intentions are driving the emphasis on one value over another? How do distortions in meaning risk producing hollow norms?

Or consider a company debating surveillance software for remote work:

- **Normative stance**: Employees ought to accept monitoring as a condition of employment.
- **Axiological concern**: Efficiency is valuable, but so is trust – which takes precedence?
- **Minalogical inquiry**: What does 'trust' actually mean in this culture? Is monitoring driven by fear, care or control? How are these intentions shaping which values are emphasised and which obligations are imposed?

Seen this way, Minalogy and normativity are not rivals but interdependent. Normativity provides guidance and Minalogy ensures that guidance is grounded in authentic significance rather than ideology or performance. Together, they safeguard coherence. Norms and values are not arbitrary, but rooted in *Mina* – the existential why that holds integrity in place.

This relationship matters for sustainability. Norms and values on their own can dictate obligations, but without *Mina*, they risk becoming hollow compliance or performative ideals. When framed through Minalogy, however, they gain ontological depth. They connect what we deem worthwhile with the deeper purposes that make those commitments authentic, durable and transformative. In this way, Minalogy strengthens the pathways to sustainability, ensuring that what ought to be is anchored in why it matters.

Conclusion

Minalogy does not replace intention. It prepares the foundation by clarifying why things matter – grounding meaning in *Mina* (existential significance) and ensuring its expression (language, stories, frameworks) carries substance rather than sentiment. In this way, Minalogy ensures that meaning does not remain an abstract impression, but becomes a lived orientation. Through Minalogy, we move beyond what something means in words to what it signifies in essence. This ensures that when intention does arise, it is carried by substance rather than sentiment.

Intention rarely emerges fully formed. It often begins as a want, a fragile desire, or a restless sense that things cannot stay the same. Minalogy provides the discipline to test these impulses. Does the meaning we attach align with authentic purpose, or is it a distortion of convenience, ideology or performance optics? By distinguishing *Mina* from the shifting interpretations we construct, Minalogy equips us to refine significance before crystallising it into commitment.

Because meaning is the first step, its coherence determines everything that follows. Without it, strategy becomes performance and action collapses into noise. But with it, the chain of vision, mission, goals, objectives, tasks and actions gains substance and momentum. And by testing *Mina* through the lens of the UOSI, we safeguard it from collapsing into sentiment, ideology or propaganda, ensuring it remains a foundation strong enough to build upon. This includes testing Mina against normativity – the domain of what ought to be. Norms and values on their own can drift or distort, but when grounded in *Mina*, they carry ontological weight and become authentic guides for coherent action.

In all these ways, Minalogy ensures that meaning does not remain an abstract impression, but becomes a lived orientation – one capable of sustaining leadership, performance and systemic integrity. This coherence also sharpens our ability to respond to dysfunction. Where the SSC exposes patterns of breakdown, Minalogy clarifies why repair matters. Together, they prevent reform from becoming reactive or hollow and prepare the way for intention to emerge with depth.

The next chapter, *From Desire to Direction – The Sources of Intention*, explores how raw longings mature into grounded intention, and how intention becomes the compass strong enough to organise goals, objectives, tasks and actions. If this chapter prepared the soil – cultivating meaning through Minalogy and testing it through UOSI – the next is where the seed of desire is planted, clarified and cultivated into intention.

CHAPTER 47

From Desire to Direction – The Sources of Intention

Meaning without intention is like a seed left on a windowsill. It may hold infinite potential, but unless it is planted, nurtured and given direction, it will never be brought to life. In the previous chapter, we crossed the bridge from sense-making to meaning-making through Minalogy, clarifying why things matter to us and what they call for. We also examined how coherence develops through five stages: sense-making gives rise to meaning-making, which takes form as intention, directs decision-making, and eventually finds expression in the reality we live out. Now we turn our focus to intention itself.

This chapter asks: How do the sources from which intention arises shape its quality and trajectory? Intention is often mistaken for a goal or plan. In reality, it is not primarily a mental construct but an ontological practice – the orientation of your Being towards a chosen possibility. Before any policy is written or a strategy is drafted, intention has already set the trajectory. Where that trajectory originates – in clarity or distortion, sovereignty or coercion, authentic care or inherited scripts – makes all the difference.

In exploring the sources of intention, we will distinguish authentic sources from distorted ones, examine how bad faith corrodes coherence, and show why normativity – the alignment of axiology, values, ethics, morality and virtue – provides the compass that determines the quality of an intention.

By the end of this chapter, you will see that not all intentions are equal. Two people can aim for the same result yet generate radically different outcomes, because what matters most is not only *what* they intend, but *where* that intention comes from.

Sources of intention: Authentic vs distorted

Where an intention arises from is just as important as the intention itself. The same outward commitment – say, to grow a business, strengthen a relationship or create a sustainable infrastructure plan – can either regenerate or corrode, depending on its source.

When intention arises from an authentic source, it carries coherence. Authentic intention is born of clear awareness rather than distortion. It aligns with discerned meaning rather than shallow goals. It is grounded in sovereignty, chosen freely rather than imposed by coercion or pressure. Most importantly, it flows from Being itself – from who and how you are being – rather than from performance or appearances.

In contrast, when intention emerges from a distorted source, it carries fracture from the start. Distorted intentions often arise from fear or scarcity, shaped by avoidance or survival rather than vision. They may be set for reasons of performance, appearances or compliance – to appease others, perform for show or satisfy cultural expectations. At times, they come from inherited narratives, the stories handed down by family, society or institutions that are adopted without question. And at their most corrosive, they are rooted in bad faith – the deliberate misalignment between stated values and lived choices, often used for manipulation or self-deception.

The difference between these sources is not merely intellectual, it is ontological. Recognising the source of an intention requires meta-awareness, authenticity and the courage to confront one's shadows. Without this inquiry, it is easy to confuse a distorted intention for an authentic one, because they often look identical on the surface. Both can be expressed with passion, written into strategies or embedded into policies. Yet over time, only authentic intentions generate coherence and trust. Distorted ones, however clever or well-packaged, eventually corrode the systems they are meant to sustain. Consider the following examples.

Personal health

Two people might both set the intention to 'get fit'. On the surface, the commitments look the same. But if one arises from an authentic source – a desire for vitality to be present with their family, freely chosen and aligned with care – it generates coherence. If the other arises from a distorted source – fear of judgement, pressure to conform or the need to perform – it produces anxiety, burnout or resentment. The outcomes diverge, not because of the words of the intention, but because of the source.

Organisational growth

A company might set the intention to 'expand into new markets'. When this is anchored in authentic purpose – serving more people with products that genuinely improve their lives – the growth strengthens trust. But when the same intention is driven by distorted motives – fear of losing status, pressure to appease investors or appearances for the sake of their quarterly reports – it breeds hollow promises and eventual decline.

The quality of intention: Normativity in action

Even when an intention arises from an authentic source, it is not automatically sound. Two people can declare the same intention, yet the outcomes may differ dramatically because the quality of their intentions is different. What gives an intention quality is not passion or eloquence, but its *normative grounding*. Normativity provides the compass that determines whether an intention is worthy, coherent and sustainable.

The first dimension to consider here is **axiology**, which asks whether the end is truly worth pursuing. In other words, does the goal itself have value? Does it elevate human dignity, ecological integrity, truth or flourishing? Or does it simply chase applause, metrics or quarterly numbers? An intention to 'expand market share' may look impressive, but if the highest value served is prestige or profit at any cost, drift will follow. In contrast, an intention to 'create products that genuinely simplify lives' carries intrinsic worth that can orient decisions even under pressure.

From axiology we move to **values**, which translate abstract worth into lived priorities. The coherence of an intention is visible in how time, attention, money and authority are actually allocated. A leader who proclaims a value of 'wellbeing' but normalises burnout undermines their own intention. The same is true of governments that proclaim to value diversity and inclusion, yet fail to direct any funding towards that value. Authentic intentions are tested here: the calendar, the budget and the trade-offs reveal whether values and intentions truly align.

The third dimension is **ethics**, which examines whether the means are consistent with the ends. A good outcome pursued through manipulative or coercive methods corrodes both the goal and the person pursuing it. Ethical quality can be tested with the following simple questions: Would this still feel just if I was on the receiving end? Could this decision be made transparent without evasion or shame? What externalities will it create, and who will bear the cost? High-quality intentions are those whose methods remain justifiable when scrutinised, not only when celebrated.

The fourth dimension is **morality**, which considers the communal codes and norms that an intention will normalise if enacted. Every intention, once embodied, sets a precedent. A couple's intention to handle conflict with respect, if repeated, cultivates a culture of trust in their household. An organisation's intention to prioritise transparency, if sustained, shapes its workplace norms for years to come. Conversely, intentions set in the name of expediency may normalise cynicism or shortcuts. Morality reminds us that intentions do not just shape outcomes; they shape the invisible codes of culture.

Finally, there is the dimension of **virtue**. Every intention places a weight on the one who carries it. A commitment to transparency requires courage; a commitment to repair requires humility; a commitment to stewardship requires temperance. Without the necessary virtues, even the most carefully worded intention collapses under its own weight. This is why intention is not only about what you aim for, but also about *who you must become* in order to carry it. The Being Framework offers a map for this inner development, reminding us that intention and virtue cannot be separated.

Taken together, these five dimensions form the normative scaffolding of intention. They are not abstract ideals, but practical safeguards. An intention rooted in axiology, aligned with lived values, carried out through ethical means, mindful of its cultural impact and supported by the necessary virtues has the strength to endure. Without this grounding, even authentic intentions can fracture. However, with it, intentions become not just private resolutions, but trustworthy compasses capable of orienting lives, organisations and societies toward coherence.

Guarding against bad faith

So far, you have learned that every intention carries a quality – not only in what it seeks to achieve, but in how honestly it reflects our Being. When intentions arise from distorted sources, they create fractures. But when distortion is coupled with self-deception or manipulation, something deeper takes hold – bad faith.

As explored earlier in this book, bad faith is not simple dishonesty. It is the deliberate misalignment between stated values, declared intentions and lived behaviour. It shows up when people, organisations or societies communicate one intention while enacting another.

At the personal level, bad faith may look like someone declaring an intention to 'prioritise wellbeing' while continuing to say yes to every demand for approval. In relationships, it appears when a partner proclaims 'openness and honesty' but hides resentment or maintains a private agenda. Within organisations, bad faith thrives when leaders commit to 'diversity and inclusion' while tolerating a toxic, male-dominated workplace culture. And at the societal level, it is visible when governments sign climate agreements with great fanfare while expanding fossil fuel projects.

In all these cases, the problem is not unmet intentions, but inauthentic ones. The fracture is built in from the start. The spoken intention comforts, but the lived pattern corrodes trust. Over time, coherence collapses because there was nothing genuine to sustain it.

This is why intention setting must always include an integrity check. Without it, even the most eloquent statements risk becoming tools of performance optics rather than compasses of coherence.

The alignment test

Before committing to an intention, ask yourself three questions:

1. **Source** – Is this intention arising from authentic awareness, or am I concealing a shadow?
2. **Congruence** – If I enacted this fully, would it align with my values, ethics and vision – or would it compromise them?
3. **Accountability** – Am I willing to be held responsible for this intention, even when it is costly or inconvenient?

If the answer to any of these is no, the intention is vulnerable to bad faith. Refine the source before you proceed.

Practising alignment: a short review cycle

Intention isn't set-and-forget. It needs revisiting under pressure, drift and new information. Use this one-page cyclical practice to ensure your intentions are (and remain) aligned and coherent.

Define (once, then refine):

1. **End** – What good is being pursued, and why is it worthy?
2. **Means and limits** – What methods will you use, and what won't you do, even under pressure?
3. **Norm** – If repeated, what will this intention normalise in your life, organisation or culture?
4. **Virtues** – Which qualities of character must you practise to carry this intention well? (e.g. patience, courage or humility)
5. **Repair** – How will you notice dysfunction and make it right?

6. **Test** – What clear sign will tell you this intention is drifting? (e.g. if staff turnover rises, if I avoid the gym for two weeks, if public trust falls in surveys).

Run the cycle: Act → Review → Adjust → Recommit.

Once the layers are defined, they need to be kept active and coherent through regular practice.

- **Weekly (10 minutes):** Review your six layers. Ask yourself: *What's working? What's slipping?* Make one small adjustment and recommit.
- **Quarterly (30 minutes):** Step back. Check whether your time, money and activity are still allocated in line with your intention. Run a quick UOSI scan:
  - Integrity – Is this still aligned with my values and Being?
  - Modulation – Am I adapting without losing direction?
  - Disintegration – Are shadows or distortions creeping in?
  - Architectonic – Is the whole system holding together?
- **When something slips:** Don't just patch the surface. Go back to the layer that failed (end, means, norm, virtues, repair or test). Fix the foundation, then move forward.

The goal is not perfection but coherence – intentions that can withstand scrutiny, hold under pressure and generate trust over time.

Conclusion

Intention is not a plan dressed up as resolve. It is an ontological practice – the orientation of our Being towards a chosen possibility. In this chapter, we have seen that the source of intention matters as much as the intention itself. When it arises from authentic awareness, discerned meaning, sovereignty and Being, it carries coherence. However, when it arises from distortion, fear, performance or bad faith, it fractures from the start.

We also explored how the quality of intention depends on its normative grounding. Axiology, values, ethics, morality and virtue provide the scaffolding that distinguishes intentions that endure from those that collapse. Coupled with a practical alignment cycle, these safeguards ensure that intentions can be tested, refined and sustained, even under pressure.

The key lesson is simple: not all intentions are equal. They may look alike on paper, but only those that arise from authentic sources and are normatively sound can generate coherence, trust and sustainability.

The next chapter builds on this foundation. Having clarified where intention comes from and how its quality is secured, we now follow its flow forward. As we have seen, intention is both the bridge that carries meaning forward and the compass that orients us within possibility. But a compass alone does not move us. The next step is commitment – the moment when direction is lifted out of possibility and bound to accountability. In the following chapter, we trace how intention moves through the layers of coherence into commitment, and what it takes to hold those commitments steady under pressure.

CHAPTER 48

The Flow of Coherence – From Meaning to Action

Intention does not appear fully formed. It begins as something smaller, often fragile – a want, a longing, a restless sense that life cannot remain as it is. Desire is the raw material of direction, but without care, it can scatter into distraction or be captured by fear, ego or convenience. To become intention, desire must be clarified, anchored in meaning and tested for coherence.

As we saw in the previous chapter, the source of an intention shapes its quality. Here, our focus shifts first to development – how fragile desire matures into grounded intention, a compass strong enough to carry significance forward. From there, we trace the flow of coherence across the continuum from meaning to action, examining how fractures can be diagnosed and restored. Finally, we turn to the decisive threshold where intention becomes commitment, and how that commitment is sustained under pressure through integrity and leadership.

At its heart, commitment is more than making promises. It's about carrying them forward into action and sustaining them through the inevitable tensions of life and leadership. Sometimes this requires a precise intervention, a decisive act that restores coherence. At other times, it requires shared responsibility, where the weight of commitment does not rest on one person alone but is carried collectively. Commitment is where authenticity is tested. Without it, intentions drift into rhetoric or performance. But with it, they gain the strength to endure.

Intention in motion

Through its anatomy, mechanics and topology, we have seen that intention is not a passing wish, fleeting desire or vague ambition. It is a structural compass – a directional force that shapes how human beings and other systems orient themselves through time. Yet a compass is never read in isolation. It only makes sense in relation to the map it serves. In the same way, intention is always nested within a broader architecture that links the deepest sources of meaning in our Being with the smallest, most concrete actions of everyday life.

In the context of transformation and sustainability, the role of intention as a structural compass becomes even more pronounced. Sustainability is never achieved through technology alone, nor through policies, metrics or external incentives. It requires *intentionality* – the inner alignment that determines whether our actions reinforce coherence or accelerate collapse. Without intentionality, transformation becomes cosmetic, driven by ego, trends or pressures rather than by integrity. But when intentionality is present and coherent, it acts as the silent architecture beneath every enduring system – holding vision accountable, anchoring mission and ensuring that strategies, goals and behaviours remain tethered to meaning.

This broader structure is not a matter of choice; it is a phenomenological fact. Every human being, regardless of culture or circumstance, cares about something. And when we care enough, our concern crystallises into intention – the directional posture of our Being. Yet care and intention alone are not sufficient. For fulfilment to occur, our intentions must find expression through layers of vision, mission, goals, objectives, tasks and, ultimately, the actions that constitute our lived conduct. Each of these layers acts as a hinge between inner orientation and outer enactment.

Because intention is a compass, the question, *What is my intention?* is inseparable from *What is my intention aligned with?* It is here that coherence either stabilises or fractures. To see how fragile desire matures into grounded intention – strong enough to carry coherence forward – we now turn to the developmental arc.

From wish to grounded intention – The developmental arc

Even when fractures are repaired, intention itself is never static. It begins in a fragile state, often little more than a want or restless longing. Left unexamined, that longing can scatter into distraction or be hijacked by fear, ego or convenience. But if nurtured, it can mature into a grounded intention – a compass strong enough to hold coherence under pressure.

The developmental arc of intention moves through three stages:

- **Wish** – The raw material of direction. A simple desire, statement or hope. For example, 'I want to get fit' or 'I wish our workplace felt different.' At this stage, nothing is yet anchored. It is possibility in its most unformed state.
- ***Primoris*** [91] – The uprising of Being. This is the threshold moment when tolerating the status quo becomes impossible – the 'enough is enough' spark. *Primoris* is what prevents desire from drifting endlessly. It ignites movement.
- **Grounded intention** – The clarified compass. This is desire anchored in meaning, tested against coherence and stabilised so that it can reliably organise goals, objectives and actions. Grounded intention is where the arc stabilises into direction.

Take, for example, someone who wishes to improve their health. At first the intention is vague: 'I should exercise more.' *Primoris* erupts when exhaustion or illness creates a breaking point: 'I cannot keep living this way.' If this spark is tied only to fear or shame, drift will return. But if it is re-anchored in meaning – *'I want vitality so I can be fully present with my family* – it matures into a genuine intention. That intention can then cascade into goals, objectives, tasks and actions that reinforce the original meaning.

---

91   From the Latin *primus* ('first' or 'foremost'); used here to represent the moment of ignition within the ontological continuum of transformation. It is the uprising of Being – the point where the implicit meaning within one's *Mina* demands expression and no longer tolerates incoherence or stagnation.

This arc shows that intention is not simply declared – it is cultivated. It moves from fragility into coherence only when meaning steadies it, integrity tests it and commitment anchors it into practice. Without this work, even polished strategies decay because they are tethered to optics rather than truth.

A 10-step process

The movement from wish to grounded intention is not automatic. It unfolds step by step, each stage clarifying and stabilising the last until coherence is possible. A practical process can help bring this arc into focus:

1. **Name the wish** – Begin with the raw material. Say plainly what is wanted, without justification or polish. 'I want to feel well again.' 'I want my team to trust me.' At this stage, honesty is more important than refinement.

2. **Reveal the motive** – Ask: 'Why this? Why now?' Is the wish rooted in care, service and purpose, or in fear, ego and convenience? The integrity of this answer determines everything that follows.

3. **Recognise *primoris*** – Notice the moment when the status quo becomes intolerable. *Primoris* is the uprising of Being, the inner refusal to remain trapped in drift or distortion.

4. **Tie it to meaning** – Anchor the uprising in something larger than preference. Ask: 'Why does this matter beyond me?' Link it to *telos* – the deeper purpose that serves dignity, truth or flourishing.

5. **Draft the intention** – Shape the first expression: 'My intention is to [direction] in [domain] with [virtues] in service of [meaning].' At this point, the wish crystallises into direction.

    - Example: 'My intention is to nurture my health with discipline and kindness, in service of living with vitality and presence.'

6. **Test for coherence** – Check whether the intention aligns with the rest of your Being – your values, roles, timing

and relationships. If the body resists or your commitments unravel, refine until alignment stabilises.
7. **Commit with clarity** – Define non-negotiables: the practices, rituals or boundaries that will hold the intention in place. Bring it into the open where appropriate – coherence thrives with transparency, not secrecy.
8. **Translate into goals and objectives** – Broaden the compass into directional goals, then sharpen them into measurable objectives. This step gives the intention a map rather than leaving it as a declaration.
9. **Design tasks and actions** – Break objectives into tangible steps. Anticipate drift by setting small contingencies: 'If I miss one week, then I reset the following Monday.'
10. **Review and refine** – Regularly trace the continuum back to meaning. Ask: 'Does this still matter? Am I carrying it with integrity?' Small adjustments here prevent fractures later.

Together, these steps stabilise the fragile wish into a grounded intention – one capable of orienting perception, filtering priorities and organising behaviour. With intention stabilised, we can now turn to how coherence flows from meaning through to action.

The flow of coherence

To see how intention carries coherence into practice, we need to trace its movement from depth to surface – from the unseen foundations of meaning through to the visible actions of everyday life.

Meaning →Vision → Mission → Intention → Goals → Objectives → Tasks → Actions

This continuum can be visualised as an iceberg or pyramid. The base represents the deep, unseen source of significance (*Mina*), while the tip shows its visible expression in the world.

The flow of coherence represents the Developmental Dimension of the tri-dimensional Fulfilment Pyramid, which is explored in detail in the next chapter. It is here that intentions are grounded in authentic meaning. The flow of coherence stabilises the compass of coherence to ensure intentions gain depth, purpose and resilience from meaning all the way through to our actions.

Coherence begins in the depths of Being, where meaning (*Mina*) takes form. From there, it rises through vision, mission, intention, goals and objectives until it reaches the outermost layer of enactment in tasks and actions. When this continuum holds, coherence moves fluidly from inner significance to outward expression. But when any layer fractures, meaning loses traction and activity collapses into noise or performance.

- **Meaning** sits at the base of this structure. It is the reservoir of *Mina* – the raw *why it matters*, the existential depth from which significance, purpose and direction arise.
  - *Mina* is the depth of meaning – the unseen current that orients our values, choices and systems.
  - **Expression** is the articulation of that depth – the words, gestures, symbols and structures that make *Mina* communicable and actionable.

  Together, *Mina* and expression form the foundation upon which every higher layer depends. From this depth, coherence ascends through the next successive layers.

- **Vision** imagines what could exist if meaning were expressed – it paints the horizon of possibility.
- **Mission** translates that vision into function – what we are here to do in service of what matters.
- **Intention** acts as the compass of coherence – the inner commitment that aligns perception and behaviour with meaning.
- **Goals** transform intention into broad domains of focus and aspiration.
- **Objectives** bring those goals into measurable form, creating accountability and direction.
- **Tasks** organise these objectives into rhythm and sequence.
- **Actions** are the surface expression of coherence – the visible tip of the iceberg, the lived proof of alignment between depth and deed.

In this architecture, coherence flows upward from depth to surface, yet it also cycles back downward. Every action either reinforces or erodes the integrity of the structure beneath. When the continuum is intact, meaning infuses every level with clarity and purpose. However, when the link between depth and surface is lost, activity becomes disconnected from significance, and coherence dissolves.

Why Mina is needed in the flow of coherence

The refinement of meaning into *Mina* and expression is not a technicality, but a necessity. It keeps the flow of coherence anchored in depth rather than dissolving into abstraction.

Without *Mina*, expression risks collapsing into hollow slogans or semantics. Without expression, *Mina* remains ineffable, inaccessible to collective life. Together, they ensure meaning is both profound and actionable.

This distinction also resolves the overload problem. In earlier treatments, 'meaning' carried both the existential *why* and the linguistic articulation. By naming *Mina* as the depth and expression as its symbolic form, clarity is restored. *Mina* provides ontological weight while expression gives it social presence.

The implications are immediate:

- **Climate policy:** Technical targets without *Mina* reduce sustainability to paperwork. *Mina* – justice between generations, preservation of life and care for the earth – restores depth and durability.
- **Organisations:** Slogans or branding without *Mina* are reduced to image management. *Mina* – dignity of work, service to humanity or enabling thriving – sustains legitimacy and coherence.
- **Intimacy:** Words and gestures without *Mina* risk becoming mechanical. *Mina* – trust, belonging and growth – gives them vitality and resilience.

In summary, *Mina* is not an optional addition, but the foundation of meaning itself. Expression makes it shareable, but *Mina* safeguards its depth. The flow of coherence depends on this inseparability. *Mina* anchors while expression carries. When intentions and visions are anchored in *Mina*, they draw from a depth that makes fulfilment not only possible, but sustainable and enduring.

Tangible examples

To see how this flow unfolds in practice, the following examples illustrate how meaning, vision, mission, intention, goals, objectives, tasks and actions play their part in various domains. The distinction between each layer may seem subtle, but they are essential: meaning anchors significance; vision imagines possibility; mission defines role; intention sets direction; goals identify broad aims; objectives bring accountability; tasks organise the work; and actions embody it in the moment.

Intimate relationships

At the level of **meaning**, intimacy is grounded in the desire to love and be loved authentically. Love here is not a fleeting mood or desire, but the deeper significance of human dignity expressed through a relationship. From this meaning arises a **vision** of a partnership marked by trust, safety and mutual growth – an imagination of what the relationship could become if love was fully expressed.

That vision translates into a **mission** – to nurture a partnership that strengthens both parties and enriches their shared life. Mission answers the question: *What is our role in serving this vision?* This mission is carried forward through **intention** – the commitment to show up with openness, care and compassion, especially in times of conflict. Intention ensures the mission does not remain abstract, but becomes a posture of Being.

Once intention is clarified, it generates **goals** – strengthening emotional intimacy and deepening mutual understanding. Goals point to the broad domains of growth. From these flow **objectives**, such as weekly check-ins to share feelings and needs – concrete, time-bound commitments that make the pursuit of goals accountable. **Tasks** then organise these objectives into practice: scheduling dedicated time; planning open conversations; and creating rituals of appreciation.

Finally, everything rests on **action**. In the smallest moments – such as pausing to listen deeply during a heated argument rather than shutting down or retaliating – coherence is either embodied or fractured.

Love is the why. Vision imagines what that love could become. Mission defines the role of the relationship in nurturing that vision. Intention commits to openness and care. And goals, objectives, tasks and actions give love its lived expression.

Organisations

At the level of **meaning**, organisations exist to serve a purpose greater than profit. Purpose is the anchor that gives work its deeper significance, shaping why the organisation exists at all. From this emerges a **vision** – a picture of the positive impact the organisation could have if that purpose were fully expressed. Vision imagines possibility, inspiring people with what could be.

That vision translates into a **mission**, the declaration of role and function. Mission defines how the organisation will serve its vision in concrete terms. This mission is then carried forward through **intention** – the commitment to pursue the vision with integrity, consistency and care. Intention ensures the mission does not remain a slogan, but becomes a lived orientation.

From intention arise **goals**, which give the organisation a broad direction, such as expanding into new markets or improving employee wellbeing. Goals then take shape as **objectives** – specific, measurable commitments like launching a new service line within 12 months or reducing workplace injuries by 20 per cent.

Tasks organise these objectives into coordinated efforts – meetings, project plans, milestones – while **actions** bring them to life in the everyday: a phone call returned; a promise honoured; or a problem solved with care.

Serving a greater purpose than profit is the 'why'. Vision imagines what that meaning or purpose could become in the world. Mission defines the role of the organisation in serving that vision. Intention commits to integrity in how the work is carried out. And goals, objectives, tasks and actions give meaning its lived expression.

Society

At the level of **meaning**, society exists to uphold human dignity and enable people to flourish together. This meaning provides the ground from which a **vision** can emerge, painting the picture of a society where dignity is upheld and people are able to flourish together.

From this vision arises a **mission** – to organise collective life in ways that serve the wellbeing of all. Mission defines the role of laws, institutions and cultural practices in nurturing that vision. Carried forward through **intention**, society commits to embodying values such as justice, fairness and care in how people live together. Intention provides the compass that prevents mission from being reduced to rhetoric.

From intention come **goals**, such as reducing inequality, promoting education or strengthening public trust. These translate into **objectives** – measurable commitments like passing a new policy, building a school or funding community services. **Tasks** organise these objectives into coordinated programs and initiatives, while **actions** appear in the smallest expressions of civic life: a citizen voting; a neighbour helping another; or a leader acting with integrity.

Upholding human dignity and enabling people to flourish together is the 'why'. Vision imagines what a flourishing society could become. Mission defines the collective role in nurturing that vision. Intention commits to justice, dignity and care in how we live together, while goals, objectives, tasks and actions give meaning its lived expression.

These examples show how intention threads through every layer of human life, from the most intimate to the most systemic. They also reveal that coherence is never automatic. It must be cultivated, and it can just as easily unravel.

Identifying and restoring fractures in coherence

So far, we have traced how coherence flows from meaning through to action. But coherence is not a given. It is fragile, and at times it fractures. Understanding where and how those fractures occur is essential if intention is to remain trustworthy.

Intention plays a crucial role here. Because it acts as a compass, intention quickly reveals whether our direction remains aligned with meaning or has drifted into distortion. Yet intention alone cannot diagnose the whole picture. For that we need the architecture of coherence, which shows how misalignment at one layer inevitably ripples both upward and downward.

- A couple who declare love, but act with contempt fracture coherence between meaning and action.
- An organisation that proclaims purpose, but exploits staff fractures coherence between mission and tasks.
- A society that enshrines dignity in principle, but denies it in practice fractures coherence between vision and lived reality.

In each case, the words may remain intact, but the flow has broken somewhere along the continuum.

When outcomes collapse into incoherence, the question is not only *What went wrong?* We also need to ask, *Where did coherence break down?* By tracing backwards – through actions, tasks, objectives, goals, intention, mission, vision and meaning – the fracture point can be identified. Once located, the work of restoration becomes possible.

Example: A healthcare organisation

A hospital declares its mission is to 'put patients first'. On paper, this aligns with the meaning of care and dignity. Yet budget cuts drive staff to exhaustion, patients experience neglect and the mission statement begins to ring hollow. The fracture is not only at the level of action (overworked staff), but further up the line in intention (prioritising financial expedience over patient dignity). By tracing backwards, leaders can locate the true break in the continuum – where mission and intention no longer align with meaning – and begin the work of restoration.

Restoring coherence: a simple process

Once a fracture has been identified, the path forward is rarely about total reinvention. More often, it is about *realignment*. A practical way to restore coherence is to move step by step, from surface to depth, to find the broken link, then from depth to surface to reset the flow.

1. **Locate the fracture** – Trace the continuum downward from the visible tip to the base (actions → tasks → objectives → goals → intention → mission → vision → meaning). Identify the layer where alignment first broke.
2. **Re-anchor in meaning** – Ask: *What does this still mean? Why does it matter?* Without this re-grounding, repairs will be cosmetic.
3. **Reset intention** – Clarify the directional posture that now carries the re-anchored meaning. Name it explicitly so it can re-orient choices.
4. **Cascade adjustments** – Redesign goals, objectives, tasks and actions so they once again rise from meaning through intention into practice.

This process is less about fixing outcomes and more about repairing flow. By restoring the link that failed, the entire continuum can carry coherence again – from the most abstract purpose to the smallest gesture of action.

In the case of the healthcare organisation, this meant more than improving bedside manner. It required re-anchoring the mission in its authentic meaning of care and dignity, resetting intention around patient wellbeing rather than financial expedience, and then cascading that orientation forward into revised objectives (safe staffing ratios, rest breaks), redesigned tasks (sustainable rosters, realistic workloads) and concrete actions (ensuring staff could give attentive care). Only by repairing the flow at its true fracture point could the mission regain coherence.

Tracing the continuum shows how intention carries coherence upward from meaning into action. But coherence alone does not guarantee endurance. For intention to hold, it must be lifted out of possibility and bound into responsibility. This is the turning point – where intention becomes commitment.

The turning point – When intention becomes commitment

Intention, even when grounded and coherent, is only a compass – and a compass must be picked up and followed if it is to serve its purpose. Commitment is the moment where possibility crystallises into promise. The true shift happens at the turning point where intention becomes commitment – when direction is anchored in responsibility, time and accountability.

For an individual, the turning point occurs when a private intention is formalised. Saying, 'I want to nurture my health' remains an intention until you schedule regular exercise, sign up for a program or tell a family member or friend for accountability. The decision to bind the direction to concrete responsibility makes it a commitment.

For a couple, commitment arises when shared intentions are carried into lived rhythm. The declaration, 'We intend to spend quality time together' becomes a commitment when a weekly date night is set, protected in the calendar and treated as non-negotiable.

In organisations, commitment takes shape when intentions are resourced. A company may declare a value of 'employee wellbeing', but it only becomes commitment when policies are enforced, budgets allocated and leaders held accountable for outcomes.

At the societal level, commitment is visible when rhetoric turns into binding decisions. A government may declare, 'We will reduce emissions', but their declaration only becomes a commitment when laws are passed, targets enforced and institutions recalibrate around them.

Across these examples, the pattern is consistent. Commitment lifts intention beyond the realm of possibility and anchors it in lived accountability. It transforms direction into obligation – not as a burden, but as the necessary binding that gives intention its strength to endure.

Commitment as a way of being

The commitments we make are the specific promises, agreements or contracts we enter into – to ourselves, to others, to organisations or to society. They are tangible and, at times, negotiable. But behind these specific commitments lies something deeper – commitment as a way of being.

In ontological terms, this is a distinction between *what we do* and *how we are being*. Commitment as a way of being is the posture we bring to every promise. It is the quality of wholehearted engagement that makes a commitment trustworthy, even when circumstances change. Without this posture, promises remain brittle. You can write them into policies, declare them in speeches or etch them into contracts, yet they fracture when pressure mounts. Conversely, when commitment as a way of being is present, even imperfect commitments are carried with integrity because the person or system embodies dedication at its core.

> ### Being Framework Ontological Distinction of Commitment[92]
>
> *Commitment* is being dedicated to someone, something, a particular promise or cause that you *care* more about than anything that may stand in the way. When you are committed, you care wholeheartedly, are considered willing, dependable, trustworthy and loyal. You fulfil and honour the promises you make and appropriately demand the same of others.
>
> A **healthy relationship with commitment** indicates that when you put your mind to something, you are all in and stay engaged until the expected outcome is fulfilled. You prioritise, working consistently and diligently towards the fulfilment of the outcome without giving up. Others may consider you dependable and focused on the things you give your word to.
>
> An **unhealthy relationship with commitment** indicates that you may often struggle to fully invest in and maintain relationships or fulfil your agreements. You frequently procrastinate and may avoid

---

[92] Tashvir, A. (2021) *Being – The Source of Power* (p. 317). Sydney: Engenesis Publications.

> making promises or taking on projects or ventures, even those you consider to be beneficial for you. You may avoid any discomfort associated with fulfilling your promises. Others may be hesitant to count on you or give you significant responsibility, which may be detrimental to your relationships and career. You may often refuse to provide specific and timebound promises, lack clarity and be lenient with your responses, or resort to excuses. Alternatively, you may commit to whatever comes your way, regardless of the workability, and may make unrealistic promises without due consideration.

This distinction explains why two people – or two organisations or institutions – can make the same commitment and produce radically different results.

- A politician may promise sweeping reform, but if their posture is opportunistic rather than committed, the promise dissolves when their power is threatened.
- A startup founder may commit to their venture, but if their way of being is more about personal recognition than genuine dedication, they will abandon it when obstacles arise.

In contrast, a leader who embodies commitment as a way of being sustains their promises, even under strain, because their dedication is anchored in who they are, not in convenience or applause.

Therefore, commitment is not simply about what we pledge. It is about *who and how we are being* in relation to those pledges. The commitments we make give shape to our lives, relationships and systems. But commitment as a way of being determines whether those promises hold, can be trusted, and whether they build the integrity on which sustainability depends.

How intention becomes commitment

If intention is the compass, commitment is the moment we choose to walk in its direction. The movement from one to the other is not automatic. It requires deliberate steps that bind orientation to responsibility. Four stages mark this transition:

1. **Discernment** – Testing the intention against meaning, sovereignty and Being. Is this what truly matters? Does it align with my deepest values, or is it shaped by fear, ego or convenience? Discernment ensures that what we commit to is worthy of commitment.
2. **Declaration** – Lifting the intention out of the private realm and voicing it in a way that creates accountability. Declaration transforms 'I want' into 'I will', signalling to ourselves and others that a line has been crossed into a commitment.
3. **Alignment** – Organising resources, relationships and systems so that the commitment can be enacted. Without this, declarations collapse into rhetoric. Alignment ensures time, money, energy and authority flow in the direction of the commitment.
4. **Embodiment** – Living the commitment consistently, even when it is inconvenient. At this stage, commitment, as a way of being, sustains the promise. It is no longer dependent on motivation or enthusiasm, but carried through posture, integrity and presence.

Together, these stages explain how intention turns into commitment. The shift is not a single moment, but a progression that combines clarity, voice, structure and embodiment.

Example: Nurturing health

An individual begins with the intention: 'I want to nurture my health with discipline and kindness.'

- With **discernment**, they test this intention against meaning, recognising it is not about appearances, but about living with vitality to be fully present for their family.
- Through a stated **declaration**, they share their intention with a close friend and sign up for a program, moving from private wish to accountable promise.
- Through **alignment**, they rearrange their calendar to include exercise sessions and adjust their budget to cover healthier food and activities.

- Through **embodiment**, they show up week after week, even on days when motivation falters, sustaining the commitment through presence and discipline.

In this way, the movement from intention to commitment is not a single leap, but a sequence. Where any stage is skipped, the promise remains brittle and the risk of fracture increases. But when all four are present, commitments gain the strength to endure, carrying intention from possibility into lived accountability.

Why commitment matters for authentic sustainability

Commitment is the hinge between direction and endurance. It is the safeguard that prevents intentions from drifting into rhetoric or performance. When individuals, organisations, institutions or societies avoid commitment, they remain fragile. Their words ring hollow, their strategies falter under strain, and their systems corrode from within. But when intention matures into genuine commitment, anchored in a way of being, it becomes capable of carrying coherence through disruption.

This is why commitment matters for authentic sustainability. It is not enough to set intentions or even design strategies. Unless those intentions are bound by responsibility, accountability and integrity, they fracture at the first sign of pressure. But with commitment, systems gain the resilience to endure, recalibrate and remain trustworthy over time.

Holding the centre

In every system – whether a relationship, a community or an organisation – commitments are not tested in calm conditions, but in moments of tension and strain. When pressure builds, when drift begins or when coherence falters, the question is not whether intentions were authentic, but whether they can be sustained. This is the work of holding the centre, remaining anchored in meaning and integrity while guiding people back into alignment.

In organisational settings, this often calls for intervention – not heavy-handed control, but small, decisive acts that reset balance.

The power of these acts lies in four qualities: immediacy (meeting the moment as it arises), minimalism (using no more force than necessary), neutrality (serving coherence rather than ego), and restoration (realigning the group).

Consider a leadership team in conflict. A debate begins to spiral into personal attacks and tension rises. Rather than letting it escalate, the managing director calmly pauses the discussion and names the shared purpose. 'We're here to design what serves our clients best – let's bring the focus back there.' It takes less than a minute, yet it resets the group. The act is immediate, minimal, neutral and restorative.

Such interventions are not techniques, but expressions of Being. They rely on courage to step into tension, discernment to sense what truly needs intervention, confidence to act without hesitation, and assertiveness to apply just enough force without tipping into control. When these qualities are present, leadership interventions are experienced not as domination, but as relief.

However, no leader can carry commitments alone. A team or organisation that depends solely on one person for stability is fragile. Sustainable leadership distributes responsibility. Stability is offered so people feel anchored, but responsibility is shared so they remain engaged and accountable. In this way, commitments become co-owned rather than imposed.

Ultimately, sustainability is not the absence of disruption, but the presence of attuned modulation. It is the art of holding the centre without crushing the group, of sharing responsibility without weakening integrity. When this balance is struck, commitments endure. They are no longer brittle promises, but resilient patterns of behaviour – carried not by enthusiasm or pressure, but by the integrity of the whole system.

Conclusion

Intention begins as a fragile desire before being clarified through meaning and stabilised into an orienting compass. Yet its strength is not proven until it crosses the threshold into commitment. Commitment is where possibility crystallises into promise, where direction is anchored in responsibility and accountability, and where authenticity is tested under pressure.

In this chapter, we first followed the developmental arc by which desire matures into grounded intention. We then traced the flow of coherence from meaning through vision, mission, intention, goals, objectives, tasks and actions (the Developmental Dimension of the Fulfilment Pyramid). When every layer holds alignment, coherence cascades naturally into practice. However, when fractures emerge, the flow falters. By diagnosing and repairing the broken link, coherence can be restored. Grounded intention, reinforced by commitment, ensures that meaning carries all the way into lived action.

We have also seen that commitment is not sustained by the exertion of personal will alone. It requires integrity, leadership and the courage to hold the centre while sharing responsibility. When these qualities are present, commitments cease to be brittle promises, becoming resilient patterns instead. They endure, not because of enthusiasm or external pressure, but because they are carried by the integrity of the whole system.

Commitment anchors intention in accountability, but fulfilment is the true measure of whether it endures. The next chapter turns to this question of fulfilment – how intentions, once committed to, are carried forward, sustained and realised in ways that hold coherence over time.

CHAPTER 49

The Architecture of Fulfilment – The Fulfilment Pyramid

Why fulfilment matters

Up to this point, we have seen that intention is more than just another step between meaning and action. It translates the abstract into the practical. Without intention, meaning remains lofty but inactive. But with it, goals, objectives, tasks and actions can all be tethered to significance. Yet intention alone is not the end of the story. The true test is whether intentions are fulfilled – whether they are sustained, embodied and carried into reality without fracturing along the way.

This is what fulfilment measures – not just what we set out to do, but how deeply intention infuses the act itself. The same behaviour – a phone call, a family dinner, a run in the park – can either feel hollow or become an act of coherence, depending on whether intention is carried through to its fulfilment. Fulfilment ensures that alignment between meaning, vision, mission, intention and practice does not remain theoretical, but is lived, day by day.

Consider a start-up. Its meaning lies in enabling fairness and opportunity – the belief that every small business deserves the chance to flourish, regardless of size or resources. Its vision is a world where no enterprise is excluded from modern digital markets. Its mission is to design and deliver affordable, user-friendly platforms that level the playing field. The intention is to engage with each customer, not as a transaction, but as a partner in growth. From there, goals might be to expand market reach across three regions, objectives to acquire 5,000 new SME users, and tasks to run workshops or launch a referral program. Fulfilment is realised when this intention reaches all the way into action – a support agent listens with patience, problem-solves creatively and restores trust. The same action – customer support – could be hollow if the intention were merely to close the ticket. With the coherent intention of partnership, the action becomes part of fulfilling the organisation's ultimate meaning.

The same is true in a family. Meaning may be defined as a life of dignity, care and mutual flourishing. Vision is a family culture where each member feels safe, valued and encouraged to grow. Mission becomes the nurturing of bonds and resilience across generations. Intention is to show up for one another with consistency and sincerity, even in small moments. Goals might be to create stronger family rhythms of togetherness, objectives to establish a weekly family dinner, and tasks to plan meals or keep schedules clear. Fulfilment occurs in the action itself. Despite being tired after a long day at work, a parent chooses to put away their phone at the table and ask their child about the highlight of their week. The meal could easily be a perfunctory routine, but the intention to deepen presence and connection transforms it into an act of coherence with the family's meaning.

This reveals why intention is distinct from goals or objectives. A goal is what we want to achieve. An objective is how we measure progress. But intention is how we show up in the act itself. Take something as ordinary as going for a run. The action may be identical in motion, yet fulfilment depends on the actual intention: to improve health and longevity; to compete and win; to clear the mind; or to spend quality time with a friend. The run is the same, but the intention alters its significance, its fulfilment and whether it coheres with one's deeper purpose (*telos*) and meaning, including meaning's deeper existential layer of *Mina*.

When meaning, vision, mission, intention, goals, objectives, tasks and actions align, life becomes coherent. Each action is more than activity – it brings a sense of dignity and fulfilment, as the smallest actions echo the larger direction of one's Being. However, when the flow is broken – when intention is forgotten or neglected, when goals detach from meaning, or when actions are divorced from intention – noise replaces coherence. People feel busy but hollow, successful yet unfulfilled, active but unanchored.

The examples above show how intention comes alive when carried into action. Yet sustaining that coherence over time requires more than isolated choices. Commitment anchors intention in accountability, but fulfilment is where its true weight is revealed. Many commitments are made with sincerity, yet they falter because they are not embedded in practice or sustained over time. Fulfilment requires more than resolve. It calls for intention to be *instated into conduct*, reinforced by systems and sustained by deeper forces of integrity, effectiveness and trust.

In this chapter, we examine how that transition occurs. We begin with the **Fulfilment Pyramid**, a tri-dimensional model that shows how intention matures across three interlocking architectonic dimensions: the Developmental, the Phenomenological and the Relational. From there, we turn our attention to **instatement**[93] – the process by which commitments are translated into behaviours, structures and cultural norms that give them durability. Instatement is the point at which intention ceases to be fragile or episodic.

Fulfilment is achieved, not because enthusiasm is maintained, but because coherence is embedded – in habits, institutions and relationships strong enough to hold direction, even when pressure mounts. Ultimately, instatement is the stage where direction is established and expanded in our shared reality – where everything converges into outcomes, results and consequences. It is the moment when intention is actualised into reality-shaping and world-building.

---

93 Based on the 'Instatement Continuum', a model within *Minalogy*, a body of work currently being developed by this author.

The Fulfilment Pyramid

Why do so many commitments, made with genuine sincerity, fail to materialise into lasting outcomes? Why do governments, organisations and even individuals so often begin with enthusiasm, only to lose coherence, momentum or trust along the way? The problem is not always with the intention itself. More often, it lies in the absence of structures that can carry an intention from a fragile declaration into a durable reality. The Fulfilment Pyramid addresses this gap – not as a theoretical embellishment, but as a practical necessity.

What is the Fulfilment Pyramid?

The Fulfilment Pyramid was first introduced in *Human Being – Illuminating the Reality Beneath the Facade* as a phenomenological model that shows how care matures into intention, intention depends on integrity and effectiveness, and effectiveness culminates in fulfilment.[94] The model also reveals how awareness of the constituent parts of our Being is essential to maintain and sustain integrity itself. In this way, care, intention, awareness, integrity and effectiveness interlock, ultimately culminating in fulfilment.

While that model captures the pathway at the level of the individual, it does not account for the developmental work required to form intention in the first place, nor the relational and systemic scaffolding needed to sustain it over time.

In this broader discourse on sustainability, the Fulfilment Pyramid has been re-envisioned as a tri-dimensional structure that maps how intention must be developed, enacted and sustained if it is to create enduring impact.

---

94 Tashvir, A. (2022) *Human Being: Illuminating the Reality Beneath the Facade*. Sydney: Engenesis Publications, p. 3.

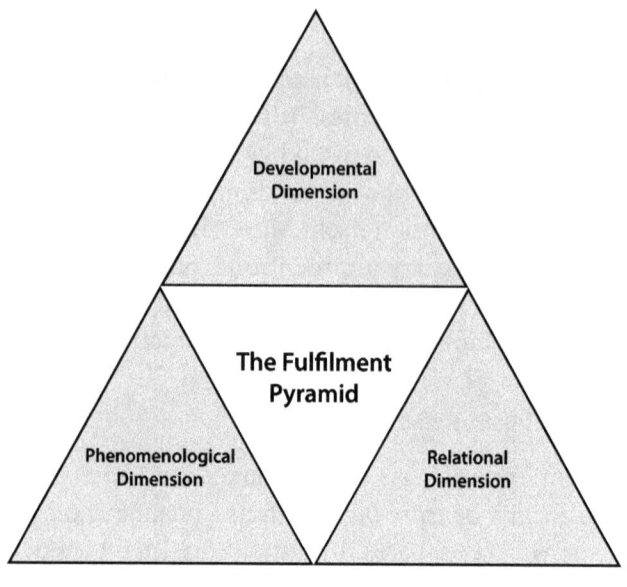
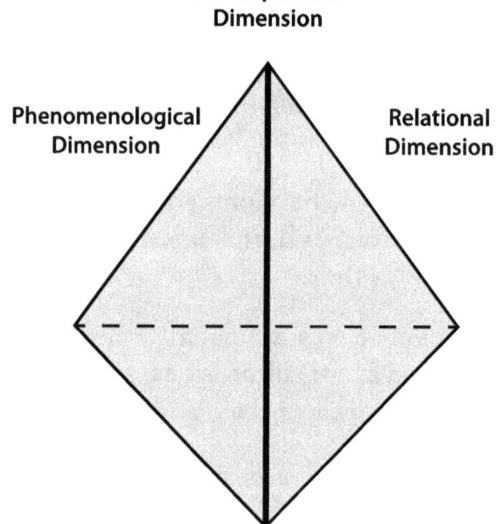

Figure 12 – The Fulfilment Pyramid.

Together, these three dimensions transform fragile commitments into durable, fulfilled intentions. When one of these dimensions is absent, commitments remain episodic – inspiring at first, but easily fractured by pressure, competing demands or short-term expedience. However, when they interlock, intention becomes systemic – a force capable not only of guiding individuals, but also of shaping organisations, cultures and societies towards coherence and sustainability.

In the context of the Authentic Sustainability Framework (ASF), the Fulfilment Pyramid is both diagnostic and prescriptive – a way to understand why commitments falter, and a guide for how they can endure over time and through challenges for the benefit of future generations.

At the same time, the Systemic Subversion Cycle (SSC) reveals what happens when these dimensions are absent. Each phase of dysfunction mirrors a missing foundation of fulfilment. This makes the Fulfilment Pyramid not just a model for fulfilment, but also a direct response to systemic breakdowns.

From diagnosis to reconstruction and enduring fulfilment

The SSC exposes how commitments falter when coherence breaks – promises unravel, exploitation rises and inertia calcifies dysfunction. Yet the cycle also points directly to where interventions are needed. Each phase corresponds to a gap the Fulfilment Pyramid is designed to close. These gaps correspond to the same points where cycles of entrenchment take hold: when intention is shallow, when enactment loses integrity, or when structures fail to sustain coherence.

- When breakdown and disorder appear, it signals that the **Developmental Dimension** has been neglected – intentions were never grounded in authentic meaning.
- When exploitation and incoherent enactment dominate, it reveals fractures in the **Phenomenological Dimension** – integrity and effectiveness were sacrificed.
- When inertia and repetition calcify across generations, it shows the absence of the **Relational Dimension** – no relational scaffolding was in place to sustain coherence.

By reading the SSC through the Fulfilment Pyramid, leaders can move from diagnosis to reconstruction. Instead of reacting to dysfunction piecemeal, they can ask: *Which dimension of fulfilment is missing here?* This reframes the cycle, not as inevitable decline, but as an invitation to rebuild coherence systemically – from meaning clarified, to integrity enacted, to relational and structural scaffolding sustained.

Unpacking the dimensions of fulfilment

The Fulfilment Pyramid is more than a conceptual model. Each of its three dimensions represents a distinct discipline that must be cultivated if commitments are to endure. Taken together, they show that fulfilment is not simply about resolve or effort, but about how intention is formed, how it is enacted in practice, and how it is carried across time and systems.

Fulfilment is never the product of intention and effort alone. Instead, it requires three distinct but inseparable dimensions oriented by the UOSI's Architectonic Sphere:

- **The Developmental Dimension** – Oriented by **meta-awareness**, this dimension ensures intention is grounded in authentic meaning rather than reactivity or superficial desire. It represents the flow of coherence, as explained in the previous chapter.
- **The Phenomenological Dimension** – Oriented by **systemic integrity**, this dimension ensures intention is enacted with integrity and effectiveness rather than ungrounded or superficial effort.
- **The Relational Dimension** – Oriented by **sustained effectiveness** and **normativity**, this dimension ensures fulfilment is not only durable, but also aligned with ethical and cultural codes.

Let's now turn our attention to each dimension in turn to see how they work individually and how, together, they form the architecture of enduring fulfilment.

The Developmental Dimension – Grounding intention in authentic meaning

Intention is often treated as if it already exists, as though people naturally know what they want and are ready to act on it. However, as we have already seen, intention must be deliberately developed. It begins as desire – fragile and unfocused – and must be clarified and matured through the flow of coherence before it can stabilise into a compass strong enough to orient and guide behaviour.

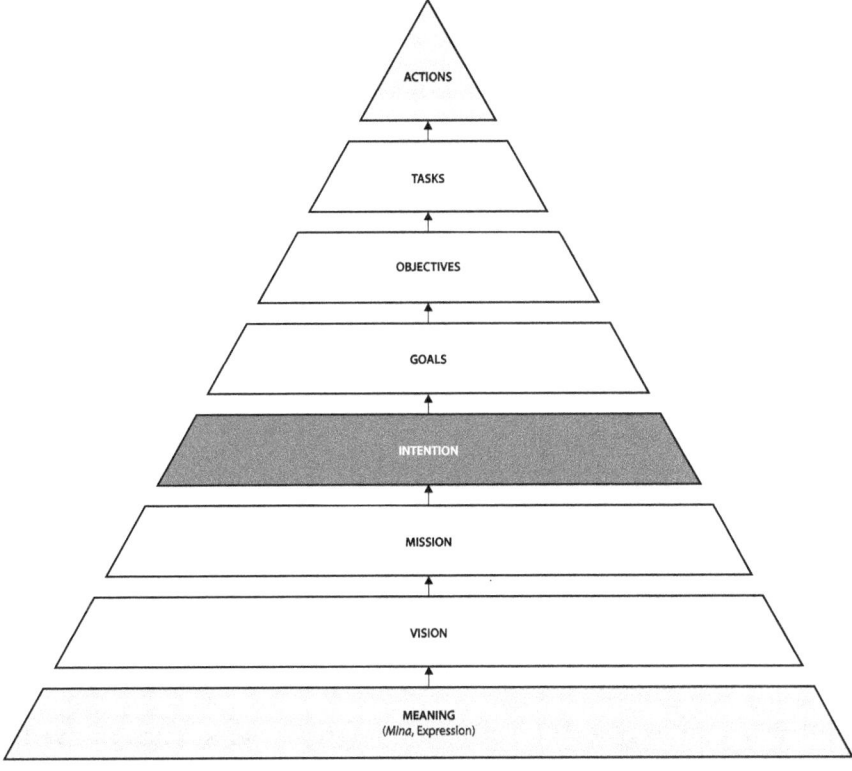

Figure 13 – The Fulfilment Pyramid's Developmental Dimension.

The Developmental Dimension is oriented by **meta-awareness**. Without it, a vision hardens into ambition without discernment, and missions drift into incoherence or opportunism. Meta-awareness ensures that what is being developed as intention is genuinely grounded in meaning and not driven by bias, trends or short-term impulses.

This dimension stabilises the compass of coherence:

- **Meaning (including *Mina*)** – The ultimate *why*, the orienting horizon that gives significance.

- **Vision** – An imagination of what meaning looks like when expressed.
- **Mission** – The declaration of one's role in service of that vision.
- **Intention** – The compass of coherence, a posture of Being that commits to a direction.
- **Goals** – The broad domain of focus and aspiration.
- **Objectives** – Brings those goals into measurable form, creating accountability and direction.
- **Tasks → Actions** – Translate intention into reality – tasks structure the path and actions embody it through visible, coherent execution.

Without this developmental foundation, intentions risk being hollow, incoherent or performative. But with it, they gain depth, purpose and resilience.

When grounded intention stabilises, it crosses the threshold from development to embodiment – the point at which the Phenomenological Dimension begins.

The Phenomenological Dimension – From intention to fulfilment (the lived translation of meaning into action)

Intention on its own is insufficient; it must be embodied in lived reality through conduct if it is to be fulfilled. This dimension highlights the phenomenological law: when care matures into intention, it naturally seeks fulfilment. But only when integrity and effectiveness are strong enough to generate momentum does intention stabilise into results that honour the meaning from which it arose.

Phenomenologically, fulfilment is the lived experience of wholeness – when what we care about is pursued with integrity and brought into being. What sustains this enactment is **systemic integrity**: the principle that coherence must hold not only within the self, but also across actions, teams and institutions. Systemic integrity ensures that effectiveness is not just immediate performance, but continuity of alignment, preventing the erosion of fulfilment by hidden fractures. **Moods** and **Primary Ways of Being** can either support or sabotage coherence. **Integrity** ensures intention is not fractured, while **effectiveness** translates commitment into results.

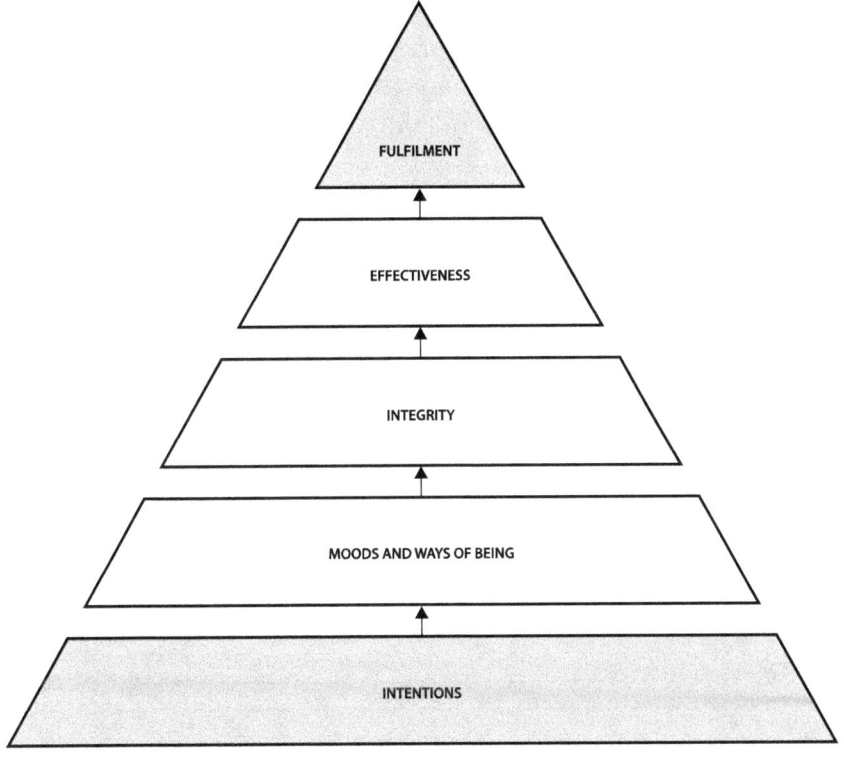

Figure 14 – The Fulfilment Pyramid's Phenomenological Dimension.

- **Intention** – The orienting commitment of Being.
- **Moods and Primary Ways of Being** – Dispositions that stabilise or destabilise coherence.
- **Integrity** – Alignment of inner architecture with the meaning from which intention arose.
- **Effectiveness** – Capacity to translate intention into outcomes.
- **Fulfilment** – The lived experience of wholeness when what we care about is pursued coherently and brought into being.

Without integrity, effort fails to gain momentum and eventually fractures. Without effectiveness, effort fails. But when both are present, momentum builds, intention is enacted and fulfilment becomes possible.

The Relational Dimension – Sustaining coherence systemically

Even when intentions are well-developed and enacted with integrity, they cannot endure in isolation. Intentions live within relationships and structures that either support them or allow them to corrode. This dimension is oriented by **sustained effectiveness** and **normativity**, ensuring fulfilment is both durable and ethically aligned.

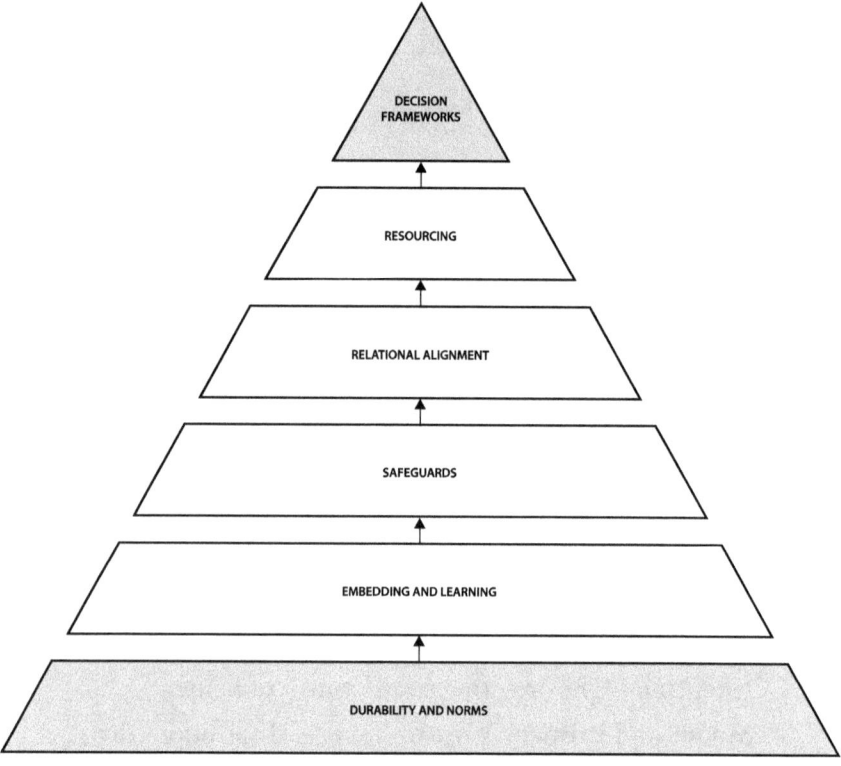

Figure 15 – The Fulfilment Pyramid's Relational Dimension.

The Relational Dimension unfolds through a set of reinforcing layers that sustain coherence over time:

- **Durability and norms** establish ethical and procedural foundations that make fulfilment last without fatigue, ensuring legitimacy and continuity.
- **Embedding and learning** institutionalise coherence through rituals, policies and reflective feedback loops so fulfilment is not person-dependent but systemic.

- **Safeguards** preserve intention by protecting sovereignty and resisting coercion, keeping systems free from corruption and drift.
- **Relational alignment** maintains trust, candour and psychological safety, allowing commitments to hold across time and teams.
- **Resourcing** allocates time, energy and capital fairly, maintaining the capacity to enact intentions sustainably.
- **Decision frameworks** clarify roles, responsibilities and escalation paths, transforming moral clarity into operational coherence.

Together, these layers form the scaffolding that carries intention forward. Where they are absent, even sincere commitments decay. But where they are present, intention becomes sustainable – a force that endures across relationships, organisations and generations.

To recap:

- The **Developmental Dimension** shapes raw desire into intention grounded in authentic meaning. Without it, commitments stay hollow or reactive – e.g., a climate pledge made for PR rather than genuine purpose.
- The **Phenomenological Dimension** enacts intention with integrity and effectiveness. Without it, commitments remain wishful or collapse in practice – e.g., a reform announced, but sabotaged by incoherent execution.
- The **Relational Dimension** provides the scaffolding (durability and norms; embedding and learning; safeguards; relational alignment; resourcing; and decision frameworks) that sustains fulfilment over time. Without this scaffolding, commitments corrode under pressure – for example, the abandonment of a wellbeing policy when budgets tighten.

Together, these three dimensions ensure intentions are formed with depth, enacted with coherence and sustained with durability.

The interrelationship between the three dimensions

Having explored each dimension individually, and how each aligns with the architectonic qualities of meta-awareness, systemic integrity and sustained effectiveness, we can now see how they interconnect to form one living architecture.

The Fulfilment Pyramid is often perceived as a linear flow: from meaning → expression → intention → commitment → action. However, in practice, it unfolds across three interdependent dimensions. These dimensions reveal how fulfilment is not merely a sequence of internal events, but a multidimensional phenomenon of development, embodiment and relational coherence.

1. The Developmental Dimension – Clarity of intention (meaning anchored)

The Developmental Dimension concerns the formation and maturation of intention. It is where your internal architecture evolves through a process of reflection, discernment and the progressive alignment of your motives with your deeper meaning (*Mina*). Intention, in this sense, is not an impulsive wish, but a cultivated orientation of Being. It arises through the developmental process of clarifying your purpose, values and inner drivers. The previous chapter zoomed in on this dimension through the flow of coherence.

The outcome of the Developmental Dimension and its flow of coherence is **clarity** – a deep understanding of what matters and why. Without clarity, intention drifts, becoming reactive or performative. However, with clarity, intention becomes deeply anchored in meaning and ready to be enacted.

2. The Phenomenological Dimension – Coherence of conduct (Being embodied)

Once intention is anchored in meaning, it must be embodied through conduct. The Phenomenological Dimension is where intention takes shape in lived experience – how you show up, decide, act and interact. This is the realm where the Being Framework becomes operative: where authenticity, integrity, care, responsibility and other Aspects of Being transform intention into observable behaviour.

Here, fulfilment is not an abstract pursuit, but a lived phenomenon. The outcome is **coherence** – the alignment between inner intention and outward expression. It's when your conduct, attitudes and choices mirror the integrity (wholeness) of your Being, revealing whether the developmental clarity has translated into existential embodiment.

3. The Relational Dimension – Fulfilment beyond the individual

The Relational Dimension extends fulfilment beyond the individual. It is where your meaning and conduct find resonance within shared, organised and tangible systems, such as teams, institutions, communities and enterprises. This dimension binds fulfilment to the logistics of real life: resourcing, management, decision frameworks and the architecture that sustains coherence across time, people and contexts.

While the Developmental and Phenomenological Dimensions refine clarity and conduct, the Relational Dimension ensures those qualities endure and scale. It translates inner integrity into collective functionality. Fulfilment only becomes sustainable when intention is anchored in structures and systems that uphold and reinforce it.

In this way, fulfilment matures from being an individual phenomenon to becoming a systemic state of coherence – one that integrates logistics, governance, culture and relationships. It represents the capacity to sustain integrity across time and complexity. The outcome is **harmony** – a living equilibrium between ourselves, others and the systems we collectively inhabit, where intention, conduct and structure reinforce one another in service of shared meaning.

To recap:

Fulfilment represents the systemic maturity of coherence – the point at which meaning is clarified, intention is embodied, and integrity is sustained through structure.

- The **Developmental Dimension** shapes raw desire into grounded intention anchored in authentic meaning.
- The **Phenomenological Dimension** enacts that intention through coherent conduct and lived integrity.

- The **Relational Dimension** ensures those qualities endure, embedding them into relationships, governance and culture so they can withstand pressure and time.

Together, these dimensions transform fulfilment from a fleeting emotional state into a living architecture of sustainability – one where what matters most is not only pursued, but sustained.

Examples

1. Leadership – Leading through a crisis

Developmental Dimension: A leader faces a sudden crisis that threatens the organisation's stability. Instead of reacting impulsively, they pause to reconnect with meaning, asking, 'What truly matters here beyond appearances or short-term optics?' Through introspection and values alignment, they clarify their intention: to act with integrity, transparency and care for their people while preserving the organisation's purpose.

Phenomenological Dimension: They embody this intention through conduct – communicating honestly, making themselves available, remaining calm and modelling ethical decision-making. Their actions are coherent with their internal clarity, creating trust through presence rather than performance.

Relational Dimension: To make this coherence sustainable, they establish decision frameworks for crisis escalation, redistribute workloads (resourcing) to avoid burnout and establish psychological safety and resilience meetings (relational alignment) to ensure team members remain candid and connected. Through these tangible structures, fulfilment moves from personal clarity to collective harmony.

2. Organisational – Building a culture of authentic sustainability

Developmental Dimension: An organisation re-examines why it exists beyond profit. Through collective reflection and stakeholder dialogue, it defines a meaningful intention – to solve real human problems through ethical entrepreneurship. This establishes the clarity of purpose that informs the organisation's strategies.

Phenomenological Dimension: Leaders and teams embody that purpose by integrating sustainability into daily operations – ethical sourcing, responsible product design, transparent communication and genuine care for employee wellbeing. Conduct becomes an expression of meaning.

Relational Dimension: To ensure this integrity persists systemically, the organisation builds safeguards against greenwashing, creates embedding and learning loops (such as impact reviews and purpose-aligned routines), defines resourcing protocols to distribute time and capital fairly and implements decision frameworks linking purpose to measurable outcomes. Consequently, fulfilment evolves from aspiration to a sustained system of coherence.

3. Personal – Rebuilding trust in a relationship

Developmental Dimension: After a conflict, one partner reflects deeply to understand the meaning behind their reactions. They realise that fear and pride masked their genuine intention to connect. As a result, they refine their intention towards honesty and care.

Phenomenological Dimension: They begin to embody this intention through conduct – communicating openly, taking responsibility and demonstrating patience instead of defensiveness. Over time, their actions become consistent with their clarified intention.

Relational Dimension: Together, they create tangible structures to sustain harmony: setting aside weekly check-ins (relational alignment), establishing safeguards, such as agreed boundaries for respectful communication, and balancing resourcing of time and attention so neither feels neglected. Over time, these practical systems transform emotional insight into a living, reliable pattern of trust.

Having seen how the three dimensions apply across leadership, organisational and personal contexts, we can now observe how they interlock within a single, integrated system.

Case study: A sustainable education initiative

Imagine a community launching an initiative to improve access to quality education.

- **Developmental Dimension**: The intention begins with meaning – the recognition that education expresses the inherent dignity and potential of human beings. A vision forms of a community where every child can flourish. A mission is declared to build accessible schools and equip them to serve local needs. Intention crystallises as a compass: 'We will provide education that nurtures both knowledge and character.' Goals, objectives, tasks and actions then cascade – from setting enrolment targets to training teachers and building classrooms.
- **Phenomenological Dimension**: To succeed, the initiative must enact this intention with integrity and effectiveness. If resources are misallocated or shortcuts are taken, the effort fractures. But when financial transparency is maintained, when teachers are empowered, and when results are measured not only by test scores, but also by student wellbeing, the system holds. Fulfilment is then experienced. The community sees young lives transformed and trust in the initiative deepens.
- **Relational Dimension**: For the initiative to endure, it must be embedded in systemic support. This means parents trust the schools, governments provide stable funding and cultural norms affirm education as a priority. At this level, intention cannot stand alone – it must be carried within a relational field that honours Being. When trust and sovereignty are also present, the community safeguards the intention, allowing it to mature beyond the enthusiasm of its founders. In this way, the intention becomes more than a project. It becomes a generational force, sustained by systems and relationships that keep reshaping futures long after the original leaders have moved on.

In summary, the three dimensions of the Fulfilment Pyramid show that fulfilment is never the product of a single act or moment. It requires:

- **Development**, so that raw desire stabilises into intention grounded in meaning;

- **Enactment**, so that intention is carried through integrity and effectiveness into lived reality; and
- **Relational scaffolding**, so that intention is not left fragile or episodic, but becomes sustainable across time and generations.

When any one of these dimensions is absent, fulfilment collapses. Development without enactment breeds hollowness. Enactment without relational integrity produces fragility. Relational scaffolding without development hardens into conformity. But when all three are present, intention becomes systemic – a force capable of orienting individual lives, organisations and societies towards coherence and authentic sustainability.

Instatement – From commitment to enduring coherence

The Fulfilment Pyramid provides the architecture, while instatement provides the mechanics – embedding intention into habits, structures and norms so coherence remains intact when conditions shift. For coherence to endure, commitment must move beyond words and take root in lived reality. This move is known as **instatement**: the embedding of intention into rhythms of behaviour, organisational structures and cultural norms. It is the point where a commitment is no longer held only by memory, enthusiasm or leadership pressure, but becomes sustained through embodied practice.

Just as seeds require soil, water and climate to grow, commitments require systems that support their enactment. Promises written into speeches or policies may inspire, but without supporting structures they collapse under the weight of competing demands. Instatement provides that support, ensuring intentions are not left fragile or episodic, but instead gain resilience through repetition, reinforcement and systemic integration.

Instatement happens at multiple levels. Personally, it looks like building routines, habits and practices that embody intention in daily life – protecting time for health, shaping conversations with integrity or creating boundaries that sustain energy. Organisationally, it takes the form of policies, processes and cultural norms that make the intended direction practical and repeatable. Societally, instatement becomes visible in laws, institutions and shared traditions that embed values like fairness, dignity and sustainability into the fabric of collective life.

When instatement is weak, intentions remain fragile – inspiring in words, but inconsistent in practice. This creates drift, cynicism and, eventually, breakdown. But when instatement is strong, intentions gain durability. They are carried not only by individual willpower, but by supportive systems that normalise coherence. In this way, instatement is less about dramatic declarations and more about cultivating environments where doing the right thing becomes the easiest, most natural thing.

In each case, instatement closes the gap between what is declared and what is lived. It ensures that intention does not remain episodic or fragile, but becomes resilient through repetition, reinforcement and systemic integration. When intention is instated, it begins to reshape conduct, institutions and cultures.

Example: Workplace culture

Consider an organisation that declares its intention to 'prioritise employee wellbeing'. Without instatement, this may result in motivational posters, occasional workshops or ad hoc wellbeing days – gestures that sound good, but fail to shift the daily experience of staff. The intention remains fragile because it is not anchored in practice. In contrast, when the intention is instated, it becomes woven into the organisation's structures. Workloads are realistically designed, managers are trained to notice early signs of burnout, budgets are allocated to health initiatives and cultural norms reward balance rather than overwork. Over time, wellbeing is no longer a slogan, but a lived reality. The intention has taken root because systems, habits and norms sustain it.

Applying the Fulfilment Pyramid: A step-by-step guide

The Fulfilment Pyramid is not only conceptual, but operational. The following guide translates its three dimensions into a practical framework that can be readily applied by an individual, a team or an organisation. It includes phased steps, tools and mini-examples to help move from commitments declared to commitments fulfilled.

Phase 1 – Developmental Dimension

Shape raw desire into coherent intention grounded in meaning via the flow of coherence.

Clarify meaning and vision

- **Meaning statement** (one sentence): Why does this matter?
- **Vision** (one paragraph): What would you, your relationship, team or organisation look like if that meaning was expressed?

Example – Personal (health):

- **Meaning statement:** Health matters because it allows me to serve others with energy and presence.
- **Vision:** If this meaning was expressed, I would live with vitality, free from preventable illness. My days would be marked by steady energy, clarity of thought and resilience under pressure. I would have rhythms of sleep, exercise and nutrition that enable me to flourish personally and support others without burning out.

Declare mission and intention

- **Mission** (one sentence): What role will be taken in service of the vision?
- **Intention** (one sentence): 'When I/we [act], it is done so with [disposition] in service of [meaning].'

Example

- **Mission:** My role is to develop sustainable habits that protect and strengthen my body so I can live and serve with vitality.
- **Intention:** When I exercise, it is done with steadiness in service of health as the foundation for a life of contribution.

Translate into direction

- **3 goals** – broad aims aligned to intention.
- **For each goal:** Write 2–4 objectives – measurable commitments.
- **For each objective:** Note the key tasks and actions.

Example

Goals:

1. Improve sleep quality
2. Build a consistent exercise routine
3. Improve daily nutrition

Objectives (2–4 per goal)

- **Sleep quality:** Average 7.5 hours per night within 90 days.
- **Movement:** Exercise 4x weekly (2 cardio, 2 strength).
- **Nutrition:** Eat 5+ wholefood meals per week, reduce processed sugar by 50%.

Tasks and actions

- Set lights-out routine (phone outside bedroom, 10 pm cutoff).
- Join the local gym and book sessions into the calendar.
- Prep weekly meal plans and shop for wholefoods each Sunday.

Meta-awareness checks

- **Bias scan:** What pressures, trends or incentives could distort intention?
- **Coherence test:** Does every goal objectively serve the intention and vision? If not, remove or rework.

Example

- **Bias scan:** Am I pursuing health for appearance or comparison, instead of vitality and service?
- **Coherence test:** Do all goals directly serve my meaning and vision of sustainable vitality?

Quick tool – The Fulfilment Canvas (one page)

- Meaning • Vision • Mission • Intention
- 3 Goals • Objectives • Key Tasks • First Actions
- Risks to Coherence • Mitigations

Example

- **Meaning:** Health sustains my capacity to serve and live with vitality.
- **Vision:** A life lived with energy, clarity, and resilience.
  Mission: Cultivate sustainable habits that strengthen body and spirit.
- **Intention:** Exercise with steadiness in service of health as the foundation for contribution.
- **Goals:** Sleep, movement, nutrition.
- **Objectives:** 7.5h avg sleep; 4x weekly exercise; 5+ wholefood meals/week.
- **Actions:** Set bedtime routine; book gym sessions; prep meals.
- **Risks to Coherence:** Overcommitment, comparison, neglecting rest.
- **Mitigations:** WIP limit of 2 habits at a time; focus on vitality, not appearance.

Phase 2 – Phenomenological Dimension

Enact intention with integrity and effectiveness until it is felt as fulfilment.

Integrity alignment

- **Primary Ways of Being:** Commitment, Responsibility and Empowerment
- **Undermining habits:** Performative and defensive. For example, 'I'm fully committed' to a fitness goal while secretly cutting corners (performative), or deflecting feedback about poor training habits by blaming time or stress (defensive).
- **Boundary conditions:** No fad diets; no training through injury.

Effectiveness design

- **Success signals (leading indicators):**
  - Morning energy rating (1–5).
  - Resting heart rate trend.
  - Consistency of weekly workouts.
- **Metrics (outcome measures):**
  - Sleep average of 7.5 hours.
  - Four workouts per week sustained over 3 months.
  - 50% reduction in processed sugar intake.
- **Feedback loops:**
  - Daily journal entry (energy + sleep).
  - Weekly review with partner.
  - Monthly check-in with GP/trainer.

Enactment rhythm

- **Weekly (30 min):** Review intention, check signals, adjust tasks.
- **Monthly (90 min):** Assess integrity breaches, effectiveness gaps, adjust plan.
- **Quarterly (half-day):** Revisit Meaning–Vision–Mission, refine goals, remove what no longer serves.

Micro-reconfiguration protocol

- If **integrity** breaks: Name it (e.g., skipped sleep for late-night scrolling), reset boundary and reinforce alignment.
- If **effectiveness** stalls: Simplify objective, change method or add capability.

Quick tool – Integrity and Effectiveness Scorecard (1–5 scale)

- Integrity kept in decisions.
- Integrity kept under pressure.

- Actions aligned with intention.
- Leading indicators trending positively.
- Outcomes achieved without burnout.

(Anything ≤3 triggers a reconfiguration conversation.)

Phase 3 – Relational Dimension

Build the scaffolding that sustains fulfilment across time and context.

Durability and norms

- **Sustained effectiveness:** Health practices are designed for long-term viability, not short bursts of willpower. Routines like balanced meals, regular sleep and steady movement are kept realistic so they can be maintained across seasons of life.
- **Normativity:** Health choices must remain consistent with personal values and ethics. Vitality is pursued, not for image or vanity, but for contribution, balance and care for myself and others.

Embedding and learning

- **Rituals:** Bedtime routine (phone out, lights dimmed), Sunday meal prep.
- **Policy-in-practice:** Weekly 'no work after 7pm' rule to protect rest.
- **Onboarding story:** 'For me, health isn't about image but vitality. I sleep deeply, eat well and move regularly so I can bring my best to my work, my relationships and the things I care about. Every small action – from putting my phone away before bed to cooking nourishing meals and taking a walk at the end of the day – is part of sustaining the energy I need to contribute meaningfully. These rhythms aren't about perfection or quick fixes. They are about building a life that is steady, balanced and durable – one where I feel strong enough to serve others, resilient enough to adapt, and grounded enough to stay true to what matters most.'

Safeguards

- **Sovereignty clause:** Health choices are not compromised for appearance or peer pressure.
- **Protection mechanism:** No unsustainable 'quick fixes' or products that erode long-term health.

Relational alignment

- **Candour and safety norms:** Weekly check-in with partner on energy, stress and routines.
- **Repair path:** If routines slip, acknowledge openly, reset and restart with one small step.

Resourcing

- **Allocations:** 5 hours/week for exercise; $X/week for healthy food and gym membership.
- **Guardrails:** No more than two habit changes at once to prevent overload and burnout.

Decision framework

- **Roles and responsibilities:** Use a simple RACI (Responsible, Accountable, Consulted and Informed) for the sleep goal. Responsible = self; Accountable = partner (to notice patterns); Consulted = GP/trainer; Informed = family.
- **Escalation path:** If persistent sleep disruption occurs, consult GP.

Quick tool – Relational Checklist

- **Norms intact** → Are my actions consistent with my deeper values of vitality, contribution and care?
- **Durability tested** → Are my routines sustainable when life shifts, for example when I'm under stress, travelling and across changing seasons?
- **Check-ins scheduled** → Do I have weekly and monthly check-ins to reflect and recalibrate?

- **Policies embedded** → Have I created personal 'policies' (e.g., phone out of the bedroom, no work emails after 9 pm)?
- **Safeguards in place** → What boundaries protect my energy and prevent unhealthy trade-offs?
- **Relational alignment** → Are my relationships reinforcing or undermining my health goals?
- **Resources realistic** → Are my time, energy and budget aligned with my health commitments?
- **Roles clear** → Who supports or shares responsibility for my health? (e.g., doctor, partner, personal trainer, accountability buddy)

Putting it together – 30-60-90 day plan (personal health example)

Days 0–30: Form and focus

- Complete Fulfilment Canvas
- Run first bias scan
- Define indicators and outcome metrics
- Establish weekly + monthly cadences
- Draft RACI and resource plan

Days 31–60: Enact and learn

- Focus on 1–2 objectives only
- Use scorecards weekly
- Log integrity breaches and reconfigurations
- Finalise trust norms, define repair pathways and establish capacity guardrails.

Days 61–90: Embed and scale

- Institutionalise 2 rituals (bedtime routine, Sunday prep).
- Share onboarding story with family/household.
- Run quarterly review: retire what no longer serves, re-align resources and refresh intention.

Conclusion

Commitment marks the threshold where intention is tested, but it is *instatement* – the process of embedding commitments into lived systems – that gives them the strength to last. Without being anchored in behaviour, structures and culture, even the most authentic commitments remain fragile.

The Fulfilment Pyramid shows why this matters. Fulfilment is not achieved by effort alone, but by the integration of three dimensions: the developmental work of forming intention, the phenomenological work of enacting it through integrity and effectiveness, and the relational scaffolding that allows it to endure. These dimensions are not linear stages, but interdependent forces that together form a living architecture of coherence – linking inner clarity, embodied conduct and systemic support into one continuum.

Each dimension carries its own cascade of layers and is oriented by deeper architectonic qualities: meta-awareness, systemic integrity, sustained effectiveness and normativity. Remove one dimension and fulfilment collapses. Neglect its orienting quality and coherence corrodes over time. But when all three interlock under these qualities, intention matures into fulfilment and becomes a systemic force that shapes individuals, organisations and societies toward coherence and authentic sustainability.

The Fulfilment Pyramid is not only constructive, but also diagnostic. Read through the lens of the Systemic Subversion Cycle (SSC), it exposes where commitments falter – lack of developmental grounding, fractures in enactment, or absence of relational scaffolding. Used together, the SSC and Fulfilment Pyramid offer both diagnosis and reconstruction: one reveals where coherence has broken, while the other provides the architecture for repair and renewal.

The practical guides included here – from canvases and scorecards to scaffolding checklists – are designed to ensure this model moves beyond abstraction. They show that fulfilment is not a distant ideal, but a disciplined practice: forming intention with depth, enacting it with coherence, and sustaining it across systems and generations.

The question now is not only how intentions and commitments are formed, but how we discern whether they are genuinely generating coherence or drifting into performance and pretence. The next chapter takes up this challenge, examining how fulfilment can be measured, recognised and validated as the lived evidence of authentic sustainability.

CHAPTER 50

Gauging Authentic Sustainability

By now, you will be familiar with the Unified Ontology of Systemic Integrity (UOSI) and its 16 qualities. You have seen them in theory, explored their anatomy and noticed how they show up across systems, including yourself. But knowing a framework is one thing. Applying it in your life is another.

This chapter opens the door to that practice. This isn't about perfection or polished answers. It's about equipping you with a way to gauge the health of a relationship or a human-designed system through the lens of authentic sustainability – even if that process is sometimes subjective or incomplete.

Later, in Part VIII, you will be introduced to a dedicated ontometric assessment tool[95] – the Sustainability Profile – that makes this process more structured and less prone to bias. But for now, the aim

---

95   A diagnostic instrument used to evaluate the degree to which a system, organisation or individual expresses key ontological qualities, such as those mapped in models like the Unified Ontology of Systemic Integrity (UOSI), which outlines 16 fundamental qualities of coherence. Each quality is assessed based on its observable distinctions and patterns, allowing a structured view of how integrity, modulation and systemic integrity manifest in practice. The purpose of such a tool is not to measure traits, but to reveal the ontological configuration and health of a system.

is to understand the challenges associated with gauging the authentic sustainability of any system – from individuals and relationships to organisations, institutions, communities and societies – and practise with the distinctions themselves. Along the way, you'll also learn to spot when a quality is not merely inconsistent or underdeveloped, but distorted – the shadows that quietly undermine sustainability.

Why gauging authentic sustainability matters

Authentic sustainability depends on more than strategies, resources or technologies. Its strength lies in the often-invisible fabric of relationships – how people trust, align, adapt and sustain integrity together. Whether you are an individual seeking coherence in your life, a couple strengthening your relationship, a team leader shaping culture, a founder building a start-up, a policymaker weighing reform, an activist designing a movement or a journalist investigating systemic dysfunction, the same challenge arises: How do you know if the system is truly sustainable?

In earlier chapters, we unpacked the underlying ontology of each of the 16 UOSI qualities through the Ontological Triad Schema (OTS) – anatomy, mechanics and topology. That work was not merely theoretical, it provided the scaffolding for practice.

Now, as we begin gauging authentic sustainability, we return to these qualities to see how they can be applied diagnostically. The task is no longer just to know what trust or adaptability is in an ontological sense, but to ask: How do these qualities show up in ourselves and the systems we are part of? Where are they healthy, where are they fractured, and what are the consequences?

This is where the 16 qualities of systemic integrity become practical. Each quality acts as a diagnostic lens. It won't hand you a neat score out of 10, but it will sharpen your questions, reveal hidden fractures and turn vague impressions into grounded observations that can guide more coherent action. Before we return to the UOSI, let's consider the inherent limitations of self-assessment.

The barriers of self-assessment

Looking at systems from the inside is never neutral because the lenses we use are shaped by the same dynamics we are trying to evaluate. Before you practise gauging authentic sustainability, it's important to acknowledge the inherent limitations of self-assessment:

- **Error-prone** – It's easy to misread signals, especially where blind spots exist. You might confuse surface harmony with genuine trust, or mistake temporary results for systemic effectiveness.
- **Biased** – Every assessment is filtered through your desires, fears, history and loyalties. As human beings, we often protect what we are attached to and downplay evidence that threatens our preferred narrative.
- **Subjective** – Two people can assess the same situation differently and both feel 'right'. Sustainability is not experienced uniformly. Our cultural background, upbringing, roles and personal dispositions all shape how we perceive it.
- **Fragmented** – Systems are complex. Focusing on one or two qualities in isolation, such as adaptability or effectiveness, can distort the picture if the other qualities are neglected.
- **Time-consuming** – Working deeply with all 16 qualities requires discipline. Without a structured process, it can feel overwhelming, leading to superficial scans or abandoned attempts.

These barriers do not invalidate the act of gauging authentic sustainability. Rather, they highlight the need to approach it with humility, discipline and openness. Even imperfect attempts have value. They stretch perception, bring shadows into view and invite dialogue where silence might otherwise hide fractures. More importantly, they make sustainability tangible – shifting it from an abstract ideal into something that can be observed, questioned and strengthened.

The following sections take two qualities – trust and adaptability – and show how the anatomy, mechanics and topology you studied earlier can now be used as practical lenses. By working through them in this way, you will see how the ontology translates directly into lived diagnosis and action.

Let's begin with trust because it is so foundational to every relationship – personal, organisational or systemic.

1. Trust

Ontological distinction

Trust is the structural orientation that enables people and systems – from individuals and relationships to organisations, institutions and cultures – to remain open, relational and functional in the presence of risk, uncertainty and dependency. It is not simply about whether you are 'trustworthy' – it's also about your willingness to engage in trust by choice. Trust does not depend on certainty, but on coherence, goodwill and alignment being actively sustained. It shapes how you carry yourself, how others experience you, and how any system cooperates and endures in the face of challenge.

A **healthy relationship with trust** indicates that you are able and willing to be open – emotionally, relationally and ideologically – while discerning whether that openness can genuinely be received and reciprocated. You are neither naive nor cynical. You participate in trust as a living dynamic – extending it thoughtfully, repairing it when broken, and withdrawing it when necessary, without collapsing into defensiveness. Trust becomes part of your presence and reputation so that others experience you as transparent, congruent and reliable. In the context of manufactured systems, healthy trust manifests as psychological safety, transparent feedback loops, distributed leadership and adaptive resilience. It reduces friction, fuels innovation, accelerates progress and fosters long-term sustainability.

An **unhealthy relationship with trust** indicates that you are either blindly optimistic or chronically suspicious. On the one hand, being overly trusting makes you naive or compliant, leaving you vulnerable to exploitation. On the other hand, pervasive distrust makes you guarded and defensive, unable to collaborate or sustain openness. Manufactured systems mirror these extremes by overregulating, enforcing conformity or becoming performative in place of genuine cooperation. Over time, sustainability erodes – not because competence is absent, but because trust is lacking or broken. Without trust, everything must be managed, controlled and surveilled – nothing can naturally thrive and evolve.

Gauging trust in practice

To gauge trust in any system, start with a simple diagnostic scan:

- **Choose your context** – Identify the system you want to examine, for example: your marriage, your founding team or a government policy such as Australia's 5% deposit scheme for first homebuyers.
- **Ask** – What does trust feel like here? Do people withhold or speak openly? Are ruptures repaired or left unresolved?
- **Scan for signals** – Healthy trust feels like transparency, reliability, repair and reciprocity. Fractured trust shows up as secrecy, defensiveness or rigid control structures compensating for missing trust.
- **Examine the consequences** – What becomes unsustainable if trust is weak? In couples, it may be emotional safety; in a start-up, collaboration; and in housing policy, public trust in institutions.

This quick scan gives you a first impression. To deepen your understanding, move through the Ontological Triad Schema (OTS) lenses.

Anatomy – The structural components

Trust is not built on sentiment alone. It rests on a structural foundation that makes coherence possible in the face of uncertainty, dependency and vulnerability. These components function like the beams of an invisible scaffold:

- **Openness** – The willingness to disclose, depend and risk vulnerability. Without openness, relationships default to transaction or control.
- **Consistency** – The repeated congruence of words, actions and follow-through. Even small inconsistencies can erode trust over time.

- **Benevolence** – The presence of goodwill and non-malicious intent. Reliability without benevolence may feel hollow and transactional.
- **Ontological alignment** – A deeper sense of congruence between values, Being and lived reality. Trust often breaks down when something feels 'off', even if outward behaviour appears correct.
- **Continuity** – The ability of trust to sustain coherence over time. Without continuity, trust becomes fragile and reactive.

Applied lens: When assessing trust in a system, ask yourself: Is openness welcomed or suppressed? Is consistency reliable, or do actions drift from words? Is goodwill genuine, or does reliability feel hollow and transactional? Do values, Being and lived reality align, or is there hidden dissonance? Is trust continuous over time, or does it collapse after ruptures?

Mechanics – The living dynamics

Trust is not static. It evolves through relational processes that either deepen or erode coherence:

- **Activation** – Trust begins with a risk, an initial act of openness or reliance. Without that seed, trust cannot grow.
- **Feedback calibration** – Every act of openness generates feedback. Was it respected or ignored, met with integrity or dismissal?
- **Trust drift** – Trust rarely breaks in a single moment. It shifts through micro-confirmations or micro-ruptures – small signals that accumulate over time.
- **Compounding trust** – Healthy trust compounds when consistency and care reinforce each other, freeing systems from constant monitoring and control.
- **Recalibration** – When trust is broken, systems face a threshold. Will coherence be rebuilt with transparency and accountability, or will suspicion harden into defence?

Applied lens: Trace your context through these dynamics. Where and how did trust first activate? How has feedback on openness been handled – has it been respected, dismissed or ignored? Are small ruptures accumulating over time, or are they being repaired? Is trust compounding through care and consistency, or is suspicion building? When trust is broken, is recalibration attempted with transparency, or does distrust harden?

Topology – The feedback loops

The elements of trust interdependently condition one another, forming recursive loops that sustain or corrode coherence:

- **Openness ↔ Consistency** – Openness is reinforced by reliability. But when met with inconsistency, mistrust quickly grows.
- **Consistency ↔ Benevolence** – Reliability alone is not enough. Goodwill ensures trust feels relational rather than mechanical, where rules are followed out of a sense of obligation rather than trust.
- **Benevolence ↔ Ontological alignment** – Benevolence holds weight only when aligned with deeper coherence of values and Being.
- **Ontological alignment ↔ Continuity** – Alignment across time confirms whether trust is stable or merely performative.
- **Continuity ↔ Openness** – Each act of openness is shaped by memory. Trust strengthens when past vulnerability is respected, but shrinks when ruptures remain unrepaired.

Applied lens: Focus on one loop – for example, Openness ↔ Consistency – and explore how it operates in practice. Does openness result in reliability or inconsistency? Such loops often explain why trust silently strengthens or corrodes.

Bringing it together – A step-by-step guide

By working with the OTS, you can shift trust abstraction to something assessable and actionable. Here's a practical sequence you can use:

1. **Choose your context** – Identify the relationship or system.
2. **Quick scan** – Ask what trust feels like, look for signals and note the consequences.
3. **Map the anatomy** – Check which structural components (openness, consistency, benevolence, alignment and continuity) are present or fractured.
4. **Trace the mechanics** – Follow the dynamics: activation, calibration, drift, compounding and recalibration.
5. **Explore the topology** – Examine key feedback loops to see what's reinforcing coherence and what's driving dysfunction.
6. **Identify ruptures or shadows** – Notice distortions (naivety, suspicion or over-control).
7. **Intervene** – Decide where repair, reinforcement or recalibration is needed.

Viewed this way, trust is no longer a vague sentiment, but a living architecture you can read, question and strengthen – the foundation of authentic sustainability.

Emergent qualities and patterns

When coherent and integrated, trust yields:

- **Relational resilience** – Openness and reliability sustain connection even through rupture.
- **Psychological safety** – People feel free to speak, create and take risks without fear of exploitation.
- **Compounding cooperation** – Small acts of reliability and care reinforce one another, reducing the need for control.
- **Transparent alignment** – Words, actions and values converge, creating congruence that is felt and trusted.
- **Durable continuity** – Trust carries forward across time and challenge, sustaining long-term coherence.

However, when distorted, trust devolves into:

- **Naive compliance** – Over-trusting without discernment, leaving systems open to manipulation.

- **Chronic suspicion** – Default defensiveness and guardedness erode collaboration.
- **Performative trust** – Surface displays of openness mask deeper control or self-interest.
- **Overregulation** – Control structures multiply to compensate for missing trust.
- **Fragmented reliability** – Inconsistencies and broken promises weaken continuity and stability.

Trust is not merely a sentiment, but a structural intelligence of sustainability. It is the architecture that allows systems to cooperate, innovate and endure without excessive force or surveillance. Authentic trust sustains openness in the presence of risk. It makes cooperation breathable – flowing naturally rather than under pressure – turning uncertainty from a threat into a pathway for shared sustainability.

Now let's look at another example: the modulating force of adaptability.

2. Adaptability

Ontological distinction

Adaptability is your capacity to recalibrate in response to change without losing coherence. It is not about being agreeable or compliant. Instead, it's about remaining attuned to context while anchored in your ethical and ontological centre: your deeper sense of truth, coherence and what ultimately matters. Adaptability enables systems – whether personal, relational or institutional – to respond to evolving conditions, not by resisting change, but by shaping it with discernment, intelligence and purpose. It is not softness or passivity, but a generative posture of sustainable responsiveness. Adaptability enables transformation without fragmentation – growth that preserves coherence rather than breaking it apart – and evolution without self-erasure.

A **healthy relationship with adaptability** indicates that you can shift behaviours, perspectives or strategies in the presence of new information or altered circumstances while remaining true to your values, purpose and Being. You are responsive without being reactive, flexible without being formless. You can evolve in ways that honour continuity, enabling resilience, creativity and sustained relevance. In relationships and leadership, this posture fosters trust and agility without sacrificing coherence.

An **unhealthy relationship with adaptability** indicates that you fall into one of two extremes. On one side, it shows up as chronic morphing – changing yourself constantly to avoid discomfort, rejection or tension. This people-pleasing collapses coherence and erodes trust, leading to identity diffusion and instability. On the other side, it manifests as rigid resistance – mistaking stubbornness for strength and refusing necessary change even when coherence demands it. In both cases, adaptability is distorted, either abandoning integrity for harmony or clinging to familiar habits or appearances at the cost of evolution. Leaders under this influence become inconsistent, rigid or untrustworthy – not because values are absent, but because their expression lacks continuity.

Gauging adaptability in practice

To gauge adaptability, begin with a quick diagnostic scan:

- **Choose your context** – Identify the domain of change: a new market, a relationship transition, or a societal upheaval. For example, climate and energy reform in Australia requires governments to adapt to global decarbonisation pressures while balancing domestic realities.
- **Ask** – How is adaptability showing up here? In a couple, do roles get renegotiated when circumstances shift? In a start-up, can the team pivot without abandoning its purpose? In policy, is a response grounded in discernment or swinging between rigidity and over-promise?
- **Scan for signals** – Healthy adaptability looks like curiosity, learning cycles and transparent transition plans. Fractured adaptability shows up as denial of change, rigid clinging to the old or hasty reactive pivots.
- **Examine the consequences** – If adaptability is weak, what becomes unsustainable? In couples, it is growth; in business,

relevance; and in policy, the credibility of long-term planning. In climate reform, adaptability grounded in coherence sustains both ecological integrity and public trust, whereas rigidity or reckless swings erode confidence and stability.

This broad scan opens the door to clarity. To refine it further, we turn to the OTS lenses.

Anatomy – The structural capacities

Adaptability consists of five structural capacities that enable recalibration without fragmentation:

- **Context awareness** – The capacity to read the field accurately. This quality senses internal and external shifts and interprets their meaning. Without context awareness, change becomes premature, delayed or misdirected.
- **Fluidity** – The flexibility of non-essential structures. This quality allows expression and organisation to shift without betraying essential coherence. Without fluidity, change produces brittleness and overwhelm. However, with excess fluidity, identity diffuses.
- **Responsiveness** – The integration of feedback into learning and iteration. Signals are received and metabolised rather than resisted or ignored. Without responsiveness, systems become brittle; however, with unfiltered responsiveness, they ricochet.
- **Anchoring** – The connection to values, purpose and Being. Anchoring prevents adaptation from becoming submission and gives direction to change. Without anchoring, modulation collapses into appeasement.
- **Reconfiguration** – Generative redesign under pressure. Structures, strategies or postures are reconfigured in real time to remain viable and meaningful. Without reconfiguration, systems repeat patterns or perform cosmetic pivots.

Applied lens: Map these capacities in your chosen context. Is context awareness superficial or distorted? Where does form refuse to bend? Where does feedback fail to land? Where is anchoring absent or performative? Where does change remain cosmetic?

Mechanics – The modulation loop

Adaptability is a living, recursive process. It assesses, adjusts and re-orients through dynamics that either reinforce coherence or corrode it:

- **Stimulus encounter** – A condition shifts; something no longer fits. Awareness is sparked.
- **Pattern-disruption recognition** – The system recognises that a familiar form or behaviour is now mismatched. Without this recognition, inertia persists.
- **Anchored reassessment** – The system re-references its centre. What matters? What must remain? What can be reimagined? This quality protects against de-anchoring – the subtle drift that leads to fragmentation and loss of coherence.
- **Reconfiguration** – A considered change of structure, strategy, tone or posture is enacted without losing the centre.
- **Integration** – Outcomes are metabolised as learning into practice and Being, completing the loop and raising baseline coherence.

Applied lens: Trace your context through this loop. Was the change or disruption clearly recognised? Was the mismatch between old patterns and new conditions openly acknowledged, or brushed aside? When reassessing, was the response grounded in core purpose and values, or driven by appeasement and fear? Did the adjustments bring real structural change, or were they mostly cosmetic? Was the outcome absorbed as sustainable learning, or did the system simply revert to old habits?

Topology – The recursive couplings

Adaptability's qualities are interdependent, forming loops that determine whether change leads to renewal or erosion:

- **Context awareness ↔ Fluidity** – Seeing clearly enables flexibility, which expands what can be seen. Without awareness, fluidity flails and without fluidity, awareness overwhelms.

- **Fluidity ↔ Responsiveness** – Willingness to change form keeps the system receptive to feedback, and integrated feedback guides which forms to change. Fluidity without responsiveness becomes chaos, while responsiveness without fluidity breeds anxiety.
- **Responsiveness ↔ Anchoring** – Feedback must pass through the lens of purpose. Anchoring filters signals so shifts do not cost identity. Without anchoring, feedback commands. Without responsiveness, anchoring calcifies.
- **Anchoring ↔ Reconfiguration** – Grounded centres generate coherent creativity. Reconfiguration without anchoring fragments, while anchoring without creativity repeats.
- **Reconfiguration ↔ Context awareness** – New forms alter the field. Ongoing sensing tests fit and completes the modulation cycle, preventing one-off pivots from stalling.

Applied lens: Choose one loop, such as responsiveness ↔ anchoring. Are shifts guided by core values, or are signals dictating identity? Such couplings reveal why adaptation evolves sustainably or corrodes into distortion.

Bringing it together – A step-by-step guide

Adaptability becomes assessable when approached structurally. Here's a practical process:

1. **Choose your context** – Identify the domain of change.
2. **Quick scan** – Ask how adaptability is showing up, note signals and examine consequences.
3. **Map the anatomy** – Assess the five capacities: awareness, fluidity, responsiveness, anchoring and reconfiguration.
4. **Trace the mechanics** – Follow the modulation loop: encounter, recognition, reassessment, reconfiguration and integration.
5. **Explore the topology** – Look at the interrelationships to see where change is sustainable or eroding.
6. **Identify distortions** – Note extremes of rigidity, reactivity, morphing or appeasement.

7. **Intervene** – Decide how to strengthen coherence: reinforce anchoring, broaden awareness or improve reconfiguration.

Authentic adaptability sustains presence in flux. It makes coherence breathable, turning change from a threat into a pathway for regeneration.

Emergent qualities and patterns

When coherent and integrated, adaptability leads to:

- **Resilient evolution** – Change emerges organically, not disruptively.
- **Ontological creativity** – New expressions arise without distortion.
- **Agility without fragility** – Responsiveness without breakdown.
- **Presence in flux** – Groundedness amid shifting conditions.
- **Intelligent flexibility** – Discernment, not panic, drives change.

However, when distorted, adaptability devolves into:

- **Chronic inconsistency** – Nothing stable, everything conditional.
- **Identity diffusion** – Shape-shifting erodes self and culture.
- **Compulsive agreement** – Yielding to avoid tension.
- **Reactive morphing** – Motion without discernment.
- **Eroded boundaries** – External pressures endlessly redraw the self.

Adaptability is not a soft skill, but a structural intelligence of sustainability. It is what allows systems to recalibrate without losing coherence, to evolve without erasing themselves. Authentic adaptability makes coherence breathable, turning change from a threat into a pathway for regeneration.

Everyday practices for gauging authentic sustainability

How can you meaningfully gauge the health of your relationships or your own systemic integrity without a formal assessment tool? The key is not to seek a perfect score, but to engage in a structured inquiry that makes the invisible visible.

Here are some practical approaches you can begin today:

1. Use the ontological distinction

Each of the UOSI's 16 qualities comes with a clear ontological distinction, which includes how a healthy and an unhealthy relationship with the quality manifests. Choose one quality at a time and ask:

- How is this showing up in my life, my relationship or my organisation?
- Which signals of health are visible? Which signs of fracture are present?
- What consequences flow from the way this quality is currently expressed?

Even a 10-minute reflection on one quality each week can radically sharpen your awareness.

2. Apply the OTS lens

To deepen your reflection, run the quality through the three OTS lenses:

- **Anatomy** – What structural components are strong, weak or missing?
- **Mechanics** – How are the dynamics of this quality playing out over time? Are they reinforcing coherence or driving erosion?
- **Topology** – Which feedback loops are sustaining health, and which are compounding dysfunction?

This process turns the quality into a living diagnostic map rather than a static description.

3. Anchor your reflection in writing

You can use a simple worksheet to structure your thinking. For each quality, note down:

- **Context** – The system or relationship you are assessing (e.g. family, partnership, team).
- **Observation** – The behaviours, practices or dynamics you notice.
- **Impact** – What becomes possible or erodes when the quality is strong or weak.
- **Next step** – One action you can take to strengthen integrity here.

This exercise helps shift the assessment from vague impressions into concrete, trackable insights.

4. Compare perspectives

Invite another person – a partner, team-mate or peer – to reflect with you. Compare your perceptions and notice where they align or diverge. Often, the differences are more revealing than the answers themselves. Gauging in this way becomes a shared practice: it surfaces hidden assumptions, deepens dialogue and strengthens trust.

5. Look for patterns over time

Don't expect a single reflection to tell the whole story. Instead, repeat the process periodically. Are you seeing the same fractures reappear? Are you noticing gradual improvements? Sustainability is not static. Gauging it means tracking the rhythms of growth, strain and renewal.

6. Translate insights into practice

Remember that reflection is not an end in itself. Once you have identified a weak quality, choose one small practice to strengthen it. For example:

- If trust feels brittle in your team, commit to transparent weekly check-ins.

- If adaptability is distorted by rigidity, experiment with one flexible practice, such as rotating meeting leadership.
- If sovereignty feels compromised, re-examine which commitments are truly yours and which are inherited.

By linking reflection to concrete action, the process becomes regenerative rather than purely diagnostic.

Sharpening your awareness

The discipline of gauging systemic health through the lens of authentic sustainability won't produce a neat metric, as explained earlier. However, it will sharpen perception, bring shadows into view and equip you to act with greater clarity. To recap:

1. Start with the ontological distinction, including its healthy and unhealthy expressions.
2. Place it in your context – personal, relational, organisational or societal.
3. Run it through the OTS lenses to see its structure, dynamics and loops.
4. Ask probing questions that reveal coherence or dysfunction.
5. Observe the consequences. What becomes sustainable, and what begins to erode?
6. Reflect and adjust – Decide what shifts or commitments are needed.

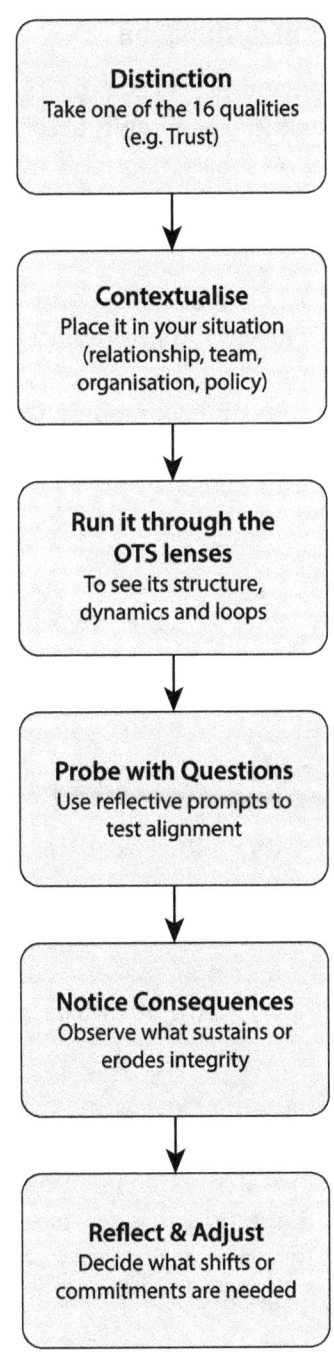

Figure 16 – Gauging systemic health through the lens of authentic sustainability.

Shadows as architects of dysfunction

The work of perception and practice prepares you for the next step – recognising when qualities are not only absent but distorted. These distortions are the shadows that unobtrusively sustain dysfunction. Left unexamined, they become self-reinforcing, feeding entrenchment and disintegration.

Shadows are not a moral category of 'good versus bad'; they are structural distortions. However, they often wear the mask of virtue: a government may frame control as security; an organisation may frame exploitation as innovation; or an individual may frame fear as responsibility. Without a healthy relationship with meta-awareness, these distortions are sustained by cultural narratives and unquestioned assumptions.

Within the Disintegration Sphere, shadows operate alongside misery, suffering and entrenchment. Whether invisible or denied, they are cracks in the foundation. You cannot build coherence on top of them and expect sustainability to hold. This is why authentic sustainability requires you to not only gauge what is healthy, but also expose and work on your shadows where they exist.

Crafting alternatives – Regeneration, not reaction

Once shadows have been identified, the task is not merely to reject or oppose them, but to re-create the patterns, systems and ways of being they distorted – this time from a place of coherence. Diagnosing distortion is only half the work; the other half is crafting what should take its place.

The process of crafting alternatives must be regenerative, not reactionary. Reactionary alternatives are born of opposition to the shadow and create mirror distortions – cynicism against naivety, chaos against control. Authentic, regenerative alternatives are born of alignment with Being and integrity. They are not about what you are against, but what you are for.

In an organisation trapped in control and fear, the alternative is not chaos or 'freedom at any cost', but a regenerative culture of trust, responsibility and aligned autonomy.

In a society where sustainability has been reduced to metrics, the alternative is not rejecting measurement, but grounding it in meaning and integrity.

Authentic alternatives regenerate – they do not simply invert the distortion.

A practical process for shadow work and crafting alternatives

1. Expose the shadow

    - Use the UOSI to map where distortion lives.
    - Leverage meta-awareness and the Nested Theory of Sense-making to uncover the hidden narratives and assumptions sustaining them.

2. Discern the impact

    - Trace how the shadow sustains dysfunction and erodes integrity.
    - Identify what the shadow is really protecting (often fear or control).

3. Return to authentic awareness

    - Anchor back into what is true beyond the distortion.
    - Practise separating surface narrative from deeper reality using the sense-making filters introduced earlier.

4. Align with Being

    - Ask: What way of being would sustain the alternative?
    - Use distinctions from the Being Framework – such as commitment, courage and resourcefulness – to clarify the regenerative posture required.

5. Craft the alternative

    - Build from discerned intention, not reaction.
    - Ensure the alternative regenerates integrity across all four spheres of the UOSI.

6. Embodiment and iteration
   - Embed the alternative as a lived commitment, not just a policy.
   - Use modulation – patience, adaptability, tolerance and surrender – to refine over time.

Shadow work in practice

South Africa – Truth and Reconciliation Commission (TRC)

At the end of apartheid, South Africa faced a profound systemic shadow arising from decades of institutionalised racial oppression. The easy path would have been revenge or denial. Instead, the TRC exposed the shadow publicly through testimony. Victims voiced their suffering. Perpetrators confessed to atrocities. The process was painful, imperfect and incomplete, as many injustices went unaddressed, reparations were uneven and deeper economic inequalities remained, but it shattered denial and began the long work of collective reckoning.

The alternative crafted was not to erase the past, nor to retaliate, but to regenerate through acknowledgement and amnesty conditioned on truth-telling. The TRC embodied the UOSI's principles: exposing the shadow (Disintegration Sphere); returning to truth (authentic awareness); holding systemic perspective through meta-awareness (Architectonic Sphere); and crafting a path to renewal (Modulation Sphere).

This did not resolve every fracture, but it demonstrated that sustainability begins with confronting shadows openly and designing alternatives rooted in integrity rather than vengeance.

Patagonia – Reframing consumerism

Patagonia, an American retailer of outdoor recreation clothing, equipment and food, confronted the shadow of consumerism – the contradiction between selling clothing and protecting the environment. Instead of denying this tension, the company acknowledged it openly. Their *'Don't buy this jacket'* campaign invited customers to reflect on consumption itself.

The regenerative alternative was not to close their doors, but to ground their business in transparency, repair programs, environmental activism and commitments like donating profits to conservation. In this way, Patagonia embodied the UOSI's principles: exposing the shadow of contradiction (Disintegration Sphere); facing it with authentic awareness rather than denial; holding systemic perspective through meta-awareness (Architectonic Sphere); reinforcing integrity through practices of transparency and stewardship (Integrity Sphere); and continually adapting its model through repair programs and activism (Modulation Sphere).

By working through each of these dimensions, Patagonia built credibility, loyalty and a culture aligned with authentic sustainability – proving that even within consumer capitalism, businesses can regenerate coherence rather than collapse into hypocrisy.

Shadows and authentic sustainability

Authentic sustainability is not the absence of shadows. It is the capacity to see and work with them without fear or denial. A system that claims to have no shadows is either lying or blind. A system that can identify and regenerate beyond its shadows is a system capable of true sustainability.

This is why shadow work must sit at the heart of any sustainability discourse. Without it, you end up reinforcing the very dysfunction you are trying to resolve.

To move from recognition to regeneration, ask yourself:

- Where in your life or organisation are shadows masquerading as virtue?
- Which of your current commitments may be sustaining a shadow rather than integrity?
- Are you willing to see the narratives that keep the shadow in place, even if they are culturally or personally convenient?
- What alternative would regenerate integrity rather than simply oppose the shadow?

Conclusion

Authentic sustainability is not supported by appearances or metrics alone. It is strengthened – or corroded – in the daily health of the UOSI's 16 qualities. The more clearly you learn to read them, the more capable you become of intervening where coherence is faltering and nurturing the conditions that allow systems to endure.

The process of gauging authentic sustainability also means identifying and confronting shadows along the way. Shadows are uncomfortable to face because they demand more than just analysis; they demand *transformation*. They require you to confront not just the external system but yourself – your own ways of being, your own intentions, your own complicity. Yet they also hold the key to regeneration. When you learn to see and move beyond them, you stop sustaining dysfunction and start crafting systems capable of authentic sustainability.

As noted at the start of this chapter, we will return in Part VIII with the Sustainability Profile – a structured ontometric assessment tool that helps address bias, error and subjectivity. However, there is no need to wait. By working with the UOSI's 16 qualities now – observing signals, discerning fractures and exposing shadows – you are already sharpening your awareness, making adjustments as you go and cultivating the discipline that will make any future measurement more meaningful and effective.

Having diagnosed and deconstructed how coherence functions and how dysfunction takes hold, the next step is reconstruction – rebuilding sustainability itself on solid ontological ground. The following chapter introduces the **Reconstructive Ontology of Sustainability (ROS)**, which integrates the full body of work you have explored so far into a living paradigm that bridges analysis and design. It marks the turning point from understanding sustainability to *reconstructing* it.

CHAPTER 51

The Reconstructive Ontology of Sustainability (ROS)

Authentic sustainability is not a checklist, a green policy statement or a marketing campaign adorned with recycling slogans and images of trees. It is a way of being – an embodied orientation that infuses every choice, interaction and system we engage with. At some point, sustainability must stop being something we *do* and become something we *are*.

In the previous chapter, you learned to gauge sustainability by observing the health of the UOSI's 16 qualities. That assessment, supported by the diagnostic lens of the Systemic Subversion Cycle (SSC), reveals where coherence is strong and where dysfunction has taken hold. But assessment and diagnosis alone are not enough. To move from awareness to design, we must rebuild the very architecture through which sustainability operates.

This chapter introduces the **Reconstructive Ontology of Sustainability (ROS)** – a key component of the Authentic Sustainability Framework (ASF) – and the CCC model, which describes the movement from content to clarity to conduct and is integral to the process of sustainable reconstruction. Far from just another model or checklist, ROS integrates all the ontological, epistemological and practical strands developed so far – the Being Framework, metacontent, the Nested Theory of Sense-making, the Unified Ontology of Systemic Integrity (UOSI), Minalogy and the Transformation Methodology – into a living, systemic paradigm for authentic sustainability in action.

Why ROS emerges here

If sustainability were merely about actions, projects and measurable outcomes, we would have solved it by now. We have more reports, mandates, audits and conferences on sustainability than ever before in history. And yet ecosystems are still collapsing, trust in institutions continues to erode, inequality keeps widening and cultures are fracturing more rapidly. The very concept of sustainability has been diluted into empty slogans.

Why? Because all those efforts focus on content – the data, the strategies, the tasks – without attending to the metacontent through which they are interpreted or considering how awareness transforms into coherent action. They focus on *what to do*, but not on *how we are making sense of what we do* or *how meaning evolves into meaningful conduct*. They chase metrics while ignoring the ontological ground of Being from which action emerges.

Critical Theory and Postmodernism taught us how to deconstruct. They revealed the power structures, hidden assumptions and ideological distortions behind our institutions. That work was necessary because it cleared the ground. But deconstruction without reconstruction on ontological foundations is merely critique without a practical solution. ROS is the deliberate rebuilding of sustainability on ontological ground. It asks: *if not sustainabilism, then what?* The question is not merely what to reject, but what to rebuild – and how.

ROS is a systemic, ontological framework that reconstructs sustainability on the foundations of Being, integrity, sense-making, meaning-making and modulation. It integrates the full body of work described in this book into a coherent paradigm for authentic sustainability in action. The Systemic Subversion Cycle (SSC), while not part of ROS itself, operates in parallel as its diagnostic counterpart – revealing where coherence erodes and where reconstruction must begin.

Reconstruction does not mean starting from scratch. It means reconfiguring the architecture we already inhabit – much like restoring a heritage building with new foundations and reinforced beams. That's why the entire authentic sustainability discourse has been constructed on solid ontological foundations.

The need for a solid foundation is why we turned to:

- **Metacontent** – Without understanding that all content is interpreted through various lenses, we cannot see why well-intentioned efforts go awry. A sustainability report may look robust, but if the organisation's metacontent equates 'growth' with extraction or 'success' with compliance rather than care, genuine responsibility and integrity, then the report is nothing but theatre.
- The **Nested Theory of Sense-making** – Misalignment begins with fractured sense-making from the outset. A distorted paradigm or an unexamined story quietly drives decisions that ripple through entire systems. Without the ability to locate which layer of sense-making is breaking down, we remain reactive and blind. Metacontent matters, but it needs structure. The Nested Theory of Sense-making provides that structure.
- **Minalogy** – Sense-making alone gives clarity, but clarity is not meaning. We can understand climate change data perfectly and still fail to act. What mobilises us is *Mina* – the deeper 'why' that attributes significance to what we see, tethers facts to purpose and connects intention to our lives and the system we are engaging with.
- The **Being Framework** – Transformation is not secured by knowledge or metrics, but by who we are being. If responsibility, authenticity and integrity are absent or distorted in leaders, even the best sustainability plans will collapse into dysfunction.
- The **Unified Ontology of Systemic Integrity (UOSI)** – Systems are sustained neither by random forces nor rigid compliance checklists. They are sustained by coherence across the UOSI's four spheres – Architectonic, Integrity,

Disintegration and Modulation. Without this, sustainability becomes fragile.
- The **Transformation Methodology** – Awareness without application is impotence. Transformation requires iterative movement between seeing, embodying and recalibrating.

Taken together, these frameworks were never ends in themselves. They were scaffolds leading to this moment: a reconstructive ontology. ROS not only critiques the distortions of sustainabilism – the performative, prescriptive forms of sustainability – but reconstructs a living architecture through which integrity is sustained and authentic sustainability can emerge and endure. Consider the foundational elements as threads forming the tapestry of ROS – a reconstructive ontology that moves us from content to clarity to conduct, from knowing to being, and from blueprint to practice.

The CCC model – Content → Clarity → Conduct

The flow from content to clarity to conduct (the CCC Model) runs like a hidden current flowing through ROS. Without this progression, we drown in content, mistake clarity for action or collapse into performative conduct. ROS ensures the movement from one to the next is coherent and regenerative.

Think of sustainability as a river. Traditional models treat the river as an engineering problem – build a dam here, dredge a channel there, measure the water levels. But if the source upstream is poisoned, all downstream interventions are futile. ROS is not about rearranging the rocks downstream; it's about healing the river at the source.

Using the river metaphor:

- **The source** = Being (Being Framework) and intention (flow of coherence – Fulfilment Pyramid)
- **The stream** = Sense-making (Metacontent + Nested Theory of Sense-making)
- **Tributaries** = Meaning-making (Minalogy)
- **The riverbed** = Systemic Integrity (UOSI)

- **Flowing water** = Transformation Methodology (Being Framework)
- **The current within the water** = CCC model (Content → Clarity → Conduct)
- **The destination** = Authentic sustainability (Conduct)

Conduct – The living expression of coherence

Within this river analogy, conduct is both the movement and the destination – the living expression of coherence as it flows from Being into action. It begins at the source, where the **Being Framework** establishes the ontological foundation through authenticity, integrity and responsibility – the essential *precondition* for conduct to emerge – and the **Fulfilment Pyramid's** Phenomenological Dimension anchors intention in Being. From there, the river flows into sense-making through **metacontent** and the **Nested Theory of Sense-making**, clarifying perception and understanding – the *enabling* ground for conduct. The tributaries of **Minalogy** infuse the stream with meaning and significance, providing the *motivation* that energises conduct. As the river moves, it is held and shaped by **Systemic Integrity (UOSI)** – the *stabilising structure* that ensures conduct remains coherent and ethically sound.

The flowing water, representing the **Transformation Methodology**, is where conduct is *in motion* – the process through which awareness becomes embodiment and insight becomes practice. Within this flow, the CCC model (Content → Clarity → Conduct) acts as the *regulating current* – the rhythm that keeps perception, discernment and action aligned through continuous cycles of reflection and recalibration. Finally, all these forces converge at the destination: **authentic sustainability**, where conduct reaches its *realised form* – coherence made visible, sustainability no longer performed but lived.

How meaning evolves into coherent conduct

ROS operates at the systemic level, rebuilding the architecture of sustainability from the ground up. Yet within every act of reconstruction, a subtler movement unfolds – the inner motion through which meaning becomes coherent conduct. This movement is captured by the CCC model, which describes how awareness transforms into coherent action.

Where ROS establishes the ontological foundation for sustainable systems, the CCC model reveals the micro-mechanics of transformation occurring within every individual, team or structure. It ensures that sustainability is not reduced to external reform, but is anchored in inner coherence within every person operating within a given system.

Exploring the movement from content to clarity to conduct in more detail will clarify why ROS leverages it in the reconstruction process to achieve authentic sustainability – the coherent conduct we are aiming for.

- **Content** refers to all that exists and all that we encounter – the data, events, narratives and experiences that fill our world.
- **Clarity** is achieved through disciplined sense-making, as described in the metacontent discourse and the Nested Theory of Sense-making. It is the refinement of perception into understanding – the moment when distortion gives way to discernment.
- **Conduct** is the embodiment of Being in action – sustainability as lived practice, not just articulated goals. It's when clarity takes shape as behaviour, practice or a systemic pattern.

This same current – Content → Clarity → Conduct – flows through ROS. ROS provides the macro-architecture – it reconstructs the foundations of sustainability across systems by integrating Being, metacontent, the Nested Theory of Sense-making, Minalogy, the UOSI and the Transformation Methodology. The CCC model provides the micro-mechanics within that architecture – the dynamic by which meaning flows through each system, from individuals and teams to organisations, institutions, communities and societies.

Dimension	CCC Model	ROS Framework
Scale	Micro – the inner process of transformation within individuals and teams	Macro – the systemic reconstruction of sustainability across entire systems
Focus	The movement from perception to understanding to embodiment	The architecture that ensures such movement sustains integrity over time
Function	Diagnoses and refines the sense-making process to prevent distortion	Rebuilds ontological coherence so that sense-making can remain sustainable
Outcome	Clarity-led conduct – local coherence in action	Authentic sustainability – systemic coherence at scale and across contexts

Table 30 – The Interrelationship Between the CCC Model and ROS.

In this way, the CCC model is to ROS what breath is to conscious life – a rhythmic, intentional process that sustains vitality. Each act of seeing clearly, discerning meaning and acting coherently becomes a deliberate reconstruction that keeps the macro-architecture of ROS alive and adaptive.

How the CCC model is embedded in the flow of ROS

ROS moves systems from **content** (awareness of what is) to **clarity** (understanding through sense-making and meaning-making) to **conduct** (sustainability as embodied practice). The CCC model mirrors this movement, but applies it internally within every layer of a system – individuals, relationships, teams, organisations, institutions and societies.

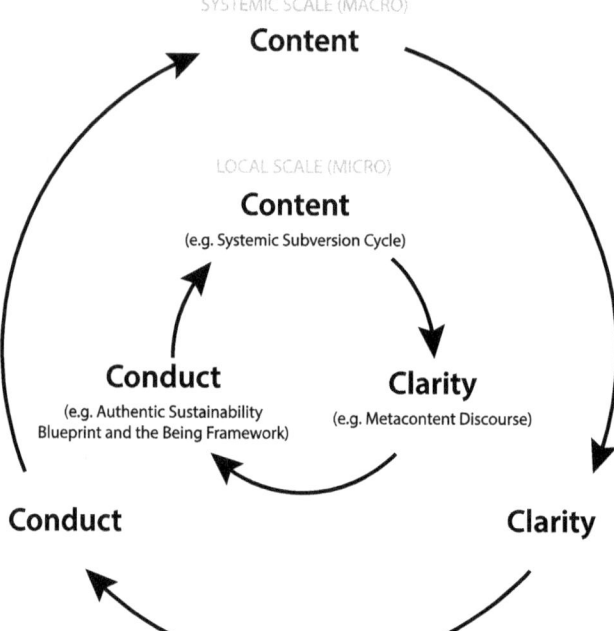

Figure 17 – The ROS Model showing the flow from content to clarity to conduct as the regenerative current of authentic sustainability.

The CCC model functions as the inner rhythm of ROS – the recurring heartbeat that converts reconstruction into regeneration. Each time a person, team or organisation moves from confusion to discernment to authentic action, the system as a whole becomes more coherent.

The bridge between discernment and design

In practical terms, the CCC model forms the bridge between discernment and design within ROS.

- **Content** corresponds to the ontological and diagnostic clarity provided by the Unified Ontology of Systemic Integrity (UOSI) and the Systemic Subversion Cycle (SSC) – identifying what is present and where dysfunction lies.
- **Clarity** corresponds to the reconstructive intelligence of ROS itself – interpreting reality through metacontent, meaning and systemic integrity.

- **Conduct** corresponds to the execution of the Authentic Sustainability Blueprint – the translation of reconstruction into sustained practice.

Ultimately, the CCC model ensures that reconstruction is not theoretical, but continually enacted through the cyclical movement described in the Transformation Methodology – reception, perception, conception, reflection, embodiment and recalibration.

The following examples make the relationship between the CCC model and ROS tangible.

Example 1: Organisational – The inauthentic sustainability report

A global retail company launches a comprehensive sustainability strategy: carbon-neutral goals, recyclable packaging, supplier audits and glossy annual reports. Externally, it looks like progress. However, internally, staff morale is falling. The sustainability team feels unheard, operational managers see the program as bureaucracy, and senior leadership quietly views it as reputational insurance.

In the context of the CCC model:

- **Content** abounds – Data, targets and compliance frameworks.
- **Clarity** is missing – Each department interprets 'sustainability' differently: marketing sees image management, operations sees cost control, HR sees culture initiatives.
- **Conduct** becomes performative – Reports are published, but behaviour remains unchanged.

ROS identifies this as a structural incoherence – the system has ample content and activity, but lacks clarity and alignment at the level of Being. Through the CCC movement within ROS, reconstruction begins:

- **Content** is re-mapped through its metacontent using the Nested Theory of Sense-making – redefining what 'sustainability' actually means.

- **Clarity** is cultivated via collective reflection using Minalogy. The organisation articulates its authentic *Mina*: 'To enrich life through dignity and trust in every transaction'.
- **Conduct** is re-designed and executed through the Authentic Sustainability Blueprint – integrating this *Mina* into procurement, customer communication and both leadership and staff training.

As a result, employees and customers begin to experience coherence between the organisation's words and actions. Decision-making aligns with a shared purpose, and sustainability ceases to be a reporting exercise, becoming the company's operating ethic instead.

This example highlights how the CCC model functions as the micro-movement within ROS – turning abstract reconstruction into lived coherence. Without the flow from Conduct to Clarity to Conduct, ROS would remain an abstract ideal.

Example 2: Societal – Bad faith in policy-making

A government launches a sweeping reform agenda aimed at restoring economic stability and social cohesion. New laws are drafted, agencies restructured and communication campaigns rolled out. Billions are spent on consultation, technology and compliance. Yet two years later, public trust in institutions is at an all-time low. Citizens feel unheard, policymakers feel unappreciated and both accuse each other of bad faith. Despite good intentions and technical rigour, the system is unravelling.

In the context of the CCC Model:

- **Content:** There is no shortage of information – reports, data and legislative drafts flood the public domain.
- **Clarity:** Narratives diverge – citizens interpret reforms as self-serving politics, while policymakers see public resistance as ignorance or apathy.
- **Conduct:** Implementation fragments – one department over-communicates promises it cannot fulfil, another withdraws in fear of backlash and reform fatigue spreads.

ROS reveals that the system's ontological foundation is fractured. There is activity but no coherence between meaning, intention and conduct. The policy apparatus has content without clarity and action without shared significance. Embedding the CCC model within ROS enables reconstruction across all three levels:

- **Content:** Information is re-contextualised through a metacontent analysis – recognising that 'trust' means different things across the social spectrum – to citizens, it signals fairness and voice; to policymakers, it means legitimacy and continuity.
- **Clarity:** Through Minalogy, policymakers, media and civic representatives co-articulate a shared *Mina* – 'To govern with dignity and transparency, ensuring that policies serve the common good rather than factional interest.'
- **Conduct:** The Authentic Sustainability Blueprint translates this clarity into participatory structures – transparent feedback mechanisms, public review forums and policy scorecards co-designed with citizens. Once the Blueprint is executed, success is measured not just by legislative output, but by the restoration of confidence, dialogue and mutual accountability.

Within months, tone and behaviour shift. Citizens begin distinguishing between disagreement and distrust. Policymakers communicate intentions rather than slogans. The same reforms, once resisted, now evolve through co-ownership.

By operating as ROS's inner current, the CCC model transformed a technocratic system into a relational architecture of coherence, where policy-making is no longer a performance of authority, but a living dialogue grounded in shared meaning and integrity.

Why the CCC model is indispensable to ROS

These examples reveal that ROS provides the architectural capacity for reconstruction, but the CCC model provides the metabolic flow that keeps that architecture alive. Without the CCC model, ROS would risk becoming intellectual or static – a design without life. And without ROS, the CCC model would lack the systemic reinforcement needed to endure. Together, they ensure that sustainability is not just engineered but *embodied* – reconstructed both in the architecture of systems and in the conduct of those who live within them.

The contrast between applying ROS, including its internal CCC model, and engaging in performative action can be seen across every scale:

- **In organisations:** Restructuring culture so that integrity, care and responsibility are rewarded alongside profit is ROS in action. In contrast, publishing a glossy sustainability report without the required application is sustainabilism.
- **In governance:** Redefining value around regenerative flourishing is ROS in action. Setting carbon targets while subsidising extraction is sustainabilism.
- **In families:** Modelling care, integrity and responsibility in daily choices is ROS in action. Preaching sustainability while living in contradiction is sustainabilism.

When engaging with any system, from a personal relationship to your team, ask yourself, *where are my actions performative and where can reconstruction begin?* Then use ROS's six interlocking parts – metacontent, the Nested Theory of Sense-making, Minalogy, the Being Framework, the UOSI and the Transformation Methodology – to flow from Content to Clarity to Conduct (authentic sustainability).

Preventing drift using the discipline of ROS

A sustainable system is not one that never wavers, but one that knows how to return to coherence. After all, even the best intentions fail. To sustain coherence over time, ROS must be lived as a discipline. The framework prevents drift when vigilance and motivation fade by embedding modulation – the discipline of continual recalibration.

Consider a company that commits to reducing its environmental footprint. In the first year, enthusiasm is high, targets are met and the team feels energised. By year three, competing priorities and subtle complacency have set in. Energy audits are delayed, new hires haven't been trained in the original sustainability values, and cost-cutting starts to override long-term commitments. Drift has begun.

Instead of responding with punitive enforcement or rebranding, a modulated approach recognises the early signs and uses them as feedback. Leadership initiates reflective dialogue across departments, revisits the organisation's 'why', and re-aligns systems with its original intentions. The focus isn't on returning to the old plan but restoring coherence. Within months, small course corrections – retraining, transparent progress dashboards, renewed communication around purpose – regenerate momentum. The plan evolves and the culture realigns.

In this way, modulation becomes the heartbeat of sustainability. It transforms drift from a threat into a signal – an invitation to adapt while staying true to purpose.

Conclusion

ROS provides the architecture, but its strength can only be proven once executed. Every system, policy and culture is ultimately animated by the ways of being of the human beings within it. Without reconstruction at the level of the individual, systemic reconstruction remains theoretical.

To make reconstruction *living*, ROS relies on the inner current described by the CCC model – Content → Clarity → Conduct. This model ensures that every act of reconstruction is metabolised into coherence – translating awareness into understanding and understanding into practice. It is the pulse that keeps ROS alive across scale and context – from individuals and teams to organisations, institutions, communities and societies.

So in practice, the work of sustainability begins not in institutions, but in *people* – in the integrity of our daily choices, commitments and responsibilities. When both the principles of ROS and the movement of the CCC model are embodied at this level, they provide the living foundation upon which coherent systems can be designed.

The next step is to envision what those coherent systems could become and to translate that vision into structured, lived practice. The following chapter introduces the **Authentic Sustainability Blueprint** – the framework that gives reconstructed ontology tangible form through disciplined envisioning and design. It shows how authentic sustainability can be envisioned, designed and embodied across all domains – transforming reconstruction into coherent conduct and living practice.

CHAPTER 52

From Vision to Blueprint – Designing Sustainable Futures

Meaning anchors purpose. *Mina* carries that purpose deeper, answering why it matters and what significance it holds – giving direction its weight and centre of gravity. Expression brings that significance to the surface, articulating it in a way that can be understood and acted upon. Analysis provides clarity, distinguishing what is real from what is assumed. Intention sets the trajectory by directing energy and focus. Commitment carries that trajectory into sustained action. Shadow work clears distortions that would otherwise fragment coherence. Through ROS, we have reconstructed the foundations of sustainability itself – rebuilding its architecture on a solid base of Being, integrity, coherent sense-making and purposeful direction through *Mina*. The natural question that follows is: what comes next? How do we give that reconstruction tangible form in practice?

This chapter marks the transition from foundation to form – from the reconstructed ontology of sustainability established through ROS to the design of its living architecture. The process begins with envisioning the next coherent version of a system – whether personal, relational, organisational or societal – and culminates in the creation of the **Authentic Sustainability Blueprint**, which translates that vision into practice.

Envisioning and blueprint design are not separate exercises. Vision articulates what coherence could become, and the Blueprint translates that direction into structure and practice. Envisioning without a plan risks becoming idealism or theatre, while a plan without vision collapses into rigid tasks disconnected from Being and systemic coherence. Together, vision and blueprint form the hinge between reflection and practice.

Where ROS reconstructs a coherent foundation, the Authentic Sustainability Blueprint designs the structure that rests upon it – bridging the space between ontology and practice. By the end of this chapter, you will see how the UOSI's qualities, the recognition of shadows and the cultivation of Being converge in a disciplined process. This process moves you from discerning a regenerative vision to building the living Blueprint that can sustain it across systems and contexts at every scale – personal, organisational, institutional, cultural and societal. It prepares the ground for what follows in Part VIII, where design becomes lived embodiment and sustainability is carried into action.

What do we mean by 'envisioning'?

Systems do not sustain themselves by accident. They sustain themselves by design – whether that design is intentional or inherited. If you do not envision the next version, you will unconsciously replicate the old one. Envisioning is not about drafting slogans or projecting fantasies. It is the disciplined discernment of the next version of a system that sustains integrity, honours Being and creates the conditions for authentic sustainability. The absence of discerned envisioning is one reason so many reforms fail – they fight dysfunction without articulating what regeneration looks like.

Authentic envisioning is not a branding exercise, but a structural, ontological act. It asks not only what outcomes you want to achieve, but what the system must *become* to sustain integrity over time. The Blueprint then provides the architecture that grounds this vision in reality – a living structure that aligns Being, intention and modulation into coherent practice.

Avoiding idealism

Vision statements often collapse into abstraction or performance. They sound inspiring, but are not anchored in Being or systemic coherence. They become decorative slogans while the underlying system remains unchanged.

Authentic envisioning avoids this trap by anchoring itself in:

- **Discernment** – Seeing what must be sustained or transformed based on authentic awareness, not wishful thinking.
- **Being** – Asking *who and how we must be* to sustain the envisioned system.
- **Integrity** – Ensuring the envisioned version aligns with the four spheres of the UOSI.
- **Modulation** – Recognising that envisioning is not a fixed destination, but a dynamic orientation.

In this way, envisioning avoids drifting into fantasy. It becomes a disciplined practice that connects aspiration and reality, shaping a future that can sustain integrity rather than merely describe it.

The envisioning discipline

Envisioning is not a matter of wishful thinking. It is a disciplined practice that takes an intention, grounds it in reality and then gives it form as a living vision. From there, the vision must be held in Being, designed for modulation and translated into commitment. This process ensures that envisioning is not a tokenistic, aesthetic or symbolic exercise, but a structural one designed to shape a future that sustains integrity across systems and contexts.

1. Ground your intention in reality

Begin by grounding your intention in what is true. Use the UOSI and the Nested Theory of Sense-making to map both the structural state of the system and the narratives colouring how you see it. Don't skip the shadows – if you avoid confronting them, your intention will unconsciously replicate them.

Analogy: Painting a masterpiece on mouldy walls may look beautiful for a time, but the decay beneath will always resurface. True envisioning begins with restoration, not decoration, so what is created can genuinely last.

Example: A business envisioning its 'green future' must first confront its reliance on supply chains that are not yet sustainable. Acknowledging this dependence allows it to plan authentic transition steps and communicate transparently. Skipping this stage only masks the shadow with sustainability slogans, creating the appearance of change while leaving the underlying distortion intact.

2. Discern the core intention

Intention is the compass that directs the vision. It defines the deeper purpose – the 'why' – that must orient future design. This is where *Mina*, the depth layer of meaning, comes into play. It carries significance and anchors intention so it is more than a preference or desire. Once your intention is grounded in reality, clarify what the system must genuinely serve.

Ask: What is the authentic intention this system must serve? Align that intention with sovereignty, trust and Being so it carries ontological weight rather than reactive desire.

Example: A family might discern their intention as 'nurturing dignity and resilience across generations', while a business might articulate it as 'creating genuine value without exploiting people or nature'.

3. Shape the vision

If intention sets the compass and *Mina* clarifies the 'why', vision gives that intention its form. This step is about describing not only outcomes, but also the structures, relationships and ways of being required for the system to serve its authentic intention. A vision shaped in this way is not decorative or aspirational – it regenerates coherence across the four spheres of the UOSI: Architectonic, Integrity, Disintegration and Modulation.

Example: Instead of an organisation aiming vaguely for 'higher revenue', the shaped vision might be: 'flat, participative structures, transparent decision-making and a culture of trust that enables sustainable value creation – which in turn translates into higher revenue.'

4. Anchor in Being

Use the Being Framework to identify the ways of being needed to sustain the envisioned system. Which qualities must be cultivated individually and collectively, for example: authenticity, vulnerability, courage, responsibility and commitment?

Example: A social movement may realise that courage and resourcefulness are just as critical to its endurance as funding or strategy. Without them, even the best-resourced initiatives lose coherence under pressure.

5. Design for modulation

Rigid visions are fragile. In contrast, living visions are resilient because they can bend without breaking. Build flexibility and renewal into the design so it can evolve through feedback and changing conditions.

Analogy: A tree survives not by resisting the wind, but by swaying with it while staying rooted.

Example: A local council envisioning urban regeneration creates flexible zoning policies that can evolve with community needs, rather than locking in regulations that quickly become outdated.

6. Translate into commitment

A vision without commitment is nothing but optics. Translate the envisioned version into lived commitments that reshape practice and culture. Commitment is where vision becomes real.

Example: A start-up that envisions participative leadership commits to shared decision-making structures and transparent feedback loops, ensuring the vision is embodied rather than rhetorical.

Envisioning across scales

The discipline of envisioning applies at every level of human systems. Whether you are shaping the next version of your life, an organisation or society itself, the same movement holds: ground intention in reality; discern the core compass; shape the vision; anchor it in Being; design for modulation; and translate it into commitment. What changes is the scale and the context.

- **Personal** – Envisioning the next version of your life is not about drafting a list of goals, but about aligning Being, intention and coherence across your relationships, health, contribution and work. What does the 'next version of you' look like when integrity is your compass?
- **Organisational** – Envisioning the next version of a business means designing for authentic value creation, participative leadership and trust rather than short-term optics or compliance with ESG checklists. Patagonia's culture of environmental repair is an example of a living vision at this scale.
- **Societal** – Envisioning the next version of society requires moving beyond reactionary politics or performative sustainability. It means designing systems grounded in sovereignty, regenerative economics and integrity in governance. South Africa's Truth and Reconciliation process, while not perfect, was a step towards envisioning a society willing to face shadows and craft alternatives.

At each scale, the question remains the same: What must the system become to sustain integrity over time?

Integrating shadow work into envisioning

Shadows do not disappear when you imagine a better future. They adapt and try to follow you. A business that ignores its exploitative practices will reproduce them in its next strategy. A government that avoids naming corruption will carry it into its reforms. A relationship that avoids broken trust will find the fracture re-emerging in new forms.

This is why authentic envisioning cannot bypass shadow work. The next version of a system is not shadow-free; it is *shadow-aware*. To be sustainable, a vision must consciously account for the distortions that will try to replicate themselves.

Integrating shadow work into envisioning means:

- **Exposing** the distortions that have shaped the current system.
- **Discerning** what they protect – often fear, control or denial.
- **Designing alternatives** that regenerate integrity rather than simply invert the shadow.

An authentic vision is not only aspirational; it is regenerative. It names what must be carried forward, what must be transformed, and what must no longer be sustained.

The living vision

An authentic vision is never static. It is not a fixed picture of the future, but a living orientation that evolves through feedback, awareness and modulation. It is designed to bend and recalibrate while staying rooted in integrity and *Mina*. In contrast, a rigid vision is fragile. It shatters the moment conditions change.

The purpose of a living vision is not to predict every detail of what lies ahead, but to sustain coherence as the system navigates change. It provides direction without rigidity, anchoring the system in Being while allowing continual adaptation.

Examples:

- A company that envisions 'building participative structures and a culture of trust' may discover, through practice, that its original structure needs to evolve. Because the vision is living, it adjusts without abandoning its core intention.

- At a societal level, New Zealand's Wellbeing Budget shows how a national vision can remain alive. The shift from GDP to wellbeing measures was not a one-off declaration – the indicators have been refined and debated over time, keeping the vision intact while adapting its expression.
- On a personal level, someone who envisions 'a life anchored in contribution and family' might change careers multiple times, but each new choice is tested against that core compass, ensuring continuity without rigidity.

In this way, the living vision becomes both an anchor and a compass. It ensures the system does not merely survive disruption, but evolves in alignment with Being and systemic coherence.

Carrying the vision forward

The discipline of envisioning only becomes powerful when it is carried into the next stage. A vision must not remain an inspiring picture. It must become the ground on which coherent action is built.

As you hold your living vision, ask yourself:

- What is the next version of the system you are part of – personal, organisational, cultural or societal?
- Are you envisioning from a place of authentic awareness or fear, optics or inherited narratives?
- Which ways of being must you cultivate to sustain the envisioned version over time?
- How will you design for modulation and renewal rather than fixed outcomes?
- Which shadows are most likely to follow your vision, and how will you prevent them from being replicated?

These questions prepare the ground for the next step: translating your vision into a living framework of practice – the Authentic Sustainability Blueprint, where design becomes the vessel through which regeneration is enacted.

From vision to Blueprint

Up until now, we have been layering insights like building blocks. You have learned to analyse systems with discernment. You have moved from sense-making to meaning-making through Minalogy. You have set intentions rooted in sovereignty and authenticity. You have explored the ontological weight of commitment and faced the shadows that distort systems. And you have envisioned the next version of what sustainability must look like in your context.

All of this has prepared the ground. But vision alone risks becoming abstraction, while plans without vision collapse into empty routines. Where envisioning gives direction, a blueprint gives it structure. The **Authentic Sustainability Blueprint** is where everything converges – the insights of analysis, the clarity of meaning, the strength of intention, the weight of commitment and the vigilance of shadow work – into a living framework that can be acted upon. It is the pivot point where reflection turns into practice, ensuring that authentic sustainability does not remain an idea, but becomes a way of life.

This is not a project management template, nor is it a business strategy in disguise. It is the translation of everything we have explored into a *strategic framework* that you can carry into your life, your team, your organisation, or even your society. It is about creating a coherent plan that can sustain integrity over time – not because it has the best spreadsheets, but because it is grounded in Being, aligned with intention and designed for modulation.

Why most plans fail

Most plans are written in good faith, but collapse under pressure because they lack ontological grounding. They focus on tasks, metrics and timelines while ignoring Being, integrity and systemic coherence. The failure is not usually incompetence or lack of effort. It is that the plan itself is disconnected from the deeper architecture of sustainability.

Think of a government promising a 'green transition', but drafting a plan driven only by numbers and deadlines. Without addressing the shadow of dependency on fossil fuel industries, or without cultivating public trust in institutions, the plan is brittle. It might look impressive on paper, but it cannot hold.

Or consider a couple deciding to 'spend more time together' as their plan to heal a struggling relationship. They schedule weekly date nights, but never address the underlying shadows of avoidance or broken trust. The plan is well intentioned, but hollow.

These examples show why authentic sustainability requires more than activity or aspiration. A plan must be rooted in Being, aligned with intention and designed to regenerate integrity across systems. Otherwise, it becomes theatre – a script that collapses as soon as reality (including shadows) intrudes.

The Authentic Sustainability Blueprint avoids these traps by embedding vision in structure, coherence in practice and modulation in design.

What is the Authentic Sustainability Blueprint?

Unlike a static document or a project management template, the Authentic Sustainability Blueprint is a *living framework* that translates vision into orientation and orientation into practice. Instead of simply measuring activity and output, the Blueprint integrates the full depth of this body of work. At its foundation, it translates sense-making into meaning through Minalogy, ensuring that every Blueprint is grounded in significance before it is tested by practice or safeguarded through diagnostics that test for dysfunction.

Alongside the Blueprint sits the Systemic Subversion Cycle (SSC), which acts as its diagnostic companion. Where the Blueprint designs for coherence, the SSC exposes patterns of erosion. Used together, they ensure that sustainability is not only envisioned and structured, but also protected from the drift of dysfunction.

This living framework is where insights converge into structure. It aligns:

- **Analysis** – Mapping the current state through the UOSI and exposing shadows.

- **Meaning** – Translating sense-making into purpose through Minalogy (meaning-making).
- **Intention** – Setting ontologically-aligned intentions rooted in sovereignty and discernment.
- **Commitment** – Sustaining the weight of those intentions through Being.
- **Shadow work** – Identifying distortions and regenerating beyond them.
- **Vision** – Articulating the next coherent version of the system.
- **Action structure** – Embedding practices, commitments and feedback loops that make the vision tangible.

The Authentic Sustainability Blueprint is not a plan you write once and file away. It is a living architecture designed for modulation, flexible enough to adapt to shifting conditions while anchored in coherence. In this way, the Blueprint ensures that sustainability does not remain a concept but becomes a lived orientation – a way of being and acting that allows truly sustainable systems to emerge.

Building the Blueprint: A step-by-step guide

The Authentic Sustainability Blueprint is built through a sequence of steps that mirror the architecture of authentic sustainability itself. Each step draws on the distinctions you have already encountered, weaving them into a coherent process that translates vision into practice.

Step 1: Analysis: map the current state

Begin with what is true now. Use the UOSI to map the structural state of the system across all four spheres (Architectonic, Integrity, Disintegration and Modulation), and the Nested Theory of Sense-making (metacontent) to clarify how reality is being perceived across its layers. This means surfacing the narratives colouring your perspective, distinguishing objective facts from subjective interpretations, and noticing the intersubjective meanings that shape collective understanding. Identify shadows and points of coherence as you go. For example:

Personal life: Notice how your health, relationships and work align (or misalign) with your deeper intentions. Perhaps you have strong adaptability but weak patience, constantly jumping from one idea to another.

Organisational: A startup founder can map where trust is strong (open communication among co-founders), but where sovereignty is weak (decisions dominated by one voice).

Societal: A government might see that while it has strong legal frameworks (integrity), it suffers from shadows of inauthenticity in political leadership, eroding public trust.

This step is about looking reality in the eye, without any illusions.

Step 2: Translate into meaning

Use Minalogy to define the deeper purpose of the system. Ask: What is this system for beyond survival or performance? For example:

- **Personal**: Instead of 'I want to earn more money', you might uncover that the deeper purpose is 'to create stability that allows me to nurture my family and contribute to my community.'
- **Relational**: A couple may move from 'we need to stop fighting' to 'our relationship exists to cultivate dignity, safety and joy for both of us.'
- **Organisational**: A business pivots their mission from 'increase market share' to 'enrich people's lives by designing products that promote trust, creativity and wellbeing.'

Meaning anchors the plan in authenticity.

Step 3: Set discerned intentions

Align intentions with sovereignty, trust and Being. Avoid reactive goals. Ensure intentions serve authentic sustainability.

- **Personal**: Instead of reacting to burnout with the intention to 'quit my job', an individual may discern a deeper intention: 'to cultivate balance and resilience so I can sustain both my wellbeing and my contribution to the organisation.' Anchored in sovereignty and authenticity, this intention reorients life choices around coherence rather than escape.

- **Organisational**: An organisation facing pressure to cut costs might resist the shadow of fear and instead set the intention to 'design sustainable value-creation that honours both financial resilience and employee dignity.'
- **Societal**: An activist might shift from 'fighting corruption' to 'building cultures of transparency and trust in governance.'

This step is where intention crystallises into orientation.

Step 4: Align Being and commitment

Use the Being Framework to identify which qualities are required to sustain the intentions and turn them into commitments. Integrate the Transformation Methodology to redesign Being where necessary.

- **Personal**: An individual may realise that improving their health requires more than routines. It depends on embodying commitment to stay consistent, proactivity to anticipate challenges, resilience to recover from setbacks, and empowerment to take ownership of their wellbeing.
- **Relational**: A couple may see that sustaining dignity and joy in their relationship depends on embodying authenticity, responsibility and courage, rather than relying only on scheduled time together.
- **Organisational**: A leader may recognise that delivering on their organisation's vision requires vulnerability and compassion, not just strategy and technical skill.

This step ensures the plan rests on *who and how we are being*, not just what we are doing.

Step 5: Integrate shadow work

Map systemic and Being shadows. Design alternatives that regenerate integrity rather than oppose the shadow.

- **Personal/Relational**: An individual recognises a shadow of avoidance in their relationship – withdrawing during conflict to preserve a sense of control. Instead of reacting in defence, they regenerate by cultivating courage, vulnerability and authenticity, practising open dialogue even when it feels uncomfortable.
- **Organisational**: A tech startup acknowledges its shadow of overwork and burnout. Instead of reacting by eliminating ambition, it regenerates by cultivating adaptability and trust, redesigning work rhythms around sustainability.
- **Societal**: A political reform movement recognises its shadow of righteous indignation. Instead of collapsing into cynicism, it regenerates by building dialogue practices that honour dissent.

Shadows do not disappear by ignoring them. They must be integrated, which can only be achieved by confronting and regenerating beyond them.

Step 6: Shape the vision

Craft a living vision that balances discernment, authenticity and modulation. Ensure it aligns across all four spheres of the UOSI.

- **Personal**: A young professional might envision not just 'a better job', but 'a career that sustains integrity, autonomy and meaningful contribution.'
- **Organisational**: A business envisions not only scaling, but doing so by deepening trust with staff, customers and society.
- **Societal**: A community envisions not just 'reducing inequality', but 'a culture where dignity and sovereignty are systemic realities.'

Vision is not fantasy. It is imagination disciplined by coherence.

Step 7: Create the action structure

Translate the vision into practical steps, commitments and feedback loops. Embed modulation so the plan evolves with reality.

- **Personal**: A Blueprint might set intentions around health (purpose-driven care for one's body), relationships (daily practices of authenticity), and work (aligning projects with meaning rather than only money).
- **Organisational**: Quarterly reviews are not just KPI check-ins, but moments of meta-awareness: 'Are we still aligned with our authentic intention?'
- **Societal**: Citizens and policymakers embed feedback loops – public forums, audits and dialogue structures that recalibrate vision against lived reality.

This final step ensures the Blueprint does not sit in a drawer. It lives – adapting with reality while preserving coherence.

Together, these steps form more than a checklist. They are a disciplined way of weaving analysis, meaning, intention, Being, shadow work, vision and action into a coherent whole. When worked through diligently and consistently, the process ensures the Blueprint is not a static plan, but a living architecture, constantly recalibrating through modulation while preserving integrity. In this way, it becomes the hinge between aspiration and practice – ensuring that authentic sustainability is not just imagined, but embodied and enacted across all systems and contexts.

The Blueprint in action across various domains

The Authentic Sustainability Blueprint is versatile. Its strength lies in the way it adapts across scales – personal, relational, organisational and societal – while holding the same ontological architecture. In every domain, it provides a living structure that keeps coherence at the centre while responding to context.

Personal

For an individual, the Blueprint becomes a living plan for one's life. It is not a to-do list of goals, but a systemic orientation that aligns health, relationships, contribution and work with deeper intention.

Example: A professional might realise that their career cannot be sustained by ambition alone. By mapping the current state, setting discerned intentions and aligning Being qualities like commitment, resilience and authenticity, they design a Blueprint that sustains vitality, nurtures family life and grounds career decisions in meaning rather than performance alone.

Relational

At the level of couples, families or close partnerships, the Blueprint can clarify shared intention and cultivate structures that sustain dignity, trust and joy.

Example: A couple moves beyond 'stop arguing' as their aim. Instead, they design a living Blueprint for their relationship that anchors it in authenticity, responsibility, vulnerability and courage. Their commitments include shared practices of dialogue, rituals of connection and feedback that keep the relationship aligned with their deeper purpose.

Organisational

For organisations, the Blueprint is a regenerative strategy that integrates value creation, culture and long-term resilience. It shifts the focus from compliance or quarterly optics to systemic coherence.

Example: A business may embed its Blueprint in participative leadership, transparent decision-making and regenerative supply chains. Quarterly reviews become opportunities for meta-awareness, asking not only 'Are we hitting targets?', but 'Are we still aligned with our authentic intention?' In this way, the organisation sustains trust with staff, customers and the wider community.

Societal

At the societal level, the Blueprint serves as a framework for governance and reform that honours sovereignty, trust and systemic renewal. It ensures reforms are not reactive fixes, but regenerative designs.

Example 1: New Zealand's wellbeing budget is one illustration. By reframing national success away from GDP alone and towards wellbeing indicators, it attempted to embed systemic coherence beyond economics. Though imperfect, it shows how a societal Blueprint can orient policy towards authentic sustainability.

Example 2: In Australia, debates around housing affordability highlight the risks of plans that lack ontological grounding. The government's low deposit scheme for first homebuyers, for instance, was framed as increasing access to ownership. But without addressing systemic shadows – such as supply constraints, inflated prices and intergenerational inequity – the plan risks eroding trust in reform itself. An Authentic Sustainability Blueprint approach would go beyond short-term incentives to design a regenerative housing system that strengthens social housing, aligns financial policy with sustainability, and ensures reforms enhance sovereignty and trust rather than undermine them.

Embedding Being into the Blueprint

A plan without Being at its centre is a hollow shell. The Authentic Sustainability Blueprint is not sustained by structures or strategies alone. Its lifeblood is the qualities of Being that animate every action, decision and relationship. Commitment, authenticity, courage, vulnerability, responsibility and other ontological aspects of Being give weight and coherence to the plan.

Embedding Being means ensuring that the Blueprint is not just about *what* we do, but *how we are being* as we do it. It is about cultivating the postures and ways of being that can sustain the intentions and structures over time. Without this anchor, the Blueprint risks becoming a performance – impressive on paper, but fragile in practice.

Think of Being as the foundation that holds the plan together. Strategies can shift, actions can change, but if the underlying ways of being are coherent, the system retains its integrity.

Examples

- **Personal:** An individual may set a Blueprint intention around nurturing family life and sustaining meaningful work. To embody this, they must cultivate responsibility (showing up reliably for loved ones), resilience (withstanding setbacks without collapse) and authenticity (living congruently with values, rather than performing for approval).

- **Relational:** A couple may design a Blueprint for dignity and joy in their relationship. This is sustained not only by external rituals, but by qualities of Being such as vulnerability, courage and adaptability – qualities that enable trust to be repaired and renewed.
- **Organisational:** A leader guiding their team through change may discover that their Blueprint will succeed, not because of technical strategies alone, but because they embody commitment, compassion and integrity, setting the tone for the culture they want to sustain.

Being is not decoration – it is the lifeblood of the Blueprint. Individuals align their personal ways of Being with the plan. Organisations design culture, leadership and decision-making around ontological coherence. Societies structure governance and policy to sustain sovereignty, trust and authenticity.

Embedding Being gives the Blueprint its foundation, but foundation alone is not enough. Systems must also move, flex and evolve with the currents of reality. This is where modulation enters. If Being anchors the Blueprint in coherence, modulation ensures it can bend without breaking, recalibrating in response to change while staying true to its centre.

A blueprint designed to adapt with change and the realities of life

Sustainability is never a final state to be reached once and for all. It is an ongoing, intentional practice of transition and renewal. A living plan is not designed merely to execute tasks, but to adapt, recalibrate and evolve in response to reality as it unfolds. This is why the Modulation Sphere must sit at the heart of the Authentic Sustainability Blueprint.

Think of a jazz band. Harmony is sustained not by rigidly following a score, but by listening, adjusting and improvising together, while staying anchored in the key and rhythm. In the same way, the Blueprint sustains coherence by allowing systems to bend without breaking and evolve without losing their centre.

A static plan dies the moment conditions change. However, a *modulated* plan preserves integrity through transitions, ensuring that authentic sustainability is carried forward by responsiveness grounded in Being.

Examples

- **Personal**: An individual designing their Blueprint around health and wellbeing adapts when life shifts, such as parenting demands or a change in workload. Rather than abandoning their intention, they modulate practices – shorter exercise sessions and new routines of rest – while staying anchored in resilience and commitment.
- **Organisational**: A company committed to regenerative supply chains encounters disruption when a key material becomes scarce. Instead of reverting to short-term fixes or compromising its values to cut costs, it recalibrates by seeking collaborative innovation – investing in research partnerships and alternative materials guided by the Blueprint's core commitments to trust, transparency and sustainability.
- **Societal**: A government embeds wellbeing indicators into national planning. As new data reveals unexpected stresses (such as climate migration or mental health crises), the plan evolves – not by discarding the wellbeing framework, but by recalibrating policies to sustain coherence across changing conditions.

In this way, modulation ensures that the Blueprint remains alive. It does not lock systems into rigid pathways, but equips them to navigate disruption with integrity, translating vision into practice that can endure. With modulation at its core, the Authentic Sustainability Blueprint becomes not only a plan for today, but a living architecture that sustains coherence across time and change.

The Authentic Sustainability Blueprint – A practical guide

This guide distils the Blueprint into a series of phases and tools you can apply in any system – personal, organisational or societal. It is not a checklist to be followed mechanically, but a living process designed to be adapted, tested and renewed.

Purpose – Translate vision into a living plan that is grounded in meaning, carried by Being, protected from shadows and designed to adapt.

Phase 0 – Scope and stakes

- **System**: Personal, relational, organisational or societal
- **Horizon**: 12–18 months for the first Blueprint cycle
- **Non-negotiables**: Ethical boundaries and must-keeps you will not trade off

Output

A one-line scope, timeframe and three non-negotiables.

Example

A couple agrees their Blueprint will focus on strengthening their relationship over the next 12 months. Their three non-negotiables are: no dishonesty; no unresolved conflict left unspoken for more than a week; and preserving time together despite busy schedules.

Phase 1 – Ground reality

Use the UOSI and the Nested Theory of Sense-making to gain clarity over the current situation.

Steps

- Map the four spheres: Architectonic, Integrity, Modulation and Disintegration.
- Name shadows clearly (no euphemisms). What are they protecting?
- Separate facts, interpretations and shared narratives.

Outputs

- **Reality map:** 6–10 bullet point truths about the current state
- **Shadow inventory:** 3–5 precise distortions and their costs

Distortion check

Invite one trusted person to quickly challenge your map. Prompt them with:

- 'What am I refusing to see?'
- 'What am I assuming that might not actually be true?'
- 'Am I making anything sound better than it really is?'

Example

The couple articulates their current reality, sharing a list of truths: 'We communicate openly most of the time, avoid money conversations and feel distant during periods of high stress.' Shadows include avoiding financial talks (protecting a fear of conflict) and one partner shutting down emotionally when stressed (protecting a fear of rejection).

Phase 2 – Mina to intention

Anchor the plan in significance before determining its structure.

Steps

- *Mina* **statement:** Write one sentence on why this matters.
- **Expression:** Write a short paragraph translating *Mina* into shared language.
- **Intention:** Write one Being-focused sentence: 'When we [act], we do so with [Being] in service of [*Mina*].'

Outputs

- Mina statement
- Expression paragraph
- Intention sentence

Distortion check

Review your wording and ask:

- 'Am I choosing any words to look good instead of being honest?'

- 'Would I say this the same way in private as in public?'
- 'Does this truly reflect our values, or is it for optics?'

Example

- **Mina statement:** 'Our relationship matters because it nurtures dignity, love and growth for both of us.'
- **Expression:** 'We are partners who care deeply for one another and want our relationship to be a place of safety, joy and resilience.'
- **Intention:** 'When we navigate challenges, we do so with vulnerability and compassion in service of our shared dignity and love.'

Phase 3 – Shape the living vision

Steps

- Write one paragraph per UOSI sphere showing what 'good' looks like.
- Name what must be carried forward, transformed and stopped.

Outputs

Vision page – 4 short paragraphs plus a 'keep–change–stop' table.

Pitfall to avoid

Avoid drafting outcome wishlists without naming the structures and ways of being that make them possible.

Example

- **Architectonic Sphere** – 'We sustain our partnership with rhythms of weekly connection.' **Integrity Sphere** – 'We remain truthful even when uncomfortable.'
- **Disintegration Sphere** – 'We stop ignoring financial stress and face it together.'
- **Modulation Sphere** – 'We adapt rituals as life shifts.'

Phase 4 – Being and commitments

Design the inner posture (ways of being) that will carry the plan.

Steps

- Select 3–5 ways of being required now (e.g., courage, responsibility, authenticity, vulnerability and adaptability).
- Write a commitment statement for accountability: 'We commit to [practice] even when [pressure point].'

Outputs

- Being established
- Commitment clauses
- Boundary conditions set.

Fracture check

Name two ways of being that would fracture the plan. Ask: 'If we showed up this way, would it undermine everything we are working towards?'

Example:

- **Ways of being:** Courage, steadiness and authenticity.
- **Commitment statement:** 'We commit to speaking truthfully, even when we fear conflict.'
- **Boundary condition:** 'We will not raise our voices in anger.'
- **Distortion check:** An unhealthy relationship with vulnerability and compassion.

Phase 5 – Modulation design

Make the plan breathable so it can bend without breaking.

Steps

Set your rhythms: Agree when you'll check in (weekly, monthly, quarterly).

Define your signals of health: 3–5 early signs (leading indicators) and 3–5 outcomes that matter most.

Establish your guardrails – Boundaries that protect integrity and prevent breakdown under pressure.

Outputs

- **Rhythm plan:** Your agreed check-in and review cycle.
- **Signals of health:** A short list of early signs and outcomes you'll track.
- **Guardrails:** Clear boundaries you won't cross, even under strain.

Repair guide

When things falter, follow these simple protocols:

- **If integrity is breached:** Name it → repair it → change the method.
- **If effectiveness stalls:** Simplify the goal → adjust capacity → re-sequence the work.

Example

- The couple agrees to a weekly check-in and a quarterly reflection. Their signals of health include: frequency of open conversations (leading indicator) and feeling more connected (outcome). Their guardrail: No major decisions without at least one night of reflection.

Phase 6 – Action structure

Turn vision into goals, objectives, actions and tasks.

Steps

- Define 3 goals aligned to intention.
- Define 2–4 objectives per goal with measures and clear roles.
- Allocate time, energy and resources realistically.

Outputs

- Goal–objective map
- Roles and responsibilities list
- Resource plan.

Example

- **Goal** – strengthen connection.
- **Objective** – one weekly date night.
- **Measure** – 80% consistency.
- **Roles** – both responsible; either partner can schedule.
- **Escalation** – if missed 3 weeks in a row, revisit priorities.

Phase 7 – Protections, embedding and learning

Make coherence durable.

Steps

- **Agree on protections**: Rules or boundaries that keep the relationship safe and fair.
- **Choose rituals and policies**: Two regular practices and two simple rules that embed your intention into daily life.
- **Write the foundation story**: A short (about 120 words) story that explains why this system matters and how you want to show up in it. In an organisational setting, this would be your onboarding story.
- **Decide on transparency**: What you will share openly, when and with whom.

Outputs

- Protections list
- 2 policies + 2 rituals
- Foundation story
- Transparency plan.

Example

- **Protections** – 'We will not hide debt or financial decisions from one another.'
- **Rituals** – monthly budgeting night, weekly gratitude practice.
- **Foundation story** – 'Our relationship exists to honour dignity, love and growth. We want it to be a place of honesty, joy and resilience. Even in difficulty, we commit to speaking truthfully, supporting one another and protecting the trust that makes us strong.'
- **Transparency** – 'We will share financial updates with each other every month, be open about stress levels during weekly check-ins, and talk honestly about personal wellbeing instead of bottling things up.'

Phase 8 – Pilot and iterate

Test your plan in small cycles before expanding.

Steps

- Start with just 1–2 objectives so you don't overload yourselves.
- Try them for a short cycle (e.g., two weeks at a time).
- After each cycle, pause to reflect. Did this strengthen integrity and bring you closer to your intention, or did it add strain?

Outputs

- A simple backlog of what you're trying.
- Short reviews of what worked and what didn't.
- A change log showing how you adjusted along the way.

Pause points

Agree on three clear signs that mean it's time to stop and rethink.

Example

- The couple decides to trial a weekly date night and a monthly budgeting night. After two weeks, they reflect on how each felt. Pause points include: repeated cancellations, resentment creeping in or conversations feeling consistently shallow.

Phase 9 – Scale and renew

Grow what works, let go of what doesn't and recalibrate as life changes.

Steps

- Every few months, pause and review your Blueprint together.
- Ask: 'What practices are helping us stay close and aligned? Which ones feel heavy or aren't working?'
- Keep and expand the practices that build integrity and trust.
- Adjust or retire the ones that no longer serve you.
- Refresh the vision if your circumstances shift significantly.

Outputs

- A short review note capturing what you'll keep, change or stop.
- A 'retain–retire–replicate' list to guide the next cycle.

Example

After three months, the couple conducts a review:

- Weekly date nights improved connection → Keep and expand.
- Budgeting nights helped, but felt draining → They realiscd the tone had become too serious and numbers-focused, so they'll change the format to be shorter and more conversational.
- A shared hobby project became stressful → Differing expectations and time pressure turned it into a chore, so they decide to retire it for now.

They agree to refresh their vision when their work schedules change later in the year.

30–60–90 day plan

Days 0–30 – Form and ground

- Complete your reality map, shadow inventory and *Mina-*intention plan.
- Draft your vision page and choose 3-5 ways of being to guide you.
- Define 3 goals, 4–6 starting objectives and simple signals of health.
- Set rhythms and guardrails; agree on who makes which decisions.

Days 31–60 – Pilot and learn

- Start with 1–2 objectives you can realistically trial.
- Test them for short cycles (e.g., two weeks each), using the repair guide if things go off track.
- Finalise protections and add two simple rules plus two rituals that embed your intention.
- Write your foundation story and agree on a transparency plan.

Days 61–90 – Embed and scale

- Quarterly UOSI review; retire or refresh as needed.
- Expand to the next objective only if leading indicators improved and integrity held.
- Lock the weekly and monthly rhythm plan; schedule the next renewal.

Authentic Sustainability Blueprint – Worksheet

Meaning and intention

- *Mina* (why this matters): _____
- **Expression (Meaning expressed as shared language):** _____

- **Intention:** 'When we _____, we do so with [Being] in service of [Mina].'

Vision – Four Spheres

- **Architectonic:** _____
- **Integrity:** _____
- **Modulation:** _____
- **Disintegration:** _____

Ways of being and commitments

- **Ways of being (3–5):** _____
- **Commitment clauses:** _____

Goals and objectives

- **Goals (3):**

    1. _____
    2. _____
    3. _____

- **Objectives (with measures and roles):** _____
- **Escalation path (if objectives are missed):** _____
- **Non-negotiables (boundaries you will not trade off):** _____

Indicators and rhythms

- **Leading (early signs):** 1) _____ 2) _____ 3) _____
- **Outcomes (results):** 1) _____ 2) _____ 3) _____
- **Rhythm plan:**
    - Weekly: _____
    - Monthly: _____
    - Quarterly: _____

Protections and Embedding
- **Protections (boundaries):** _____
- **Policies & Rituals (2+2):** _____
- **Foundation story (≈120 words):** _____

Resources
- **Time:** _____
- **Energy:** _____
- **Capital:** _____
- **Work-in-progress limit:** _____

Learning and renewal
- **Pause points (3 signs to stop/rethink):**

    1. _____
    2. _____
    3. _____

- **First trials (objectives to test first cycle):** _____

Conclusion

Authentic sustainability is not an outcome you can purchase or a performance you can stage. It is a way of being and building that keeps integrity at the centre while conditions keep shifting. In this chapter, you learned how to take the step that prevents dysfunction and drift by translating a living vision into the Authentic Sustainability Blueprint. This architecture holds *Mina*, Being, intention and modulation together so practice can stay grounded, aligned and coherent, even when tested.

The Blueprint is not another plan to file away, like a business plan that sits in a drawer. It is the ground you can stand on when conditions change, and the instrument you can tune as you learn. Its strength does not come from perfect forecasts or dense spreadsheets, but from ontological alignment: meaning before motion, Being before doing, and modulation before momentum. Held this way, structures serve life instead of constraining it.

This chapter showed how vision and the Blueprint work together – vision articulates the next coherent version of a system and the Blueprint translates that vision into practice. By moving through its phases – grounding reality, clarifying *Mina* and intention, shaping vision, embedding commitments, designing for modulation and testing through practice – you saw how coherence can be made durable across personal, relational, organisational and societal systems.

In this way, the Authentic Sustainability Blueprint becomes more than a plan. It is a living architecture for translating discernment into design and vision into practice – ensuring sustainability is not just imagined, but structured, tested and sustained through change.

From blueprint to practice – Integrating the architecture of authentic sustainability

Part VII has traced the pathway from insight to design – showing how the journey towards authentic sustainability moves from analysis to application and finally into a living blueprint to shape a sustainable future.

We began by uncovering the **UOSI's emergent forces** – the structural elements that drive systems toward coherence or dysfunction. Using this framework, we learned how to analyse systems, revealing both their strengths and fractures. From there, we examined **meta-awareness** and **metacontent** to sharpen perception and distinguish reality from narrative distortion, and we applied the **Systemic Subversion Cycle (SSC)** to diagnose how dysfunction and collapse take root when vigilance is absent.

With this analytical foundation in place, we turned to **Minalogy**, translating sense-making into meaning and giving sustainability its compass – the *why* that anchors every intention. We then followed the upward **flow of coherence** from meaning, vision, mission and intention to goals, objectives, tasks and actions, which represents the Developmental Dimension of the **Fulfilment Pyramid**. This tri-dimensional model reveals how enduring fulfilment in all aspects of life – personal, organisational, institutional and societal – relies on the application of all three of its dimensions – developmental, phenomenological and relational.

From there, the focus shifted from diagnosis to reconstruction. The **Reconstructive Ontology of Sustainability (ROS)** unified all prior frameworks into a coherent architecture grounded in Being, integrity, sense-making and meaning-making. ROS marked the threshold between understanding and reconstruction – the moment when analysis becomes creation.

Finally, we learned how to gauge authentic sustainability by reading the health of the UOSI's 16 qualities in practice, while confronting the shadows that corrode integrity unless exposed and regenerated. The journey culminated in the discipline of envisioning and the **Authentic Sustainability Blueprint** – the tool that translates reconstruction into design, creating a living framework that is adaptable through modulation while remaining firmly anchored in *Mina* and systemic integrity.

Connecting the frameworks to form one living process

To conclude Part VII, let's recap how all these frameworks and tools connect under the umbrella of the Authentic Sustainability Framework (ASF) so you can see how they are one living process rather than a series of isolated resources.

The Systemic Subversion Cycle (SSC), the Reconstructive Ontology of Sustainability (ROS), the Unified Ontology of Systemic Integrity (UOSI), the Fulfilment Pyramid and the Authentic Sustainability Blueprint are not parallel models. They are sequential expressions of the same regenerative logic embodied within the Authentic Sustainability Framework (ASF). Each reveals a distinct movement within the wider process of authentic sustainability: from seeing, to rebuilding, to embodying, to designing, and to practising coherence.

- **The SSC** provides the *diagnostic lens*, exposing how coherence erodes through distortion, drift and subversion.
- **ROS** provides the *reconstructive foundation*, rebuilding systems on ontological ground – Being, integrity,

sense-making, meaning-making and modulation. It weaves together the major frameworks introduced throughout the book – the Being Framework, metacontent, the Nested Theory of Sense-making, Minalogy, the UOSI and the Transformation Methodology – into one coherent paradigm for authentic sustainability in action.

- **The UOSI** provides the *standards of coherence*, ensuring what is reconstructed remains ethically, structurally and systemically sound.
- **The Fulfilment Pyramid** carries that coherence inward, showing how meaning flows through intention, commitment and conduct until it becomes enduring fulfilment in lived reality.
- **The Authentic Sustainability Blueprint** gives that coherence outer form – turning vision into living systems, rhythms and feedback loops that adapt without losing integrity.

Seen through the lens of the ASF, these frameworks form one continuous movement, each stage preparing the next and sustaining coherence across scales of human activity – from the individual to the societal.

Diagnosis (SSC) → Reconstruction (ROS) → Coherence (UOSI) → Flow (Fulfilment Pyramid) → Form (Blueprint) → Practice (Embodiment)

One continuous workflow

In practice, the movement is straightforward:

- **See clearly** – Use the SSC and UOSI to map reality, reveal subversion and name shadows precisely.
- **Discern meaning** – Articulate *Mina* and its expression so that significance precedes strategy.
- **Align intention** – Set discerned intentions rather than reactive goals.
- **Embody integrity** – Establish the requisite ways of being and convert them into lived commitments.

- **Shape coherence** – Form the living vision across the four spheres of the UOSI, defining what the next coherent version must become.
- **Design the architecture** – Weave together the insights of ROS into a living design (Authentic Sustainability Blueprint) where form and purpose, structure and rhythm, evolve together in structural coherence.
- **Do the work** – Translate the architecture into action: goals, objectives, roles, pilots and feedback loops.
- **Sustain coherence** – Review with the UOSI and the Blueprint; scale what works, renew what doesn't, and maintain vigilance through modulation.

From design to action

Design, no matter how elegant, is only potential until it becomes lived. The real test of sustainability begins when frameworks meet friction – when vision is expressed through conduct, decisions, and relationships that must hold coherence under real-world pressure.

Part VIII opens that next phase. Here we move from blueprint to practice – from preparation to embodiment. These final chapters explore how the architecture of the ASF becomes a lived reality: how systems – ourselves and the systems we engage with and inhabit – are tested, adapted and renewed through modulation. The focus now shifts from designing sustainable futures to *inhabiting* them – carrying coherence into practice, translating principle into performance, and regenerating integrity through every cycle of change.

Blueprints sketch the path. But only practice makes it real.

PART VIII

From Plan to Practice — Executing Authentic Sustainability

A blueprint is only potential until it is lived. Insight without embodiment remains a concept. Intention without enactment remains a promise unfulfilled. The work of sustainability demands more than clarity and design. It demands the courage to carry them into action.

This final part of the book is where the architecture we have built so far is tested in real life. It is where sustainability stops being an intellectual exercise and becomes a lived reality. Here, we cross the threshold from plan to practice.

Execution is rarely a straight line. In the context of authentic sustainability, it is a living process in which every action reshapes the system it touches. Success lies not in control, but in sustaining coherence through change. To achieve this, we must learn to act with integrity, modulate with discernment, and embody the qualities of Being that can hold the weight of authentic sustainability.

In the chapters that follow, we integrate the full body of work – the ontologies, frameworks and distinctions developed so far – into lived application. We begin with the human being, the most significant unit of sustainability, then ground our practice with the UOSI as our compass. From there, we introduce the Sustainability Profile, a practical tool for gauging systemic health and linking observation directly to transformation. This profile provides a way to measure what matters. Next, we apply the Transformation Methodology in action, explore modulation as the art of sustaining coherence through disruption, and expand the field of application from individuals and relationships to institutions, all the way to humanity itself.

Part VIII takes us from strategy to execution – from designing sustainable systems to practising them in real conditions, where coherence is maintained through modulation and continual renewal. It asks not only what you will design, but how you will live – and what kind of future your Being and actions will make possible for your own life and for generations to come.

CHAPTER 53

From Blueprint to Practice – The Leap into Action

A plan, no matter how insightful or beautifully crafted, remains solely potential. It serves as a necessary map to show what might lie ahead, but it does not guide us on how to navigate and enter that terrain. The moment you move from planning to action is the moment when sustainability stops being a theory and becomes a lived reality. This is the leap that separates conceptual work from embodied change.

In Part VII, we reconstructed the very foundations of sustainability through the Reconstructive Ontology of Sustainability (ROS), envisioned the next coherent version of systems and translated that vision into design through the Authentic Sustainability Blueprint. But a blueprint on its own is lifeless. Without embodiment, it gathers dust, like so many reports and strategic plans in boardrooms and government offices.

Now we cross the threshold. This chapter is not about adding more analysis. It's about stepping into the terrain – taking the architecture you have built and translating it into practice.

Why execution fails without ontology

Most execution frameworks focus on strategy, tasks and measurement. They assume that if you break a plan into steps and hold people accountable, action will follow. But as you have seen throughout this book, sustainability is not sustained by checklists. It is sustained by Being.

Execution fails when it tries to bypass ontology. You cannot implement authenticity, integrity or regeneration as procedures. They must be lived as ways of being. Without that ontological grounding, execution collapses into compliance, performance optics and short-term outputs.

Consider a government that maps out a bold climate roadmap. On paper, it looks impeccable: clear targets, metrics and policies. Yet if the underlying intention is driven by fear of political backlash or optics rather than integrity, the execution will sustain dysfunction rather than enable transformation.

Or think of a startup. Two co-founders draft a visionary plan for their venture. The pitch deck is flawless. But if trust between them is fractured, no funding round, growth strategy or product roadmap can make the venture sustainable. The plan unravels because the ontology of the team – their collective Being – was never aligned.

From knowing to doing – It starts with you

The gap between knowing and doing is not a lack of discipline. It is a lack of embodiment. You can understand systemic integrity intellectually and still sustain dysfunction if your way of being has not shifted. This is why the first step of execution is not action. It is alignment.

Put simply, authentic sustainability begins with you. This is not a self-help slogan; it is a systemic reality. Systems are sustained through the beings within them. If your way of living, relating and working cannot maintain coherence, no policy, plan or strategy will. A family that burns out while trying to 'live sustainably' is not sustainable. An organisation that preaches sustainability while corroding the wellbeing of its people is not sustainable. A society that sacrifices the dignity of its citizens for short-term stability is not sustainable.

So, before you act, pause to consider who and how you must be to sustain this action – how your team or organisation must be as a collective to carry the blueprint forward, and what this demands in terms of trust, sovereignty and integrity. These questions are not philosophical luxuries; they are the entry point into effective practice.

When coherence is embodied personally, it can scale authentically into organisations, communities and societies. Therefore, the leap into action must begin not with doing more, but with *being aligned* – ensuring every step you take is grounded in integrity.

Being – The architecture beneath our personal and collective conduct

Governments, organisations, families, communities and societies are all mirrors reflecting the beings who inhabit and sustain them. That's why it is impossible to build a sustainable system on the foundation of fragmented Being. No matter how elegant the design, no matter how well-funded the initiative, if the human beings within it are distorted in their orientation, the system itself will fracture. This is why authentic sustainability must begin with the human being. This is not merely a philosophical preference; it's a systemic necessity.

Most sustainability efforts focus on policy, technology or process. They assume that if you 'fix' the structure, the system will be sustainable. But structures are created and run by people. The best governance model collapses if leaders are driven by fear. The most effective corporate strategy disintegrates if teams are paralysed by inauthenticity or resentment.

It is we human beings who demand systems. It is we who design them, implement them, adhere to them, subscribe to them, follow them, refine them, critique them, challenge them and, ultimately, transform them. It is all a human affair. We are the ones who give birth to these systems – particularly the manufactured, man-made and constructed ones – and it is we who keep them alive.

Yet not all systems are human inventions. Some are natural, existential or ontological in origin – such as the laws of nature, the dynamics of ecosystems, or the fundamental principles that science seeks to uncover rather than create. In relation to these systems, our awareness and humility determine the integrity of our interaction. This is where surrender becomes vital – the recognition that certain systems are not ours to control but to understand, align with and serve through coherence rather than domination.

For all these reasons, sustainability collapses when it is treated as a project rather than a posture of Being. Systems do not fail because they lack procedures. They fail because they lack coherence in the ways of being of the human beings that engage with them. While engagement within systems inevitably involves procedures, coherence does not arise from the procedures themselves. It arises from the posture of Being through which those procedures are enacted. Procedure shapes form while Being shapes essence. A process can be efficient yet incoherent if the consciousness animating it is misaligned.

As we have learned, Being is not personality, skillset or behaviour. It is the underlying ontological posture from which all actions and decisions emerge. It is the architecture beneath our conduct. When your Being is aligned with integrity and authentic awareness, everything you build carries that alignment into the world. A simple act – like setting a workplace policy or negotiating with a partner – can ripple coherence across an entire system. But when Being is distorted, dysfunction is embedded in every choice. Fear masquerades as prudence, control masquerades as care and pride masquerades as confidence.

This is why the first step in executing your Authentic Sustainability Blueprint is not to act but to align. The essential question becomes: *Who and how must I be for this plan to endure and be truly sustainable?* For leaders of teams, the next logical question is: *Who and how must my people be to achieve an authentically sustainable outcome?*

Leveraging the Being Framework

Having explored how the essence and Being of human beings underpin every system we create or engage with, it becomes evident that authentic sustainability must begin there. As one of the four qualities within the Integrity Sphere, Being encompasses both the essence of our *whatness* – our essential nature – and, more importantly, *how we are being*, individually and collectively, in relation to these essential qualities. Through this lens, we can see why grounding any pursuit of sustainability in the Being Framework[96] is vital. It provides the ontological structure that ensures alignment between who we are, what we build and how we sustain it.

The Being Framework's 31 Aspects of Being are not abstract virtues or aspirational slogans to pin on an office wall. They are ontological levers – qualities that, when embodied, determine whether intentions can endure as lived commitments.

Take authenticity, for example. Without it, sustainability efforts devolve into theatre – glossy reports, staged photo opportunities and empty words. When you have a healthy relationship with authenticity, your actions align with your intentions, preventing performative sustainability.

Or consider responsibility. A healthy relationship with this Primary Way of Being turns intention into daily ownership. Without responsibility as a way of being, commitments slip into compliance – tasks done because someone said so, not because they are anchored in Being.

Care grounds sustainability in genuine regard for life, people, the systems you engage with and the world. Without care, efficiency replaces empathy and sustainability is reduced to a box-ticking exercise.

Integrity is the force that holds coherence between values, choices and systemic structure. Discernment (as part of awareness) sustains integrity when complexity tempts you towards shortcuts or illusion.

---

96 Tashvir, A. 2021 *Being – The Source of Power.* Engenesis Publications: Sydney.

Each Aspect of Being is like a load-bearing beam in the architecture of sustainability. Remove one and the structure weakens. Distort another and cracks appear.

Diagnosing and refining your way of being

Alignment begins with awareness. To sustain authentic sustainability, you must first see how your current way of being supports or undermines coherence. The **Being Profile**[97] serves as your diagnostic companion at this stage. This assessment tool maps where your relationship to the 31 Aspects of Being is coherent and where it is distorted.

For example, you might value responsibility, but relate to it through guilt – taking on too much, compensating for others and eventually burning out. Or you may reject vulnerability, mistaking it for weakness, when in truth, its absence prevents trust and collaboration. The Being Profile makes these dynamics visible, turning blind spots into pathways for regeneration.

When used alongside your Authentic Sustainability Blueprint, the Being Profile becomes a mirror. It shows which ways of being must evolve to sustain your intentions and which shadows threaten to distort them. In this way, it ensures that execution begins from ontological alignment rather than performance.

You cannot sustain authentic sustainability while your Being is entangled in shadows. To ignore them is to build on a foundation of sand. The goal is not to eliminate shadows, but to *integrate* them – to reclaim the energy they conceal and redirect that energy towards coherence. This process transforms reaction into response and distortion into discernment.

By making the terrain visible, the Being Profile allows you to map which qualities are present, which are underdeveloped, and which shadows are silently distorting your execution.

---

[97] Tashvir, A. 2021 *Being – The Source of Power* (Part 3, Ch 1). Engenesis Publications: Sydney.

From awareness to embodiment

Execution begins where awareness becomes practice. Once you have mapped your relationship with each of the 31 Aspects of Being and exposed your shadows, the next step is to apply the **Transformation Methodology**[98] to move from observation to redesign, embedding new postures of Being that will support you to sustain your Blueprint over time.

In practical terms:

1. **Assess** – Map your current relationship to key Aspects of Being.
2. **Discern** – Identify which aspects must strengthen to sustain your Blueprint.
3. **Transform** – Use conscious practice, coaching and feedback to embody the new posture.
4. **Embed** – Integrate the qualities into daily life – in meetings, relationships, decisions and self-care.
5. **Recalibrate** – Review regularly, using reflection or dialogue to detect drift and restore coherence.

Through this cycle, alignment stops being a momentary exercise and becomes a lived rhythm – the heartbeat of sustainable practice.

From individual to collective Being

While execution begins within the individual, it cannot stop there. The same ontological principles apply collectively. Organisations that seek coherence need to map the Being of their culture, leadership and teams. Societies that aspire to thrive do so by examining their collective ways of being – how governance, policy and cultural norms arise from shared ontological qualities like trust, responsibility and discernment.

Authentic sustainability is never just technical; it is always ontological. Systems are sustained not by their procedures or plans, but

---

[98] Tashvir, A. 2021 *Being – The Source of Power* (Part 3, Ch 2). Engenesis Publications: Sydney.

by the quality of Being that animates them. No blueprint, policy or structure can outlast the coherence of the people who bring it to life.

Before moving into systemic execution, pause to consider:

- Which Aspects of Being are most alive within you or your team right now?
- Which may be underdeveloped or distorted?
- How might these qualities shape, strengthen or sabotage the system you are building?

These questions are not philosophical abstractions. They are the foundation of practical sustainability – the ground on which every coherent system stands.

Execution as an ontological shift

Execution is not simply behavioural change; it is a systemic and ontological shift. Embodiment expands from the individual to the collective, requiring alignment across three dimensions that mirror the architecture of sustainability itself:

- **Being alignment** – Ensuring your way of being can carry the weight of your intentions and commitments.
- **Systemic integrity** – Ensuring the systems and structures you are acting upon are aligned with the Unified Ontology of Systemic Integrity (UOSI).
- **Modulation** – Designing action that can adapt and sustain itself across time and complexity.

Example:

Think of a hospital introducing a new patient-care model. If doctors and nurses don't embody qualities such as responsibility, resourcefulness and compassion (**Being alignment**) on an individual level, the model will not hold. If the institution's policies, culture and resource flows are not aligned with the UOSI's principles of integrity and trust (**systemic integrity**), the reform collapses into paperwork. And if the rollout is rigid, unable to recalibrate as staff adapt and unexpected challenges emerge (**modulation**), the initiative fractures.

When all three elements are present, the system regenerates itself – remaining coherent and sustaining better patient outcomes as conditions evolve and layers of complexity build over time. Together, these dimensions form the living architecture of execution, ensuring that practice becomes a regenerative act rather than a one-off enactment.

Being, systemic integrity and modulation underpin every act of execution. The next step is to translate all three into daily practice through your Authentic Sustainability Blueprint.

Translating the Authentic Sustainability Blueprint into practice

The Authentic Sustainability Blueprint you built in the last chapter is not a finished product. It is a living structure waiting to be embodied. The leap into action requires you to translate that Blueprint into practice.

This is where Being, systemic integrity and modulation come to life through application and embodiment. The following steps translate these dimensions into tangible action – turning your Authentic Sustainability Blueprint from concept to coherent conduct and lived reality:

- **Align Being** – Use the Being Framework to ensure your Being sustains the Blueprint. Identify which of the 31 qualities of Being must be cultivated or strengthened to support your commitments.
- **Anchor commitment as a way of being** – Move from intention to embodied commitment. Anchor commitment not as a list of tasks, but as a way of being that holds steady even when conditions shift.
- **Design feedback loops** – A sustainable plan evolves. Build structures that allow you to learn and adjust in real time. Use modulation to keep the plan alive and adaptive.
- **Act iteratively** – Avoid the trap of waiting for perfection. Start small, learn, adapt and recalibrate as you go. Authentic sustainability is built through continuous recalibration, not one-off interventions.

Think of a policymaker shaping education reform. Instead of announcing a rigid 10-year plan, they embed cycles of feedback from teachers, students and parents, recalibrating as conditions evolve. Or a family wanting to live more sustainably. Instead of upending their lifestyle overnight, they begin with one change – shifting how they manage food waste – and gradually expand from there. In both cases, small gradual steps to change result in sustainability becoming a living practice – one that acts, adjusts and regenerates coherence over time.

Example – Embedding the Blueprint in a business

A mid-sized Australian architecture firm commits to embedding authentic sustainability into its culture.

- **Align Being:** The firm's partners identify that the qualities of authenticity, responsibility, higher purpose, commitment and resourcefulness must underpin every project.
- **Anchor commitment as a way of being:** Rather than issuing new sustainability policies, they begin weekly reflection circles where staff share how their daily decisions reflected (or missed) those qualities.
- **Design feedback loops:** They establish 90-day modulation reviews – short sessions to recalibrate project methods, budget priorities and team wellbeing against their meaning, including their *Mina* ('why') statement: *'We design spaces that restore human connection to the environment.'*
- **Act iteratively:** Each quarter, they pilot one small change, such as switching suppliers, redesigning waste systems and trialling new materials, learning from the results before scaling up.

Within 18 months, sustainability isn't just a policy and plan; it's the firm's operating rhythm. Staff describe a tangible shift in morale and trust, and clients notice the coherence between message and delivery.

Exercise: Translating your Blueprint into practice

1. **Review your Blueprint** from Chapter 52. Choose *one* goal or commitment that feels most urgent or resonates with you.

2. **Align Being:** Identify at least three Aspects of Being that must be strengthened for this goal to be fulfilled.
3. **Anchor commitment as a way of being:** Write one sentence that translates this goal into a way of being that holds, even when challenged (e.g., *'When I lead my team, I do so with patience and accountability, even under pressure.'*).
4. **Design a feedback loop:** Decide how you will know if coherence is holding (e.g., weekly reflection, peer feedback or quick check-ins).
5. **Take one micro-action** within the next 48 hours that embodies this commitment. Record what changed.

(Tip: start small. Sustainability scales through repetition, not intensity.)

The role of modulation in execution

As mentioned earlier, execution is rarely a straight line. It is a living process of transition – from intention to action, from plan to reality, from order to renewal. Every implementation phase carries both motion and resistance. For this reason, modulation is essential. It is the capacity to guide transitions without losing coherence – to keep purpose steady while form and circumstance evolve.

In practice, modulation means cultivating the ability to:

- Anticipate resistance and design for it,
- Hold space for denial while sustaining direction, and
- Move between stability and change without fracturing integrity.

From a leadership perspective, modulation is not about being kind, altruistic or benevolent. It is not a moral gesture, but an existential, ontological and practical one. Some may wish for team members to leave their personal anxieties at the door and don a mask of professionalism when faced with a challenging situation. That is neither authentic nor reflective of reality. Modulation is not babysitting or emotional indulgence. It is acting from truth rather than illusion – recognising that feigned coherence only breeds disappointment later.

In the end, customers do not care about the origin of someone's anxieties; they care about their experience. A person representing an organisation inevitably carries their state of Being into every interaction. To deny this is to design on false assumptions – systems that may appear stable, but are fundamentally incoherent.

A leader who cannot modulate will either push too hard, creating fracture, or wait too long, allowing dysfunction to entrench. In contrast, a leader who does modulate becomes a steward of sustainability – adjusting rhythm, pacing and focus with precision and courage.

Example – Leadership modulation in practice

During a major digital transformation, a public-sector leader notices staff anxiety rising. Instead of forcing rapid compliance (rigid execution) or delaying rollout (avoidance), she applies the modulating forces of patience, tolerance, adaptability and surrender to guide the transition – knowing that people don't experience their team's intentions; they experience their state of being in action.

- **Patience** allows her to slow the pace without losing momentum, resisting pressure for instant outcomes.
- **Tolerance** helps her hold discomfort and ambiguity without rushing to fix it, creating open forums for honest dialogue.
- **Adaptability** enables her to re-sequence milestones, form pilot teams and deliver small visible wins that rebuild trust.
- **Surrender** frees her from rigid expectations, accepting that some elements will evolve unpredictably and that coherence is more important than control.

Within a year, the implementation is complete – not without challenge, but without collapse. Retention improves, burnout falls and morale stabilises. Through modulation, the leader proves that sustainability is carried not by control or speed, but by sustained coherence through times of challenge and change.

Applying modulation in your own practice

Modulation in execution begins with conscious awareness of transition. When a project, relationship or system starts to shift, the question is not *how to control it,* but *how to move with it without losing your centre.*

Try this simple rhythm:

1. **Identify the live transition** – Name what is shifting and where resistance sits.
2. **Select the quality to lead with** – Patience, tolerance, adaptability or surrender.
3. **Intervene minimally, observe deeply** – Apply the smallest effective intervention, then sense how the field responds.
4. **Review and recalibrate** – Reflect on what changed, what held steady and what needs further adjustment before continuing.

Over time, this rhythm turns execution from a mechanical process into a living one. Modulation brings flexibility without drift and stability without rigidity. It transforms turbulence into learning and performance into regeneration.

The practical art of mastering modulation will be covered in more detail in Chapter 57. For now, remember that every act of execution is also an act of transition. How you move through those transitions determines whether your system merely functions, or truly sustains itself.

Conclusion

The leap from planning to action requires a shift from intellectual understanding to ontological embodiment – carrying what you've learned so far as a way of life rather than a set of concepts. This is where authenticity is tested, integrity is embodied and sustainability ceases to be an idea and becomes lived reality.

This chapter marked the threshold between design and enactment – where the blueprint comes alive through Being, coherence and modulation in motion. The chapters that follow take us deeper into this lived terrain.

Although authentic sustainability begins with you and every other human being, it does not end there. The same discipline of coherence must be built into the systems, relationships and structures that carry your work forward. In the next chapter, we turn to the Unified Ontology of Systemic Integrity (UOSI) – the framework that anchors execution in structural coherence and systemic trust.

CHAPTER 54

Leveraging the UOSI – The Compass of Execution

You've aligned who and how you must be for authentic sustainability to take form. The next step is ensuring that your actions, systems and relationships stay aligned as they unfold. Execution does not test ideas; it tests integrity. The Unified Ontology of Systemic Integrity (UOSI) provides the compass to navigate this test, keeping movement coherent as your Authentic Sustainability Blueprint enters real life.

Execution is not a neat sequence of tasks on a Gantt chart or a project that begins and ends once a checklist is complete. It is alive. Every action reshapes the system you are acting upon, often in ways you cannot predict in advance. That is why implementation cannot be treated as a one-off event or rollout. It must be guided by a framework that sustains coherence while allowing for adaptation and renewal.

The UOSI is that framework. It is the architecture and compass that prevent execution from becoming a reactive scramble. As you move from plan to action, the UOSI ensures the living process remains anchored in coherence.

Up to this point, the UOSI has served as a diagnostic lens – to analyse systems, reveal shadows and imagine the next version of what could be. That work was critical. But in execution, the UOSI shifts roles – it becomes a live compass, not just a conceptual map.

Think of it like navigation at sea. A map helps you plot the route. But once the ship is moving, you need a compass to keep adjusting your course in real time. Winds change, tides pull and storms appear. Without that live instrument, you drift. The UOSI plays that role during execution, ensuring that every decision, structure and adjustment remains aligned with Being, integrity and authentic sustainability.

This shift is not optional. Many well-designed plans fail, not because they were poorly conceived, but because execution drifted from integrity over time. Without a live ontological anchor, action becomes fragmented, reactionary and misaligned with the deeper intentions that birthed it.

Applying the four spheres

The strength of the UOSI lies in its four spheres – **Architectonic, Integrity, Disintegration** and **Modulation**. These are not abstract categories, but live dimensions of orientation that keep execution coherent as systems evolve. Each offers a distinct vantage point through which to read and realign the field of action.

Together, they form a compass for execution – one that ensures your Authentic Sustainability Blueprint doesn't just move forward, but does so in alignment with purpose, ethics, resilience and adaptability.

The Architectonic Sphere

This is the governing dimension of the UOSI – the sphere that orients the entire system, ensuring your *'why?'* and *'to what end?'* are aligned with your actions. Guided by four meta-factors – meta-awareness, systemic integrity, sustained effectiveness and normativity – the Architectonic Sphere is where discernment becomes design and responsibility becomes architecture. These forces form the compass and moral backbone of any system, from a person to a global institution.

In execution, the Architectonic Sphere ensures that your actions are not just efficient but meaningful – that structure, rhythm and design serve the deeper coherence of the system rather than mere momentum.

The Integrity Sphere

The Integrity Sphere provides the inner scaffolding that holds everything together when complexity increases. It governs the relational and ethical dimensions of execution, ensuring that *how* things are done remains consistent with *why* they are done. Its four regulating forces – intention, trust, sovereignty and Being – keep relationships, commitments and decisions anchored in authenticity and coherence.

In practice, the Integrity Sphere sustains trust under pressure and prevents noble goals from collapsing into performance or pretence. It reminds you that sustainability without integrity is only theatre.

The Disintegration Sphere

Every system encounters breakdowns. The Disintegration Sphere helps you read them before they spread. It reveals where coherence is weakening, showing whether misalignment is emotional, structural or ethical. Its four components – shadows, misery, suffering and entrenchment – mark stages where dysfunction begins to normalise itself.

In execution, the Disintegration Sphere isn't about blame but clarity. By recognising where energy is leaking or truth is being avoided, you can intervene early and restore coherence with structural intelligence rather than reacting.

The Modulation Sphere

The Modulation Sphere governs systemic coherence during times of change and pressure – the capacity to bend without breaking and to evolve without losing your centre. Its four regulators – patience, tolerance, adaptability and surrender – stabilise systems through change, allowing coherence to renew rather than collapse.

In execution, modulation determines whether transitions become regenerative or destructive. It enables individuals, teams, organisations and societies to navigate disruption with composure and courage – leading without coercion, transforming without breaking and growing without betraying what matters.

Personal example – Navigating a career transition

You've been offered a new role in another city. The news is both exciting and disruptive. It represents a significant promotion and salary increase, but accepting it would mean uprooting your family. Should you take the role? Applying the four spheres keeps your decision coherent.

- **Architectonic Sphere:** You clarify your deeper *why* – not just professional advancement, but aligning your work with meaning, purpose and wellbeing.
- **Integrity Sphere:** You discuss the offer openly with your partner and children, weighing its pros and cons together to ensure everyone's sovereignty and trust are honoured in the process.
- **Disintegration Sphere:** You notice early signs of strain – tension at home, self-doubt or fatigue – and treat them as feedback about pace and support, not as failure.
- **Modulation Sphere:** You apply patience to slow the timeline, tolerance to hold uncertainty, adaptability to explore hybrid options and surrender if the move proves misaligned with your shared coherence.

Instead of forcing an outcome, you create conditions for a decision that sustains both purpose and relational integrity.

Community example – Implementing a new preventative-care model

A regional health department introduces a community-based program designed to reduce hospital admissions.

- **Architectonic Sphere:** Leaders revisit purpose before rollout, ensuring the program serves long-term wellbeing rather than short-term cost savings.

- **Integrity Sphere:** Trust and sovereignty are built through early consultation with clinicians, patients and local councils, so the initiative becomes a co-created architecture rather than a directive.
- **Disintegration Sphere:** When staff exhaustion and communication gaps appear, leaders recognise them as signs of systemic strain, not personal failure, and realign workflows and resourcing accordingly.
- **Modulation Sphere:** When external funding delays create pressure, the team slows some targets (patience), hosts open forums to surface concerns (tolerance), adjusts schedules to maintain progress (adaptability), and releases outdated KPIs that no longer serve coherence (surrender).

Within a year, the model stabilises. Stress decreases, trust rises, and measurable health outcomes improve – proof that coherent execution regenerates rather than depletes.

Organisational example – Redesigning a sales model for sustainable growth

A mid-sized consumer goods company seeks to redesign its sales function. While quarterly targets are being met, relationships with customers have become transactional, employee turnover is high, and the pressure to perform is leading to burnout. The leadership team recognises that sustainable sales require systemic coherence rather than short-term success.

This example takes the exploration a step further by contextualising not only the four spheres of the UOSI, but also the quad components within each sphere, demonstrating how all 16 qualities function in practice within a specific commercial context. By examining the sales model through this lens, you can see how coherence is maintained operationally – how every meta-factor, regulator and dynamic within the four spheres contributes to a system's capacity to evolve, adapt and sustain integrity in real-world execution.

Architectonic Sphere: Leaders revisit the underlying purpose of sales, ensuring that revenue generation serves the company's broader mission of creating value and trust with customers rather than merely extracting profit. Targets and incentives are redesigned to reward long-term partnerships, ethical engagement and repeat customer satisfaction.

- **Meta-awareness:** Leaders reflect on how sales decisions are made, identifying hidden assumptions behind 'growth at all costs'.
- **Systemic integrity:** They ensure alignment between purpose, structure and outcomes – that what is promised in the sales pitch can genuinely be delivered.
- **Sustained effectiveness:** KPIs are balanced between short-term performance and long-term customer relationship quality.
- **Normativity:** The team discusses not only what can be sold, but what *ought* to be sold – aligning offerings with ethics, genuine need and value.

Integrity Sphere: Sales managers rebuild the relational foundation through trust, sovereignty, intention and Being. The focus shifts from persuasion to authenticity – listening to clients' real needs, maintaining transparency and honouring commitments. Team members are encouraged to take ownership of their results while staying grounded in integrity and care.

- **Intention:** Each salesperson aligns their motive with genuine service rather than manipulation or pressure.
- **Trust:** Transparency in pricing and delivery rebuilds credibility with customers and within the team.
- **Sovereignty:** Salespeople are empowered to make principled decisions without fear of being punished for honesty.
- **Being:** The presence and authenticity of each team member become central to the customer experience – who they are matters as much as what they sell.

Disintegration Sphere: When warning signs appear – such as manipulative selling tactics, declining morale or miscommunication between sales and delivery teams – leaders treat them as indicators of systemic strain rather than personal failure. They address misalignments in incentives, restructure workloads and clarify expectations to restore coherence.

- **Shadows:** Aggressive tactics and inflated promises are recognised as symptoms of a fear-based culture, not dismissed as 'necessary'.
- **Misery:** Leaders notice the emotional fatigue beneath high performance and address its root causes.
- **Suffering:** Difficult conversations are held to surface hidden frustrations and broken trust.
- **Entrenchment:** Rather than defending 'how we've always done things', the team acknowledges outdated methods and prepares to evolve.

Modulation Sphere: When market conditions shift or new technologies disrupt the landscape, the sales team applies patience to pace decisions, tolerance to engage differing opinions, adaptability to refine strategies and surrender to release outdated targets that no longer serve coherence.

- **Patience:** When revenue dips temporarily during transition, leadership resists panic, allowing new systems to take root rather than forcing premature results.
- **Tolerance:** Divergent views between the sales, marketing and operations teams are discussed openly, allowing productive dialogue instead of reactive blame.
- **Adaptability:** The team refines sales strategies based on evolving customer behaviour and market conditions without losing sight of their core purpose.
- **Surrender:** Outdated KPIs and rigid sales scripts are released, making space for authentic engagement and regenerative growth.

Within a few quarters, sales performance becomes stable and regenerative. Customer loyalty deepens, staff retention improves and the company becomes known as an ethical, relationship-driven business – proof that coherence and sustainability in sales generate growth that endures.

Exercise

Choose one project, decision or transition you are currently navigating. Use the four UOSI spheres to bring clarity and coherence to your next step.

1. **Architectonic Sphere:** Revisit your *why*. Does this action or decision serve a coherent purpose, or has it drifted into reaction or routine?
2. **Integrity Sphere:** Examine how intention, trust, sovereignty and Being are operating. Are voices being heard? Are your choices aligned with shared intentions and authentic care?
3. **Disintegration:** Identify early signs of strain, such as fatigue, avoidance, miscommunication or cynicism. What are these symptoms revealing about the system's alignment or capacity?
4. **Modulation:** Apply at least one modulating force – patience, tolerance, adaptability or surrender – to restore balance. Which of these qualities is most needed right now?

Write one simple adjustment for each sphere. Together, these four moves form your *execution compass* – keeping your Authentic Sustainability Blueprint alive, grounded and regenerative as it moves from intention into lived reality.

Applying the UOSI across scales

The same structural logic applies whether you're leading yourself, a team, an organisation or a society. The coherence or distortion of any whole reflects the Being of its parts. Applying the UOSI across these scales ensures alignment is not lost as systems expand in scope and complexity.

At the **individual level**, the UOSI helps you sustain coherence between who you are, what you do and why you do it. A professional working through burnout might use the Architectonic Sphere to clarify purpose, the Integrity Sphere to rebuild trust and self-sovereignty, the Disintegration Sphere to notice patterns of overextension and the Modulation Sphere to restore rhythm through patience and adaptability. Rather than chasing balance as a fixed formula, you learn to live systemically – continually re-balancing in response to changing circumstances and allowing your energy, relationships and commitments to remain coherent and alive through adaptation.

In **organisational execution**, the UOSI becomes the backbone of strategy and culture. It prevents the common trap of having values written on walls, but not lived in corridors.

- The **Architectonic Sphere** aligns mission and design – ensuring the organisation's structure reflects its true purpose and ethical coherence.
- The **Integrity Sphere** shapes the relational field – trust, sovereignty, intention and Being across leadership and teams.
- The **Disintegration Sphere** reveals structural blind spots — toxic norms, misaligned incentives or unexamined habits that corrode the system from within.
- The **Modulation Sphere** sustains adaptability – enabling change without collapse and continuity without stagnation.

A business that integrates the UOSI into execution does not simply deliver quarterly outputs. It creates an organisation that can renew itself – one that weathers crises without losing its core and grows without collapsing its foundations.

At a **societal level**, the UOSI becomes a framework for policy, governance and cultural renewal. It helps societies avoid reactionary policymaking – the kind that patches crises while planting seeds for the next.

- The **Architectonic Sphere** clarifies what a society is truly sustaining – prosperity, wellbeing or short-term growth.
- The **Integrity Sphere** safeguards trust between citizens and institutions – the invisible currency of democracy.
- The **Disintegration Sphere** exposes collective shadows – polarisation, apathy or institutional decay – so they can be addressed rather than denied.
- The **Modulation Sphere** enables societies to evolve through transition – managing economic, environmental and cultural change without implosion.

Applied this way, the UOSI restores continuity across generations, enabling a civilisation that can renew itself rather than perpetually rebuild after every crisis. Consider climate transitions. A society that pushes aggressive carbon targets without attending to the Being of its people may fuel resentment and backlash. In contrast, a society that addresses climate, economy and cultural values in coherent alignment is far more likely to sustain change over decades.

UOSI-driven execution – Practical steps

1. **Anchor in the Blueprint** – Start with your Authentic Sustainability Blueprint. Map its intentions via the UOSI's four spheres to ensure coherence from the start.
2. **Define pathways** – Translate those intentions into tangible action steps, ensuring each is anchored in Being and integrity and designed with modulation in mind.
3. **Live assessment** – Use the UOSI as a live diagnostic tool during execution. Continuously assess where actions or behaviours are drifting from integrity and recalibrate in real time using the Modulation Sphere's four causal forces of patience, tolerance, adaptability and surrender.
4. **Integrate feedback loops** – Build reflection and renewal into the system so recalibration becomes ongoing, not crisis-driven. For example, a family might hold monthly dialogues while a company might embed reflective practices into quarterly reviews.
5. **Align personal and systemic Being** – Ensure that your ways of being sustain systemic action. An organisation cannot embody care if its leaders treat themselves with neglect. A society cannot embody integrity if its citizens are rewarded for opportunism.

The genius of the UOSI is that it transforms execution from a project into a *regenerative cycle*. It allows systems to adapt, refine and sustain themselves over time. Instead of forcing systems into rigid structures that eventually break, it builds in the capacity for self-renewal.

This is what distinguishes authentic sustainability from performative implementation (sustainabilism). The latter produces reports and narratives, but collapses under pressure, while the former evolves with the living system it seeks to sustain.

Ask yourself:

- Am I using the UOSI as a live compass during execution, or only as a planning tool?
- How aligned are my current actions with the four spheres of systemic integrity?
- Am I building modulation and renewal into my execution, or am I rigid in my execution?
- How am I integrating personal Being into systemic execution?

Conclusion

The Unified Ontology of Systemic Integrity (UOSI) transforms execution from a series of tasks into a living system of coherence. It ensures that movement remains anchored in integrity, adaptability and meaning – that every decision, structure and adjustment stays aligned with the deeper purpose your Authentic Sustainability Blueprint was designed to serve.

Yet coherence in action is not enough. To sustain it, we must also *see* it – not through compliance checklists or vanity metrics, but through instruments that reveal the real state of systemic integrity as it evolves. Without feedback, even the most coherent systems drift and without insight, even the most ethical intentions stagnate.

Part VII explored ways to gauge sustainability and systemic integrity. But it also revealed the inherent limits and biases of doing so without a structured measurement tool. This is where the **Sustainability Profile** comes in. More than a mechanism of measurement, it serves as a mirror, reflecting whether the architecture you have built is holding or fracturing under pressure.

In the next chapter, we explore how to measure what truly matters. You'll discover how the Sustainability Profile moves measurement beyond performance and into practice – turning data into dialogue, reflection into responsibility and awareness into transformation.

CHAPTER 55

Measuring What Matters – The Sustainability Profile

We live in an age obsessed with measurement. We measure GDP, literacy rates, emissions, staff engagement, customer satisfaction and even happiness. The assumption is simple: if you can measure it, you can manage it. Yet despite this abundance of data, reports and dashboards, our ecosystems continue to collapse, our institutions fracture, and trust in leadership and the system we engage with erodes.

The issue is not that we measure, but *how* we measure and, more importantly, *why*. Too often, measurement has become performative – a theatre of reassurance rather than a practice of renewal. Dashboards are built to appease stakeholders rather than provoke reflection. Reports are produced to prove compliance rather than reveal the truth. Metrics promise objectivity, but without integrity of purpose, they conceal as much as they illuminate.

The Sustainability Profile was developed to shift measurement from optics to ontology and from data collection to discernment. It does not seek to prove success or failure through a scorecard, but to reveal the quality of relationship a person, team or larger system has with the 16 qualities of systemic integrity that make authentic sustainability possible. It was never designed as a management instrument;

it is a mirror. And like all mirrors, its purpose is not to flatter, but to reflect reality – how things really are.

This chapter explores how the Sustainability Profile emerged as part of the Authentic Sustainability Framework (ASF), how it functions as a structured way of measuring coherence and integrity, and how it can be used to sustain the coherence of any system at any scale, from personal to societal. You will also be introduced to its unique and crucial advancement in delivering measurement reliability: the Vulnerability Index, which reflects how authentically a person engages with the assessment itself. To understand the purpose of the Sustainability Profile, we must first revisit what makes reliable measurement so difficult in the first place.

A shared mirror that aligns what we think we see with reality

Although gauging authentic sustainability without a formal assessment tool is possible using the distinctions of the 16 qualities of systemic integrity as diagnostic lenses, that process brings various limitations we can't ignore:

- Bias – We interpret systems through our own filters.
- Blind spots – Shadows often hide beneath stories of virtue.
- Inconsistency – Two people can see the same context differently.
- Inefficiency – Working through all 16 qualities rigorously is time consuming.
- Drift – Without a structured baseline, we lose track of progress or regression.

The Sustainability Profile was created to address these challenges. It takes the same foundation – the Unified Ontology of Systemic Integrity (UOSI) and its 16 qualities – and translates it into a structured, repeatable and shareable form. The tool doesn't replace discernment or leadership; it strengthens them. It offers a shared mirror that brings people into collective clarity, enabling insight that conversation alone can't always reach.

In essence, the Profile does for sustainability what calibration does for instruments: it ensures that what we *think we see* aligns with *what is actually happening.* It transforms integrity from an intuition into something visible, sharable, discussable and, most importantly, actionable.

Why traditional assessment tools fall short

For much of human history, we've gauged the health of people, teams and societies through observation, intuition and dialogue. While these modes of discernment are natural and valuable, they are also inherently limited. Human judgement, even when guided by insight, remains prone to bias, projection and subjective distortion. Our sense-making is influenced by emotional investment, relational tension and unconscious preferences that colour what we see and how we interpret it.

In practice, assessing the health of our relationship with ourselves and others – and by extension, the systems we design, lead or give life to – is often inconsistent, confronting and unreliable. It depends heavily on perspective, bias and willingness to be transparent. In organisations, this plays out daily. Leaders interpret feedback through the lens of their own identity. Teams shape surveys around what they think executives want to hear. Whole systems learn to perform coherence rather than live it. Without a shared language or structure for seeing clearly, evaluation depends as much on perception and politics as it does on truth. The result is often an incomplete or distorted understanding of systemic health.

Traditional assessment tools, even the sophisticated ones, rarely resolve this. Most are built on psychological or behavioural models that measure outputs and appearances rather than underlying coherence. They tell us how people act, what they prefer, or what they think of themselves. But what they don't tell us is how authentically their inner architecture sustains integrity within themselves and the systems they inhabit.

Even data-driven instruments can be distorted by self-presentation. When people try to 'look good', appear consistent or align with expectations, results reflect performance rather than authenticity. The tool ends up capturing how a person wishes to be seen, not how they are *being*.

The consequence is familiar: reports filled with descriptive statistics but little insight; graphs that show satisfaction without revealing sincerity; and dashboards that measure activity without illuminating alignment. In short, most metrics capture what can be seen rather than what sustains coherence.

Recognising these limitations, the challenge was to design a tool capable of bringing structure, reliability and depth to the practice of gauging authentic sustainability – a way to move from intuitive observation to ontometric precision.

The Sustainability Profile was developed to meet this challenge. It's a tool designed to reveal the deeper patterns of systemic integrity that shape how individuals, collectives and the larger systems they engage with actually function.

From observation to ontometric precision

Observation and intuition have always been the starting points of wisdom. They help us notice patterns, feel the texture of systems and sense whether something is coherent or not. Yet even the most perceptive observer is limited by perspective. What we call 'insight' is often shaped by emotion, habit and partial information. Without structure or shared language, what one person sees as healthy, another might perceive as problematic.

The Sustainability Profile is a purpose-built ontometric assessment tool that bridges the gap between intuition and precision. The word 'ontometric' simply means measuring the state of being – assessing not what someone or something does, but *how they are being*. By measuring the coherence of a system's internal architecture, the Profile allows us to perceive what intuition can sense but cannot consistently measure or describe.

With its ontometric precision, the Sustainability Profile extends the practice of reflection and gauging authentic sustainability into the realm of rigour. It transforms subjective impression into structured discernment, allowing leaders, teams and communities to see the invisible architecture shaping their outcomes.

How the Sustainability Profile works

Having established why traditional measurement falls short – and how the Profile introduces ontometric rigour – we can now explore how it functions in practice. The Sustainability Profile measures how coherently an individual or collective (such as a team, organisation or community) relates to the UOSI's 16 qualities, along with one additional construct: the Vulnerability Index. Together, these 17 measures form a comprehensive picture of systemic coherence, adaptability and sustainability.

Unlike conventional diagnostics that focus on performance or preference, the Sustainability Profile reveals relationship quality – how integrity and coherence are expressed through intention, trust, adaptability, sovereignty and other fundamental qualities within the UOSI. It does not ask what people do, but *how they are being as they do it* – the ontological foundation beneath every action, choice and interaction.

How the tool is structured

The Profile is a structured questionnaire consisting of a comprehensive set of short, plain-language statements. Each statement invites reflection on how the respondent experiences or expresses one of the 16 systemic qualities – or their relationship with vulnerability – in real situations. For example, a statement might seek to reveal how easily one maintains trust during disagreement, or how confidently one upholds sovereignty in collaborative settings.

Responses are rated on a sliding scale from *strongly disagree* to *strongly agree*. The simplicity of each statement conceals its depth, with every statement designed to elicit reflection on the lived alignment between inner architecture and outward behaviour.

Behind the scenes, an algorithm aggregates these responses into a set of scores, each ranging from 1–10. The results are then mapped across the four spheres of the UOSI, revealing the system's overall pattern of coherence:

Sphere	Qualities Measured
Integrity	Intention, Trust, Sovereignty, Being
Modulation	Patience, Tolerance, Adaptability, Surrender
Disintegration	Shadows, Misery, Suffering, Entrenchment
Architectonic	Meta-awareness, Systemic Integrity, Normativity, Sustained Effectiveness

Table 31 – The qualities measured for each UOSI.

Each sphere contributes a unique lens on systemic health. Together, they reveal how coherence is maintained or lost as individuals and collectives evolve through change, stress and renewal.

Reading the results

The output of the Sustainability Profile is presented as a visual report that highlights:

- **Strengths** – areas of high alignment and systemic coherence
- **Fractures** – weak or distorted relationships between qualities
- **Inconsistencies** – gaps between intention and practice
- **Trends** – how relationships with each quality evolve over time

These insights are not designed for judgement or comparison, but for clarity and renewal. The purpose is not to generate a score to improve upon, but a mirror to engage with. A strong score is not necessarily 'better'; it simply reflects stability in that relationship. A lower score signals an opportunity for inquiry and growth, and should be received positively.

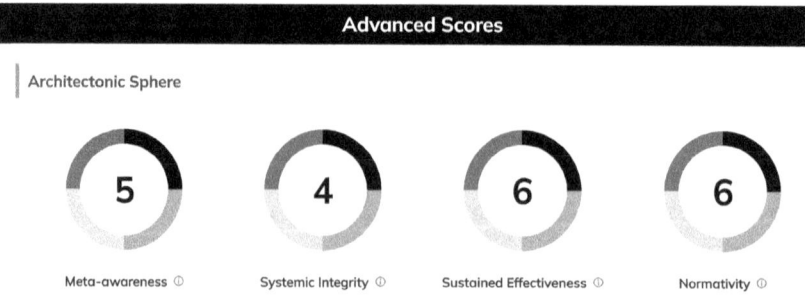

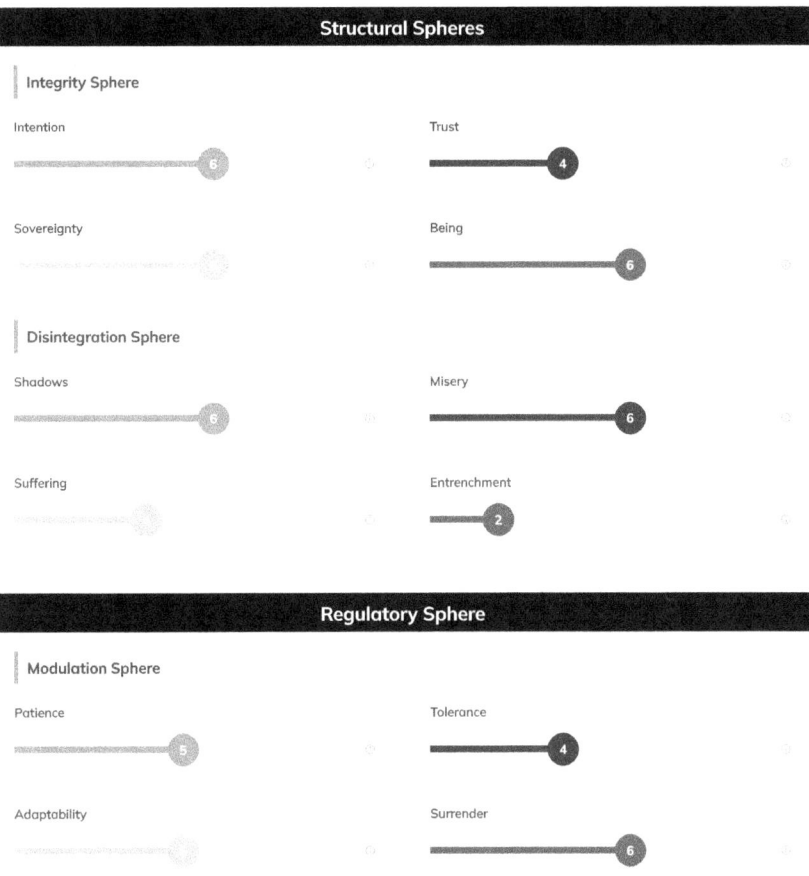

Figure 18 – Example output from the Sustainability Profile: patterns of coherence and disintegration.

Interpretation: From insight to action

Insight alone is not transformation. What matters next is how the data is interpreted and translated into meaningful action.

The Sustainability Profile includes two interpretive layers:

1. **Generic distinctions** – A clear explanation of each quality and how it manifests in healthy and unhealthy forms (the ontological distinctions articulated in Parts 3–6 of this book). These act as philosophical anchors for understanding the data.

2. **Score-specific insights** – Tailored interpretations based on individual or collective results, offering context-specific reflections and developmental pathways.

While the Profile can be completed independently, it reaches its full depth through a debrief conversation with a trained practitioner accredited in the Authentic Sustainability Framework. In these sessions, data becomes dialogue. Practitioners help participants explore their results, identify patterns and translate awareness into tangible action or cultural reform.

Revealing patterns of coherence and disintegration, the output is not a judgement, but a revelation. For example:

- A **team** may discover strong scores on **trust** and **intention** but weak scores on **sovereignty**, suggesting that while purpose and connection are clear, individuals may hesitate to exercise authorship or take initiative.
- A **community** may score high on **patience** but low on **adaptability**, showing that while there is steadiness through change, community members struggle to recalibrate when new realities demand it.
- An **organisation** may score well on **systemic integrity** but poorly on **normativity**, revealing operational coherence but a lack of clarity around what is ethically worthy or valuable over time.

The point is not to boast about strengths or panic about weaknesses. It's to ask: *What do these results reveal about the work we must do to restore alignment, coherence and systemic integrity over time?*

What makes the Sustainability Profile unique?

Where most diagnostic tools assess surface-level outcomes – behaviour, satisfaction or performance – the Sustainability Profile measures the *ontological foundation* that sustains them. It moves beyond perception into pattern recognition: seeing not just what happens, but why it happens that way.

In doing so, it provides a shared language and structure for discussing and working towards systemic integrity – not as a moral virtue or management concept, but as a measurable property of systemic coherence.

Figure 19 – Each question invites reflection on how coherence is expressed in action and relationship.

Also unique to the Sustainability Profile is an index that measures each respondent's authentic engagement with the tool, as explained below.

The Vulnerability Index – Measuring authentic engagement

No assessment tool, no matter how well designed, is immune to distortion. Even with a coherent framework, the way people *engage* with an assessment profoundly affects its reliability. Some respond openly and truthfully while others – often unconsciously – manage impressions, soften discomfort or protect their self-image. Without accounting for this, even the most sophisticated measurements can be misleading.

The Vulnerability Index was developed to address this problem. It measures not only *what* people report, but *how* authentically they engage with the process of reporting itself. In other words, it reveals the degree of openness, courage and congruence a person brings to their self-reflection. When completed by a collective, such as a team or a Board of Directors, the Vulnerability Index is averaged across all respondents in that group.

Vulnerability, in this context, is not emotional exposure for its own sake. It is the structural capacity to remain transparent and grounded when facing the possibility of being seen – to let truth be visible even when it feels uncomfortable. An individual or a collective with a healthy relationship with vulnerability can confront incoherence without denial or collapse. They can acknowledge limitations without losing integrity.

Vulnerability Index – An ontological measure of reliability in assessment

The **Vulnerability Index** refers to the degree to which an individual or collective engages with openness, congruence and authenticity when responding to the Sustainability Profile. It does not measure vulnerability as a personality trait, but as a *systemic posture* – the structural integrity of one's relationship with truth when being seen. Whether that visibility brings approval, judgement or discomfort, the Vulnerability Index reveals how truthfully a person, team or organisation allows reality to surface without resorting to performance, concealment or self-justification.

A **high Vulnerability Index** reflects a healthy and authentic engagement with the assessment process. It indicates that the individual or group remained open to seeing themselves as they are – acknowledging incoherence without collapse, receiving insight without defensiveness and allowing difficult truths to emerge. Such openness reflects both humility and courage, balancing exposure with composure. At the collective level, this translates into a culture where transparency strengthens trust, feedback fuels learning and coherence becomes self-correcting.

A **low Vulnerability Index** signals guardedness or image management – a reluctance to confront contradiction or risk exposure. Responses may appear polished or reflective, but lack genuine self-revelation. Teams or organisations in this state often display performative agreement, cautious dialogue or avoidance of tension for fear of conflict or disapproval. Leaders may unintentionally reward conformity over candour, reinforcing a climate of superficial harmony. Over time, this erodes psychological safety and prevents meaningful renewal.

In this way, the Vulnerability Index functions as a reliability gauge within the Sustainability Profile – clarifying how sincerely and coherently the data represents lived reality. High vulnerability enhances validity while low vulnerability signals distortion. Therefore, it ensures that the measurement of systemic coherence is grounded not only in one's response, but in the authenticity with which it is revealed.

How the Vulnerability Index works

For each of the 16 systemic qualities, the Profile includes three additional questions designed to assess openness. These questions explore how willingly you – or your team – reveal your real relationship with that quality, and whether you respond from a place of honesty or self-protection. Each question is rated on a five-point scale and aggregated into a Vulnerability Index Score for that specific quality.

When the Sustainability Profile is completed by a group – such as a leadership team, department or board – the collective Vulnerability Index reveals the group's overall openness in engaging with truth, not just the tendencies of any one member. In essence, it measures the *collective posture* towards authenticity: whether the culture encourages candour and curiosity or leans towards guardedness and self-preservation.

The 16 vulnerability scores (one per UOSI quality) are then averaged and converted into an overall Vulnerability Index Score. This score functions as a *meta-metric* – a structural measure of authenticity. A high Vulnerability Index Score indicates that you or your group engaged with the Profile sincerely, making the overall data trustworthy and stable. A lower score does not imply dishonesty. It simply signals caution or guardedness, reminding both the participant and the interpreter that some results may reflect performance rather than presence and authenticity.

When viewed alongside the main Profile scores, the Vulnerability Index introduces a vital layer of reflexivity. It allows you – or your team – to see not only what your relationship with integrity looks like, but also how truthfully that relationship was revealed. By making the act of measurement itself transparent, the Index ensures that your Sustainability Profile reflects both *what* was said and *how authentically* it was expressed.

In this way, the Vulnerability Index transforms the Profile from a simple self-assessment into a mirror of systemic coherence – one that reveals the integrity of both individuals and collectives. The depth of insight it offers is directly proportional to the depth of honesty brought to the process.

Figure 20 – The overall Vulnerability Index Score.

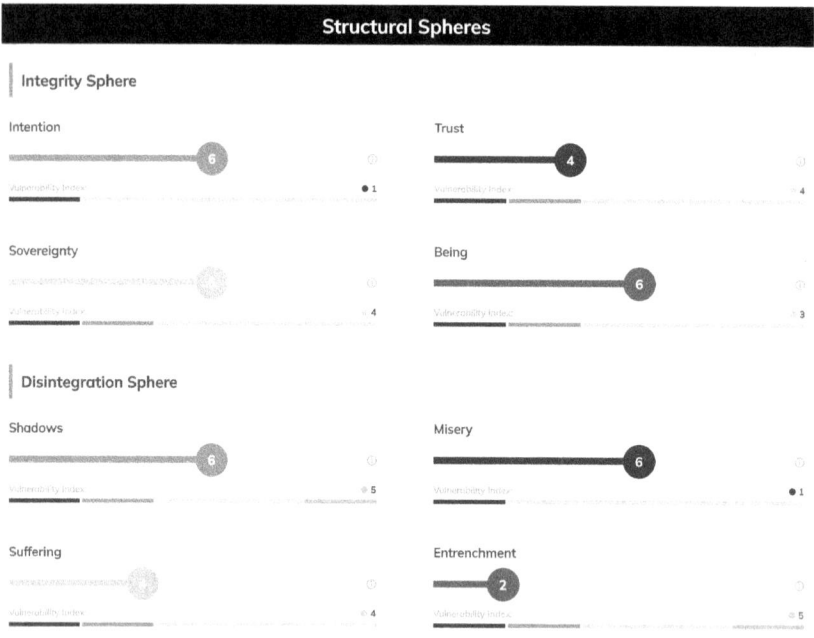

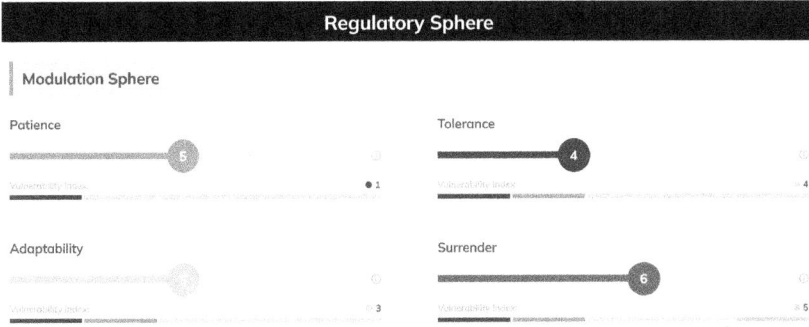

Figure 21 – A Vulnerability Index Score is shown for each quality measured.

Why factoring in the Vulnerability Index matters

Although traditional psychometric tools recognise bias in theory, they rarely account for the full spectrum of defensiveness, fear of exposure or image management that shapes real-world responses, particularly in organisational and leadership contexts. Research across multiple disciplines has shown that self-report instruments, while convenient and scalable, are inherently vulnerable to social desirability bias and impression management, where individuals consciously or unconsciously tailor their responses to appear competent, trustworthy or socially acceptable. Even when researchers attempt to model or statistically adjust for such distortions, traditional Likert-scale formats remain susceptible to the subtle effects of self-presentation, fatigue and contextual pressure.[99]

This distortion becomes even more pronounced in leadership and organisational settings. Research involving executives and senior leaders has found that responses are often filtered through the lens of organisational culture and social desirability rather than emerging from unguarded self-awareness. Leaders consciously shape their answers to preserve credibility and alignment with institutional expectations. This highlights a broader limitation: while most

---

99 Based on findings from van de Mortel, T. F. (2008) 'Faking it: Social desirability response bias in self-report research', *Australian Journal of Advanced Nursing*, 25 (4), pp. 40–48; and Kreitchmann, R. S., Abad, F. J., Ponsoda, V., Nieto, M. D. and Morillo, D. (2019) 'Controlling for response biases in self-report scales: Forced-choice vs. Likert formats', *Frontiers in Psychology*, 10, p. 2309.

psychometric systems acknowledge bias as a theoretical concern, few adequately measure or correct for the deeper ontological variables – such as fear, defensiveness and the desire for control – that underpin distorted self-representation.[100]

The Sustainability Profile's Vulnerability Index directly addresses this gap. Rather than assuming uniform sincerity or self-awareness, it measures the relational integrity between the respondent and the assessment itself – how openly and authentically a person engages with the process. In doing so, it transforms vulnerability from a confounding variable into a diagnostic lens, revealing how truthfully an individual or collective relates to themselves and to the act of being seen.

In ontometric science, reliability arises not from statistics alone, but from coherence between what is measured and how it is measured. The Vulnerability Index embodies this reflexive quality, allowing interpreters to discern the difference between genuine and performed coherence – between integrity as a lived reality and as an image. This reflexive layer enhances both interpretive precision and ontometric reliability. It ensures that results reflect authentic engagement rather than performance, and that what is measured can be genuinely trusted. With this dimension in place, the assessment becomes self-aware – capable of revealing not only patterns of coherence, but also the quality of truth within them.

Relationship with the Being Framework

The Vulnerability Index shares its philosophical roots with the Being Framework[101], which defines vulnerability as one of the 31 Aspects of Being. In the Being Profile, vulnerability describes how a person *is being* when faced with exposure or risk – their lived posture in the moment. It is existential and experiential.

In the Sustainability Profile, the Vulnerability Index operates at a systemic level. It measures how authentically that same quality of

---

100 Based on findings from Densten, I. (2011) 'The impact of organisational culture and social desirability on Australian CEO leadership', Doctoral dissertation, University of New South Wales.
101 Tashvir, A. 2021 *Being – The Source of Power*. Engenesis Publications: Sydney.

vulnerability is maintained across all 16 dimensions of systemic integrity.

Aspect	Vulnerability (Being Framework)	Vulnerability Index (Sustainability Profile)
Nature	A quality of Being	A systemic measure of relational openness
Focus	How you are when feeling exposed	How you reveal your relationship with the 16 qualities when feeling exposed
Function	Develops authenticity, humility and presence	Diagnoses coherence, defensiveness and impression-management
Expression	Existential and experiential	Structural
Outcome	Trust, integrity and authenticity	Clarity, alignment and systemic reliability

Table 32 – The difference between vulnerability in the Being Framework and the Sustainability Profile's Vulnerability Index.

The Being Profile measures vulnerability as one of the 31 Aspects of Being within the Being Framework. In the Unified Ontology of Systemic Integrity (UOSI), the quality of Being within the Integrity Sphere encompasses all 31 Aspects of Being, including vulnerability.

In contrast, the Vulnerability Index within the Sustainability Profile does not assess vulnerability as an inherent quality of Being. Instead, it functions as a meta-indicator – a measure of reliability and authenticity in how a person or collective engages with the assessment process and the Sustainability Profile itself, providing insight into the sincerity and self-awareness they brought to that process. So, in the Sustainability Profile, the Vulnerability Index is used solely as an indicator of reliability and authenticity in the participant's responses. It reveals the degree to which one's relationship with the 16 systemic qualities of the UOSI is expressed sincerely when completing the tool.

Viewed together, the Being Profile and the Sustainability Profile (including its Vulnerability Index) operate in harmony. They bridge micro and macro coherence between how an individual sustains integrity within themselves and how that coherence extends outward into the systems they design, inhabit and influence.

From measurement to movement

The Sustainability Profile was never intended to end with a report. Its real power begins after the data is revealed – when numbers, insights and reflections are brought into conversation. Measurement, in this sense, is only the doorway. What follows is dialogue, discernment and deliberate movement toward coherence.

When viewed this way, the Profile becomes far more than an assessment. It becomes a practice of seeing – a structured ritual of truth-telling that invites us to confront how we are actually functioning. Whether used by an individual, a leadership team or an entire organisation or community, the data becomes a mirror that speaks back: *this is how you/we are being.*

But mirrors alone don't change behaviour. What transforms a system is what happens next – how that reflection is received, discussed and enacted. When the data moves from being a static result to a dynamic conversation, it turns insight into energy for renewal. This is what we call *the movement* – the translation of awareness into adaptive action.

When used authentically, the Profile triggers a living cycle of transformation:

- **Revelation** – Seeing what is usually denied or distorted — the absence of trust, the weakness of adaptability or the erosion of sovereignty.
- **Dialogue** – Bringing those revelations into conversation, where stakeholders interpret them together, make sense of them and own the implications.
- **Commitment** – Turning awareness into lived responsibility — decisions, promises and intentions that align with integrity.
- **Transformation** – Redesigning structures, practices and cultures so that commitments are embodied in reality.
- **Modulation** – Sustaining those shifts over time — recalibrating as contexts change and preventing drift into old patterns.

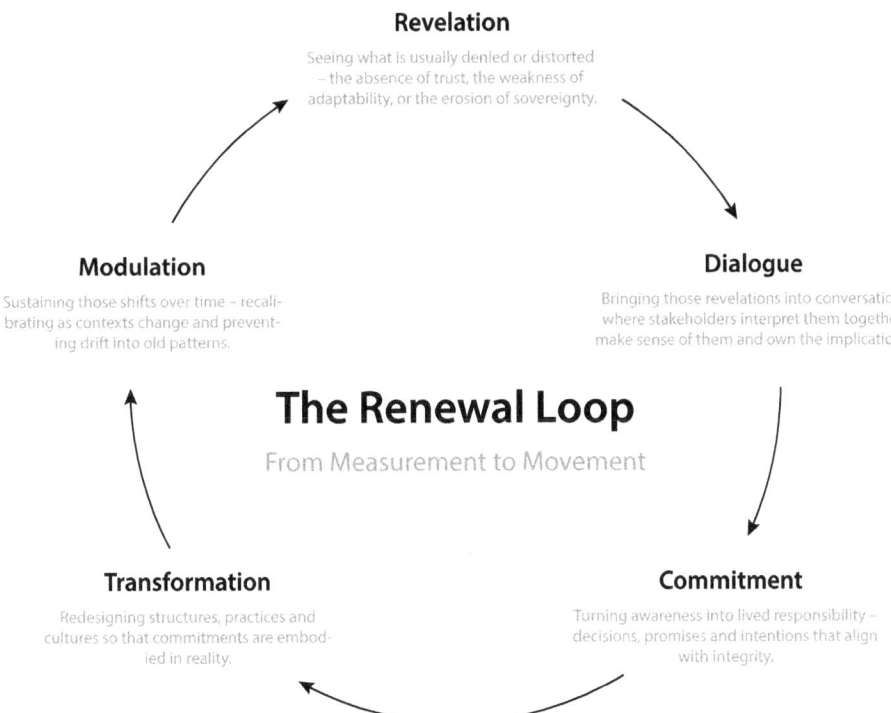

Figure 22 – The Renewal Loop: from measurement to movement.

When this process is embedded in practice, measurement becomes a rhythm of renewal. The Profile shifts from being a report to an *engine of transformation* – a discipline that keeps coherence visible, dialogue continuous and integrity alive in motion. In real-world settings, this rhythm unfolds through a sequence of reflection, dialogue, design and recalibration. The next chapter explores how to execute this transformation process methodically – the frameworks, disciplines and decision structures that translate awareness into tangible, regenerative action.

Application across domains

The Sustainability Profile is versatile, making it valuable across a wide range of contexts. Whether applied to individuals, teams, organisations or societies, its purpose is the same: to reveal how integrity, adaptability and coherence are actually being lived.

The assertion here is that how we, as individuals, relate to these qualities – how we think, feel and act within a team, organisation, community, society or governing body – will ultimately manifest in the very systems we design, implement or participate in. In this sense, every collective outcome is a reflection of the relational quality of its participants.

Consider the following examples:

- **Individuals and families** – A couple might use the Profile to explore how trust, Being and adaptability show up in their relationship. It offers a shared mirror that moves conversation beyond blame into systemic patterns, turning personal conflict into insight about how coherence is sustained or lost.
- **Organisations and teams** – A business might use the Profile to assess whether its culture sustains normativity, meta-awareness and authenticity, or whether it has slipped into performative busyness. A corporation could apply it to surface where sustainability efforts are rooted in optics rather than integrity.
- **Communities and collectives** – A local council might use the Profile to examine whether community forums genuinely empower residents (sovereignty), foster mutual trust and allow decisions to evolve coherently – or whether participation has drifted into surface-level consultation with little real influence.
- **Governments and institutions** – A national government could apply the Profile to evaluate whether its policies uphold integrity, respect sovereignty and demonstrate adaptability in response to social and environmental change. Rather than measuring success solely by efficiency or growth, the Profile reveals whether governance structures sustain trust, responsiveness and ethical alignment over time.
- **Global systems** – International bodies could use the Profile as a shared ontological map for collaboration – assessing whether global initiatives embody systemic integrity and normativity rather than being driven by national self-interest or short-term advantage. In doing so, the Profile provides a

framework for aligning diverse cultures and nations around coherence, ethics and mutual stewardship.

In each case, the Profile does not dictate the answers. It provides the lens through which better questions can be asked, leading to proactive, targeted and regenerative action.

Case studies – The Profile in practice

The following examples demonstrate how the Sustainability Profile functions in real-world contexts:

1. Personal and relational context – Rebuilding trust within close relationships

Elena noticed growing strain in her closest relationships. Conflicts with her partner escalated quickly and she often withdrew to avoid further hurt. Completing the Sustainability Profile revealed low scores in **trust, tolerance** and **surrender**, and a moderate Vulnerability Index, indicating guardedness in self-revelation.

Through her debrief with an accredited Authentic Sustainability Framework practitioner, Elena recognised that her defensiveness masked a deeper fear of rejection. Supported by her practitioner, Elena began practising small shifts: naming when she felt unsafe; allowing discomfort instead of suppressing it; and rebuilding trust through steady transparency. Over time, her relationships deepened and became more reciprocal. The Profile acted as both a mirror and a roadmap, transforming personal tension into an opportunity for coherence and authentic connection.

2. Leadership – Strengthening organisational coherence

Marcus is the founder and CEO of a fast-growing technology company. While he is proud of the business's commercial success, he has been sensing growing internal misalignment. Each member of his leadership team completed the Sustainability Profile and their scores were averaged as a collective. The results revealed strong **sustained effectiveness** and **adaptability** but weaker **systemic integrity** and **normativity**, signalling that the company was delivering results at the expense of ethical and relational alignment.

The group's combined Vulnerability Index was low, showing reluctance to speak openly. With support from a trained practitioner, Marcus facilitated conversations about the gap between declared values and lived practice. The process sparked cultural renewal: transparent communication; recalibrated incentives; and a rediscovered sense of shared purpose. Within months, staff turnover dropped and morale improved. The Sustainability Profile became the catalyst for restoring trust and coherence at scale.

3. Societal and NGO context – Aligning compassion with structure

Asha, a program director in a humanitarian NGO, faced tension between her team's moral drive and the organisation's structural capacity. The Sustainability Profile, completed across leadership and field teams, revealed high scores for **intention** and **suffering** but low **systemic integrity** and **patience** scores, with a wide variation in Vulnerability Index Scores across departments. The data exposed a classic pattern in purpose-driven organisations – overextension without structural coherence.

Asha used the findings to redesign rhythms of reflection and boundary-setting. The NGO implemented clearer communication loops, realistic pacing and shared decision-making processes. As burnout decreased, impact stabilised. Through the Profile, the organisation saw that authentic sustainability requires as much care for the system as for the mission itself.

Preventing drift and sustaining coherence

Even the most coherent systems drift over time. Success breeds familiarity, structures harden into habits and the pressures of survival often eclipse the deeper work of renewal. Without regular reflection, integrity erodes quietly – not through collapse, but through the slow normalisation of subtle misalignments.

The Sustainability Profile was designed to make this drift visible before it collapses into dysfunction. When revisited periodically, it provides a rhythm of recalibration – a way to check whether commitments made in the name of integrity are still being lived in practice. By revisiting the Profile at intervals, you can see whether commitments are holding, whether shadows are creeping back in, or whether new fractures are forming. In this way, it creates a rhythm of reflection and recalibration, preventing collapse into complacency and ensuring that sustainability remains a living, adaptive practice.

Used in this way, the Profile becomes less an instrument of measurement and more a discipline of maintenance. It allows individuals, teams and organisations to see how coherence evolves, how trust withstands pressure, and how adaptability holds during times of change and challenge. By observing how the system's relationship with each of the 16 qualities shifts over time, leaders can anticipate where renewal is needed and prevent entrenchment before it takes hold.

Drift does not mean failure. It simply indicates where the system has outgrown its current form or where fatigue has dulled attention. When seen through this lens, every new Profile reading becomes a map for refinement. For example:

- A leadership team might discover that **sovereignty** and **trust** have weakened since the last assessment, signalling that decision-making has become overly centralised.
- A community group may notice higher **patience** but lower **adaptability** scores in this round, revealing that stability has become stagnation.
- A government department might see a drop in **meta-awareness** and **normativity**, indicating that processes have replaced purpose.

In each case, the invitation is the same: to realign before repair becomes reinvention.

When the Profile is used cyclically, it embeds a living rhythm of reflection into the culture. The act of measuring becomes part of how the system learns, breathes and evolves. Coherence is sustained not through control, but through attentiveness – the willingness to pause, listen and recalibrate. Chapter 57 reveals how to master modulation – the art of sustaining integrity through movement – so that drift becomes not a threat, but a teacher, guiding renewal through every cycle of change.

Conclusion

The Sustainability Profile is far more than a measurement tool. It is part of a broader philosophical and practical architecture that translates the distinctions of the UOSI into a structured, tangible practice. It moves sustainability out of theory and into the lived rhythm of leadership, governance and daily life.

Without such a mirror, sustainability risks dissolving into rhetoric and aspiration. But with it, coherence becomes visible, measurable and actionable through a process that honours complexity while grounding action in reality. The Profile provides the rhythm of reflection and recalibration that prevents drift and transforms measurement from theatre into transformation.

The Profile is not about comparison or judgement. It is not about proving who performs better or worse. It's about who and how you and others are *becoming*. It offers leaders, teams, organisations, institutions, communities and nations a shared awareness and language for aligning decisions and actions with integrity – and a rhythm for maintaining coherence over time.

Measurement becomes meaningful only when it provokes reflection rather than reassurance – when data becomes dialogue and dialogue becomes movement. That is the deeper purpose of the Sustainability Profile: to reveal what is real; to renew what has drifted; and to restore alignment through continual engagement with truth. Its companion, the Vulnerability Index, strengthens this process by ensuring ontometric reliability – confirming that what is being measured is not performance, but authentic engagement. Together, they enable measurement to evolve into discernment and discernment into regenerative movement.

Consider where measurement is still treated as theatre rather than transformation in your personal life, organisation or any other system you are engaging with. What might a mirror of your relationship with the 16 UOSI qualities reveal? And how could genuine dialogue around those insights reshape your commitments and keep coherence alive over time?

Used authentically, the Sustainability Profile ensures that sustainability remains a living practice rather than a performed ideal. It is here, in the ongoing application of the Profile, that authentic sustainability begins to walk on its own legs. This sets the stage for the next chapter, where we turn from measurement to execution, exploring the methodology and mechanics that bring transformation fully to life in practice.

CHAPTER 56

Executing Transformation – The Methodology in Practice

Sustainability without transformation is an illusion. You simply cannot sustain what has not first been transformed. A system that is misaligned at its roots cannot be 'maintained' into coherence. It must evolve or it will decay. This is why the Transformation Methodology[102] sits at the very heart of execution. It is the living engine that turns lofty intentions into embodied change, translates blueprints into lived reality, and enables regeneration rather than stagnation.

Authentic sustainability is not about maintaining systemic integrity. It's about *sustaining* it. Maintenance preserves dysfunction as much as it preserves integrity. True sustainability is about enabling systems – whether personal, organisational or societal – to regenerate, realign and continuously transform in coherence with Being and systemic integrity.

Think of a garden. You cannot simply freeze a flower once it has bloomed to preserve its beauty. If you try to 'maintain' it through control or fixation, it will wither. True sustainability is not about preservation or checklist maintenance; it's about attunement. A

---

[102] Tashvir, A. 2021 *Being – The Source of Power* (Part 3, Ch 2). Engenesis Publications: Sydney.

garden thrives only when we respond authentically to what it needs – warmth, water, light and renewal – not as we wish it to be, but as it is. The gardener's role is not to dominate nature, but to surrender to its laws, to the way things are. Likewise, systems endure not through force or artificial balance, but through coherence with the underlying order of existence – the first principles and bedrock upon which all meaning and authenticity rest.

In this body of work, sustenance and maintenance are closely connected, yet their essences diverge. Understanding this distinction is crucial for executing transformation well. Maintenance, when stripped of authentic awareness, becomes an act of force – the attempt to preserve what we desire, even when it no longer belongs to the rhythm of life. It is the grasping of form without attending to essence, the illusion of control disguised as care. We maintain what we fear to lose, often at the cost of what must evolve.

Sustenance transcends maintenance. It is maintenance transformed by consciousness – the act of preserving not through coercion, but through coherence. To sustain is to be in dialogue with what's real, not in battle with it. It means recognising that what endures does so not because we hold it tightly, but because we serve its becoming.

Therefore, the distinction is subtle but vital. Maintenance fixes; sustenance listens. Maintenance seeks permanence; sustenance honours impermanence. In the framework of authentic sustainability, we are invited to move beyond the maintenance of appearances towards the sustenance of truth – to nurture systems, relationships and structures in fidelity with the way things are, not merely the way we wish them to be.

This is why the Transformation Methodology is indispensable. It ensures that transformation is not random, reactive or left to chance, but is guided by structure and intention. It enables us to intervene consciously in our lives, organisations and societies, turning disruption into renewal rather than collapse.

The six-step Transformation Methodology presented here is not a standalone invention, but a contextualised application of the deeper Being Framework Transformation Methodology, woven together with the Unified Ontology of Systemic Integrity (UOSI) to serve the broader aim of authentic sustainability. It brings together the inner and outer dimensions of change, translating deep ontological principles into a clear, practical pathway for execution.

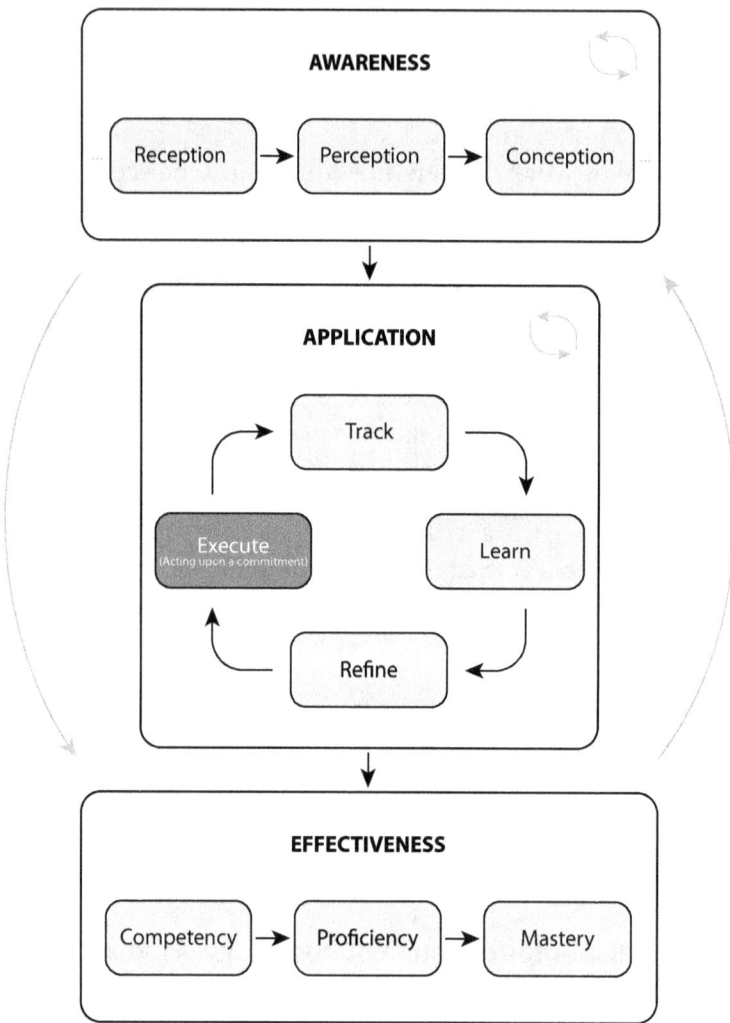

Figure 23 – The Being Framework Transformation Methodology™.

The Transformation Methodology – A six-step process

As mentioned, the process outlined here draws its strength from the Being Framework and the UOSI. Together, they ensure that transformation remains coherent – personal in its origin, systemic in its reach and regenerative in its rhythm. The six steps that follow are not linear boxes to tick, but living movements that feed into one another, forming an ongoing practice of alignment, renewal and evolution.

1. Generate awareness through assessment

Transformation begins with awareness because you cannot shift what you cannot see with clarity. Use tools like the UOSI, the Being Profile[103] and meta-awareness practices to assess the current state, identifying:

- What is working?
- Where are the fractures?

For example, in an organisation, assessment may reveal that 'burnout' may not stem from workload, but from a culture that equates worth with productivity. Seeing this reframes the challenge from efficiency to Being. Here, the UOSI offers the structural mirror through which coherence and fracture can be seen clearly.

2. Map the deeper structures (ontological mapping)

Once awareness is established, the next step is mapping the deeper structures. How do the UOSI's four spheres – Architectonic, Integrity, Disintegration and Modulation – reveal the field of coherence and distortion? What ways of being are sustaining the current state? What intentions – conscious or unconscious – are driving behaviour? Which systemic patterns keep repeating themselves?

At a personal level, you might notice that a fear of failure underpins your career choices. At an organisational level, a manager might realise that their decisions always revert to control rather than collaboration, revealing an ontology of mistrust beneath procedural issues.

3. Identify shadows

Every system carries shadows – distortions of Being, such as fear disguised as responsibility or ego disguised as confidence. Within the Disintegration Sphere, shadows mark the early stages of systemic

---

103 Tashvir, A. 2021 *Being – The Source of Power* (Part 3, Ch 1). Engenesis Publications: Sydney.

decay. The key is to identify them early to prevent fragmentation before it embeds. In this step, you bring them into the light. Shadows are not failures to be hidden; they signal where transformation is needed most.

For example, a government promoting 'stability' might actually be entrenching fear-based control. Recognition of that shadow opens the possibility for renewal.

4. Redesign Being and systems

This is the creative heart of the methodology. Here, you realign your ways of Being with the intentions of your Authentic Sustainability Blueprint and redesign the structures that hold them. Guided by the UOSI's Architectonic and Integrity Spheres, you bring ethical coherence, systemic integrity and sustained effectiveness into alignment and redesign the structures that hold them – the cultural norms, workflows, feedback loops and decision mechanisms that translate inner alignment into external expression.

At a personal level, this could mean committing to authenticity over performance. At an organisational level, it might mean reconfiguring governance so that responsibility and sovereignty are shared. At a societal level, it might mean rethinking policy around regenerative flourishing rather than GDP.

5. Commit and embody

Designs on paper are only potential. Transformation doesn't take root until intentions are embodied as lived commitments. Here, modulation begins to play a central role – patience to stay the course, tolerance to hold discomfort, adaptability to respond to feedback and surrender to release control when truth demands it. Commitment means shifting from 'What we say we value' to 'How we are being in real time matters.'

At a personal level, this might look like setting aside a few minutes each evening to reflect on how your actions aligned (or didn't) with integrity throughout the day – writing what you noticed, what felt incoherent and one thing you'll recalibrate tomorrow. A Being

Framework Transformation Methodology Conception Worksheet is a simple yet effective tool to use here.[104]

Conception Worksheet

How does this relate to me? What's in it for me? Why should I care or bother?

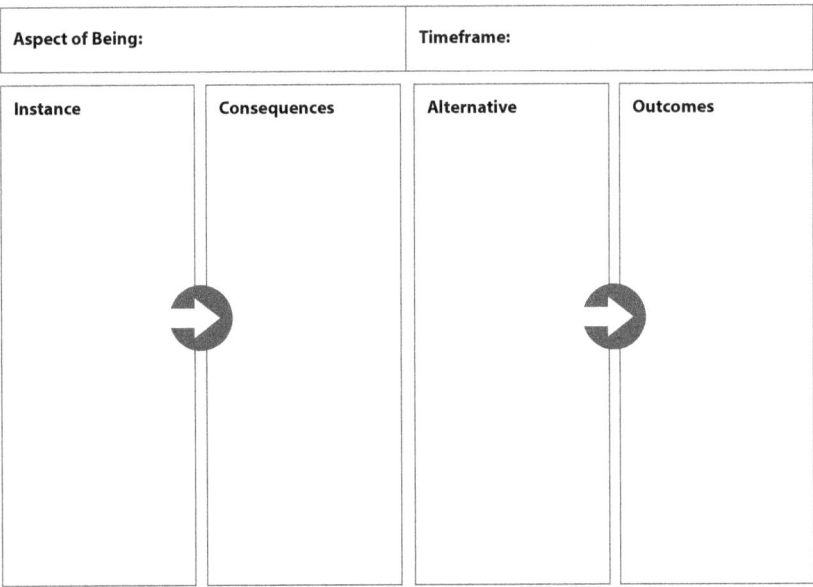

Figure 24 – The Being Framework Transformation Methodology Conception Worksheet.

Designed to gradually progress you to a higher degree of awareness and effectiveness, the Worksheet supports you to not only clarify your thinking around the area you wish to transform, but also shape a deeper conception of it, making adjustments as you go.

At an organisational level, this step could be embedding care into performance metrics so that culture and wellbeing are not 'soft extras' but core deliverables. At a societal level, it might mean ensuring that policies are not only passed, but enacted in civic life through education, enforcement and shared responsibility.

---

104 Tashvir, A. 2022 *Human Being – Illuminating the Reality Beneath the Facade* (pp. 45–53). Engenesis Publications: Sydney.

6. Refine iteratively

No transformation is ever finished. Systems live in perpetual motion, which means feedback must be built in so that transformation never hardens into rigidity. Modulation again becomes the sustaining rhythm – patience, tolerance, adaptability and surrender ensure that transformation never hardens into rigidity.

Refinement is not repetition; it is evolution – learning, adjusting and re-embodying again and again. Just as a musician tunes their instrument before every performance, leaders, organisations and societies must continually recalibrate and refine to stay in harmony with coherence.

At an individual level, this might involve a monthly reflection on your Being Profile or using your Conception Worksheet to focus on an increasingly narrow timeframe with a goal of eventually being able to respond to the first signs of breakdowns in coherence in real time. At an organisational level, it could be a quarterly recalibration of culture, strategy and practice. At a societal level, it might be ongoing civic engagement that evolves policy through dialogue rather than sporadic elections.

Applying the Methodology in practice

With the Transformation Methodology's six movements as your guide, the next step is to bring them to life in real systems – personal, organisational and societal – where transformation takes shape through lived practice. Each domain reveals how the methodology unites inner and outer work, shifting ways of being while redesigning the structures that express them.

Personal systems

Transformation at the personal level begins with honesty. It requires seeing how your inner architecture – beliefs, fears, habits and ontological postures – shapes the reality you live in.

Imagine the following financial scenario. Despite earning well, you experience constant anxiety about where the next dollar is coming from and how to keep putting food on the table.

- Start by **generating awareness through assessment**. Is this truly about money or about your relationship with security and control?
- **Ontological mapping** might reveal a story inherited from childhood scarcity.
- The **shadow** could be fear disguised as prudence.
- **Redesign** may involve aligning financial choices with care and generosity rather than hoarding.
- **Commitment** could take the form of shared transparency around spending and saving.
- **Iterative refinement** might mean revisiting your budget monthly, observing when old fears return and consciously recalibrating.

In this way, transformation shifts from fixing problems to reconfiguring Being. Your relationship with money becomes an expression of coherence rather than a reaction to fear.

Organisational systems

At the organisational level, transformation becomes the art of aligning culture, leadership and structure with integrity.

Imagine a company experiencing high staff turnover. Despite competitive salaries and strong performance, people are leaving faster than they can be replaced.

- Start by **generating awareness through assessment**. What's really driving the exodus? The data might point to burnout, but deeper reflection reveals a culture that equates worth with output.
- **Ontological mapping** exposes an underlying pattern of extraction – people treated as resources rather than participants.
- The **shadow** could be performance masquerading as purpose.
- **Redesign** may involve redistributing workloads, embedding care as a strategic priority and reshaping decision-making processes to share responsibility and sovereignty.

- **Commitment** might mean leaders being committed to modelling the change – leaving on time, taking breaks and acknowledging wellbeing as a metric of success.
- **Iterative refinement** could include regular feedback loops, ongoing cultural audits and recalibrating strategy as conditions evolve.

Transformation at this level shifts the organisation from performance to purpose and from extraction to regeneration. Workplaces become environments where integrity and care are not aspirational values, but operational realities.

Societal systems

At the societal level, transformation must extend beyond policy reform to systemic renewal. This requires collective honesty about the paradigms shaping civic life and the courage to realign them.

Take climate policy. Despite ambitious targets and abundant reporting, emissions keep rising.

- Start by **generating awareness through assessment**. What's really at play beneath the metrics?
- **Ontological mapping** reveals that the underlying ontology remains *growth at all costs*, where the economy is treated as separate from ecology.
- The **shadow** might be sustainability language masking extractive practice – greenwashing dressed as progress.
- **Redesign** may involve reorienting policy frameworks around regenerative wellbeing rather than GDP, integrating social, environmental and economic coherence.
- **Commitment** shows up through education, transparent governance and active civic participation, ensuring that policies live in practice rather than on paper.
- **Iterative refinement** requires continuous dialogue – updating strategies, recalibrating incentives and responding to emerging realities rather than waiting for electoral cycles.

When transformation operates this way, societies move from crisis management to regenerative continuity and stewardship, capable of adapting without losing coherence or trust.

Across all domains – personal, organisational and societal – the Transformation Methodology provides a rhythm for renewal. It keeps coherence visible and alive, ensuring that transformation is not a one-off project, but an ongoing expression of integrity in motion.

Conclusion

Transformation is not a one-time project or event. It is a living process – a continual cycle of learning, adjustment and renewal. Systems that treat transformation as an ongoing rhythm rather than a milestone are the ones that stay coherent over time.

This is why the final step of the Transformation Methodology – iterative refinement – is not the end of the process, but the beginning of its continuity. Just as a forest renews itself through changing seasons, sustainable systems remain alive by returning regularly to reflection and recalibration. Transformation becomes part of their identity – something they do naturally, not occasionally.

To keep transformation alive, return to these guiding questions:

- Am I treating transformation as a project, or as a living process?
- How aligned is my current way of being with the six steps of this methodology?
- Where are shadows still shaping my decisions or actions?
- How am I embedding feedback and refinement into my personal, organisational or societal systems?

When reflection becomes habit, transformation becomes continuous. Through this process, awareness leads to action, action leads to learning, and learning leads to renewal – the essence of authentic sustainability.

In the next chapter, we turn to the Modulation Sphere – the art of sustaining transformation through change and uncertainty. You'll learn how to master the modulation process by navigating tension, absorbing disruption and preventing drift in action, so transformation remains steady and coherent through every transition. After all, authentic sustainability is not simply maintained, but sustained through continuous transformation and modulation.

CHAPTER 57

Modulation and Mastering Transitions

When people talk about sustainability, they often imagine stability – keeping systems balanced, preserving resources and maintaining harmony. But authentic sustainability is not about preservation. It is about *modulation* – the art of sustaining coherence, especially through times of uncertainty and upheaval.

To recap, modulation is the intentional movement between coherence, disruption and renewal – the rhythm through which systems remain integrous while evolving. It's about remaining *alive* when challenges arise, pressure mounts and conditions evolve – because that's life. Every system – personal, organisational or societal – is in a constant state of flux. Systems that merely remain static eventually decay. But systems that modulate stay coherent and relevant. The question is not whether transitions will happen, but whether they will happen intentionally or by default. Without modulation, change becomes a reaction, rather than proactive regeneration.

Authentic sustainability depends on the art of modulation. While planning, measurement and transformation give a system its architecture, modulation gives it breath. It is what allows leaders, teams and communities to absorb shocks, realign purpose and move forward without losing their centre.

In practice, modulation transforms execution from a rigid plan into a living process – one capable of adjusting pace, direction and focus while remaining true to their purpose and deeper meaning (*Mina*). Modulation is the capacity to guide these transitions consciously, sustaining integrity through change rather than clinging to false stability. This is why the Modulation Sphere is so critical to authentic sustainability.

Modulation is not about controlling outcomes. It's about maintaining integrity through movement. This requires:

- **Awareness** – seeing transitions as they begin, not just when they are complete.
- **Discernment** – knowing when to stabilise and when to disrupt.
- **Being alignment** – sustaining authenticity and integrity through uncertainty.
- **Systemic coherence** – ensuring the parts shift without losing the whole.

Without modulation, systems either become rigid and entrench or collapse into disintegration. But with modulation, they remain adaptive, regenerative and coherent through change.

The four regulators of modulation

You will recall that the Modulation Sphere is governed by the four regulating forces of patience, tolerance, adaptability and surrender. Each acts as a distinct 'muscle' of integrity, governing how a system moves through transition. Just as a muscle needs conscious, deliberate exercise to remain healthy, the same is true with the modulating forces – your relationship with each one can be healthy or unhealthy (distorted).

- **Patience**, when healthy, regulates *endurance* and the pace of change. It allows time for reality to surface and wisdom to mature before decisive movement. *Distortion:* Too little patience becomes impulsive reactivity; too much becomes stagnation and avoidance.

- **Tolerance**, when healthy, regulates the *variance* a system can hold. It permits difference, tension and pressure without collapse. *Distortion:* Too little tolerance breeds impatience and blame; too much dissolves boundaries into permissiveness.
- **Adaptability**, when healthy, regulates *recalibration* and purposeful change. It enables evolution of form while preserving essence. *Distortion:* Too little adaptability creates rigidity; too much leads to formless drift where purpose erodes.
- **Surrender**, when healthy, regulates *wise yielding* and letting go. It is not defeat, but the release that restores movement when control becomes constriction. *Distortion:* Too little surrender traps energy in a constant state of struggle; too much becomes resignation.

Together, these four regulators form the inner mechanics of sustainability in motion. They determine whether a person, relationship, team, organisation, institution or society can bend without breaking – whether it can learn, recalibrate and renew without forfeiting coherence.

Used consciously, they keep systems alive across time and complexity. But when used unconsciously or in a distorted manner, they entrench dysfunction: impatience exhausts; intolerance fractures; rigidity hardens; and false surrender abandons what still needs care. Therefore, mastering modulation begins not with control, but with *awareness* of which regulator the moment requires.

Reading transitions in real time

Transitions rarely announce themselves. They begin as subtle shifts in tone, energy or direction long before anyone names them. Modulation begins by learning to *read* those signals and respond with the lightest effective touch.

Earlier, we described this movement as a lemniscate ∞ loop. On one side sits **integrity** (coherence under pressure), on the other **disintegration** (loss of coherence). The path between them runs through the Modulation Sphere. The more skillfully you engage patience, tolerance, adaptability and surrender, the more often the loop returns to coherence as **reintegration** rather than spiralling into collapse.

The four regulators – patience, tolerance, adaptability and surrender – are the steering instruments that guide a system through this loop. Each transition tests which one must take the lead.

The modulation micro-check

When you sense tension building, be it during a meeting, a conversation at home or a policy debate, pause for a micro-check. This quick four-step scan brings an unconscious transition into your conscious awareness and turns modulation from theory into immediate practice.

1. **Name the transition:** What is happening here? What is this tension arising from and suggesting? Is it a challenge, is it flagging a necessary change or is it suggestive of an overload?
2. **Select the regulator** – Lead with the quality that the moment most calls for – patience, tolerance, adaptability or surrender.
3. **Intervene minimally** – Use the least intervention required to restore coherence – a pause, a question, a boundary or a reframing.
4. **Re-sense** – Observe whether the field relaxes or tightens. If tension persists, shift to a different regulator and repeat the process.

This quick scan can be done privately in seconds or collectively by a team. With practice, it becomes an instinctive rhythm: awareness → discernment → minimal action → sensing. The aim is not to perfect the system, but to keep it alive and learning.

Signs of healthy modulation

Leaders and teams that modulate well tend to display certain signature traits:

- Decisions emerge at a *natural* pace rather than from panic or paralysis.
- Difference is expressed without personalisation or breakdown.

- Adaptations are framed as learning, not as failure.
- Letting go is done with clarity, grace and a sense of rational closure, not resentment.

These are not personality traits, but systemic behaviours arising from modulation in action.

Common pitfalls

Even experienced leaders can slip into distortion when the pressure rises:

- **Over-control:** Trying to stabilise everything at once – the loop jams and energy stagnates.
- **Over-speed:** Moving so fast that insight cannot metabolise – learning is lost.
- **Over-tolerance:** Refusing to name dysfunction – coherence quietly erodes.
- **Over-correction:** Introducing unnecessary or excessive change – stability fractures and the system remains in perpetual flux.
- **Over-surrender:** Confusing acceptance with apathy – momentum dies.

Each distortion signals which regulator has been over- or under-used. The good news is that awareness enables recalibration before dysfunction hardens into entrenchment.

Practical application – Mapping modulation as a lemniscate flow

Try using the lemniscate as a visual tool during your next planning or review meeting. Sketch the ∞ symbol on a page. Label the left curve *Integrity* and the right *Disintegration*. In the centre, write *Modulation*.

As a team, reflect on a recent project. Mark points along the loop where conscious transitions (modulations) occurred – when patience stabilised the system, when adaptability renewed it, when tolerance permitted pressure and tension without collapse, and when surrender cleared the way for a better approach. Do the same for instances of dysfunction, for example, when too little patience triggered a knee-jerk reaction.

This simple exercise using the lemniscate flow visual keeps the language of modulation alive and shared. You can apply it in any scenario – personal, professional or societal.

Applied modulation across various domains

The principles of modulation hold true across every scale of human systems – from the individual navigating life choices, to the organisation steering collective purpose, to the society negotiating change at scale. The pattern remains the same: disruption is inevitable; coherence is optional. The difference lies in how consciously transitions are modulated. Consider the following scenarios.

Personal modulation – Sustaining coherence through change

Healthy modulation doesn't always produce the outcome you first imagined. It produces the outcome that *sustains integrity*. By consciously working with the four regulators, you avoid reactive disruption and turn an unconscious transition into a conscious, regenerative process — one that strengthens coherence rather than straining it.

Scenario – Leadership fatigue and renewal

After years of sustained pressure, a CEO begins noticing the early signs of burnout – irritability, decision fatigue and waning creativity. The temptation is to push harder or withdraw completely. Modulation offers another path – to adjust the rhythm without losing their centre.

- **Patience** – Pause before introducing new initiatives and allow space for recovery and clarity to emerge.
- **Tolerance** – Hold the discomfort of slowing down while the team maintains momentum. Accept variance without guilt.
- **Adaptability** – Redistribute responsibilities, delegate key tasks and experiment with new rhythms of rest and work.
- **Surrender** – Release the illusion of being indispensable. Trust others to carry the vision forward for a while.

Healthy modulation allows for regeneration without collapse. In this case, it allows the leader to breathe, recover and realign, emerging stronger and more coherent than before.

Organisational modulation – Leading systems through pressure

Scenario – Product quality crisis in a scaling company

A defect in a newly released product has been detected by multiple customers. Social media is heating up. Two paths cross your mind as leader: denial and overreaction. Your role in this situation is not simply to 'fix the issue' but to restore trust and coherence through the turbulence.

- **Patience** – Give yourself time to stabilise and gather all verified facts before responding publicly.
- **Tolerance** – Hold the cross-functional heat without scapegoating so information continues to flow.
- **Adaptability** – Form two teams: a rapid containment squad and a redesign group. Adjust your communication tone daily as data unfolds.
- **Surrender** – Retire a much loved but flawed component, apologise with grace and redirect resources towards regeneration.

In practice, modulation looks like deliberate pacing, transparent information flow, structural recalibration and graceful release. The crisis becomes a living workshop in coherence under pressure, demonstrating that sustainability is not what happens during times of stability, but what survives with integrity when tested.

Practice – The modulation cadence for meetings

Embed modulation awareness into your organisational rhythm:

1. **State of mind check** – A quick scan of energy, focus and readiness.
2. **Name the transition type** – Is this a challenge, a divergence or a sign that change is needed?

3. **Choose a lead regulator** – For example, 'Today, I will lead with tolerance to hear all perspectives on the problem at hand before making any decisions.'
4. **Close with a restorative modulation** – A single, neutral act that resets coherence before moving forward – a pause, a slow, deep exhalation or moment of gratitude for next-step clarity.

Over time, these micro-practices normalise modulation as a collective behaviour. It becomes part of how the organisation operates, learns and recalibrates in real time.

Culture signal

Encourage team leaders to narrate modulation choices aloud. For example:

'We waited 48 hours before responding, demonstrating patience. We listened to three alternative proposals, demonstrating tolerance. We adjusted the rollout plan, demonstrating adaptability. We ended a partnership that no longer aligned with our values, demonstrating surrender.'

Such narration teaches the team to see modulation as a conscious discipline.

Societal modulation – Sustaining reform without entrenchment

Scenario – Policy reform under polarisation

A government intends to reform the energy market. Push too hard and opposition doubles. Move too slowly, and the grid falters. Modulation transforms reform from a reactive pendulum into a regenerative process.

- **Patience** – Stage reforms over time, sequencing implementation while pre-committing to review milestones.
- **Tolerance** – Create participatory forums that genuinely hold opposing views rather than performative consultations with people whose opinions align with the government's.
- **Adaptability** – Tailor policies regionally while maintaining national coherence.

- **Surrender** – Retire a symbolic but counterproductive legacy scheme to redirect resources towards what actually works.

By engaging modulation at this scale, governments model coherence rather than polarisation. The same pattern that steadies a leader's team also steadies a society. Each regulator becomes a civic virtue: patience as deliberation; tolerance as pluralism; adaptability as innovation; and surrender as humility.

Community practice – Civic modulation circles

Imagine quarterly gatherings where citizens, local businesses, NGOs and public officials reflect together on their community's transitions. Each participant identifies one act of patience, one of tolerance, one of adaptability and one of surrender that has advanced collective wellbeing. These commitments are published – not as propaganda, but as living indicators of civic coherence. Over time, such practices build shared language, mutual responsibility and trust – the infrastructure that generates authentic sustainability.

Modulation scales infinitely

Whether you are leading yourself, your organisation or your nation, the same principles apply:

- Stay conscious of transition.
- Choose the appropriate regulatory force (patience, tolerance, adaptability and surrender).
- Reconfigure, applying minimal intervention.
- Observe and learn.

The field may change, but the rhythm remains the same – awareness, discernment, action, observation and learning. This is the living anatomy of sustainability in motion.

Practising and training modulation

Modulation is not mastered by theory alone. It must be felt, practised and refined until it becomes a systemic reflex – a way of being that keeps coherence alive, even in turbulent times. The task of practice is therefore twofold: to make the unconscious conscious; and to cultivate the capacity to hold pressure without losing coherence.

Making the unconscious conscious

Most transitions first appear as small signals rather than crises. Those who sense these early tremors prevent disruption from becoming disintegration. Modulation training begins by sharpening perception across three channels.

- **Somatic** – Notice what the body reveals before the mind interprets. Observe breath, heartbeat, temperature and muscle tension. Ask: *Where is reactivity showing up in my body and what is it asking of me?*
- **Relational** – Pay attention to the micro-shifts in tone, pacing and openness during interactions. Is the relational field between people tightening or expanding?
- **Systemic** – Read the wider feedback loops: decision cycle times, re-work rates, staff turnover, customer sentiment and civic trust. What do these indicators say about coherence or drift?

When leaders learn to read across these channels, modulation becomes anticipatory rather than reactive.

Awareness alone is not enough. Once we can see transitions, we must build the stamina to stay present within them. This second task involves strengthening our capacity for steadiness under tension – to be with or hold conflict, uncertainty and delay without collapsing into reaction. The following guardrails and training methods develop that endurance in practice.

Guardrails – Avoiding distortions

Every modulation force (regulator) can over- or under-express itself. The purpose of guardrails is not to constrain movement, but to prevent distortion from eroding integrity.

Regulator	Distortion Pattern	Antidote / Re-alignment
Patience	*Impatient activism* – constant urgency that burns people and systems	Slow the first 5% of the decision to save the last 95% of re-work.
Tolerance	*Boundless tolerance* – confusing openness with permissiveness	Name non-negotiables early. Tolerance has edges.
Adaptability	*Shapeless adaptability* – pivoting until purpose dissolves	Re-anchor in the ontological centre – who and how you are – before flexing form.
Surrender	*Defeatist surrender* – calling avoidance 'acceptance'	Distinguish functional surrender to truth from collapse into resignation.

Table 33 – How guardrails prevent distortion from eroding integrity.

Guardrails give modulation structure without rigidity. They remind practitioners that integrity lies between fixation and drift.

Training modulation as a capability

Like any discipline, modulation strengthens through repetition and reflection. The following practices help translate awareness into habit.

1. The 30-day modulation journal

Each day, capture one moment in which you used each regulator. Two brief lines per entry – context and effect. By day 30, patterns will appear: which regulator you overuse; which you neglect; and how your field responds.

2. The 4x4 pre-mortem

Before any major change, ask the following short questions, each beginning with:

If this fails because we lacked...

- Patience, what did we miss?
- Tolerance, what did we miss?
- Adaptability, what did we miss?
- Surrender, what did we miss?

Then, ask the inverse:

If this fails because we over-extended…

- Patience, what did we delay or avoid naming?
- Tolerance, what dysfunction did we permit?
- Adaptability, what stability did we compromise?
- Surrender, what responsibility did we abandon?

Convert the answers into safeguards before launching the initiative. This simple calibration exercise ensures modulation remains balanced – preventing both deficiency and excess from distorting coherence.

3. Restorative modulation interventions

When tension rises, deliver a minimal, neutral, restorative act that recentres the field.

Examples:

- A deliberate silence that resets pacing (**patience**)
- A boundary that protects sense-making (**tolerance**)
- A reframing that unlocks motion (**adaptability**)
- A clean stop that releases sunk cost (**surrender**)

4. The Sustainability Profile loop

Revisit your Sustainability Profile periodically. Use it to correlate quantitative indicators (performance, wellbeing, turnover and trust) with qualitative reflections from your journal. For example, where patience scores fall, look for increasing error rates and conflict. Where surrender scores are low, expect burnout or rigidity. This feedback loop grounds modulation in evidence rather than perception.

Advanced practice – Applying modulation in the field

Earlier in Part VIII, you were introduced to the rhythm of modulation in execution. Here, that rhythm evolves into lived practice – a method for translating awareness into coherence under real-world pressure.

Choose one live transition in your professional sphere – something already in motion. It might be a leadership restructure, a new product launch, a funding shortfall, a partnership renegotiation or a team morale issue. Keep it real. Modulation can only be learned in the field. Then work through the following sequence, ideally with your team or a trusted peer.

Step 1. Identify the transition

- What is shifting?
- Where is the system under pressure?
- What signals of disintegration or renewal are visible?

Step 2. Select the lead regulator

- Which of the four qualities – patience, tolerance, adaptability or surrender – is most needed right now?
- Record your choice and reasoning.

Step 3. Design a minimal intervention

Choose one act small enough to test, yet visible enough to shift energy. It could be delaying a decision, setting a boundary, having an honest conversation or deliberately letting go of something.

Step 4. Review and recalibrate

- After 24–48 hours, notice what changed. Did coherence increase? Did tension ease? What was learned?
- Over 30 days, track your experiences. Which regulator do you overuse? Which do you avoid?

These observations reveal your modulation signature – the pattern by which you sustain or lose coherence under pressure. Modulation mastery begins here, by recognising the pattern, not judging it. Each cycle offers both data and development – evidence of what shifted and practice in holding integrity while things move.

Case studies

The following brief case studies demonstrate when modulation made the difference.

Health system surge response

During a sudden hospital surge, administrators postponed non-critical procedures (**patience**), maintained open communication and emotional steadiness amid rising tension (**tolerance**), cross-trained staff across departments (**adaptability**) and retired outdated paperwork protocols (**surrender**). Quality of care and service held under pressure and the system's integrity survived the chaos.

Civic transition done well

A city shifting its transport mix staged changes over multiple seasons (**patience**), tolerated temporary inconvenience through open dialogue (**tolerance**), adapted designs block-by-block (**adaptability**) and surrendered a politically popular but harmful subsidy (**surrender**). Public trust rose with each transparent iteration.

Corporate culture reset

After a trust breach, a company paused expansion (**patience**), widened listening channels to include dissenters (**tolerance**), adapted incentives to reward integrity, not optics (**adaptability**), and released a star executive who refused to align (**surrender**). Output dipped briefly, then surpassed prior highs with lower friction.

These patterns show that modulation is structural, not stylistic. The same regulators that govern an individual's composure sustain hospitals, corporations and cities.

Embedding modulation into daily life

Make modulation a normal part of everyday life:

- **In one-to-ones:** Ask, 'Do we need patience, tolerance, adaptability or surrender right now?'

- **In design reviews:** Specify not only *what* will be delivered, but *how* the team will modulate when uncertainty appears.
- **In budgeting:** Keep a 'modulation reserve fund' – time and budget set aside for pilot testing and the graceful surrender of whatever no longer serves.
- **In culture:** Celebrate visible modulation choices as much as outcomes.

When practised collectively, modulation becomes the atmosphere of sustainability – a field where systems breathe, learn and renew together without collapsing or calcifying under pressure.

Conclusion

Modulation completes the architecture of authentic sustainability. It turns design into movement and insight into lived rhythm. Without it, even the most elegant Blueprint hardens into structure. But with modulation, the structure breathes.

In practice, modulation is not an event but a posture. It begins the moment awareness meets tension and continues until coherence is renewed. Every pause, boundary, adjustment or release is a small act of regeneration – the work of holding integrity through change.

When embodied across scales, modulation becomes culture. A leader pauses before reacting, a team listens through discomfort, a city reforms without fracturing, and a society learns to deliberate without polarising. Each act of modulation ripples outward, teaching systems to evolve without losing themselves.

Ask yourself:

- How do you currently navigate transitions in your life or work – by default or by design?
- Which regulator do you tend to overuse and which do you avoid?
- Where do you sense entrenchment in your system and which regulator would loosen it?

- How will you embed modulation practices into your life over the next quarter?

Authentic sustainability is not a fixed state. It is a living modulation – the capacity to stay coherent amid continual movement, to regenerate rather than merely preserve, and to turn every transition into an opportunity for renewal. In mastering modulation, you learn not only how to sustain systems, but how to live sustainably within them.

CHAPTER 58

Expanding Sustainability – The Ripple Effect

Authentic sustainability cannot remain confined to personal life or organisational practice. If the work stops there, it becomes self-referential, sustaining a small island of coherence in a sea of systemic dysfunction. For sustainability to live, it must expand outward into the greater systems – communities, governance, economies, cultures and the human story itself.

The ripple effect of Being

Every action you take is not isolated. Being ripples outward. A single authentic commitment influences the immediate environment, which in turn influences larger systems. When scaled intentionally, this ripple becomes the foundation of renewal. This is why authentic sustainability starts with you. However, it doesn't end with you. Systems are not abstractions; they are living networks of relationships and actions. When your Being aligns with integrity and regeneration, it naturally shapes those networks.

To keep those ripples authentic, always consider the following whenever you scale:

1. **Ontological alignment** – Is this action emerging from who and how you are being, not from an image of who you wish to appear to be?
2. **Systemic integrity** – Does this decision strengthen or erode coherence? Check every decision against each of the UOSI's four spheres.
3. **Regenerative intention** – Will my actions result in outcomes that keep creating conditions for sustainability?

Authenticity, not performance

The wider the audience, the greater the temptation to perform. Performative activism, virtue signalling and glossy reports detached from meaning erode trust. The antidote is authenticity – the alignment between inner posture and outer action.

Before launching a campaign, passing a policy or scaling a program, pause to ask:

- What quality of Being animates this action — authenticity, responsibility, care or courage?
- Which UOSI Sphere is being strengthened — Architectonic, Integrity, Disintegration or Modulation?
- How will this action measurably improve lives?

If these questions cannot be answered with conviction, the initiative may serve performance more than purpose.

Governance and policy – Designing for coherence, not control

Policy is a lever that shapes collective reality. Without systemic integrity, it becomes a tool of entrenchment. Acting upon governance with authentic sustainability means:

- **Embedding trust and sovereignty** into policy frameworks – mechanisms that decentralise relevant authority, improve transparency and enable informed consent.
- **Using the UOSI** to test bills and programs. Will it increase or erode the four spheres over time?

- **Holding the Being of the leader to account** – not only for their outcomes, but for the ontological posture through which power is exercised.

Practical applications

For each proposed policy, map the intended outcomes across all four Spheres of the UOSI:

Example: A data-privacy statute designed through authentic sustainability principles might:

- Align the architecture of technology, law and civic education systems to uphold coherence across domains. (**Architectonic Sphere**)
- Guard personal sovereignty by embedding transparent data-use consent and enforceable rights. (**Integrity Sphere**)
- Identify and dismantle shadow interests or exploitative data practices that erode trust. (**Disintegration Sphere**)
- Phase compliance over time to avoid systemic shock and allow adaptation through iterative review. (**Modulation Sphere**)

This integrated mapping process ensures the law's architecture, intention, integrity and adaptability remain coherent as the system evolves.

In terms of modulation, an example without it would be sweeping energy reform rushed to meet electoral optics, producing backlash. A better approach would be a phased reform with pre-announced milestones, regional pilots and sunset clauses for legacy subsidies. Trust increases when transparency and repair mechanisms are embedded from the start.

Economic Systems – From extraction to regenerative value

Economics is a cultural phenomenon that reflects collective Being. Acting upon economic systems for authentic sustainability requires reframing value itself.

- **Redesign value creation** around long-term coherence rather than short-term extraction.
- **Integrate integrity** into enterprise and policy – wealth generation that enhances sovereignty and trust, not dependency and a lack of transparency.
- **Modulate structures** to enable adaptation without collapse.

Practical applications

Regenerative profit and loss

Add two non-financial but decision-critical ledgers to traditional profit and loss. For example:

- *Integrity capital* – trust levels, repair rates and stakeholder consent.
- *Renewal capital* – soil health, skills development, social cohesion and shared knowledge.

Attach executive incentives to both. Each 'ledger' corresponds to a UOSI dimension: **integrity** through ethical operation; **architectonic** through holistic reporting structures; **disintegration** through visibility of erosion; and **modulation** through cyclical recalibration.

Circular contracts

Design contracts that anticipate change and embed regeneration. Include take-back and repair clauses, secondary markets and clear modulation triggers that allow agreements to flex under stress without compromising integrity.

Each clause strengthens a different Sphere of the UOSI:

- **Architectonic Sphere:** Aligns agreements with ethical norms, systemic awareness, coherent design and enduring effectiveness.
- **Integrity Sphere:** Maintains trust, transparency and respect for sovereignty in relationships between parties.
- **Disintegration Sphere:** Exposes and removes exploitative, obsolete or contradictory clauses that corrode coherence.

- **Modulation Sphere:** Provides adaptive review and renewal cycles to maintain relevance as conditions evolve.

Example – Regenerative manufacturing

A mid-sized manufacturer recognised that its supply chain, though efficient, was eroding trust and resilience over time. Leadership committed to redesigning the entire value chain through the lens of authentic sustainability, aligning each stage with the four spheres of the UOSI.

They began with the **Integrity Sphere**, introducing open supplier audits and transparent procurement processes that rebuilt trust between partners and customers. Next came the **Architectonic Sphere**, expressed through cooperative worker ownership – a structural shift that embedded fairness, systemic awareness and shared responsibility into the company's architecture.

To ensure the system could evolve over time, they applied the **Modulation Sphere**, redesigning products with modular components that extended lifecycles and allowed for ongoing adaptation without waste.

Finally, they addressed the **Disintegration Sphere** by instituting continuous improvement reviews that surfaced inefficiencies, contradictions and emerging shadows before they could corrode coherence.

At first, margins dipped as the company invested in new systems and retraining. But within 18 months, trust stabilised, retention increased and profitability returned – stronger, more consistent and far less volatile. The value chain had become not just sustainable, but *regenerative* – a living example of how coherence, once designed and embodied, compounds over time.

Cultural narratives – Shifting the invisible architecture

Culture decides what feels possible, valuable and true. It is the hidden architecture that shapes how societies imagine progress, success and belonging. Acting upon cultural narratives is important and delicate work because stories do not merely describe systems – they *sustain* them. To change a system, you must also shift the stories it tells about itself.

Authentic sustainability in culture begins with awareness. Use **the Nested Theory of Sense-making** to name the dominant stories and surface the shadows embedded within them – what they glorify, what they exclude and what they silence. Employ **Minalogy** to reconstruct meaning without erasing difference. Then, introduce **Being-aligned narratives** – stories that normalise trust, sovereignty and authentic purpose rather than fear, control or competition.

Practical applications

Narrative mapping sessions

Host cross-community circles where participants explore the stories they live by about work, home, dignity, care and the future. Plot where each narrative sustains or erodes the UOSI Spheres:

- **Architectonic:** Which cultural structures and values these stories uphold.
- **Integrity:** Whether they cultivate trust and authenticity.
- **Disintegration:** Where they perpetuate distortion or fear.
- **Modulation:** How they can evolve without rupture.

Such mapping sessions make the unseen visible, turning culture into a conscious field of design.

Cultural prototyping

Commission art, media or micro-rituals that embody emerging meanings. Instead of one grand gesture, use small, consistent signals that modulate public awareness over time. Each prototype operates as a micro-system of coherence:

- **Architectonic:** Reinforces ethical and systemic alignment.
- **Integrity:** Honours truth and representation.
- **Disintegration:** Acknowledges pain and contradiction without collapsing into cynicism.
- **Modulation:** Evolves meaning through iterative feedback.

These prototypes allow culture to learn in motion – to expand what is possible without coercion.

Re-authoring language

Words shape worlds. Retire words and phrases that commodify people – such as referring to citizens as 'consumers' or employees as 'resources' – and replace them with vocabulary that conveys care, dignity and responsibility. This re-authoring restores the moral architecture of language (**architectonic**), rebuilds trust (**integrity**), dissolves reductionism (**disintegration**) and enables ongoing cultural renewal (**modulation**).

Communities as living systems

Communities are where the personal and the systemic converge. They are close enough for people to feel impact, yet large enough to shape societal direction. Authentic sustainability takes root here first – in the places where belonging meets responsibility.

To act upon communities authentically:

- **Align leadership with Being** – Select and develop leaders for integrity, care and responsibility.
- **Use the UOSI as a design map** for neighbourhood forums, councils or dispute resolution models that preserve coherence across diverse needs.
- **Embed regenerative practices** through repair networks, shared infrastructure, local apprenticeships and citizen-science projects that restore both environment and trust.

Practical applications

Local Authentic Sustainability Blueprint

Co-create community plans that name intentions, articulate the qualities of Being to cultivate, and design UOSI-aligned pathways across domains such as energy, mobility, food, safety and learning.

- **Architectonic:** Create structures that link these domains coherently.
- **Integrity:** Centre trust-based decision-making and transparency.

- **Disintegration:** Surface local shadows, such as inequity, exclusion or resource imbalance, before they fracture coherence.
- **Modulation:** Phase implementation through pilot programs and review cycles.

When community design aligns with the four spheres, local change becomes self-sustaining.

Modulation drills

Hold quarterly civic gatherings where residents practise the four regulators – **patience** for listening, **tolerance** for difference, **adaptability** for creative options and **surrender** for closure. Instead of publishing only what was decided, also share what was *learned*. This practice normalises civic reflection and strengthens the integrity and modulation while reducing the risk of disintegration through polarisation.

Case study – A riverside town's renewal

After a series of major floods, a riverside town realised that recovery plans focused solely on engineering defences were no longer enough. The council invited residents, local businesses and environmental experts into a series of modulation-aware forums to design a longer-term, living response.

Through this process, residents agreed on a staged retreat – a phased relocation program for the most flood-exposed homes, supported by grants, land-swap options and community-led relocation planning (**surrender**). During this emotionally charged process, the community practised **tolerance** by holding conflicting needs and timelines – allowing space for differing opinions, economic worries and generational attachments to land while decisions matured. To distribute the strain fairly, they introduced work-sharing arrangements that balanced rebuilding, prevention and relocation projects across the workforce.

At the same time, new adaptive zoning allowed for raised walkways, floating gardens and amphibious micro-businesses such as kayak hire, cafes and boat repair hubs (**adaptability**). Finally, the council embedded a five-year review cycle to reassess risks, update zoning and evaluate progress before the next flood season (**patience**).

Over several years, insurance premiums stabilised, new investment returned and residents reported a stronger sense of trust and agency. The town didn't just survive the floods – it learned to live with the river, becoming more coherent, adaptive and resilient than before.

Collective responsibility and agency

Acting upon greater systems is not about imposing a grand vision from above. It's about awakening collective agency and responsibility, supporting all stakeholders to see themselves as co-creators of sustainability rather than passive recipients of it. Authentic sustainability happens when leadership becomes distributed – when the responsibility for integrity and renewal is shared across the network.

Your personal Authentic Sustainability Blueprint is the thread you bring to the larger tapestry. Each decision, however small, sends ripples outward – the supplier standard you hold firm on, the transparent communication you model, the hiring choice you refuse to compromise, the public apology you make and follow with action. These acts may seem small or routine, but together they weave coherence across a wider system.

Leadership, in this context, means moving from control to *collective stewardship* – cultivating environments where others can act with the same clarity and care. When sustainability becomes everyone's work, not just the 'sustainability officer's', coherence compounds.

The following examples translate this principle into practical, role-specific guidance. They are not formulas, but prompts for self-reflection and design. The key is to adapt each pattern to your situation while staying grounded in Being, systemic integrity and modulation.

The policymaker

Working within governance systems, the policymaker's central task is to keep reform anchored in coherence rather than optics, ensuring that good intent translates into sustainable structure.

- **Map proposals across the UOSI Spheres** – Ensure the policy strengthens structural wisdom and long-term design principles (**Architectonic**), preserves trust and sovereignty (**Integrity**), acknowledges and transforms existing dysfunctions without blame (**Disintegration**), and builds adaptive capacity to learn and evolve over time (**Modulation**).
- **Convene multi-perspective sense-making sessions before drafting** – Include practitioners, citizens and critics to surface blind spots early and ground policy in lived experience.
- **Build modulation into the policy process** – Design every reform with built-in review cycles, pilot phases and sunset clauses to enable adaptation without loss of coherence.
- **Publish the Being commitments of leadership alongside the legislation** – Communicate transparently how those responsible will embody integrity, humility and care during implementation.

Taken together, these steps shift governance from command-and-control to *learning-and-adapting* – transforming policy from a rigid decree into a living system that evolves with the people it serves.

The founder or CEO

For a founder or CEO, authentic sustainability is not a department, initiative or marketing angle. It is the way the organisation exists and evolves. The leader's primary role is to embed coherence into both the culture and the commercial system so that purpose, people and performance move as one.

- **State your ontological centre clearly** – Articulate, in plain language, *who and how we are being together.* This becomes the anchor for every strategic and operational decision. When employees, partners and investors can name and feel that centre, alignment becomes natural rather than enforced.
- **Tie incentives to integrity and renewal capital, not just profit** – Measure success across financial and non-financial dimensions: trust, staff wellbeing, repair rates, knowledge growth and community contribution. Reward those who build long-term coherence rather than short-term output.

- **Train every manager in modulation** – Equip leaders at every level with the ability to sense and respond to transition. Teach the four regulators – patience, tolerance, adaptability and surrender – as a language for decision-making. A modulating organisation can flex under pressure without losing integrity.
- **Gauge authentic sustainability periodically or measure it using the Sustainability Profile** – Track how the organisation is maturing across the four spheres. If using the Sustainability Profile, treat it as a story of evolution, not a compliance scorecard.

When leadership matures to this level of systemic coherence, the organisation's culture begins to think and feel with the leader. However, sustaining such coherence requires more than strategic alignment – it depends on how ideas, perspectives and awareness circulate within the organisation. A leader may set the ontological centre, but the collective must continually participate in refining, questioning and re-interpreting it as the organisation evolves.

This is where solicitation of ideas and participative leadership become essential. These practices ensure that coherence is not maintained through authority or compliance, but through shared discernment and authentic contribution.

Solicitation of ideas and participative leadership

Solicitation of ideas refers to the practice of intentionally inviting, gathering and engaging with diverse perspectives to enrich understanding, innovation and collective discernment. In this body of work, it is not a performative display of inclusivity or an attempt to crowdsource truth. Rather, it is an ontological practice of humility. It reflects the willingness to transcend the limits of one's own perspective and worldview, and to access the deeper insight embedded in others' lived experience.

Within the metacontent discourse and the UOSI, solicitation of ideas functions as an instrument of authentic awareness and systemic coherence. It acknowledges that no individual – however wise or experienced – possesses complete access to truth. By engaging others

– not to confirm one's biases but to expand one's cognitive horizon – the process itself becomes an act of integrity.

In Minalogical terms, it sustains the field of *Meaning-in-Relation* – the shared *Mina* that arises when intention, perception and understanding interact authentically. Therefore, solicitation of ideas is both epistemic and ethical: it keeps systems alive through exchange; invites transformation without coercion; and turns listening into a mode of leadership.

From a leadership perspective, solicitation of ideas naturally evolves into **participative leadership** – a mode that goes beyond distributed authority or delegated tasks. Participative leadership is not about merely assigning responsibilities; it is about cultivating contributors rather than subordinates. It invites individuals to think, discern and co-create, rather than simply comply or execute. In this view, leadership becomes a living ecology of participation, where each person's Being, awareness and sense of ownership are activated in service of the whole.

Leaders accustomed to a more directive or authoritarian style may resist this approach, dismissing it as inefficient or idealistic. Yet such resistance often points not to a flaw in the philosophy, but to a misalignment within the system itself. When dialogue feels slow, unproductive or overly dependent on the leader's control, it may reveal that the team has been assembled for obedience rather than contribution. In such cases, the work is not to abandon participation, but to refine who participates and how – beginning with the leader's own appetite for coherence in recruitment, development and succession.

Tools such as the Being Profile and the Sustainability Profile can assist leaders in discerning the relational and ontological readiness of team members – revealing how they relate to qualities like trust, sovereignty, adaptability and authenticity. Building a participative culture depends on assembling people who can hold these qualities responsibly, so that authority becomes situational rather than habitual, and directive leadership is used intentionally rather than reflexively.

Discernment remains essential in this process because not every decision requires consultation, and not every moment is suited to dialogue. Participative leadership demands sensitivity to timing and trust – the ability to recognise when the circle should open for collective reflection and when it must close for decisive action. This is not indecision disguised as inclusion; it is coherence expressed through responsiveness.

Participative leadership also requires mutual trust. The leader must trust the team's capacity to contribute meaningfully, and the team must trust the leader's capacity to act decisively when needed. Practised authentically, solicitation of ideas and participative leadership form a dynamic continuum that transforms leadership from control into stewardship, from command into coherence.

In this framework, leadership itself is a relational act of attunement. Solicitation of ideas keeps leadership connected to truth beyond the self, while participative leadership ensures others are empowered to engage with that truth actively. Together, they create systems that think, feel and act in alignment – systems where people are not merely managed, but invited to participate in meaning itself. This deeper mode of leadership transforms decision-making from control into collaboration, and from efficiency into systemic intelligence.

The community organiser

Communities are where sustainability becomes visible – where people experience the real impact of systems every day. Acting upon communities means turning shared values into shared structures, where regeneration is not a project, but a way of living together.

- **Co-create a local Authentic Sustainability Blueprint** – Bring residents, local businesses, educators, service providers and council representatives together to name shared intentions and clarify non-negotiables. Identify the qualities of Being the community wants to strengthen – such as responsibility, care and reliability – and map these to tangible initiatives using the Developmental Dimension of the Fulfilment Pyramid to check the flow of coherence.

- **Build regenerative infrastructure, not just programs** – Establish shared assets that enable continuity: tool libraries, repair cafés, seed exchanges, learning hubs and community gardens. These create physical expressions of mutual care and reduce dependence on extractive systems.
- **Normalise constructive tension** – Teach community members to hold difference without division. Use the four regulators – patience, tolerance, adaptability and surrender – to navigate competing priorities, such as economic growth versus environmental protection, or heritage versus innovation.
- **Celebrate small regenerative wins** – Make progress visible. Honour each act of repair, inclusion or restoration, whether it's a youth-led clean-up, a revived creek bed or a more equitable local hiring policy. Visibility reinforces meaning and strengthens trust.

When communities operate this way, they stop waiting for outside solutions and start becoming their own regenerative ecosystems. Shared responsibility replaces blame. Diversity becomes an asset, not an obstacle. And sustainability ceases to be a slogan. Instead, it becomes the story people live by.

The journalist, educator or artist

Culture is the hidden infrastructure of sustainability. It shapes what people believe is possible, acceptable and worth pursuing. Journalists, educators and artists occupy the front line of this cultural field. Their work determines whether societies evolve through meaning or collapse through distortion.

- **Reveal distortion with care, not contempt** – When exposing injustice, misinformation or systemic shadow, aim to clarify rather than humiliate. Contempt deepens polarisation while care invites reflection. True cultural repair happens when truth is told in a way that keeps dignity intact.
- **Tell layered stories** – Connect the visible to the invisible, the personal to the systemic. Help people see how everyday choices, such as those relating to energy, consumption, work

or education, ripple through the larger architecture of life. Use the Nested Theory of Sense-making to weave perspectives without disregarding difference.

- **Create participatory formats** – Invite your audience to be co-authors rather than spectators. Design lessons, exhibitions, performances or articles that ask, *'What part of this story is mine to carry?'* Participation transforms consumption into contribution.
- **Model integrity in process** – How the story is told matters as much as what it says. Transparency, humility, proper attribution and consent all signal coherence in action. When these qualities are embodied, the work itself becomes regenerative.

Artists, teachers and storytellers don't simply reflect culture; they modulate it. Through their tone, method and message, they can expand the collective field of perception, revealing new ways to live, work and belong. Culture changes not through argument, but through resonance. Every truthful word, image or lesson restores coherence to the social fabric.

Guarding against common breakdowns

Every movement towards authentic sustainability will inevitably face turbulence. As systems evolve, the same forces that generate growth can also produce distortion. Recognising these breakdowns early allows leaders to re-enter coherence before dysfunction becomes culture.

The following highlights some common breakdowns to be aware of and ways to restore coherence.

- **Performative scale** – When visibility outpaces integrity. This looks like glossy campaigns, impressive metrics and public declarations with little substance beneath them. Performative scale is seductive because it wins applause in the short term. The remedy is traceability: a clear line from Being to action to feedback. Every initiative should be able to answer, 'How did this come about, what did it change in the world, and how do we know?'

- **Technocratic overreach** – Clever designs that ignore human texture. Systems built from spreadsheets alone eventually collapse under the weight of their abstraction. To prevent this, begin every design with narrative mapping and participative sense-making. Listen before building. A system – whether an organisation, community or government body – that can hear itself through honest feedback and participation will correct course faster than any external model or consultant ever could.
- **Centralised fragility** – When coherence depends on one person, one process or one platform, the whole system becomes fragile. Power concentrated in a single node creates vulnerability disguised as control. The antidote is distributed integrity – shared principles, distributed practice and light coordination across semi-autonomous parts. A distributed system breathes. It can absorb failure and still stay whole.
- **Rigid timelines** – Schedules that serve optics instead of rhythm. When deadlines are set to satisfy external expectations rather than internal readiness, trust erodes. Modulation clauses – pauses, milestone reviews and pivot points – allow projects to move at the speed of coherence, not panic. A slower, steadier rhythm often achieves far more enduring change.

None of these breakdowns signal failure. They are signs that **modulation** has been lost. When noticed and named, they can be converted into renewal through the modulation process. Each re-entry into coherence strengthens the capacity to sustain integrity under greater complexity.

Case study – A technical college's sustainability initiative breaks down and then recalibrates

A regional technical college set out to 'go green'. The first attempt looked promising – solar panels were installed, promotional materials appeared across campus, and a sustainability week drew local media attention. The initiative was applauded, but it soon became clear that visibility had outpaced integrity (performative scale). Within months, enthusiasm waned, workloads grew and staff engagement fractured.

The program began to feel like a compliance exercise rather than a genuine cultural shift.

The reset came when a newly appointed director reframed the initiative through the UOSI. Instead of asking *What should we do?*, she asked, *Who and how must we be to sustain this?* To explore this, the leadership team applied the UOSI's four spheres:

- **Architectonic Sphere** – Leadership clarified the normative intent: sustainability as an ethical stance, not a publicity exercise. Planning began with meta-awareness – seeing the college as a living system within a broader social and ecological ecosystem – and ensuring that structures, governance and policies were coherent and capable of long-term effectiveness.
- **Integrity Sphere** – The director opened decision-making to community review. Staff, students and industry partners joined procurement and resource-management discussions. Clear intentions were declared for each initiative, Being (personal and collective) was recognised as part of accountability, trust was rebuilt through transparency, and sovereignty was honoured by giving all stakeholders a genuine voice, not symbolic consultation.
- **Disintegration Sphere** – Instead of hiding breakdowns, staff were encouraged to surface them early. A failed waste-management pilot was discussed openly: the shadow dynamics (shame, blame); the small 'daily miseries' in workflow; and pockets of entrenchment ('we tried that once and it didn't work') were named without humiliation. Cross-departmental teams were then formed to design systemic repairs that reduced friction and prevented suffering from compounding into culture.
- **Modulation Sphere** – The college launched a six-month circular-economy pilot with deliberate pauses for reflection and recalibration. Faculty and students practised patience in sequencing, trust in those closest to the work to propose adjustments, adaptability in redesigning processes mid-stream, and surrender when an idea proved incoherent in practice.

The college also adopted the **Sustainability Profile** as an assessment tool, tracking its living relationship to intention, trust, sovereignty and Being.

Two years on, operational costs had fallen, collaboration increased and staff retention improved. More importantly, students began initiating their own sustainability projects, faculty reported renewed purpose, and the wider community trusted the process even when outcomes fluctuated. This was no longer a 'green campaign'; it was coherence in motion. The system had learned to see its shadows without collapse, to act from Being and sovereignty, and to modulate change with patience, trust, adaptability and surrender. Sustainability stopped being an event and became a way of being.

Conclusion

Authentic sustainability matures when coherence expands beyond the self — when what begins as personal integrity and organisational practice ripples outward into collective renewal. Every act of authenticity, every decision made in trust or courage, sends a signal into the wider field. Over time, those ripples form a living fabric of sustainability that shapes culture, policy and shared systems of value.

Each sphere of the UOSI plays a role in this expansion:

- The **Architectonic Sphere** establishes the moral and structural blueprint that ensures our designs serve life rather than image.
- The **Integrity Sphere** anchors every choice in intention, trust, sovereignty and Being.
- The **Disintegration Sphere** reminds us that progress requires honesty – the willingness to meet shadows, misery, suffering and entrenchment without collapsing into them.
- And the **Modulation Sphere** ensures continuity through change – cultivating patience, trust, adaptability and surrender as the active muscles of sustainability in motion.

Throughout this chapter, you've seen how these principles move from concept to reality – in governance, enterprise, culture and community.

Each domain, when aligned ontologically, becomes a field of renewal. The policymaker transforms regulation into evolution. The founder turns commerce into coherence. The community organiser converts tension into collective capacity. The educator or artist reawakens cultural meaning.

Now the question turns to you.

- Where does your Authentic Sustainability Blueprint naturally intersect with greater systems right now?
- How can you ensure that your influence scales without diluting integrity?
- Which sphere or regulating force most needs strengthening in your own context?
- And what will you measure and narrate so that coherence remains visible — not as perfection, but as honesty in motion?

As you consider these questions, remember that systemic transformation is not built through pressure alone. It grows through *participation* – through each person, organisation and institution choosing to act from Being rather than performance, and to move with integrity through disruption rather than around it.

The work ahead is not about building new doctrines. It is about *embodying* the architecture of authenticity so fully that sustainability no longer requires persuasion – it becomes the natural rhythm of our shared life.

The chapters that follow bring this entire body of work to life, demonstrating how the frameworks, distinctions and tools explored so far converge in practice. The next chapter examines a commercial ecosystem, revealing how coherence reshapes leadership, culture and commerce from the inside out. Through this example, you'll see how the Authentic Sustainability Framework moves from concept to execution and how transformation unfolds through diagnosis, reflection, reconstruction and renewal.

A subsequent chapter extends this lens to a societal scale, showing how the same frameworks can be leveraged to analyse and regenerate complex systems such as healthcare, education, the economy and governance. In doing so, it reveals how authentic sustainability operates not only within organisations, but within the very architectures that shape civilisation itself.

CHAPTER 59

Coherence by Design – Applying the ASF

Throughout Part VIII, we have explored the practical dimensions of translating the ontological architecture of authentic sustainability into methods, tools and practices that restore coherence across human systems. Each model, ontology and methodology serves a distinct yet interconnected function. Together, they form a regenerative cycle of awareness, diagnosis, reconstruction, embodiment and continuity. This chapter brings those elements together, showing how the entire Authentic Sustainability Framework (ASF) functions as one living architecture in action. Let's begin with a recap:

- **Unified Ontology of Systemic Integrity (UOSI)** – Defines the 16 systemic qualities that make coherence observable, measurable and designable within any human system.
- **Systemic Subversion Cycle (SSC)** – Diagnoses where coherence is weakening or breaking down, revealing the patterned nature of dysfunction and its causes.
- **Reconstructive Ontology of Sustainability (ROS)** – Provides the method for rebuilding alignment once subversion is visible, integrating integrity, meaning and design into renewed coherence.

- **Sustainability Profile** – Translates the ontological qualities of the UOSI into measurable indicators, allowing both individuals and collectives to assess and track their relationship with systemic integrity.
- **Fulfilment Pyramid** – Bridges meaning and conduct, showing how coherence is lived experientially across the developmental, phenomenological and relational dimensions.
- **Authentic Sustainability Blueprint** – Embeds coherence structurally, ensuring that governance, operations and culture evolve as one living, self-correcting system.

These components are not steps to be followed mechanically, but forces to be *intentionally orchestrated*. When applied together, they form a regenerative loop – from awareness to assessment, from reconstruction to fulfilment, and finally, to the living continuity of coherence by design.

The following case study demonstrates how the ASF can be applied as a unified architecture to regenerate coherence within a real-world commercial ecosystem. While this example focuses on a business context, the same process can be adapted across domains – from personal relationships and education to community and governance. It reveals that authentic sustainability is not a theory to learn, but a tangible, relevant and deeply practical practice to live by. When the architecture of integrity, meaning and coherence is consciously applied, systems at every scale – individual, organisational and societal – can regenerate from within and be sustained with minimal intervention.

Case study – Rebuilding a business for authentic sustainability

A four-year-old mid-sized technology company was born from a bold idea – to create an AI-driven analytics platform that helps SMEs better understand and serve their customers. Its founding purpose was clear and deeply human: to enhance connection through intelligent design. The product had passed rigorous testing and early adoption phases with strong customer feedback.

Yet, despite a promising trajectory, the organisation found itself struggling. Beneath the surface of innovation and optimism, fractures had begun to appear. A key member of the leadership team – the Head of Customer Experience – resigned unexpectedly, citing burnout and growing misalignment around the company's direction. A new operations leader was brought in from a large corporate background. Within months, their process-heavy management style clashed with the start-up's creative culture.

At the same time, the external environment shifted. A surge of generative AI tools entered the market, rapidly commoditising features that once set the company apart. Internally, teams began to rely on these same AI systems to manage customer communication. What began as a cost-saving measure soon diluted the human touch that had built the brand's reputation. Customer service became inconsistent, responses felt robotic and complaints began to rise.

By the time revenue started to dip, the founders were exhausted. Their once-cohesive team had split into factions – those championing efficiency and automation versus those fighting to preserve the company's human-centred values. Decision-making grew reactive. Trust eroded. Several staff resigned.

Drawing on their healthy relationship with vulnerability, responsibility and authenticity – made visible recently when they conducted a **Being Profile** assessment – the co-founders acknowledged that the problem was not simply operational or technical – it was structural. They reached out to a trusted adviser, seeking clarity beyond conventional performance metrics.

Step 1. Diagnosis

Using the **Systemic Subversion Cycle (SSC)**, the adviser helped the leadership team diagnose what was really going on beneath the surface. The company was caught in the Escalation and Fractures stage of the cycle – a point where dysfunction had become self-reinforcing. The early signs had been ignored: blurred roles, poor communication and misaligned priorities. Rumours and defensiveness filled the gaps left by absent leadership clarity.

Through this diagnosis, the co-founders could finally see that the dysfunction was not random but patterned. The business had drifted into the same subversion loop that undermines many growing enterprises, losing coherence under the weight of fear, fatigue and misplaced efficiency. Recognising this pattern marked the turning point. The path forward would no longer be about fixing isolated issues, but about restoring the conditions for integrity and systemic coherence to re-emerge.

Step 2. Assessment – Revealing the architecture through reflection

With the pattern of dysfunction now visible through the Systemic Subversion Cycle, the next step was to make coherence measurable. The adviser introduced the **Sustainability Profile**, the ontometric tool within the Authentic Sustainability Framework that translates the principles of the Unified Ontology of Systemic Integrity (UOSI) into tangible assessment.

Each member of the leadership team completed a Sustainability Profile to evaluate where coherence was strong, where it had weakened and how alignment could be restored. The results revealed striking asymmetries across the four spheres of systemic integrity.

Within the **Integrity Sphere**, *intention* and *trust* scored lowest. Leaders had become fixated on survival metrics, losing touch with the original meaning that had animated the business. *Sovereignty* – once a defining feature of the team's creative freedom – had eroded under rigid processes introduced during the leadership transition. Yet *Being* remained partially intact: the founders still held a sincere desire to do good, even if they no longer knew how.

The **Modulation Sphere** showed uneven results. *Patience* and *tolerance* were present but strained, reflecting the tension between urgency and exhaustion. Some leaders were adapting too quickly, bending to trends without reflection, while others resisted change altogether.

The **Disintegration Sphere** revealed pockets of *suffering* rather than full *entrenchment* – a sign that while dysfunction had taken hold, there was still capacity for renewal. Importantly, the team's willingness to see and name these issues was itself a sign of integrity beginning to reassert itself.

Their relatively low **Vulnerability Index Score** mirrored reality on the ground, with some leaders often defending choices or rationalising results. But through facilitated dialogue, these defences softened.

At the adviser's recommendation, the process was extended to the **customer service team**, whose role represented the company's public interface. Their profiles painted a different but complementary picture: *high aspiration, low alignment.* Team members deeply valued the company's purpose, but felt disconnected from leadership decisions and overwhelmed by automation.

In their **Modulation Sphere**, *adaptability* scored lowest. Staff had responded to rapid technological change with oscillating extremes – overcompensating with scripted efficiency or resisting new systems entirely. *Patience* and *tolerance* were depleted, reflecting mounting fatigue.

In the **Disintegration Sphere**, the signs were clearer: *misery* was present in language like 'We're running on fumes', while *entrenchment* was evident through phrases such as 'It's always been this way.' Yet beneath the frustration was a relatively high score for Being within the **Integrity Sphere** – reflecting that ways of being like care, compassion and love prevailed. If reconnected to the company's deeper meaning (*Mina*), this could become the foundation for renewal.

Seeing these two sets of results side by side provided the leadership team with their first true mirror. The issue was not a lack of talent, care or commitment; it was *coherence*. Each group held fragments of integrity, but the system as a whole had fallen out of alignment.

This revelation changed the tone of the organisation. The leadership team stopped trying to manage behaviour and began redesigning the architecture that shaped it. For the first time in months, staff reported feeling heard. The company had finally moved from diagnosing dysfunction to understanding how to regenerate coherence.

Step 3. Reconstructing coherence

With the organisation's structural imbalances now visible, the adviser introduced the next phase: rebuilding through the **Reconstructive Ontology of Sustainability (ROS)**.

The process began with a single clarifying question: *Why does this enterprise exist, and what is it here to sustain?* Through guided dialogue, the founders and their leadership team revisited the organisation's *Mina* – its deeper meaning and purpose. They quickly realised that what had started as a vision to enhance human connection through intelligent design had quietly shifted into a pursuit of efficiency through automation.

This insight reframed everything. Rather than adding new processes, the leadership team began to re-anchor the company in its original essence of *connection and service*. Every decision was now filtered through this renewed meaning. If a policy, tool or system didn't support coherence between purpose, people and product, it was either redesigned or released.

To understand the human and cultural architecture beneath these patterns, the adviser introduced a **metacontent analysis** using the **Nested Theory of Sense-making**. Together, the leaders explored the underlying narratives and perspectives shaping behaviour within the organisation and in the market. They discovered two dominant stories:

1. Internally, 'We're falling behind' had replaced 'We're pioneering change', and
2. Externally, customers perceived the company as becoming 'just another tech brand'.

These insights revealed the invisible meaning structures driving disconnection – and where coherence needed to be rebuilt.

Next, every team within the business completed a **team Being Profile** to reveal their collective relationships with the Being Framework's 31 Aspects of Being, including the shadows. This step brought visibility to the underlying patterns of Being influencing the company's culture – traits like *care* and *compassion* remained strong, but shadows revealed an unhealthy relationship with Aspects of Being like *authenticity, resilience, proactivity* and *confidence*. Leaders realised that the way each person was being – their posture, awareness and integrity – shaped not only their own performance, but also the dynamics, decisions and coherence of the entire organisation.

Using the **Transformation Methodology** and its Conception Worksheet process, each team member, including leaders, began working on their own individual shadows. These structured reflections helped translate awareness into transformation. The process became deeply personal yet collectively reinforcing – as individuals grew in awareness, effectiveness and integrity, team dynamics stabilised and collaboration began to flow again.

At this point, the adviser introduced the **CCC Model** (Content → Clarity → Conduct) to embed coherence into daily behaviour. Within the flow of ROS, the CCC Model serves as a bridge from awareness to practice. The leadership team used this model internally within each department, allowing every layer of the system – individuals, teams and the company as a whole – to move from content to clarity, and from clarity to coherent action. It became a shared rhythm of reconstruction: seeing, understanding and embodying coherence in practice.

At a systems level, the adviser guided the leadership team to integrate these insights structurally:

- **Communication pathways** were rebuilt to encourage openness and shared understanding.
- **Decision rights** were redistributed to restore creative sovereignty across teams.
- **Customer experience protocols** were redesigned to bring the human element back into every interaction.

One of the most transformative shifts came from rethinking the company's relationship with technology itself. Instead of letting digital systems replace human presence, staff used them to create more meaningful moments of contact, such as scheduling real check-ins after online interactions or adding brief personal follow-ups that re-humanised the customer experience. Customer satisfaction began to recover – not because the technology changed, but because the *intent* behind its use had.

As coherence was reconstructed, the organisation began to feel different. Meetings became more reflective than reactive. Teams that once felt silenced now felt seen. The company had stopped managing dysfunction and started cultivating integrity. By rebuilding from meaning outward, the enterprise began to stabilise – not through control, but through coherence.

Step 4. Embedding alignment

Reconstruction had given the company a renewed sense of clarity and purpose. But sustaining that coherence required translating insight into ongoing, embodied practice. To achieve this, the adviser introduced the **Fulfilment Pyramid**, focusing on how coherence expresses itself across three dimensions – Developmental, Phenomenological and Relational.

Developmental Dimension – At the developmental level, fulfilment began with meaning and growth. Each leader paused to reconnect with *why* they were here – not just to deliver outcomes, but to cultivate coherence within themselves and their teams. This shift from performance to purpose became the inner stabiliser for leadership through uncertainty. Team leaders began opening meetings by articulating a shared intention: *'Let's focus on what truly matters here and how we can act in alignment with that.'* This grounded every action in values and *Mina*.

Phenomenological Dimension – At the experiential level, intention was translated into conduct. Leaders practised being fully present and calm in high-pressure situations, modelling integrity through tone, language and behaviour. Instead of using authority to impose direction, they created space for open dialogue and reflection. This embodied presence set a new tone across the organisation – coherence was no longer a concept, but a felt experience.

Relational Dimension – At the relational level, fulfilment moved from personal clarity to collective harmony. The leadership team recognised that sustaining coherence required adequate resourcing, clear frameworks and relational safety. They restructured workloads to avoid burnout, redistributed responsibilities to balance capability, and established psychological safety check-ins where staff could speak openly about tension or fatigue.

Weekly **Relational Fulfilment Sessions** became part of the company rhythm, structured around three simple reflections:

- *Are we aligned in meaning?* (Do we still understand why this matters?)
- *Are we aligned in intention?* (Are we aiming in the same direction?)
- *Are we aligned in conduct?* (Are our actions matching our words?)

This practice brought relational coherence to life. Teams that once operated in silos began collaborating naturally, sharing insight and supporting one another through shifting demands. Adequate resourcing ensured that alignment wasn't just emotional but practical – time, energy and capability were balanced so fulfilment could be sustained without exhaustion.

Externally, the same principles began to shape customer relationships. Rather than relying solely on data or automation, service teams engaged customers with renewed authenticity – listening, empathising and responding with both efficiency and humanity. The company's purpose of *enhancing human connection through intelligent design* was once again being lived, not just stated.

Through these three dimensions, the Fulfilment Pyramid turned alignment into flow:

- Meaning anchored purpose.
- Intention aligned action.
- Commitment translated coherence into conduct.

Together, these created a living rhythm – fulfilment not as an endpoint, but as a continuous movement of integrity between people, purpose and system.

Step 5. Designing continuity

With fulfilment now flowing through all three dimensions – developmental, phenomenological and relational – the organisation's next task was to ensure that these new rhythms would endure. The adviser guided the leadership team through the creation of an **Authentic Sustainability Blueprint** – a living design for embedding coherence into every layer of structure, governance and decision-making.

The blueprint process began by mapping the interdependencies between purpose, process and people. The team examined each system – from strategy and innovation to resourcing, leadership and customer engagement – asking one unifying question: *Does this design sustain coherence or erode it?*

Where the Fulfilment Pyramid focused on *how alignment is lived*, the Blueprint focused on *how it is maintained*. It translated the relational and developmental insights of fulfilment into operational architecture – ensuring that what had been learned in practice became repeatable, measurable and self-sustaining.

New governance rhythms emerged organically:

- **Quarterly reflection cycles** replaced rigid annual reviews, keeping the organisation adaptive and current.
- **Cross-functional calibration sessions** became a space to align meaning, intention and conduct across departments.
- **Resourcing maps** were established to monitor capability and wellbeing, ensuring that sustainability was supported, not stretched.
- **Integrity metrics** were embedded alongside financial ones – regularly measuring intention, trust, sovereignty and Being as key indicators of health.

The adviser emphasised that the Blueprint was not a static plan but a *dynamic architecture*: it evolved as the organisation evolved. It provided guardrails for decision-making while maintaining flexibility for innovation and change.

In summary, the Blueprint brought together everything the organisation had learned into one coherent movement of regeneration:

1. **Diagnosis:** Using the **SSC** and the **UOSI**, the organisation revealed the structural forces driving dysfunction.
2. **Assessment:** Through the **Sustainability Profile**, it measured coherence and vulnerability, identifying where alignment was strong and where it had weakened.

3. **Reconstruction:** Applying **ROS**, it rebuilt the organisation's architecture on ontological foundations of integrity, meaning and Being.
4. **Fulfilment:** Through the **Fulfilment Pyramid**, it brought coherence to life across the developmental, phenomenological and relational dimensions.
5. **Continuity:** Finally, through the **Authentic Sustainability Blueprint**, it translated all of this into a living design – a structure capable of sustaining alignment, adaptability and systemic integrity through ongoing change.

The impact was profound. The company no longer viewed turbulence as a sign of failure, but as an invitation to recalibrate. Teams had a shared method for engaging complexity rather than fearing it. When another industry disruption occurred months later, the organisation did not descend into crisis. It activated its frameworks, reviewed alignment, adjusted resourcing and moved forward with calm precision.

For the co-founders, the transformation was both structural and personal. What began as an effort to rescue a business had become a model for regenerative leadership. Profitability returned, but more importantly, trust, creativity and wellbeing flourished. The company had learned to sustain coherence by design – not through control or performance, but through a living architecture grounded in authenticity, integrity and systemic alignment.

Conclusion

Coherence is not a state to be achieved, but a rhythm to be lived. It breathes, renews and responds – much like life itself. The Authentic Sustainability Framework is not a collection of methods or checklists; it is a living architecture that evolves through the awareness and integrity of those who apply it. Each ontology, distinction and tool becomes meaningful only when brought to life through one's way of being – when the inner posture of authenticity and care animates the form, turning concepts into lived coherence.

As seen in the case study, the movement from dysfunction to regeneration is not linear but cyclical – a continual process of perceiving, realigning and renewing coherence. The **Systemic Subversion Cycle** reveals where fragmentation begins. The **Reconstructive Ontology of Sustainability** shows how meaning and design come back into alignment. The **Fulfilment Pyramid** and **Authentic Sustainability Blueprint** translate coherence into lived rhythm and structure, while the **Sustainability Profile** makes it measurable and narratable over time. Together, they form a constellation of instruments that bring awareness into motion.

This demonstrates that authentic sustainability is not built by enforcing order, but by cultivating harmony – the movement of truth through design, where purpose becomes structure, structure becomes rhythm, and rhythm becomes culture. In such systems, alignment is not demanded; it emerges. Leadership, in this context, is not about control but attunement – designing coherence into the very relationships, rhythms and decision-making structures that shape how people think, work and evolve together.

The same process applies across scale. Whether within an individual, a team, an organisation or a civilisation, coherence unfolds through the same regenerative flow: from awareness to assessment; from reconstruction to fulfilment; and finally into continuity. The principles do not change – only their context and expression. What shifts is the scope of stewardship, not the architecture of coherence itself.

In the next and final chapter of Part VIII, this architecture meets the full complexity of society – revealing how the same ontological framework that restores coherence within individuals and organisations can also illuminate, diagnose and regenerate the vast systems that shape our shared future.

CHAPTER 60

Leveraging the ASF as a Systemic Lens for Analysis and Renewal

In the previous chapter, we saw the entire Authentic Sustainability Framework (ASF) brought to life through a business case study. That application revealed how coherence can be designed, measured and renewed within an organisational ecosystem – demonstrating that authentic sustainability is not an abstract philosophy but a living architecture in motion.

This chapter shifts the focus from application to leveraging – from demonstrating the ASF in practice to learning how to use it to assess, diagnose and restore coherence within any human system across any domain. To make this tangible, the framework has been contextualised here within one of the most universal and revealing domains of all – care, and particularly healthcare.

While healthcare is used as the contextualised example, the same method can be applied to evaluate and renew any human-designed system from a sustainability perspective. It demonstrates how the ASF provides a consistent way to perceive where coherence breaks down, discern why it happens and guide renewal from within – whether in communities, industries, institutions or entire societies.

Care touches every human being regardless of status, wealth or circumstance. It is both intimate and systemic, encompassing every layer of human organisation: from governance and policy to ethics and economics, from medical practice to technological innovation, from compassion to institutional design. By its very nature, the healthcare system brings together policymakers, practitioners, engineers, entrepreneurs, ethicists, financiers, academics, educators, patients and loved ones – each participating in an intricate web of service. It is both deeply personal and unavoidably collective.

In the pages ahead, we will not merely discuss care, but use it as both lens and method – a living example through which you can explore how the ASF reveals and renews sustainability across diverse systems and contexts.

This chapter is written as a reflection, not a manifesto. It invites you to look beyond political and economic debates and to see sustainability through a new lens – not merely as a question of systems, but of Being. Its purpose is to help you shift from ideological to ontological thinking, from analysing structure to recognising the deeper architecture of existence itself.

By the end of this chapter, you may find yourself not only thinking differently about the systems you inhabit and engage with, but *sensing* their coherence – or lack thereof. The intention is not to leave you with theory, but with transformation – a realignment that reconnects intellect with integrity, policy with purpose and structure with soul.

If you are a practitioner, policymaker or leader, this chapter offers a moral and structural compass – a way to discern where coherence breaks down and how it might be restored. If you are a reflective reader, it offers a bridge between the systemic and the sacred, showing that sustainability depends not only on resources or reform, but also on the moral quality of the consciousness that animates them.

At its deepest level, this exploration is about rekindling reverence for life – a reminder that to sustain is not to preserve for preservation's sake, but to honour meaning.

Care as a reflection of civilisation's coherence

Few domains reveal a civilisation's moral and systemic health more vividly than its care for life, its response to suffering, and its spirit of service. Care is where philosophy becomes tangible – where coherence, or its absence, shows itself in how societies heal, nurture and honour one another.

In an age of astonishing medical progress – where humanity has decoded the genome, engineered organ transplants and built machines that prolong life longer than ever before – a sobering paradox remains. We have never been so capable yet so incapable of providing effective care.

Globally, societies are caught between two realities. On the one hand, we have abundance: advanced technology, intricate procedures and vast networks of professionals dedicated to healing. On the other, we have fragmentation: exhausted practitioners, inaccessible services, spiralling costs and citizens who, despite living in the most medically advanced era, still feel unseen, unheard and inadequately cared for.

This paradox reveals something profound: the crisis of care is not a crisis of capacity, but of coherence. It is not that we do not know *how* to care; it is that the systems we have built no longer reflect *why* we care.

Behind every failing structure lies a dissonance between intention, meaning and conduct – the three coordinates of coherence that determine whether a system sustains life or merely manages its symptoms. When these coordinates fall out of alignment, healthcare becomes a transaction rather than a vocation, a service industry rather than an expression of stewardship.

Modern civilisation's struggle with healthcare is, therefore, not a failure of intelligence or infrastructure, but a deeper disorder – an ontological one. We have treated health as a technical problem while neglecting its moral and existential architecture. We have reduced care to logistics and efficiency, forgetting that what makes a system sustainable is not its machinery, but its humanity – the consciousness of those who design, govern and participate in it.

This chapter looks beneath ideology and economy – beyond the binaries of privatisation and nationalisation – to ask a more fundamental question:

What makes a system of care coherent, sustainable and humane, regardless of the 'ism' it belongs to?

In pursuing this question, we will see that sustainability, at its core, is not about resource allocation or political preference. It's about alignment – the degree to which a society's systems, values and human beings are congruent with truth, integrity and meaning.

From this perspective, care is not simply an outcome of governance or economics; it is a moral indicator of how a civilisation understands itself. The state of a society's healthcare system mirrors the state of its soul.

Beyond the ideological divide

When we speak about healthcare systems, public discourse often collapses into familiar binaries – the state versus the market, socialism versus capitalism, centralisation versus freedom. Each side champions its preferred model as the 'ultimate solution', pointing to the failures of the other as proof of its own superiority. Yet despite their differences, they continue to produce the same symptoms: inefficiency, alienation and erosion of trust. Why? Because the underlying problem is not structural, but ontological.

Ideologies, by their very nature, capture only a fragment of truth and mistake it for the whole. A market-based model celebrates freedom, innovation and choice – all of which are valuable – but when unmoored from ethical responsibility and collective purpose, it can turn care into commerce and compassion into currency. In contrast, a state-controlled model aspires to equality and accessibility – noble intentions indeed – yet when detached from responsiveness, personal agency and trust, it becomes stagnant, bureaucratic and dehumanising.

Though polar opposites in design, both systems can fail in remarkably similar ways when they lose touch with meaning. The market forgets *why* it serves, while the state forgets *for whom* it serves. In both cases, the human being – the very subject of care – becomes obscured behind process, policy and profit.

To understand how to create a sustainable healthcare system, we must move beyond ideology and step into the realm of ontology – from the system we run to how we are *being* within it. For even the most virtuous ideology will collapse if inhabited by individuals and institutions out of alignment with integrity, truth and purpose.

A sustainable system is not one that is purely capitalist or socialist, centralised or distributed. It is one that maintains coherence between its intentions, actions and outcomes – where care is both efficient and humane, structured and adaptive, principled yet alive.

When the focus shifts from ideology to ontology and from argument to awareness, sustainability ceases to be a contest of models and becomes an expression of *Being* – of how a civilisation holds itself in relation to life, truth and one another.

The mirror of care – A study in contrasts

Across the world, a striking duality can be observed. In some societies, the healthcare system operates like a finely tuned marketplace – efficient, innovative and competitive – yet deeply divided by wealth and access. In others, healthcare is guaranteed as a universal right – accessible, equal and state-funded – yet burdened by inefficiency, fatigue and the quiet erosion of care.

Though outwardly different, these two models mirror one another in their dysfunction. In the first, abundance exists without coherence – abundance of tools, technology and treatment, but scarcity of compassion, continuity and trust. In the second, equality exists without vitality – a well-intentioned promise of universality that struggles under the weight of bureaucracy and diminishing responsiveness.

Neither model is sustainable. One celebrates autonomy but neglects meaning. The other enshrines the collective good but forgets sovereignty. One idolises freedom but breeds inequality. The other guarantees fairness but suffocates initiative. Both are expressions of imbalance, reflecting a civilisation's distorted relationship with integrity, responsibility and truth.

In the market-driven model, healthcare becomes commodified. Constrained by profit margins and the ever-present fear of legal consequence, practitioners often serve the system rather than the human beings they are called to serve. Patients are treated as customers, their healing measured in transactions and outcomes rather than presence and empathy. The system thrives economically but withers existentially.

In the state-driven model, healthcare becomes bureaucratised. Practitioners, while liberated from market pressure, often drown in protocols, compliance and systemic fatigue. The intention to serve everyone ends up serving no one deeply. The system functions, but without a soul.

Both models are reflections of the same underlying phenomenon – a civilisation's fractured coherence. Nowhere is this fracture more critical than in systems of care, where the consequences are measured not in profits or policies, but in human suffering. When a society's sense of purpose, ethics and *Being* loses alignment, the rupture manifests everywhere – yet it is felt most acutely in how we care for life itself.

Viewing the healthcare system as a mirror held up to the soul of a civilisation, we can see whether a society's priorities arise from authentic meaning or from fear, vanity and convenience. The question is no longer which system works better, but what truth lives at the heart of its people – the hidden variable that determines whether a system truly sustains life or merely prolongs it.

Sustainability as a moral and ontological state

Behind every system that thrives and every system that collapses lies a lurking variable[105] that cannot be seen in policy documents,

---

105 A lurking variable is a hidden or unobserved factor that influences both the independent and dependent variables in a statistical relationship, creating a false or misleading association between them. In other words, it is an unseen variable that 'lurks' in the background, potentially confounding causal interpretation.

economic models or institutional blueprints. It is the quality of Being of those who participate in, design and govern that system.

No amount of funding or reform can compensate for the absence of moral coherence in those people. A system's sustainability is not determined solely by its resources or structure, but by the alignment between its intention, integrity and meaning. When these three are in harmony, even limited resources can yield remarkable results. But when they fracture, abundance itself becomes a source of decay.

Sustainability, in this sense, is not an engineering challenge, but a moral and ontological one. The Authentic Sustainability Framework positions it as a state of coherence between what a system intends, what it does and what it signifies. This coherence cannot be legislated or incentivised. It must be cultivated through awareness, responsibility, authenticity and stewardship.

A society that approaches healthcare with the genuine intention of preserving life, dignifying human beings and honouring our shared humanity naturally creates systems that regenerate themselves. Practitioners act from meaning, not merely from obligation. Citizens engage not as entitled recipients, but as co-stewards of the common good.

When a system's intention becomes contaminated by vanity, politics or fear, care loses its moral centre. Practitioners perform without presence, institutions operate without conscience and citizens demand without contribution. Such systems become self-referential, serving their own continuity rather than the wellbeing of those they were created to serve. This is why two societies with identical infrastructures can produce radically different outcomes: one sustains coherence through authentic intention; the other disintegrates through appearance and fear.

At its essence, sustainability is not about survival – it's about alignment with reality. Systems that reflect reality – the truth of interdependence, dignity and ethical stewardship – endure and evolve. However, systems that deny or distort reality inevitably collapse, no matter how sophisticated their architecture. Therefore, sustainability is a moral phenomenon expressed through systemic behaviour – a mirror of collective Being, revealing how consciousness translates into structure and purpose.

Illuminating the architecture beneath the facade

Every healthcare system – whether market-driven, state-administered or hybrid – is more than an infrastructure of policies and institutions. It is a living expression of collective consciousness: the visible outcome of the intentions, values and moral logic that animate it. When coherence prevails, healthcare embodies stewardship and trust. When it fractures, the same system becomes bureaucratic, exploitative or fatigued.

The Authentic Sustainability Framework provides a way to map this coherence, beginning with diagnosis using the Systemic Subversion Cycle (SSC).

The Systemic Subversion Cycle in healthcare – How coherence breaks down

As you have learned, the SSC provides the diagnostic lens through which we can identify where and how a system has drifted from alignment. It reveals the recurring pattern by which structures designed to serve life begin, often unconsciously, to serve themselves.

In healthcare, this decay seldom appears as a single collapse. It unfolds gradually – through habit, pressure and rationalisation – until incoherence becomes invisible, normalised as 'just the way things are'. The SSC allows leaders, practitioners and policymakers to locate the phase their system is in and to discern what form of intervention is needed before moving into reconstruction and renewal.

In the context of healthcare, the SSC unfolds through its four interdependent phases as follows:

1. Distortion – When purpose gives way to performance

Distortion begins when the founding intention of care – the preservation of life and dignity – is quietly replaced by surrogate aims, such as efficiency, compliance, reputation management or optics. The language shifts from *'Are we helping this person?'* to *'Have we met our target?'* Purpose remains declared but no longer embodied.

2. Escalation – When urgency replaces discernment

Once distortion becomes normalised, strain compounds. Burnout rises, fear spreads and crises become routine. Systems chase activity to prove relevance, mistaking motion for progress. When this happens, the human being – practitioner or patient – becomes an object of throughput rather than presence.

3. Fracture – When trust disintegrates

As escalation persists, relationships fragment. Clinicians blame administrators, administrators distrust clinicians, while patients lose faith in institutions. Communication collapses, silos form and goodwill is replaced with self-preservation. The system ceases to behave as one coherent organism and becomes a network of competing survival zones instead.

4. Entrenchment – When dysfunction hardens into identity

Entrenchment is the point at which incoherence becomes culture. Failing processes are defended, critique is treated as disloyalty and appearance replaces substance. For example, an emergency department may persist with chronic overcrowding and excessive wait times, defending the situation as 'normal seasonal pressure' rather than addressing deeper structural issues, such as staffing shortages, inefficient triage systems and bureaucratic delays that compromise timely care. The system still functions, but it loses its capacity for self-correction. Its moral pulse weakens even as its machinery runs.

The SSC enables diagnosis before prescription. It helps leaders and practitioners see where the system's coherence is failing – whether at the level of purpose (distortion), rhythm (escalation), relationship (fracture) or culture (entrenchment).

Without this ontological map, reform efforts remain superficial – adding new processes on top of outdated, dysfunctional versions. The SSC prepares the ground for systemic renewal by revealing what must be restored and where.

It is from this point of diagnosis that we can move into examining the deeper anatomy of coherence through the UOSI to understand how the four spheres and their underlying quad qualities form the living architecture of sustainable systems.

While the SSC reveals how coherence unravels through distortion over time, the UOSI enables us to observe the architecture of that coherence itself – the structural forces that sustain or destabilise it within living systems.

Applied to healthcare, the UOSI serves as both mirror and compass. It illuminates the systemic anatomy beneath surface performance – showing where integrity is sustained, where modulation falters, and where structures have become misaligned with their founding purpose.

In the following sections, we explore each sphere through the lens of care – showing that sustainability is not the outcome of any political ideology, but of the inner coherence of these ontological forces.

The Integrity Sphere – The moral core of care

At the heart of every sustainable system lies integrity – the alignment between intention, trust, sovereignty and Being. These four causal qualities form the moral bloodstream through which coherence flows. They determine whether care remains an act of stewardship or degenerates into an act of performance. Let's consider each causal quality of integrity through the lens of care.

Intention – The source of coherence

Intention is the moral compass of the healthcare system – the reason it exists and the purpose it serves. When intention arises from genuine meaning – from the sincere desire to preserve life and uphold dignity – coherence follows. But when intention becomes self-serving, political or performative, dissonance spreads through every layer.

When a healthcare system is animated by authentic intention, it doesn't just heal bodies and minds; it generates faith in the system itself.

Trust – The social currency of integrity

Trust is the invisible foundation of care. It allows patients to surrender vulnerably, practitioners to act with sovereignty and leaders to serve transparently. In trust-rich healthcare systems, truth flows naturally – transparency and accountability emerge not from compulsion, but from character. However, in trust-poor healthcare systems, fear becomes the operating principle, and bureaucracy multiplies as a substitute for faith.

Whether publicly funded or privately managed, a healthcare system's success depends on an unspoken covenant of goodwill – the assumption that others act sincerely. Without it, every interaction becomes a negotiation rather than a relationship.

Sovereignty – Freedom within responsibility

Sovereignty represents the dignity of self-governance aligned with ethical order. A healthcare system that suppresses sovereignty through over-regulation suffocates responsibility, while one that idolises it without boundaries breeds entitlement.

Sustainability emerges only where freedom and responsibility coexist – where individuals act with conscience and autonomy rather than compliance and control. The paradox is simple: the more a society honours sovereignty, the less control its systems (including healthcare) require.

Being – The root of integrity

All integrity begins and ends in Being – the state of inner coherence from which individuals act. A healthcare system can rise no higher than the consciousness of those who inhabit it. Practitioners without empathy, leaders without humility or citizens without gratitude will unconsciously shape institutions in their own likeness.

When individuals within the system embody authenticity, responsibility, care and compassion, coherence becomes self-reinforcing. But when they are driven by fear, pride or apathy, disintegration is inevitable. Therefore, integrity is not a policy, but a state of consciousness expressed collectively.

The Disintegration Sphere – The 'dark' side of care when its forces are ignored

Disintegration is the gradual erosion of coherence – the slow collapse of awareness into habit, fear or denial. Within systems of care, this erosion often unfolds beneath the surface, long before it becomes visible through crises or measurable through statistics.

Referring to this sphere as the 'dark' side does not imply malevolence. The word 'dark' here means that which is not yet illuminated by awareness – the territory of the unknown, the unseen or the unacknowledged. Darkness in this sense is neither negative nor shameful. It is the fertile ground in which renewal begins once light is brought to it.

The Disintegration Sphere reveals how coherence unravels through its four interdependent dynamics – shadows, misery, suffering and entrenchment. Each represents a different expression of distortion, disconnection or strain within a system – and each, when engaged consciously, offers a path to regeneration rather than collapse.

A healthy relationship with these dynamics does not mean escaping them, but learning to engage them truthfully and responsibly.

Shadows – Distortions and misalignments

Shadows are the unseen distortions that form when good intentions become disconnected from truth. In a healthy relationship with shadows, individuals and systems stay open to feedback and willing to see what has been hidden. A practitioner who invites peer review or a leader who welcomes critique is illuminating shadows rather than defending them. Awareness turns distortion into data, restoring coherence through humility and reflection.

Misery – The spectrum of discomfort to adversity

Misery refers to the broad continuum of hardship – from daily stress and fatigue to crisis and catastrophe. A healthy relationship with misery means recognising it as information, not as identity. Rather than avoiding discomfort or denying strain, a system listens to it as feedback. For example, when practitioners acknowledge emotional exhaustion instead of hiding it behind professionalism, they create the opportunity for genuine repair. When this happens, misery becomes a messenger for recalibration, not a mark of failure.

Suffering – The subjective and intersubjective experience of misery

Suffering is how sentient beings experience misery – internally and relationally. It is the human face of disintegration. A healthy relationship with suffering means being present to it without being consumed by it. In healthcare, this could look like practitioners who remain compassionate in the presence of pain rather than emotionally numbing themselves. Systemically, it means acknowledging collective distress and responding with empathy and structure rather than denial or avoidance. Suffering, when met consciously, deepens wisdom and restores compassion to the system.

Entrenchment – The edge of collapse

Entrenchment arises when rigidity replaces reflection – when systems, relationships or individuals defend dysfunction rather than transform it. A healthy relationship with entrenchment recognises it as a threshold moment – a signal that transformation is both necessary and possible. When a hospital acknowledges that its bureaucracy has become unsustainable and chooses reform over resistance, entrenchment becomes the doorway to renewal. It is at the point of almost breaking that systems rediscover their capacity to evolve.

Seen this way, the Disintegration Sphere is not the realm of failure, but of *revelation*. It is where the unseen becomes visible and the rigid becomes fluid. It is not the absence of light, but the invitation to bring light to what has been neglected. When engaged with awareness, courage and humility, the so-called 'dark' side of care becomes the crucible through which coherence is reborn.

The Modulation Sphere – The flow of responsiveness

Where integrity provides stability and disintegration reveals fracture, modulation represents movement – the capacity of a system to remain alive through change. In healthcare, modulation is the art of responsiveness – the ability to adapt without losing coherence, to evolve without abandoning purpose.

Sustainability in the context of care is not achieved by controlling change, but by engaging with it consciously. A healthcare system that cannot bend will break. One that bends without structure will lose form. Modulation is the rhythm between these extremes – the living pulse that keeps coherence dynamic rather than rigid.

The Modulation Sphere expresses this rhythm through its four causal qualities: patience, tolerance, adaptability and surrender. Together they determine whether a healthcare system responds to tension constructively or collapses beneath its weight.

Patience – The space for understanding

Patience allows a system to hold tension without resorting to premature action. In the complex realm of healthcare, it is the pause that prevents panic – the willingness to observe before intervening.

Impatient systems chase results at the cost of reflection, mistaking activity for progress. In contrast, patient systems allow insight to mature and trust that meaningful change emerges through understanding, not haste.

Tolerance – The strength to withstand discomfort

Tolerance is the system's ability to endure contradiction, uncertainty and discomfort without resorting to suppression or reaction. In healthcare, it is the capacity to face moral complexity, competing needs and human imperfection without collapsing into blame or fatigue.

When tolerance is absent, systems become fragile and reactive. But when present, it allows compassion to coexist with accountability, and reform to coexist with respect.

Adaptability – The capacity to evolve coherently

Adaptability is the system's ability to recalibrate in response to change without losing its structural integrity. In healthcare, this means embracing innovation, policy reform and evolving social needs while staying anchored to the deeper purpose of care.

Rigid systems resist adaptation and eventually become obsolete, while chaotic systems adapt reactively and lose coherence. In contrast, sustainable healthcare systems evolve intelligently, discerning what must change and what must remain as is.

Surrender – The wisdom of alignment

Surrender is the capacity to yield to what is real without resignation. In healthcare, surrender means trusting truth more than control – allowing the evidence of lived experience, not ideology, to guide reform.

Systems that cannot surrender cling to what once worked, mistaking familiarity for safety. However, systems that willingly surrender recognise when the form must change to preserve the essence.

Through patience, tolerance, adaptability and surrender, coherence remains alive within healthcare systems. Modulation transforms tension into rhythm, allowing care to remain responsive, humane and whole amid the inevitability of change.

The Architectonic Sphere – The design of conscious systems

If integrity forms the heart of coherence, disintegration its shadow, and modulation its rhythm, then the Architectonic Sphere provides its moral compass – the framework through which consciousness becomes design.

In healthcare, this is where values, awareness and ethics crystallise into policies, institutions and culture. It is where the moral and systemic architecture of care takes visible form.

The Architectonic Sphere reveals how societies organise their collective awareness into living systems. Its four causal forces – meta-awareness, systemic integrity, sustained effectiveness and normativity – determine whether the structure serves life or subjugates it.

Meta-awareness – The awareness of awareness itself

Meta-awareness is the system's capacity to observe itself. In healthcare, it is the ability of practitioners, leaders and institutions to reflect on their own assumptions and recognise how prevailing narratives shape behaviour and outcomes.

In the language of the metacontent discourse[106] and its Nested Theory of Sense-making, meta-awareness represents the upper layers of reflection – the capacity to step outside immediate content and perceive the meta-content that informs perception, policy and practice. It is the awareness of the stories, mental models and paradigms through which a system interprets itself.

Without meta-awareness, ideology hardens into dogma. Policies are repeated without question and procedures replace purpose. However, with meta-awareness, reform becomes renewal and learning becomes self-corrective.

When healthcare systems cultivate meta-awareness, they evolve consciously. They remain humble in the face of complexity, aware that medicine is not just a science of treatment, but a mirror of meaning.

Systemic integrity – The coherence of the whole

Systemic integrity reflects the degree to which a system's purpose, structure, behaviour and outcomes remain coherently aligned. In healthcare, it is not limited to moral virtue or professional ethics. It concerns whether the entire architecture of care operates in integrity with its stated purpose.

When purpose and practice drift apart, fragmentation sets in. Protocols multiply, communication falters and bureaucracy replaces coherence. The result is not necessarily unethical behaviour, but systemic incoherence – a misalignment between what the system claims to serve and what it structurally sustains.

A healthcare system with systemic integrity is one where each layer – from policy to patient care – functions in a rightful relationship to the whole, ensuring that design, decision and delivery reinforce one another. Integrity in this sense is dynamic, not dogmatic; it evolves with changing needs while remaining anchored in coherence. When

---

106 Tashvir, A. 2024 *Metacontent – The intellectual Substrates for Sense-making*. Engenesis Publications: Sydney.

systemic integrity prevails, trust, adaptability and sustainability arise naturally – not as outcomes to be enforced, but as the lived expression of a system that knows why it exists and acts accordingly.

Sustained effectiveness – Longevity through learning

Sustained effectiveness is the capacity of a system to endure by evolving. It is the ability to learn without losing essence – to adapt methods while preserving meaning.

A healthcare system that measures success only in quarterly metrics or short-term outcomes loses sight of its moral horizon. True effectiveness is generational: it measures continuity of care, the transmission of wisdom, and the resilience of trust.

When systems stop learning, they begin dying – even if their machinery still runs. In contrast, sustainable systems renew themselves continuously, integrating experience into wiser forms of practice.

Normativity – The moral architecture of sustainability

All coherence rests upon normativity – a society's living conception of what is right, good and worthy. In healthcare, it defines what a community believes it owes to human life. A civilisation that regards health as a public service naturally organises care inclusively, while one that treats it as a commodity divides access by privilege.

Normativity establishes the invisible *ought-to-be* that shapes every policy and decision. When it erodes, systems drift into moral relativism – efficient perhaps, but empty at the core. Ethics is not decoration. It is the architecture of coherence itself.

Normativity reveals how faithfully a system's structures embody its stated values. In healthcare, it asks whether the ethical principles proclaimed at the top – compassion, dignity and equity – are truly reflected in the daily actions of those on the front line. When intention and implementation diverge, dissonance spreads – rules multiply, trust erodes and bureaucracy fills the space once held by purpose.

A system achieves normative coherence not through uniformity, but through alignment – when every layer, from policymaker to practitioner, moves in rhythm with the same moral compass. When normativity prevails, coherence becomes the invisible scaffolding of care.

When meta-awareness, systemic integrity, sustained effectiveness and normativity align, structure becomes wisdom. Institutions serve life rather than image, and systems act as extensions of consciousness rather than instruments of control. Through the Architectonic Sphere, sustainability becomes visible – not as ideology, but as design in service of meaning.

Integrity beyond the 'isms'

Across all four spheres, one truth prevails: authentic sustainability transcends ideology because it is grounded in ontology. A healthcare system may call itself free, fair or universal, yet if its intention, trust, sovereignty and Being are fragmented, it will disintegrate regardless of its political or economic model.

When shadows are acknowledged, misery understood and entrenchment released, disintegration becomes renewal. When patience, tolerance, adaptability and surrender are cultivated, modulation becomes evolution. When meta-awareness, systemic integrity, sustained effectiveness and normativity align, structure becomes wisdom.

When coherence prevails in this way, ideology dissolves into essence. What remains is a civilisation that cares, not because it is instructed to, but because it remembers what it means to be human.

The human element – The role of Being in systemic care

Every structure, no matter how sophisticated, is an extension of the consciousness that created it. Therefore, the sustainability of any healthcare system is inseparable from the state of being of those who participate in it – practitioners, policymakers, leaders and citizens alike.

No policy can sustain what the collective Being of a society refuses to uphold. Where there is integrity in people, coherence emerges in systems. However, where distortion in people prevails, fragmentation multiplies in the institutions those people inhabit.

The Being Framework[107] provides a lens through which this dynamic can be understood. It reveals that every individual expresses a blend of healthy and unhealthy ways of being – patterns that either foster coherence or quietly corrode it.

When healthcare practitioners embody constructive ways of being such as authenticity, compassion, vulnerability, integrity and responsibility, coherence breathes through every interaction. Even amid constraint, their presence restores trust and meaning. But when destructive ways of being dominate, expressed as apathy, pride, entitlement, deceit or cynicism, dysfunction becomes inevitable.

A healthcare practitioner who performs without presence, a citizen who demands without stewardship or a leader who governs without sincerity each contributes to systemic decay. The state of being, therefore, is not a private affair; it is a public determinant of coherence.

Every act of care, every policy and every interaction carries an invisible moral vibration. It either strengthens or weakens the system's ethical architecture. A society filled with entitled citizens will always require more regulation. But a society grounded in responsible citizens will self-regulate.

This is why reform efforts that focus solely on structure fail repeatedly. They attempt to correct symptoms without transforming the source – the collective Being of those within the greater system, including the citizens reliant on it. True sustainability arises not when systems are optimised, but when people who inhabit and engage with them are transformed.

In every act of healing, the Being of the caregiver precedes the act itself. A practitioner grounded in authenticity transmits coherence through presence alone. Their words, gestures and silences carry

---

107 Tashvir, A. 2021 *BEING – The Source of Power*. Engenesis Publications: Sydney.

restorative power. Conversely, one operating from fear, resentment or fatigue may perform flawlessly according to protocol, yet leave patients unseen.

The same principle applies to leadership. A leader's Being sets the moral tone of the entire system. A leader anchored in integrity and vulnerability infuses the organisation with trust and responsibility. But one driven by control or vanity propagates the same distortions throughout their hierarchy. Therefore, a system can never transcend the consciousness of its leaders. Ultimately, sustainability depends on the inner development of those who sustain it.

The Being Framework is not merely psychological; it is ontological. Psychology studies the mind – thoughts, emotions and behaviour – often treating them as phenomena to be managed or improved. In contrast, ontology concerns the nature of existence itself – the deeper structures from which thought, emotion and behaviour arise. Where psychology seeks to understand what a person thinks or feels, ontology inquires into the state of being that gives rise to those thoughts and feelings. The Being Framework operates at this ontological level, revealing that sustainable transformation cannot occur by adjusting surface behaviour alone. Instead, it requires coherence at the level of existence itself.

The Being Framework also links personal evolution to systemic health. A society that invests in cultivating conscious practitioners, leaders and citizens is, in essence, investing in its own sustainability. For it is not technology or policy that preserves coherence, but the human quality behind them. When the Being of individuals is aligned with sincerity, empathy and purpose, the system self-corrects. But when it is distorted by fear, convenience or pride, no reform can save it.

Ultimately, coherence within people must root itself in coherence beyond them. The inner architecture of Being finds stability only when it is anchored in something deeper than itself – in meaning. Just as Being shapes how systems are sustained, meaning determines *why* they are sustained. From here, we move from ontology at the personal level to ontology at the systemic level, the realm of *Minalogy* – where value, purpose and dignity become the moral foundations of sustainable care.

Meaning, Minalogy and the ontology of dignity

At the deepest level of every sustainable system lies an invisible architecture – the moral and axiological foundation that gives intention its orientation and conduct its integrity. Without it, even the most coherent flow of processes eventually collapses into emptiness.

This foundation is meaning, and the discipline that studies its structure and dynamics, as we have learned, is **Minalogy** – the systematic study of how meaning, value and purpose cohere across realities.

Meaning is not merely psychological or cultural; it is ontological. It defines the relationship between existence and significance – between what *is* and what *matters*. It answers not only *what* we do, but *why* it is worth doing. When this deep, existential meaning (*Mina*) and its expression become distorted, every downstream layer – intention, conduct and outcomes – loses coherence.

The minalogical dimension is the moral root of sustainability. It determines the ethical realism upon which systems of care, education, governance and economy are built. A civilisation's conception of meaning reveals what it believes about the human being. If it perceives a person merely as a collection of cells, transactions or economic units, then care becomes conditional, mechanistic and disposable. But if it perceives human beings as carriers of inherent dignity and reflections of consciousness, then care becomes sacred.

Dignity, in this sense, is not granted by law; it is recognised as an ontological truth. It asserts that to sustain life is not a utility, but a moral act. Therefore, a sustainable healthcare system is not one that simply prolongs existence, but one that affirms the *worth* of existence itself.

From this vantage, sustainability becomes inseparable from moral realism. Ethics cannot be reduced to preference or cultural habit. It must rest upon a coherent understanding of what is good, right and worthy across time and circumstance. When this understanding is lost, relativism corrodes meaning, and systems drift into performative morality – acting as if they care while serving convenience.

Minalogy restores coherence to this moral architecture. It situates meaning, not as sentiment but as structure – the living logic that binds intention to truth. It reminds us that sustainability is not the endurance of function, but the continuity of significance.

In the context of healthcare, this distinction is profound. A sustainable healthcare system is not one that merely provides medical attention. It is one that expresses reverence for the mystery and worth of life. It treats healing as a sacred act, not a commodity. It honours both science and soul, efficiency and empathy. Such a system functions not out of obligation, but out of recognition – the recognition that life, in all its forms, possesses inherent value.

Where meaning is shallow, healthcare systems become transactional. Where meaning is profound, they become transcendent.

Ultimately, the sustainability of care – and of civilisation itself – depends on whether meaning is anchored in moral truth or diluted by convenience. When the essence of life is revered, coherence follows naturally. But when it is reduced to utility, coherence dissolves.

When meaning fractures, systems lose their orientation and drift from their moral centre. To restore coherence, they must not only rediscover what is worthy, but also learn how to return to it. This is the work of the **Reconstructive Ontology of Sustainability (ROS)** – the disciplined process of renewal.

The dynamics of renewal – ROS in the context of healthcare

If the Unified Ontology of Systemic Integrity (UOSI) reveals the anatomy of coherence and the Systemic Subversion Cycle (SSC) exposes its pathology – how coherence erodes and dysfunction becomes systemic – the Reconstructive Ontology of Sustainability (ROS) offers the pathway to renewal by charting the path of return. This is the disciplined process through which systems realign with their ontological centre.

In the context of healthcare, ROS begins with truth-telling: the willingness of leaders and practitioners to see fragmentation not as failure, but as *feedback*.

To recap, the ROS process unfolds in four recursive movements:

1. **Recognition** – Seeing the fracture clearly without blame and understanding how distortion became normalised.
2. **Reconnection** – Returning to the founding meaning (*Mina*) and authentic intention of the system – why it exists, whom it serves and what it honours.
3. **Realignment** – Redesigning structures, relationships and decision-making processes so that purpose, policy and practice once again mirror one another.
4. **Reintegration** – Embedding coherence into conduct, allowing the system to self-correct through continuous feedback and reflection.

Within this movement, the **CCC Model (Content → Clarity → Conduct)** operates as ROS's living mechanism. It ensures that insight does not stagnate in reflection, but flows into renewed action – that awareness matures into design, and design into conduct.

Applied to healthcare, this reconstructive movement transforms reform into regeneration. Rather than endlessly restructuring budgets or departments, leaders engage in ontological renewal – re-anchoring care systems in their deepest purpose. Hospitals become places not merely of treatment, but of coherence. Policies cease to be reactive fixes and instead become moral expressions of understanding.

When viewed together, the SSC, the UOSI and ROS reveal the full living cycle of sustainability:

- The SSC shows how coherence decays through distortion, denial and fragmentation.
- The UOSI reveals the structural anatomy of coherence itself – the 16 systemic qualities that make integrity, adaptability and meaning observable and measurable within any system.
- ROS shows how coherence regenerates through recognition, reconnection and reintegration.

Every sustainable system must understand all three – how coherence unravels, what sustains it and how it can be restored. To heal without understanding how illness forms is to repeat it; to diagnose without knowing what health consists of is to misjudge it; and to see what is broken without reconstructing it is to despair. In this light, healthcare becomes not only the service of healing, but also a metaphor for how all systems can rediscover coherence and renew life from within.

ROS shows us how systems rediscover coherence. Yet restoration is not the end of the journey. For coherence to be sustained, it must become embodied and repeatable through time. The **Fulfilment Pyramid** illustrates this living continuity – how renewed meaning flows through intention into practice, and practice into enduring structures of care.

The Fulfilment Pyramid in healthcare – Sustaining intention across systems of care

In healthcare, as in all living systems, intention does not emerge fully formed. It begins as something subtle – a longing, a restlessness, a felt sense that something must change. Desire provides the initial movement; but without refinement, it can scatter into distraction or be captured by ego, fear or convenience.

For intention to mature, it must pass through a process of clarification – anchored in meaning, tested by coherence and expressed through conduct. This developmental movement is referred to in this body of work as the Flow of Coherence – the dynamic through which purpose travels from its origin in meaning to its embodiment in action.

The Fulfilment Pyramid reveals this flow in structural form. It shows how intention must be developed, enacted and sustained if it is to become durable and real across time. In healthcare, this matters because care cannot remain an abstraction. It must be held in practice under stress, repeated across teams, protected in policy and carried forward across generations. Without that, the system would drift into performance and appearance, and citizens experience that drift as abandonment.

To recap, the Fulfilment Pyramid unfolds across three interdependent dimensions:

- **The Developmental Dimension** – How intention is formed and stabilised in authentic meaning.
- **The Phenomenological Dimension** – How that intention is enacted through conduct, integrity and effectiveness.
- **The Relational Dimension** – How coherence is structurally sustained across teams, institutions, budgets, governance and time.

These are not 'soft culture' on one side and 'operations' on the other. They are the architecture of fulfilment itself. In the context of healthcare, when any one dimension is missing, we see what so many modern systems of care reveal: sincere declarations that never result in lived reality.

Just as importantly, these three dimensions correspond directly to the dynamics of breakdown mapped in the Systemic Subversion Cycle (SSC), and to the path of reconstruction mapped in the Reconstructive Ontology of Sustainability (ROS). When a healthcare system is in distortion, escalation, fracture or entrenchment, it is almost always because one or more dimensions of fulfilment have collapsed. And when that same system finds its way back to coherence, it is doing the work of ROS – recognition, reconnection, realignment and reintegration – to restore these dimensions and bring the intention of care back into embodied practice.

Let's examine each dimension in the context of the healthcare system:

The Developmental Dimension – Forming and stabilising intention in care

The Developmental Dimension asks the most honest question in healthcare: *What is the real intention of this system?* Not the slogan. Not the press release. Not the political promise. The actual intention.

In a coherent healthcare system, intention is not assumed; it is developed, clarified and anchored in meaning (*Mina*) before being allowed to steer policy, protocol or funding. This is crucial, because if the developmental work is shallow, the entire system will be built on convenience, optics or fear rather than truth.

In healthcare, the Developmental Dimension is where a society – and the institutions through which it cares for the vulnerable – defines its moral centre in explicit terms. It is where the system sincerely answers:

- Why do we exist?
- Who are we here to serve?
- What does dignity actually mean in practice?
- What are we unwilling to trade off, even under pressure?

If these answers are not made conscious, the system drifts. We see it everywhere: *'patient-centred care'* on the wall, but throughput targets in the meeting; *'care for all'* in the charter, but quiet rationing in practice; *'wellbeing of staff matters'*, while burnout is normalised as professional maturity. That is developmental failure – the failure to stabilise intention in meaning before it enters policy and process.

When intention is underdeveloped or performative, the SSC's first phase – **distortion** – ignites. The original purpose of care is quietly replaced by surrogate motives: funding optics; waiting-list metrics; political defensiveness; legal risk minimisation; and institutional reputation. The words remain noble, but the living compass has already shifted.

In contrast, when the Developmental Dimension is healthy, intention in care is grounded in authentic meaning and articulated transparently. The system can say, without posturing:

> 'We exist to uphold dignity in the face of human vulnerability. We will prioritise preserving life, relieving suffering and protecting the worth of each person. We refuse to become an industry of throughput.'

From there, that intention is allowed to cascade through policy design, clinical standards, triage logic, workforce training, budget priorities and even the way a receptionist greets a frightened family at 2 am in an emergency department.

This is the first test of fulfilment in healthcare: *Is the intention that supposedly guides this system actually anchored in meaning – or is it already entangled with vanity, self-protection and institutional survival?* If it is the latter, the collapse has already begun.

When leaders in care return to that original meaning – through **recognition** ('we have drifted'), **reconnection** ('this is why we exist') and **realignment** ('we are redesigning around that meaning') – they are doing the work of ROS. That is healthcare's pathway out of distortion and towards renewal. Therefore, authentic developmental work is the first act of reconstruction.

The Phenomenological Dimension – From intention to conduct in the act of care

The Phenomenological Dimension is where intention stops being a statement and becomes a way of showing up. This is the lived translation of intention into conduct – the moment where care either becomes coherent and humane or collapses into performance, fatigue and quiet moral injury.

In healthcare, this is the domain of:

- The clinician at the bedside.
- The nurse in triage in the 14th hour of a double shift.
- The surgeon who chooses to take her time to explain a procedure in detail to a terrified family.
- The community health worker who remains the only point of trust for someone failed by institutions.

Phenomenologically, fulfilment is not measured in procedural completion alone ('the test was ordered' or 'the form was filed'). It is measured as **coherence**: *Did the way we acted honour the intention we claimed? Did we preserve dignity? Did we act with presence, responsibility and care? Did effectiveness serve meaning or replace it?*

This is where the Being Framework is critical. Systems do not deliver care – *people* do. And people do not express policy. They express their state of being.

Constructive ways of being like authenticity, responsibility, compassion, presence, courage and commitment generate coherence even in strained systems. A practitioner who slows down for 90 seconds to see the human being in front of them restores a kind of trust that no policy can manufacture. That is coherence transmitted through Being.

In contrast, destructive ways of being such as entitlement, indifference, cynicism, superiority, resignation, defensiveness and performative compliance generate incoherence, even in well-funded systems. A practitioner who is technically excellent but emotionally absent leaves suffering unacknowledged. A manager who operates from vanity rather than stewardship poisons entire teams. That is fragmentation transmitted through Being.

When constructive Being is present, integrity and effectiveness align. Care is delivered with both competence and compassion. However, when destructive Being dominates, the system enters **escalation** – the second SSC phase. Pressure rises, presence wanes and everyone retreats into metrics and risk language because it feels safer than the truth.

Here, integrity and effectiveness become the two guardrails of phenomenological fulfilment:

- **Integrity** means the conduct of the system reflects the intention grounded in meaning. 'We said we honour dignity and we are actually honouring dignity.'
- **Effectiveness** means that conduct produces real outcomes: wounds heal, communication clarifies and suffering lessens.

Without integrity, effectiveness becomes cruelty. Without effectiveness, integrity turns sentimental. Both are common failure modes in modern healthcare. When this breakdown occurs, **fracture** emerges – the third phase of the *Systemic Subversion Cycle (SSC)*. Practitioners stop trusting leadership, leadership stops trusting practitioners, and patients stop trusting the institution. Each begins to operate for survival rather than service.

At this point, coherence cannot be restored through process correction alone – it requires conscious reconstruction. The **Reconstructive Ontology of Sustainability (ROS)** must be intentionally activated to begin the work of renewal. When someone has the courage to say, *'This isn't who we said we are,'* that act becomes **recognition** – the first movement of reconstruction. When followed by **reconnection** (*'This is why we exist'*) and realignment (*'We will change processes, workloads, staffing, escalation paths and communication norms to reflect that'*), phenomenological coherence can be restored.

Therefore, professional burnout is not just an HR issue, but an ontological indicator – evidence that intention can no longer flow into conduct without moral injury. What appears as a staffing crisis is, in truth, a coherence crisis.

The Relational Dimension – Sustaining coherence through structure, rhythm and stewardship

Even when intention is clear and conduct is sincere, coherence will not last unless it is structurally held. That is the work of the Relational Dimension.

The Relational Dimension asks: *Can this care system sustain coherence over time, across teams, across governments, across budget cycles and leadership changes – or is it dependent on a few heroic individuals who will eventually collapse?*

This is where fulfilment becomes systemic rather than episodic. It shows up in:

- Staffing models that don't burn people out to the point where compassion dies.
- Escalation pathways that protect rather than punish truth-tellers.
- Budgets that reflect what dignified care actually costs.
- Governance that shields clinical judgement from political optics.
- Alignment across disciplines so that primary care, hospitals and community services act in concert, not competition.

The Relational Dimension is oriented by **sustained effectiveness** and **normativity.** Sustained effectiveness means the system can keep delivering care without degrading itself. It has feedback loops, rituals and rhythms that preserve quality and trust. Normativity is the moral architecture – the living sense of 'what we owe each other'. It defines what human beings deserve and which lines cannot be crossed.

Without a healthy Relational Dimension, systems enter **entrenchment** – the fourth SSC phase – where dysfunction becomes identity. Chronic understaffing is rationalised, delays are renamed 'process' and people stop believing change is possible. When this happens, incoherence becomes culture.

This is also where most reform fails – because it tries to fix processes without restoring relational scaffolding. Without sustained effectiveness and normativity, the system digests reform and nothing changes.

When consciously held, this dimension is where ROS's final movement – **reintegration** – becomes real. It manifests as:

- Rostering rules that make safe staffing non-negotiable.
- Mental-health support being treated as infrastructure, not charity.
- Escalation channels that feed directly into policy.
- Cross-sector planning that replaces competition with coherence.
- Explicit 'guardrails of dignity' that cannot be bargained away.

This is not project management. This is the relational scaffolding that lets intention live across time. When missing, systems die while appearing to function. But when present, sustainability becomes a lived property of care itself.

Fulfilment in healthcare is not 'Did we deliver a service?' It is: *Did our stated intention – grounded in meaning and anchored in dignity – travel all the way into conduct, and did that conduct gain the structures it needs to survive pressure, politics, fatigue and time?*

The Fulfilment Pyramid allows us to see and assess this. It shows where coherence is failing to carry, where intention has stopped travelling, and where reconstruction must begin.

A healthcare system does not become sustainable through ideological argument. It becomes sustainable when:

- Intention is re-grounded in meaning and made explicit.
- Conduct is brought back into integrity and effectiveness through the quality of Being.
- Scaffolding is built to hold coherence through stress, time and hierarchy.

That is fulfilment in care. That is what it looks like when care becomes sustainable, not merely available.

Conclusion

At its deepest layer, sustainability is neither a technical phenomenon nor a managerial process. It is the continuity of meaning – the enduring coherence between what a civilisation holds as true, how it intends to act, and how it conducts itself through time.

Nowhere is this more evident than in the systems through which we care for life itself. A healthcare system is not sustained by infrastructure alone, but by the integrity of meaning that animates it – the moral rhythm between why it heals, how it serves, and what it becomes.

All sustainable systems share one defining characteristic: they align meaning, intention and conduct into a coherent moral rhythm. When this alignment holds, life flourishes. When it fractures, systems decay – no matter how efficient or well-funded they appear.

This can be expressed as a simple yet profound ontological equation:

$$\text{Meaning} \times \text{Intention} \times \text{Conduct} = \text{Coherence}$$
$$\text{Coherence} \times \text{Time} = \text{Sustainability}$$

Meaning provides direction. Intention provides movement. Conduct gives form. When these dimensions are congruent, coherence becomes self-sustaining. But when even one collapses, the whole system begins to unravel. A society may possess abundant medical knowledge, resources and technology, yet still decline if it loses meaning. It may reform endlessly, yet repeat the same patterns if its intentions are not anchored in truth. It may act with urgency, but without coherence, it will exhaust itself in the name of progress.

Sustainability in healthcare, therefore, is not achieved through scale, regulation or innovation alone. It arises from harmony between the inner and outer, between consciousness and conduct, between the moral and the mechanical. In this sense, sustainability is a spiritual act disguised as systemic design – an agreement between Being and Becoming, between purpose and practice. When a healthcare system's meaning is anchored in truth, its intentions serve coherence and its conduct expresses integrity. But when meaning becomes distorted, intention is corrupted, and conduct becomes a parody of purpose.

The greatest threat to sustainable healthcare is not scarcity, but forgetting what it means to be human and what truly matters – why we care, why we heal and why we serve. Remembering restores coherence. It reconnects care to purpose and purpose to Being. To sustain is to remember meaning through time – to hold coherence across generations so that what is built continues to serve life rather than merely perpetuate itself. A sustainable healthcare system does not exist to survive; it exists to uphold significance. It is not about permanence, but continuity of purpose.

Although explored here through the lens of healthcare, this same logic applies to every domain of civilisation – education, governance, economy and the environment. The Authentic Sustainability Framework offers a way to reveal where coherence endures and where it has fractured, across any system that shapes human life. For wherever meaning, intention and conduct fall out of alignment, sustainability begins to erode. And wherever they reunite, renewal becomes possible.

In the end, sustainability – in healthcare and beyond – is not a destination. It is *a way of being*.

EPILOGUE

The Bright Horizon – Humanity Beyond Sustainabilism

There comes a moment in every long journey when the horizon shifts. What once appeared as a distant possibility begins to take shape, not as a mirage, but as a landscape we can genuinely walk towards. This chapter is that moment. It is not about methods, models or frameworks – though they have been our faithful companions throughout. It is about the future that becomes possible when those methods are lived, when the frameworks are embodied, and when sustainability ceases to be a concept we chase and becomes a reality we inhabit.

In this final chapter, we lift our gaze to the wider horizon – exploring what humanity beyond sustainabilism might look like. When the principles explored throughout this work are not merely practised but lived, when islands of coherence begin to connect across disciplines, cultures and generations, a different kind of future becomes possible. Not one managed by control or fear, but shaped by wisdom, trust and the quiet, enduring rhythm of regeneration.

Leaving sustainabilism behind

For decades, the world has been weighed down by what we have called *sustainabilism* – the performative version of sustainability. It has filled shelves with reports, flooded organisations with dashboards, and reduced care into targets, audits and slogans. Sustainabilism has sought to manage life as though it were a balance sheet, stripping meaning from words like renewal and integrity until they rang hollow, emptied of their original power.

But this is not another critique of systems. It is an unveiling of the deeper coherence beneath them – a call to remember what sustainability was always meant to serve.

We now stand at the threshold of something different. Humanity beyond sustainabilism is not a world that abandons structure; it is a world that reclaims structure with *integrity*. It is a civilisation that no longer performs sustainability but *is* sustainability – where Being, intention, meaning and overall systemic integrity align so deeply that regeneration becomes second nature, woven into every relationship and institution.

This moment marks a turning point in our collective evolution: from performance to presence; from control to stewardship; and from sustainabilism to authentic sustainability.

The vision moving forward

Picture this:

> A child in a rural village, a leader in a bustling metropolis, a farmer on the land and a scientist in a lab – all participating in the same conversation. Not about slogans, but about stewardship. Policies crafted not to appease markets or ideologies, but to serve life itself. An economy that measures wealth not in consumption, but in flourishing; not in extraction, but in renewal. Communities where diversity is not managed, but is celebrated as part of coherence – where disagreement does not fracture, but strengthens the collective.

This is not a world free of challenges. Floods will still come, markets will still shift and conflicts will still emerge. But it is a world where challenge itself becomes regenerative, because systems are designed to adapt, modulate and transform challenge into growth.

This is not a utopia sketched on paper, but a return to reverence – a world where stewardship replaces control and systems exist in fidelity to life itself. It is the natural consequence of systems that sustain their integrity. When trust is lived, when intention is an authentic expression of deep existential meaning (*Mina*), and when Being is aligned, coherence ripples outward until it becomes the norm in our culture, economy and society. Such a world begins not with declarations, but with coherence lived at every scale.

This horizon emerges when we stop fighting shadows with more shadows and instead bring light to the roots of dysfunction. It is not achieved through force, but through coherence – the quiet power of alignment that restores meaning to our collective life.

At the heart of this vision is not a model or a policy. It is Being. Systems do not sustain themselves; the beings within them do. Humanity beyond sustainabilism is not a political future, but an ontological one, shaped by the state of being we each bring to the systems we inhabit.

Authentic sustainability at the scale of humanity is nothing more, and nothing less, than billions of people choosing to live in alignment with integrity, sovereignty and care. This is why our journey began with Being, and why it ends here as well.

The Unified Ontology of Systemic Integrity, the Nested Theory of Sense-making and Minalogy all converge on a simple truth: systemic renewal is the outward expression of inner coherence. A civilisation becomes coherent only to the extent that its people are.

Being is the seed of every sustainable system. It's the invisible architecture from which coherence takes form. When individuals embody integrity, humility and compassion, those qualities permeate the structures they touch. But when fear, pride or indifference prevail, those distortions replicate through policy, leadership and culture.

Therefore, the future of sustainability does not depend on how much we know, but on who and how we are being.

From blueprint to horizon

Your Authentic Sustainability Blueprint is not just a personal plan. It is a thread in a much larger tapestry. When lived collectively, these blueprints weave together into a civilisation where sustainability is not a department or a project, but a way of existing.

The horizon is not built by declarations. It is built through the quiet consistency of ordinary choices made with extraordinary coherence:

- A company redesigns its value chain, not for compliance, but for care.
- A community chooses dialogue over division.
- A family aligns its wealth and wellbeing with long-term regeneration.
- An individual chooses integrity over convenience in a quiet, unseen moment.

Each decision becomes a small architecture of coherence. This is how the tapestry is woven – one deliberate thread at a time. Such choices may seem insignificant, yet collectively they are the living proof that philosophy can transform reality. They demonstrate that coherence is not a theory but a practice, not an aspiration, but a way of being made visible through action.

Translating coherence into practice

Authentic sustainability begins with observation, but matures through reflection. Before applying the framework at scale, it is vital to recognise where coherence – or its absence – already lives within your current context, whether that be your organisation, workplace, community or personal life.

These reflections are not diagnostic checkboxes, but invitations for awareness. They are meant to orient you towards the ontological centre of the systems you engage with – to see beneath activity and outcome to the alignment between meaning, intention and conduct.

A coherent practitioner, policymaker or leader does not impose order but cultivates it. They understand that sustainability is not maintained by control, but by coherence. Their task is not to command alignment, but to embody it – to ensure that integrity flows through relationships, structures and transitions alike. In this way, leadership becomes stewardship and coherence becomes culture.

Seen in this context, leadership is not a position of control, but a practice of coherence. A leader's task is not to enforce alignment but to nurture it – to create conditions where meaning, intention and conduct flow congruently through the systems they influence.

In this ontology, leadership is where philosophy becomes practice. It is a form of stewardship that perceives the organisation as a living field rather than a machine. Dysfunction, in such a view, is rarely the fault of individuals, but the symptom of misaligned design, trust or purpose.

A coherent leader listens deeply to the rhythm of their system and responds with the regulating forces of modulation – patience, tolerance, adaptability and surrender – rather than panic, coercion or blame. In doing so, they embody the very qualities that sustain integrity through change.

In the context of sustainability, leadership is an act of attunement. It requires presence, humility and courage – the willingness to hold tension without collapse, to respond from integrity rather than fear, and to allow coherence to become not merely a concept, but a culture.

Ask yourself:

- Where do I notice patterns of dysfunction or fatigue repeating themselves despite surface-level solutions?
- Which quality within the Integrity Sphere – intention, trust, sovereignty or Being – feels most alive, and which one feels depleted or reactive?
- In moments of tension, do I respond with awareness and adaptability, or with defence and control?
- How does my relationship with vulnerability influence the reliability of my perception and decisions?

- If my organisation, team or community were to complete the Sustainability Profile today, what might it reveal about our collective coherence?
- What would reconstruction look like if guided by meaning rather than metrics?

Use these reflections not as critique, but as calibration. Coherence does not demand perfection; it requires sincerity. As you engage with these questions, you will begin to see that systems do not change because we fix them; they change because we begin to see them clearly.

Ultimately, sustainability is not a technique but a state of awareness: a living coherence moving through every design, decision and interaction. It invites each of us – leaders, practitioners and citizens alike – to participate as conscious stewards of systems that sustain life through integrity.

Scaling authentic sustainability – From individual to society

The same ontological architecture that governs coherence within a person also governs it within teams, organisations and societies. Systems differ in size and complexity, but not in essence. When coherence is cultivated at one level, it reverberates through all others, shaping how meaning, intention and conduct take form across the whole.

So, while sustainability begins with the individual, it does not end there. It is expressed through relationships, institutions and cultures that reflect the same structural integrity that first emerges within Being.

Micro – The individual

At the personal level, authentic sustainability begins in awareness. Through frameworks such as the Being Profile and the Fulfilment Pyramid, individuals learn to align their meaning, intention and conduct. Self-awareness becomes systemic awareness; how one leads the self determines how one participates in larger systems. Every deliberate act of integrity – however small or unseen – strengthens the coherence of the whole.

Meso – The collective

Within teams, organisations and communities, sustainability becomes a shared rhythm. The Sustainability Profile, ROS and the Authentic Sustainability Blueprint translate ontological principles into collective practice. At this scale, coherence turns into culture – a way of designing relationships, decision-making and governance that regenerates rather than extracts. Leadership becomes stewardship, performance becomes integrity in motion, and collaboration becomes the living expression of trust.

Macro – The society

At the civilisational level, sustainability becomes both a philosophical compass and a moral architecture, as discussed at length in the previous chapter with the healthcare example. It reframes governance, economics and education from control to coherence, recognising that systemic wellbeing cannot be legislated; it must be cultivated. When applied through education, policy-making and collective leadership, the Authentic Sustainability Framework becomes a regenerative structure for civilisation itself – one in which systems of care, commerce and culture evolve through the same ontological laws that govern the coherence of Being.

Across all three scales, one truth prevails: systems thrive when they align with integrity, meaning and Being. The coherence that begins within the individual extends outward through every structure we create, forming a continuum from self-awareness to systemic renewal. This is how sustainability scales – not by replication, but by resonance.

Walking towards the new horizon

Authentic sustainability is not a destination to arrive at, but a way of being to embody. What lies ahead is not certainty, but possibility – a possibility sustained by courage, humility and the willingness to shape systems that serve life rather than merely preserve themselves.

The work of the preceding pages was preparation – to offer an ontology that honours Being, a framework that sustains coherence, and a language through which awareness can become transformation. Yet the real work begins now – in the living expression of these ideas.

It begins in the way you speak in your next conversation, design the next policy or project, model integrity when no one is watching, and hold systems steady through modulation rather than control.

Every deliberate act of coherence, however ordinary it may seem, is a thread in a greater tapestry. Each moment of integrity contributes to the quiet architecture of renewal. The tapestry of a sustainable civilisation is not woven in boardrooms or declarations, but in daily choices made with awareness.

What we sustain, we sanctify. When meaning flows through intention and conduct, sustainability becomes the natural rhythm of life itself.

So, as you step beyond these pages, carry this with you. Sustainability is not found in policies or plans. It emerges through the way you live, in the systems you touch, and in the Being you embody. The horizon is already forming. Walk towards it with patience, integrity and courage.

In the end, what sustains us is not progress but coherence – the living rhythm between what we know, what we intend and how we act. Civilisations rise and fall by this rhythm, as do families, organisations and lives. Yet beneath the rise and fall, something endures: the pulse of meaning that calls us back to integrity. To sustain is to remember – to remember why we build, why we care, why we choose to serve life rather than merely survive it.

And from this remembrance arises hope – not the naive kind that denies difficulty, but the steady kind that endures through it. Hope born of coherence, humility and truth. Hope that knows renewal is possible because Being itself is regenerative.

When coherence becomes our way of being, sustainability ceases to be a task. It becomes a truth lived faithfully, humbly and together – the quiet continuity of meaning that carries humanity beyond sustainabilism into its next becoming.

APPENDIX

Authentic
Sustainability
Framework
White Paper

Background

This work was not conceived within a program nor confined to a single environment. Its roots stretch far deeper. It is grounded in years of philosophical inquiry, ontological investigation and reflection on the nature of human beings, systems and civilisation itself.

It evolved through observing organisations, institutions and societies – both thriving and collapsing – and through questioning why some endure with coherence while others fracture under pressure. It matured in dialogue with leaders, academics, entrepreneurs, policy-makers and ordinary people navigating real constraints and complexity.

It was shaped by lived experience: building ventures, supporting founders, guiding leaders and witnessing the gap between what many call 'sustainability' and what truly endures.

The frameworks in this book emerged first through contemplation, discernment and structured sense-making – long before any formal program existed. Practice did not give birth to the ideas. It was where they were tested, sharpened and strengthened. Programs and real-world engagements became crucibles in which philosophical clarity met lived reality, and each iteration revealed what was essential, what was insufficient, and what must evolve.

This background matters because the work you hold is neither theory imagined in isolation nor methodology reverse-engineered from workshops. It is the product of an integrated path – part philosophical, part empirical, part experiential – grounded in an unwavering commitment to understanding what sustains human systems and how we can steward them responsibly.

With this foundation established, the work entered periods of structured application and review, allowing theory and practice to inform – but not collapse into – one another. Each environment served a different purpose, and each revealed insights that strengthened the coherence, depth and usability of the frameworks.

This work stands at the intersection of philosophy, ontology, systems thinking and lived organisational practice, and is offered not as a method to follow, but as a lens through which to think, act and build.

Summary – How this Work was Developed

For readers seeking a concise overview of the methodology and development of this body of work, the following summary outlines its key elements and context.

What this work is

A coherent, practice-ready body of philosophy and tools for building authentically sustainable systems. It integrates:

- **Philosophical ontology** – Being Framework™, metacontent and its Nested Theory of Sense-making, Minalogy.
- **A unifying systemic framework** – The Authentic Sustainability Framework (ASF) and its core Unified Ontology of Systemic Integrity (UOSI).
- **Practical diagnostics and methods** – Sustainability Profile™, Systemic Subversion Cycle (SSC), Reconstructive Ontology of Sustainability (ROS) and the Fulfilment Pyramid.

The work aims to deliver a lens and pathway leaders can use to design, implement and refine systems that endure, beginning with who and how they are being.

Why it was built

- To move beyond 'sustainabilism' (performative, compliance-driven efforts) towards **authentic sustainability** (integrity-driven, lived, regenerative).
- To address recurring realities leaders face – reactivity rather than proactivity, burnout, fragile cultures, volatile revenue and fragmented execution.
- To ground sustainability in who we are being, how we make sense of things, and how integrity aggregates across people, teams and structures.

Where it came from

- Years of philosophical inquiry into human beings, systems and civilisation.
- Direct organisational practice – venture building, executive coaching and analysis of thriving and failing systems.
- A deliberate blend of philosophical depth and practical impact.

How it was developed

Two interwoven streams:

1. **Philosophical theorisation** – Clarifying first principles, ontological distinctions and systemic qualities.
2. **Practical application** – An evolutionary process based on iterative testing and refinement with leaders, teams and organisations.

This produced a body of work that is rigorous without detachment and practical without superficiality.

Program context

- Six program cycles involving 48 leaders representing various nationalities and cultures – founders, SME owners, managers and corporate team leaders.

- Each cycle combined conceptual input with live application to real business dilemmas.
- Structured note-taking, feedback loops, debriefs and interviews informed the evolution of the Authentic Sustainability Framework (ASF) and its refinement.
- Senior facilitators with corporate, entrepreneurial and coaching backgrounds ensured translation from concept to practice.

Outcome: Clearer language, stronger tools, repeatable methods for assessing and cultivating systemic integrity – the keys to authentic sustainability.

Ontometric data and practitioner dialogue

- ~5,000 Being Profile® assessments completed across multiple countries, industries and demographics.
- Anonymised practitioner dialogues with trained coaches revealed recurring patterns. **Convergent signal:** Many leaders and teams were trapped in reactivity and burnout. The root issue was ontological – ways of being, sense-making and meaning-making – not procedural.

Key tools and frameworks

- **Being Framework™** – A comprehensive model of 31 qualities of Being that shape performance, leadership, effectiveness and culture.
- **Metacontent and the Nested Theory of Sense-making** – A multilayered framework explaining how sense-making shapes coherent perception, decision-making and action.
- **Minalogy** – A philosophical discourse that defines purpose, clarifies value and identifies what is genuinely worth sustaining.
- **Unified Ontology of Systemic Integrity (UOSI)** – A systemic model comprising 16 interrelated qualities distributed across four spheres.

- **Sustainability Profile™** – An ontometric instrument that maps a system's relationship to the UOSI qualities and produces a Vulnerability Index for assessing coherence and fragility.
- **Systemic Subversion Cycle (SSC)** – A diagnostic model that reveals the recurring pathways through which systems drift into dysfunction, entrenchment and collapse.
- **Reconstructive Ontology of Sustainability (ROS)** – A regenerative framework that guides systemic renewal and realignment beyond critique, restoring coherence through conscious reconstruction.
- **Fulfilment Pyramid** – A developmental model that illustrates how intention matures into fulfilment through three interdependent dimensions: developmental (growth of capability and consciousness), phenomenological (awareness and lived experience) and relational (interaction and alignment with others). Together, these dimensions provide a practical blueprint for translating clarity of purpose into coherent action and realised outcomes – fulfilment as the lived result of aligned execution.

Methodology at a glance

Paradigmatic stance: Pragmatic, interpretive–constructivist, with a critical dimension.

Methods blended as appropriate:

- Philosophical ontology (conceptual development and coherence testing)
- Phenomenology (lived experience of leaders and teams)
- Adapted grounded-theory principles (inductive patterning from field data)
- Action-research cycles (six iterations)
- Interpretive case analysis (historical and contemporary examples)

Data sources: Session notes, debriefs, participant feedback, facilitator observations, reviewer input, follow-up interviews, comparative expert dialogues and cross-case studies.

Validity, transparency and confidence

Rigour was maintained through multiple complementary measures:

- **Triangulation** – Drawing on diverse data sources and perspectives.
- **Iterative refinement** – Recalibrating models and tools after each program cycle.
- **Practitioner review** – Incorporating critique from experienced executive coaches and external reviewers.
- **Longitudinal check** – Confirming continuity and applicability with returning participants.
- **Coherence testing** – Ensuring philosophical clarity aligned with observed systemic outcomes.
- **Privacy** – Analysing only aggregate patterns to protect participant confidentiality.

Confidence in the findings arises from three interrelated foundations:

- **Analytic generalisation** – Insights apply where ontological conditions align, rather than through statistical generalisation.
- **Practice validation** – The frameworks have been tested and refined within real organisations under real constraints.
- **Philosophical coherence** – First principles are integrated across contexts, allowing the concepts to travel and remain valid in varied settings.

What this is not

- A laboratory-style, positivist or statistically generalisable study.
- A prescriptive script guaranteeing outcomes.
- A rebrand of managerial jargon.

Scope and limits

- Human systems are complex, emergent and relational. Therefore, precision is contextual and pragmatic, not absolute.
- Measurement within this work is ontometric, concerned with relationships to qualities rather than mechanical quantification.
- The framework itself is living and will continue to evolve through further application, calibration and critique.

Bottom line (for busy readers)

- **Problem:** Performative sustainability (sustainabilism) collapses under pressure because it overlooks the ontology of people and systems.
- **Response:** A philosophically grounded, practice-proven framework that makes authentic sustainability assessable, discussable and cultivable.
- **Evidence:** Six program cycles, approximately 5,000 Being Profile® assessments, practitioner dialogues, expert reviews, internal applications and cross-case analyses.
- **Use it for:** Orienting leadership, diagnosing fragility, guiding renewal and sustaining coherent performance over time.

Introduction

The purpose of this Appendix is to provide a transparent and structured account of how this body of work – the Authentic Sustainability Framework (ASF) and its constituent parts, including its core Unified Ontology of Systemic Integrity (UOSI) – came into being. The frameworks and tools did not emerge in isolation or descend from theory alone. Their development was iterative: grounded in philosophical construction and refined through multiple forms of lived organisational practice across diverse contexts.

From the outset, the foundation is philosophical. Philosophy is the discipline best equipped to interrogate meaning, ontology and ethics – the structures beneath human action and systemic order. However, this is not philosophy for its own sake. The philosophical lens clarifies problems and structures solutions, while practice tempers and validates those insights. The orientation has remained consistently focused on usability in the lived world, where leaders face real constraints and consequential decisions.

This Appendix is part of that transparency. *Sustainabilism – Exposing the Sustainability Illusion* critiques the dominant approach to sustainability – referred to in this work as 'sustainabilism': prescriptive, scripted, compliance-driven and performative versions of sustainability. The critique matters because this paradigm routinely fails to meet the realities leaders, teams, organisations, institutions and societies actually face.

Throughout this work, sustainability extends beyond its conventional environmental focus. It refers to the enduring capacity of human beings, organisations, institutions and societies to operate with systemic integrity (coherence) and the conditions for adaptability and long-term flourishing.

Before any frameworks were applied in structured programs, they were the outcome of years of philosophical inquiry and organisational practice. This earlier work explored human beings, systems and civilisation through two interwoven streams:

- **Philosophical theorisation** – Clarifying first principles, ontological distinctions and systemic qualities; and
- **Practical application** – Venture building, executive coaching and analysis of thriving and failing systems to refine what consistently worked in practice.

This deliberate blend of philosophical depth and practical impact laid the foundation for what would later become the Authentic Sustainability Framework (ASF) and the Unified Ontology of Systemic Integrity (UOSI).

Building on that foundation, the frameworks were further shaped through direct engagement across multiple applied contexts – including leadership and coaching practice, internal organisational implementations, comparative case analyses and, among these, six carefully facilitated program cycles involving 48 leaders representing diverse nationalities and cultures. These programs provided a structured environment in which to test and refine the constructs within the real-world complexities of business – revenue, delivery, talent, cohesion, risk and resilience.

Across multiple iterations and contexts, new models were created, tested, refined and tested again. Input from leaders, facilitators and external reviewers helped shape the UOSI and refine the ASF, deepening the link between theory and practice to ensure the frameworks were both coherent and usable. Early prototypes of a sustainability assessment tool (including spreadsheet-based pilots) later evolved into an ontometric instrument called the **Sustainability Profile™**, capable of mapping a team's or individual's relationship with various systemic qualities.

Crucially, the work has been reviewed beyond any single program setting. Interviews and dialogues with policy-makers, governance experts, senior executives and academics, together with historical and contemporary analyses of governments and global organisations, ensured that the new frameworks resonate across all levels of human systems – from the micro (individual) and meso (organisational) to the macro (institutional and societal).

The central premise is that authentic sustainability begins with the integrity of individuals and teams and scales upward – from leadership orientation and culture into organisational, societal and global domains. Top-down mandates without this grounding are precisely the illusion critiqued in this book.

Accordingly, the purpose of this Appendix is transparency, explanation and credibility. What follows documents the evolution of an emergent and iterative body of work, shaped through philosophical inquiry and tested through multiple real-world applications. The leadership program cycles are presented not as the origin or entirety of this development, but as one of several environments in which key insights surfaced – insights that revealed the limitations of existing frameworks and catalysed the evolution of what ultimately became the Authentic Sustainability Framework (ASF) and its constituent parts.

Philosophical Grounding and Practical Imperative

At the heart of this body of work lies a philosophical orientation. Philosophy has always been concerned with first principles: what is real, why it matters, and how human beings ought to live and act. It is the discipline most suited to interrogate meaning, ethics and ontology, and to reveal the deeper structures that shape human behaviour and systemic coherence.

When applied to sustainability, philosophy asks questions that conventional organisational frameworks often overlook: What do we mean by sustainability? What is its nature? What makes it authentic rather than performative? How do we understand integrity, not as a moral slogan, but as a systemic quality?

Notably, while this inquiry has been philosophically grounded from the outset, it has also been practically driven. The intention was never to create abstract models for academic discussion, but to develop frameworks capable of withstanding the complexity of lived organisational life. Each model, distinction and framework was designed for expression in the real world, where leadership pressures, competing priorities and systemic fragility test ideas to their limits.

The two streams introduced earlier – philosophical theorisation and practical application – operated in constant dialogue. Philosophy provided depth and coherence; practice revealed relevance and limitations. Each acted as a mirror for the other, ensuring that theory remained grounded and practice remained principled.

In practical terms, this meant engaging deeply with the real challenges leaders face. Sustainability was approached not as an aspirational ideal or compliance requirement, but as a tangible necessity – steady revenue generation, delivery reliability, team cohesion, ethical decision-making and cultural resilience under pressure. These are the everyday conditions that determine whether a system endures or fragments.

The philosophical grounding provided the interpretive lens for these challenges. The **Being Framework** illuminated how a leader's qualities and orientations directly influence the sustainability of their organisation. **Metacontent** and its **Nested Theory of Sensemaking** revealed how leaders' assumptions and sense-making layers shape strategic clarity or distortion. And **Minalogy**, the discourse of meaning, value and purpose, exposed the moral and axiological foundations of leadership, clarifying why people act, what they pursue, and whether those pursuits sustain or corrode coherence.

Together, these discourses created a structure through which practice could be examined, refined and evolved. Philosophy provided the depth to see beneath the symptoms; practice provided the feedback to ensure that insight translated into action. Each informed and tempered the other. This same dynamic underpinned what later emerged as the Authentic Sustainability Framework (ASF) and Unified Ontology of Systemic Integrity (UOSI).

The work is grounded in a pragmatic interpretive–constructivist orientation, integrating philosophical ontology, phenomenology, and applied qualitative inquiry. Rather than relying on controlled laboratory methods or detached observation, the frameworks emerged and evolved through cycles of practical engagement, reflection and refinement, ensuring that each theoretical advance was tested against lived experience.

The result is a body of work that is both philosophically coherent and practically validated. It does not seek to prescribe behaviour, but to reveal the ontological structures through which coherence, integrity and sustainability can emerge. Philosophy gives it depth; practice gives it life.

Insights from Ontometric Data and Practitioner Dialogue

It is important to highlight that this body of work did not emerge solely from observation and dialogue, but also from structured ontometric insights derived from earlier research into the study of human beings. Prior to shifting the focus from Being to sustainability, extensive work had been undertaken using a mature assessment instrument – the Being Profile® – grounded in the Being Framework. Through this lens, the research examined how human beings engage in life and with others, in work and participation more broadly, and how their relationship with core qualities such as authenticity, responsibility, courage, assertiveness and care influences performance, leadership and effectiveness.

This body of insight provided a comprehensive foundation. However, it soon became evident that leadership capability, while essential, was not sufficient. To achieve sustainability that endures, it is necessary to understand not only how individuals are being within themselves and with others, but also who and how they must be to demand, design, implement, participate in and refine systems beyond themselves – including relationships, teams, organisations, institutions and societies. Authentic sustainability requires qualities beyond competence – qualities that enable continuity, coherence and collective stewardship.

This recognition marked a significant shift in the trajectory of the work – from mapping the metacontent of human beings (the focus of the Being Framework) to mapping the metacontent of sustainability. This shift ultimately led to the development, testing and iterative refinement of the Authentic Sustainability Framework (ASF) and its core Unified Ontology of Systemic Integrity (UOSI). In essence, the inquiry evolved from exploring individual and team performance to identifying the specific ontological capacities required for the long-term viability of systems at every scale. It is not a matter of mechanical processes alone, but of the ecology of human existence – how human beings are being with one another and with the systems they shape and inhabit.

Alongside philosophical inquiry and practical programs, a substantial body of ontometric data informed the development of this work. Through the Being Profile – the Being Framework's ontometric assessment tool – close to 5,000 profiles had been completed at the time of commencing this work by professionals and leaders from diverse countries, industries, demographics and cultural backgrounds. The tool measures the health and quality of one's relationship with 31 foundational qualities of Being, each of which influences performance, effectiveness and decision-making.

These profiles were not examined in isolation. Insights emerged through anonymised aggregate patterns, supported by extensive discussions with trained practitioners and coaches who worked with participating leaders in confidential contexts. No individual's privacy was ever compromised; rather, recurring themes surfaced through practice-based observation, reflective dialogue and systemic analysis.

Across contexts, a consistent pattern became evident: many leaders and teams were operating in a state of persistent firefighting. Burnout, reactivity, crisis-driven decision-making and the absence of sustainable progress were not anomalies but recurring conditions. The lack of sustainability was not merely organisational or procedural – it was ontological. Many individuals were capable and committed, yet constrained by ways of being that could not sustain coherence, resilience and continuity under pressure.

The ontometric data did not stand alone as evidence. Instead, it formed one stream of insight – a recurring signal that reinforced what was already being observed through lived practice, philosophical inquiry and historical analysis. These patterns highlighted the need for a framework that addresses sustainability at its root: the Being, sense-making and meaning-making capacities of individuals and the systems they create, inhabit and influence. Collectively, these insights reinforced the conclusion that a more authentic and enduring approach to sustainability was not only valuable, but increasingly urgent.

Integration with the Existing Body of Work

The frameworks and methods presented in this Appendix did not emerge in isolation. They evolved from years of philosophical inquiry and practical development that preceded any formal testing environments. When these constructs were later applied in real-world contexts, the intent was not merely to test pre-formed theories, but to explore how existing philosophical insights could be translated, adapted and expanded through lived engagement.

This integration of philosophy and application reflects the methodological core of the work: sustainability and systemic integrity cannot be understood through abstract reasoning alone, nor through practice divorced from principle. Each must inform the other in a continuous cycle of reflection, experimentation and refinement.

Foundational discourses

Before the emergence of the Authentic Sustainability Framework (ASF), three major philosophical discourses had already been developed through extensive research and application. Together, they provided the conceptual and ontological base from which the ASF gradually evolved:

- **The Being Framework** – A comprehensive model of human ontology identifying 31 qualities of Being that influence how individuals lead, decide and relate. This framework offered a way to understand not only *what* people do, but *how* they are being in the process. It emphasised that sustainable performance arises from integrity in one's way of being, not merely from competence or skill.

- **Metacontent and the Nested Theory of Sense-making** – A body of work examining the perceptual and interpretive layers through which people construct meaning and make decisions. Leaders often operate within unexamined assumptions and inherited frames of reference. The Nested Theory maps these layers – from broad purpose and worldview down to concrete tasks – showing how distortions at higher levels can cascade into systemic dysfunction below.
- **Minalogy** – The discourse of meaning, values and purpose, which provides the moral and axiological foundation underlying human conduct and systemic coherence. While the Being Framework reveals *how one is being* and metacontent explains *how one perceives*, Minalogy addresses *why one acts at all* – anchoring leadership in authentic purpose rather than ambition, ideology or convenience. It helps leaders discern what is genuinely worth sustaining, grounding decision-making in moral realism and existential clarity.

These three discourses are interdependent. Together, they enable a more complete understanding of human systems: how Being, sense-making, values and purpose coalesce to produce either coherence or fragmentation. They were not designed as abstract theories, but as practical instruments for reflection and transformation – lenses through which leaders could interpret and influence their lived environments.

From foundational discourses to an integrated framework

As these philosophical models matured through years of practice in leadership, coaching and organisational contexts, their interconnections became increasingly evident. Patterns that surfaced through ontometric data, practitioner dialogue and program experience revealed that individual and team-level insight alone could not resolve the systemic challenges of sustainability. This recognition catalysed the gradual evolution of a new, integrated framework – one capable of addressing coherence and systemic integrity across multiple levels of scale.

Over successive cycles of application and reflection, insights from the Being Framework, Metacontent and Minalogy converged and crystallised into what eventually became known as the **Authentic Sustainability Framework (ASF)** – a coherent system integrating the ontological, phenomenological and systemic dimensions of sustainability.

The ASF ultimately brought together several key components:

- **The Unified Ontology of Systemic Integrity (UOSI)** – The structural backbone of the framework, mapping 16 interrelated systemic qualities (including those drawn from the Being Framework) across four spheres: Architectonic, Integrity, Disintegration and Modulation.
- **The Systemic Subversion Cycle (SSC)** – A diagnostic model exposing how systems drift into dysfunction, entrenchment and collapse, highlighting the importance of early recognition and intervention.
- **The Reconstructive Ontology of Sustainability (ROS)** – The regenerative dimension of the ASF, integrating the Being Framework, Metacontent, Minalogy and the Transformation Methodology™ to guide systemic renewal.
- **The Sustainability Profile** – An ontometric assessment tool that maps a system's relationship to the 16 UOSI qualities and generates a Vulnerability Index, enabling structured reflection, diagnosis and development.
- **The Fulfilment Pyramid** – A developmental model illustrating how intention matures into fulfilment across three interlocking dimensions – Developmental, Phenomenological and Relational – ensuring coherence from purpose to practice.

Together, these elements form a living, interdependent architecture for cultivating, assessing and sustaining systemic integrity across individuals, organisations and societies. They did not appear fully formed; they emerged organically through iterative cycles of philosophical inquiry, practical engagement and reflection, each layer of insight building upon the one before it.

Practical and philosophical interdependence

The interplay between theory and practice is central to the integrity of this work. Philosophy provides the clarity and depth to reveal hidden dynamics; practice provides the environment where those insights are tested, challenged and refined. Each tempers the other. Without philosophical structure, practice risks devolving into reactive fixes and managerial jargon; without practical grounding, philosophy risks irrelevance.

As the early frameworks and distinctions were applied across diverse contexts – executive coaching, venture development and leadership engagements – the reciprocal relationship between Being, sense-making, meaning-making and purpose became increasingly evident. These experiences revealed both the power and the limits of existing models, preparing the ground for the next phase: the emergence of a more integrated, systemic framework that could address sustainability and integrity across multiple levels of scale.

Beyond the individual: Systemic reach

The practical application of these ideas soon extended beyond the realm of individual transformation. Leaders were encouraged to see how their ways of being, sense-making and meaning-making shaped the systems around them – how personal coherence (or its absence) cascaded into team culture, organisational strategy and collective performance.

This widening systemic lens connected insights across the micro (individual), meso (organisational) and macro (institutional and societal) levels, demonstrating that sustainability is not confined to personal or organisational success, but arises through alignment across all three. These realisations helped to crystallise the need for a framework that could integrate human ontology with systemic structure – a need that would ultimately give rise to the Authentic Sustainability Framework.

From integration to application

By the time a structured leadership program was established, the philosophical architecture and foundational discourses were already well developed, and the early contours of the ASF were beginning to take shape. The program provided a critical environment for bringing these evolving ideas into concentrated practice. It offered a living laboratory where leaders could engage with the work directly, apply emerging distinctions to live organisational challenges and contribute insights that, in turn, informed and accelerated the frameworks' refinement.

In this way, the program did not *create* the frameworks; it *catalysed their evolution* – translating philosophical clarity into lived experimentation and allowing the work to mature through the realities of practice.

The following section outlines how this evolutionary process unfolded within a structured leadership program – one of several environments through which the frameworks were progressively developed, tested and refined in practice.

The Program Context

The leadership program served as one of several developmental environments through which this body of work evolved. It was not the origin of the ideas, but a structured setting in which existing philosophical and ontological constructs could be brought into direct engagement with lived organisational realities. The purpose was not to trial a completed theory, but to explore how established frameworks could illuminate practice – and how practice, in turn, could expose the gaps that theory alone could not resolve.

In this sense, the program functioned as a living laboratory – a dynamic context where the **Being Framework**, **Metacontent** (and its **Nested Theory of Sense-making**) and **Minalogy** were applied, observed and refined through experience. These frameworks were not presented as abstract teachings, but as practical instruments that enabled leaders to interpret their challenges and examine the relationship between their ways of being, perceiving and acting.

As these applications unfolded across multiple cohorts, recurring patterns began to surface. Certain challenges could be addressed effectively through awareness of Being and sense-making, while others revealed deeper systemic dynamics that these frameworks alone could not fully account for. It was through this recognition – and through the lived experiences of the participants – that the seeds of the **Authentic Sustainability Framework (ASF)** and its **Unified Ontology of Systemic Integrity (UOSI)** began to form.

For example, a director struggling with team cohesion was encouraged to look beyond tactics to the qualities of Being they were embodying in that process. A founder grappling with inconsistent revenue examined not only their business model, but also the underlying metacontent shaping their assumptions about customers, markets and value creation. Through these inquiries, leaders discovered how philosophical distinctions could directly illuminate practical decisions – and, in doing so, they also revealed where further conceptual integration was required.

Program design and purpose

The program was designed to create the conditions for translating philosophy into lived organisational practice. It brought together a diverse cohort of leaders – founders, business owners, executives and managers – representing a wide range of industries, organisational sizes and cultural contexts. Across six program cycles, 48 participants from various continents – Australia, Europe, Africa, Asia and the Middle East – engaged in intensive dialogue and applied experimentation.

Each cycle combined conceptual input with real-time exploration of business and leadership dilemmas such as revenue volatility, operational stability, cultural cohesion, leadership consistency and systemic resilience. The program's design enabled leaders to test new distinctions within their live organisational environments and to observe the immediate consequences of their shifts in perception and behaviour.

In the early cycles, the frameworks applied centred on the **Being Framework™** and **Metacontent**, including its **Nested Theory of Sense-making**. These constructs offered powerful insight into personal and team dynamics, yet their application consistently revealed a deeper systemic gap: the challenge of creating truly sustainable, enduring systems could not be resolved solely through individual transformation or improved leadership awareness.

While each participant's context was unique, the unifying question remained constant: *How can sustainability be lived as systemic integrity, rather than performed as compliance?*

This recognition set in motion the next phase of the work. Drawing on feedback and observation from the first four cohorts, development began on what would become the **Unified Ontology of Systemic Integrity (UOSI)** – a synthesis that mapped the qualities required for coherence and regeneration at the systemic level. The fifth program cycle marked the first introduction and structured testing of these emerging distinctions, while the sixth cycle, which included three returning participants, constituted the first full application of the **Authentic Sustainability Framework (ASF)** in practice.

Target participants

Participants were carefully selected for their relevance to the inquiry. They included:

- Founders and established startup owners navigating growth and scalability.
- SME directors and business owners seeking systemic stability.
- Executives and mid-level managers in NGOs and not-for-profits balancing resource constraints with mission-driven complexity.
- Team leaders of agile units within larger corporations managing delivery, culture and adaptability.

This diversity ensured that insights could be drawn from multiple sectors, organisational maturities and cultural contexts. In the earlier cohorts, this variety enabled the Being Framework and metacontent to be examined across a broad spectrum of lived realities. As the work evolved, the same diversity became instrumental in testing the emerging distinctions of the UOSI and, later, the full ASF. This progression allowed participants within each phase of the program to explore the frameworks' coherence, adaptability and systemic relevance within their real organisational contexts.

Thematic focus

Although participants worked in varied industries, they shared a common pursuit: to make sustainability real and actionable within their organisations. For them, 'sustainability' had tangible meanings such as:

- **Steady and consistent revenue generation** – Avoiding cycles of rapid growth followed by instability.
- **Reliable lead generation and customer acquisition** – Reducing dependence on sporadic opportunity.
- **Consistent delivery and operational effectiveness** – Ensuring that value promised to customers was reliably fulfilled.
- **Team cohesion and development** – Building cultures where individuals grew, contributed and remained engaged.
- **Decision-making on dilemmas** – Navigating the normative and practical challenges of hiring, firing, delegating and developing people.
- **Regenerative organisational culture** – Establishing practices that could endure and adapt rather than collapse under pressure.

The unifying thread across all cases was the pursuit of **authentic sustainability** – not as a compliance exercise or strategic performance, but as a lived, relational and systemic capacity to endure, adapt and regenerate.

Rigour and iteration

Each program cycle balanced conceptual depth with practical application, serving simultaneously as a workshop for leaders and a field experiment for the evolving frameworks. Across iterations, participants applied distinctions from the Being Framework™ and the Metacontent discourse to live organisational challenges. The insights and feedback gathered through these engagements directly informed the development of the Authentic Sustainability Framework (ASF) and sharpened the ontological distinctions that would later form the Unified Ontology of Systemic Integrity (UOSI).

The program was conducted with methodological rigour and adaptive design. Structured documentation of all sessions was maintained, continuous feedback loops were embedded, and formal online interviews were introduced to capture longitudinal reflections. Each cohort informed the next, enabling a process of systematic refinement.

Feedback was treated not as an afterthought, but as a core design element. Leaders were encouraged to provide candid reflections on what resonated, what felt abstract, and what required further development. Facilitators recorded these insights in real time, identifying where the translation from concept to practice succeeded and where recalibration was required.

The final iteration, involving nine leaders – six new participants and three returning – provided a valuable longitudinal perspective. As the first program cycle in which the ASF was applied in full, it enabled validation not only of immediate effects, but also of the continuity and coherence of the work over time.

This iterative design was supported by a dedicated facilitation team that played an essential role in bridging philosophy and practice, ensuring that every concept was tested, translated and refined through lived organisational engagement.

Collaboration with facilitators

The program was brought to life through the contribution of two key facilitators, Jacqueline Hofste and Ariya Chittasy, whose expertise was central to translating philosophical constructs into lived engagement with leaders. Together, they formed a triad of inquiry, practice and facilitation that enabled the work to reach and influence real organisations.

The role of facilitation

In this context, facilitation was not concerned with delivering a pre-packaged curriculum or managing logistics. Rather, it required inhabiting the frameworks – embodying the ontological distinctions drawn from both the Being Framework and the emerging Authentic Sustainability Framework (ASF) – and guiding leaders as these constructs were applied to their organisational realities.

The facilitators functioned as interpreters, practitioners and co-inquirers, maintaining the delicate balance between philosophy and practice. Their role was to ensure that leaders were neither overwhelmed by abstraction nor constrained by oversimplification.

Jacqueline Hofste

Jacqueline brought deep experience from the corporate world, having led multi-location distributed teams and managed PMOs in organisations such as Citect and Schneider Electric while overseeing a €40 million program budget. Her background gave her an acute understanding of complexity, scale and the pressures of leadership in large systems.

After transitioning from corporate environments to SMEs, Jacqueline gained a dual perspective – combining an appreciation of global structures with insight into the agility and constraints of smaller enterprises. Holding a Master's degree in Physics, she blended scientific rigour with human-centred leadership.

In the program, Jacqueline's role was to bridge these worlds. Her facilitation style combined structure with empathy and ensured that philosophical models were made relevant to leaders navigating the everyday realities of sustainable growth and organisational coherence.

Ariya Chittasy

Ariya brought a complementary perspective. With a background in psychology, business development and commercialisation – and as Director of Engenesis Ventures – he was deeply familiar with the entrepreneurial environment. Having advised and trained more than 800 startups and founders, Ariya understood the pressures of innovation, growth and leadership under uncertainty.

His facilitation combined psychological insight with commercial acumen. Drawing on his knowledge of the Being Framework, he helped leaders translate ontological distinctions into concrete business practices. Ariya challenged assumptions, illuminated how metacontent shaped strategic and interpersonal dynamics, and consistently drew leaders back to the link between internal orientation and external results.

A collaborative approach

A collaborative approach was adopted, creating a multi-dimensional facilitation environment. Philosophical and architectural coherence was maintained throughout the program to ensure that each engagement remained anchored in systemic integrity and lived application.

Corporate depth, scientific method and human-centric leadership were contributed by Jacqueline Hofste, while Ariya Chittasy brought entrepreneurial pragmatism, psychological insight and commercial strategy.

Through this collaboration, leaders were exposed to a synthesis of perspectives – philosophy made practical, corporate discipline infused with humanity and entrepreneurial energy informed by ontological clarity. This blend enabled the frameworks to be taught, experienced and embodied rather than merely explained.

Reviewer collaboration and practical validation

The development of the program was further strengthened by collaboration with seasoned practitioners who participated as reviewers and reflective contributors. Their role was to observe, engage and provide grounded feedback based on extensive experience with executives and leadership teams across multiple industries.

Among these contributors, John Smallwood and Aydin Yassemi each played a role.

John Smallwood is a C-suite coach, facilitator and mentor with extensive experience as a CEO across multiple industries and countries. An ontologically trained high-performance coach, he has led businesses with turnovers exceeding USD $250 million across Europe, Australia and Asia. His depth of executive experience and systemic awareness brought invaluable perspective to the program's leadership dynamics.

Aydin Yassemi is a senior leadership facilitator, Thrive Coach and organisational development expert with more than 30 years of cross-cultural experience. Trained in biophysics at UC Berkeley, his career spans research at Lawrence Berkeley Labs, international development projects with the GEF and UNDP, and the co-founding of three small businesses. He has delivered leadership and coaching programs for global corporations and UN agencies, combining analytical rigour with human-centred development.

Both John and Aydin participated in full program iterations, engaging deeply with the material and providing candid reflections on how the evolving frameworks resonated in real organisational contexts. Their insights helped refine language, pedagogy and facilitation methods, ensuring that the program's philosophical depth was matched by practical accessibility and measurable impact.

Beyond these reviewers, additional practitioners contributed behind the scenes – reviewing materials, observing sessions and ensuring relevance across industries. This network of reviewers formed a vital feedback loop between philosophical architecture and practical embodiment, validating that the new frameworks were both conceptually rigorous and experientially transferable.

Impact on the development of the work

The facilitators were not simply delivering a curriculum; they were active participants in the evolution of this body of work. Through facilitation, they observed how leaders engaged with the emerging models, where resistance was encountered, and where breakthroughs occurred. These observations were continually integrated into the ongoing evolution of the frameworks, shaping their structure and language over time.

When participants struggled with abstract distinctions, the facilitators worked to translate these ideas into language and practices that resonated with lived organisational realities. When leaders applied the concepts in unanticipated or innovative ways, those insights were captured and fed back into subsequent refinements. In this way, the facilitation team acted as a conduit between practice and philosophy, sustaining a two-way flow of discovery and validation.

The facilitators' diverse professional backgrounds added both credibility and depth to the process. Leaders recognised that they were not only engaging with philosophical inquiry, but with practitioners who understood the operational realities of leadership, business and transformation. This combination of philosophical rigour and grounded facilitation ensured that the program was neither theoretical nor superficial, but a rigorous, iterative exploration of sustainability and systemic integrity in practice.

This collaborative dynamic became instrumental in advancing the work. It created a bridge through which insights from lived engagement continually informed conceptual development. This laid the groundwork for the next phase of analysis: observing what shifted in leaders, teams and organisations as philosophy evolved into practice.

Observed outcomes for leaders

While every leader's journey was unique, common themes emerged:

- Increased capacity to systemise and optimise their businesses.
- Deeper awareness of how their own Being and sense-making shaped outcomes.
- More intentional approaches to decision-making and team development.
- Greater discernment between performative actions and authentic practices.
- Recognition that sustainability is not a static goal, but an ongoing process of coherence and adaptation.

Emergence and refinement of the ASF

As the program cycles unfolded, insights drawn from participants, facilitators and lived organisational experimentation progressively coalesced into what would become the Authentic Sustainability Framework (ASF) – a coherent architecture unifying and extending the ontological models developed throughout the broader body of work.

The framework did not appear fully formed. It evolved through multiple iterations as patterns identified in earlier cohorts revealed systemic gaps that could not be addressed solely through the Being Framework and Metacontent. Each cycle added conceptual and practical depth, leading to the formulation and subsequent refinement of several key components:

- **Unified Ontology of Systemic Integrity (UOSI)** – The structural backbone of the ASF, mapping 16 systemic qualities (including those drawn from the Being Framework) across four spheres: Architectonic, Integrity, Disintegration and Modulation.

- **Systemic Subversion Cycle (SSC)** – A diagnostic model identifying how systems drift into dysfunction, entrenchment and collapse, emphasising the importance of early recognition and intervention.
- **Reconstructive Ontology of Sustainability (ROS)** – The regenerative dimension of the ASF, integrating the Being Framework, Metacontent, Minalogy and the Transformation Methodology™ to guide systemic renewal.
- **Sustainability Profile™** – An ontometric assessment tool mapping a system's relationship to the 16 UOSI qualities and generating a Vulnerability Index for structured reflection, diagnosis and development.
- **Fulfilment Pyramid** – A multidimensional model illustrating how intention matures into fulfilment across three interlocking dimensions – Developmental (growth of capability and consciousness), Phenomenological (awareness and lived experience) and Relational (interaction and alignment with others). These dimensions collectively translate clarity of purpose into coherent action and realised outcomes – fulfilment as the lived result of aligned execution.

Together, these elements form a living, interdependent framework – an evolving architecture for cultivating, assessing and sustaining integrity across individuals, organisations and societies. None were imposed from the top down; each emerged organically through the interplay of philosophical reflection, practical experimentation and real-world adaptation.

Significance for the broader body of work

The program context was not incidental; it was formative. Without it, the frameworks might have remained theoretical. Instead, they were confronted with the lived realities of organisational life – tested against real-world constraints, challenges and diverse interpretations. This process refined language, clarified concepts and validated the frameworks' systemic coherence.

However, the program was not the sole source of this evolution. In parallel, the frameworks continued to be developed through philosophical study, cross-disciplinary inquiry and broader fieldwork with leaders, scholars and practitioners. Together, these multiple streams ensured that the ASF and its constituent parts, including the central UOSI, emerged as both philosophically grounded and practically verified.

Research Methodology and Approach

This work is not presented as a traditional academic study, nor as a product of laboratory research or institutional peer review. Rather, it follows a rigorous philosophical and practice-grounded development process. To support transparency for readers familiar with research conventions – without misrepresenting the nature of the work – this section outlines the paradigmatic stance and methodological approaches that shaped the development of this body of work.

The methodology integrates ontological inquiry, lived organisational practice and interpretive qualitative methods, enabling the emergence, refinement and validation of the frameworks in real contexts rather than theoretical isolation.

By integrating ontology, phenomenology, grounded theory, action research and case study analysis, this work occupies a unique space within academic traditions. It aligns most closely with traditions of practical philosophy, organisational phenomenology and interpretive social science. Its contribution lies in bridging the gap between philosophical ontology and practical leadership, offering a framework that is both intellectually rigorous and practically usable.

1. Paradigmatic stance

The work is grounded in a pragmatic, interpretive–constructivist orientation, incorporating a critical dimension where appropriate.

- **Interpretivist** – Understanding how leaders make meaning of sustainability and system dynamics in lived organisational settings.
- **Constructivist** – Acknowledging that knowledge and understanding arise through collaborative processes of reflection and inquiry with leaders, rather than being objectively found or imposed from outside.
- **Pragmatic** – Prioritising what works in practice and produces coherent, sustainable outcomes in real systems.
- **Critical** (secondary) – Interrogating dominant sustainability narratives and exposing performativity, reductionism and institutional blind spots.

This pragmatic interpretivist–constructivist stance aligns with the ontological nature of the work: the inquiry concerns how human beings *are being* and how they *act* within systems, and how meaning, integrity and sustainability arise in lived contexts.

2. Methods and methodological logic

The development of the frameworks drew on complementary qualitative and philosophical methodologies:

No single method could encompass the philosophical, phenomenological and organisational layers at play. Sustainability – understood here as systemic integrity – is emergent, relational and lived. Accordingly, philosophical inquiry needed to meet lived practice – and lived practice, in turn, had to inform philosophical clarity.

Method	Application
Philosophical Ontology	Conceptual development of the Being Framework, metacontent (Nested Theory of Sense-making), Minalogy and the Authentic Sustainability Framework (incorporating the Unified Ontology of Systemic Integrity, the Systemic Subversion Cycle, the Reconstructive Ontology of Sustainability, the Sustainability Profile and the Fulfilment Pyramid); articulating distinctions of Being, meaning and systemic integrity.
Phenomenology	Considering leaders' lived experience, emotional landscapes, constraints and meaning-making in real organisational practice.
Grounded Theory Principles	Inductive pattern recognition from cohort engagement, feedback and case notes; iterative refinement of concepts based on emergent insights – not the full Grounded Theory procedure.
Action Research Cycles	Iterative application environments – including structured leadership programs and broader organisational engagements – functioned as cycles of intervention, reflection, learning and recalibration. Through these iterative processes, the ASF and its constituent components emerged and evolved, shaped by continual feedback from real-world contexts.
Interpretive Case Analysis	Historical and contemporary sustainability examples analysed for patterns, failures and contrasts.

Table 34 – Methods and methodological logic.

3. Data, validity practices and analysis

Data sources included:

- Program session notes and structured reflection records (from multiple cycles).
- Participant feedback across six cohorts and other organisational applications.
- Facilitator observations and debriefs.
- Follow-up interviews with selected participants.
- Internal organisational application within Engenesis.
- Comparative review across external expert dialogues.
- Historical and contemporary case studies.

Validity and reliability

Validity was established through multiple complementary approaches:

- **Principle Application:** Triangulation across multiple data sources – including leaders, facilitators, external reviewers and case studies.
- **Iterative Refinement:** Six program cycles, with recalibration and adjustment following each iteration.
- **Practitioner Review:** Experienced master coaches and facilitators participated as reviewers throughout complete program cycles.
- **Longitudinal Check:** Returning participants validated the continuity, coherence and practical efficacy of the frameworks over time.
- **Coherence Testing:** Ensuring that philosophical clarity aligned with observable systemic outcomes in lived organisational contexts.

The orientation of the research was analytic and practice-based rather than statistical. Validity therefore rests on *coherence, lived relevance* and *sustained applicability* across diverse contexts of use, rather than on controlled or exclusively program-bound measures.

Data analysis

Data analysis followed a **hermeneutic approach**, interpreting data within the broader philosophical and ontological frameworks that underpin this body of work. Feedback and lived experiences were not treated as isolated variables but as interpretive texts – sources of meaning through which the structures of coherence, fragmentation and renewal could be discerned.

This interpretive process enabled the identification of recurring themes, ontological patterns and systemic insights that directly informed the emergence and evolution of the Authentic Sustainability Framework (ASF). The frameworks were not imposed *a priori* but developed through iterative interpretation and synthesis, shaped by the lived realities of leaders and organisations.

In parallel, a **comparative analysis** was conducted across cohorts to distinguish enduring structural patterns from context-specific phenomena. This method ensured that the ASF and its constituent components reflected systemic dynamics observable across multiple environments, rather than being products of isolated cases or single iterations.

4. Scope and limits

This methodology does not claim the predictive precision of the natural sciences. The phenomena under study – Being, systemic integrity and sustainability – are inherently complex, non-linear and emergent. Accordingly, the findings are interpretive and developmental, not prescriptive or predictive. The purpose of the research was not to formulate universal laws, but to generate ontological frameworks and practical insights that enable leaders to shape and sustain coherent, adaptive and enduring systems – whether organisational, institutional or societal.

In short, this work does **not** claim:

- Statistical generalisability
- Controlled-environment replicability
- Positivist causal certainty

Its strength lies in:

- **Analytic generalisation** – Frameworks transfer effectively where ontological and systemic conditions align.
- **Practice validation** – Insights tested and refined in lived contexts with leaders and organisations.
- **Ontological clarity** – Focused on Being, meaning and systemic coherence rather than surface behaviour or mechanistic correlation.

In essence, this is philosophical-ontological, practice-grounded research, not positivist science. It privileges depth, coherence and lived usability over numerical abstraction – seeking understanding of how sustainability emerges and endures, rather than prediction of how it behaves.

Data Gathering and Iterative Refinement

From the outset, the development of this body of work was approached not as a single act of creation, but as an iterative, evolutionary process. Each cycle of practical application generated new insights, feedback and opportunities to refine and strengthen the emerging Authentic Sustainability Framework (ASF) and its Unified Ontology of Systemic Integrity (UOSI). The guiding philosophy was clear: theory must be tested through practice, and practice must be illuminated by theory. Only through repeated cycles of application, reflection and refinement could the work mature into a framework that is both rigorous and usable.

Systematic documentation

Every program iteration was accompanied by structured documentation. Sessions were not treated informally but recorded with precision – capturing both the dynamics of facilitation and participants' responses in real time. These records formed a living archive, enabling longitudinal analysis of how leaders engaged with the frameworks, where they experienced breakthroughs, and where points of abstraction or misalignment arose.

Over time, distinct patterns became visible. Certain challenges recurred across cohorts – dilemmas around team culture, inconsistency in revenue generation and the tension between long-term vision and short-term demands. Others were unique to particular industries or organisational contexts. By systematically distinguishing between recurring systemic patterns and context-specific variations, the work gained both depth and adaptability, allowing refinements to be grounded in lived organisational realities rather than theoretical conjecture.

Feedback loops

Feedback was not treated as an afterthought, but embedded into the design of each program from the outset. Participants were encouraged to offer candid reflections on what resonated, what felt abstract, and what required further refinement. These reflections were captured both in real time and through structured debriefs following each session.

As the programs evolved, **formal feedback mechanisms** were progressively introduced. Online discussion forums enabled participants to share ongoing reflections and provide live commentary as their understanding deepened. In later iterations, in-depth online interviews were conducted to capture richer qualitative insight into how leaders were interpreting and applying the evolving frameworks within their organisational contexts.

Facilitators played a vital role in maintaining these feedback loops. Through close observation of participant engagement and direct conversations with those seeking deeper dialogue, they surfaced both the strengths of the emerging frameworks and the areas where translation into practice required refinement. Their insights ensured that each iteration remained grounded, coherent and responsive to lived organisational realities.

Iterative refinement across contexts and cohorts

The iterative nature of the work meant that no two applications – whether program-based or within separate organisational settings – were identical. Each cycle built upon the learnings of the previous one. When a distinction proved too abstract, it was clarified in the next iteration; when a tool proved cumbersome, it was simplified and recalibrated; and when a concept generated deep resonance, it was expanded and more deliberately integrated into subsequent applications.

The final leadership program cycle was particularly significant. It involved nine leaders – six new participants and three returning from earlier cohorts – providing an invaluable longitudinal lens. The returning participants offered perspective not only on immediate outcomes, but on the enduring relevance and coherence of the frameworks over time. Their reflections validated the integrity of the work across iterations and contributed to the ongoing refinement and evolution of the Authentic Sustainability Framework (ASF) and its Unified Ontology of Systemic Integrity (UOSI), both of which continue to develop through lived application.

Data beyond numbers

It is important to emphasise that the data gathered was not merely quantitative. This was not a laboratory experiment with controlled variables and numerical metrics. The data was qualitative, phenomenological and relational. It captured the lived experiences of leaders navigating complex organisational realities.

This does not make the data less rigorous. On the contrary, it makes it more authentic. Sustainability is not reducible to a formula. It is about human beings, with all their limitations, aspirations, emotions and decisions. The richness of qualitative data – stories, reflections, dilemmas and breakthroughs – provided insights that no spreadsheet could capture in isolation.

Validation through practice

Through this iterative process, the ontological distinctions of the Unified Ontology of Systemic Integrity (UOSI) and its associated frameworks were not only refined but empirically grounded in lived organisational experience. Their validity was demonstrated through direct application to real leadership challenges, including:

- Stabilising revenue streams.
- Navigating talent acquisition and offboarding.

- Cultivating regenerative organisational cultures.
- Sustaining the inner coherence of leaders alongside the coherence of their organisations.

Consistently, the results affirmed the relevance and applicability of the frameworks – though always with nuance. The distinctions did not offer prescriptive or formulaic solutions; rather, they provided structured ways of perceiving, interpreting and acting that enabled leaders to generate authentic, context-specific responses. This validation through practice differentiated the work from conventional management models by demonstrating that sustainability, when grounded in systemic integrity, must be lived and enacted rather than imposed or performed.

From notes to theory

The iterative refinement process also informed the philosophical evolution of the work. Notes and feedback were never treated as raw data to be archived; they were engaged philosophically – interpreted through ontological and phenomenological lenses – and woven into the ongoing development of theory. In this way, practice did not merely *test* theory; it *shaped* it.

This methodological loop – from theory to practice, practice to insight, insight to reflection, and reflection back to theory – gave the work both depth and resilience. It ensured that the resulting frameworks were not speculative abstractions, but *lived constructs*, forged in the crucible of real experience.

Perhaps the most important outcome of this process is that the work remains alive. It is not frozen in a final form. Just as each cohort shaped its evolution, future engagements will continue to refine and extend it. This openness to iteration is itself an expression of authentic sustainability – the recognition that systems endure not by clinging to rigid forms, but by adapting, learning and regenerating.

Testing the Sustainability Profile (Ontometric Tool)

One of the most significant practical outcomes of the iterative applications and testing environments was the development of the **Sustainability Profile** – an ontometric tool designed to measure an individual's or team's relationship with the 16 qualities articulated in the Unified Ontology of Systemic Integrity (UOSI). This tool provided a way to bring structure, measurement and reflection into what had previously been a purely qualitative domain.

The first version of the Sustainability Profile existed as a relatively simple prototype built in an Excel spreadsheet. Participants responded to structured questions designed to reveal their orientation towards the 16 systemic qualities, each nested within the four-layered construct of the UOSI. The tool then produced indicative results, highlighting areas of coherence, fragility or dysfunction.

This early prototype represented a critical milestone. It made the abstract tangible. Leaders could see, in structured form, a reflection of how they and their teams were relating to systemic qualities like trust, adaptability, tolerance, integrity, patience and sustained effectiveness. For many, this externalised what had previously been felt, but not named – the hidden dynamics shaping their organisations.

Iterative testing, calibration and refinement

The Sustainability Profile was tested and refined across a range of controlled and applied contexts. Closed groups were invited to engage with the tool, reflect on their results, and provide structured feedback. Six test cases included internal teams within Engenesis, ensuring that the tool was examined in both internal and external environments.

Developing an ontometric tool is not a straightforward process. Unlike instruments in the physical sciences that can be calibrated against objective standards, ontometric tools engage with human beings – with their perceptions, orientations and lived experiences – making calibration inherently more complex.

Each testing cycle revealed opportunities for recalibration. Certain questions proved overly abstract and were simplified to enhance clarity. Scoring thresholds were adjusted to more accurately reflect lived organisational realities, and the feedback report structure was refined to make insights clearer and more actionable. Over time, data comparison across groups revealed consistent patterns that strengthened confidence in the tool's validity. When anomalies appeared, they were examined carefully: were they artefacts of measurement, or did they reveal deeper truths about a team's orientation?

This reflective calibration ensured that the tool did not drift into reductionism. It remained sensitive to the complexity of human beings while still offering structured insights. With each iteration, the Sustainability Profile advanced in reliability, coherence and usability, deepening its alignment with the Authentic Sustainability Framework (ASF) and its Unified Ontology of Systemic Integrity (UOSI).

Purpose of measurement

The Sustainability Profile was designed not as a prescriptive instrument, but as a reflective one. Its purpose was never to categorise leaders or teams as 'good' or 'bad', nor to provide formulaic solutions for success. Rather, it was intended to function as a mirror – enabling participants to observe and understand their relationship with systemic qualities more clearly.

For instance, a team might discover that while it demonstrated strong adaptability, it exhibited fragility in trust. Such insights were not prescriptive diagnoses, but invitations to reflect: How might the team's current ways of being contribute to fragmentation in trust? What practices could be cultivated to strengthen trust without diminishing adaptability?

By providing reflections of this nature in a clear, structured form, the tool enabled leaders and teams to move beyond abstract aspirations of systemic integrity towards a concrete awareness of where coherence was present and where fragility or dysfunction prevailed.

Observed impact

Across the six test cases, as well as within broader program cohorts, the Sustainability Profile demonstrated measurable impact. Leaders reported heightened awareness of systemic qualities previously overlooked, while teams used the results to initiate deeper conversations about culture, performance, systemic integrity and sustainability – discussions that had not been possible before.

Within Engenesis, the internal application of the tool revealed areas in which teams could strengthen coherence and clarify shared sense-making. This process proved both humbling and invaluable, underscoring that the body of work was not something imposed upon others, but something lived, tested and refined internally through practice.

Challenges of measurement

The development of the Sustainability Profile also revealed the inherent challenges of measurement within this domain. Unlike engineering or software development, where calibration can achieve precision and replicability, sustainability concerns human beings – entities of perception, emotion and meaning-making. Measurement in such a context is necessarily interpretive rather than mechanical.

Accordingly, exactitude was neither possible nor the goal. The emphasis was on functional accuracy – generating insights that could empower reflection and intentional, adaptive action. The tool was therefore designed to balance structure with sensitivity: to illuminate systemic qualities without reducing human complexity to numerical abstraction.

Through this approach, the Sustainability Profile maintained fidelity to its ontological purpose – providing clarity and coherence while honouring the nuanced, evolving nature of human systems.

A living, evolving and integrated instrument

The long-term vision for the Sustainability Profile has been to develop a refined digital instrument fully integrated within the broader body of work – a mature ontometric tool capable of serving leaders and teams at scale. It operationalises the Unified Ontology of Systemic Integrity (UOSI), enabling the measurement and reflection of systemic qualities in lived organisational contexts. In doing so, it bridges philosophical ontology and organisational reality, ensuring that the UOSI functions not merely as a theoretical construct, but as a framework enacted in practice.

In this way, the tool embodies the defining characteristics of authentic sustainability – emergent, iterative and grounded in lived experience. The early prototypes provided the initial foundation, revealing both potential and limitations. Subsequent iterations built upon this groundwork, enhancing reliability, usability and systemic impact.

Therefore, the Sustainability Profile remains a living instrument that is continuously refined through application, dialogue and feedback. As leaders and teams engage with it, the tool itself evolves, sustaining coherence between philosophical depth and practical relevance.

The Nature of the Work – Philosophy Meets Phenomenology

It is necessary to be clear about the nature of this body of work. As the domain of sustainability and systemic integrity involves human beings – conscious, social, emotional and meaning-making entities with vast subjective depth – to treat sustainability as if it can be reduced to a formula or engineered into existence through a scripted process would be a fundamental misrepresentation of its nature. For this reason, philosophy and phenomenology provide the foundation for this work.

The philosophical dimension

Philosophy is critical to this body of work because it offers the tools to examine and query meaning, ethics and ontology – to ask questions about what is real, what matters, and how we ought to live. Without philosophy, sustainability collapses into superficial slogans and narrow compliance checklists. Philosophy allows us to step back, examine assumptions and articulate distinctions that make hidden dynamics visible.

More than theory, philosophy is also a practical necessity for authentic sustainability. For example, the Being Framework, which is fundamental to this work, is a philosophical model of human ontology that identifies 31 qualities of Being, each of which shapes how individuals perform, decide and relate. These qualities are ontological distinctions that illuminate why leaders act the way they do, and how those ways of being ripple outward into organisational culture and systemic outcomes.

In parallel, the metacontent discourse – also core to the authentic sustainability conversation – examines how human beings construct and interpret meaning. Leaders are often unaware of the underlying metacontent informing their decisions: their assumptions about markets, people, value and purpose.

Minalogy, the discourse of meaning, value and purpose, complements these lenses by addressing the moral and axiological foundations of human conduct. It explores how individuals discern what is genuinely worthwhile and how those judgements shape individual and collective behaviour. Through this inquiry, leadership becomes grounded in authentic purpose rather than ambition, ideology or convenience. Minalogy invites leaders to clarify what is truly worth pursuing, anchoring decisions in moral realism and existential coherence rather than performative success.

By surfacing these interrelated layers of Being, sense-making and meaning-making, philosophy exposes blind spots, broadens perspective and expands the possibilities for more conscious and effective decision-making.

The phenomenological dimension

If philosophy provides the lens, phenomenology provides the ground. Phenomenology is concerned with lived experience – how human beings encounter and interpret the world as it appears to them. It recognises that human beings are not passive observers, but active participants, always engaged in meaning-making.

This perspective is essential for sustainability. A leader does not simply implement strategies; they live them, interpret them, and embody them. A team does not simply follow processes; it experiences them, negotiates them, and responds to them. Sustainability emerges not from abstract plans, but from lived practices, from the way people show up, decide and relate in real time.

Phenomenology also acknowledges that human beings are emotional and social. Decisions are not made by rational calculation alone. They are shaped by moods, trust, fear, hope and relationships. Any comprehensive and meaningful framework for sustainability must take these dimensions into account.

Why philosophy and phenomenology matter for sustainability

Sustainability is often misrepresented as a technical or managerial challenge – something that can be solved simply by introducing better processes, stricter compliance or more advanced tools. While these are important, they are insufficient. At its core, sustainability is about systemic integrity – about the coherent alignment of human beings, teams, organisations and other systems with the realities they face and the purposes they pursue.

This makes sustainability fundamentally a human question. Every system, no matter how complex, is ultimately animated and maintained by human choices, relationships and values. The patterns that sustain – or destabilise – a system emerge from how people think, feel, decide and act within it. When integrity erodes in individuals or groups, no amount of technical optimisation can restore coherence. Conversely, when people act with awareness, responsibility, care and alignment, even flawed structures can renew themselves.

To sustain anything – an ecosystem, a business, a culture, a society – we must first understand what it means to be human within it. How are leaders *being* in the face of challenge? How are teams *relating* to one another? How are organisations *making sense* of their environment? These are ontological and phenomenological inquiries, not technical ones. They reveal that sustainability begins not in policy, but in presence – in the lived quality of how we inhabit, interpret and respond to the systems we create.

By bringing **philosophy** and **phenomenology** together, this work avoids two common distortions that limit the effectiveness of sustainability efforts.

1. **Reductionism** – The tendency to treat sustainability as a purely technical or mechanical problem, as though human

systems could be engineered into balance through metrics, controls and procedural efficiency alone. This approach may produce short-term order, but it often suppresses the very adaptability and relational intelligence that genuine sustainability requires.

2. **Abstraction** – The inclination to frame sustainability as an intellectual or ideological construct detached from lived experience. In this mode, sustainability becomes a discourse of concepts rather than a discipline of practice, valued for its rhetoric but disconnected from human reality.

This work seeks to move beyond both. It situates sustainability where it actually belongs: in the lived experience of human beings who are both limited and capable, rational and emotional, individual and collective. It recognises that sustainability is not something done *to* systems, but something enacted *through* the quality of human engagement within them.

By grounding sustainability in the realities of perception, relationship and meaning-making, the integration of philosophy and phenomenology allows it to be understood not as a problem to solve, but as a condition to cultivate – one that must be continuously interpreted, embodied and renewed.

Methodological orientation

The overall philosophical and phenomenological orientation shaped the methodology of the entire project. The goal was never to devise a formula for success or a prescriptive model to impose on leaders and organisations. Rather, the inquiry was approached as a disciplined journey of discovery – one that demanded both surrender and agency, reflection and participation.

Imagine a leader and their team rowing a boat across the ocean. The ocean represents the larger forces – markets, societies, histories and natural systems – that no leader can control. The waves rise and fall, the currents shift, and storms appear without warning. Leaders cannot command the ocean. What they can do is row in unison with their team – in rhythm, with harmony and discipline. In doing so, they align with forces larger than themselves while still exercising intentional agency.

This metaphor captures the interplay of phenomenology and philosophy. Phenomenology is the ground – the ocean of lived reality that must be encountered directly, without illusion or denial. Philosophy is the lens – the structure through which meaning, rhythm and direction are discerned. Together, they make sustainability possible: a practice of navigating complexity with awareness, coherence and purpose, even when the destination is never fixed and the journey never ends.

A living orientation

Recognising the nature of this work also clarifies that it is not a static or closed system that claims finality, but a *living body of work* – coherent, adaptive and continually evolving. While it provides a clear and rigorous pathway, its strength lies in its flexibility: it invites ongoing interpretation, reflection and renewal as conditions change. Like the leaders and teams it serves, it matures through practice, dialogue and refinement.

This orientation mirrors the very essence of authentic sustainability. Sustainability is not a static end-state to be achieved once and for all. It is an ongoing process of coherence, adaptation and regeneration. By grounding the work in philosophy and phenomenology, it remains aligned with this reality – rigorous without rigidity, structured without sterility and always attuned to the lived experience of human beings.

Regenerative agriculture analogy

One of the most useful analogies for understanding authentic sustainability is found in the practice of regenerative agriculture. Unlike industrial farming, which seeks short-term yield through extractive practices, regenerative agriculture focuses on cultivating soil health, biodiversity and ecosystem vitality. It does not attempt to control nature with rigid formulas, but works with natural processes, encouraging life to flourish through small, iterative and cumulative actions.

This analogy is particularly powerful because it mirrors the philosophy behind this body of work. Sustainability in organisations and systems is not about extracting as much as possible in the shortest amount of time, nor is it about imposing rigid scripts from the outside. It is about cultivating conditions under which resilience, regeneration and long-term viability can emerge.

Extractive versus agricultural regenerative models

Traditional industrial agriculture is a fitting metaphor for the performative, compliance-driven version of sustainability critiqued in this body of work as *sustainabilism*. In agriculture, extractive practices may produce impressive short-term yields, but they degrade the soil, reduce biodiversity and create long-term fragility. The land may appear productive for a time, but beneath the surface, it is being hollowed out.

In organisations, the same dynamic is at work. Leaders who chase immediate revenue at the expense of culture, prioritise compliance over coherence or burn out their people to meet short-term targets may appear successful in the moment. These extractive methods often seem easier and more efficient at first, but they come at a hidden cost. In contrast, regenerative approaches require greater effort and discipline in the short term – investing in trust, capability and shared purpose rather than extracting performance. Yet over time, this investment compounds. Like fertile soil, regenerative systems become increasingly self-sustaining, delivering stable, high-quality outcomes without exhausting the people or resources that sustain them.

In regenerative agriculture, farmers plant cover crops, rotate fields, use compost and work in harmony with natural cycles. The soil becomes richer with each season, able to sustain life without constant artificial inputs. Similarly, authentic sustainability in organisations arises when leaders cultivate coherence, adaptability, trust and regenerative culture – building systems that grow stronger, not weaker, through systemic integrity.

The power of small, iterative actions

Regenerative agriculture demonstrates that transformation does not come from dramatic interventions, but from cumulative, consistent actions. Adding organic matter to the soil, encouraging microbial life and reducing tillage may seem insignificant in isolation, but together they create profound change.

The same is true for organisations. Authentic sustainability is not achieved through grandiose strategies announced at board meetings or glossy sustainability reports that overpromise and under-deliver. It emerges from small, consistent practices – simple actions that, when sustained, shift the character of a system:

- A leader taking time to reflect before making a difficult decision, even when under pressure to act quickly.
- A team committing to honest dialogue about values and priorities, especially when opinions diverge.
- An organisation choosing long-term trust with customers over short-term gains.
- A culture that transforms mistakes into learning through open feedback loops rather than concealing errors, fostering defensiveness and eroding trust.

Just as soil becomes fertile through countless small contributions of organic matter, organisations become sustainable through countless small acts of integrity, discernment and regeneration.

Working with, not against, natural forces

A key lesson from regenerative agriculture is the importance of working *with* natural forces rather than attempting to control them. Farmers who rely on chemical interventions and monocultures enter a constant struggle to maintain productivity. In contrast, those who align with natural cycles enable nature to become a partner in regeneration and resilience.

The same principle applies in organisations. Leaders operate within complex systems shaped by human motivations, social dynamics, cultural narratives and economic conditions. These forces cannot be commanded into submission, but they can be understood, aligned and leveraged. Effective leadership recognises that progress depends not on resistance to these dynamics, but on *working with them* – designing structures and practices that channel their energy towards coherence and sustainability.

Just as ocean currents cannot be controlled, but can be navigated, organisational forces cannot be dictated, but can be directed through awareness and alignment. Authentic sustainability arises when leaders stop seeking to dominate complexity and learn to align or move in concert with it instead.

Transformation through aggregation

Perhaps the most important lesson of regenerative agriculture is that transformation occurs through aggregation. No single intervention restores the soil; it is the accumulation of many small, aligned practices over time that rebuilds fertility and resilience. Farmers know that regeneration requires patience and persistence, not quick fixes or single-point solutions.

The same is true for systemic integrity. Sustainability is not achieved through one program, one framework, or one charismatic leader. It emerges when individuals, teams and organisations make countless small, iterative moves towards coherence and renewal. Together, these actions create durable, system-wide transformation.

This understanding calls for humility. Regenerative agriculture does not promise instant results, and neither does authentic sustainability. The value of this work lies in resisting the pressure to over-promise or reduce transformation to a guaranteed formula. Instead, it offers a framework for cultivation – a disciplined approach that honours both human agency and the greater forces beyond our control. Sustainability, like fertile soil, cannot be commanded; it must be cultivated, tended and renewed through consistent practice.

Beyond the Program – Broader Validation

While the six program cycles provided an immediate context in which the work was tested and refined, they were never its sole source of validation. From the outset, it was recognised that for the frameworks to hold credibility and weight, they needed to be examined from multiple vantage points. Sustainability and systemic integrity cannot be confined to the operational level of SMEs, startups or NGOs; they extend into the macro dynamics of governance, policy and global institutions.

Accordingly, the development of the Authentic Sustainability Framework (ASF) and its central Unified Ontology of Systemic Integrity (UOSI) was accompanied by broader validation efforts, incorporating structured interviews, expert dialogues and comparative case analyses across diverse contexts.

Expert review and dialogue

A wide range of experts contributed to the validation of the frameworks through structured interviews and dialogues. These engagements included:

- **Policy-makers and governance leaders** – Individuals operating within complex public decision-making environments, where sustainability is frequently treated as a political or bureaucratic ideal.

- **Senior executives and organisational leaders** – Those responsible for leading large teams, divisions and organisations, whose perspectives ensured that the frameworks resonated beyond the SME context.
- **Academics and researchers** – While not the primary audience of the work, their participation provided an additional layer of intellectual critique and validation.

Insights drawn from these interactions confirmed what the program context had already revealed: that sustainability, when treated as a scripted or performative compliance exercise, consistently fails to generate substantive, effective and enduring results.

Leaders across sectors expressed frustration at the persistent gap between sustainability rhetoric and lived organisational reality. Across these conversations, a shared recognition emerged – that meaningful sustainability requires grounding in integrity, Being and systemic coherence, rather than in compliance or performative display.

Complementing micro with meso and macro

In addition to interviews and dialogues, an extensive examination was undertaken into how sustainability and systemic integrity have been approached by governments and global organisations. The analysis encompassed major institutions such as the United Nations, the World Economic Forum and other global governance bodies, as well as national governments across a range of contexts.

Both historical and contemporary cases were studied to trace patterns in how leaders and organisations navigated crises, pursued long-term objectives or succumbed to systemic dysfunction. This multi-level analysis – spanning the micro (individual and team), meso (organisational) and macro (institutional and societal) domains – provided a broader empirical and philosophical foundation for understanding the conditions under which systems sustain or disintegrate.

For example:

- **Historical analysis** revealed how empires, corporations and social movements rose or fell according to the integrity of their sense-making and decision-making. The pattern was consistent across time and context. When integrity in vision and leadership diminished, decline followed. However, when it endured, systems adapted and evolved. For example, the Roman and Ottoman empires each thrived when coherence and strategic clarity were strong, yet faltered when these qualities eroded. Once industry leaders, corporations such as Kodak, Nokia and HTC lost relevance as coherence and adaptive capacity eroded. Social movements showed the same dynamic: enduring civil-rights coalitions sustained momentum through coherence and shared purpose, while many revolutionary efforts failed when integrity fractured. Across these diverse systems, integrity proved the decisive factor between endurance and collapse.

- Similarly, **contemporary case studies** revealed how global institutions, corporations and governments continue to struggle with sustainability when they overlook the ontological and phenomenological dimensions of human beings. When decision-making is detached from lived experience, policies become performative and strategies lose traction. Many initiatives remain technically sophisticated, yet fail to engage the values, motivations and relational dynamics that determine whether systems can actually sustain themselves. In contrast, the most effective organisations and programs are those that recognise human coherence as the foundation of systemic coherence. They integrate purpose with process, align culture with strategy, and create conditions where accountability and adaptability can coexist.

These studies provided not only critique, but also comparative validation. They demonstrated that the gaps identified in the modern sustainability discourse are not new; they are recurring patterns. By situating the work within this broader historical arc, the frameworks gained depth, resilience and legitimacy.

The findings also reinforced the central critique. Many large-scale initiatives lacked metacontent – they failed to interrogate the assumptions and frames underlying their policies. As a result, they produced scripted programs, compliance-driven frameworks and performative actions that often did more to signal virtue than to generate authentic sustainability.

By contrasting these macro-level failures with the micro-level successes observed in program cohorts and other applied contexts, the work was able to highlight the importance of starting from the ground up. Authentic sustainability emerges not from top-down mandates but from the aggregation of integrity within individuals and teams, scaling upward into organisations and societies.

The inclusion of these broader validation efforts ensured that the work did not remain confined to a single setting. While the experiences of 48 leaders across six programs provided rich and authentic data, they could not capture the full spectrum of sustainability challenges. By integrating perspectives from policy-makers, executives, academics and cross-sectoral case studies of governments and global organisations, the inquiry expanded its lens and confirmed the universality of the underlying dynamics.

This multi-layered validation demonstrated that the issues faced by startup founders and SME directors are structurally similar to those faced by governments and international institutions. The difference lies in scale, not essence. In both contexts, sustainability falters when it is reduced to compliance and performance, yet flourishes when it is grounded in integrity, Being and systemic coherence.

Documenting these broader validation efforts is essential for transparency. The work has not been developed in isolation, nor within an echo chamber. It has been tested, critiqued and refined through sustained engagement with practitioners and systems operating at different levels of complexity and influence.

This breadth of inquiry does not imply finality or completeness. On the contrary, it underscores that the work remains a living body of practice and philosophy – one that continues to evolve as new insights emerge and conditions change. What it does establish, however, is that the frameworks presented in this body of work are not speculative abstractions. They are grounded in sustained engagement with reality across multiple strata – the micro-level of individuals and teams, the meso-level of organisations and the macro-level of societies and institutions – forming a coherent architecture that links human integrity with systemic sustainability.

Global Sustainability Literature and Practitioner Discourse

The evolution of this work was not confined to internal programs or isolated inquiry. In parallel, deep engagement occurred with global sustainability discourse through direct exposure to academic, institutional and practitioner perspectives. This engagement included participation in, and contribution to, formal scholarly work published by Springer within edited volumes focused on sustainability, organisational transformation and leadership.

Contributions were made to two major Springer volumes within the broader *Sustainable Organization* and *3-P Model* body of literature:

- *Transforming Public and Private Sector Organizations: Implementing Sustainable Purpose, Travelling Organization and Connectivity for Resilience,*[108] in which a connection between the Being Framework and the Three-Pillars Model was explored; and

- *The Sustainable Organization: How Organizations Address*

---

108 Wollmann, P. & Püringer, R. (eds.) (2022) *Transforming Public and Private Sector Organizations: Implementing Sustainable Purpose, Travelling Organization and Connectivity for Resilience.* Cham: Springer.

the 17 UN SDGs Using the 3-P Model,[109] where metacontent, identity and inclusion were examined through an ontological and systemic lens.

Broader validation of the need for a new, ontologically grounded approach capable of addressing the shortcomings of existing paradigms was further supported through engagement with international sustainability literature and practitioner discourse. Participation in peer-reviewed publications and collaboration with global scholars provided additional perspectives on how sustainability is being interpreted and operationalised across organisational, governmental and societal contexts.

Engagement with these scholarly and practitioner communities offered exposure to a diverse range of perspectives and methodologies across the global sustainability and organisational transformation landscape. Through these exchanges, interaction occurred with a wide spectrum of authors, advisors and practitioners working across public, private and social sectors. The collective effort represented within this body of work reflected strong intention, rigorous inquiry and genuine care for the future of organisations and society, while also highlighting the limitations of prevailing sustainability practice – reinforcing the necessity for a deeper foundation.

Across this landscape, a recurring pattern was observed. While many sustainability initiatives originated from sincere concern and compelling intent, they were often vulnerable to drift, distortion and performativity once operationalised. This pattern appeared not only in scholarly and organisational frameworks but also within global policy environments. Reviews of instruments such as the United Nations Sustainable Development Goals (SDGs) and analyses of government policies across multiple jurisdictions revealed similar tendencies.

What emerged repeatedly was not an absence of intelligence, commitment or goodwill, but the persistent challenge of implementation when sustainability is approached primarily through mechanistic,

---

109 Wollmann, P., Pemler, D. & Ndrevataj, M. (eds.) (2025) *The Sustainable Organization: How Organizations Address the 17 UN SDGs Using the 3-P Model*. Cham: Springer. Available at: https://link.springer.com/book/9783031895487

metric-driven or compliance-oriented lenses. When sustainability frameworks become procedural scripts rather than lived orientations, they risk detaching from the ontological foundations of enduring systems – how human beings are being, how they make sense, how they relate and how they steward what they build.

This observation does not represent a critique of the ideals themselves – many of which carry substantial merit – but of the recurring pattern through which they are translated into practice. These findings collectively validated the need for a framework capable of reconnecting sustainability efforts with the human, relational and systemic dimensions that sustain them. Without grounding in the human ecology of sustainability, institutional efforts can inadvertently reinforce fragility, bureaucracy and performative alignment, even while intending to cultivate resilience, responsibility and regeneration.

It was through this combination of scholarly participation, extensive literature review and lived observation that the need for a deeper ontological foundation became clear. The gap was not one of ambition or intelligence, but of the absence of a sufficiently human-centred, meaning-grounded and integrity-based foundation capable of holding the complexity of human experience and systemic life.

The Authentic Sustainability Framework (ASF) and the Unified Ontology of Systemic Integrity (UOSI) were, therefore, developed and positioned not as a rejection of global sustainability efforts, but as a response to the clearly validated need for such an ontological foundation – a means of deepening, supporting and safeguarding the intent behind these initiatives so they may be realised authentically in lived practice rather than diluted into performance or compliance.

Distinction from 'Sustainabilism'

The breadth of validation undertaken for this work reaffirmed its central insight: that the prevailing sustainability paradigm remains trapped in performative, compliance-driven modes that neglect the human and systemic realities upon which genuine regeneration depends. To make this distinction explicit, this section contrasts *sustainabilism* with *authentic sustainability* – the very gap this body of work was designed to bridge.

Throughout this book and its supporting body of research, a deliberate distinction is drawn between what is termed *sustainabilism* and what is presented as *authentic sustainability*. This distinction is not semantic; it is essential. It clarifies the limitations that the work seeks to overcome and exposes why many existing approaches to sustainability fail to generate meaningful, enduring results.

What is sustainabilism?

Sustainabilism refers to the prevailing paradigm of sustainability as it is often practised and promoted by large institutions, governments and corporations. It is marked by a number of recurring features:

- **Compliance-driven mandates** – Framing sustainability as a set of procedural obligations designed to satisfy regulators, investors or stakeholders, while neglecting how these

measures impact both the people within the organisation and the broader systems of which it is a part.
- **Performative signalling** – Glossy reports, public commitments and marketing campaigns designed more to project virtue than to produce authentic change.
- **Scripted frameworks** – Top-down models that dictate what organisations should do, regardless of context, without engaging the lived realities of the people within them.
- **Fragmented thinking** – Treating sustainability as an isolated initiative or department rather than an integrated expression of systemic integrity.

This version of sustainability may look impressive on paper. It often produces charts, metrics and certifications. Yet beneath the surface, it is depleted and devoid of integrity. Like industrial agriculture that yields abundant crops while exhausting the soil, *sustainabilism* extracts compliance and performance without cultivating genuine resilience or regeneration.

Why it fails

The failure of *sustainabilism* is not merely technical; it is ontological. It fails because it does not engage with human beings as they truly are – limited in rationality, yet emotional, social and capable of meaning-making. By reducing sustainability to procedures, scripts and compliance frameworks, it overlooks the very source of authentic sustainability: the integrity of people and the systems they inhabit in their lived reality.

Such approaches are often blind to interdependence. They may implement initiatives that appear beneficial within one organisation, sector or nation, yet fail to consider their unintended consequences across other systems. The result is progress in isolation – success in one domain purchased at the expense of coherence in another.

This is why so many sustainability initiatives collapse into contradiction. Organisations proclaim commitments, yet struggle internally with inconsistent delivery, disengaged employees and fragile cultures. Governments announce ambitious targets, yet fall short in practice because the systemic integrity required to achieve them is lacking. *Sustainabilism* promises transformation, but delivers performance theatre – a facade of progress masking the absence of lived integrity.

From sustainabilism to authentic sustainability

In contrast, authentic sustainability – as articulated through the Authentic Sustainability Framework and its central Unified Ontology of Systemic Integrity (UOSI) – begins from a different foundation. It is not imposed from the outside, but cultivated from within. It does not treat sustainability as a checklist, but as an emergent property of systemic integrity and regeneration across individuals, teams, organisations and institutions.

Its features are the inverse of *sustainabilism*:

- **Integrity-driven orientation** – Sustainability rooted in alignment between what people say, what they do, and how they are being.
- **Lived experience** – Sustainability as something felt and practised in day-to-day decisions, not merely reported in documents.
- **Bottom-up emergence** – Sustainability that arises from the aggregation of countless small, authentic actions, rather than from top-down mandates.
- **Systemic coherence** – Sustainability integrated into the very fabric of how organisations function, rather than isolated as a separate initiative.

Where *sustainabilism* extracts, authentic sustainability regenerates. Where *sustainabilism* performs, authentic sustainability transforms.

The role of the UOSI

The Unified Ontology of Systemic Integrity (UOSI) provides the structural foundation for authentic sustainability. By identifying 16 systemic qualities nested within four layers – Architectonic, Integrity, Disintegration and Modulation – it offers a coherent framework for understanding how sustainability emerges in practice. Rather than prescribing what organisations must do, it illuminates the qualities they must develop and maintain a healthy relationship with.

This is a crucial difference. Mandates and scripts attempt to dictate behaviour. Ontological frameworks reveal structures of Being and systemic integrity, empowering leaders to act with discernment and agency. Rather than compliance and performance, the UOSI invites coherence and transformation.

Implications for leaders and organisations

For leaders, the distinction between *sustainabilism* and authentic sustainability is more than conceptual. It is profoundly practical. Choosing *sustainabilism* means chasing compliance, reporting and optics, often at the expense of real coherence. In contrast, choosing authentic sustainability means committing to the often slower, cumulative work of cultivating integrity within oneself, one's team and one's organisation.

For organisations, this distinction determines whether sustainability will be a hollow slogan or a lived reality. Those that champion *sustainabilism* may win short-term approval, but risk long-term fragility. However, those that embrace authentic sustainability may struggle with complexity in the short term, but build resilience, trust and regeneration over time.

Conclusion – A Work in Motion

The purpose of this Appendix has been to provide transparency – to show how this body of work came into being, how it has been tested and refined, and why it carries credibility. Too often, frameworks and theories are presented as if they emerged fully formed, detached from the processes that shaped them. Here, it has been made clear that *Sustainabilism* and the *Authentic Sustainability Framework (ASF)*, including its central *Unified Ontology of Systemic Integrity (UOSI)*, are not abstract constructs, but the result of years of philosophical inquiry, practical engagement, iterative refinement and validation across multiple contexts.

At its core, this body of work reflects a dual commitment. On the one hand, it is grounded in philosophy – in the ontological, ethical and phenomenological exploration of what it means to be, to lead and to sustain. On the other, it is anchored in practice – tested with leaders, teams and organisations confronting the real challenges of sustainability on a daily basis. Neither philosophy nor practice alone would have sufficed: philosophy provided depth, coherence and clarity, while practice provided reality, relevance and impact. Together, they gave rise to a body of work that is both rigorous and usable.

Iterative development in context

The development of this work cannot be separated from the program context in which it was applied and refined. Across six cycles, 48 leaders engaged with the frameworks, testing them within their businesses, teams and organisational realities. Their feedback, challenges and breakthroughs informed ongoing evolution. Notes were taken, interviews conducted and feedback loops embedded. Prototypes such as the *Sustainability Profile* were created, tested and recalibrated. Each cycle added depth and resilience to the ontometric tool, ensuring that the work did not remain theoretical, but was continually forged through lived experience.

Equally important were the contributions of facilitators Jacqueline Hofste and Ariya Chittasy, whose diverse backgrounds and practical insights enabled the translation of philosophy into organisational reality. Their collaboration demonstrated the interdependence of theory and practice, with their observations directly informing subsequent refinements to the frameworks.

Beyond the program

Validation extended well beyond the program context. Structured interviews with policy-makers, executives and academics, alongside studies of governments and global organisations, provided meso- and macro-level perspectives. Case studies – both historical and contemporary – revealed recurring patterns of success and failure in sustainability practice. These broader inquiries confirmed what the program data had already shown: sustainability falters when reduced to compliance and performance, and flourishes when grounded in integrity, Being and systemic coherence.

Distinguishing authentic sustainability

The distinction between *sustainabilism* and *authentic sustainability* lies at the heart of this work. *Sustainabilism* represents the prevailing paradigm of compliance-driven, performative sustainability – glossy on the surface, hollow underneath. In contrast, *authentic sustainability* emerges from the aggregation of countless small acts of systemic integrity and regeneration. It is cultivated from the bottom up, not mandated from the top down.

The frameworks developed through this body of work – the Authentic Sustainability Framework (ASF) and its core Unified Ontology of

Systemic Integrity (UOSI), together with the Being Framework, Metacontent and its Nested Theory of Sense-making, and Minalogy – provide the architecture for this cultivation. They do not prescribe behaviour, but illuminate the ontological and systemic qualities that enable discernment, coherence and regeneration across contexts.

A living body of work

Authentic sustainability is not a fixed destination, but an ongoing process. Systems endure not by clinging to rigid forms, but by adapting, regenerating and aligning with the forces within and around them. Likewise, this body of work remains alive – open to refinement, responsive to feedback and adaptive to new conditions.

The metaphor of regenerative agriculture applies here once again. Just as soil becomes fertile through countless small contributions of organic matter, this work grows richer through iterative engagement. Each leader who applies it, each organisation that tests it, and each critique that challenges it adds to its vitality. The work is not a static product to be consumed but a living framework to be cultivated.

The ontometric tools developed through this process, such as the Sustainability Profile, will continue to evolve through practice. Each iteration, informed by real-world data and lived application, allows for further calibration, refinement and validation.

By the time of this book's completion, more than 100 Sustainability Profiles had been completed. Their findings are being reviewed and integrated into the next cycle of calibration, continuing the ongoing practice of testing, refining and strengthening the tool through real systems, real leaders and real demands. In parallel, the UOSI and its 16 systemic qualities are now being systematically measured, and a cohort of practitioners is in active training to apply this instrument in support of professionals, leaders and organisations.

This continuous process embodies the very principle of sustainability it advocates: learning, adapting and renewing through lived experience.

Transparency and credibility

This Appendix documents the development process to ensure transparency and establish credibility. The work did not emerge in isolation; it was shaped through rigorous philosophical inquiry, applied engagement with leaders across industries, collaboration with facilitators, validation through expert review and case studies, and ongoing iterative refinement.

Transparency is essential in a field often characterised by overstatement. Many sustainability initiatives promise certainty or rapid solutions to inherently complex challenges. This work takes a different approach. It recognises that sustainability demands humility, adaptability and a willingness to engage deeply with complexity. Its credibility rests on this foundation – on a disciplined commitment to coherence rather than claims of control, and to cultivation rather than prescription.

Moving forward

As this body of work continues to evolve, its relevance will depend on how it is lived. Frameworks hold value only when embodied – when leaders, teams and organisations apply them within their own contexts, test them through experience and adapt them to emerging challenges.

This conclusion is therefore not an endpoint, but an invitation: for leaders, organisations and communities to engage with the frameworks, to explore their practical implications, and to contribute to their ongoing refinement. It is an invitation to move beyond *sustainabilism* and towards **authentic sustainability** – not as rhetoric, but as a lived, regenerative practice.

References

Argyris, C. (1993) *Knowledge for Action: A Guide to Overcoming Barriers to Organizational Change*. San Francisco: Jossey-Bass.

Argyris, C. and Schön, D.A. (1996) *Organizational Learning II: Theory, Method, and Practice*. Reading, MA: Addison-Wesley.

Ashby, W.R. (1956) *An Introduction to Cybernetics*. London: Chapman & Hall.

Bertalanffy, L. von (1968) *General System Theory: Foundations, Development, Applications*. New York: George Braziller.

Biermann, F., Pattberg, P., van Asselt, H. and Zelli, F. (2009) 'The Fragmentation of Global Governance Architectures: A Framework for Analysis', *Global Environmental Politics*, 9(4), pp. 14–40.

Boochani, B. (2018) *No Friend but the Mountains: Writing from Manus Prison*. Translated by O. Tofighian. Sydney: Picador.

Boulding, K.E. (1956) 'General Systems Theory—The Skeleton of Science', *Management Science*, 2(3), pp. 197–208.

Braun, W. (2002) 'The System Archetypes', in *The Systems Modeling Workbook* (pp. 1-26). https://www.albany.edu/faculty/gpr/PAD724/724WebArticles/sys_archetypes.pdf

Brosschot, J.F., Pieper, S. and Thayer, J.F. (2005) 'The Perseverative Cognition Hypothesis: A Review of Worry, Prolonged Stress-related Physiological Activation, and Health', *Journal of Psychosomatic Research*, 58(1), pp. 163–169.

Churchman, C.W. (1968) *The Systems Approach*. New York: Delacorte Press.

Complexity Science Hub Vienna (n.d.) *Crisis and Complexity*. Available at: https://csh.ac.at/research/research-topic/social-complexity-collapse/ (Accessed: 14 September 2025).

de Beauvoir, S. (2009) *The Second Sex*. Translated by C. Borde and S. Malovany-Chevallier. London: Vintage Books.

Deci, E.L. and Ryan, R.M. (1985) *Intrinsic Motivation and Self-determination in Human Behaviour*. New York: Springer. Available at https://doi.org/10.1007/978-1-4899-2271-7 (Accessed 10 September 2025).

Densten, I. (2011) *The Impact of Organisational Culture and Social Desirability on Australian CEO leadership*. PhD thesis, UNSW.

Donovan, P. (2023) *What is Profit-Led Inflation?* UBS GWM, 16 March. Available at http://joseluisoreiro.com.br/site/link/332ed4a1c501e1d8970217df6e74fc78101f27a3.pdf

Esquivel, V. (2016) 'Power and the Sustainable Development Goals: A feminist analysis', *Gender & Development*, 24(1), pp. 9–23. Available at doi: 10.1080/13552074.2016.1147872 (Accessed 10 September 2025).

Fahrig, L. (2003) 'Effects of Habitat Fragmentation on Biodiversity', *Annual Review of Ecology, Evolution, and Systematics*, 34, pp. 487–515.

Foucault, M. (1991) *Discipline and Punish: The Birth of the Prison*. London: Penguin Books.

Foucault, M. (1998) *The History of Sexuality: Volume 1 – The Will to Knowledge*. London: Penguin Books.

Franey, J. (2025) 'World Bank Bureaucrats Accused of 'Hypocrisy' Over Jet Flights to UN Climate Confab', *New York Post*, 12 March. Available at: https://nypost.com/2025/03/12/business/world-bank-bureaucrats-accused-of-hypocrisy-over-jet-flights-to-un-climate-confab/ (Accessed: 14 September 2025).

Frankl, V.E. (2004) *Man's Search for Meaning*. Rev. edn. London: Rider.

Fromm, E. (1942) *Escape from Freedom*. New York: Farrar & Rinehart.

Good Governance Institute (2021) *Lean Governance: Evidence-based Governance for Better Outcomes*. London: GGI.

Heidegger, M. (2010) *Being and Time*. Translated by J. Stambaugh, revised by D.J. Schmidt. Albany: SUNY Press. (Orig. 1927).

Hickel, J. (2020) *Less is More: How Degrowth Will Save the World*. London: William Heinemann.

Hofste, J. (2024) 'Navigating the Unknown in Organizations: And How to Read the Respective Organizational Capabilities', in Wollmann, P., Stricker, L. & Pemler, D. (eds). *Reading an Unknown Organization: Leaders in New Roles Thriving in Challenging Environments with the 3-P-Model Mindset*. Cham: Springer, pp. 221–244. Available at: https://link.springer.com/chapter/10.1007/978-3-031-67408-2_11 (Accessed: 20 October 2025).

Holling, C.S. (1973) 'Resilience and Stability of Ecological Systems', *Annual Review of Ecology and Systematics*, 4(1), pp. 1–23.

Hughes, B.B., et al. (2011) *International Futures (IFs) Version 7.00: User's Guide*. Frederick S. Pardee Center for International Futures, University of Denver. Available at: https://korbel.du.edu/wp-content/uploads/2015/04/International-Futures-IFs-Training-Manual.pdf

Inner Development Goals Initiative (2021) *The Inner Development Goals*. Available at: https://www.innerdevelopmentgoals.org (Accessed: 14 September 2025).

Kegan, R. and Lahey, L.L. (2009) *Immunity to Change*. Boston, MA: Harvard Business Press.

Kim, I-B., Lee, J-H. and Park, S-C. (2022) 'The Relationship Between Stress, Inflammation, and Depression', *Biomedicines*, 10(8), Article 1929.

Lansing, J.S. and Kremer, J.N. (1993) 'Emergent Properties of Balinese Water Temple Networks: Coadaptation on a Rugged Fitness Landscape', *American Anthropologist*, 95(1), pp. 97–114. Available at: https://anthrosource.onlinelibrary.wiley.com/doi/abs/10.1525/aa.1993.95.1.02a00050 (Accessed: 10 September 2025).

Lin, K., Wang, H., Chen, Y. and Zhang, L. (2023) 'Understanding Embodied Effects of Posture', *Behavioural Sciences*, 5(2), Article 30.

Lomborg, B. (2015) *The Nobel Laureates' Guide to the Smartest Targets for the World: 2016–2030*. Kindle.

López-Castro, T., Saraiya, T., Zumberg-Smith, K. & Melara, R. (2019) 'Association Between Shame and Posttraumatic Stress', *Journal of Clinical Psychology*, 75(9), pp. 1659–1671.

Lyotard, J-F. (1984) *The Postmodern Condition: A Report on Knowledge*. Manchester: Manchester University Press.

Maturana, H.R. and Varela, F.J. (1980) *Autopoiesis and Cognition: The Realisation of the Living*. Dordrecht: D. Reidel.

Mayer, R.C., Davis, J.H. and Schoorman, F.D. (1995) 'An Integrative Model of Organizational Trust', *Academy of Management Review*, 20(3), pp. 709–734.

Morin, E. and Kern, A.-B. (1993) *Terre-Patrie*. Translated by Catherine M.G.L. Duport 2000. Paris: Éditions du Seuil.

Newman, M.E.J. (2010) *Networks: An Introduction*. Oxford: Oxford University Press.

Nietzsche, F. (2002) *Beyond Good and Evil*. Translated by J. Norman. Cambridge: Cambridge University Press. (Orig. 1886).

Project Management Institute (n.d.) *Disciplined Agile Toolkit: Lean Governance*. Available at: https://www.pmi.org/disciplined-agile (Accessed: 14 September 2025).

Rahman, F. (1975) *The Philosophy of Mulla Sadra*. Albany: State University of New York Press.

Ravi, M., Miller, A.H. and Michopoulos, V. (2021) 'Immunology of Stress and the Impact of Inflammation on the Brain and Behavior.', *BJPsych Advances*, 27(3), pp. 158–165.

Raworth, K. (2017) *Doughnut Economics: Seven Ways to Think Like a 21st-Century Economist*. London: Random House Business.

Ryan, R.M. and Deci, E.L. (2000) 'Self-Determination Theory and the Facilitation of Intrinsic Motivation, Social Development, and Well-Being', *American Psychologist*, 55(1), pp. 68–78. Available at: https://doi.org/10.1037/0003-066X.55.1.68 (Accessed 7 September 2025).

Sartre, J-P. (2003) *Being and Nothingness*. Translated by H.E. Barnes. London: Routledge. (Orig. 1943).

Scaled Agile (n.d.) *Lean Portfolio Management*. Available at: https://scaledagileframework.com/lean-portfolio-management/ (Accessed: 14 September 2025).

Schäfer, I., Lass-Hennemann, J., Rosner, R., Friese, M. & Plichta, M.M. (2022) 'Clinical Manifestations of Body Memories', *Frontiers in Neuroscience*, 16, Article 9138975.

Soliman, A. (2024) Academics Say Flying to Meetings Harms the Climate – But They Carry on. *Nature News*. Available at https://www.nature.com/articles/d41586-024-02965-7 (Accessed: 9 September 2025).

Tooze, A. (2022) 'Welcome to the World of the Polycrisis', *Financial Times*, 28 October.

Tosey, P., Visser, M. and Saunders, M.N.K. (2012) 'The Origins and Conceptualisations of "Triple-Loop Learning"', *Management Learning*, 43(3), pp. 291–307.

Truth and Reconciliation Commission (1998) *Truth and Reconciliation Commission of South Africa Report*. Vols. 1–5. Cape Town: Government of South Africa.

United Nations Department of Economic and Social Affairs (2024) *The Sustainable Development Goals Report 2024*. New York: United Nations.

United Nations (Inter-agency Task Force on Financing for Development) (2024) *Financing for Sustainable Development Report 2024: Financing for Development at a Crossroads*. Available at: https://desapublications.un.org/

publications/financing-sustainable-development-report-2024 (Accessed: 14 September 2025).

Vaillant, G.E. (1992) *Ego Mechanisms of Defense*. Washington, DC: American Psychiatric Press.

van de Mortel, T.F. (2008) 'Faking it: Social Desirability Response Bias in Self-Report Research', *Australian Journal of Advanced Nursing*, 25(4), pp. 40–48.

van der Kolk, B.A. and Fisler, R. (1997) 'Memory and the Evolving Psychobiology of PTSD', *Harvard Review of Psychiatry*, 4(5), pp. 253–265.

van der Leeuw, S.E. & McGlade, J. (eds.) (1997) *Time, Process and Structured Transformation in Archaeology*. London: Routledge.

von Foerster, H. (2003) *Understanding Understanding: Essays on Cybernetics and Cognition*. New York: Springer.

Weil, S. (2002) *Gravity and Grace*. Translated by E. Craufurd. London: Routledge. (Orig. 1952).

Wiener, N. (1948) *Cybernetics: Or Control and Communication in the Animal and the Machine*. Cambridge, MA: MIT Press.

Wilber, K. (2000) *Integral Psychology*. Boston, MA: Shambhala.

Wilber, K. (2001) *Sex, Ecology, Spirituality*. 2nd edn. Boston, MA: Shambhala.

Wittgenstein, L. (2001) *Tractatus Logico-Philosophicus*. Translated by D.F. Pears and B.F. McGuinness. London: Routledge. (Orig. 1921).

Wollmann, P., Pemler, D. & Ndrevataj, M. (eds.) (2025) *The Sustainable Organization: How Organizations Address the 17 UN SDGs Using the 3-P Model*. Cham: Springer. Available at: https://link.springer.com/book/9783031895487 (Accessed: 7 September 2025).

Wollmann, P. & Püringer, R. (eds.) (2022) *Transforming Public and Private Sector Organizations: Implementing Sustainable Purpose, Travelling Organization and Connectivity for Resilience*. Cham: Springer

Works by Ashkan Tashvir

Tashvir, A. (2021) *Being – The Source of Power*. Sydney: Engenesis Publishing.

Tashvir, A. (2022) *Human Being: Illuminating the Reality Beneath the Facade*. Sydney: Engenesis Publications.

Tashvir, A. (2022) 'The Application of a New Framework: Connecting the "Being Framework" with the "Three-Pillars Model" of Organization and Leadership to Foster Transformations: A Helpful Contextualising of the "Being Framework Ontological Model" in Working with People in Organizations in Transformations', in Wollmann, P. & Püringer, R.

(eds.) *Transforming Public and Private Sector Organizations: Implementing Sustainable Purpose, Travelling Organization and Connectivity for Resilience*. Cham: Springer, pp. 137–164.

Tashvir, A. (2024) *Metacontent: The Intellectual Substrates for Sense-making*. Sydney: Engenesis Publications.

Tashvir, A. (2025) 'The Meta-content of Being and Identity: Rethinking Diversity, Inclusion, and Sustainable Organizations', in Wollmann, P., Pemler, D. & Ndrevataj, M. (eds.) *The Sustainable Organization: How Organizations Address the 17 UN SDGs Using the 3-P-Model*. Cham: Springer, pp. 85–127. Available at: https://doi.org/10.1007/978-3-031-89549-4_5 (Accessed: 20 October 2025).

Tashvir, A. (forthcoming) *Minalogy: The Ontology of Meaning and Instatement*. Unpublished manuscript.

About the Author

Ashkan Tashvir is a multidisciplinary author, philosopher and entrepreneur whose work bridges ontology, organisational design, human development, technology and systems thinking. His intellectual pursuit is not limited to observing the world but transforming it. Through a rare integration of philosophical inquiry and real-world execution, he has developed frameworks that directly advance human potential, leadership and the sustainability of systems.

His body of work includes the **Being Framework**™, an ontological paradigm for leadership, performance and effectiveness, adopted by leaders across more than 50 countries. Supported by applied tools such as the **Being Profile**®, his work enables measurable growth in individuals and organisations by illuminating the human qualities that shape – or compromise – performance, integrity and systemic resilience.

In parallel with this book, Ashkan has also led the development of the **Sustainability Profile**™ – an ontometric diagnostic and transformation tool designed to elevate how leaders and organisations assess and build sustainability at the human, cultural and structural levels. Mirroring the transformative impact of the Being Profile, it offers a practical pathway for leaders to cultivate authentic sustainability in themselves, their teams and the systems they shape.

Sustainabilism is Ashkan's fifth book, following *Being*, *Human Being*, *Becoming* and *Metacontent*. In it, he expands his inquiry from the inner structure of the individual to the architecture of institutions, economies and civilisations – revealing how human coherence, meaning and ethical grounding determine whether systems endure or deteriorate.

Ashkan's thinking is informed by Eastern, Western, Islamic and Persian philosophical traditions, as well as faith-based and scientific perspectives. Rather than taking sides, he synthesises and transcends them, offering a practical and regenerative path forward for leaders, organisations and societies. In recognition of his contributions to leadership and organisational development, he received an Honorary Doctorate in Business Administration from the Collège de Paris in 2024.

Beyond theory, he builds. Ashkan is the founder of **Engenesis** – a platform for human transformation – and **Engenesis Ventures**, a venture-building organisation shaping ventures, technologies and leadership cultures using his ontological and systemic frameworks. His work exists not only in books and philosophy, but in enterprises, economies and futures being shaped today.

Recently, Ashkan has focused increasingly on philanthropic work through **GHEST** – a stewardship-driven community on the Engenesis platform dedicated to human empowerment and sustainable transformation. Recognising that many individuals who would benefit most from his body of work may not pursue traditional commercial pathways, he created GHEST as a philanthropic channel to make these ideas, tools and developmental structures accessible to broader communities. His commitment in this realm is grounded in expanding human potential, fostering conscious and ethical participation and enabling individuals and groups to navigate uncertainty with integrity, humility and collective responsibility.

Outside his professional life, Ashkan enjoys time with his family and dogs (especially in nature), cooking, collecting, playing music and exploring the beauty and complexity of the natural world.

Pathways to Further Exploration

If this work has resonated with you and you feel called to explore it more deeply, there are ways to continue your journey. *Sustainabilism* is not only a philosophical body of work, but a living practice – applied in real-world contexts to bring greater coherence and vitality to individuals, organisations, institutions, communities, cultures and societies.

Whether you are an entrepreneur, manager, executive, educator, policymaker or someone dedicated to your community, you may find that these principles speak directly to your context, intentions and aspirations.

Visit **sustainabilism.net** to discover more about this evolving body of work. There you'll find resources, programs, events and opportunities to connect with those who are practising and teaching these principles.

These pathways are for those who wish not only to understand this work, but to embody and apply it – translating insight into practice and contributing to systems that sustain and endure for generations to come.

www.ingramcontent.com/pod-product-compliance
Lightning Source LLC
Chambersburg PA
CBHW052210090526
44584CB00019BA/2643